The Taming of Cocaine

Tom Decorte

The Taming of Cocaine

Cocaine Use in European and American Cities

VUB **UNIVERSITY** PRESS

Criminological Studies

This series publishes studies which contribute significantly to the development of the criminological sciences, through either theoretical elaborations, empirical research or criminal policy discussions.
Studies coming from other scientific disciplines can also be considered if they are relevant to the criminological domain.
The editorial board consists of academics from the criminological research institutes of the Vrije Universiteit Brussel(VUB) and the Universiteit Gent(UG).
All manuscripts are reviewed by at least two referees.

Editorial Board:

Coverillustration: The 'Snow'-capped City of Antwerp (Belgium)
Coverdesign: Danny Somers

© 2000 VUB University Press
Waversesteenweg 1077, 1160 Brussels - Belgium
Fax ++ 32 2 6292694
e-mail: vubpress@vub.ac.be
ISBN 90 5487 284 5   NUGI 661
D / 2000 / 1885 /040

For Kristien and Kaat

ACKNOWLEDGEMENTS

Over the three years I have been working on the research described in this book I have incurred many debts. First and foremost, this study would not have been possible without the support of my wife, Kristien Vingerhoets. Ever since our marriage she has had to cope with my manifold absences and my fatigue during the fieldwork phase, with my irritability and unpredictable mood swings during the phase of writing, and with my narrow-mindedness throughout the whole study. Her little notes of encouragement and her patience have helped me to complete this work. She also, in her readings of early drafts, kept the reader's viewpoint in front of me, with her insistent demands for clear and straightforward prose.

I also wish to thank my parents, Luc Decorte and Betty De Preter, and my brother Jeroen, who, among other things, encouraged me to continue at times when I did not seem to have the courage. They put up with me, they believed in me. They have my love and my eternal gratitude.

The foundations for this book lie in my work in the field of drug care, where as a student I soon learned that the natural setting is at least as important for understanding drug users' lives as the therapeutic setting. In 1992, during my apprenticeship at the Free Clinic in Antwerp, Annemie Van Cauwenberghe and Dr. Sven Todts were the best tutors I could hope for. Since then, both our professional cooperation and our friendship has grown continuously.

Prof. Dr. Em. Lode Van Outrive *(Catholic University Leuven [Belgium], Research group Police and Judicial Organisation)* and Prof. Dr. Joris Casselman *(Catholic University of Leuven [Belgium], University Centre for Psychiatry)* supervised this study. In particular, I wish to express my gratitude for the fact that they both allowed me to enjoy a maximum of academic freedom, for their sincere sympathy and understanding at times of personal grief and despair, and for their encouragement and wise criticism at better times.

Not only did Prof. Dr. Em. Lode Van Outrive invite me to be a member of his research group at the Catholic University of Leuven in September 1992, but during the subsequent years he also initiated me into the art of qualitative research. He taught me, among other things, the importance of 'non-governmental sociology' and how to integrate criminological theory and fieldwork.

Prof. Dr. Joris Casselman supervised the development of my doctoral dissertation and improved this manuscript with his expert touch. I have profited greatly from his extensive knowledge of alcohol and drug related issues. First, as supervisor of my licentiate's thesis on methadone, and later, as tutor for my doctoral thesis, it was Dr. Joris Casselman more than anyone else who put me on the road to being a drug researcher.

With Prof. Dr. Peter Cohen *(University of Amsterdam, Centre for Drug Research)* I have had many discussions on drug policy and drug research in Belgium and elsewhere. Together with the work of Dan Waldorf, Craig Reinarman, Sheigla Murphy, Norman E. Zinberg, Jean-Paul Grund, Harold S. Becker, John B. Davies, and Douglas

Acknowledgements

Husak, his work shaped my ideas and insights to a large extent. If you, reader, feel inclined to say 'that idea came from' any of those people it probably did.

Appreciation to Prof. Dr. Peter Cohen is not only due for his permission to use (an important part of) his semi-structured questionnaire, but also for his crucial assistance with the analysis of cocaine samples. I also wish to thank his junior researcher Arjan Sas for his patience and benevolent cooperation in processing the data. I have bombarded him countless times with questions on matters of detail.

Other colleagues have also helped me at various stages of my work. At various moments, Stefan Bekaert *(Catholic University of Leuven, Centre for Africa Studies)*, Bart Cambré *(Catholic University of Leuven, Research group Police and Judicial Organization)*, Frederik Maes *(Catholic University of Leuven, Centre for Educational Policy)*, Tomas Van Reybrouck *(Ghent, Centre for Alcohol and Toxicomania)*, Jean-Pol Wydoodt *(Brussels, Association for Alcohol and other Drug-related Problems)*, Dr. Sven Todts *(Antwerp, Free Clinic)* and Prof. Dr. Geert Vervaecke *(Catholic University of Leuven, Department of Penal Law, Criminal Procedure and Criminology)* read early versions of the manuscript and provided many valuable comments and suggestions.

In particular I would like to thank my former colleagues Johan Van der Borght and Wauter Van Laethem, for making the 'third floor' a boisterous and a jolly research group, and my former office-mate Bart(jes) Cambré, for his bluesy empathy, filthy jokes and sincere anti-smoking efforts. Anita Van Cleynenbreughel provided secretarial support to the project. Her constant friendliness, her flawless management of research budgets and red tape, and her delicious coffee, were a welcome relief.

I would also like to express my gratitude to Hilde Vautmans, who has helped me to locate and interview ten respondents. She has spend numerous hours 'moonlighting' after hours as a criminology student. Her moral support inspired me with confidence to complete the final product.

Nobody has read this book more closely in advance than Dr. Marc de la Ruelle, who devotedly took charge of the linguistic correction. In looking over more than 800 pages of preliminary drafts he did not neglect to point out inconsistencies and oversights in the text, but he is certainly not to blame for any errors that remain.

Chapter 13, on the quality of cocaine, could not have been written without the contribution from Dr. Crista Van Haeren *(Brussels, National Institute for Criminology and Criminalistics, N.I.C.C.)*. Martine Dethy *(Brussels, Anti-Prohibitionnist League)* has provided invaluable assistance in translating both questionnaires into French.

I also thank my new colleagues, Prof. Dr. Paul Ponsaers and Prof. Dr. Patrick Hebberecht *(Ghent University, Department of Penal Law and Criminology)*, for creating the space to finish this book, despite the workload in Ghent, and for the encouragement during the last months.

Finally, this study would not have been possible without the help of the many people who were the subjects of my research. For reasons of confidentiality I am unable to identify these genuine experts by name, but I am, nevertheless, grateful for the access they allowed me to their lives. Their attempt to break the taboo is a courageous first step towards a grounded debate on drug use. I hope their trust has not been misplaced.

Thanks are also due to the many people who helped this research by allowing me access to the various settings where potential respondents could be contacted. Similarly, identifying these people by name could harm the confidentiality of the respondents' identity. I owe a special debt to Ivo Van den Broeck who helped me in many ways, not least in sharing the many late nights of fieldwork.

Even with all that expertise I could never have written this book without regular breathing spaces with my dear friends from Bruges, Antwerp, Brussels, Mechelen, Leuven, Aalst, Ghent, Catania (Sicily), Sijsele, Mariakerke, Beernem, Lier, Loppem, Tienen, Berg, and Leiden (The Netherlands). On February, 3rd 1998 my dear friends Sebbe, Roosje, Hadewich, Stefaan and my soulmate Stefan 'Bekie' Bekaert were snatched from our midst because of reckless flying of an American army pilot. I am truly grateful for what we had, but I cannot help but think everyday of what more we could have had...

Tom Decorte
July, 31st 2000

This research was supported, in part, by grant No. G.0197.96 from the Fund for Scientific Research *(Brussels, Fonds voor Wetenschappelijk Onderzoek, F.W.O.).*

TABLE OF CONTENTS

INDEX TABLES AND FIGURES

Wherever small coding differences between the various community studies of co-caine users remain possible, we have added the symbol [♠] to tables or figures, indicating that one should be cautious with interpretation of the figures.

Chapter 4

Chapter 5

Chapter 6

Chapter 7

Chapter 8

Chapter 9

Chapter 10

Chapter 11

Chapter 12

Chapter 13

Chapter 14

Chapter 15

Chapter 16

Chapter 17

Chapter 18

Chapter 19

INTRODUCTION

The initial impetus for the present study

Anyone who takes the use and/or the abuse of drugs as a subject for scientific research faces a provocative challenge. The large variety of individual patterns of use and the complex search for an adequate and legitimate drug policy require this research to start from the most elementary propositions. But what is known about the nature and the extent of drug use in Belgium?

As far as drug epidemiology is concerned, Belgium is still in its infancy. Figures and data about drug use in general have been incomplete and fragmentary. Reasons for this are manifold: as the possession and the use of drugs (such as cocaine) are illegal and subject to a repressive policy, it is very difficult to reach and study populations of users. The result is an unknown, but presumably a high dark number. Secondly, like anywhere else, the nature and extent of (il)legal drug use are susceptible to fashions and trends. The availability, the purity and the price of drugs, the law enforcement efforts, the preventive and curative strategies, the social, (sub)cultural and economic forces at work, etc. influence the prevalence and the socio-cultural meaning of drug use. Thirdly, different epidemiological methods have yielded information on divergent subgroups of drug users, each of which may show specific characteristics of use. And there may be other subgroups that remain to be discovered...[1]

But in our view there is a more substantial explanatory factor, which has little to do with the inherent limitations of epidemiological methodology. Thorough knowledge about the nature and extent of any drug use has never been a priority for Belgian policymakers. There is even some doubt as to whether there has been a drug policy at all in Belgium... It was not until very recently that the need for a uniform registration of drug problems, for scientific research into drug use, and for an 'integrated' drug policy has been acknowledged by the Belgian government (De Ruyver & De Leenheer, 1994).

Part of the initial impetus for the present study was the observation that drug epidemiology in Belgium is scarcely out of its infancy.[2] A summary of the official statistics available and the main findings from population surveys, utilization studies and ethnographic research on cocaine use in Belgium into a mosaic configuration showed that many of the mosaic stones are still missing (Van Daele *et al.*, 1996).

First, when epidemiologists are unable to give simple answers to those who call for hard figures, politicians, journalists, and even treatment specialists and prevention officials resort to *official statistics and figures* published by the various federal and regional services and institutes, e.g. on seized drugs or drug-related deaths. Official figures, however, are very poor indicators of the nature and the extent of drug use. They contain so many limits and biases that it is both impossible and dangerous to draw general conclusions about drug use and its consequences. Official figures may tell us something about law enforcement efforts, priorities of law enforcement agencies, the hub function of Belgium in the international drug trade, prices and purity of specific drugs, the prevalence of HIV seropositivity among intravenous drug users, and even possible rises in media attention for drug-related topics... But they only show the tip of the iceberg, they are incomplete and yield few, if any, answers to questions such as whether the use of illegal drugs is increasing or decreasing? How many of the current users of any drug end up as compulsive abusers? How does drug use relate to specific life-styles, (sub)cultural characteristics, etc.?

Second, *population surveys* into the use of (il)legal drugs in Belgium are fragmentary and restricted to specific population segments or limited territorial areas (special city districts or single regions in rural areas). The indicator commonly used in this kind of research is *prevalence*: the number of drug users in a certain population at a specific time. The main recent population surveys in Belgium tend to focus on the young, especially on secondary school pupils (aged 14-18). This particular group has been studied regularly in other countries as well.[3] First of all, national and international comparison is hampered by different sampling and data collection methods. Second, these studies generally seem to support the idea that illegal drug use among young people has increased, while a closer look at the data reveals that cannabis accounts for most of it. Reported levels of lifetime experience with cocaine and heroin are generally below 1%. Furthermore, the proportion of frequent users of any drug is even smaller. And third, it must be kept in mind that school surveys (which focus on the schoolgoing young) yield information about initiation into drug use and experimental drug use by adolescents, rather than about prolonged drug use by adults (Wydoodt & Booms, 1997: 2). Again, these studies do not provide answers to questions such as: how many of the experimental users continue to use as they get older and how many youngsters start using drugs after they have left school?

Utilization studies reflect the characteristics of drug using individuals who have had contact with treatment institutions and judicial agencies. Systematic registration of data on regular users of (il)legal drugs by these agencies gives some insight into sociodemographic characteristics, the nature and the extent of (poly) drug use, sources of income, drug-related crime, changing trends in problematic drug use and so on... Clearly, the bulk of our knowledge on the nature and the extent of drug use is based on data from institutional settings such as hospitals, prisons, and treatment agencies. Respondents are primarily drawn from known, visible and easily accessible subpopulations: problem drug users demanding treatment (either voluntarily or under judicial pressure), or users identified by police or judicial agencies. Regarding the latter group, these figures yield more information about the activity of police and judicial agencies rather than about the real extent of drug use. As for the former group, utilization studies might only reveal some characteristics of those who end up in trouble (the 'worst case scenarios').

What is most striking is the complete lack of *qualitative data* on drug use in Belgium. Research that seeks to study drug users in general, and cocaine users in particular, from within their culture, rather than from outside, and to present their world as users see it, is not available. Although such an ethnographic approach, which tries to comprehend drug users' behavior from the 'native point of view', has been frequently applied in other countries, it has not been popular in this country, probably because the 'natives' concerned here have been defined as deviant by the dominant societal forces.

Only two Belgian studies have drawn their respondents partly from the ranks of the hidden population of drug users. Kinable *et al.* (1994) set up a double action research with the intent of preventing HIV risk behavior in intravenous drug users. In an attempt to make a valuable contribution to the de-marginalization of drug users, Blanquart (1996) studied the creation of a drug users' organization ('vzw DEBED') from within. By learning from users what they were doing and why they were doing it, both qualitative studies are first steps towards a better understanding of the meaning of the experience of drug use in the context of users' lives. Yet, their results do not allow to infer encompassing statements about drug users in general and cocaine users in particular. They do not shed any light on the nature and the extent of cocaine use in Belgium (or Flanders). It is clear that purely ethnographic studies, which have been lacking so far in Belgium, would provide a solid foundation for public policies that could reduce the harm caused by drugs.

In short, we have several indicators of drug use in general, although these may be biased and focused on specific groups (the young, problem drug users, intravenous drug users,...). But there is much more we do not know about drug use in general, and about cocaine and crack in particular. Findings based on the best known, most visible, accessible, and maybe most marginalized subgroups of drug users reveal only a partial picture of drug use patterns. Moreover, observing or interviewing respondents with the intent of affecting their lives in any way (helping, controlling or treating them) tends to bias research findings.

The present study makes use of an ethnographic approach which has its roots in both cultural anthropology and sociology. Clifford Geertz (1973, 1983) has argued persuasively that because human beings are suspended in webs of significance and meaning that they themselves have woven, one can comprehend their behavior best 'from the native's point of view'. With this 'thick' description, the present study wants to make an original contribution to the field of drug epidemiology by describing a sample of cocaine users from within their culture rather than from outside it, and to present their world as they see it. We wanted to offer a description of our sample from the perspective of the cocaine users themselves (*the insider's view*). These analytic descriptions may be closer to the way drug users are seen and responded to within their own sociocultural context than to the portrait painted by some health professionals, law enforcement agencies, politicians, and media reports.

General focus of the present study

Coca has been used for thousands years. Societies may change their opinions on coca(ine) over time, and have in fact often done so. What is defined as a 'drug', what forms of drug use are regarded as acceptable and unacceptable, the way in which any given drug is used, and how the use of drugs is socially controlled, are matters which have been addressed in sometimes radically different ways at different times and in different places. Furthermore, the effect and the social significance of drug use are at least partly culturally constructed. The prohibition of cocaine is a relatively recent phenomenon. Nevertheless, none of the bans on cocaine have been successful in convincing users to abstain. While the quasi-monopolized production of coca by South

American countries keeps increasing, (new) black markets are created and flourish. This conclusion leads Grund (1993: 269) to state that: *'Drugs are here and they are here to stay. Society must thus learn to live with their use, minimize the harm of use and turn it to its benefits as much as possible.'*

Still, the use of cocaine and crack is not without risks. The literature illustrates the range and seriousness of problems that accompany cocaine use or are directly caused by it. There is evidence that those who chronically use (crack) cocaine face a number of potentially serious physiological, psychological and behavioral problems. It is not, however, implied that such effects are inevitable repercussions of cocaine use. Contrary to the popular fallacy that each drug has the same effect on every user under diverse sets of conditions, many important distinctions must be considered when describing the effects of cocaine: the confluence of physiological and psychological factors, the route of drug administration, the dose, the acute and the chronic effects of cocaine, occasional, habitual or compulsive use patterns, etc... (Grinspoon & Bakalar, 1976). Therefore, individual experiences may differ from the standard descriptions of the pharmacological and physical effects of cocaine presented by numerous authors.

Moreover, as most research has been based on highly selected samples of users –i.e. those in treatment or in health care programs- they tend to represent the extremes of the continuum of cocaine users: those most at risk for physiological problems and those with health problems that are not necessarily related to their drug use. Too often, these clinical studies are used to generate prevalence rates for such problems among the general population of cocaine or crack users. From the very start, the present study has assumed a critical attitude towards this *pharmacocentrism,* which is often the subtly implicit paradigm of drug research.

Overemphasizing the pharmacological effects of any drug may lead to underestimating the importance of set and setting factors. Whether the balance between use and abuse tips to either side, depends not only on the pharmacological properties of a drug, but even more strongly on personality characteristics and socio-cultural factors. Drugs are not the root of the problems. They are the epiphenomenal expression of deeper, structural dilemmas. Self-destructive drug abuse is merely the medium for desperate people to internalize their frustration, resistance and powerlessness (Bourgeois, 1995: 319-325). Thus it is important to understand that the contemporary exacerbation of substance abuse within concentrated pockets of the population (in the U.S. and in other countries) has little to do with the pharmacological properties of the particular drugs involved.

Norman Zinberg (1984) has organized the multideterminants of drug effects into three interactive categories: set, setting and substance. Set represents the physical and hereditary characteristics of the user, his or her personality, and his or her emotions and expectations. Setting consists of the physical, social and cultural environment in which the drug use occurs. As will be shown in this study, there are countless set and setting factors that interact in producing a response to drug taking. Zinberg has also argued that it is the social setting, through its development of informal social controls, that brings the use of illicit drugs under control. Therefore, the *general focus* of this research is informal control mechanisms or self-regulation by illicit drug users. In order to understand how and why certain users have lost control over drugs, we have to tackle the all-important question of how and why many others manage to achieve control and maintain it.

Preliminary notes on crack (cocaine) or freebase

To clarify the terminology of crack cocaine and freebase we present some preliminary information on crack (or freebase) here.

Crack, also known as 'rock' or 'freebase', is (a simple variant of) cocaine (Bean, 1993: 1-10). In this form, cocaine is taken by smoking through a pipe or a similar device. Smoking crack or freebasing generates a very rapid and powerful response. The process of converting cocaine hydrochloride, the powdered or crystal form of cocaine, entails the elimination of hydrochloride through the use of baking soda or ammonia, water and heat (Shaffer & Jones, 1989: 16-17; Siegel, 1992). This process eliminates many of the contaminants that were involved in the production of cocaine. Crack presumably got its name from the crackling sound generated by the burning sodium bicarbonate. Because crack is smoked, it provides an almost instant 'rush' as it passes through the blood-brain barrier in approximately six seconds. Crack highs are 'higher' and its lows (cocaine 'crash') are lower than those of intranasally or orally ingested cocaine.

Although a sizable, albeit unknown, proportion of America's cocaine users began freebasing in the late 1970s or early 1980s, the term crack had not yet entered the lexicon (Siegel, 1982: 183-212; Williams, 1992: 9; Shaffer & Jones, 1989: 17; Inciardi, 1988: 3; Inciardi *et al.*, 1993: 6). Crack did not become recognized as a public problem until the so-called crack summer of 1986, when it was portrayed as a drug that was immediately addictive and a great menace (Erickson *et al.*, 1994: 23). Crack epidemics were soon reported in most large American cities (Belenko, 1993: 9-32). Press reports and some of the scientific literature gave the impression that it was a completely new drug. True, the distinction between freebase and crack is often confusing. While some authors make a clear distinction between both products,[4] most authors agree that the processes of converting cocaine hydrochloride, the powdered or crystal form of cocaine, into crack and into freebase are almost identical, and that both terms actually refer to the same process or at least to the same end product (De Bie & Bieleman, 1995: 8-9).[5]

The current differences between freebase and crack relate only to the manufacturer and the method of selling. If made by a dealer rather than by the users, crack can contain more adulterants, and retail dealers tend to sell crack in small, inexpensive units, often on street corners and out of crack houses (Waldorf *et al.*, 1991: 105). One of Waldorf's respondents told him that the difference between freebasing and crack use was like 'the difference between preparing a gourmet meal and going out to McDonald's'. Other authors (and other respondents) agree: crack has been marketed and sold like a fast food product, relatively consistent in quality, easy to obtain, and affordable to most consumers. Like a 'Big Mac', crack is precooked, prepackaged, relatively inexpensive, and always available in major American cities (Shaffer & Jones, 1989: 16-17; Waldorf *et al.*, 1991: 104).

In the United States, the major transformation brought about by the introduction of crack has been the change in marketing methods. Crack offered an opportunity to expand sales in unprecedented ways because it was packaged in small quantities that sold for as little as two to five dollars (Williams, 1992: 10). This allowed dealers to attract a new class of customer: the persistent poor (Williams, 1990: 24-28). Crack cocaine is commonly sold on the streets of most American major cities, and recently in smaller cities as well, as urban gangs have enhanced distribution by expanding geographically. Crack has been widely believed to be cheaper than powder cocaine, and this 'fact' has been used to help explain why in the U.S. drug problems worsened in the 1980s. However, crack is not, in fact, cheaper per pure unit than powder cocaine. Price analyses have shown that crack and powder cocaine are equally expensive, but qualitatively different (Caulkins, 1997).

In Europe, reliable data on crack consumption are still lacking in many countries despite high levels of concern. Crack smoking has emerged in certain cities in France (Domic, 1996; Boekhout van Solinge, 1996: 53-73; Institut de Recherche et Epidémiologie de la Pharmacodépendance, 1992), the Netherlands (Grund, 1993: 207-217; Kruyer, 1997: 4-9; Grund *et al.*, 1991), the United Kingdom (Shapiro, 1993; Bean, 1993; Shapiro, 1994; Leitner *et al.*, 1993) and Scotland (Ditton *et al.*, 1991; Scottish Research Group, 1993; Ditton & Hammersley, 1996), Germany (Perkonigg *et al.*, 1998; Kemmesies, 1995, 1996 and 1997), and Spain (Anta *et al.*, 1993; Diaz *et al.*, 1992; Bieleman *et al.*, 1993).[6] It is unclear for how long the practice of freebasing has been around in *Belgium,* as there are no reliable sources available. But we do know that, analogously to the drug scare in other countries, there was a short period of panic about the emergence of crack in Belgium. When the police found that the number of burglaries and other violent crimes had markedly increased in the otherwise relatively 'calm' neighborhood of Matonge (community of Elsene) in Brussels, a special task force was installed. In November and December 1993, several crack 'laboratories' were impounded, and several Africans (mainly from Zaire) were arrested.[7]

The Flemish media reported that *'in most cases, a single dose of crack is addictive',* *'crack users are very aggressive*[8], *'the police figures about the number of crack addicts in the Matonge district in Brussels predict a new, alarming trend*[9]. According to the police spokesman crack users were capable of doing insane things: *'For some months we have seen some coloured persons roam around Matonge, who are extremely agitated and who do not seem to realize what they are doing. After a hold-up by daylight (...) six police officers were needed to overpower one of the gangsters who had been smoking crack just before the hold-up. The man went on like a fearless and indomitable animal'.*[10] But after this very short period of drug scare, nothing was heard again about crack traders or users, at least not in the media or the scientific literature. At that time (late 1993), it was suggested in the media that crack (or 'putulu' as it is also called according to one newspaper article)[11] had been introduced via the Zairian community in Paris, who had known the product for some years. If that is true, it is odd that no new attempts were made by the Parisian traders to set up crack laboratories. Another valid explanation could be that the laboratories that were impounded at the end of 1993 were merely an opportunistic attempt by some small groups of individuals to commercialize the well-known practice of freebasing.

Whatever the case may be, since then media reports on crack (or freebasing) have been very scarce, and scientific research on this topic is virtually non-existent. It remains unclear whether the Belgian situation differs from other settings. One of the goals of the present study is to shed some light on the practice of smoking crack cocaine (freebasing) in Belgium, compared to 'crack' in America and England, to 'cooked coke' in the Netherlands, to 'caillous' in France, to 'basuco' in Spain and to 'crack' in Germany.

Structure of the present study

This book is organized in twenty chapters. Chapters 1 and 2 are based mainly on existing literature and constitute the *preliminary groundwork*. They present the general focus and the conceptual framework of the present study, and discuss the research methodology. Chapters 3 to 19 present the *empirical results*, and Chapter 20 offers a discussion of these findings and *general conclusions*.

This study focuses on informal control mechanisms or self-regulation by drug users. Through an overview of the literature, *Chapter one* draws up the main theoretical principles of our study. The phenomena of 'controlled use' and 'cessation of drug use' are first discussed, because they indicate that consumption of an illegal drug does not necessarily lead to 'abuse' and/or 'addiction'. A crucial factor in the controlled use of any drug, according to Norman Zinberg (*Drug, Set and Setting. The basis for controlled intoxicant use*, 1984), is the social setting, with its capacity to develop (new) informal social sanctions and rituals (informal controls), and its transmission of information in numerous informal ways. Building on Zinberg's central thesis, we explore possible determinants of these informal controls and the potentially negative effects of formal drug policy on the processes of self-regulation through Jean-Paul Grund's feedback model of self-regulation (*Drug use as a social ritual*, 1993).

After making the goals of the present study explicit, *chapter two* explains the research methodology of non-randomized snowball sampling. Apart from some theoretical considerations on this chain referral technique, we describe the sample acceptability criteria, the procedure for composing the zero stage sample, a technique for screening for biases in the nomination process, and the instruments for data collection.

In *Chapter three* the Antwerp sample (N=111) is described with general social and economic variables (age, gender, nationality, education, profession, income, marital status and living situation) and, wherever possible, compared with data from other studies. Fifty-five 'registered' or 'known' respondents (who had either been found guilty of a felony, or had been in a drug treatment program) were compared with the rest of the sample. And finally, the chapter contains some data on the respondents' social networks (i.e. of other users 'known' to them).

Chapter four presents data regarding cocaine use initiation (age at initiation, initiation into the use of other drugs, initiation company, location of first use, first route of ingestion, way of obtaining first cocaine, and dosage at initiation). The data are compared with other major community cocaine studies. To gain a better understanding of possible interactions between drug, set and setting factors, this chapter subsequently discusses the circumstances of initiation into drug use. And finally, the process of social learning related to the use of cocaine is described following the three stages of Howard Becker's classical essay 'Becoming a marihuana user' (*Outsiders*, 1963): learning the technique, learning to perceive the effects, and learning to enjoy the effects.

One of the conditions for a rational discussion of drug use is that the concept of 'use' is defined clearly, and, where possible, quantified. In *chapter five* the use of cocaine in the Antwerp sample is described with exactly the same variables as in a comparable cocaine study in Amsterdam: dose, frequency of ingestion per week, level of use, distribution of occasions of use during a week, and patterns or changes of use during the user career.

In *Chapter six* we explore six different routes of ingestion of cocaine: snorting, injecting, eating, freebasing, smoking and application on genitals. Furthermore, as most users have experience with more than one route of ingestion, this chapter discusses the factors influencing the choice of route of ingestion. Opinions about routes of ingestion can be interpreted as the equivalent of rules of use. Therefore, this chapter presents the advantages and disadvantages ascribed to snorting, injecting and freebasing by our respondents. Special attention is given to those opinions that are not based on the respondents' own experience.

Compared to other community samples of cocaine users, freebasing is a more prominent route of ingestion in our Antwerp sample. *Chapter seven* presents more detailed data about freebasing cocaine in our sample. It discusses the Antwerp freebasers' vocabulary that illustrates the conceptual confusion among users. It describes the processes of making and using freebase cocaine, the Antwerp respondents' experiences with 'freebasing' and/or 'crack', and the differences between 'crack' and 'freebase' as perceived by our respondents.

Chapter eight investigates the use of other drugs and the use of cocaine in combination with other drugs by members of the Antwerp sample and. Special attention is given to the prevalence of polydrug use in our sample. We also present some quantitative and qualitative data on suitable and unsuitable combinations of cocaine with other drugs, according to our respondents. The interviewees' accounts reflect a kind of folk model of drug effects and are interpreted as the equivalent of informal rules.

Any illegal drug is used within the context of supply and demand. *Chapter nine* presents mainly qualitative data on buying cocaine. Starting from the (subjective) experiences of users who buy their cocaine, the following issues are discussed: price variations, sources of cocaine, and location of cocaine purchase. Qualitative data on the user's knowledge on (types of) cocaine and (types of) dealers, on being ripped off, and on aggression by dealers, are discussed.

The distinction of 'good' and 'bad' quality cocaine helps the user to decide whether or not to buy from a particular dealer. Furthermore, most respondents take it for granted that the cocaine they buy or use is adulterated. In *Chapter ten* we present our data on the quality of cocaine (between August 1996 and April 1997). The chapter analyzes the opinions of our Antwerp respondents with respect to adulterants in the cocaine they use, and to the effects of amphetamines (or 'speed') in cocaine, as perceived by our respondents. The results of a test for impurities and the cocaine hydrochloride percentage in 30 Antwerp samples are shown, and an account of testing methods used by our Antwerp respondents is given.

Whereas descriptions of the negative effects (or disadvantages) of cocaine are universal, many studies on drug use tend to minimize the positive effects (advantages) of drugs. This suggests that the use of illicit drugs yields positive experiences or advantages in the beginning of a user's career only and that eventually the balance always tips to the negative effects or disadvantages. *Chapter eleven* presents data on the advantages and disadvantages of cocaine, and on the prevalence of (adverse) effects of cocaine, as perceived by our respondents.

In drug debates and in media reports it is often claimed that one line of cocaine inevitably leads to another, relentlessly in ever increasing doses. This suggests that a drug such as cocaine has the same effect on every user under different sets of conditions: physiological disturbances, health problems, and eventually, dependence and/or addiction. *Chapter twelve* presents data on respondents who report periods of abstinence (of one month and sometimes much longer), on cocaine users who seem to be able to cut back (i.e. to reduce dosage or frequency, without becoming abstinent or quitting), and on respondents who decided to quit cocaine use definively. The data contradict the inevitability of repercussions of cocaine use: the difficulties, if any, users encounter in temporarily abstaining, cutting back or quitting are not insurmountable.

Similarly, the desire ('craving') for a drug is commonly seen as an inevitable physical or pharmacological effect that may be so strong that many, if not most, people are unable to resist and continue taking the drug, in spite of negative or even life threatening consequences. It follows that the drug is assumed to exert power over a user who often becomes its victim. *Chapter thirteen* examines this mysterious desire for cocaine with two kinds of indicators. It summarizes some objective measures of desire elaborated in previous chapters. It presents our data on the subjective experience of craving by our respondents. And finally, it presents both quantitative and qualitative material on the kind of (illegal) activities our respondents engaged in to obtain (money to buy) their cocaine.

Understanding the drug experience requires more than knowledge of the pharmacology of the drug. Norman Zinberg's investigations on the social rituals and rules of drug use have shown that a person's emotional and social situation has a significant impact on drug use. Set and setting may determine not only the choice of drug itself, but also the effects of its use. *Chapter fourteen* presents data on rules of use applied by our respondents, categories of persons with whom respondents would definitely not use cocaine, and financial limits on cocaine purchase. This chapter also focuses on emotional states (sets) and situations (settings) that were reported by our respondents as (un)suitable for cocaine use and its qualitative data illustrate the set and setting factors that either facilitate or hamper respect for the personal rules of use.

All Antwerp interviewees acknowledge that some forms of cocaine use have negative consequences and others are relatively safe. The qualitative data in *chapter fifteen* illustrate the users' concepts of 'controlled' and 'uncontrolled' use, or 'risky use' and 'safe use', or 'use' and 'abuse'. First, a catalogue of indicators for controlled and uncontrolled use is constructed. Then, the process of confirmation of boundaries and informal rules through counter-examples is illustrated. Becker's ideas on the role of social learning in illicit drug use are tested again: how do people become 'controlled' users? And finally, the respondents' recommendations for a drug policy relating to cocaine are discussed.

Illicit drug use in general, and cocaine use in particular, takes place in a special social context, and those around the user often respond in particular ways. The social contexts of use thus are affected by the use, and in turn influence it. Parents, siblings, partners, fellow workers, and friends are major sources of social responses to illicit drug use, and indeed of efforts to control behavior that is judged as problematic. In the context of everyday life, the family holds a special place. *Chapter sixteen* explores the patterns of interactions between cocaine users and their family (i.e. parents and/or siblings). It discusses successively the effects of the family on the respondents' cocaine use, the effects of our subjects' cocaine use on their family life, the taboo surrounding illicit drugs within the family, the respondents' views on parenthood and illicit drug use, and the specific role of siblings. All these data are added to the general context of socialization into cocaine use.

Chapter seventeen addresses the effects of cocaine use on the respondent's relationship with his/her life companion. Both quantitative and qualitative data illustrate the positive and negative effects of cocaine on these relationships. A separate paragraph is devoted to the ambivalent reputation of cocaine as an aphrodisiac. Second, the impact of the partner on the respondent's cocaine use pattern is analyzed. Obviously, the partner of a drug user responds in some particular way to the use. His/her actions and reactions can stimulate the user to use cocaine (and other illicit drugs), to curb the drug use, or both.

Chapter eighteen discusses cocaine use at work, by using qualitative data on the function of cocaine in three occupational sectors (the hotel and catering industry, the arts-related professions, and the sex industry). It presents both quantitative and qualitative data on frequencies of working under the influence of cocaine and other substances in the Antwerp sample, on the effects of cocaine on three work-related issues: quality of work, quantity of work, and working relations with fellow workers and employers, and on the negative effects of cocaine use in the workplace. If social modeling and structural factors of the workplace act as a barrier against cocaine use in the workplace, they can be seen as mechanisms of informal social control. Qualitative data on how these factors can encourage or discourage illicit drug use are discussed.

In *Chapter nineteen* we analyse the effects of cocaine use on friendships, and the influence friends have on the respondents' cocaine use. Friends play an important role in the initiation and the development of cocaine use patterns of our subjects. The most salient findings regarding the role of friends are assembled from other chapters. Like in the other chapters, we analyze comments from respondents to other cocaine users and remarks from other users to the respondents, to illustrate informal social control among friends. Finally, the respondents' accounts about informal help among cocaine-using friends and emergency situations/overdoses are also discussed.

In *Chapter twenty* we summarize the main empirical results of our study following the three specific research goals set at the end of Chapter 1. First, the Antwerp sample of 111 experienced cocaine users is described in general terms. Then, our empirical results regarding informal control mechanisms (rituals and rules), their socialization, and the possible interaction between formal control and informal control are presented. Finally, some final reflections are made, together with some policy and research recommendations.

Cocaine use in European and American cities: major community samples

In order to check whether the people interviewed in the present study are similar in their patterns and experience of cocaine use, the empirical data of the Antwerp study are regularly compared with the findings of other community cocaine studies. In the chapters to follow, these studies are usually referred to briefly. However, there are some differences between these studies. Therefore, we present an overview of the research design of the major community studies of cocaine users since 1985 (see Table A).

Table A   Major community cocaine studies

Site	Author(s)	Date of study	N
1. Miami	Chitwood & Morningstar (1983)	1980-81	75
2. Toronto	Erickson *et al.* (1994)	1983	111
3. Australia	Mugford & Cohen (1989, 1994)	1986-87	73
4. San Francisco	Waldorf *et al.* (1991)	1986-88	267
5. Amsterdam	Cohen (1989)	1987	160
6. Scotland	Scottish Cocaine Research Group (1993, 1996)	1989-90	133
7. Toronto	Erickson *et al.* (1994)	1989-90	100
8. Turin	Merlo *et al.* (1992)	1990-91	100
9. Barcelona	Diaz *et al.* (1992)	1990-91	153
10. Rotterdam	Bieleman & de Bie (1992)	1990-91	110
11. Amsterdam	Cohen & Sas (1993)	1991	64
12. Amsterdam	Cohen & Sas (1995)	1991	108

None is identical, although some were designed with comparability in mind (especially Merlo *et al.* 1992, Diaz *et al.*, 1992, and Bieleman & de Bie, 1992). Some separate studies were carried out by the same researcher (Cohen, 1989, Cohen & Sas, 1993 & 1995) and some used questionnaires (partly) designed by others. Both the present study and the study by the Scottish Cocaine Research Group used Cohen's 1989 questionnaire, while Cohen borrowed several questions from the questionnaire used by Morningstar & Chitwood in Miami (1983).

1. MIAMI (1980-81)

CHITWOOD, D.D. and MORNINGSTAR, P.C. (1985), Factors with differentiate cocaine users in treatment from nontreatment users, 20 *International Journal of the Addictions* 3, 449-459.

This study was designed to investigate differences between patterns of use and between groups of users. The research setting was Miami and data were collected from April 1980 to June 1981. A structured interview schedule was administered to a 'purposive' sample of 95 treatment clients and 75 non-clients all of whom reported cocaine to be a primary drug of use. Treatment clients were drawn from an existing population of cocaine users who recently had entered treatment, while non treatment respondents were selected through a snowball sampling procedure designed to tap a wide variety of separate user networks. The difference in the sex ration, ethnicity and occupational level of the two user groups were not statistically significant. Cocaine dealers above the ounce redistribution level, adolescents under 18 years of age and upper class users were excluded.

2. TORONTO (1983)

ERICKSON, P.G. *et al.* (1994), *The Steel Drug. Cocaine and crack in perspective*. New York: Lexington Books.

The research challenge was to locate a group of fairly typical cocaine users in the community rather than those who had presented themselves for treatment or had been in trouble with the law. The principal criteria for selection in the study, in addition to some experience with cocaine in the last three years (i.e; at least once), were that participants must be 21 years of age and must have been employed at least six of the past twelve months. Students were deliberately excluded because as a group they are relatively detached from conventional adult roles and from community standards of drug use behavior. A total of 111 participants were obtained with the snowball sampling technique from two separate sources: personal contacts (47) and an advertising campaign (64). An in-depth interview was conducted with each respondent.

3. AUSTRALIA: SYDNEY / CANBERRA / MELBOURNE (1986-87)

MUGFORD, S.K. (1994), Recreational cocaine use in three Australian cities, 2 *Addiction Research* 1, 95-108. MUGFORD, S.K. and COHEN, P. (1989), *Drug use, social relations and commodity consumption: a study of recreational cocaine users in Sydney, Canberra and Melbourne*. Report to Research into Drug Abuse Advisory Committee, National campaign against drug abuse.

The primary goal was to gather information covering the 'how, what, when, where, with whom' questions of cocaine use. Mugford and Cohen (1989) wanted typical recreational users – that is, users who had not presented for treatment or had been arrested for a cocaine offence. The aim was to assess these typical users and determine the distinctive characteristics of their use of cocaine. To this end, data were collected through two means: a self-completed questionnaire and an open-ended in-depth interview. The overall method of sample selection involved snowball sampling from initial starting points. The snowball procedure generated a sample of 73 recreational Australian cocaine users in the cities of Sydney (40), Canberra (20) and Melbourne (13). Present or past users were accepted, although current non-users had to have used within the last eighteen months. A fairly broad definition of use was adopted. People were included even if they appeared to border either on experimental use or on compulsive-intensive use.

4. SAN FRANCISCO (1986-88)

WALDORF, D., REINARMAN, C. and MURPHY, S. (1991), *Cocaine changes. The experience of using and quitting*. Philadelphia: Temple University Press.

By far, the most comprehensive ethnographic study of cocaine users was conducted by Dan Waldorf and his colleagues Craig Reinarman and Sheigla Murphy. During the two-year study they interviewed 267 persons, including a main sample of 122 current users and 106 quitters. In addition to the main sample, they also included a follow-up sample of 21 users who were first interviewed in 1974 and reinterviewed in 1986, and a sample of 53 crack and freebase users. Respondents were traced through snowball sampling. An in-depth, life-history interview was conducted with all these respondents.

The project staff recruited and trained a number of specific people to assist them in locating and interviewing black and Latino users, women, freebasers, special occupation groups, college students, and gay men. The general focus of the study was cocaine, so subjects with other drug problems were excluded. Anyone who had used four or more ounces of distilled spirits (or the equivalent in wine, beer, or any combination) per day for at least sixty days in a row within ten years was excluded. They also excluded anyone who reported using any opiate, metamphetamine, or barbiturate daily for two weeks or more within a ten-year period prior to the interview. Persons who were in treatment, prisons, jails, or other institutions were also excluded, as were people on probation or parole. The criteria for inclusion specified both amount and length of cocaine use in the hopes of tapping the most serious or heavy users. Any person who used an average of two or more grams of cocaine per week for at least six months, or who used any amount daily for at least twelve months, was included.

5. AMSTERDAM (1987)

COHEN, P. and SAS, A. (1989), *Cocaine use in Amsterdam in non-deviant subcultures*. Amsterdam: Instituut voor Sociale Geografie.

The original goals of this investigation were to gain more insight into patterns of cocaine use among groups not normally associated with problematic drug consumption. The intention was to find out how such patterns developed, what mechanisms for controlling cocaine consumption (if any) could be observed, and if problems with cocaine use could be detected.
In the months February, March and April 1987, 160 persons with a minimum cocaine use of 25 life time instances were interviewed. Other sample acceptability criteria were: respondents should neither have been found guilty of a felony, nor should they have been in a drug treatment program at any time during the last two years. Users from so called deviant subcultures (junkies, criminals, prostitutes) were excluded. The sample was selected by means of a snowball method with random selection of the next respondents from a list of nominees made by the interviewed person. The interview schedule was half structured.

6. SCOTLAND (1989-90)

SCOTTISH COCAINE RESEARCH GROUP (1993), 'A very greedy sort of drug': portraits of Scottish cocaine users, 76-98. In: BEAN, Ph. (ed.), *Cocaine and crack. Supply and use*. New York: St. Martin's Press. DITTON, J. and HAMMERSLEY, R. (1996), *A very greedy drug. Cocaine in context*. Amsterdam: Harwood Academic Publishers.

The Scottish Cocaine Research Group (SCRG) was established in March 1989 to see whether any Scottish cocaine users existed, and, if so, whether they resembled uncontrolled high-dose American crack smokers or controlled low-dose Amsterdam snorters. It was decided to adopt the snowball method of contacting respondents, and to use a modified and translated version of Cohen's (1989) questionnaire. To qualify as a cocaine user and thus for inclusion in the study group, users had to have used cocaine at least once in the past three years. Seventeen members of the SCRG interviewed cocaine using subjects known to them or suggested by other interviewees. These interviews were conducted in Glasgow, Edinburgh, Dundee, Aberdeen, Ayr and at other Scottish locations. Some 92 respondents were contacted using the snowball method and a further 41 recruited via a Glaswegian evening newspaper.[12] Subjects obtained by the two recruitment methods were sufficiently similar to be analysed together, although the newspaper-recruited subjects tended to be younger, have lower incomes, and more of them were poly-drug users.

7. TORONTO (1989-90)

ERICKSON, P.G. *et al.* (1994), *The Steel Drug. Cocaine and crack in perspective.* New York: Lexington Books.

This time, Erickson *et al.* were interested in current users who had moved beyond the stage of experimentation to a more regular pattern of use. The principal criterion was use of cocaine at least ten times in the past twelve months. Commencing in early 1989, Erickson and her colleagues interviewed 100 users in the community and reinterviewed 54 of them one year later. The sample was recruited from adult cocaine users who lived in the metropolitan Toronto area. The major vehicle for publicizing the study was through advertisements inviting those with recent experience with cocaine, aged 18 years or older, to call a number at the Addiction Research Foundation (ARF). Despite efforts to build snowball referral chains through those responding to the advertisements, this approach produced very few additional contacts with cocaine users. Again, in-depth interviews were conducted with these respondents.

8. TURIN (1990-91)

MERLO, G., BORAZZO, F., MOREGGIA, U. and TERZI, M.G. (1992), *Network of powder. Research report on the cocaine use in Turin.* Ufficio Coordinamento degli interventi per le Tossicodipendenze.

This study has been partially funded by the European Community, and was designed for a comparative analysis of cocaine use in Turin, Barcelona and Rotterdam. The general object of the study was to gain wider knowledge of the phenomenon of cocaine use and to organize all our information thereof, both qualitatively and quantitatively, in order to define feasible policies for prevention, therapy and rehabilitation. Specific objects were: definition and identification of the different populations of cocaine users, description of their sociocultural-environmental characteristics and of their types of relation with the substance; estimate of the prevalence size in the identified populations; indications on the organization of the market structure.

Apart from a network analysis and analysis of contextual data (such as emergency room episodes, police operations, and daily newspapers), a sample of 100 cocaine users was recruited through snowball sampling. A group of six interviewers (3 men and 3 women) was formed by selecting persons who were already involved in various environments of possible contacts with users or of diffusion of substances. Each of them was a key providing access to different environments: health center for drug addiction (SER.T.), criminality, the world of art and public entertainment, social and political circles of young people, entertainment places ('targeted sampling'). The questionnaire contained two separate sections: a qualitative part (centred on the interviewee) and a quantitative part (focusing on nominees).

9. BARCELONA (1990-91)

DIAZ, A., BARRUTI, M. and DONCEL, C. (1992), *The lines of success? A study on the nature and extent of cocaine use in Barcelona.* Barcelona: Ajuntament de Barcelona.

This study has been partially funded by the European Community, and was designed for a comparative analysis of cocaine use in Turin, Barcelona and Rotterdam. The main aim of this study was to achieve a thorough knowledge about the nature and extent of the phenomenon of cocaine use in order to be able to design suitable policies for prevention and action by the health authorities based on the results of the research. A total of 18 interviewers were selected on the basis of training and experience in carrying out in-depth interviews, but also some knowledge about the drug phenomenon, their ability to relate to people and their position within the different settings with which the researchers intended to get in touch. The preferential circles of cocaine users were: elite (fashion, business, art, etc.); new urban middle class (qualified professionals, professions related to the nightlife world and other people of middle status involved in the fashion, business and art worlds); young people; criminal circles and opiate addicts; workers (middle status and middle-low status).

The main criterion for inclusion was that individuals must have used cocaine at least 5 times during the last six months or at least 25 times in their lifetime. By using the snowball method and a nominative method, a total sample of 153 cocaine users was obtained. The interviews were open and semi-directed (semi-structured). The questionnaire used consisted of a qualitative and a quantitative section. The content of both sections, in its essential aspects, was agreed by the working teams of the three cities of Turin, Barcelona and Rotterdam in order to facilitate the comparability of the results.

10. ROTTERDAM (1990-91)

BIELEMAN, B. and DE BIE, E. (1992), *In grote lijnen. Een onderzoek naar aard en omvang van cocaïnegebruik in Rotterdam.* Groningen: Intraval.

This study has been partially funded by the European Community, and was designed for a comparative analysis of cocaine use in Turin, Barcelona and Rotterdam. As in the Turin and Barcelona studies, the general object of this study was to gain wider knowledge about the nature and extent of the phenomenon of cocaine use in order to be able to design suitable policies for prevention and action by the health authorities based on the results of the research. Data were gathered through a combination of snowball sampling and targeted sampling. Targeted settings were: the world of hard drugs, youth circles, art and music worlds, world of fast money, hasj users, illegal and semi-legal circles (prostitutes, drug dealers, youth criminals), students, and sport and fitness worlds. Eventually, a total sample of 110 cocaine users was obtained. Several methods of recruitment were used: fieldwork (28% of total sample), prison (11%), key informants (7%), treatment centers (13%), advertising in local newspapers (17%) and nominated by other respondents (24%). The criteria for inclusion was that individuals must have used cocaine at least 5 times during the last six months or at least 25 times in their lifetime; and living in Rotterdam.

11. AMSTERDAM (1991)

COHEN, P. and SAS, A. (1993), *Ten years of cocaine. A follow-up study of 64 cocaine users in Amsterdam.* Amsterdam: Instituut voor Sociale Geografie.

In this report, Cohen and Sas describe 64 persons who on average started their regular cocaine use career some 6 years before they interviewed them for the first time in 1987. Seeing them for the second time in 1991, the period since first regular use had increased to ten years. The main goal of this study was to look at the development of use patterns in the original respondents since they were first seen in 1987. Cohen and Sas wanted to know if a proportion of the 1987 respondents developed problem-related patterns of use. The same interview schedule was used in 1991 as in 1987, with a few small changes. However, for those who had stopped using cocaine, a short interview schedule was designed.

12. AMSTERDAM (1991)

COHEN, P. and SAS, A. (1995), *Cocaine use in Amsterdam II. Initiation and patterns of use after 1986.* Amsterdam: Instituut voor Sociale Geografie.

This report is a sequel to the first cocaine use investigation (Amsterdam, 1987) and describes a sample of 108 persons who on average started their regular cocaine use career in 1985 or later. Main goal of this investigation was to find out whether cocaine had remained attractive to the same type of persons as found by Cohen in 1987, or that changed publicity about the drug had modified both type of users and patterns of use. Respondents were identified using a snowball sampling technique very similar to the one used in the 1987 study. To be included, individuals must have started consuming cocaine in 1986 or later, and at the time of the interview, to have used cocaine a minimum of ten occasions. In the current study, as in 1987, non-deviant cocaine users were defined as those not engaged in full-time prostitution or full-time criminal activities. So-called junkies were also excluded.

A note on references to other cocaine studies

This book is based on both semi-structured questionnaires and in-depth, life-history interviews with 111 experienced cocaine users, recruited through a chain referral technique (a more elaborate description of the methodology of this study is presented in Chapter 2). Both the present study and the study by the Scottish Cocaine Research Group used Cohen's questionnaire (1989: 129-158), who in turn borrowed several questions from Chitwood and Morningstar (1985). This semi-structured questionnaire was slightly modified and 'translated'.[13] Furthermore, we have added some open-ended questions relating to the specific goals of the present study (informal control mechanisms).

In some tables and figures in the chapters to follow, we have presented our quantitative data alongside those of the other major studies of cocaine users in European and American cities. We have tried hard to reduce the risk of coding differences to an absolute minimum, thereby lessening problems of comparability. Nevertheless, we were not able to solve all these minor coding problems. *Wherever small coding differences remain possible, we have added the symbol [♠] to tables or figures, indicating that one should be cautious with the interpretation of the figures.* Both in the text and in the tables or figures we will mostly use brief references to these studies, such as Miami (1980), San Francisco (1986-88), Toronto (1989-90), etc. The reader will notice that most of the comparative data are taken from the 1987 Amsterdam I study and the 1991 Amsterdam II study by Peter Cohen and his team from the Centre for Drug Research, because these data were more easily accessible to us.

NOTES

[1] However, recent efforts both on a national and an international level have shown great promise for a more complete and less fragmented knowledge about the nature and the extent of drug use and abuse.

[2] This does not imply that drug treatment specialists and prevention workers in the field lack sufficient expertise and knowledge about possible use and abuse of drugs in general and cocaine in particular. Our summary of available data on the nature and the extent of cocaine use can only take into account scientific and/or specialist publications.

[3] It is important to keep in mind that on both the national and the international level, comparison between different surveys is hampered by different sampling and data collection methods and by analyses which employ incompatible categories or measures. The situation is slowly improving, as more and more countries recognize the value of a consistent series of surveys repeated every few years as trend indicators, and as projects to improve comparability are beginning to pay off. This need for adequate data collection on drug use has only very recently been recognized by Belgian government officials.

[4] According to some authors, the terms 'crack' and 'freebase' refer to two different ways of production: crack is obtained by mixing cocaine with sodium bicarbonate and water, and then heating it. After cooling off, a kind of cake is formed that is broken into little rocky lumps ('rocks'). These lumps of crack are preferably heated on an aluminum foil or in a pipe, and the vapors are inhaled. Freebase, another form of smokable cocaine, is obtained through a much slower and complicated process, in which the freebase is purified with various techniques, until almost 100% pure cocaine base is obtained. See for example: INCIARDI, J.A. (1987), Beyond cocaine: basuco, crack, and other coca products, *Contemporary Drug Problems*, 461-492.

[5] See also: INSTITUTE FOR THE STUDY OF DRUG DEPENDENCE (1993), *Drug notes: cocaine & crack*. London: ISDD.

[6] See also: E.M.C.D.D.A. (1997), *Annual report on the state of the drugs problem in the European Union*, 13. Lisboa: EMCDDA.

[7] 'Mission anti-crack in Brussels' [our translation, 'Opération anti-crack à Bruxelles'], *Le Soir*, November, 30th 1993. 'Crack discovered in the Matonge district' [our translation, 'Crack ontdekt in Matonge'], *De Standaard*, December 7th, 1993. 'Crack pops up in the Matonge district' [our translation, 'Crack duikt op in Matonge'], *Het Volk*, December 3rd, 1993. 'Breakthrough of crack leads

to increase in crime' [our translation, 'Doorbraak crack leidt tot toename criminaliteit'],*Het Laatste Nieuws*, December 1st, 1993.

8 'Matonge-district in Brussels flooded with crack. Within a few weeks dozens of youngsters addicted to "the poor man's cocaine" [our translation, 'Brusselse Matongewijk overspoeld door crack. Tientallen jongeren op enkele weken verslaafd aan "cocaïne voor de armen"'], *De Morgen*, December 3rd, 1993. 'Crack pops up in the Matonge district in Brussels' [our translation, 'Crack duikt op in Brusselse Matonge-wijk'], *Gazet van Antwerpen*, December 4th, 1993.

9 'Again a crack laboratory rounded up' [our translation, 'Opnieuw crack-labo opgerold in Elsene'], *De Morgen*, December, 7th 1993. 'Eight million worth of drugs found in the district of Elsene' [our translation, 'Voor acht miljoen drugs gevonden in Elsene'], *Gazet van Antwerpen*, December, 7th, 1993.

10 Our translation. 'Crack discovered in the Matonge district' [our translation, 'Crack ontdekt in Matonge'], *De Standaard*, December 7th, 1993.

11 'Breakthrough of crack leads to increase in crime' [our translation, 'Doorbraak crack leidt tot toename criminaliteit'], *Het Laatste Nieuws*, December 1st, 1993.

12 In addition, and at various times (but mostly during early 1995) an additional 24 Scottish cocaine users were interviewed using a qualitative schedule which covered much the same ground as the main quantitative instrument. See: DITTON, J. and HAMMERSLEY, R. (1996), *A very greedy drug. Cocaine in context*, 19. Amsterdam: Harwood Academic Publishers.

13 Although Dutch ('Nederlands') is the official language in both Belgium (together with French and German) and The Netherlands, Cohen's questionnaire (1989: 129-158) required some modification: certain (particular) expressions, especially in the domain of drugs, needed 'translation'.

CHAPTER 1

THE TAMING OF COCAINE:
THEORETICAL PERSPECTIVES ON INFORMAL REGULATION OF DRUG USE

1.1. INTRODUCTION

In the present chapter, the main theoretical principles of this book and the general set of questions addressed through it are elaborated through an overview of the literature (built up as a collage of verbatim quotes). The *general focus* of this study is informal control mechanisms or self-regulation by illicit drug users. In order to understand how and why certain users have lost control over the drug or drugs they are using, we have to tackle the all-important question of how and why many others manage to tame it, that is: achieve control and maintain it.

In paragraphs 1.2 and 1.3 the concepts of 'controlled use' and 'cessation of use' are discussed, because they illustrate the existence of a wide range of patterns of use and because they indicate that consumption of an illicit drug does not necessarily lead to 'abuse' and/or 'addiction'. Indeed, in order to understand the drug experience, we have to take into account more than just the pharmacology of the drug (= 'pharmacocentrism') or the personality of the user (= 'pathologification'). Controlled users do exist and factors other than the power of the drug and the user's personality (and his/her physical condition or corporality) are at work.

Paragraph 1.4 presents Zinberg's investigations (1984) that focused on the physical and social settings in which use occurs. Embroidering on his central thesis that the social setting, with its capacity to develop (new) informal social sanctions and rituals (informal controls), and its transmission of information in numerous informal ways (§1.5), is a crucial factor in the controlled use of any drug, we shall explore possible determinants of these informal controls (§1.6) and the potentially negative effects of formal drug policy on the processes of self-regulation (§1.7), by presenting a theoretical model by Grund (1993).

Based on the literature survey on informal control mechanisms by illegal drug users presented in this Chapter and on the conclusions that were part of the initial impetus of the present study, paragraph 1.9 presents the three specific research goals of the present study.

1.2. CONTROLLED USE

1.2.1. Control over licit and illicit drugs

As we explained above, most observers from both professional and lay circles define any use of an illicit drug as 'abuse'. For them the very concept of 'controlled use' is a contradiction in terms. Yet, the generally accepted view that drug use inevitably leads to loss of control is challenged by common knowledge about varying use patterns of licit drugs such as alcohol and nicotine, and by a bulk of scientific studies on controlled use of illicit drugs. This paragraph reviews some of these studies.

Cigarette smokers have long displayed an array of use patterns (Black, 1984). Most of us know the common two-pack-a-day smoker who always seems to have a cigarette in hand, and many of us personally know how difficult it is to stop smoking. But we also know at least some smokers who smoke only after dinner, or who routinely limit the places where they smoke (not at work, not in the car, etc.) or the number of cigarettes they consume in a day.

Drinkers demonstrate similar controlled use patterns in far higher proportions than smokers. The hopeless alcoholic who drinks continually is but one pattern. By far the majority of alcohol users – and alcohol is a hard-drug!- drink in controlled ways: with meals, outside of working hours, in limited amounts, or only on ceremonial occasions such as weddings and seldom at inappropriate times. Moreover, a significant portion of persons with drinking problems who do not enter formal treatment either abstain from alcohol completely or become moderate drinkers (Humphreys *et al.*, 1995).

However, this knowledge about varying drug use patterns is not often generalized to illicit drugs. With few exceptions, most of the writing and research on drug users up to the 1970s expressed presumptions that people could not use illicit drugs in controlled ways. If the possibility of non-abusive use was acknowledged, it was usually treated as a very brief transitional stage leading either to abstinence or more probably to compulsive use. An early exception to the dominant paradigm was Howard Becker. In his classic study of the processes of becoming a marijuana user (1963), he writes: 'The user is not using the drug all the time. His use is scheduled; there are times when he considers it appropriate and times when he does not. The existence of this schedule allows him to assure himself that he controls the drug and becomes a symbol of the harmlessness of the practice. He does not consider himself a slave to the drug, because he can and does abide by his schedule (...) Test are made -use is given up and the consequences awaited- and when nothing untoward occurs, the user is able to draw the conclusion that there is nothing to fear.' (Becker, 1973: 76)

Although it was well known even then that in order to understand how control over drugs could be developed, maintained, or lost, different patterns of consumption had to be compared. This principle had long been applied to the comparative study of patterns of alcohol use (alcoholism as opposed to moderate drinking), but it was not until the mid-1970s that the existence and importance of a still wider range of using patterns became recognized by (a part of) the scientific community. Since then, a bulk of new research on controlled drug use and addiction has uncovered some surprises. A brief overview of the landmark studies is presented here.

1.2.2. Control over opiate use

The most influential work has been that of Lee Robins and her colleagues, whose research on drug use among Vietnam veterans indicated that consumption of heroin, the illicit drug that the public considers the most dangerous, did not always lead to addiction or dysfunctional use, and that even when addiction occurred it was far more reversible than was popularly believed (Robins *et al.*, 1977; Robins *et al.*, 1979). Robins estimated that at least 35% of enlisted men tried heroin while in Vietnam and that 54% of these became addicted to it. Although the success of the major treatment modalities available when these veterans became addicted cannot be precisely determined, evaluations showed that relapse to addiction within a year was a more common outcome than abstinence, and recidivism rates as high as 90% were reported.

Nevertheless, as Lee Robins and her colleagues have shown, most addiction did stop at the South China Sea. For addicts who left Vietnam, recidivism to addiction three years after they got back to the United States was approximately 12% - virtually the reverse of previous reports. Apparently it was the abhorrent social setting of Vietnam that led men who ordinarily would not have considered using heroin to use it and often become addicted to it. Yet, once outside the horrendous war setting, the pharmacological power of heroin simply did not by itself lead to an inevitable or permanent addiction. Bill Hanson's team came to similar conclusions after in-depth interviews with 124 black heroin users from the ghetto-life in Chicago, New York, Washington D.C. and Philadelphia (Hanson *et al.*, 1985).

These findings were followed by those of Norman Zinberg, a professor of psychiatry at Harvard Medical School. From 1973 to 1981 he undertook a series of related studies of people who used heroin, LSD or other psychedelics, and marihuana in controlled, non-addictive ways. Zinberg (1984) was able to demonstrate that occasional heroin users did exist, and in numbers larger than anyone had believed. He set out to learn what kinds of controls they employed to avoid the addictive patterns that had been thought inevitable. In general, Zinberg and his colleagues found that informal sanctions and controls effectively influenced many people to control their drug use and prevent problems over long periods. Because his ideas have been crucial to the initial impetus of this book, a separate paragraph is devoted to his work (see below).

Blackwell (1983) studied the characteristics of opiate users who avoided becoming chronically dependent. Tracking down long-term recreational opiate users is the ultimate challenge for outreach research. In her paper, Blackwell identifies 51 such users and divides them into three groups according to the method they employ to control their drug consumption:

*Drifters (*11 respondents, 22 %)
=   Casual users, who are relatively unimpressed with the psychotropic effects of narcotics and for whom other aspects of life compete strongly for time and resources.

*Controllers (*22 respondents, 44 %)
=   Those who respond to their strong attraction to opiates by making even stronger rules governing their use and by being aware of the effect of drug use both on themselves and other users.

Overcomers (18 respondents, 34 %)
= Those who allow the process of habituation and/or dependence to develop but become past masters or mistresses at the art of ending dependent episodes.

All three groups in her study displayed a degree of self-motivation and introspection greater than that usually attributed to dependent users first entering treatment.[1] [2]

1.2.3. Control over cocaine use

Erickson *et al.* (1994) seriously questioned media depictions of cocaine as inevitably addicting or as curable only through treatment by professionals. After reviewing an array of animal studies, clinical studies, population surveys, and community studies, they concluded that the potential for controlled cocaine use has been understated in the scientific literature. In embarking on a study of 111 cocaine users (1983), they intentionally avoided a focus on the worst cases and tapped the experiences and perceptions of the more typical users, not those whose medical problems were well documented in the treatment literature or whose criminal status in society made them already marginal. She concludes: 'In all, few participants experienced serious chronic reactions.' and '...it was precisely the possible dangerous physical, social and financial consequences of crack addiction that kept most users away from regular use. The more that users perceived risks of harm in crack use, the less they used it. Yet this user rationality is ignored in claims that crack's pharmacological powers are omnipotent.' (Erickson *et al.*, 1994: 187).

In a second study of cocaine users in the community in 1989, Erickson and her colleagues interviewed 100 users and re-interviewed 54 of them one year later. To test the popular image of crack as powerfully addicting, Cheung, Erickson and Landau interviewed 79 crack users from Toronto. They concluded: '...there was little evidence that the use of crack is necessarily compulsive. Over half of the respondents had rarely or never experienced a craving to take crack. (...) It is clear that even if compulsive use had occurred before, reduction to infrequent use or abstinence was the pattern for the majority of crack users over time...'. These users controlled their use by avoiding people and situations where cocaine would be found, by limiting the amount used or the money spent, by abstaining, or by exerting self-control (Erickson *et al.*, 1992: 82-89).

In another article, Erickson and Alexander (1989) conclude, after having summarized studies of cocaine users in the community, outside of treatment and prison: 'Most social-recreational users can maintain a fairly low use pattern over lengthy periods without escalation to addiction. Users appear to recognize the need to limit their use of cocaine, and most seem to be able to accomplish this without professional intervention.'.

By far the most comprehensive ethnographic study of (heavy) cocaine users was conducted by Waldorf, Reinarman and Murphy (1991). Their book represents a study of three groups of cocaine users: (1) a main sample of 228 users (subdivided into 122 current users and 106 quitters); (2) a follow-up sample of 21 users who were first interviewed in 1974 and re-interviewed in 1986;[3] and (3) a sample of 53 crack and freebase users. Again, the most salient finding of this study was the wide variability found in the use-abuse continuum. For both cocaine and crack users, there was no uniform progression or pattern of use. Indeed, although many developed problems because of their cocaine use, about half of the participants maintained a controlled pattern of co-caine use, some of them even for up to a decade.

Waldorf *et al.* (1991: 265-266) defined controlled use as 'regularly ingestion of (co-caine) without escalation to abuse or addiction, and without disruption of daily social functioning' or 'a pattern in which users do not ingest more than they want to and which does not result in any dysfunction in the roles and responsibilities of daily life.'[4] For example, use that results in any chronic, disruptive problems with health or work is not controlled. But in their definition, occasional nasal sniffles, irritability, or even weekend *binges* without proper eating and sleeping do not necessarily constitute loss of control any more than dehydration, headaches, and occasional nausea after nights of drinking constitute alcoholism.

They estimated that approximately 50 percent of their respondents who were using at the time of interview did so moderately and in ways that minimized negative effects and maximized positive effects. Some of these men and women had previously used the drug heavily during occasional binges or periods of daily use, but had since reas-serted and maintained control. Even many of their respondents who had quit using had always been controlled users (Waldorf *et al.*, 1991: 143). Based on their observations, Waldorf and his colleagues offered something of an ideal type of controlled users:

- Controlled users tended to be people who did not use cocaine to help them manage preex-isting psychological problems, and did not also abuse other drugs, especially alcohol.
- Controlled users generally had a multiplicity of meaningful roles, which gave them a posi-tive identity and a stake in conventional daily life (e.g., secure employment, homes, and families). Both of these factors anchored them against drifting toward a drug-centered life.
- Controlled users, perhaps because they were more anchored in meaningful lives and identi-ties, were more often able to develop, *and stick to*, rules, routines, and rituals that helped them limit their cocaine use to specific times, places, occasions, amounts, or spheres of ac-tivity (Waldorf *et al.*, 1991: 267).[5]

Waldorf *et al.* also explored the strategies and the specific steps cocaine users took to quit. Their data suggested that serious cocaine users rarely have one, overarching problem which drives them to quit, but rather a complex of several problems that in-teract in unique ways within the context of their lives. When these interacting prob-lems accumulated to the point where they seriously disrupted valued aspects of users' daily lives, most made some move to cut down, exert control, or quit. However, many of their respondents regulated their intake of cocaine so that such problems either never developed or did not accumulate to the point of disruption or unmanageability.[6]

Given that their sample was designed to exclude all but very heavy users, Waldorf and his colleagues were surprised both by the wide variety of ways in which users manage to quit, and by the relative ease with which so many managed to do so (Wal-dorf *et al.*, 1991: 271). Their strategies for doing so, moreover, were fairly common-sensical social avoidance techniques designed simply to put distance between them-selves and the drug. On the other hand, while two in five sought new non-drug-using friends as a strategy, a majority did not; most had maintained such friends throughout their cocaine careers. Friends are a crucial part of getting into cocaine use and they also may be a crucial resource for getting out of it: 'Both friends and occupational roles reaffirm non-drug identities and bond people to conventional values and life-styles. Indeed, we suspect that one reason why so many of our users could control their use and why so many quitters could quit is because they did not undergo identity transformation as, say, heroin addicts so often do.' (Waldorf et al., 1991: 273)

In 1989, Cohen reported on a study of 160 very experienced cocaine users. The original goal of this investigation was to gain more insight into patterns of cocaine use among groups normally not associated with problematic drug consumption. The intention was to find out how such patterns developed, what mechanisms for controlling cocaine consumption (if any) could be observed, and whether problems with cocaine use could be detected. Cohen found many indications that experienced cocaine users controlled their use by adhering to snorting as their route of ingestion, by keeping cocaine consumption at a moderate level, and by associating consumption to a limited number of social circumstances and emotional states. The use of freebase cocaine was not popular, and carried a negatively charged emotional connotation, like intravenous drug use (Cohen, 1989: 13-19).

Support for the hypothesis that the pharmacological characteristics of cocaine make problematic (high) use patterns inevitable was not found. On the contrary, there were no indications that this group of experienced users lost control and developed into compulsive high level users with a marginalized life style in order to support drug consumption. Yet, users were aware of many adverse effects. Cohen concluded that criminalisation was more of a threat to these users than cocaine itself.

In a second report, Cohen and Sas (1995) describe another sample of 108 persons who on average started their regular cocaine use career in 1985 or later. As in 1989, their most important conclusion was that most users seem able to control their cocaine consumption by applying various rule systems. Typically users have pre-established limits regarding the amount of drug they will use, the amount of money they will spend, who they will make purchases from, the settings in which cocaine will be consumed and who they will share the experience with. They also tend to take into account 'risky use models' to monitor their own use and define particular emotional states as appropriate or inappropriate to cocaine consumption. External controls, such as low availability and heavy risk in purchasing, play a much smaller role.

In 1993, Cohen and Sas (1993) reported on a follow-up study of 64 cocaine users, who were re-interviewed in 1991, six years after their participation in the first cocaine study (1987). They found that almost half of the participants had terminated their use of cocaine since 1987, while for the other half use had stabilized at a lower level. Only 6% (4 respondents) of their follow-up sample had sought assistance to help them control or quit using cocaine. Cohen and Sas concluded that controlled use of cocaine was a common pattern exhibited among their 64 users.

Spotts and Shontz (1980) have provided the best in-depth profile of intravenous cocaine users. Using a representative case method, they selected nine males whose preferred drug was cocaine, each depicting a different life-style. The researchers emphasized the selection of intravenous users in order to obtain sufficient data either to confirm or to refute the myths surrounding the use of cocaine in its potentially most hazardous form. The following findings are of particular interest: most users felt a powerful attachment to cocaine but not to the extent of absolute necessity; cocaine unequivocally produced euphoric effects and a sense of well-being; low-dose users felt the drug enhanced social relationships; heavy users reported the converse; all agreed that cocaine was not physically addicting; many reported temporary tolerance; users reported extreme differences in intensity between intranasal and intravenous administration;

most intranasal users reported few serious adverse effects, nasal congestion and rhinor-rhea being most common. Similarly, most intravenous users did not report severe medical complications associated with use. In fact, none had ever received emergency medical treatment for drug-related conditions.

Siegel (1985) conducted an early follow-up study of cocaine users. Initially he re-cruited 118 users for a study in 1976; 99 of them were social-recreational users using at least 1 gram per month for twelve months. Sixty-one users participated in all phases of the first four years, and fifty of these participated in a follow-up study in 1983. All users reported episodes of cocaine abstinence, while twenty-five maintained their pat-tern of social-recreational use for nine years. However, four intensified their use, while five became compulsive users, most of them freebase smokers. Most users seemed to be able to develop strategies to adequately 'detoxify' or limit their use of cocaine, without professional guidance. In general, Siegel's study suggests that most social-recreational users can maintain a low to moderate use pattern without escalating to de-pendency and that many users can essentially 'treat themselves'.

Bieleman, Diaz, Merlo and Kaplan (1993) report on an intensive study of cocaine use in the cities of Barcelona, Rotterdam and Turin. In all, 363 cocaine users in the three cities cooperated with in-depth interviews. Through snowball sampling, targeted sampling and network analysis data were collected on an additional 1,635 cocaine us-ers who were the contacts of the interviewed users. They concluded that most patterns of use are integrated (or can be integrated) in society. They present mainly the intrana-sal route of ingestion, and do not seem to be either destructive or disruptive. Cocaine use can occur over many years, often in a discontinuous pattern. Most users maintain that cocaine has not caused them problems of a physical, psychic, social or relational nature. Compulsive and problematic use of cocaine is more related to the intravenous consumers of heroin and freebasing. Those who do not use heroin and of whom the large majority has no problems with cocaine, usually solve their own problems and do not need any form of assistance.

In another paper, Kaplan *et al.* (1992) presented a theoretical definition and empiri-cal analysis of the 'casual' user of cocaine. Data were drawn from a subsample of 58 cocaine users and their cocaine-using contacts in Rotterdam. Their theoretical defini-tion was systematically related to two social context variables: (1) the scope of settings where contacts used cocaine; (2) the degree of involvement in social network relations of actual cocaine use. Scope of settings was defined in terms of the number of cocaine-using circuits contacts are drawn from: i.e. 'narrow' setting where all contacts origi-nated from one circuit while a 'wide' setting indicates contacts came from two or more circuits. Involvement was defined in terms of the percentage of contacts where the re-lation with study participants was characterized by cocaine use most or all of the time. According to their hypotheses, a 'casual user' was someone with a wide scope of set-tings of contacts' use and a low involvement in social relations with those where fre-quent use of the drug occurs. The 'compulsive user' lived in a social network where there was high involvement of use with other cocaine contacts, and a narrow scope of settings. The 'controlled user' was someone who has a low involvement of cocaine use in his or her cocaine network, but who adapted to a narrow scope of settings. Their re-sults supported the finding that compulsive use is an exception when considering co-caine.

1.2.4. Other relevant studies

Apsler (1982) makes a distinction between five different styles of controlling use. Three of the control styles involve reliance on an external standard for making the decision of how much of a substance to use. The reliance is on 1) the amount others are using; 2) a regular amount that is commonly used; and 3) the amount specified by someone else, such as a physician. Conversely, the two remaining control styles involve reliance on an internal standard: using until 1) I feel the way I want; or 2) I get a strong feeling that I should stop. Thus the internal controls require that the individual test some internal index that changes as a substance is used. Apsler found that, with few exceptions, individuals who employ internal control styles score more negatively on the dependency scales, regardless of substance, than those relying on external control styles. In other words, respondents who rely on internal controls also tend to feel that they are more dependent on substances and that the substances are more likely to cause them problems in their lives, in comparison with respondents who rely on external controls.

These results suggest that the study of drug use involves much more than simply knowing the frequency and quantity of use. The way individuals control their use of substances is at least as important a dimension of drug use as is the actual amount of the substance ingested. Similarly, Grund (1993: 92) remarks that controlled use does not necessarily have to entail lower levels of intake. In his outstanding study on the determinants of drug use management and self-regulation, Grund observes that, within his study population of heavy (and marginal) users of cocaine and heroin, stability of use levels and successful prevention and management of drug use related problems may be more appropriate indicators of control. Control may best be perceived as a multidimensional process.

So far our selective overview of scientific studies on controlled use of illicit drugs. Needless to say there are many more books, articles and papers discussing the prevalence of recreational drug use, socially integrated drug use, controlled use, casual drug use, etc. (e.g. Powell, 1973; Zinberg & Jacobson, 1976; Harding, 1980; Weber & Schneider, 1990). We have demonstrated that controlled users exist.

Sceptical readers might object that a certain degree of control over the use of some types of drugs (such as cannabis and cocaine) may be feasible, but that controlled use of other types of drugs (such as heroin or crack) is beyond the bounds of possibility. For effective control, to them, it seems crucial whether or not a substance is considered to cause physical dependence (cocaine does not, heroin does). Yet, two of the most authoritative drug studies described above (Lee Robins on Vietnam veterans and Norman Zinberg) focused on heroin 'addicts'. Both studies indicated that consumption of the illicit drug that the public considers the most dangerous does not always lead to dysfunctional use. Even compulsive users exercise some degree of control. Although it may seem obvious now, these authors were struck by the fact that even people who use too much of the drug, did not use as much as they could have.

Moreover, the comparative study of control over *different* substances, including some that are not drugs (such as sugar and other foods) has shown that a wide assortment of these substances (tobacco, caffeine, sugar and various food additives) are potentially hazardous to health (Zinberg & Harding, 1982). It appears that both the idea that illicit drugs are altogether harmful and the idea that licit drugs are altogether benign, are myths...

Before addressing the general focus of this book -how and why illicit drug users manage to achieve control and maintain it- a concise overview of literature on 'cessation of drug use' is presented in the next paragraph. In our view, the analysis of how people manage to quit illicit drug use is quite similar to the investigation of control over illicit drug use. After all, is being able to stop using drugs not the ultimate proof of mastery over the pharmacological power of a substance?

1.3. STUDIES ON CESSATION OF DRUG USE

There have been many studies on the strategies and motives of people who were able to quit using illicit drugs in a relatively autonomous or 'spontaneous' way, i.e. without any professional help. In the following non-exhaustive overview of relevant literature, we have singled out four central concepts: 'maturing out', 'natural recovery' (or 'quitting'), 'drifting out' and 'models of change' (through relapse and recovery). On the one hand, these four distinct concepts probably refer to overlapping realities, but on the other, each of these terms has its own implicit theoretical inferences and seems to be 'contaminated' by different paradigms (such as the dominant medical or clinical vision).

1.3.1. 'Maturing out'

Charles Winick (1964) was one of the first to scientifically examine the processes of termination of addiction. He analyzed the records of the Federal Bureau of Narcotics (FBN) in order to determine how many people had been registered in the FBN files during the year 1955, and how many of them had disappeared from these files by the end of 1959, either because they were dead, or because they were abstinent. Winick concluded that, even if there were a higher than normal death rate among drug addicts, the trend was clear: most of the addicts became abstinent between the ages of 23 and 37. Considering the ages when they became addicted and the duration of the addiction, he found further evidence that the later they became addicted, the shorter their addiction. Winick hypothesized that, in the case of heroin addiction, for most (perhaps two out of three) addicts, addiction was a self-limiting process: 'After some time, drug addicts go through a kind of maturing-process, and the use of hard-drugs ceases to fulfill the initial functions. Most drug users kick the habit in a 'natural' way: at a certain moment, drugs become useless in their way of life.' (Winick, 1962: 1-17)

In this maturation process addicts have learned to handle their problems (as a result of role-strain and role-deprivation which they suffer in daily life) in some other way and, in the end, the negative sides of life as a junkie become too much to carry on. The finding that the later one became addicted, the shorter the addiction, was explained by Winick by stating that the self-limitation of drug use was possibly a function of the number of years one is addicted. At the time, Winick's proposition was surprising, since the dominant opinion on drug addiction was that it was a lifetime affair. From the moment of Winick's publication, researchers have tried to gather evidence for the confirmation or for refutation of his hypothesis. While most studies have found that at least some addicts do become inactive, the results have not been consistent and the existence and conditions of the maturing out process remain controversial.

Table 1.3   Representative studies relating to maturing out of addiction [7]

Reference	Sample	Follow-up period	approx. % achieving abstinence	% deceased	% still ad-dicted
Winick (1962, 1964)	16,725 reported to Federal Bureau of Narcotics in 1953-1954	5 yr	65% not reported to F.B.N. after 5 yrs		
Hunt and Odoroff (1962)	1,912 New York City addicts discharged from Lexington in 1952-1955	1-4½ yr	10% remained abstinent during follow-up period		
Duvall *et al.* (1963)	453 Lexington addicts stratified subset of Hunt and Odoroff sample	5 yr	25% voluntarily abstinent at time of interview		
O'Donnell (1964)	266 white Kentucky addicts admitted to Lexington 1935-1959. Sample representative for the state of Kentucky.	av. 10 yr	53% of living sample abstinent or occasional users at time of interview	14%	8%
Vaillant (1966, 1970, 1973)	100 New York City addicts admitted to Lexington 1952 (50% white, 50% black)	12 yr (1966) 20 yr (1973)	57% of living sample drug-free and in community at time of interview; in 1973: 35 to 42% (inclusive 27% since 1966	14% (1966) 23% (1973)	25% (1973) 32% (1966)
Ball *et al.* (1969)	108 Puerto Rican addicts admitted to Lexington 1935-1962	Av. 13 yr	19% abstinent for 3 yr prior to interview	n.a.	40-59%
Langenauer *et al.* (1971)	97 male addicts discharged from Lexington Clinic in 1968-1969	½ yr	14%		
Chapple *et al.* (1972)	108 London addicts, 1963-1965. Max. for 2 yr in Home Office files	5 yr	23%	16%	38-47%
Stephens *et al.* (1972)	200 addicts committed to Lexington under NARA law, discharged by 1969	6 months	35% not re-addicted by end of 6-month period	64.5%	
Snow (1973)	3,655 of the addicts reported to New York City Narcotics Register in 1964	4 yr	23% inactive, i.e., not reported to Register by 1968		
Nurco *et al.* (1975)	267 addicts from Baltimore, first offenders narcotics 1952-1971	10 yr	35%	n.a.	24%
Wiepert *et al.* (1978)	575 clients of 2 clinics of heroin prescription, London, 1968-1975	1-7 yr (2/3 of sam-ple: < 5 yr)	28%	11%	52%
Gordon (1978)	60 clients London clinic 1970	4 yr	43%	15%	23%
Stimson *et al.* (1978, 1979)	128 clients (representative sample of London opiate prescription clinics), 1969	7 yr	31% (25% >2yr)	12%	48%
Harrington *et al.* (1979)	51 narcotics offenders in Tucson in 1955-1957	20 yr	2% voluntarily abstinent at time of data collection		
Maddux and Desmond (1980)	248 San Antonio drug abusers admitted to Ft. Worth Clinical Research Center 1964-1967	10 yr	22% abstinent for 3 yr prior to interview	11%	31%
Bschor *et al.* (1984)	100 ambulant treated addicts, intakes 1969-1971, West-Berlin	10-15 yr	39%	20%	38%

(Sources: Swierstra, 1987; Anglin *et al.*, 1986)

Based on two overviews by Swierstra (1987) and by Anglin *et al.* (1986), Table 1.3 summarizes some representative studies on maturing out, mainly from the United States and England. Some variation in empirical results may be due to differences in data collection procedures (analysis of official files versus interviews with the clients themselves) and the varying social contexts (European versus American data, data from the 50s versus data from the 80s). Variation in results may also be due to differences in the definition of variables. For example, definitions of the major variable, 'abstinence', varied from purist (no opiate use at all, and only moderate alcohol and soft drug use) to elastic (irregular opiate use without manifest addiction). Moreover, the 'point of measurement' varied from one study to another: the criterion for abstinence was a minimum period of one month in one study, or at least three or even five years in another. In assessing the reliability of these studies, one has to bear in mind that 'abstinence' usually meant not being addicted throughout the whole follow-up period, while 'being addicted' usually referred to a particular moment in time.

Despite these methodological problems, all authors found that many addicts had ceased addicted drug use. Some degree of support for the concept of maturing out was found. In most of these studies the notion that cessation of drug use was related to age was accepted uncritically. From all these research findings Swierstra (1987: 78-92) deduced an abstinence and mortality curve, showing a remarkably consistent empirical regularity.

Although empirical support for Winick's early work was found, his explanatory model was generally rejected for being too simple and too broad. Most subsequent authors have suggested that the natural cessation from the addiction process may depend on a large number of contextual and etiological factors. Anglin and McGlothlin (1984) developed a theoretical model for assessing the more complex conditional relationships of maturing out over time. Having analyzed a predominantly white and Chicano sample of 406 male admissions to the California Civil Addict Program, they concluded that economic or sociopathic reinforcers related to crime suppress a relationship between cessation of drug use and age (Anglin *et al.*, 1986: 233-246). Without these reinforcers, older addicts tend to mature out. But with participation in any significant level of property crime or drug dealing, older and younger addicts tended to cease addiction in similar proportions and at a lower rate than those older addicts less involved in these criminal activities.

In later analyses, Anglin and his colleagues tested the influence of other variables. Their results suggested that while high personal resource levels of the addict do not increase the probability of maturing out with the passage of time, the existence of these resources affects younger addicts, increasing the likelihood that they will cease drug use early in their addiction careers. Ethnicity was not found to play a conditional role in the time-related maturing-out process, even when considering differences in resource levels (Brecht *et al.*, 1987). A strong maturing out pattern appeared among those addicts with some period of methadone maintenance treatment. On the other hand, the effects of legal supervision (e.g. parole supervision) did not seem to be related to the maturing out phenomenon (Brecht & Anglin, 1990).

In his summary of 19 follow-up studies, Swierstra (1987) concluded that only 'close social ties' clearly facilitate abstinence. Usually, this so-called social stability implied existing ties during and after the process of cessation, such as a steady job, a stable life (e.g. a marriage) or living environment, no contact with a drug subculture, the absence of criminality in the addict's way of life, etc. Abstinence facilitating factors in the users' past were: a stable family of origin and experience with a steady job, training or education. Contrary to the findings of Anglin *et al.* (1986), Swierstra (1987) concluded that not being part of an ethnic minority did play an abstinence facilitating role.

More recently, the search for a 'deep' understanding of the course of hard drug addiction has aroused researchers' interest in the maturing out theory. We will refer to one particular study only, because it clearly illustrates the psychological implications of the concept, which we shall deal with later. Based on autobiographical interviews with 65 hard drug addicts (located through the registration of a drug treatment center), Prins (1995) described a conceptual framework of drug addiction trajectories. He stated that especially young persons who were not securely attached, or were missing one or more significant others, suffered a slowdown in the development of their personal and social identity, i.e., the process of maturing. It slowed down because of a lack of opportunity for, and support by the performance of biographical work necessary to develop and build a personal and social identity. Under the pressure of crisis situations, this biographical work will nevertheless be performed in time and the process of building one's personal and social identity will eventually progress to reach a level that enables the person to handle the problems of life without the excessive use of exogenous means such as drugs.

Prins concluded: 'The conceptual framework of a drug addiction trajectory predicts then that for those who are essentially mentally healthy, that is to say for more than two thirds of all drug addicted people, the outcome of the process will be that they eventually will reach an adequate level of personal and social identity, that is, they will mature out and subsequently escape the trajectory and regain a life free of the use of heroin, cocaine, amphetamines, LSD...' (Prins, 1995: 104)

In conclusion, there is substantial empirical evidence that under specific conditions maturing out does exist. But the theoretical explanation of maturing-out with respect to the process of becoming abstinent remains controversial. Three majors critiques can be (and have been) made towards these studies.

First, almost all of these studies focused on the (ab)use of opiates (heroin). Studies on maturing out of the use of tobacco, alcohol, cannabis, cocaine, etc. have been rare. Yet, these might tell us much more about the degree to which users of any substance can achieve a life without it. More in particular, the maturing out thesis should be submitted to a renewed evaluation in the light of the phenomenon of poly drug use.

Second, the majority of the studies summarized above related to addicts who had (had) contacts with one form or another of professional treatment. First of all, the direct effect of treatment interventions on becoming abstinent of heroin is generally extremely difficult to measure. More importantly, there is no *control group* of individuals who have never been treated professionally, to compare with the clients studied at follow-up research. Furthermore, it is not even known how many heroin users have ever been in contact with treatment agencies, and how many never have.

Third, the psychological implications of the term 'maturing out' or the idea that drug use reflects immaturity (as suggested by Prins and others) was questioned by other researchers. O'Donnell (1964) found that abstinence from opiates occurred most often as addicts aged, but he concluded that their accounts offered no support for the maturation hypothesis (cf. table 1.1.). Maddux and Desmond (1980) found that while some former addicts attributed their abstinence to maturity, the concept did not allow to account for the variety of explanations they gave for quitting. And Waldorf and Biernacki (1981) argued that recent research on the developmental stages of adults had suggested that there were several age periods in which maturation took place, rather than a single phase. In another publication, Waldorf and his colleagues concluded that most of their subjects were by all outward indications mature people when they began their cocaine use -homeowners, responsible parents, successful workers- and so could not be said to have used cocaine because of immaturity.

'[…] we found no evidence in our in-depth interviews of any progression from immaturity and drug use to maturity and cessation. Indeed, the maturing out hypothesis smuggles into scholarship on drug use an insupportable assumption about abstinence that is rooted in temperance-era moralism: that fully developed human beings do not desire to alter their consciousness with drugs.' (Waldorf et al., 1991: 236)

1.3.2. 'Natural recovery' or 'quitting'

The first systematic review of literature related to the incidence of natural recovery from heroin addiction was done by Waldorf and Biernacki (1982). They concluded that: (1) contrary to general belief, spontaneous recovery is not a rare phenomenon; and (2) untreated addicts have equal possibilities to recover as those who are professionally treated.[8] Ever since, researchers have employed various concepts to indicate cessation of drug use without any professional intervention: 'spontaneous remission', 'self-change', 'natural recovery or resolution', 'untreated remission', 'quitting'... (e.g. Sobell *et al.*, 1991; Christo, 1998). Many individuals choose not to seek treatment because they perceive themselves as having been responsible for the development of their problem and assume that they are capable of overcoming it on their own; others have negative attitudes toward treatment and also wish to avoid the labeling process (for example, alcoholic, addict) and its concurrent stigmatization. Thus, self-change does not appear to be as spontaneous as the early concepts of 'natural recovery' and 'spontaneous recovery' suggest, for a number of factors have been found to be related to the initiation of change efforts (Marlatt *et al.*, 1988).

After interviewing both treated and untreated ex-addicts, Biernacki (1986) concluded that immersion in the social world of addiction (a life-style centered on hustling, copping, and getting high) and identification with that world are important to recovery. Contrary to popular stereotypes, he found different levels of immersion and social identification, the prototypical street addict being only one of three types. The other two resembled Matza's drifting delinquents (1964) (see below): they seemed either to be passing through the heroin scene without breaking ties with the conventional world, or they were only peripherally involved with heroin and had little commitment to either the conventional or the addict world.

The experience of recovery varied with the level of immersion and identification (Biernacki, 1986). Street addicts had a difficult time overcoming their addiction because so much of their lives hinged around the addict life-style and because they were excluded from conventional society. They typically had to experience rock bottom or some existential crisis before overcoming their addiction. Once they resolved to quit they remained stigmatized and had a difficult time finding a new social identity or a niche in society where they could function comfortably. As a result they often had trouble staying off heroin. The other two types had it easier because their immersion and commitment to the life-style were tenuous or fleeting; some just walked away from heroin and simply resumed their conventional lives.

Between 1985 and 1987, Waldorf *et al.* (1991) interviewed 267 heavy cocaine users. With the exception of a few cocaine sellers along with some young, working-class users who had little attachment to conventional work, most of their cocaine quitters were *not* deeply immersed in a drug-centered life-style. This led Waldorf and his colleagues to conclude: 'More often than not our quitters decided to stop using after concluding that the increasing negative effects they were experiencing, combined with the interaction of such effects with their lives and identities, simply made continued cocaine use undesirable. Under such conditions, many of our heavy users simply walked away from cocaine with little difficulty, often by using social avoidance strategies. Yet, in contrast to Biernacki's immersed street addicts, most (particularly the untreated) had less difficulty remaining abstinent because they were neither stigmatized by nor estranged from society. Thus, they had little need for major life-style changes.' (Waldorf et al., 1991: 239)

Shaffer and Jones (1989) reviewed the available research on the intrapersonal, biological, and social factors associated with people who stop using drugs, and compared these data with their own observations of natural cocaine quitters. In their more recent study *Cocaine changes. The experience of using and quitting*, Waldorf, Reinarman and Murphy (1991) added their own extensive and valuable findings to those of Shaffer and Jones. We shall briefly summarize the findings of Shaffer and Jones (1989: 89-99) on the reasons for quitting and the coping strategies for maintaining abstinence (see also: Gekeler, 1983; MDHG, 1987; Klingemann, 1991; Buntinx *et al.*, 1992).

Reasons for quitting

The process of self-recovery is similar for alcohol, opiates, cocaine, and, to a lesser extent, tobacco users. The chief reasons for terminating the use of various substances are similar. These motivations can be grouped conveniently into physical, social and intrapersonal categories. Some aspects of the quitting and recovery experience of illicit drugs may be dissimilar to recovery from licit drug use, because of the illicit character of certain drugs.

- **Intrapersonal reasons**: Researchers have found that users describe humiliating experiences, moving cognitive or emotional incidents, or shifts in the source(s) of gratification previously associated with their drug use. Similarly, people have reported that they hit a personal 'rock bottom', experienced a sense that they had lost control over their life, had a spiritual experience, or developed a stable source of increased hope and self-esteem.
- **Physical reasons**: Researchers in every area of natural recovery have reported health reasons. Self-quitters are motivated consistently by physical concerns. The problems range from a general concern about health to more specific allergic or physical distress on the one hand and an acute threat to life on the other (Brady, 1993).
- **Social reasons**: A growing sense of commitment to a loved one or a fear of losing an important relationship (Esbensen & Elliott, 1994; Willms, 1991; Brady, 1993) are the two most common reasons cited as precursors to natural recovery. The importance of acquiring a new, close relationship to self-quitting has been noted. Also, pressure from one's family, partner, or colleagues can provide an impetus to some self-quitters. Geographical changes, legal troubles and financial hardship have been described as other social reasons for quitting.
- **Illicit character of drugs**: Erickson and Murray (1989) state that formal controls seem to be irrelevant as barriers to continuing use, which implies that legal threats are perceived to be remote. Nevertheless, quitting illicit drug use can involve fear of legal ramifications and fi-

nancial hardships that are not observed with licit drug users. Moreover, unlike tobacco or alcohol, illicit drug supplies can dry up temporarily. Occasionally, quitters referred to this dry spell as a time when they began to consider terminating their use. Furthermore, because illicit drug use often involves the illegal selling or 'dealing' of the drug, quitters often experienced a dissonance between their personal values and their observed lack of standards while dependent on their drug.

Coping strategies for maintaining abstinence

The scientific literature is consistent about the strategies reported by natural recoverers for maintaining their newly achieved sobriety. These approaches include avoidance, self-reinforcement, social support, structure building, and substitutions (see for example: Kirby *et al.*, 1995).

- **Avoidance**: The most common strategy for (maintaining abstinence and) avoiding relapse is to remove oneself from the drug-using environment (geographical moves) and to break off social relationships with those friends who continue to use drugs (changing social circles). Many quitters attempt to avoid emotional crises and therefore have to pay attention to their affective states in a way that is quite different from when they were using drugs.
- **Self-reinforcement**: Research has demonstrated that physical aversion and negative association to a drug may help maintaining abstinence. Some users have found it helpful to activate both fears of relapse and positive reasons for abstaining. Others provide evidence that if they carry on an internal dialogue on the negative aspects of drug use, they are more effective in maintaining their status as ex-users.
- **Social support**: Social support from friends and family is very important in maintaining abstinence. Quitters report that they often practice a form of self-initiated social control by asking their friends to assist them in avoiding drug-use settings, provide recovery-oriented 'sponsorship' and hold the quitter accountable for his or her behavior.
- **Structure building**: Quitters change a multiplicity of social structures to maintain drug abstinence. These changes include attempts to create new, more positive interests and acquire new friends and social identities. Consequently, these new identities help to develop new activity patterns that promote assimilation into the drug-free social environment. Building new life structures includes a wide range of activities: emphasizing relationships, careers, and social responsibilities; cultivating new forms of intellectual stimulation; emphasizing self-development (such as learning new skills, entering psychotherapy); transforming the tendency to abuse health into health-promoting activities (such as jogging, bicycling, eating health foods); and, finally, developing a spiritual relationship.
- **Substitutions:** Some quitters have reported substituting religious involvement for their drug-using behaviors. Attending Alcoholics Anonymous has been substituted for drinking (Brady, 1993), and actively supporting social causes has been substituted for opiate dependence. Chemical substitutions (food for tobacco, coffee for alcohol, and alcohol for heroin) have been reported too. This chemical substitution itself can become excessive and lead to abuse. Others encounter patterns of over- and/or under-eating, or experience excessive sexual activity. One of the most interesting substitutions can be considered self-serving in character: some cocaine quitters report new interest in acquiring enormous power, wealth and influence.

While all these studies suggest that each quitter has a unique configuration of motives for giving up drug use, the aggregate data show that psychological and physical health problems, financial strain, and pressure from significant others are especially important. As well-being, love, and money are indeed central to human existence, it is not surprising that when users are harmed in one or more of these basic realms they will be motivated to quit.

Shaffer and Jones (1989: 127-129) distinguish two types of quitters ('rock bottom quitters' and 'structure builders'), and two quitting styles ('tapering' and 'cold turkey'). 'Rock bottom quitters' are people who become immersed in the drug world and the addict life-style to the point at which virtually all aspects of 'normal life' disintegrate and they are moved to quit. 'Structure builders' are people who do not necessarily experience dislocation because of their drug use, but who set about finding activities to take its place.

Waldorf *et al.* (1991) find confirmation for this typology in their study of heavy cocaine users, while adding an important nuance: '...Many of our quitters undertook activities to help them quit that could be understood as structure building (e.g. developing new social, political, or athletic interests or changing social circles). Again, however, many had never let their cocaine use destroy existing structures and thus already had jobs, families, communities, and activities to focus on while quitting.' (Waldorf et al., 1991: 241)

Finally, Shaffer and Jones (1989: 129-131) describe people who quit 'cold turkey', i.e. suddenly and completely, and people who 'taper' their use.[9] The term *'cold turkey'* was originally used by heroin addicts detoxifying from their addiction. One of the detoxification side effects is goose bumps (or turkey bumps) and clammy skin. 'Cold turkey' has been used as a shortcut for an abrupt termination of the drug of abuse, and is often used in a negative and dramatic sense to describe detoxification techniques used by the police, prisons and certain treatment programs. The *'tapering' method* involves a gradual decrease in drug intake over a period of time. This style of drug recovery requires time. Most treatment and recovery literature regards this tapering style of cessation as a cruel delusion or a form of 'denial', while both Shaffer and Jones, and Waldorf *et al.* suggest otherwise.

These cases teach us the fallacy of maintaining a rigid adherence to a single theory and treatment perspective, such as pharmacocentrism. Addiction does not reside in drugs; it resides in human experience.[10] In spite of the physiological dependence that may be one (pharmacological) consequence of drug use, addiction is not inevitable. Furthermore, neither physiological dependence nor behavioral addiction implies that death is inevitable. The drug user can recover and regain his/her autonomy.

1.3.3. 'Drifting out'

In order to avoid connotations of psychological immaturity, disease and illness, some authors have explored other terms as a means of making sense of their data. One of those concepts is 'drifting out'. David Matza's concept of drift (1964) was a breakthrough for understanding why many young people moved in and out of delinquent or deviant behavior. Contrary to conventional social science wisdom, Matza found that most delinquents neither rejected conventional norms or values nor were they committed to any deviant ideology or way of life. They were living in circumstances (youth) that allowed them simply to drift between deviance and conformity. The concept suggests that many drug users and others defined as deviant cease their deviant acts simply because they drift back toward the conventional ways that they had never really abandoned anyway. Thus, moving from illicit drug use to abstinence need not be the result of any existential crisis or maturation.

The concept of drift has been useful in qualitative studies on users of marijuana. Henley and Adams (1973) found that cessation of marijuana use was not so much related to aging per se, but to the entry that most people eventually make into significant social statuses (such as marriage and the birth of the first child). In their study of college graduates, Brown *et al.* (1974) conclude that those who ceased marijuana use seemed to do so largely as a result of acquiring commitment to non-student roles and becoming socially isolated from marijuana users. However, they did not lose all of the values and norms distinctive of this subculture. They just seemed to have turned off.

Waldorf's (1983) study of cessation among heroin addicts found that many simply drifted away from heroin without conscious effort, apparently never having been committed to the drug or to the life-style of an addict. Similarly, Blackwell (1983) identified 11 respondents of a sample of 51 opiate users who avoided becoming chronically dependent, as 'drifters'. These were casual users who were able to control their drug consumption, who were relatively unimpressed with the psychotropic effects of narcotics and for whom other aspects of life competed strongly for time and resources.

Waldorf *et al.* (1991: 238) argue that, although the concept of drift provided them with a useful sensibility about the tenuousness of many users' commitment to cocaine use, their data did not offer strong support for the idea that their 'quitters' just drifted out of cocaine use. The vast majority of both treated and untreated quitters had made a conscious decision to stop. Many were able to walk away from cocaine relatively easily, but most had to make a point in doing so. However, their respondents were among the heaviest users in the U.S., and they suspected that many less serious users do drift out of regular use.

Finally, Waldorf et al. also used the concept of drifting to describe how many of their respondents became dealers, without being compelled or committed to dealing: 'The regular availability of supplies, a network of user friends, a modicum of start-up capital, with perhaps a higher-level dealer willing to 'front' or consign... when such conditions fell into place, some users who had been merely dealing for stash seemed to drift into dealing.' (Waldorf et al., 1991: 77)

1.3.4. Model of change: relapse and recovery

Cramer and Schippers (1994: 25-34) have reviewed 52 reports with empirical data on the process of kicking the habit. Their analysis was based on 5 overviews by other authors.[11] Based on all minimal and maximal percentages in these overviews, all data after 5, 10, 15 and 20 years after registration or end of treatment were summarized in a diagram (figure 1.3.a). Cramer and Schippers' figure shows clearly that problematic use of hard drugs decreases over the years. After 5 years significant changes can be observed. After 10 years the percentage of problematic users has decreased to around one third. One third of the total number has changed to integrated use, another third has quit using. After 20 years, approximately 20% are dead, about 20-25% remain problematic users, more than 40% are abstinent and the other 15-20% are integrated users.

One must bear in mind that these data stem from studies of cohorts of addicts recruited in treatment settings or from judicial files. Consequently, these samples are not

.epresentative for all hard drug users, since they are likely to form a negative selection from the total population (the worst case scenarios).

Clinical, biographical and ethnographical literature on quitting drug use shows that detoxification from hard drugs is best described as a process, and not as a matter of all or nothing at all (see e.g.: Casselman, 1996; Prochaska & DiClemente, 1986). This process can be compared to a spiral in which the same cycle is done several times. These cycles are successively characterized by: weighing the pros and cons of using and being clean, taking the decision to change, starting to kick the habit, and –after some time- starting to use again (relapse). During this process the nature of these considerations changes. In the first cycles the physical aspects of detoxification are most important, after that the psychological aspects, and after that the 'quality of life'.

Figure 1.3.a   Changes in drug use careers (Cramer and Schippers)

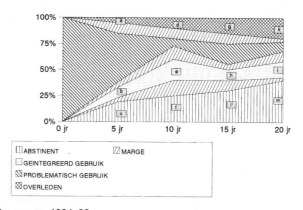

Source: CRAMER and SCHIPPERS, 1994: 32.

(a)   5-15%, based on Swierstra (1990) 10%
(b)   10-15%, supposedly based on Schneider (1988) after 10 years (e) and 20 years (h)
(c)   19-23%, based on Ladewig (1987) 19-23% and Swierstra (1990) 20%
(d)   10-20%, based on Ladewig (1987) >16%, Onstein (1987) 15%, Schneider (1988) 10-13%, Swierstra (1990) 15%, Brinkman (1985) 15-20%
(e)   20-33%, based on Schneider (1988)
(f)   25-40%, based on Schneider (1988) 25%, Swierstra (1990) 30%, Onstein (1987) 40%
(g)   15-25%, based on Ladewig (1987) >20%, Swierstra (1990) <20%
(h)   10-15%, based on Schneider (1988), after subtracting 20-25% problematic users from total number of users
(j)   30-40%, based on Swierstra (1990) 35%
(k)   20-23%, based on Schneider (1988) 20%, Swierstra (1990) 23%
(l)   15-25%, supposedly based on Schneider (1988) after 10 years (e) and 20 years (h)
(m)   40-43%, based on Schneider (1988) 40%, Swierstra (1990) 40%, Ladewig (1987), 40-43%

Cramer and Schippers (1994: 62-65) consider the process of change successful when the drug user develops a regimen (rules of life) and commitment that help him/her to control the drug use, and that create the opportunity to lead a reasonably satisfying life. The criterion for successful detoxification should be 'the quality of life' rather than complete abstinence. The authors found that the process of kicking the habit was not given enough attention in the existing treatment and self help material, and they decided to produce a booklet to support drug users in their self-control (based on the cy-clical process of quitting drug use).

Cramer and Schippers (1994) prefer the term *self-control* instead of *self-help*, be-cause the latter term is often associated with self-help organizations such as Alcoholics Anonymous and Gamblers Anonymous whose philosophy is partly based on the ad-diction-as-disease concept.[12] Cramer and Schippers consistently use the term self-control because it refers to the competence of an individual to adopt goal-oriented be-havior. Thus, self-control refers to a characteristic of an individual, or a competence to self-regulate. Self-regulation is usually seen as a cycle of processes, which includes the observation of one's own behavior and the consequences, the comparison with an in-ternal standard, the search for alternative, effective and realistic possibilities, the selec-tion of goals, the development of a behavioral plan, the execution of that behavior, and the observation of the consequences and the relation to the goals (Miller & Brown, 1991; Karoly, 1993).

The term self-control tends to have moral connotations: self-control is often seen as a valuable and wanted competence, and as an obviously individual quality. A person who does not show sufficient self-control is often blamed for it. However, the influ-ence of the setting on an individual's competence for self-control must not be ignored. As we will argue in the next paragraphs, self-regulation is as much a consequence of the incentives and restraints that operate in the social environment of the individual as it is of any battle within the individual to decide for of against adopting some specific behavior (Saunders & Alsop, 1992).

1.4. COUNTERING PHARMACOCENTRISM: SETTING

Before the 1970s it was assumed that because of their pharmacological properties, the psychedelics, heroin, and to a lesser extent, marihuana could not be taken on a long-term, regular basis without causing serious problems. The unfortunate condition of heroin addicts and other compulsive users was invoked as 'proof' of this 'pharmaco-mythology'. It was also widely held that these 'dangerous' substances were almost al-ways sought out by people with profound personality disorders. Most drug research was strongly influenced by the moralistic view that all illicit drug use was 'bad', in-evitably harmful, or psychologically or physiologically 'addictive', and that abstention was the only alternative.

As more evidence about controlled use and natural cessation of illicit drug use arose, 'it became obvious that in order to understand the drug experience, one would have to take into account not just the pharmacology of the drug and the personality of the user (the set) but also the physical and social setting in which use occurred' (Zin-berg, 1984: x). It was demonstrated that controlled users existed and that factors other than the power of the drug and the user's personality were at work.

In 1973, Zinberg (1984) offered a tripartite model for understanding drug effects: drug, set and setting. The hypotheses underlying Zinberg's project were far more con-troversial then than they would be today, and although the triangle model is often used in explanatory models nowadays, the importance of the setting-factors is still not gen-erally accepted. In the paragraphs to follow, we will summarize Zinberg's theory by collating some verbatim quotes from his works.

Zinberg contended, first, that in order to understand what impels someone to use an illicit drug and how that drug affects the user, three determinants must be considered: the drug (the pharmacological action of the substance itself), the set (the attitude of the person at the time of use, including his personality structure, and his physical condition or corporality), and the setting (the influence of the physical and social setting within which the use occurs). Because of these three determinants, the setting had received the least attention and recognition, Zinberg made it the focus of his investigation (Zinberg & DeLong, 1974).

Thus the second hypothesis, which was a derivative of the first, was that it is the social setting, through the development of sanctions and rituals, that brings the use of illicit drugs under control. The use of any drug involves both values and rules of conduct, which Zinberg called social sanctions, and patterns of behavior, which he called social rituals; they are known as informal social controls. Social sanctions define whether and how a particular drug should be used. They may be informal and shared by a group, as in the common maxims associated with alcohol use ('Know your limit'), or they may be formal, as in the various laws and policies aimed at regulating drug use (Zinberg *et al.*, 1981). Social rituals are the stylized, prescribed behavior patterns surrounding the use of a drug. They concern the methods of procuring and administering the drug, the selection of the physical and social setting for use, the activities undertaken after the drug has been administered, and the ways of preventing untoward drug effects (Zinberg, 1984: 16). Rituals thus serve to buttress, reinforce, and symbolize the sanctions.

Social controls (both rituals and sanctions) apply to the use of all drugs, not just alcohol, and operate in a variety of social settings, ranging all the way from very large social groups, representative of the culture as a whole, down to small, discrete groups (Harding & Zinberg, 1977). If the culture as a whole fully adopts a widespread social ritual, it may eventually be written into law. Small-group sanctions and rituals tend to be more diverse and closely related to circumstances.

Most of these informal rules (rituals and social sanctions) concerning controlled use are not 'conscious rules': they are usually applied unknowingly.[13] Users see these rules as a part of their personality, and not as learned social sanctions and rituals (Jansen, 1992). Some users do not identify their rules until they have violated them. In a sense, the average drug clinic attender is a victim of his or her failure to make, identify or obey adequate personal rules that govern problematic drug-related behavior.

The existence of social sanctions and rituals does not necessarily mean that they will be effective, nor does it mean that all of them were devised as mechanisms to aid control (e.g. 'booting'). 'More important than the question of whether the sanction or ritual was originally intended as a control mechanism is the way in which the user handles conflicts between sanctions. With illicit drugs the most obvious conflict is between formal and informal social controls – i.e. the illegality of the substance and the social group's approval of use' (Zinberg, 1984: 6). The decision to use, so rationally presented, conflicts with the law and so may cause anxiety to the user. Such anxiety interferes with control. It is this kind of personal and social conflict that makes controlled use of illicit drugs more complex and more difficult to achieve than the controlled use of licit drugs (Zinberg, 1984: 7).

'Of course the application of social controls, particularly in the case of illicit drugs, does not always lead to moderate use. And yet, it is the reigning cultural belief that drug use should always be moderate and that behavior should always be socially acceptable. Such an expectation, which does not take into account variations in use or the experimentation that is inevitable in learning about control, is the chief reason that the power of the social setting to regulate intoxicant use has not been more fully recognized and exploited.' (Zinberg, 1984: 7) This cultural expectation of decorum stems from the moralistic attitudes that pervade our culture. It is only at special occasions, such as a wedding celebration or an adolescent's first experiment with drunkenness, that less decorous behavior is culturally acceptable.

Zinberg further argues that this stolid attitude inhibits the development of a rational understanding of controlled use and ignores the fact that even the most severely affected alcoholics and addicts, who may be grouped at one end of the spectrum of drug use, exhibit some control in that they actually use less of the intoxicating substance than they could.

Zinberg (1984: 7-9) has argued that the cultural insistence on extreme decorum overemphasizes the determinants of drug and set by implying that social standards are broken down because of the power of the drug or some personality disorder of the user. This way of thinking, which ignores the social setting, requires considerable psychological juggling, for few users of intoxicants can consistently maintain such self-discipline. Intoxicant use tends to vary with one's age, status, and even geographical location.

He concludes 'the social setting, with its formal and informal controls, its capacity to develop new informal social sanctions and rituals, and its transmission of information in numerous informal ways, is a crucial factor in the controlled use of any intoxicant. This does not mean that the pharmacological properties of the drug or the attitudes and personality of the user count for little or nothing. All three variables -drug, set and setting- must be included in any valid theory of (controlled) drug use' (Zinberg, 1984: 14-15).

1.5. SOCIAL LEARNING: SOCIALIZATION OF INFORMAL CONTROLS

The processes through which social sanctions and controls are transferred from one individual to another, from one social group to another, and from one generation to another, vary with the legal status of the substances involved (Webster *et al.*, 1994). In most sectors of our society, both formal and informal education about licit drugs (alcohol, nicotine...) is readily available. Conversely, formal education about illicit drugs seems to exclude the possibility of discussing reasonable informal social controls that may condone use. The natural processes of social learning inevitably go on for better or for worse (Moore, 1993). The present paragraph describes the learning or internalization of social sanctions related to licit and illicit drugs and points out some important differences, again through a collage of (verbatim) quotes by several authors.

1.5.1. Social learning and licit drugs

The social acquisition of informal control mechanisms begins in early childhood. Social sanctions and rituals cannot be delivered 'ready-made' to users, nor can they be imposed through a formal policy. They originate largely through unknown processes in the social interactions between users. They are 'seen but unnoticed'; they develop gradually in ways that tally with changing socio-cultural and subcultural conditions.

Let us explore the informal regulation of alcohol use. Mechanisms by which moderate drinking is socialized in the young and maintained by the social group have been studied for Italians (Lolli *et al.*, 1958), Jews (Glassner & Berg, 1980), Chinese (Barnett, 1955), and Greeks (Blum & Blum, 1969). 'Children see their parents and other adults drink. They are exposed to acceptable and unacceptable models of alcohol use in magazines and movies and on television. Some may sip their parents' drink or be served wine with meals or on religious occasions. So, by the time they reach adolescence they have already absorbed an enormous amount of information on how to handle drink. When the adolescent tests -as most do- the limits he has learned and gets drunk and nauseated, there is little need to fear that this excess will become habitual. As he matures the adolescent has numerous examples of adult use at hand and he can easily find friends who share both his interest in drinking and his commitment to becoming a controlled drinker. Support for control continues throughout adult life.' (Zinberg & Harding, 1982:18) Adult drinking is also controlled by group attitudes about both the proper amount of drinking and the behavior when drinking. Strong disapproval is expressed when an individual violates these standards and acts in an antisocial manner.

Alcohol using rituals define appropriate use and limit consumption to specific occasions. For example, two well-known alcohol rituals are: a glass of port before the meal (as an aperitif or appetizer), glasses of beer at a student party. Positive social sanctions permit and even encourage alcohol use, but there are also negative sanctions that condemn promiscuous use and drunkenness. For example: the common invitation 'Let's have a drink' automatically exerts some degree of control by using the singular term 'a drink'. By contrast, the statements 'Tonight I'm going out and I want to get drunk' and 'What's all the fuss about just one beer?' imply that some (or all) restraints will be abandoned. Nevertheless, people will often show their disapproval towards publicly drunken individuals; the informal sanction here is: 'Know your limits'. Others will dissuade someone from driving a car when he or she is drunk, referring to both an informal social control and a formal law: 'Do not drink and drive' (Jansen, 1992: 10).

This does not mean that users never break these rules, but when they do they are usually aware of making an exception. They know, for instance, that being drunk at a wedding party or a bachelor party is acceptable behavior, but that drinking whisky-cola for breakfast would violate accepted social standards (Zinberg & Harding, 1982: 18).

Obviously, the influence of social learning on the alcohol user is not always so straightforward. Social sanctions and rituals promoting control are not uniformly distributed throughout the culture. Social rules are highly differentiated along social class, ethnic, occupational and cultural lines. These different groups need not and, in fact, often do not share the same rules. The problems they face in dealing with their environment, the history and traditions they carry with them, all lead to the development of different sets of rules (Becker, 1973: 15). Zinberg gives the example of the Irish, who lack strong sanctions against drunkenness and have a correspondingly higher rate of alcoholism (Zinberg & Harding, 1982: 18). Alcohol socialization within the family may break down as a result of divorce, death, or some other disruptive event. In some instances the influence of other variables -personality, genetic differences, as well as other setting variables- may outweigh the influence of social learning. Nonetheless, controlling rituals and social sanctions exert a crucial and distinct influence on the way most people use alcohol (Harding & Zinberg, 1977). While alcoholism is still a major public health problem, the extent of non-compulsive use of such a powerful, addictive and easily available intoxicant is remarkable. According to Zinberg and Harding (1982: 17) this can only be fully understood in terms of the rituals and sanctions that pattern the way alcohol is used.

Finally, it is interesting to see that both prevention campaigns and advertising agencies can and often do play along with the existence of social sanctions and rituals. For example, the slogan 'A Belga cigarette you never smoke alone' refers to the supposed sociability accompanying the use of this tobacco brand.

1.5.2. Social learning and illicit drugs

In contrast to alcohol, the opportunities for learning how to control illicit drug consumption are quite limited. Neither the family nor the culture normally provide long-term education models of use. The chief educational message from media, the parents, and the schools is still that reasonable, controlled use of illicit drugs is impossible. 'Our culture does not yet fully recognize, much less support, controlled use of most illicit drugs. Users are declared either 'deviant' and a threat to society, or 'sick' and in need of help, or 'criminal' and deserving of punishment. Family-centered socialization for use is not available. Parents, even if they are willing to help, are unable to provide guidance either by setting an example (as with alcohol) or in a factual, non-moralistic manner' (Zinberg, 1984: 15).

'If parents tell their children not to use drugs because they are harmful, the youngsters disregard that advice because their own experiences have told them otherwise. Their using group and the drug culture reinforce their own discovery that drug use in and of itself is not bad or evil and that the warnings from the adult world are unrealistic.' Once users discover that drugs are neither such an overpowering high nor 'instantly addicting', they tend to discount the 'official line'. What users take as extreme anti-drug warnings do not 'check out' with their experience. Ironically, this disparity seems to inoculate them against such warnings, leading many to throw away the proverbial baby with the bath water. Thus, instead of keeping people away from drugs, warnings that get discredited by personal experience leave many neophyte users open to further use.

'In the case of the mass media, most of the information provided is dramatically opposed to drug use and to the possibility of controlled drug use. Heroin consumption is viewed as a plague, a social disease.' (Zinberg, 1984: 16). Stories about bad psychedelic trips resulting in psychosis or suicide have served for years as media staples, and more recently there has been a new spate of MDMA ('ecstasy') and crack horror broadcast programs. 'Cultural opposition further complicates the development of controlled use: by inadvertently creating a black market in which the drugs being sold are of uncertain quality. As a result there are wide variations in strength and purity that make the task of controlling dosage and effect more difficult. Aside from its questionable effect on the number of drug users, the prohibition policy actively contributes to the prevailing dichotomy between abstinence and compulsive use. It makes it extremely difficult for anyone who wishes to use drugs to select a moderate using pattern.'

Although the opportunities for learning how to control illicit drug consumption are extremely limited, rituals and social sanctions that promote control do exist within subcultures of drug users. Zinberg (1984: 17-18) distinguishes between four basic and overlapping ways in which controlling rituals and sanctions function:

- Sanctions define moderate use and condemn compulsive use
  E.g.: 'Do not use every day'; 'Restrict your use to weekends'...

- Sanctions limit use to physical and social settings that are conducive to a positive or 'safe' drug experience
  E.g.: 'Use in a good place at a good time'; 'Never inject'; 'Do not use with strangers'...

- Sanctions identify potentially untoward drug effects. Rituals embody the precautions to be taken before and during use
  E.g.: 'Only use good quality'; 'Only buy from a dealer you know'; 'Do not use everything in one go'; 'Check alcohol intake when using cocaine'...

- Sanctions and rituals compartmentalize drug use and support the users' non-drug-related obligations and relationships
  E.g.: 'Only use at night or in the weekends to avoid interfering with work performance'; 'Do not use more than the pre-fixed budget allows'...

The process by which controlling rituals and sanctions are acquired varies from subject to subject. Most individuals come by them gradually during the course of their drug-using careers. In his classical essay *'Becoming a marihuana user'* Becker (1973: 41-58) describes this process of social learning in three stages: learning the technique, learning to perceive the effects, and learning to enjoy the effects.

- The first step in the sequence of events that must occur if the person is to become a user is that he must learn to use the proper (smoking) technique so that his use of the drug will produce effects in terms of which his conception of it can change. This is a result of the individual's participation in groups in which the drug is used. The individual can learn the technique by direct teaching, but often, new users are ashamed to admit ignorance and, pretending to know already, must learn through the more indirect means of observation and imitation.

- Secondly, the user must be able to point out the effects caused by the drug. He can ask more experienced users or provoke comments from them about it. Or he can pick up from other users some concrete referents of the term 'high' and apply these notions to his own experience.

- And thirdly, the user must learn to enjoy the effects he has just learned to experience. Drug-produced sensations are not automatically or necessarily pleasurable. The taste for such experience is a socially acquired one. The beginner must thus learn to redefine the sensations as pleasurable, and this redefinition occurs, typically, in interaction with more experienced users who, in a number of ways, teach the novice to find pleasure in this experience. They may reassure him as to the temporary character of the unpleasant sensations, calling attention to the more enjoyable aspects, teaching him to regulate the amount he uses, so as to avoid any severely uncomfortable symptoms while retaining the pleasant ones.

The problem is that many aspects of the social learning process concerning illicit drugs as described above, are developed in the (illicit) drug scene during a long process of casual information exchanges in informal networks - generally not based on objective information, but on users' personal experiences. For example, regarding freebasing and crack use, Waldorf et al. observe: 'We have become convinced that (...) 'learning the high' is less a process of interpreting drug effects than a process of learning the technique necessary for getting a 'real good hit'. By 'technique', we mean quite specific knowledge and equipment.(...) Across different users groups there are bound to be variations in such techniques, as well as in style, tools, and personal preferences. There is no central clearinghouse for such illicit information, and few of the details about freebasing procedures have been published in the mass media. Thus, freebasers and crack users are left to their own folk-experimental devices for testing tools or techniques.' (Waldorf et al., 1991: 112-113)

Frequently the source of such information is not traceable and for many users its validity is hard to check. Therefore, many informal control mechanisms (rules and rituals) contain rational and non-rational elements. Grund (1993: 98) also observes that myths are an important ingredient of the observed rituals, which might indicate that knowledge about certain drugs and the best ways to use them in a safe way is still underdeveloped.

'When parents, schools and the media are all unable to inform neophytes about the controlled use of illicit drugs, that task falls squarely on the new user's peer group - an inadequate substitute for cross-generation, long-term socialization. Since illicit drug use is a covert activity, newcomers are not presented with an array of using groups from which to choose, and association with controlled users is largely a matter of chance.' (Zinberg, 1984: 16). However, the peer group provides instruction in and reinforces proper use; and despite the popular image of peer pressure as a corrupting force pushing weak individuals toward drug misuse, Zinberg's research showed that many segments of the drug subculture have taken a firm stand against drug abuse (Zinberg & Harding, 1982: 19).

Regarding the role of the peer group as probably the most important source of precepts and practices for control, a final remark needs to be made. Much has been made of the importance of peer 'pressure' as a major causal factor in the onset of drug use, and illicit drug use in particular. The attraction of this explanation -highly comparable to that of the disease-model of addiction and drug abuse- is obvious: drug use is reprehensible behavior and if someone is pressured into drug use by others, the (reprehensible) behavior is not the fault of the person concerned (or according to the disease-model: if someone falls victim to the disease of addiction, the behavior is not his or her fault). Instead, the blame can be laid at the door of those influential others who are primarily responsible for leading the young person astray. Passively undergoing the pressure from others, he or she is unable to refuse.

In a well argued paper, Coggans and McKellar (1994) state that most of the data adduced in support of this hypothesis are associational and therefore provide no basis for the inference of causality. We fully agree with them that there is a need to reassert the role of the individual in his/her own development. Their motivation and choice of drug using peers should not be seen simply in terms of personal or social inadequacy. Coggans and McKellar argue that, while there is evidence to show that peer factors are associated with illicit drug use, this evidence has often been inappropriately interpreted or cited as support for peer pressure when it should have been more appropriately interpreted as evidence for peer assortment or peer preference.

If the active role of the individual drug user is ignored the role of peers, and the nature of interactions between individuals and peers, cannot be properly explained: 'It is still commonplace to hear of 'peer pressure' (coercion or persuasion to take drugs) or 'peer influence' (a vague term indicating that the impact of peers is effectively to make others take drugs), when more appropriate terms would be 'peer support' (toleration, approval or encouragement of an individual's drug-related attitudes or behavior) or 'peer assortment or preference' (favoring or choosing friends or associates over others).(...) 'peer clustering' (the coming together of young people who share similar beliefs, values and behaviors)'.

Coggans and McKellar (1994) assert that (adolescent) drug use is normative behavior and does not necessarily arise from pathological personal characteristics or from pathogenic socialization processes. In their view the peer group provides both access to drugs and a more congenial social setting for what the young person wants to do, i.e. to take drugs.[14]

Contrary to the ubiquitous belief that (licit and illicit) drugs using youngsters cause their non-using peers to take up the habit through strategies such as coercion, teasing, bullying and rejection from a desired group, several authors suggest that the influence of peer pressure has been overestimated. They observe that individuals play a more active role in starting drug use than has previously been acknowledged, because friend selection and projection may increase the association between friend and adolescent behavior (Bauman & Ennett, 1996; Ennett & Bauman, 1993; Aseltine, 1995; White & Bates, 1995). Evidence from these studies paints a picture of adolescents making active choices about many aspects of their lives, including drug use. They either seek out or avoid contexts in which drug use occurs and choose friends who, like themselves, may or may not use these drugs (Michell & West, 1996; Iannotti *et al.*, 1996; Oostveen *et al.*, 1996).

The key issue addressed by these authors is that peer pressure is inappropriate and unsupported as an explanation for drug use, and that the processes underlying the development of drug use behaviors are the same psycho-social processes that underlie both conformist and non-conformist behavior. The nature of the relationship between individuals and their peers is dynamic and reciprocal, and we certainly need to take into account both the social aspects of development and the dynamics of relationships between young people and those around them, if we want to understand the social learning processes.[15]

1.6. DETERMINANTS OF INFORMAL SOCIAL CONTROL

In his doctoral dissertation, *Drug use as a social ritual*, Grund (1993) analyses the rituals and rules that have developed in the subculture of regular users of heroin and cocaine. He also shows that both on the individual and the group level the functions and meanings of drug use rituals are multifold and intertwined, serving instrumental as well as symbolic goals. His data offer strong support for Zinberg's theory that the control of drugs is largely established by (sub)culturally based social controls -rituals and rules (or social sanctions in Zinberg's terminology)- which pattern the way a drug is used: 'Ultimately, users themselves regulate their use of intoxicants through a peer based social learning process, in which specific rituals and rules are developed as adaptations to the effects of the interaction between drug, set and setting.' (Grund, 1993: 237)

Grund agrees with Zinberg that rituals and rules are key determinants of drug use self-regulation processes. However, Zinberg's theory does not explain the intra-group variation in the ability to effectively utilize these social controls, found in Grund's study. Some users seem able to use large amounts of cocaine and heroin without or with few of the characteristic problems, whereas others -typically the down and out users- actually use very little of these (expensive) drugs, but seem most susceptible to their related (psychological) problems. Nor does Zinberg account for the multidimensional nature of self-regulation processes. Grund argues that self-regulation or control is more than limit one's intake. It equally refers to the prevention and management of drug related problems and should, therefore, be perceived as a multidimensional process. And thirdly, besides rituals and rules, his theory does not explicitly address other factors that may impact upon the effectiveness of these social controls. In that respect, Grund views Zinberg's theory as rather static. Although not invalid, the theory requires certain adaptations and elaborations to account for Grund's dissonant findings.

In an attempt to revise Zinberg's theory, Grund introduces and discusses two distinct (clusters of) factors that, in addition to the concept of rituals and rules, are thought to be essential determinants of the self-regulation processes that control drug use: drug availability and life structure. The hypothetical DARRLS-trinity-model Grund presents explains controlled use of drugs in terms of a dynamic interaction between Drug Availability, Rituals and Rules, and Life Structure (see figure 1.6).

Figure 1.6   Grund's feedback model of drug use self-regulation

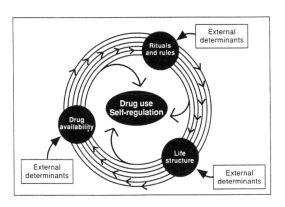

Source: GRUND, 1993: 248.

Drug availability, rituals and rules, and *life structure* form a trinity – they are interactive factors in an internally coherent circular process, in which they are themselves modulated (modified, corrected, strengthened, etc.) by their outcomes. It is a 'feedback circuit' that determines the strength of self-regulation processes controlling drug use (Grund, 1993: 248).

According to Grund, 'drug availability has a pivotal impact on the daily lives of regular users. Artificially limiting the availability of drugs may limit intake to a certain degree, but at considerable (psychosocial) expense. Apart from creating a strong economic incentive for the sale of drugs in unregulated entrepreneurial circuits, restricting availability induces and fuels a psychosocial process, which greatly multiplies the ritual value of drugs - ushering in a narrowing of focus in the user. Fixation on the drug will lead to strong limitation of behavioral expressions when the drug is craved and difficult to obtain, and to impulsive indulgence when a dose becomes available. As a result, rituals and rules relating to the drug become directed less at self-regulation and safety in the sense of health, and more at safeguarding, covering and facilitating drug use and the related activities (e.g. drug transactions). In contrast, the absence of uncertainty about the next dose liberates the user from the recurrent obsessive worries about obtaining the drugs and the necessity to chase them. Sufficient availability thus creates a situation in which rituals and rules can develop which restrain drug use and induce stable use patterns. This does not necessarily mean lower levels of drug use.' (Grund, 1993: 243) When the drugs are sufficiently available, Grund's users seem to be able to sustain high consumption levels, without developing typical drug related problems.

An equally important condition is a stable *life structure*. Citing Faupel (1987), Grund emphasizes the regular activities (both conventional and drug use related) that structure daily patterns as key determinants of life structure (Grund, 1993: 248). 'It is logical to include people's connections, commitments, obligations, responsibilities, goals, expectancies, etc. Relationships and aspirations that are demanding, and simultaneously valuable in social (e.g. affection) or economic (e.g. income) ways are equally important determinants of life structure. Regular contacts with controlled and non-users are therefore of considerable importance, as is participation in structures and activities not (primarily) driven by drug related incentives.'

Maintaining scheduled activities and fulfilling social obligations, etc. -thus maintaining a stable, high degree of life structure- requires careful management of drug consumption and related activities. Such management is dependent on the development of, and compliance with, rituals and rules. Grund argues that the climate of minimal repression of heroin use and the easy accessibility of the heroin substitute methadone have been indispensable facilitators of the social learning processes that facilitate controlled drug use. However, self-regulation processes are complicated because people continue to become socialized into heroin use in the context of a subculture that was formed under more repressive and unstable conditions, and because other drugs (cocaine, in particular) have been added to the daily use patterns (Grund, 1993: 246).

Drug availability, rituals and rules, and life structure must thus be considered a coherent constellation, according to Grund. The continuity of drug availability is dependent on the stability of life structure, which results from strict compliance to the rituals and rules regulating patterns of drug use. Availability is a precondition for the development and maintenance of regulating rituals and rules. 'Rituals and rules determine and constrain the patterns of drug use, preventing erosion of life structure. A high degree of life structure enables the user to maintain stable drug availability, which is essential for the formation and maintenance of efficient rules and rituals. Self-regulation of drug consumption and its (unintended) effects is thus a matter of a (precarious) balance of a circularly reinforcement chain.' (Grund, 1993: 248)

Grund's feedback model is circular, without being a closed and independent circuit. The three cornerstones of the trinity model are each the result of distinctive variables and processes. Price, purity and accessibility determine drug availability and are mediated by market factors and governmental policy. Rituals and rules are the product of culturally defined social learning processes, both through inter-generational, family centered socialization (mainstream culture) and through drug using peer group centered socialization (subculture). The shape and the degree of life structure are the product of the regular activities, relationships and ambitions, whether drug related, or not. General socio-economic factors and actual living conditions, personality structure and the prevalence of (non-drug related) psychosocial problems, and cultural factors may further determine life structure. Clearly, external stimuli can impact on the feedback system, in particular on its ability to support controlled and adjust uncontrolled use. And most importantly, as we will show in the next paragraph, the social definition of drugs and their users, embodied in drug policy, can be seen to affect the model at all three cornerstones.

In conclusion, Zinberg's theory does not explain intra-group variation in the ability to effectively utilize these social controls, nor does it account for the multidimensional nature of self-regulation processes. And thirdly, besides rituals and rules, the theory does not explicitly address other factors which may impact upon the effectiveness of these social controls (Grund, 1993: 238). In this paragraph, we have presented a circular feedback model of drug use self-regulation by Grund in an attempt to revise Zinberg's theory. This hypothetical model explains controlled use of drugs in terms of a dynamic interaction between Drug Availability, Rituals and Rules, and Life Structure.

1.7. INTERACTIONS BETWEEN INFORMAL AND FORMAL SOCIAL CONTROLS

In the previous paragraphs we elaborated the concept of informal control. The concept of formal control (which cannot be detached from informal social control) and the interactions between formal and informal control systems will be discussed here.

1.7.1. Formal versus informal social controls

People direct their own use of pleasurable substances and the use by other people through various forms of 'force'. This can be through the force of legislation, or more informal forms of 'force', conscious self-control or internalized self-control. These various forms of 'force' or 'control' cannot be dissociated from each other. For example, Gerritsen (1994: 1-5) states that a strict legislation leaves little space for people to regulate the use of pleasurable substances informally. Repressive laws leave no margin for experimentation and for the exploration of limits. Conversely, adequate forms of informal social control can develop more easily within a framework of more restrained legislation.

Formal and informal social controls form a continuum of which the force exerted by repressive state legislation is the one extreme: it is a formal and external form of regulation. The opposite extreme is formed by the forms of informal social control between peers and the internalized self-control people apply to their use, and which have become part of their personality through socialization (as described in the previous paragraph). [16]

The idea that drugs and self-control are a *contradictio in terminis* has generated a myriad of 'external' and 'formal' controls: religious, legislative and societal. Laws and regulations from the government and other formal organizations punish the production, distribution and use of certain drugs (oddly enough, some other drugs are accepted). In our view, not only the numerous legislative controls of the regional, national, European and international authorities should be seen as formal control. Even the network of treatment agencies and organized prevention can be interpreted as a kind of formal control. After all, they form a whole range of specialists, operating within a formally structured context, who are fully occupied with the ways people consume pleasurable substances. It is a full time job for addiction doctors, policemen, prevention workers, customs officers, etc...[17] Numerous authors have discussed the important negative effects of the 'war on drugs'; it is quite superfluous to repeat their extensive argumentation. Rather, we prefer to examine the reciprocity between the formal control (the current repressive drug policy) and the informal control mechanisms around the use of pleasurable substances.

Before we go on, it is important to note that the notion of formal control should not be interpreted too formalistically. Formal control refers not only to laws and official policies, but also to the agencies and individual agents that enact them. The effect of formal control cannot be reduced to its formalistic structures and the constitutional rules of the game, as one should also take into account the individual encounters between drug users and the enforcers of a formal policy. In essence, the drug user is never confronted with the drug laws in a direct sense; he/she always faces the law indirectly, through law enforcers. Moreover, as the Belgian drug laws incriminate a huge number of behaviors (and as so many people commit offences), the police has to make choices (select target groups and determine priorities). At this time, Devresse (Université Catholique de Louvain-la-Neuve) is studying the direct encounters between drug users and police officers through participant observation in two Brussels police forces (Devresse, 1998 and 1999). Her preliminary results illustrate how social, operational, technical and strategic factors can lead to quite different types of police intervention towards drug users.

Clearly, there are important differences between formal and informal controls. Legal rules, naturally, are most likely to be precise and unambiguous (Becker, 1973: 133). Hence the difficulty to distinguish between use and abuse of substances in legal and medical definitions. Informal and customary rules are more likely to be vague and to have large areas in which various interpretations of them can be made (cf. the social sanction 'know your limits'). Moreover, informal rules and rituals may be identical, similar or radically different from those imposed upon the individual by society, the legal or political system or religious organizations. Illicit drug users rarely have rulebooks or value systems that are completely coterminous with societal law and norms (George, 1993).

1.7.2. Interactions between informal and formal control

We suspect, however, that there is a strong connection between formal and informal control mechanisms (Gerritsen, 1994: 11-12 and 223). The formal and external state controls are part of a structural framework that needs to be filled with informal social control mechanisms, such as habits, rituals and rules, and internalized intra-psychic controls (Zinberg & Harding, 1982: 9). We strongly believe that -in the case of substance use- the interplay between both forms of social control has negative effects on the development and the (continued) existence of informal control mechanisms. We shall attempt to summarize the most important arguments.

Figure 1.7   Effects of drug policy on Grund's feedback model

Prohibition	Legalization
I. Effects on Drug Availability	
- decreased, but unstable and uncontrolled availability - unstable quality, price and sales unit - chain between producer and consumer is controlled by illegal enterprises	- stable, controlled availability - stable quality, price and sales unit - chain controlled by legal enterprises and constructive governmental regulations
II. Effects on Rituals and Rules	
- subcultural socialization (limited options, few identification models of controlled drug use)	- mainstream subcultural socialization (multiple options and identification models of controlled drug use)
- natural (e.g. inter-generational) social learning processes are obstructed	- natural social learning processes are facilitated
- rituals and rules aimed at shielding/covering drug use and safeguarding drug transactions	- rituals and rules aimed at controlling the drug use and reducing drug related harm
- more emphasis and dependence on explicit and rigid (idiosyncratic)[18] group rituals	- less explicit ritualization, rituals become less important and often empty, and are replaced by more generally applicable rules
- less stable, less general, less efficient rules	- stronger, broadly supported rules
III. Effects on Life Structure	
- increased drug (acquisition) related activities - living conditions, activities, connections, commitments, etc. are unstable - social network structure determined by (uncontrolled) drug using friends, connections, etc. - possible non drug related personality or psychosocial problems become obscured by, and intertwined with, drug related problems	- less drug related activities - living conditions, activities, connections, commitments, etc. are more stable and demanding - social network structure determined by non- and controlled- drug using connections - such problems become clear and unpolluted and, as a result, better to treat

Source: GRUND, 1993: 251-253.

Let us first return to Grund's circular feedback model of drug use self-regulation we discussed in the previous paragraph. Grund (1993: 248-254) also discusses the impact of the 'external' drug policy on his model. Exploring and comparing certain aspects of prohibition and legalization, he concludes that prohibition interferes with the natural processes underlying self-regulation. Legalization, at the other hand, is not an instant remedy for this interference, but merely paves the way for alternative drug control policies, outside of criminal law, which are expected to facilitate natural processes of self-regulation. Figure 1.7 schematically presents the effects of a formal drug policy on the feedback model of self-regulation.

Quite a few other authors have pointed out that, instead of working together to mini-mize problems, formal (repressive) controls and informal controls often work against each other.

(1) Under existing circumstances there are limits to how far informal social controls can go to prevent abuse and addiction. Neither the principle that people should limit their use nor the practices by which some have learned to do so have had a long gesta-tion period in our society. When a drug is criminalized, its use tends to be marginalized or pushed out of conventional society into deviant subcultures. In such circles few drug users place a premium on moderation; on the contrary, many look for ways to get more bang for their buck. Communication about ill effects and other risks tends to remain subterranean and therefore difficult to have any effect. By creating the preconditions for deviant subcultures of illicit drug use, our society has minimized the normative in-fluences of family, friends, and moderate users. Under such conditions, users can only slowly pass along knowledge of the drug's dangers and the ways to avoid or minimize them (Waldorf *et al.*, 1991: 154-155).

(2) Zinberg argues that, unlike those of licit drugs, the informal social control mecha-nisms of illicit drugs have not evolved rapidly enough to keep pace with their growing popularity and social use. The social rituals and sanctions that have developed for al-cohol use are not as fully developed for users of illicit drugs, such as cocaine, MDMA ('ecstasy'), heroin, etc... Again, unlike those of alcohol, and because of its illegal na-ture, the mechanisms of illicit drug control are not taught through any formalized net-works within the user's social environment (family or school systems). The capacity to regulate, e.g. cocaine use, has not been transmitted from one generation to the next, nor are social rituals and sanctions built into the users' social matrix. The usual social pre-scriptions and protections against addiction are thus less developed with illicit drugs (Zinberg, 1984: 80). This suggests that there is a higher potential for abusive use of il-licit substances. As social control mechanisms for illicit drugs become more mature, we can expect abuse and the associated adverse consequences to diminish (Shaffer & Jones, 1989).

Ideally, a society could formulate and teach the principles and practices users have developed to avoid problems and maintain control, for we believe that these possess huge untapped potential for harm reduction. However, such controlled use norms and other informal social controls remain powerless; they have not been allowed to be-come part of public discourse and culture. Cocaine has been criminalized and scape-goated. When use must be surreptitious, regulatory mechanisms are less likely to de-velop and be disseminated. For bad as well as for good reasons, parents, schools, me-dia, and government suppress information about the possibilities and procedures for controlled use. Thus, what one generation of drug users learns is difficult to transmit to the next. When social learning is impeded, the tragedies are bound to be repeated (Waldorf *et al.*, 1991: 276-277).

(3) The public learns about the disastrous results of the use of illicit drugs from widely disseminated media reports, principally on television. These presentations give the overriding impression, that such disastrous effects are the normal response to illicit drug use (Zinberg, 1984: 15-18). Those who have had personal experience with drug

use are not convinced by the media accounts and are forced into a sharply opposing position. Official warnings are perceived as the suspect propaganda of drug warriors and conservative moral crusaders rather than as potentially helpful public health information (Waldorf *et al.*, 1991: 154-155). Neither of these responses allow room either for reasonable social learning about the range of responses to the drug and how best to cope with them or for the development of social sanctions and rituals that might prevent many of the dysfunctional reactions.

Those who either withhold or distort information in order to support the current social policy, run the risk that potential users will detect this falsification and tend to disbelieve all other reports of the potential harmfulness of use. Conversely, those presenting the information that not all drug use is misuse, thus contravening formal social policy, run the equally grave risk of being interpreted and publicized as condoning use.

(4) Prohibition interferes with the natural processes underlying self-regulation. It generates and reinforces the stereotypical negative image (junkie, criminal, violent) and related behaviors, which are generally related to drug use per se (Grund, 1993: 253). Thus, deviancy amplification is another hazard of the present policy. The impact on individual personality structure of being declared deviant -'sick' and in need of treatment, or 'bad' and deserving punishment- may create a self-fulfilling prophecy (Cohen, 1984). Some users may come to accept an identity which includes an antisocial component not originally present. Others may incorporate the mainstream culture's view of them as weak and dependent, and come to feel they cannot cope without the drug, institutional care or some other support (Zinberg & Harding, 1982: 30-31).

Ostracizing heavy heroin users into asocial situations will change their ways of relating to the social world around them. One of the consequences of ostracism is that many users are no longer seen as persons towards whom normal behavior is required. In their turn heavy users will find that if they behave normally it has little effect on the way they are treated. Their behavior is met with enormous distrust. It follows that users will abandon the old rules of behavior because these are not productive for them. Abiding or not abiding by basic social rules will make little difference on their image as outcasts. So why stick to the rules? On the other hand, living the life of an outcast and pariah is extremely difficult and many are in danger of collapsing psychologically in the process. Very special kinds of adaptation are required that will in turn enhance or at least confirm the outsiders' view of the 'crazy junky' (Cohen, 1991: 59-64).

Waldorf *et al.* (1991: 277) affirm that one important reason control was possible for so many of their respondents is that they believed it was possible – i.e. that cocaine was not necessarily addicting, that it could and should be used in a controlled fashion. They had at least the beginnings of a vocabulary of controlled drug use with which to conceive and articulate normative expectations of controlled use.

Substances are never bad or dangerous in the sense that they can invalidate individual decision-making. That many people think they can is one of the tragic social constructions behind our suffering a 'drug problem'. The keystone to the addiction debate is the omnipresent idea that drugs generate dependence (George, 1993: 32-35). The classical 'addiction-as-disease' model implies the necessity of denying the existence of personality and environmental characteristics that exert sustained control over the use of drugs (Moore, 1993). This paradigm may stimulate the user's dependence of external control mechanisms. The individual is thus offered a possibility to avoid any responsibility and is supported in the idea that drug use cannot be controlled and thus should be banned or discouraged through punishment and/or treatment.

Blaming the (pharmacological properties of the) drug for any criminal or problematic behavior of drug users and/or addicts gives them the opportunity to neutralize social disapproval by others: 'In so far as the delinquent can define himself as lacking responsibility for his deviant actions, the disapproval of self or others is sharply reduced in effectiveness as a restraining influence. (...) By learning to view himself as more acted upon than acting, the delinquent prepares the way for deviance from the dominant normative system without the necessity of a frontal assault on the norms themselves.' (Sykes & Matza, 1957)

As such, the concept of addiction as a disease can lead to a state of 'learned helplessness': the supposedly absolute pharmacological dependence is replaced by a therapeutical dependence, while the drug using individual is hindered in his/her attempt to take on an active and constructive role in his/her health-related behavior (Davies, 1992: 160-161).[19] The same paradigm leaves husbands, wives, sons, daughters and other relatives of drug users in a similar hopeless position: there is nothing they can do to prevent their loved ones taking drugs excessively in the first place. The sooner they realize the matter is 'out of their hands' the better it appears for all concerned.[20]

Davies points out that the idea of addiction-as-disease is alive and well amongst many drug and alcohol abusers and their families, and in many treatment agencies, because it is highly functional (Davies, 1992). By redefining types of behavior that might otherwise be viewed in a negative light, the function of the addiction concept is to help people explain their own behavior and to give it a meaning for themselves and for those who judge them (treatment specialists, judges, etc.). This 'pathologification' helps to ensure that something that is defined as 'bad' is not also seen as done 'on purpose' (a non-volitional act), and to brush aside judgments of 'guilt' and 'responsibility'. This recasts the doer of the 'bad' thing into the role of helpless victim.[21]

The widespread 'externalisation' of control over drug use may have the effect of disempowering drug users, themselves members of the society which has adopted the 'helpless victim' myth, and, by expecting loss of control over drug use, perpetuates the self-fulfilling prophecy of addiction (George, 1993): 'The more we treat drug problems as if they were the domain of inadequate, sick or helpless people, the more people will present themselves within that framework, and the more we will produce and encounter drug users who fit that description.' (Davies, 1992: 23)

(5) The more a deviant group (i.e. deviant from the dominant behavior, norms and values) is set apart and put under pressure, the more it will profile itself as a deviant group. The more stereotypical deviant behavior, norms and values will then become emphasized and reinforced, resulting in a highly separated, intra-dependent, monofocussed subculture, whose members are very distrustful towards the mainstream culture (Grund, 1993: 26). Those who break a rule often find allies. The individual moves into a subculture of users where he learns to carry on his deviant activity with a minimum of trouble. Others have faced all the problems he faces in evading enforcement of the rule he is breaking. Solutions have been worked out (Becker, 1973: 39). Informal controls help him to minimize or avoid the negative effects of his rule-breaking behavior (the use of an illicit drug). This also consists in learning to control the drug's effects

while in the company of non-users, so that these can be fooled and the secret success-fully kept (Becker, 1973: 70). This phenomenon hinders an open discussion between drug users and non-users, thus impeding the dissemination of controlling rituals and social sanctions about drug use in general, stimulating the alienation of drug users, and amplifying deviancy.[22]

(6) As far as illicit drugs are concerned, the most obvious conflict is between the law prohibiting use and the social group's approval of use. Generally, those who seek out new drugs have strong motives for doing so: they are often perceived as social misfits or psychologically disturbed. Fearing society's disapproval, as well as its legal sanc-tion, new drug users typically experience high levels of anxiety (Zinberg, 1984: 84-90 and 111-112). Such anxiety interferes with control. In order to deal with this conflict the user may display more bravado, exhibitionism, paranoia or antisocial feelings than would have been the case if he used licit drugs. It is this kind of personal and social conflict that makes controlled use of illicit drugs more complex and more difficult to achieve than the controlled use of licit drugs (Zinberg, 1984: 7). This anxiety is also elevated because new users have little knowledge of the drug's possible effects. But as deviant drug use patterns become more prevalent and popular, knowledge about the drug and its effects increase. Misconceptions are only slowly corrected, while new ones may develop (Shaffer & Jones, 1989: 163-173).

(7) Faced with extensive and repressive laws, breaking the rule may result in extremely problematic behavior (Grund, 1993: 253; Gerritsen, 1994: 234). The conscious deci-sion to use illicit drugs, and thus to break the formal prohibition, may lead to involun-tary infractions of other social rules: 'Though the effects of opiate drugs may not im-pair one's working ability, to be known as an addict will probably lead to losing one's job. In such cases, the individual finds it difficult to conform to other rules which he had no intention or desire to break, and perforce finds himself deviant in these areas as well.' (Becker, 1973: 34). Again, the result may be self-identification as a drug user, decreasing community positive behavior, junky (or scarcity) behavior, and high levels of drug related crime and violence...

1.8. CONCLUSION

This literature survey has mainly taken the form of a collage of (verbatim) quotes of authoritative researchers such as Zinberg, Becker, Grund, Waldorf, Reinarman and Murphy, Shaffer and Jones, etc. It was made clear that political and legal responses to drug use are largely underpinned with the ubiquitous belief that illicit drugs generate dependence which, in turn, creates chaos. At the beginning of this chapter, we have ar-gued that both our common knowledge about varying use patterns of licit drugs (such as alcohol and nicotine), and an extensive array of scientific studies on controlled use of illicit drugs challenge the widely held belief that drug use inexorably tends towards loss of control.

The social setting, with its capacity to develop new informal social sanctions and rituals (informal controls), and its transmission of information in numerous informal ways, is a crucial factor in the controlled use of any intoxicant. This does not mean that the pharmacological properties of the drug or the attitudes and personality of the user are negligible. As Zinberg argues, all three variables -drug, set and setting- must be included in any valid theory of drug use. Yet, the very existence of 'controlled use', 'recreational use', 'casual use', 'maturing out', 'spontaneous recovery' and 'drifting out' reveals the fallacy of maintaining a rigid adherence to a single theory and treatment perspective, such as pharmacocentrism. Contrary to treatment and policy perspectives such as those espoused by the disease model of addiction and drug abuse -which does not recognize the existence of self-quitters because drug abuse is a disease that without outside intervention can only worsen or end in death - the data reveal significant evidence of individuals who have managed to terminate their use of drugs without formal drug treatment. *Addiction does not reside in drugs; it resides in human experience.* In spite of the physiological dependence that may be one (pharmacological) consequence of drug use, addiction is not inevitable. Furthermore, neither physiological dependence nor behavioral addiction implies that death is inevitable. It is possible to recover and regain one's independence, or in other words, to 'tame drugs'.

Zinberg argued that the processes through which social sanctions and social controls are transferred, vary with the legal status of the substances involved. In most sectors of society informal education about licit drugs is readily available. By the time we reach adolescence, we have absorbed an enormous amount of information about how to use these drugs. At the same time, most people believe that moderate use of these substances is possible, while the actual extent of non-compulsive use is remarkable.

Unlike the situation with licit drugs, the opportunities for learning how to control illicit drug consumption remain extremely limited. Neither the family, nor the school, nor the culture in general provides models for controlled use. As a consequence, the most important, but often inadequate, source is peer using groups. Despite the generally accepted idea that illicit drugs cannot be controlled and the popular image of peers as a corrupting force pushing people toward abuse ('peer pressure'), peer using groups provide instruction in controlling use (through 'peer support' processes).

The control of drugs is largely established by (sub)culturally based social controls (rituals and rules). But besides rituals and rules, there are other potential factors that impact upon the effectiveness of these social controls. Grund's feedback model suggests that other determinants of self-regulation might be drug availability and life structure. Rituals and rules, drug availability and life structure, in turn are each the result of distinctive variables and processes. External stimuli can either hinder or stimulate this feedback system, in particular its ability to support controlled and to adjust uncontrolled use.

Undoubtedly, one of the weightiest external stimuli that affect the proposed model of informal self-regulation at all three cornerstones, is the social definition of drugs and their users, embodied in formal drug policy. We believe that the current drug policy, with its mainly repressive characteristics, fails to reinforce safe use and even to a large extent obstructs the development and communication of safe standards. Formal norms may have some influence on whether people start using illicit drugs, but do not have a regulating effect on the actual use of drugs, as they do not provide instructions or rules for safe or controlled use. As a consequence, norms of controlled use are developed by users themselves through interaction and diffusion processes in, and between social groups, intrinsic to the practice of social drug use. Formal rules regarding illicit drug use not only fail to reinforce safe use, but their active enforcement even obstructs to a large extent the development and communication of safe standards.

The present forms of formal control create the preconditions for deviant subcultures of illicit drug use, generates and reinforces the stereotypical negative image (junkie, criminal, violent) and related behaviors, which are generally associated with drug use per se, and may thus create a self-fulfilling prophecy. Current drug policy hinders a more open discussion between drug users and non-users, thus impeding the dissemination of controlling rituals and social sanctions about drug use in general, and stimulating the alienation of drug users and amplifying deviancy. The normative influences of family, friends, and moderate users are minimized, while knowledge of the drugs' dangers and ways to avoid them is passed along slowly. Furthermore, the conflict between the law prohibiting use and the social group's approval of use, may cause personal and social conflicts (anxiety) that make controlled use of illicit drugs more complex and more difficult to achieve than that of licit drugs.

The initial impetus of this book (as explained in the general Introduction) was the conclusion that drug epidemiology in Belgium is scarcely out of its infancy: (1) most indicators of drug use in general are biased and focused on specific groups (the best known, most visible, accessible and maybe most marginalized subgroups of users); and (2) there is a complete lack of qualitative studies that seek to comprehend drug users' behavior from the 'native point of view'. Based on the literature survey on informal control mechanisms by illegal drug users presented in this Chapter, we can now formulate three specific research goals:

(1) To locate a minimum of 100 experienced cocaine users, preferably from non-institutionalized, non-captive[23] and hidden populations, and from the metropolitan area of Antwerp;

(2) To provide a 'thick' description of social rituals and rules (the informal controls) and the processes through which these are transferred;

(3) To initiate the identification of those factors related to current formal drug policy that might (de)stabilize self-regulation and controlled use.

NOTES

[1] Therapeutically, the 'protective' characteristics that distinguish the survivors have been used productively in the treatment of the casualties, using techniques such as motivational interviewing and relapse prevention training. These treatment strategies seek to increase mastery and control (which manifests itself in the non-problematic use of both illicit and licit drugs), generate valued alternatives to drug-centered behavior and increase insight by challenging denial. Cf. MILLER, W.R. and ROLLNICK, S. (1991), *Motivational interviewing*. New York, London: Guilford Press. MARLATT, G.A. and GORDON, J.R. (eds.) (1985), *Relapse prevention: maintenance strategies in the treatment of addictive behaviors*. New York: Guilford Press. MARLATT, G.A. and GORDON, J.R. (1980), Determinates of relapse: implications for the maintenance of behavioral change, in DAVIDSON, P.O. and DAVIDSON, A.M. (eds.), *Behavioral medicine: changing health lifestyle*.

New York: Brunner/Mazel. VAN BILSEN, H. and VAN EMST, A.J. (1989), Motivating heroin users for change, in BENNETT, M.G. (ed.), *Treating Drug Abusers*, Tavistock: Routledge.

2   Personal control and responsibility are key themes in the therapeutic use of 'motivational interviewing'. This popular method of counseling has suggested that clients need to believe they have a significant degree of control over their behavior if they are to make progress. Haynes and Ayliffe used a locus of control questionnaire to establish whether active misusers really believed they had less personal control than non-misusers. They found that active substance misusers are likely to have comparably higher external locus of control of behavior scores than non-misusers. HAYNES, P. and AYLIFFE, G. (1991), Locus of control of behaviour: is high externality associated with substance misuse, 86 *British Journal of Addiction*, 1111-1117.

3   See also: MURPHY, S., REINARMAN, C. and WALDORF, D. (1989), An 11-year follow-up of a network of cocaine users, 84 *British Journal of Addiction*, 427-436.

4   Compare with the definition of Weber and Schneider: 'Unter kontrolliertem Gebrauch illegaler Drogen verstehen wir eine bewußte und autonom eingeleitete Gebrauchsvariante, die keine ausschließlich drogenbezogene Lebensführung impliziert.' WEBER, G. and SCHNEIDER, W. (1990), Herauswachsen aus der Sucht: Kontrollierter gebrauch illegaler Drogen und Selbstheilung, 22 *Kriminologisches Journal*, 647-657.

5   See also p. 42.

6   Similarly, White and Bates present data from a non-clinical sample showing that many adolescents and young adults, who have experimented with or continually used cocaine for some time, self-initiate cessation before developing serious life problems. WHITE, H.R. and BATES, M.E. (1995), Cessation from cocaine use, 90 *Addiction*, 947-957.

7   References to the literature reviewed in this table are included in our general bibliography. Another summary of most of these studies is found in: CHRISTO, G. (1998), A review of reasons for using or not using drugs: commonalities between sociological and clinical perspectives, 5 *Drugs: education, prevention and policy* 1, 59-72.

8   Still, it must be acknowledged that cessation through natural recovery and cessation through formal treatment are difficult to compare and that there is a need for thorough comparative studies. WALDORF, D. and BIERNACKI, P. (1982), Natural recovery from heroin addiction: a review of the incidence literature, 173-182 in ZINBERG, N.E. and HARDING, W.M., *Control over intoxicant use. Pharmacological, psychological and social considerations.* New York: Human Sciences Press.

9   Cf. two possible pathways out of drinking problems without professional treatment, as described in: HUMPHREYS, K., MOOS, R.H. and FINNEY, J.W. (1995), *loc. cit.*, 427-441.

10 Orford *et al.* suggest that neuroadaptation, tolerance and withdrawal, often thought to be central to the process of addiction, may in fact be of comparatively little importance. ORFORD, J., MORISON, V. and SOMERS, M. (1996), Drinking and gambling: a comparison with implications for theories of addiction, 15 *Drug and Alcohol Review*, 47-56.

11 LADEWIG, D. (1987), Katamnesen bei Opiatabhängigkeit, 55-69. In: KLEINER, D., *Langzeitverläufe bei Suchtkrankheiten.* Berlijn/Heidelberg: Springer-Verlag. SWIERSTRA, K. (1987), *loc. cit.*, 78-92. SWIERSTRA, K. (1990), *Drugscarrières: van crimineel tot conventioneel.* Academisch Proefschrift Rijksuniversiteit Groningen. Groningen: Onderzoekscentrum voor Criminologie en Jeugdcriminologie. ONSTEIN, E.J. (1987), Heroïneverslavingscarrières. Hoe is het beloop in de tijd? Heeft therapie effect? Zijn er prognostisch gunstige factoren?, 29 *Tijdschrift voor Psychiatrie*, 516-525. SCHNEIDER, W. (1988), Zur Frage von Ausstiegschancen und Entwicklungsmöglichkeiten bei Opiatabhängigkeit, 34 *Suchtgefahren*, 472-490. TIMS, F.M., FLETCHER, B.W. and HUBBARD, R.L. (1991), Treatment outcomes for drug abuse clients, 93-113. In: PICKENS, R.W., LEUKEFELD, C.G. and SCHUSTER, C.R. (eds.), *Improving drug abuse treatment.* Washington: NIDA Research Monograph 106. TIMS, F.M. (1993). *Drug abuse treatment outcomes: two decades of research.* Lecture October Meeting Gelders Centrum voor Verslavingszorg. Arnhem.

12 See also Stanton PEELE's publications on these organizations.

13 Cf. the 'habitus'-concept of Pierre Bourdieu. See: LAERMANS, R. (1984), Bourdieu voor beginners, 18 *Heibel* 3, 21-48. BOURDIEU, P. *et al.* (1965), *Un art moyen*, 22. Paris: Minuit. BOURDIEU, P. (1980), *Le sens pratique.* Paris: Minuit. BOURDIEU, P. (1970), *La réproduction*, 64. Paris: Minuit.

14 Users choose mainly friends that use illegal drugs too. That is consistent with Erickson's finding that most cannabis users screen off themselves from social disapproval by others (non-users). ERICKSON, P.G. (1989), Living with prohibition: regular cannabis users, legal sanctions, and informal controls, 24 *The International Journal of the Addictions*, 175-188.

15 (Unintended) peer support effects have recently been acknowledged as a central feature of prevention projects and outreach work. Cf. BARENDREGT, C. and TRAUTMANN, F. (1996), *With little help from my friends. A survey on non-intentional peer-influences among drug users*. Utrecht: NIAD; TRAUTMANN, F. and BARENDREGT, C. (1994), *European Peer Support Handbook. Peer support as a method for AIDS prevention among IDU's*. Utrecht: NIAD. LEVY, J.A., GALLMEIER, C.P. and WIEBEL, W. (1995), The Outreach assisted peer-support model for controlling drug dependency, 25 *Journal of Drug Issues*, 507-529.

16 Cf. the distinction Norbert Elias makes between 'Fremdzwang' and 'Selbstzwang'. ELIAS, N. (1990), *Het civilisatieproces. Sociogenetische en psychogenetische onderzoekingen*, 239-345. Aula Paperback: Het Spectrum. In his theory of civilization, Elias departs from the fact that human beings are thrown together: they live together in 'figurations'. The genetical equipment of mankind is not such that these figurations are fixed for once and for all: they are subject to changes and through these changes the whole human way of life changes. The restrictions people impose themselves (similar to what we have called 'informal control'), stem from the figurations in which they live; the pressure they impose on themselves (*Selbstzwang*) is a direct continuation of the pressures they feel others impose on them (*Fremdzwang*). Elias describes how these various forms of pressure coming from other people are remolded into self-constraints; how the regulation of the whole inner life of emotions, impulses and drives becomes gradually more universal, steady and stable. These self-constraints have partly the appearance of conscious self-control and partly that of automatically functioning habits. Theoretically, Elias' ideas can also be applied to the phenomenon of drug use/abuse. The present study seeks to describe various forms of self-constraint and how these can evolve over time...

17 On the political use of the phenomenon 'drug addiction' by the police, see for example KAMINSKI, D. (1996), Approche globale et intégrée: de l'usage politique des drogues, 240. In: DE RUYVER, B., VERMEULEN, G., DE LEENHEER, A. and MARCHANDISE, T. (eds), *Veiligheids- en medisch-sociale benadering: complementair of tegengesteld? Drugbeleid 2000*. Antwerpen/Brussel: Maklu Uitgevers/Bruylant. *'Si la police veut rester (selon l'obligation légale qui leur en est faite mais aussi selon les priorités qu'elle se donne) un acteur dominant dans le domaine particulier de la lutte contre la drogue, elle doit (comme dans l'ensemble du travail judiciaire de la police) prouver en même temps l'efficacité et l'inefficacité de son action. Ce paradoxe est le moteur de la rhétorique du manque de moyens. Les fléaux sont les secteurs idéaux pour que cette rhétorique batte son plein: le fléau de la drogue est évidemment très important et tout qui lutte (...) est légitimé dans l'importance de son action même si (et surtout si) c'est une goutte d'eau dans l'océan.'* See also KAMINSKI, D. (1990), *loc. cit.*, 179-196.

18 Idiosyncracy = way of thinking or behaving that is peculiar to a person; personal mannerism.

19 See also: CRAMER, E. and SCHIPPERS, G. (1994), *op. cit.*, 23. Cramer and Schippers developed a self-control program starting from the assumption that addictive behavior is a form of learned and functional behavior, and thus can be 'unlearned'.

20 Moreover, an individual's beliefs concerning his/her own problem are important variables influencing the client's response to treatment programmes. See: KEENE, J. and RAYNOR, P. (1993), Addiction as a 'soul sickness': the influence of client and therapist beliefs, 1 *Addiction Research* 1, 77-87.

21 The classical concept of 'addiction' might even be a functional explanation of drug use for the professional enforcers of the present formal-repressive control system. According to Becker, the enforcers of formal control systems are not necessarily committed to the content of the rules, but only to the fact that the existence of those rules provides them with employment and a *raison d'être: 'In justifying the existence of his position, the rule enforcer faces a double problem. On the one hand, he must demonstrate to others that the problem still exists: the rules he is supposed to enforce have some point, because infractions occur. On the other hand, he must show that his attempts at enforcement are effective and worthwhile, that the evil he is supposed to deal with is in fact being dealt with adequately. (..) We may also note that enforcement officials and agencies are inclined to take a pessimistic view of human nature. If they do not actually believe in original*

sin, they at least like to dwell on the difficulties in getting people to abide by rules, on the characteristics of human nature that lead people toward evil.(...) It is not too great a stretch of the imagination to suppose that one of the underlying reasons for the enforcer's pessimism about human nature and the possibilities of reform is that fact that if human nature were perfectible and people could be permanently reformed, his job would come to an end.' BECKER, H.S. (1973), *op. cit.,* 156-158.

22 Cf. Becker's statement: 'The final outcome of a moral crusade is a police force.' BECKER, H.S. (1973), *op. cit.,* 163.

23 The term 'captive' is from Becker. BECKER, H.S. (1970), Practitioners of vice and crime, 30-49 in HABENSTEIN, R.W. (ed.), *Pathways to data.* Aldine. A 'captive audience' is a group of people who are, in a sense, forced to become involved in a given research activity by virtue of their obligatory position in some social position, or by virtue of their easy accessibility, such as inmates of prisons, students or pupils in a classroom, or institutionalized drug users. BLACK, J.A. and CHAMPION, D.J. (1976), *op. cit.,* 265-326.

CHAPTER 2

METHOLOGICAL DESIGN

2.1. INTRODUCTION

In chapter 1, we elaborated the *general focus of our research*, i.e. informal control mechanisms or self-regulation by illegal drug users. The present chapter deals with the *methods of data collection and analysis*. The subsequent paragraphs discuss the research methodology: non-randomized snowball sampling (or chain referral techniques).[1] In the area of deviant behavior, drug use and addiction in particular, snowball sampling was used to gather materials for studies now thought of as classics in the field.[2] In spite of the widespread use of chain referral sampling in qualitative sociological research, little has been written specifically about it. Few general textbooks on research methods and techniques devote more than a paragraph to descriptions of non-probability sampling (such as quota sampling, purposive or judgmental sampling...) in general, and snowball sampling in particular, and the problems these entail (Arber, 1993; Blalock, 1979; Black & Champion, 1976). This chapter explores the process of snowball sampling, and describes and analyses its procedures.[3] A separate issue addressed here is the generalizability of data that the snowball method can yield (the 'problem' of representativeness).

2.2. THEORETICAL CONSIDERATIONS ON SNOWBALL SAMPLING

Sample surveys can be categorized into two very broad classes on the basis of how the sample was selected, i.e. probability samples and non-probability samples. A probability sample has the characteristic that every element in the population has a known, non-zero probability of being included in the sample. A non-probability sample is one based on a sampling plan that does not have this feature. Because every element has a known chance of being selected in probability sampling, the reliability of the resulting population estimates can be evaluated. This provides insight into how much value can be placed on the estimates. In non-probability sampling, the reliability of the resulting estimates cannot be evaluated (Levy & Lemeshov, 1991). The major disadvantage of non-probability sampling is that we can obtain no valid estimate of our risks of error. Therefore, statistical inference or generalizations to a larger population are not legitimate and should not be made (Blalock, 1979: 571-573).

Nevertheless, non-probability samples are used quite frequently, for two main reasons. First, to gather sufficient data for an accurate estimation of correlates of current drug abuse, randomized sampling in the general population would require a very large sample. Probability sampling is a time-consuming and expensive procedure. Due to organizational or financial constraints, this is often not feasible (Wiebel, 1990).

And secondly, (epidemiological) research in the field of drug use has been confronted with the problem of the low social visibility of the target group (Watters & Biernacki, 1989). Given the societal view on cocaine use as deviant behavior and consequently the potential legal and social sanctions imposed on such behavior, respondents may either be hesitant to cooperate or tend to avoid morally or socially undesirable answers (Hendriks *et al.*, 1992: 13). Because of the 'hidden' nature of non-institutionalized drug use, it has been found extremely difficult to identify and specify the correct universe to be studied (Heckathorn, 1997).

In the general introduction of this book it was argued that both household and school surveys as well as monitoring systems that focus on specific target groups (drug abuse treatment admissions, drug-related police arrests, etc.) tend to miss important segments of the drug using population.[4] These so-called secondary indicator data sources are limited to 'captive' groups that may not compare to the total population of drug users (Van de Goor *et al.*, 1994: 33-34; Watters & Biernacki, 1989). Specific groups of (non-institutionalized) drug users may be underrepresented in surveys. For example, treatment-based surveillance systems incorporate by definition only drug users who have experienced physical, employment, legal, social, or psychological problems in relation to their drug use, and fail to include the non-problematic or controlled drug user. A related and equally fundamental critique on survey studies is their heavy reliance on statistically significant relations, which can lend a false understanding of causality and may not at all reflect the reality of every day life.

When referring to hidden populations of drug users, the implication is that they are hidden from formal systems of social service and control (Van de Goor *et al.*, 1994: 36). Although illegal drug use is often portrayed as an anonymous and retreatist activity, many (ethnographic) studies have shown that no drug user remains completely hidden or unknown, and that any drug user will always be part of some social network (Arber, 1993: 74). One of the most common forms of access to hidden populations of drug users is based on the essentially social nature of drug use. It is known as *chain referral sampling* or *snowball sampling* (Goodman, 1961). It involves asking known drug users to identify and/or introduce the researcher to drug-using friends and acquaintances, thereby attempting to move from known to unknown drug users and to generate a sample of hidden users.[5]

Thus, the social ties between the drug user and his/her partner, friends, acquaintances, colleagues, and even dealer(s) provide a way of selecting and contacting subjects for study in populations otherwise very difficult to target. The main problem is the extent and the sources of bias in such samples (Erickson, 1979: 299). Theoretically, random sampling designs (through which new respondents are randomly selected from a list of nominees by the known respondent) are preferable to non-random samples,[6] because they are grounded in a probabilistic theory which provides a formal model of selection and selection bias, as well as the practical tools to infer from sample to population (Hendriks *et al.*, 1992: 17). Although one can never be sure that a random sample is truly representative of the population from which it is drawn, at least the 'laws of chance' can be applied to estimate bias parameters. Non-random sampling designs lack the advantage of such a theory and its tools.

2.3. METHODOLOGY OF THE PRESENT STUDY: NON-RANDOM SNOW-BALL SAMPLING

As the best way to select a cross-section of users who are as representative as possible, we started to trace respondents using a snowball sampling procedure with randomized sequences. We recruited four cocaine users who met the intake criteria (snowball chain A).[7] At the end of the first interviews (in August 1996), these respondents were asked to mention all persons they knew who had used cocaine at least 25 times (i.e. a sample acceptability criterion taken over from Cohen, see below). Respondents were asked to write the initials, age, gender and profession of these people on a list... [8]

In a 'normal' course of events, the interviewer would then proceed to select randomly two nominees from this list, one to be the next respondent in a chain of referrals and one for reserve. It was planned to ask the interviewee to contact the first randomly selected nominee, to ask for cooperation preferably by telephoning while the interviewer was still there. Random selection from each respondent's list of nominees would lessen the possibility of respondent preference.

However, an unforeseen difficulty arose during these first four interviews. Each time a respondent was asked to mention all cocaine users he/she knew, we were confronted with a blunt refusal, and in one case a slightly aggressive rejection. None of these first four respondents was willing to mention any other cocaine user, not even if they were asked to write down only the initials, age and gender of the persons involved. Instead, all of them suggested that they would first talk to potential respondents, and let us know a few days or weeks later whether these people were willing to cooperate. It seemed to us that the illegal status of cocaine -and consequently the constant fear of discovery and prosecution- seriously hampered the successful application of a randomized snowball sampling procedure (see also: Heckathorn, 1997: 178-179).[9] Obviously, these cocaine users did not want to implicate other users in the research without first having obtained their informed consent. Giving names or even initials to a relatively unknown researcher just seemed too risky to them.

Because of these difficulties in finding and contacting respondents (and consequently our fear of being left with too small a sample), we decided to omit the randomization in the selection of nominees, and to interview each person who had been contacted by the respondent and who was willing to cooperate. However, it must be noted that after 6 months of intensive fieldwork, it became clear that a random sampling design would have been feasible from the start, if only a lengthier phase of developing trust with the target population had been possible. Within the given organizational and financial constraints of this study, it would have taken several more months to obtain a sample of the size we have recruited now (with a non-random sampling design, and after 9 months of intensive fieldwork). In conclusion, we felt that a random sampling procedure would have been possible if the research budget had been such to allow fieldwork over a longer period, or to recruit and train fieldworkers.

Of course, our choice for a non-randomized sampling design has serious drawbacks. We are aware that the naming of other people who share a certain characteristic (cocaine use), is not a random process, and that the first ('zero stage') respondent who is contacted to start the snowball, tends to be not randomly selected. Instead, naming others may be heavily influenced by factors such as the social (or geographical) distance between the namer and the named. Rapoport (1957 and 1979) distinguished the following formal sources of bias that can be expected to operate in social networks:

1. The *social distance* between pairs of individuals: clearly, the probability of one individual being connected to another is a function of the social distance between the individuals.

2. The *'island model'*: there may be several subsets of individuals among which the connection probabilities are random, but between which the connections have finite probabilities.

3. *Overlapping acquaintance circles*: although several subsets of individuals exist without any connections between them, the entire population can be connected by way of individuals being members of more than one subset.

4. *Reciprocal or reflexive bias*: a connection from an original individual to a target individual enhances the likelihood of a connection from the target person back to the original person.

5. *Force field bias*: because of certain characteristics (e.g. popularity) some individuals have a greater likelihood of being targeted than others.

6. *Sibling bias*: if A names B and C, then B and C are likely to name each other.

In short, our choice for a non-random sample design implied that we were unable either to lower the possibility of respondent preference, or to exclude the chance of being referred to nominees on the basis of unknown interviewee criteria, such as the ones identified above (Black & Champion, 1976).

2.4. THE 'PROBLEM' OF REPRESENTATIVENESS

Given the limits of our non-random sampling design, objections may be raised concerning the 'representativeness' of our sample. In paragraph 2.6 we describe our efforts to select many zero sample respondents as possible. The eventual snowball consisted of 25 different entrances (or chains). In paragraph 2.7 a technique of screening our snowball sampling data for bias is presented to provide the reader with cumulative insight into the nature of the snowball sampling process. Some general objections may be countered as follows.

A common critique of ethnographic research is that by studying small samples its findings are of little value because they are not generalisable. In our view, the choice of a small sample represents a trade-off between studying cases in depth or breadthwise. Ethnography usually sacrifices the latter for the former; while survey research does the reverse. In sacrifying depth, survey researchers may run the risk of losing relevant information or misunderstanding key features of the cases being studied (Van de Goor *et al.*, 1994: 34-35). In sacrifying breadth, ethnographers may lose possibilities for easy generalization (Watters & Biernacki, 1989). Advocates of quantitative survey research and of ethnographic fieldwork have contested each other's scientific status, but we believe this debate simply to be an issue that involves value judgments, in which people may disagree simply because they have different values (Schofield, 1993).

It cannot be stressed too much that the present study does not aspire to make inferences from a sample of 111 cocaine users to the total population of illegal drug users. In order to gather epidemiological knowledge we have tried to select as many zero sample respondents as possible (see paragraph 2.6.3) and to screen the snowball sampling procedure for biases (see paragraph 2.7). However, our aim is *not* to generalize to some larger whole or aggregate of cases of which our case forms part, as a prerequisite in assessing such generalizations is to know the identity of the larger aggregate. The purpose of this study is not to test a series of predetermined hypotheses on a representative sample that will allow for extrapolation to the whole population. Rather, it is to explore and analyze the social and psychological processes that help to tame cococaine and bring about its controlled use.

Many descriptions, evidential claims and conclusions presented in this book will seem concurrent with conclusions drawn by other authors. Referring to other studies on cocaine use and on informal regulation of illegal drug use, we can provide descriptive information about (controlled) cocaine use in Antwerp that is typical in some relevant aspects of the larger drug using population.

As we are concerned with making theoretical inferences rather than with empirical generalization, our sample is not required to be representative (Arber, 1993). It cannot be ignored that the illegal status of some drugs has led to a situation in which nobody really knows the total population of drug users. Consequently, the reader must try and estimate the most likely total population of drug users and consider the likely validity of our sample in generalizing for that population.

It has been suggested that ethnographic research suffers from a lack of precision as a result of the absence of quantification. But ethnography does not intrinsically reject quantification. Indeed, the present study employs quantification (through structured questions, to gain the same information from all the participants), together with open-ended questions, designed to explore the perspectives of the persons involved. However, precision is not always of overriding importance. Large and obvious differences may be reported in relatively imprecise ways without loss. Furthermore, there is the danger of over-precision: insisting on precise quantitative measures may produce figures that are more precise than can be justified given the nature of the data, and that are therefore misleading.

Rather than generalizing the findings of this book to the larger population of drug users ('empirical generalization'), our aim is to draw theoretical conclusions ('theoretical inference'). These claims are universal in scope: they refer to a range of possible cases rather than to a finite set of actual cases. As stated above, our fieldwork and our combination of structured and open-ended questions were designed to offer a description from the perspective of the cocaine users themselves (the insider's view) and to illuminate the theoretical issue of controlled use in general, and more specific the genesis, the existence and the application of informal control mechanisms (the 'taming' of cocaine).

To conclude, the aim of the present study is primarily qualitative and descriptive. Snowball sampling (or chain referral) offers clear practical advantages in obtaining information about a phenomenon that is difficult to observe, and that involves a sensitive and illegal issue. Since our study focuses on the description of new or unknown phenomena, the generalizability of the findings is of a lesser concern.[10] It follows that less stringent criteria are required in the snowball sampling procedure (Hendriks *et al.*, 1992: 22).

2.5. SAMPLE CRITERIA FOR EXCLUSION AND INCLUSION

During our search for literature on the subject of informal control mechanisms, we came across three cocaine studies by Peter Cohen and his colleagues at the University of Amsterdam.[11] In 1987, they interviewed 160 persons in Amsterdam with a minimum cocaine use of 25 lifetime instances (Cohen, 1989). In 1991, a follow-study of 64 cocaine users from this sample was completed (Cohen & Sas, 1993). And in the same year, Cohen and Sas (1995) interviewed another 108 experienced cocaine users.

First of all, the original goal of Cohen's investigations was similar to ours, namely to gain more insight into patterns of cocaine use among groups normally not associated with problematic drug consumption and to find out what mechanisms for controlling cocaine consumption were applied. Moreover, a comparison of the results of cocaine studies in neighboring countries (Belgium and the Netherlands) may well reveal interesting observations. Therefore, in order to make our sample as comparable as possible to Cohen's first study, we defined *identical* sample acceptability criteria (Cohen, 1989: 23):

1. The general focus of the study was *cocaine.* We told potential respondents that cocaine was our main interest, and that we were looking for people who had experience mainly with cocaine, or who considered cocaine to be their main drug (or drug of preference).
2. A *minimum lifetime experience of 25 instances* of cocaine was required for inclusion in the sample. This entry level was chosen to exclude very recently initiated users or experimental users from our database of experienced users.
3. For the same reason, respondents had to be *at least 18 years old* to be included.
4. Respondents should *not have been found guilty of a felony.*
5. Respondents should *not have been in any drug treatment program.*

The latter two exclusion criteria were chosen to locate a group of fairly 'typical' cocaine users in the community rather than those who had presented themselves for treatment or who had been in legal difficulties. Both sample exclusion criteria were also used because the location of at least 100 experienced cocaine users, preferably from non-institutionalized, non-captive and hidden populations, was one of the prerequisites of the present study. Representative surveys of the population tend to identify few cocaine users, whereas studies of those in treatment include more heavy users and therefore overestimate the extent of problems from cocaine use.

However, the respondents were not informed of the latter two exclusion criteria. Thus, after completing our interviews we found out that some of them had been convicted and/or had participated in a drug treatment program. But as will be shown further, what was initially considered a shortcoming turned out to be an advantage for illuminating some theoretical issues.[12]

2.6. COMPOSITION OF THE ZERO STAGE SAMPLE

In theory, a main source of bias determining the snowball sample is bias in the composition of the zero stage sample. In other words, the individuals who start the snowball chains should be selected at random (Spreen, 1992: 49). In practice, it is of vital importance to obtain as many different entrances as possible.

It has already been stated that in research in hidden populations, the application of a full random model or other types of probability sampling is often not feasible. Concerning the zero stage sample, the researcher often has no better option than to rely on the 'face validity' of a tentative map to judge its representativeness. For descriptive purposes, the zero stage sample must at least be grounded in a tentative model of the distribution of the phenomenon under study over types of individuals, places and time (Braunstein, 1993; Hendriks *et al.*, 1992: 23). For example, (controlled) cocaine use may be more likely to occur among certain age/gender/ethnic groups, in specific areas or sites of the city of Antwerp, or at specific times.

Based on a review of earlier research on cocaine use in other European and American cities,[13] on registered data from the city's institutions (police, hospitals, drug abuse treatment...) and on our own knowledge, a provisional 'map' of the occurrence of cocaine use in Antwerp was developed (see also: Watters & Biernacki, 1989: 416-430). Naturally, this tentative map was partly based on assumptions that may have been incorrect, and it was therefore regarded as just a vehicle to 'get the study started'. Moreover, these milieus often overlap each other. The initial model was to identify possible target groups according to the following two criteria: (1) a map of possible cocaine use in professional categories; and (2) a geographical map of cocaine use in Antwerp.

2.6.1. Identifying and selecting target groups

Based on foreknowledge of social groups/professional categories in general and of cocaine users in Antwerp in particular, the initial map of the present study was as follows:[14]

1.	street junkies	7.	hooligans
2.	prostitutes and escort services	8.	large discotheques
3.	professional criminals	9.	the Jewish milieu (diamond traders)
4.	artists/actors/musicians	10.	other important ethnic milieus in Antwerp
5.	restaurant/bar/hotel staff	11.	medical and paramedical professions
6.	pupils and stuudents	12.	youth centers

Some of these professional categories or social groups, such as the street junkies, the prostitutes and escort services and the professional criminals were explicitly eliminated as target populations, because the research aimed at obtaining information about the least 'visible', least 'known' (i.e. 'registered' or 'institutionalized'), least 'studied' and least 'marginalized' subpopulations of cocaine users.

Similarly, we have argued that since most information on drug users derives from either experimenting youngsters or extreme cases (worst case scenarios) because these are convenient to locate, and they may not apply to the majority of users. Thus, categories such as pupils and youth clubs were left out because we wanted to create a database of experienced cocaine users, at the exclusion of young 'experimenters'.

And finally, all ethnic minorities remained underrepresented in the snowball sample, simply because we failed to gain access to them. Although intensive efforts were made throughout the fieldwork, our efforts to relate to the Jewish, Moroccan, Irish, South American or other ethnic milieus remained unsuccessful.[15] For instance, we met one Jewish diamond trader who told us many stories about cocaine use among (Jewish) diamond merchants, but he was unwilling to participate in the interviews, or to nominate other respondents.

2.6.2. Tentative geographical map of research sites

Another way of mapping the occurrence of cocaine use in Antwerp was based on existing knowledge about the geographical distribution of natural congregation sites of cocaine users.[16] Although drug users are not confined to a particular part of the city and drugs such as heroin and cocaine can be bought in many neighborhoods, there are obviously some areas with heightened drug activity. On the basis of prior experience in the Antwerp drug scene,[17] these areas had been identified beforehand.[18] Furthermore, there are some areas where window and street prostitution is quite visible.[19]

As we wanted to assemble data on cocaine users who did not belong to the most visible and most marginalized subcultures frequenting these well known areas of prostitution and copping zones, these natural congregation sites were *excluded* both as strategic research sites for the present study and as sites for the selection of the zero sample respondents. Throughout our fieldwork we visited these areas only occasionally.

In fact, from the onset of this study we decided to start the survey by immersing ourselves into the *Antwerp nightlife scene* rather than to select specific zones to make contacts with cocaine users. Bearing in mind cocaine's reputation as a party drug, and the descriptions offered by scientific literature on its recreational use (e.g. Hendricks, 1992; Mugford, 1994; Ditton & Hammersley, 1994), we assumed the popular bars, cafes and discotheques in Antwerp to be the natural congregation sites of many cocaine users. Thus, in August 1996, we started hanging out at entertainment centers (see also: Power, 1989). After gaining access to some social networks of cocaine users, we were often invited to join respondents in other bars and dance halls, and occasionally at private parties and private homes. At the end of our fieldwork, in April 1997, we had become a regular visitor to five large dance halls (including three discotheques in the city center) and about fifteen popular bars in the inner city. With the exception of one dance hall, all these venues were located outside the prostitution and drug copping areas.

2.6.3. Location of zero stage respondents

In theory, the total sample size should be sufficiently large to ensure reasonable representativity (Hendriks *et al.*, 1992: 23). The best way to achieve this is by starting with a relatively large zero sample rather than by requiring a larger number of nominees per person. Although representativity was not a main goal, much effort was directed toward selection of as many zero sample respondents as possible. After all, gaining epidemiological knowledge was one of the goals of this study. The snowball sample finally obtained consisted of 25 different entrances (+ chain A, which contains the four pilot interviews). Figure 2.6.a shows an overview of the snowball chains.

A major problem of the snowball sampling method or chain referral technique is the selection of the first respondents (zero stage). This paragraph describes how the 25 zero stage respondents (chain B to Z) were located. But first, the use of locators in the snowball sampling procedure of this study needs to be dealt with. Most authors find it fruitful to use both paid and unpaid persons to help locate new respondents and start additional referral chains (e.g. Wiebel, 1990; Griffiths *et al.*, 1993). First, because finding respondents on the basis of theory and foreknowledge often restricts the initiation of referral chains to those areas that the researcher is already aware of and that are easily accessible.

Second, as a result of their past or present situations, certain persons have greater accessibility and knowledge about a specific area of life than do others. These persons can develop referral chains more easily because they may already be aware of potential respondents or may be more likely to have others reveal their potential to them. The financial restraints of the present study did not allow for hiring paid locators or research assistants. But some of the (initial) respondents became de facto research assistants, since they managed to make contacts for possible interviews more efficiently than me. They also helped to allay the suspicion that the researcher might be connected with law enforcement agencies or treatment institutions.

- In August 1996 we started our fieldwork by re-establishing old contacts with two individuals we had met in 1994 during a previous research project on safety and private surveillance in discotheques (Van Laethem *et al.*, 1995). Both persons were still working in a discotheque and knew many of their customers well enough to assist us in locating and addressing potential respondents. These entries led to two snowball chains (C and Z).

- Secondly, we made use of our personal contacts with the staff of two low threshold treatment institutions in Antwerp to make contacts with drug users who were willing to take us to some bars, or to potential respondents. These contacts led to snowball chains D, F, H and N.[20]

- Six further snowball chains were initiated through our personal friends, colleagues or acquaintances. These key informants were carefully instructed about the criteria for sample acceptability. These contacts led to snowball chains G, J, K, L, U, and V.

- After several months of fieldwork, we also succeeded in establishing approving relationships with high-status indigenous individuals in the nightlife scene. These contacts facilitated direct rapport with many group members, and led to snowball chains B, E, I, M, Q, R, S, W, X, and Y.

- Unlike other studies, our project had insufficient resources to recruit and train people to assist us in locating and interviewing cocaine users. Fortunately, we were able to recruit a recently graduated sociologist who knew other networks of cocaine users. She initiated three snowball chains through her acquaintances (O, P and T), leading to 10 respondents.

Figure 2.6.a   Overview of snowball chains

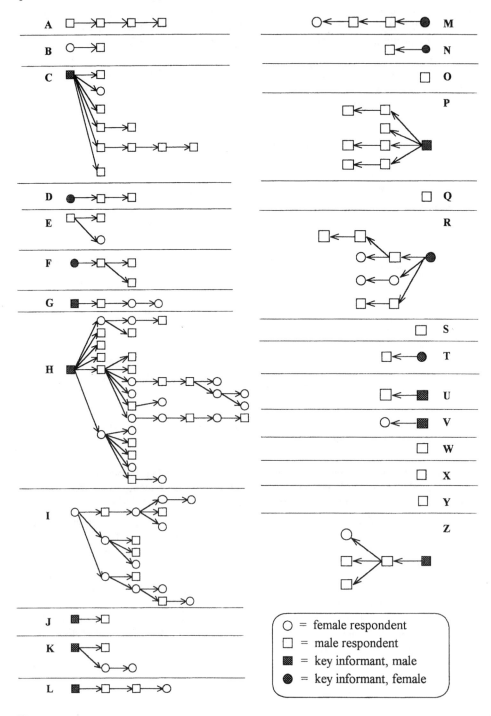

2.6.4. Overview of snowball chains

The Antwerp sample of 111 cocaine users interviewed between August 1996 and April 1997 can be grouped in 26 different snowball chains (see figure 2.6.a).

- Six of the 26 chains (O, Q, S, W, X, and Y) were limited in length to the 'starter', i.e. they consisted only of zero stage respondents (23.1%);
- Five of the 26 chains (J, N, T, U, and V) were initiated by non-using key informants, and led to only one respondent (19.2%);
- In general, 10 chains (A, B, E, I, O, Q, S, W, X, and Y) were initiated through actual cocaine users (38.5%) and 16 chains (C, D, F, G, H, J, K, L, M, N, P, R, T, U, V, and Z) were initiated through non-using key informants (61.5%).
- Eighteen chains (A, C, E, G, H, J, K, L, O, P, Q, S, U, V, W, X, Y, and Z) were initiated through male respondents or key informants (69.2%) versus 8 chains (B, D, F, I, M, N, R, and T) through female 'starters' (30.8%).
- Chains where one respondent is followed by one other respondent only are called 'linear chains'. Our sample contains 17 linear chains, if the chains that are limited to the 'starters' are included (A, B, D, G, J, L, M, N, O, Q, S, T, U, V, W, X, and Y). Three chains are bi-linear (E, F, and K), i.e. two nominees are the next respondents in a 'forked' chain.
- Six chains are 'multilinear' (C, H, I, P, R and Z): i.e. certain respondents have led to more than two new respondents. Because the risk of several kinds of bias is obvious for these chains, a closer look at the 'starters' provides more insight in these snowballs:

Chain C: A high status indigenous individual who had been working in the hotel and catering business for more than 20 years initiated this chain. He contacted several potential respondents, with whom he had different relations. Some of them were friends he met regularly in the nightlife scene, others used to be customers in his discotheque, and others clearly were mere acquaintances he nevertheless convinced to take part in the interview. Participant observation in the nightlife scene showed clearly that only 2 of the 5 respondents he contacted really knew each other.

Chain H: This chain was initiated by a staff member of a low threshold treatment agency in Antwerp. He was informed extensively about the goal of the present study, and contacted 6 people. Although initially none of these 6 individuals seemed to know each other, several indications were subsequently found that most of the respondents from this chain frequented the same scene.

Chain I: This chain was initiated by a 26-year-old female cocaine user, who was working in a bar. She contacted three people: two girls who according to her used to be close friends more than 5 years ago, but 'had drifted away because they had other interests'. The third person she contacted belonged to a distinct group of friends she had been frequenting the last few years.

Chain P: A 35-year-old friend of the second interviewer initiated this chain. He knew two colleagues who used cocaine, and he also recruited two more respondents from his personal circle of friends. He assured us that the two colleagues and the two friends did not know each other at all.

Chain R: This chain was initiated by a 27-year-old female researcher. She contacted three of her friends, who in turn contacted other people. Although these people clearly belong to very distinct professional categories (2 actors, 1 graphic designer, 1 journalist, 1 social worker, 1 scientific worker, 1 computer programmer and 1 student), fieldwork provided indications that the respondents from this chain knew each other.

Chain Z: This chain was initiated by a 36-year-old male bartender. He contacted a regular customer of his bar, who in turn contacted three friends. Obviously, these 4 respondents frequented the same bar, but fieldwork provided indications that only two of them actually knew each other.

- The longest chain consisted of 7 persons (including the zero stage respondent, who was a non-user) or 6 waves (a 'wave' is the step from one respondent to the next in the chain). The average length of the snowball chains equaled 3.1 respondents, or 2.1 waves (if the non-using 'starters' are included). The average length of the snowball chains equaled 2.3 cocaine users, or 1.3 waves (if the non-using 'starters' are excluded).

- The two interviewers differed substantially in average lengths of their snowball chains: the average length of the snowball chains interviewed by us equaled 3.2 respondents (or 2.2 waves), whereas the average length of the snowball chains of the other interviewer equaled 2.3 respondents (or 1.3 waves), if the non-using 'starters' are included. Another remarkable difference between both interviewers is that the female sociologist interviewed 9 male cocaine users, whereas the (male) author interviewed 61 male and 41 female cocaine users. Although other clear differences might be found (for example regarding other demographic characteristics or specific features of their cocaine use), the effect should be rather limited as 91.9% of all the respondents were interviewed by the same (male) interviewer.

- If the non-using zero stage key informants are included, the average number of new respondents nominated by a previous respondent was 1.2. If the non-using zero stage key informants are excluded, the average nominations made by respondents was halved to 0.6. The average number of respondents nominated by non-using key informants was 2.0, which was markedly higher. These figures illustrate the importance of a few key informants to gain access to the target population. Although some of them did *not* use cocaine, their greater accessibility and knowledge about drug use in general and cocaine use in particular, helped us to develop referral chains.

2.7. SCREENING FOR BIASES IN THE NOMINATION PROCESS

Having acknowledged the limits of the non-random sampling design at the zero level, we will screen our final sample in this paragraph for bias at the further level (the nomination process). Theory suggests that the targets of the nominators should be equiprobable, i.e. having an equal chance of being drawn (Hendriks *et al.*, 1992: 83).

With respect to the nomination process, there are several ways to screen the snowball sampling data on the occurrence of bias. For example, insight into the mechanisms of the nomination process can be obtained by investigating different snowball chains. Table 2.7.a provides an analysis of the five largest snowball chains of the Antwerp sample (chains C, H, I, P, and R), comparing mean age, male-female-ratio, occupational background, route of ingestion, level of use during the three months prior to the interview, prevalence of opiate use (combined with cocaine), treatment contacts and self-reported deviance.

Table 2.7.a - Comparison of 5 snowball chains

	Total sample N=111	Chain C N=10	Chain H N=32	Chain I N=17	Chain P N=7	Chain R N=8
Mean age	29.2yrs	30.7yrs	29.6yrs	27.7yrs	27.6yrs	25.9yrs
% of male respondents	63.1%	90.0%	46.9%	35.3%	100.0%	62.5%
Occupation						
-unemployed	16.2%	-	21.9%	5.9%	-	-
-arts-related professions	18.0%	10.0%	9.4%	41.2%	42.9%	37.5%
-hotel and catering	16.2%	50.0%	12.5%	11.8%	-	-
-students	9.9%	-	15.6%	5.9%	-	25.0%
Route of ingestion (LTP)						
- snorting	99.0%	100.0%	96.9%	100.0%	100.0%	100.0%
- freebasing	72.1%	60.0%	87.5%	70.6%	28.6%	62.5%
- injecting	24.3%	-	50%	17.6%	-	-
Route of ingestion (LMP)						
- snorting	53.2%	50.0%	43.7%	70.6%	57.1%	87.5%
- freebasing	17.1%	10.0%	31.2%	5.9%	-	12.5%
- injecting	7.2%	-	18.75%	-	-	-
Level of use last 3 months						
-none	18.9%	30.0%	18.8%	23.5%	14.3%	-
-low	64.9%	40.0%	62.5%	58.8%	71.4%	100.0%
-medium	10.8%	10.0%	15.6%	11.8%	14.3%	-
-high	5.4%	20.0%	3.1%	5.9%	-	-
Opiate use						
- life time prevalence	63.1%	10.0%	84.4%	52.9%	28.6%	62.5%
- last 2 weeks preval.	17.1%	-	31.2%	-	-	-
- combined with coke	21.6%	-	53.1%	17.6%	-	37.5%
No treatment contacts	79.3%	100.0%	59.4%	94.1%	85.7%	100.0%
No convictions	47.7%	20.0%	37.5%	70.6%	57.1%	75.0%
No illegal activities	73.0%	90.0%	56.25%	76.5%	85.7%	100.0%

Some major differences between these 5 snowball chains can be observed in this table:[21]

- The mean age of the respondents of **chain C (N=10)** is 30.7 years, which is higher than in the chains H, I, P and R, and higher than the mean age of the total sample. It is an almost exclusively male subsample (90%). Half of this sample's respondents work in a hotel/bar/restaurant; none is unemployed or a student. Compared to chain H, P and R, and to the total sample, the prevalence of freebasing as a route of ingestion (both for lifetime prevalence and for last month prevalence) is relatively low.[22] None of the respondents of this chain have ever tried injecting cocaine. The proportion of ex-users and high level users (at the time of the interview) is higher. In comparison to the other chains and to the total sample, the prevalence of opiate use (combined use with cocaine included) is markedly low. None of the respondents report treatment contacts, and only 1 individual reports illegal activities to obtain (money for) cocaine. Nevertheless, 80% of chain C has been convicted for a felony at least once.

- The mean age in **chain H (N=32)** is higher compared to the total sample, and to chains I, P and R. There are relatively more female respondents, as well as more unemployed and students. The prevalence of injecting and freebasing is rather high in this chain (when including both lifetime prevalence and last month prevalence). Nevertheless, the pattern of respondent's level of use at the time of the interview is quite similar to the pattern found in the total sample. Opiate use is clearly more prevalent compared to the total sample, and to other chains. This chain shows the lowest proportion of respondents who report no treatment contacts and no illegal activities to obtain (money for) cocaine. Compared to the total sample, more respondents have been convicted for a felony.

- **Chain I (N=17)** shows a relatively high proportion of female respondents. A considerable proportion of respondents (41.2%) works in arts-related professions. The pattern of life time prevalence of different routes of ingestion resembles the one found in the total sample, although snorting seems to be the most prevalent route of ingestion at the time of the interview. The prevalences of opiate use, treatment contacts, convictions and illegal activities are all lower than in the total sample.

- **Chain P (N=7)** is an exclusively male subsample. About 43% have an arts-related profession. The prevalence of freebasing as a route of ingestion is the lowest compared to the other chains, and to the total sample. None of these respondents has ever injected cocaine, or combined it with opiates. Compared to chains C, H and I, and to the total sample, the proportion of low level users at the time of interview is high. The same holds for the proportion of respondents of this chain who report no treatment contacts, no convictions, or no illegal activities.

- The mean age of **chain R (N=8)** is relatively low (25.9 years). About one quarter of this chain are students; more than one third have an arts-related profession. None of these respondents has ever injected. All respondents are low level users at the time of the interview. A considerable proportion (37.5%) combines cocaine with opiates, but none of them reports treatment contacts or illegal activities to obtain (money for) cocaine.

Thus, the comparison of the five largest snowball chains of the Antwerp sample (chains C, H, I, P, and R) on a number of variables shows some important differences. We are aware that most first ('zero stage') respondents who were contacted to start the snowball, were not randomly selected. We admit that our study did not quite succeed in avoiding this kind of bias.

Yet, other factors may influence the nomination process as well. For excample, the island model (see above) implies that within the population of cocaine users several subgroups of users may exist within which the likelihood to be nominated may be random, but the limited connections between different subgroups may result in a finite, and rather small, nomination probability across subgroups. For example, cocaine users may form connected, or closed subgroups that can be described by preferred route of ingestion. If this were the case, then the nominees would be quite likely to prefer the same route of ingestion as the nominator, and the probability within a snowball chain to cross from cocaine users who prefer snorting over to cocaine users who prefer injecting will be rather small. The implicit consequence of this bias is that -unless the selection of zero stage respondents is carefully weighed- cocaine users who prefer a different route of ingestion have a much smaller probability to be included in the subsequent stages of the snowball sample than cocaine users preferring the same route of ingestion as the (zero stage) nominator.

In general, a snowball sampling procedure carries the risk of recruiting respondents who are -in unknown, but still systematic ways- similar to the person who nominated them, which in turn may result in a biased sample (Hendriks *et al.*, 1992: 86).[23]

Indeed, we did find some similarity bias in the nomination process. Relative similarities between respondents and their nominees were found for injecting as a route of ingestion, prevalence of heroin use, combined use of heroin and cocaine, treatment experience and self-reported deviance. In short, the snowball sampling procedure may have resulted in a slightly biased sample as a consequence of the non-random recruitment of nominees. However, as stated above, the aim of this book is 'theoretical inference' rather than empirical generalization. Our efforts were directed towards detection of all relevant information and key features of informal control mechanisms in cocaine users, rather than towards generalizability of the findings to the population of all cocaine users.

2.8. INSTRUMENTS AND DATA COLLECTION

Previous research activities with drug-using groups in the natural setting focused on the congregation areas frequented by drug users during the course of their daily activities. Such sites commonly included drug-copping areas, shooting galleries, prostitution strolls, public parks and streets (e.g. Bourgeois, 1995; Grund, 1993; Hammersley & Ditton, 1994; Power *et al.*, 1995; Ratner, 1993; Sterk-Elifson & Elifson, 1993; Waldorf, 1977). After gaining access to the people frequenting these places, field observations are possible all day and night. If the target group is compulsive, marginalized, and often visible, participant observation at any moment of the day is feasible. But if the targeted populations are recreational or controlled users, who are not marginalized at all (i.e. who have a regular job, a family, etc.), participant observation becomes difficult. These populations tend to be less easy to follow during their daily course of activities (Braunstein, 1993: 131-140).

Therefore, our preliminary fieldwork consisted mainly of 'hanging out' at those places where non-marginalized cocaine users tend to meet regularly: the nightlife scene. At first, an additional advantage of this method seemed to be that the researcher's presence did not need any legitimization: he was just another partygoer. Our immersion in the Antwerp nightlife scene offered interesting possibilities for locating and establishing contacts with potential respondents in a friendly yet non-intrusive manner, but it proved to be impossible to observe the target population on a daily basis. However, it was possible to observe people during their regular nights out.[24]

Through *participant observation* we established contacts that would lay the foundations for a more formal interview situation (Power, 1989: 43-52). Participant observation was primarily used as an enabling process for the setting up and completion of a required number of interviews. It was also used to gain access to a variety of different networks of drug users, to nurture relationships of trust so that new introductions would be forthcoming, and to acquire an insider's view of a group of cocaine users.[25]

Our primary objective was to achieve an understanding of social processes by interviewing in detail and at length, and on more than one occasion (Arber, 1993). After establishing preliminary contacts with potential respondents during field observations, we asked them whether they were willing to participate in a double interview:[26]

1. *A semi-structured questionnaire.* This included questions about initiation of use, level of use, patterns of use over time, temporary abstinence and decreased use, methods of use, use of cocaine with other drugs, purchase of cocaine, circumstances of use, advantages and disadvantages of use, presence of adulterants, opinion about cocaine, dependency, using cocaine at work, and general data about the respondent. In order to obtain comparable data, about 80% of the questions of the semi-structured interview were taken over from Cohen's first cocaine study in Amsterdam (1989: 129-158). See also the questionnaire in Appendix.

2. *An open biographical interview.* Respondents were asked to tell their life story in their own words. The interviewer used a protocol listing the respondent's youth, family relations, school career, initial experiences with drugs, relations with peers, drug career, occupational career, intimate relationships, control over drug use, treatment experiences, contacts/encounters with the police, involvement with dealers, cocaine and sex, cocaine and aggression, and rules about cocaine use.

Both interviews took place at different moments, usually with a time interval of two to three weeks. Respondents were asked to set the date and place for the interviews to their own preference. On average, each interview took two hours. About half of the first interviews took place at the respondents' homes, the rest at another agreed place. Almost three-quarters of the second interviews took place at the respondents' homes.

Between August 1996 and April 1997 the author of this book conducted 101 first interviews (semi-structured questionnaires) and 97 second interviews (open biographical interviews). A recently graduated sociologist (female) was recruited to conduct both interviews with 10 respondents. Participants were paid 2,000 Belgian francs after completion of the second interview. This *payment of subject fees* was intended as an indication of the value of the data being collected and as an acknowledgment of the value of the time subjects were expected to dedicate to the research protocol, rather than as a financial bait for potential respondents (see: Power, 1989). Moreover, our assumption that people who could afford a cocaine habit from their normal wages, would not be easily tempted to give up their anonymity for a relatively small fee, proved to be right for the majority of our respondents.

With the exception of three biographical interviews, all interviews were recorded on tape with the participants' informed consent. Transcriptions were done by the author and some personal friends. Great pains were taken to exert stringent control over the literal transcriptions of the tape recordings. After transcription, the tapes were destroyed and the data were made anonymous. The data from the semi-structured questionnaires were statistically handled with Spss Version 7.0™.[27] The data from the open biographical interviews were handled with QSR NUD*IST Version 4.0[28], a software program that allowed to link our quantitative data from Spss with our qualitative data.[29] All coding and analyses were performed by the author.

2.9. CONCLUSION

Traditionally, (epidemiological) research on drug use has been confronted with low social visibility of the target group. Given the societal view on cocaine use as deviant behavior and hence the potential legal and social sanctions, it has proved extremely difficult to identify and specify the correct universe to be studied. The present study uses the *chain referral sampling* or *snowball sampling* technique, based on the essentially social nature of drug use (i.e. the presence of social ties between the drug user and his/her partner, friends, acquaintances, colleagues and even dealers). Theoretically, random sampling designs (through which the known respondent randomly selects new respondents from a list of nominees) are preferable to non-random samples, because the 'laws of chance' can be applied to estimate bias parameters. But because of difficulties in finding and contacting respondents (and consequently being left with too small a sample), we decided to omit the randomization in the selection of nominees, and instead to interview each individual who had been contacted by the respondent and who was willing to cooperate. To make our sample comparable to Cohen's first study (1989), we defined identical sample acceptability criteria.

Concerning the zero stage sample, a provisional 'map' of cocaine use in Antwerp was developed, based on existing knowledge. This initial model was meant to identify possible target groups according to two criteria: (1) a map of possible cocaine use according to professional categories; and (2) a geographical map of cocaine use in Antwerp. Clearly, the first ('zero stage') respondents for the present study were not randomly selected. Some of the professional categories or social groups, such as the street junkies, the prostitutes, escort services and professional criminals were explicitly eliminated as target populations, because we wanted to obtain information about the least 'visible' and least 'marginalized' subpopulations of cocaine users. Natural congregation areas such as well-known drug copping zones and areas of prostitution were *excluded* as strategic research sites for the same reason. Secondary school pupils and youth clubs were left out because we wanted to create a database on experienced cocaine users, at the exclusion of young 'experimenters'. And finally, ethnic minorities remained underrepresented in the snowball sample, simply because the researcher did not succeed in gaining access to them.

Plunging into the Antwerp nightlife scene started the survey. Bearing in mind cocaine's reputation as a party drug, we assumed that the popular bars, cafes and discotheques in Antwerp were the natural meeting places for many cocaine users. Although representativity was not a main goal, much effort was directed toward the selection of as many zero sample respondents as possible. Through some old contacts with inhabitants, colleagues, friends, but even more through the establishment of approving relationships with high-status indigenous individuals in the nightlife scene, we finally obtained 25 entrances. After establishing preliminary contacts with potential respondents during field observations, we asked them whether they were willing to participate in a double interview: a *semi-structured questionnaire* and an *open biographical interview*.

Obviously, our choice for a non-randomized sampling design had important drawbacks. To provide the reader with cumulative insight into the nature of the snowball sampling process, we made a comparison of different snowball chains. We assume that the naming of people who share a certain characteristic (cocaine use) is not a random process. As a rule, a snowball sampling procedure has the inherent risk of recruiting respondents who are -in unknown but still systematic ways- similar to the person who nominated them, which in turn may result in a *biased sample*. This chapter provided ample proof that one disadvantage of our method is that it almost certainly includes only respondents within a few connected networks of individuals. Undoubtedly, there were other networks of contacts that were not covered by this study. Yet, this does not lessen the *validity* of the findings presented in the following chapters, for the following reasons.

This book does not pretend to make inferences from the sample of 111 cocaine users to the total population of illegal drug users, because a first requirement in assessing such generalizations is to know the identity of the larger aggregate. Rather than generalizing the findings of the present study to the larger population of drug users ('empirical generalization'), it is our aim to draw theoretical conclusions ('*theoretical inference*'). In other words, the aim of the present study is primarily qualitative and descriptive. Thus, the generalizability of the findings is of a lesser concern. It is clear then, that less stringent criteria are needed in the snowball sampling procedure.

Even if more stringent criteria were applied in the snowball sampling procedure, one can never be sure that a random sample is truly representative of the population from which it is drawn. First of all, the possible sources of bias we described above may not at all be so strong. Certain tendencies may be a mere reflection of population parameters. Moreover, theories about snowball sampling procedures presuppose a fixed number of selected nominees per respondent, and an equal non-response (see: Hendriks *et al.*, 1992: 32).

And finally, one can never be sure that the selection of zero stage respondents reflects the factual population (which is unknown). In our view, it was more important that our sample showed great variability (or diversity), since the focus of our research is primarily on the description of new or unknown phenomena and on generating hypotheses about these phenomena. Regarding (features of) cocaine use, the next chapters are bound to show considerable variation within our sample of cocaine users. Chapter 3 provides more insight in the (variance in) basic demographic characteristics of our Antwerp sample of 111 cocaine users.

NOTES

1   The terms 'snowball sampling method' and 'chain referral technique' will be used alternately.

2   It was used in LINDESMITH's original study of opiate addiction (1968) as well as in BECKER's work on marijuana users (1966). These are only two of a large number of studies in deviance that utilized the chain referral method. Some references: BECKER, H.S. (1966), *Outsiders: studies in the sociology of deviance*. New York: Macmillan. LINDESMITH, A.R. (1968), *Addiction and opiates*. Chicago: Aldine. ATKYNS, R.L. and HANNEMAN, G.J. (1974), Illicit drug distribution and dealer communication behavior, 15 *J. of Health and Social Behavior*, 36-45. FELDMAN, H.W. (1977), A neighborhood history of drug switching, 249-278 in WEPPNER, R.S. (ed.), *Street ethnography: selected studies of crime and drug use in natural settings*. Beverly Hills, CA: Sage. HARDING, W., ZINBERG, N., STEMACK, S. and BARRY, M. (1979), Formerly addicted-now-controlled opiate users, *Int. J. of Addictions*, 14. HANSON, W., BESCHNER, G., WALTERS, J. and BOVELLE, E. (1985), *Life with heroin: voices from the inner city*. Lexington, MA: Lexington

books. For a discussion of major community cocaine studies using snowball sampling methods or chain referral techniques, see the general introduction.

3   The methodological and ethical problems that emerged in the course of using the chain referral method are discussed in a forthcoming publication: DECORTE, T. (2000), A qualitative study of cocaine and crack in Antwerp (Belgium): some ethical issues, in E.M.C.D.D.A. (ed.), *Understanding and responding to drug use: the role of qualitative research* (forthcoming). Lissabon, E.M.C.D.D.A.

4   See Introduction, p. 1-3.

5   Discussing the utility of snowball sampling in the context of drug use research, BIERNACKI and WALDORF stated that this method is particularly applicable when the focus of study is on a sensitive issue, possibly concerning a relative private matter, and thus requires the knowledge of insiders to locate people for study. Given its illegal status, cocaine use can clearly be considered 'a private matter'. To prevent discovery and prosecution, cocaine users have to hide their cocaine related activities. BIERNACKI, P. and WALDORF, D. (1981), Snowball sampling problems and techniques of chain referral sampling, 10 *Sociological Methods and Research*, 141.

6   Unless of course the aim of a given research is to examine a phenomenon in very specific subgroups of the total population (targeted sampling).

7   See figure 2.6.a, p. 68.

8   We wanted to trace respondents using exactly the same snowball sampling procedure with randomized sequences, as Cohen did in his study of Amsterdam cocaine users. COHEN, P. (1989), *Cocaine use in Amsterdam in non-deviant subcultures*, 23-24. Amsterdam: Instituut voor Sociale Geografie, Universiteit van Amsterdam.

9   A research team from Paris experienced the same difficulties. INGOLD, R., TOUSSIRT, M., PLISSON, T, and RAGOT, V., *Paris individual report on cocaine: notes and observations*, 51-58 in HENDRIKS, V.M., BLANKEN, P., and ADRIAANS, N.F.P. (1992), *op. cit.*, 16.

10 Nevertheless, we have tried to screen our snowball sampling data for bias, to provide the reader with a cumulative insight into the nature of the snowball sampling process (see paragraph 2.7).

11 See also Introduction, p. 13, 16, 17 and Chapter 1, p. 24.

12 See Chapter 3, p. 86-93.

13 See Introduction, p. 10-17.

14 This pre-knowledge was partly based on the author's personal experiences, both professionally (see note 17) and privately (observations among friends), and on the review of relevant scientific literature in the years preceding the present study.

15 Unfortunately, financial constraints prevented us from recruiting (native) fieldworkers with the right status (and knowledge of language) to gain access into these sensitive and sometimes closed environments.

16 See note 14 and 17.

17 The author of the present study worked for a period of four months in the FREE CLINIC, a low threshold drug treatment center in Antwerp.

18 These areas comprise the following streets and squares: *De Conincksplein, Provinciestraat, Statiestraat, St.-Jansplein, Dambruggestraat, Franklin Rooseveltplaats...*

19 Two areas of window prostitution (the *Schipperskwartier* and the *Korte en Lange Winkelhaakstraat*) and an area of street prostitution (the blocks between the *Franklin Rooseveltplaats* and the *St. Jansplein*).

20 After completing 111 interviews, it became clear that many of the respondents from these snowball chains did not comply with our sample acceptability criteria, although we explicitly mentioned these key informants that we were not interested in cocaine users from so-called deviant subcultures ('junkies', prostitutes).

21 Because of the small numbers involved, statistical significance was not tested.

22 For an extended discussion of this particular route of ingestion in the Antwerp sample, see Chapter 7, p. 175-195.

23 One way to investigate similarity bias in the nomination process is to relate some specific characteristic of the nominator to the corresponding characteristic of the persons he/she nominated. Since similarity, social distance, geographic distance, etc... are integral aspects of relations between people, there are no absolute criteria for determining whether these aspects unacceptably influence the characteristics of the total snowball sample. Notwithstanding this lack of 'cut-off points', investigation of the data may provide some insight in this matter.

24 Which afterwards proved to be the preferable environment for cocaine use for many of our respondents. See Chapter 14, p. 312-315.

25 The following books were consulted: BILLIET, J.B. (1990), *Methoden van sociaal wetenschappelijk onderzoek: ontwerp en dataverzameling*, 259-313. Leuven/Amersfoort: Acco. SILVERMAN, D. (1993), *Interpreting qualitative data. Methods for analysing talk, text and interaction*, 30-58. London: Sage. FOSTER, P. (1996), Observational research, 57-93. In: SAPSFORD, R. and JUPP, V. (eds.), *Data collection and analysis*. London: Sage.

26 In preparation of the double interviews, the following authors were consulted: HOLSTEIN, J.A. and GUBRIUM, J.F. (1995), *The active interview*. Qualitative research Methods series No. 37. London: Sage. SILVERMAN, D. (1993), *op. cit.*, 90-143. WILSON, M. (1996), Asking questions, 94-120. In: SAPSFORD, R. and JUPP, V. (eds.), *Data collection and analysis*. London: Sage. BILLIET, J.B. (1990), *op. cit.*, 159-210.

27 Statistical Package for the Social Sciences.

28 NUD*IST stands for Non-numerical Unstructured Data Indexing Searching and Theorizing, a registered trademark of Qualitative Solutions Research Pty Ltd. For a discussion of software packages for qualitative analysis, see RICHARDS, T.J. and RICHARDS, L. (1998), Using computers in qualitative research, 211-245 in DENZIN, N.K. and LINCOLN, Y.S., *Collecting and interpreting qualitative materials*. London: Sage Publications.

29 To choose a computer program for qualitative data analysis, we consulted: MILES, M.B. and HUBERMAN, A.M. (1994), *Qualitative data analysis*, 311-317. London: Sage. BURGESS, R.W. (ed.) (1995), *Computing and qualitative analysis*. London: JAI Press. WEITZMAN, E.A. and MILES, M.B. (1995), *Computer programs for qualitative data analysis: a software sourcebook*. Thousand Oaks, CA: Sage. RICHARDS, T.J. and RICHARDS, L. (1994), *loc. cit.*, 445-462.

CHAPTER 3

GENERAL CHARACTERISTICS OF THE SAMPLE

3.1. INTRODUCTION

Some general data on the age, gender, nationality, education, profession, income, marital status and living situation of the Antwerp sample are presented in this chapter (§3.2, §3.3 and §3.4). The data on demographic characteristics of the Antwerp sample will be compared extensively with the Amsterdam 1987 sample (and sometimes the Amsterdam 1991 sample).[1] Brief references will also be made to other community cocaine studies.[2]

Although two of the sample acceptability criteria were that respondents should neither have been found guilty of a felony, nor have been in a drug treatment program, after completing the interviews it appeared that 55 respondents scored on either of these variables. We decided not to eliminate these 'registered' or 'known' respondents,[3] but to use them to our advantage and compare them with the rest of the sample (§3.5).

In the previous chapter the choice of a non-randomized snowball sampling design was explained by our difficulties to find and contact respondents. Respondents simply did not want to implicate other users without their informed consent.[4] Conversely, respondents were willing to indicate *how many* other users were personally known to them. The data about numbers of 'known'[5] and 'risky' users are presented in §3.6.

3.2. AGE, GENDER AND NATIONALITY

3.2.1. Age

The age of the respondents varies between 19 and 64 years, with a mean of 29.16 years (S.D. = 6.84).[6] More than 60% of the respondents are between 26 and 35 years old, while 22.5% are between 21 and 25 years of age (see Figure 3.2.a). Adolescents (i.e. under 18 years) are not part of our sample, because one of the sample acceptability criteria was that respondents should be at least 18 years old.[7] But even the number of respondents in the age category of less than 21 years is low (2.7% of the total sample).

Two explanations are possible: it might be an effect of our selective recruitment of respondents in the Antwerp nightlife, as we were forced to limit our visits to only some of the dozens of discotheques and bars. Youngsters are likely to frequent other places than those we visited, or at other points of time. Secondly, our aim was to find experienced cocaine users, and experience increases with age. Looking for young and at the same time experienced users would probably have been more time consuming and perhaps even more difficult (because we were 27 at the time of the interviews).

Fig. 3.2.a   Age distribution of the 1997 Antwerp sample at the time of interview, in % (N=111)

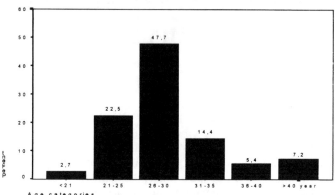

Both mean age and age distribution in the Antwerp sample are not markedly different from findings in other community studies of cocaine users. The average mean age of all these samples is 28.7 years.[8] The majority of respondents in all these samples are between 20 and 35 years of age. Compared to most other community samples, the proportion of 26 to 30 year-old respondents in the Antwerp sample is larger, whereas the proportions of respondents younger than 25 years and those older than 31 years are somewhat smaller.[9] Almost half of our respondents was between 26 and 30 years of age.

3.2.2. Gender

Of the interviewed cocaine users, 36.9% are female and 63.1% male (see table 3.2.b). The mean age of the male respondents is 30.2 years, that of the female respondents 27.4 years, which constitutes a statistically significant difference.[10] In the 26-30 years category the proportion of male respondents is more than twice as large as the proportion of female respondents. We also asked our respondents to estimate the male and female percentages of the other cocaine users they knew.[11] There is a striking agreement between the Amsterdam I sample, the Amsterdam I estimates, the Antwerp sample and the Antwerp estimates.[12]

Table 3.2.b   Male-female ratio in the 1987 Amsterdam I sample and the 1997 Antwerp sample (with respondents' estimate, and list of nominees), in %

| | Amsterdam I (1987) | | Antwerp (1997) | |
| | Sample N=160 | Estimates N=158 | Sample N=111 | Estimates N=109 |
Gender				
Male	60	62	63.1	62.8
Female	40	37	36.9	37.2
Total	100	99	100	100.0

These percentages do not differ very much from those in other major community co-caine studies.[13] The proportion of male respondents fluctuates between 52.7 and 81%. The average proportion of male respondents over all these samples is 67.8%, and the average proportion of female respondents 32.2%. In short, the data of the present study and of other cocaine community studies yield a consistent trend: approximately one third of all cocaine users in these samples are women, and two thirds are men. We be-lieve that this consistency reflects a real trend in the total population of cocaine users.

3.2.3. Nationality

Nearly all our respondents are white (98.2%), and the majority of the interviewed co-caine users were born in Belgium (89.2%). Additionally, the sample contains 4 persons of Dutch nationality (including 1 originally from Surinam and 1 from Indonesia), 2 from France, 1 from Ireland, 1 from Mexico, 1 from Morocco, 1 from Germany, 1 Belgian born in Germany, and 1 from England. Similarly, the majority of the parents of the respondents were born in Belgium (84.7% of the mothers, 82% of the fathers).[14] Although this seems consistent with most other community samples of cocaine users (except in the San Francisco and the Rotterdam studies), [15] it is likely that these data reflect sampling biases rather than trends in the actual population.

3.3. EDUCATION, PROFESSION AND INCOME

3.3.1. Education [16]

One third of our sample are studying for or have a university degree or a non-university college of further education (the so-called 'A1-level').[17] Seventy-six re-spondents (71%) in our sample have obtained their degree (versus 55% of the Amster-dam I sample and 39% of the Amsterdam II sample). Twelve percent are still studying (versus 18% of the Amsterdam I sample and 31% of the Amsterdam II sample), but it should be noted that 2 of these Antwerp respondents are in employment while study-ing.

Table 3.3.a   Educational level in the 1997 Antwerp sample [18]

| Educational level | Antwerp (1997) | | | | |
	%	N	Finished	Studying	Quit
Elementary school (LO)	10.8	12	67%	-	33%
Lower Vocational School	9.0	10	60%	-	40%
Lower Technical School (A3)	9.0	10	90%	-	10%
Lower High school	5.4	6	50%	-	50%
Higher Vocational school	5.4	6	66%	17%	17%
Higher Technical school (A2)	19.8	22	82%	18%	-
High level High school	7.2	8	100%	-	-
Non univ. Polytechnic college (A1)	19.8	22	68%	23%	9%
University	13.5	15	47%	20%	33%
Total	**100.0**	**111**	**71%**	**12%**	**17%**

International comparisons of the educational data of community cocaine studies are extremely difficult because of different school systems and grades. In short, compared to the Amsterdam sample, the educational level of the Antwerp sample is lower: the proportion of respondents with a university education is somewhat smaller, and the proportion of semi- and unskilled people is probably larger.[19] This is undoubtedly an effect of our non-randomized snowball sampling procedure. Most of these low skilled respondents are part of chain H, a snowball chain initiated by a staff member of a low threshold treatment agency.[20] However, compared to other cocaine community samples the Antwerp sample contains a relatively high proportion of people with a university education (including non-university college of further education).[21]

3.3.2. Profession

A wide variety of professions is represented in our sample: social workers, market vendors, people employed in or owning hotels/restaurants/bars (i.e. the hotel and catering industry), car dealers, computer experts, workers in socio-cultural training, students, cover girls, unskilled workers, bouncers, tele-marketeers, tutors, electrotechnicians, electro-mechanics, artists (actor, dancer, director, painter, sculptor, musician, architect), hair dressers, industrial engineers, lawyers, fashion designers (couturier), skilled workers, cooks, scientific workers, programmers, account managers, journalists, therapists, beauticians, photographers, police officers, house wives, travel agents, saleswomen, students,...

An overall comparison of the figures in table 3.3.b with data from other major community studies in an international context is very difficult because of different occupational classification systems. However, between our sample and the 1987 Amsterdam I sample, four groups of professions are perfectly comparable: 1) 18.0% of our sample work as artists or in *art related professions* (musician, painter, photographer, interior designer, journalist[22]). In the Amsterdam I sample, a considerably larger proportion of 26.9% for this group was reported; 2) 9.9% of our sample are *students* (versus 6.9% of the Amsterdam I sample); 3) 16.2% of our sample works in *hotels/restaurants/cafés* as waiters, cooks or owners, while Cohen found a smaller proportion of 10.0% in his Amsterdam I sample; and 4) 16.2% of our respondents are *unemployed* (versus 11.9% of the Amsterdam I sample).[23]

Compared to other community samples of cocaine users, the proportion of respondents working as artists or in art-related professions is relatively low,[24] whereas the proportion of respondents working in bars-hotels-restaurants is relatively high.[25] Like in most other studies, students make up around 10% of our sample.[26] And compared to the Amsterdam sample, the proportion of unemployed respondents is rather high, but compared to most other community studies, it is rather low.[27]

Table 3.3.b   Professional level of the 1997 Antwerp sample

Antwerp 1997		
Professional level	**N**	**%**
Low occupational level		
1. Unskilled and untrained worker/assistant	2	1.8
2. Skilled and trained worker with A4-level certificate (in employment)	9	8.1
Middle Low occupational level		
3. Skilled worker with A3-level certificate (in employment)	18	16.2
4. Small businesspeople without employees	4	3.6
5. Self-employed craftsmen without employees	1	0.9
6 Self-employed market gardeners and small farmers	-	-
7. Employee (level junior clerk)	4	3.6
8. Employee (level senior clerk)	2	1.8
9. Employees in education/ technicians with A3 or A2 level certificate	6	5.4
Middle occupational level		
10. Employees on A1 level	13	11.7
11. Self-employed people with A1 level certificate	1	0.9
Middle High occupational level		
12. Employees with university level certificate	4	3.6
13. Medium-sized and large businessowners (with 1 to 5 employees)	2	1.8
14. Medium-sized and large market gardeners and farmers (with 1 to 5 employees)	-	-
15. Senior officials	1	0.9
16. Professionals without own practice	1	0.9
High occupational level		
17. Owners of companies of 5 to 20 employees	1	0.9
18. Senior officials, executive staff members, managers	-	-
19. General managers of companies with 20 to 100 employees	-	-
20. Professionals with own practice	2	1.8
21. Higher academic professions	-	-
22. Directors/managers of companies with more than 100 employees	-	-
Other		
23. Artistic profession (actor, director, musician, sculptor)	10	9.0
24. Unemployed	13	11.7
25. On disability benefit	5	4.5
26. Housewife/houseman	1	0.9
27. Student	11	9.9
Total	**111**	**100.0**

3.3.3. Income

The median of net income in our sample is between 40,000 and 50,000 Belgian francs per month (see Figure 3.3.c). 37.8% of our sample have some form of income from social benefits.[28] This category includes: 27 people with unemployment benefit, 6 people living from a subsistence level benefit; 8 people with a disability benefit, and 1 person with an orphan's allowance. One respondent draws a pension.

27.9% of our sample have a net income of 50,000 Belgian francs or more (ca US $1,400). The income of 3 out of 10 respondents does not exceed 30,000 Belgian francs (ca. US $845).

Figure 3.3.c   Net income per month in the 1997 Antwerp sample, in %

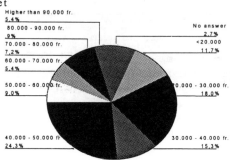

It is particularly difficult to recode data from other community cocaine studies for comparison as none of the raw data are available. In their attempt at comparison, Ditton and Hammersley (1996: 27) decided that the only consistent break point is that of those earning either more or less than £10,000 gross per annum. It was impossible to recode our data (because £10,000 per annum is an equivalent of approximately 47,500 Belgian francs per month). Moreover, a thorough comparison would need to take into account indexing of wages and fluctuations in purchasing power.

3.4. MARITAL STATUS, HOME ENVIRONMENT AND CHILDREN

3.4.1. Marital status and home environment

The majority of our respondents are unmarried (86.5%). Of the fifteen respondents who were married, 9 respondents (8.1 %) are now divorced, while 6 (5.4%) are still married. In comparison to most other community studies of cocaine users the proportions of married and divorced respondents in the Antwerp sample are relatively low. [29]

Almost half of our respondents (45.9%) have had a partner for longer than one year. About 17% of the Antwerp sample have had a partner for less than one year and 37% have no partner at the time of the interview.[30]

Table 3.4.a   Partner and home environment in the 1997 Antwerp sample, in %

| | Antwerp (1997) | | | | |
| | Home environment (%) | | | | |
Partner	N	Alone	With partner	Other	Total
No	41	56.1	-	43.8	99.9
< 1 year	19	42.1	36.9	21.0	100.0
> 1 year	51	17.7	72.5	9.8	100.0
Total	**111**	**36.0**	**39.6**	**24.3**	**99.9**

The proportion of our respondents living alone (36.0%) is almost half of the proportion found in the 1987 Amsterdam I sample (62.7%). Our categories of 'living with a partner' (either married or unmarried) and 'other'[31] are much larger than in the A'dam I sample.

After cross-tabulating 'partner' and 'home environment', we find that 37 respondents (33.3%) or one third of our sample live with a partner with whom they have a steady relationship (more than one year). One fifth of our total sample (20.7%) have no partner and live alone.[32]

Comparison with other major community cocaine studies (see Figure 3.4.a) shows no consistent trends. [33] The proportion of married and divorced respondents in the Antwerp sample is relatively small, and the proportion of single respondents relatively large. Yet, the proportion of respondents living with a partner in the Antwerp sample is higher than in all other community samples. This discrepancy can be explained by the fact that many respondents live with a partner with whom they have a steady relationship, but prefer not to marry (their marital status being 'unmarried' or 'single'). Indeed, many young people prefer (informal) cohabitation to marriage in a 'traditional' sense. Moreover, general social and cultural factors may help to explain discrepancies between various community studies.

Figure 3.4.a   Comparison of home environment in six community cocaine studies [♠]

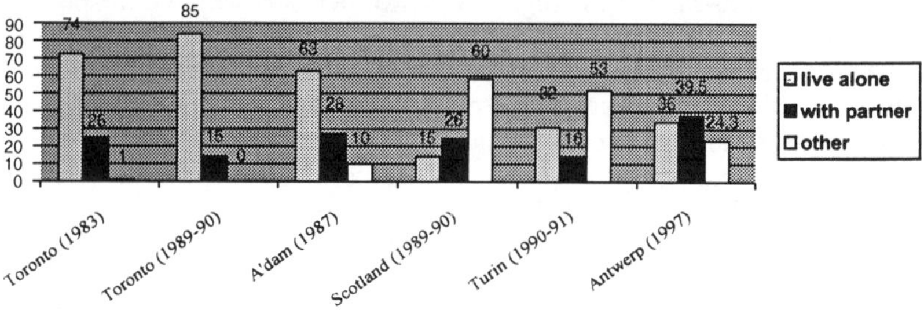

3.4.2. Children

Twenty-three respondents have one or more children (20.7%). Sixteen of these respondents live with their partner and their children. Four individuals have children who live elsewhere (in two cases with their mother, in two cases because they are independent). Three respondents have children who live with them and children who live elsewhere.[34]

Table 3.4.b   Children and home environment in the 1997 Antwerp sample, in %

| Children | Antwerp | | | | |
| | | Home environment | | | |
	N	Alone	With (ex)partner	Other	Total
None	88	39.8	29.5	30.8	100.1
Living at home	16	-	100.0	-	100.0
Living somewhere else	4	100.0	-	-	100.0
Both at home and elsewhere	3	33.3	66.7	-	100.0
Total	**111**	**36.0**	**39.6**	**24.3**	**99.9**

Almost one in five of the Antwerp respondents have children at home. Compared to the Amsterdam II sample (1991), this is a relatively high proportion.[35] Few other major community cocaine studies report on children of respondents, except for Waldorf *et al.*, who mention that 27.2% of their sample had under-age children living in their household (San Francisco, 1986-1988). The equivalent of this proportion in the Antwerp sample would be 17.1%, which is considerably lower.

3.5. 'REGISTERED' VERSUS 'NON-REGISTERED' RESPONDENTS

Two of the sample acceptability criteria were that respondents should neither have been found guilty of a felony, nor have been in a drug treatment program at any time. Apart from the instruction that we were not interested in 'junkies', these exclusion criteria were not mentioned to the respondents. As we explained earlier, it was often not possible to check whether potential respondents scored on either of these variables.[36]

After completing 111 interviews we found that 46 persons had been convicted (41.4%) and that 22 persons had participated in a drug treatment program (19.8%). Thirteen respondents score on both variables. We decided not to eliminate these respondents from the sample, mainly because this sub-sample of cocaine users can be regarded as a sub-sample of 'registered', 'known', or 'captive' respondents. Through their contacts with treatment institutions and/or the judicial system these respondents probably form part of the population traditional surveys and secondary indicators of drug (ab)use draw their raw data from. A comparison with the other, non-registered respondents can thus yield interesting information.

In the following paragraphs, the sub-sample of 55 'registered' respondents is analyzed for variables such as level of use, proportion of ex-users, income level and route of ingestion.

3.5.1. Treatment contacts

Twenty-two respondents (about one fifth of the total sample) reported ever having been in contact with drug treatment agencies or with medical doctors for a drug problem. Almost three quarters of them had participated in a treatment program for heroin problems (see table 3.5.a). Two respondents asked for help concerning an alcohol problem; two others with reference to amphetamines.

Table 3.5.a.   Treatment contacts in the 1997 Antwerp sample [*]

	Antwerp	
	Treatment	
	N	% of total sample
For heroin	16	14.4
For alcohol	2	1.8
For cocaine	2	1.8
Other	2	1.8
Total	**22**	**19.8**

[*] More than one answer per respondent was possible

Twelve of these respondents belong to snowball chain H, 3 to snowball chain F, 2 to snowball chain L. Snowball chains D, I, N, P and Y each contain one 'treated' respondent. We strongly suspect that the construction of our sample may be biased in the sense that some snowball chains -especially chain F and H- were restricted to specific subsets of users in which the proportion of respondents having been in contact with treatment facilities is probably higher than in other subsets (or 'subcultures').[37]

The sub-sample of 22 'treated' respondents was checked on variables such as age, gender, level of use and route of ingestion (see table 3.5.b). Compared to the sub-sample of respondents who had never been in treatment and to the total sample, the mean age of the 'treated' respondents is slightly but not statistically significant higher (29.9 years).

The proportion of female respondents in the 'treated' sub-sample is lower (31.8%) than in the total sample, although not statistically significant. When looking at the level of use during the period of heaviest use,[38] the proportion of high level users in the 'treatment' sub-sample is significantly higher compared to the 'untreated' sub-sample and the total sample. As to the level of use during the three months prior to the interview, the proportion of high level users and medium level users in this sub-sample is higher. Although we might expect that users who have been in treatment, and therefore probably have experienced severe problems with drugs, are more likely to quit, the proportion of ex-users among these 'treated' respondents is lower.

Clearly, the route of ingestion is an important factor in differentiating between 'treated' and 'untreated' respondents: 54.5% of the 'treated' users were injecting cocaine during their period of heaviest use, versus 18.0% of the 'untreated' respondents. This difference is statistically significant. During the three months prior to the interview, 36.4% of the respondents ever having been in treatment versus 8.1% of the 'untreated' respondents, were using intravenously. The proportion of 'treated' respondents who were freebasing during their period of heaviest use (18.2%) is significantly smaller compared to both the 'untreated' sub-sample (24.7%) and the total sample (23.4%).

Table 3.5.b. Comparison of cocaine users having been in treatment with the rest of the sample and with the total sample (Antwerp, 1997)

		Antwerp		
		'Treated' users N=22	**'Untreated' users N=89**	**Total sample N=111**
Age		29.9 years	29.0 years	29.2 years
Gender		31.8 % female	42.0 % female	36.9 % female
Level of use%	low	4.5	25.8	21.6
during	med	22.7	30.3	28.8
top period [(1)]	high	72.7	43.8	49.5
Level of use%	low	54.5	67.4	64.9
during	med	22.7	7.9	10.8
last 3 months	high	9.1	4.5	5.4
before interview	none	13.6	20.2	18.9
%i.v. use top period (N) [(2)]		54.5 (12)	9.0 (8)	18.0 (20)
%i.v. use last 3 months (N)		36.4 (8)	1.1 (1)	8.1 (9)
% free base top period (N) [(3)]		18.2 (4)	24.7 (22)	23.4 (26)
% free base last 3 months (N)		18.2 (4)	12.4 (11)	13.5 (15)

[(1)] Levene's test for equality of variances: F=8.296, P=0.005. T-test for equality of means: t-value=-2.712; df=109, p=0.008 (2-tailed).

[(2)] $\chi 2$=24.862; df=2; p<0.001.

[(3)] $\chi 2$=24.862; df=2; p<0.001.

Comparison with other community cocaine studies is difficult because of differences in the questionnaires. In some studies respondents were asked whether they had ever been in contact with treatment centers for cocaine-related problems.[39] For example, in Barcelona (1990-91) only 8% of the respondents and in Turin (1990-91) 16% of the sample had made use of the services offered by drug assistance agencies. In Rotterdam (1990-91), a larger number of respondents had contacted the services (38%). Only 1.8% of the Antwerp sample had sought formal help for cocaine-related problems... In the Scottish study (1989-90) respondents were asked if they had had any medical or other treatment in the previous three years. For cocaine use only 3% said yes, and for other drug use only 22% affirmatively. 74% of the Scottish sample had had no treatment at all the last three years. And finally, Waldorf *et al.* (1991: 208) asked all quitters in their San Francisco sample (1986-88) whether they had had any formal treatment: 28.3% had been 'treated'. Among our ex-users, 10% had been 'treated'.

3.5.2. Convictions for felonies

Forty-six respondents (41.4% of the total sample) reported ever having been convicted for a felony.[40] Table 3.5.c shows that more than half of the convicted respondents had been arrested for drug *possession*. From the qualitative interviews we know that most of these respondents had been arrested for possession of cannabis. One third of the convicted respondents had been arrested for drug dealing, and about 40% had been convicted for crimes against property.

Within the sub-sample of convicted respondents, the mean number of convictions per respondent were 1.3. Two respondents reported having been convicted for three or more felonies: both had been convicted for drug possession, drug dealing and crimes against property. Note that one of them is part of snowball chain H, the other of snowball chain F, which again indicates that these two snowball chains generated respondents from a specific subset of probably more problematic and/or marginal users. Eleven respondents had been convicted for two different felonies, usually drug dealing and drug possession. Thirty-three respondents (about half of the sub-sample) had been convicted for one felony only (usually drug possession).

Table 3.5.c   Convictions in the 1997 Antwerp sample [*]

Antwerp (N=46)			
Convicted for	**N**	**% of total sample**	**% of convicted persons**
Drug possession	26	23.4	56.5
Drug dealing	14	12.6	30.4
Crimes against property	18	16.2	39.1
Crimes against persons	2	1.8	4.3
Other	1	0.9	2.2
Total	61	41.4	100.0

[*] More than one answer was possible

Of the 46 respondents reporting one or more convictions of a felony, 18 belonged to snowball chain H (56.3% of this chain), 7 to snowball chain C (70% of this chain) and 5 to snowball I (29.4% of this chain). Again, this might indicate a bias effect of our snowball sampling procedure.

As for treatment history, comparison with other community cocaine studies is again difficult because of differences in the questionnaires. Few of these studies do report data on the respondents' arrest histories. Waldorf *et al.* (1991: 294) report that 58.3% of their total sample had never been arrested as adults on any charge (San Francisco, 1986-88). Less than one in four had any adult conviction. Only 21.9% had ever been incarcerated in prison or jail (and for very short stays only). In the Scottish study (1989-90) only 3 respondents (2% of the Scottish sample) had been convicted for cocaine use, and 14% for other drug use only. 81% of this sample had had no convictions at all the last three years.

In short, both the data from these community cocaine studies and our own suggest that sustained cocaine use does not necessarily entail a criminal life-style or subculture. Thus criminal contacts are far from inevitable. Moreover, although all cocaine users break drug laws against possession (and sometimes sales) regularly, only one in four to one in five (for different samples) fail to stay out of legal trouble.

Having been convicted does not indicate a criminal career, however. Conversely, not having been convicted at all does not indicate a non-criminal life-style. We also asked our respondents a complete set of questions to find out how often cocaine users would engage in illegal behaviors.[41] Comparison of these data on self-reported deviance with the data on convictions shows some discrepancies (see table 3.5.d).

Table 3.5.d. Cross-tabulation of convictions and reported illegal activities in the 1997 Antwerp sample, in % of total sample (and N)

	Antwerp (N=111)			
	No illegal activities	1-3 illegal activities	> 3 illegal activities	Total
Never convicted (N)	45.0 (50)	9.9 (11)	3.6 (4)	**58.6 (65)**
Ever convicted (N)	27.9 (31)	6.3 (7)	7.2 (8)	**41.4 (46)**
Total (N)	**73.0 (81)**	**16.2 (18)**	**10.8 (12)**	**100.0 (111)**

Fifty respondents (45.0% of the total sample) reported no illegal activities, and had never been convicted for a felony. Of the 46 respondents who reported ever having been convicted for a felony, 31 reported no illegal activities to obtain (money for) cocaine. 58.1% of these 31 respondents had been convicted for drug possession, 19.4% for drug dealing, 25.8% for crimes against property and 6.5% for crimes against a person. Of the 65 respondents who had never been convicted for a felony, 15 reported illegal activities to obtain (money for) cocaine. The illegal activities most mentioned were: running con games or swindling (by 66.7% of these 15 respondents), shoplifting (46.7%), theft in a face-to-face-situation, forging checks, and stealing from friends (33.3% each).

These inconsistencies may have various explanations, and one should not derive any simple conclusions about possible (causal) relations between drugs (or cocaine) and criminality. The least we can say is these figures reflect different life-styles. Some of our interviewees had been convicted for a felony that had nothing to do with (obtaining money for) cocaine. These people may have been pursuing a 'criminal career', apart from their cocaine use. Other users avoided illegal activities (to obtain money for cocaine), but were unlucky to be caught for illegal drug possession. Police actions are perceived as 'out of all proportions' and 'excessive' by these respondents, because they were just carrying small quantities, usually cannabis. Still, others did engage in illegal activities (such as shoplifting or running con games) in order to obtain money for cocaine, and were eventually caught in these acts.

Table 3.5.e shows the results of a comparison of the respondents who had been convicted for a felony with the sub-sample of users that had never been convicted and with the total sample. The average age of 'convicted' respondents is significantly higher (30.8 years) compared to the total sample and the sub-sample of 'non-convicted' respondents (28.0 years). Among the sub-sample of 'convicted' respondents, the proportion of female users (22.6%) is significantly lower than among the users that had never been convicted for a felony (47.7%). During the period of heaviest use (top period), the proportion of high level users is significantly higher for the sub-sample of 'convicted' respondents (63.0%) than for the 'non-convicted' respondents (40.0%).

Table 3.5.e. Comparison of cocaine users having been convicted for a felony with the rest of the sample (Antwerp, 1997)

		Antwerp		
		Users convicted N=46	**Users not convicted N=65**	**Total sample N=111**
Age [1]		30.8 years	28.0 yrs	29.2 years
Gender (% of female resp.) [2]		22.6 %	47.7%	36.9 %
Level of use%	low	13.0	27.7	21.6
during	med	23.9	32.3	28.8
top period [3]	high	63.0	40.0	49.5
Level of use%	low	52.2	73.8	64.9
during	med	10.9	10.8	10.8
last 3 months	high	10.9	1.5	5.4
before interview	none	26.1	13.8	18.9
%i.v. use top period (N) [4]		32.6 (15)	7.7 (5)	18.0 (20)
%i.v. use last 3 months (N) [5]		13.0 (6)	4.6 (3)	8.1 (9)
% free base top period (N)		26.1 (12)	21.5 (14)	23.4 (26)
% free base last 3 months (N)		19.6 (9)	9.2 (6)	13.5 (15)

[1] Levene's test for equality of variances: F=3.323, P=0.071. T-test for equality of means: t-value=-2.164; df=109, p=0.033 (2-tailed).

[2] $\chi 2$=5.298; df=1; p=0.021.

[3] Levene's test for equality of variances: F=0.914, P=0.341. T-test for equality of means: t-value=-2.559; df=103.744, p=0.012 (2-tailed).

[4] $\chi 2$=14.238; df=2; p=0.001.

[5] $\chi 2$=10.977; df=3; p=0.012.

The same holds for level of use during the three months prior to the interview (although not statistically significant). Both for the top period and the last three months, the proportion of respondents who were using intravenously is significantly higher among the 'convicted' respondents compared to the sub-sample of 'non-convicted' respondents. The same holds for freebasing as a route of ingestion (although not statistically significant).

3.5.3. 'Registered' versus 'non-registered' respondents

After completing his 160 interviews in 1987, Cohen (1989) also found that 13 persons had been convicted for a felony, and that 7 had participated in a drug treatment program. Two respondents scored on both variables. The most important differences between this total group of 18 persons (Cohen called them the 'deviant' group) and the rest of the 1987 Amsterdam sample were level of cocaine use during their top period (which was very much higher with the 'deviant' group), and the proportion of females (which was much lower). Intravenous use during their top period was higher (for the 'deviant' group), but not significantly (Cohen, 1989: 28).

In the paragraphs above, we analyzed the sub-sample of 22 respondents who had been in a drug treatment program and the sub-sample of 46 respondents who had been convicted for a felony separately. In this section, we will compare the total group of respondents who scored on either of these two variables with the rest of the Antwerp sample. As already mentioned, we prefer not to label this group as 'deviant', but rather as 'registered', 'known', or 'captive' respondents (see table 3.5.f).

Table 3.5.f   Comparison of 'registered' cocaine users with the rest of the sample and with the total sample (Antwerp, 1997)

		Antwerp		
		'Registered' N=55	**'Non-registered'** N=56	**Total** N=111
Age		30.3 years	28.0 years	29.2 years
Gender [1]		29.1% female	48.2% female	36.9 % female
Level of use%	low	12.7	30.4	21.6
during	med	27.3	30.4	28.8
top period [2]	high	60.0	39.3	49.5
Level of use%	low	54.5	75.0	64.9
during	med	14.5	7.1	10.8
last 3 months	high	9.1	1.8	5.4
before interview	none	21.8	16.1	18.9
% i.v. use top period (N) [3]		32.7 (18)	3.6 (2)	18.0 (20)
% i.v. use last 3 months (N)		16.4 (9)	- (-)	8.1 (9)
% free base top period (N) [4]		23.6 (13)	23.2 (13)	23.4 (26)
% free base last 3 months (N)		18.2 (10)	8.9 (5)	13.5 (15)

[1] $\chi 2=4.276$; df=1; p<0.05.
[2] Levene's test for equality of variances: F=1.333, P=0.251. T-test for equality of means: t-value=-2.594; df=106.999, p=0.011 (2-tailed).
[3] $\chi 2=17.832$; df=2; p<0.005.
[4] $\chi 2=17.832$; df=2; p<0.005.

The mean age of the 'registered' respondents (30.3 years) is higher compared to the 'non-registered' respondents (28.0 years), but not statistically significant. Like Cohen, we find that the proportion of female respondents is much lower in the group of 'registered' respondents' (statistically significant). In the period of heaviest use the proportion of low level users is much lower in the 'registered' group, while the proportion of high level users is significantly higher (similar to Cohen's findings).[42] Intravenous use during their top period is significantly higher (32.7%) with the 'registered' group (statistically significant).[43] Similarly, the prevalence of freebasing is higher in this group, both during their period of heaviest use (statistically significant) and for the three months prior to the interview (not significant).

A possible interpretation of the discrepancies between mean age of 'registered' (30.3 years) and 'non-registered' respondents (28.0 years) is that the latter group is still in an earlier phase of their cocaine using career. Proponents of the implicit theory of cocaine gradually producing dependency would then assume that, as these younger, non-registered users continue to use, they will gradually use more and experience higher levels of use during later periods, maybe even start using cocaine intravenously... According to this theory, were we to interview them a few years later, they might report drug treatment contacts or convictions as well (and thus eventually be registered too). If we look at the average length of the cocaine using career (by subtracting the age at first year of regular use from the age at the time of interview)[44] for both groups, we find that the average length of career for 'registered' users is 7.7 years, versus 5.2 years for the 'non-registered' users.[45] However, the discrepancies can also be attributed to coincidence, as they are not statistically significant.

3.6. NETWORKS OF COCAINE USERS

It was already explained why asking the respondents to nominate specific persons and to specify their profession, age, gender, etc. was not feasible.[46] Due to the repressive climate in Belgium, snowball sampling with randomized sequences was not possible within a realistic time budget. What we did ask our respondents was to indicate how many other users they *knew* personally.[47] Unsurprisingly, all respondents reported knowing other cocaine users. In table 3.6.a, under the heading of 'known users' percentages are given of respondents who know 0 users, 1-5 users, etc.. Under the heading of 'risky users' the percentages are given of respondents who know 0 risky users, 1-5 other risky users, etc...

Table 3.6.a   Number of cocaine users 'known' to respondents and number of 'risky' cocaine users known to respondents, in the 1987 Amsterdam I sample and the 1997 Antwerp sample, in %

Number of users	Amsterdam I (1987)		Antwerp (1997)	
	'Known' N=160	'Known as risky' N=160	'Known' N=109	'Known as risky' N=109
0 users	-	35.0	-	31.5
1-5 users	7.5	42.5	4.5	44.1
6-10 users	21.9	11.3	17.1	8.1
11-25 users	29.4	3.8	30.6	7.2
>25 users	38.1	4.4	45.0	3.6
No answer	*3.1*	*3.1*	*2.7*	*5.4*
Total	**100**	**100**	**100.0**	**99.9**

We can see that our respondents report more 'known' users than the respondents from the 1987 Amsterdam sample: 21.6% of our respondents know 1 to 10 other users (versus 29.4% of the Amsterdam I sample); 30.6% of our sample know between 11 and 25 other users (comparable to the 29.4% of the Amsterdam I sample); and 45.0% of the Antwerp sample know more than 25 other users (versus 38.1% of the Amsterdam I sample).

The average number of other users per respondent is 49, which is much higher than the 37 in Amsterdam I. Both in the present study and in the Amsterdam study, these high averages are raised (biased) by respondents who claim to know a high number of other users (100, >100, 200, 250, 1,000). Although these answers seem exaggerated and thus unreliable, they are consistent with the fact that many of the Antwerp respondents were recruited through participant observation in the Antwerp nightlife, and more specifically in discotheques. By leaving out the respondents claiming to know more than 100 cocaine users -as Cohen did- the average lowers to 25, which is near to the Amsterdam finding of 30 (Cohen, 1989: 35).

Of all respondents, 63.1% report knowing 'risky users' of cocaine, which is next the figure in the 1987 Amsterdam sample (64%). In Amsterdam, an average of 8 risky users known per respondent was found, while we find 5.5 risky users known per respondent. If we leave out again those 16 respondents that claim to know 100 or more other cocaine users, this average drops to 4 risky users per respondent. Compared to the 'known' number of other users (average: 25), barely 16% of cocaine users (n=4) are seen as 'risky' users by our respondents. If we calculate this for all the respondents who answered this question (including those with 'exaggerated' answers), we find that only 11.2% of the known cocaine users are thought of as 'risky' by our respondents. Cohen (1989: 35) found an average of 20% users regarded as 'risky' by his 1987 Amsterdam respondents.

In short, the respondents from the Antwerp sample report more 'known' users than the respondents from the 1987 Amsterdam sample. However, our respondents regard only 11.2% of the known cocaine users as 'risky'.

3.7. CONCLUSION

In the previous sections the Antwerp sample was described with some general social and economic variables and, where possible, compared with data on these variables from other studies. Neither mean age (29.2 years) nor age distribution in the Antwerp sample are markedly different from findings in other community studies of cocaine users (average 28,7 years). The majority of respondents in all community samples are between 20 and 35 years of age. Almost half of our respondents were between 26 and 30 years of age.

The data of the present study and of other cocaine community studies yield a consistent image: approximately one third of all cocaine users in these samples are women. It is plausible that this consistency reflects a real trend in the total population of cocaine users. Nearly all our respondents are white, the majority of the interviewed cocaine users were born in Belgium and have the Belgian nationality. Adolescents and ethnic minorities are almost completely absent in our sample. Although this seems consistent with most other community samples of cocaine users, it is more likely that these data reflect sampling biases rather than trends in the population itself.

As to the general level of education, one third of our sample are students or have a university degree, while about one fifth of the total sample is unskilled. Compared to the Amsterdam sample, the educational level of the Antwerp sample seems lower. However, compared to other cocaine community samples the Antwerp sample contains a relatively high proportion of people at university level. Furthermore, the proportion of respondents working as artists or in art-related professions is relatively low, whereas the proportion of respondents working in bars-hotels-restaurants is relatively high. Like in most other studies, students make up around 10% of our sample. And compared to the Amsterdam sample, the proportion of unemployed respondents is rather high, but compared to most other community studies, it is rather low.

Financially the respondents do not belong to the upper scales of the community: almost 40% have some form of income from social security benefits. Almost one third has a net income of 50,000 Belgian francs or more (ca US $1,400). The income of 3 out of 10 respondents does not exceed 30,000 Belgian francs (ca. US $845). About one third of the respondents are living with a partner with whom they have a steady relationship (more than 1 year). One fifth of the sample has no partner and lives alone. Almost 80% of the respondents have no children. In comparison to most other community studies of cocaine users the proportions of married and divorced respondents in the Antwerp sample are relatively low.

Having found that 49.5% of the sample either had been in a drug treatment program or had been convicted for a felony (or both), we decided to compare this sub-sample of 55 'registered' respondents with the rest of the ('non-registered') sample.

About one fifth of the Antwerp sample reported ever having been into contact with drug treatment agencies or with medical doctors for a drug problem, usually for problems associated with heroin use. Only two respondents sought formal help concerning cocaine-related problems. As the proportion of respondents having been in contact with treatment facilities is concentrated in chains F and H, we believe that there has been a bias effect in the construction of the sample. However, our data are consistent with other community studies on cocaine users in that they show a majority of respondents not having had any contact with drug treatment facilities (with the exception of the Rotterdam sample). Comparison of the 'treated' and 'untreated' respondents shows statistically significant differences for level of use during the period of heaviest use (more high level users among 'treated' respondents) and for route of ingestion during the period of heaviest use (more intravenous use and less free basing among 'treated' respondents).

Sixty-four respondents report ever having been convicted for a felony. More than half of them had been caught for drug possession (usually cannabis). One third had been arrested for drug dealing, and about 40% had been convicted for crimes against property. Again, indications were found that particular snowball chains have generated respondents from a specific subset of probably more problematic and/or marginal users. However, the data from other community cocaine studies and our own data suggest that sustained cocaine use does not necessarily entail a criminal life-style or subculture. Moreover, only one in four to one in five (for different samples) fail to stay out of trouble with the law. Inconsistencies between the data on self-reported deviance and those on convictions reflect different life-styles. Some cocaine users who have been convicted for a felony, may have been pursuing a 'criminal career', apart from their cocaine use. Some users avoided illegal activities (to obtain money for cocaine), but had been unlucky to be caught for illegal drug possession. Still others had engaged in illegal activities in order to obtain money for cocaine, and had eventually been caught in these acts.

Comparison of the 'convicted' and 'not convicted' respondents shows statistically significant differences for mean age (higher for 'convicts'), gender (less female respondents among 'convicts'), level of use during the period of heaviest use (more high level users among 'convicts') and for route of ingestion during period of heaviest use (more intravenous use and more free basing among 'convicts') and during the three months prior to interview (idem). Furthermore, some inconsistencies are found after comparing the data on convictions with those on self-reported deviance. Among this sub-sample of 'convicted' respondents, we also find some differences between types of felonies: the proportion of respondents using at high levels during their period of heaviest use, and the proportion of respondents using intravenously during that period are markedly higher for the subgroups of respondents having been convicted for drug dealing, and property crimes/violence, compared to respondents who were convicted for drug possession/use only.

Furthermore, the 'registered' respondents (those who either had been in a drug treatment program or who had been convicted for a felony) were compared with the rest of the Antwerp sample. Like in the Amsterdam I sample, statistically significant differences were found for gender (a smaller proportion of female users among 'registered' respondents), for level of use during period of heaviest use (more high level users among 'registered' respondents) and for route of ingestion during period of heaviest use (more intravenous use and more free basing among 'registered' respondents). A reasonable explanation for these findings is that treatment agencies and the like are more likely to see the 'worst case scenarios' than the moderate or controlled users.

And finally, the respondents' social networks were examined. Participants were asked to indicate how many other ('risky') users they personally knew. After leaving out the supposed exaggerations, we find that the average number of other users known by our respondents is 25. Only 11.2% of the 'known' cocaine users are seen as 'risky' by our respondents, whereas Cohen found an average of 20% users seen as risky by his 1987 Amsterdam respondents.

NOTES

1   For the comparative data in this Chapter, see: COHEN, P. (1989), *Cocaine use in Amsterdam in non-deviant subcultures*, 28-36. Amsterdam: Instituut voor Sociale Geografie. COHEN, P. and SAS, A. (1995), *Cocaine use in Amsterdam II. Initiation and patterns of use after 1986*, 21-36. Amsterdam: Instituut voor Sociale Geografie.

2   For the comparative data in this Chapter, see: ERICKSON, P.G. *et al.* (1994), *The Steel Drug. Cocaine and crack in perspective*, 93-95 and 165-167. New York: Lexington Books. WALDORF, D., REINARMAN, C. and MURPHY, S. (1991), *Cocaine changes. The experience of using and quitting*, 288-290. Philadelphia: Temple University Press. DITTON, J. and HAMMERSLEY, R. (1996), *A very greedy drug. Cocaine in context*, 23-29. Amsterdam: Harwood Academic Publishers. MERLO, G., BORAZZO, F., MOREGGIA, U. and TERZI, M.G. (1992), *Network of powder. Research report on the cocaine use in Turin*, 57-63. Ufficio Coordinamento degli interventi per le Tossicodipendenze. DIAZ, A., BARRUTI, M. and DONCEL, C. (1992), *The lines of success? A study on the nature and extent of cocaine use in Barcelona*, 105-111. Barcelona: Ajuntament de Barcelona. BIELEMAN, B. and DE BIE, E. (1992), *In grote lijnen. Een onderzoek naar aard en omvang van cocaïnegebruik in Rotterdam*, 26-31. Groningen: Intraval.

3   'Known' means here: 'known to the authorities, or probably integrated in official statistics'.

4   See Chapter 2, p. 61.

5   'Known' means here: 'known to the respondents'.

6   Compared to Cohen's data (1989) from his 1987 Amsterdam sample, there are only small differences: the age of his respondents varied between 21 and 53 years, and the mean age was 30.4 years (S.D. = 5.8).

7   See Chapter 2, p. 64-65.

8   Mean ages found in other major community cocaine studies were: 29.4 years (Toronto, 1983), 27.6 years (Sydney/Canberra/Melbourne, 1986-87), 27.2 years (Toronto, 1989-90), 30.5 years (San Francisco, 1986-88), 24 years (Scotland, 1989-90), 29.0 years (Turin, 1990-91), 28.9 years (Barcelona, 1990-91) and 29 years (Rotterdam, 1990-91). For exact references, see footnote 4 and 5. Thus, our data are fairly consistent with those from Amsterdam, Toronto, Turin, Barcelona

and Rotterdam. The lower mean age for Scotland was explained by the authors by the comparative recency of sampling (?), and the newspaper recruited portion, which was markedly younger (Ditton & Hammersley, 1996: 23).

9   This is the case for the Toronto samples (1983 and 1989-90), the Amsterdam samples (1987 and 1991), the Barcelona sample (1990-91) and the Rotterdam sample (1990-1991).

10   T-test: t=2.062; df=109; p=0.042 (2-tailed).

11   As a third way of establishing the male-female ratio Cohen (1989) calculated the percentages from the lists of nominees. As explained above, we were unable to ask our respondents to nominate other possible cocaine users in the way Cohen and his colleagues did. See Chapter 2, p. 66-67.

12   Cohen (1995) does not report on respondents' estimates in his report on the Amsterdam II study.

13   For exact references, see note 1 and 2.

14   It must be noted that we did not try to recruit respondents from nationalities other than the Belgian, as it was not a specific goal of this study, and it did not affect core questions of this research. Moreover, fieldwork taught us that access to the various allochthonous subcultures living in the city would be very difficult. Valid scientific research on culture specific differences in drug use (and informal control mechanisms) would take a lot of time, and probably require researchers or interviewers familiar with the foreign language and culture. Especially for the Antwerp setting, specific ethnographic studies of the Irish, Moroccan, Turkish, Dutch, Jewish, Russian (or from other countries of the former Eastern bloc) and South American subcultures would be of great interest.

15   Hardly any specific data on nationality and ethnicity are reported in the other major community cocaine studies. However, most authors suggest that their samples are almost exclusively white (Toronto, 1983 and 1989-90), Scotland (1989-90), Turin and Barcelona (1990-91). There are two exceptions. Waldorf *et al.* (1991) report proportions of 15.8% black and 8.8% Latino respondents (San Francisco, 1986-88), and Bieleman and de Bie (1992) report that 12% of the Rotterdam sample (1990-91) have a non-Dutch nationality (Surinam, Antillean, Indonesian, Moluccan, Cape Verdean, etc.). For exact references, see note 1 and 2.

16   Because of the complexity of the Belgian school systems and those in other countries, as well as substantial differences in organization and names of the different curricula and levels, a thorough comparison of the educational levels of the Antwerp sample and the other community based samples would lead us too far. We will confine our analysis of these data to some brief observations.

17   This is probably less than Cohen's findings in both his Amsterdam samples (1989 and 1995) , because some degrees (such as social worker, industrial engineer, etc...) are taken at non-university colleges in Belgium, while in the Netherlands these are taken at so-called Higher Vocational Schools (HBO).

18   The distinctive categories 'still studying', 'finished' and 'quit' were taken over from Cohen's study (1989).

19   For example, the categories of 'elementary school' and 'lower vocational school' make up 19.8% of our sample, which can be (carefully) compared with the category 'elementary and lower vocational school (LBO)' in both Amsterdam samples (both app. 5%).

20   See Chapter 2, p. 69.

21   Only higher degrees (university level) can be plausibly compared: 27% of the first Toronto (1983) sample, 13% of the second Toronto (1989-90) sample, 32.5% of the San Francisco sample (1986-88), 27% of the Scottish sample (1989-90), 16.2% of the Turin sample (1990-91), 13.1% of the Barcelona sample (1990-91), and 6% of the Rotterdam sample (1990-91). For exact references, see note 1 and 2.

22   Whether a journalist is an art-related profession may be under discussion, but for the sake of comparison we chose to define the category of 'artists and/or art-related professions' exactly as Cohen did (Cohen, 1989: 31).

23   Cohen & Sas (1995) did not report on professions for their 1991 Amsterdam II sample.

24   Compared to the Barcelona sample (20.3%) and the Amsterdam 1987 sample (26.9%), the proportion of Antwerp respondents working in *art-related jobs* is rather low.

25   Diaz *et al.* (1992) reported on some other professional categories for the Barcelona sample (1990-91), as did Bieleman and de Bie (1992) for the Rotterdam sample (1990-91). 7.8% of the Barcelona sample had a job in the nightlife (discotheques, bars), versus 12% of the Rotterdam sample. As stated above, the proportion of respondents working in *hotels/restaurants/bars* in the Antwerp sample was higher (16.2%).

26   Proportions of *students* are: 8% in the second Toronto sample (1989-90), 11% in the Australian sample (1986-87), 7.9% in the San Francisco sample (1986-1988), 10% in the Turin sample (1990-91), 11.1% in the Barcelona sample (1990-91), and 7% in the Rotterdam sample (1990-91). Students probably make up approximately one tenth (between 7 and 11%) of the total population in the community.

27   Proportions of *unemployed respondents* are: 26% in the first Toronto sample (1983), 13% in the second Toronto sample (1989-90), 8% in the Australian sample (1986-87), 7.5% in the San Francisco sample (1986-1988), 17% in the Turin sample (1990-91), 4.6% in the Barcelona sample (1990-91), and 51% in the Rotterdam sample (1990-91). No unequivocal trend can be observed here: the proportion of unemployed fluctuates from 4.6 % (Barcelona) to 51% (Rotterdam). These differences may be attributed to biases in the samples. The proportion of unemployed respondents in the Antwerp sample is rather low.

28   In the 1987 Amsterdam sample, 31% have some form of income from social benefits (Cohen, 1989: 32). Cohen & Sas do not report about this for the 1991 Amsterdam II sample.

29   International comparison with other community cocaine studies is possible if all data are recoded into three categories (married, single and divorced). No specific data were available for the Scottish sample (1989-90), and the Barcelona and Rotterdam samples (1990-91). An overall comparison between the other community studies yields the following: 1) the proportion of married respondents ranges from 0% (Australia, 1986-87) to 19.7% (San Francisco, 1986-88), with an average of 11.2%; 2) the proportion of single respondents ranges from 74.8% (Toronto, 1983) to 86.5% (Antwerp, 1997), with an average of 80.4%; and 3) the proportion of divorced respondents ranges from 7% (Amsterdam, 1989) to 15.3% (Toronto, 1983), with an average of 11.5%. For exact references, see note 1 and 2.

30   Cohen's findings for the 1987 Amsterdam I sample are very similar: 47.% of hisd respondents have had a partner for longer than one year, ca 14% have had a partner for less than one year, and 38.6% have no partner at the time of the interview (Cohen, 1989: 33).

31   Our category of 'other' in both table 3.4.a and 3.4.b includes: 13 persons who live with their parents, 2 persons officially residing with their parents, but in fact living in a student home, 10 people living with friends and 2 people with no permanent address or home.

32   In his 1987 Amsterdam sample, Cohen (1989) found these proportions in the reverse order.

33   Compared to both Toronto samples (1983 and 1989-90) and the Amsterdam I sample (1987) the proportion of respondents living alone is markedly smaller; whereas the category of 'other' is larger. Compared to the Scotland sample (1989-90) and the Turin Sample (1990-91), the proportion of respondents living alone is clearly higher, whereas the proportion of 'other' is smaller. For exact references, see note 1 and 2.

34   In his report on the Amsterdam I sample, Cohen (1989) does not report on the presence of children in the home of his respondents.

35   For the Amsterdam II sample Cohen (1995) reports that only 5 percent of the respondents in the snowball sample live at home with children (compared to 10% of the respondents in a population sample and 31% of 20-40 year old in the general population). He concluded that cocaine use in Amsterdam in 1991 occurs mainly among persons who choose not to care for children, at least at the present time. In our sample, 21 respondents have children at home (including two respondents who have raised their children at home until they were self-supporting). This means 18.9% of the total Antwerp sample (i.e. almost one fifth) chose to care for children...

36   See Chapter 2, p. 64.

37   It must be noted that snowball chain H was initiated by a staff member of a low threshold treatment agency in Antwerp. He was informed extensively about the goal of the present study and contacted 6 people. During fieldwork several indications were found that most of the respondents from this chain frequented the same locations. See Chapter 2, p. 69.

38 Levels of use were defined as low (less than 0.5 gram per week), medium (between 0.5 and 2.5 gram per week) and high (more than 2.5 gram per week). See Chapter 5, p. 138.

39 For exact references, see note 1 and 2.

40 Seven other respondents reported only having been convicted for (minor) traffic offenses. These were not included in the subsample of 'convicted' respondents.

41 See Chapter 13, p. 297-301.

42 The same holds for the three months prior to the interview, although not statistically significant.

43 Another way of testing this would be to check whether the groups of 'registered' respondents and 'non-registered' respondents differed significantly for life time prevalence ('yes' or 'no') of 'injecting' and 'free basing' as a route of ingestion. Here too, we found statistically significant differences.

44 See also Chapter 5, p. 141-142.

45 t-value=-3.015; df=105, p=0.003.

46 See Chapter 2, p. 61.

47 An exact definition of what it means to 'know' people was not given to respondents. Especially in the nightlife scene, 'to know' some one might mean anything. If the interviewer was asked what he meant by 'knowing people', he'd specify that the respondent should at least know someone by name (not just someone's face). Similarly, an exact definition of 'risky users' was not given. When asked for more clarification, the interviewer would refer to other adjectives such as 'dangerous', 'hazardous', 'problematic' or 'uncontrolled'.

CHAPTER 4

INITIATION INTO COCAINE USE

4.1. INTRODUCTION

In this chapter we present our data regarding cocaine use initiation: age at initiation (§4.2), initiation into the use of other drugs (§4.3), initiation company (§4.4), location of first use (§4.5), first route of ingestion (§4.6) and way of obtaining first cocaine (§4.7). We also discuss dosage at initiation (§4.8). Information about the circumstances surrounding initiation into drug use and its influence on subsequent behavior may be pivotal in understanding interactions between drug, set and setting factors. Paragraph 4.9 contains our findings regarding respondents' experience with cocaine before first use and the information on cocaine available to them before first use (i.e. discouraging and/or encouraging information).

And finally, the process of social learning around the use of cocaine is described in §4.10 (cf. Chapter 1). During the second interview, we asked our respondents how they had learned to use cocaine, and whether they had had any guidance or supervision. Following the structure of Becker's (1973) classical essay *'Becoming a marihuana user'*, the process of social learning is described in three stages: learning the technique, learning to perceive the effects, and learning to enjoy the effects. Again the data of the Antwerp sample will be compared with both Amsterdam samples[1] and some other major community cocaine studies.[2]

4.2. AGE AT INITIATION

The mean age at which our respondents consumed their first cocaine was 20 years (N=111; range: 12-38 year; S.D.: 4.54). In their 1991 sample, Cohen and Sas (1995) found an average age of initiation into cocaine use of 22.4 years, which was similar to the one found in their 1987 sample (22.0 years).[3] Both in the Amsterdam samples and in the Antwerp sample, a large proportion of users were initiated before their 20th birthday (see table 4.2.a.), although a majority of all three samples had their first cocaine experience well after they had finished secondary school (usually after their 17th birthday). More than two in three respondents of the Antwerp sample were 18 years or older at initiation (68.5% of the total sample).[4]

The data on mean age at initiation from the Antwerp sample are quite consistent with findings from other major community studies of cocaine users.[5] Proportions of respondents who started using cocaine before they were 20 years old, of respondents who started using cocaine between 21 and 25, and of respondents who started using at the age of 31 years or older (3.6%) are comparable to those found in other studies. The Antwerp sample is only different from other studies in that the proportion of respondents who first used cocaine before they were 21 years old (61.3%) is markedly higher, and the proportion of respondents who first used cocaine between 26 and 30 years old (3.6%) is markedly lower.

Table 4.2.a   Age at initiation of cocaine use, in three samples

Age	Amsterdam I 1987		Amsterdam II 1991		Antwerp 1997	
	N	%	N	%	N	%
< 16 yr	7	4.4	8	7.4	9	8.1
16 – 20 yr	64	40.0	35	32.4	59	53.2
21 – 25 yr	53	33.1	40	37.0	35	31.5
26 – 30 yr	28	17.5	16	14.8	4	3.6
> 30 yr	8	5.0	9	8.3	4	3.6
Total	160	100.0	108	99.9	111	100.0
Mean	22.1		22.4		20.0	

4.3. INITIATION INTO THE USE OF OTHER DRUGS

Like Cohen, we were also confronted with a failure to find cocaine users under twenty years, while 61.3 % of our respondents reported their age of initiation was under 20.[6] Cohen (1989: 37) suggested that variable factors such as drug fashion, availability, the price of cocaine and the way of selecting respondents could play a role. We can largely agree with this. Not only did we specifically search for experienced cocaine users (with an inclusion criterion of at least 25 times of use), our data also suggest that at least for our Antwerp sample, use of cocaine is strongly related to going out and socializing behavior. It might be that other drugs, such as MDMA ('ecstasy') and amphetamines ('speed'), have become more available or fashionable than cocaine among the younger participants in the nightlife. Despite the fact that the price of cocaine has significantly decreased over the last two decades, it still is relatively more expensive than MDMA or amphetamines. Moreover, our qualitative interviews revealed that most of our respondents had tried other fashionable nightlife drugs *before* they tried cocaine for the first time.

Table 4.3.a shows the number of drugs used by our respondents before they were initiated into cocaine. If we look at the illicit drugs only (alcohol and tobacco are excluded), we find that cocaine was the first illicit drug for only one respondent. Almost 60% of the total sample report having experimented with at least three other types of illicit drugs before starting with cocaine. Naturally, if we look at all types of drugs (including alcohol and tobacco), the average number of drugs experimented with before initiation into cocaine is higher. More than 90% of the total sample reports having experimented with three to six other types of drugs before using cocaine for the first time.

Table 4.3.b shows the types of drugs used by the respondents before they started using cocaine. Almost all the Antwerp respondents had used alcohol and tobacco and cannabis before they first used cocaine. More than half of them had used LSD and amphetamines, while one in four had used MDMA before trying cocaine.

Table 4.3.a   Number of drugs used before cocaine initiation, in the 1997 Antwerp sample

Number of drugs prior to cocaine	All drugs [1]		Illicit drugs [2]	
	N	% of total sample	N	% of total sample
0 drugs	-	-	1	0.9
1 drug	-	-	21	19.6
2 drugs	3	2.8	20	18.7
3 drugs	19	17.8	39	36.4
4 drugs	22	20.6	18	16.8
5 drugs	35	32.7	5	4.7
6 drugs	21	19.6	2	1.9
7 drugs	4	3.7	1	0.9
8 drugs	2	1.9	-	-
9 drugs	1	0.9	-	-
Total [3]	107	100.0	107	99.9

Antwerp (1997) spans the "All drugs" and "Illicit drugs" columns.

[1] Types of drugs included are: alcohol, tobacco, cannabis, hallucinogens, opiates, hypnotics, sedatives, solvents, MDMA and amphetamines.

[2] Types of drugs included are: cannabis, hallucinogens, opiates, hypnotics, sedatives, solvents, MDMA and amphetamines. Tobacco and alcohol are excluded.

[3] N=107 because four respondents could not be retraced for the second interview.

Table 4.3.b   Type of drugs used prior to cocaine, in the 1997 Antwerp sample

Type of drugs prior to cocaine	N	% of total sample [2]
Alcohol	105	98.1
Tobacco	101	94.4
Cannabis	102	95.3
LSD	58	54.2
Opiates	17	15.9
Hypnotics	11	10.3
Sedatives	12	11.2
Solvents	23	21.5
MDMA ('XTC')	27	25.2
Amphetamines ('speed')	62	57.9

Antwerp (1997) N=107 [1] spans the header.

[1] N=107 because four respondents could not be retraced for the second interview

[2] Percentages do not add up to 100 because more than one answer was possible

Our data are fairly consistent with findings from other cocaine studies in European and American cities. All authors report that the vast majority of their respondents did not, metaphorically speaking, lose their virginity on cocaine.[7][8] Most were seasoned drug users, first of alcohol and later of marijuana. Hallucinogens such as LSD tended to be used next, and the prescription drugs (stimulants, tranquilizers, and barbiturates) were likely to follow in the fifth or sixth positions. Interestingly, the position of cocaine was nearly always last, regardless of the number of other drugs ever used (Waldorf *et al.*, 1991: 22; Erickson *et al.*, 1994: 172; Mugford, 1994: 95-108).[9] The respondents from the Antwerp sample typically reported a very similar sequence of drugs.[10]

In other words, from the data from our own sample and those from other cocaine studies, a first conclusion that can be drawn is that most users experiment with a wide variety of drugs. The population(s) under study are essentially multi-drug user ones. Second, it is relatively safe to conclude that most users start with alcohol and/or tobacco, then move on to cannabis and later to other (illicit) drugs. Thus, the onset of licit drug use generally precedes the onset of illicit use in normal population samples. Cocaine and heroin are usually the drugs into which initiation comes last. The classical 'stepping stone' theory (or 'domino theory') suggested that alcohol, tobacco and cannabis were gateway drugs to more dangerous drugs such as cocaine and heroin, because drug users are always looking for 'kicks', and because alcohol, tobacco and cannabis eventually do not yield sufficiently strong effects (through tolerance and addiction). Although it still is an implicit assumption taken for granted by the general public and by many policy makers, scientists have since long renounced the pharmacological variant of this theory (Lenson, 1995).[11] Explanations for this data on sequences of drug use must be based on social factors (setting) rather than on pharmacological or drug-related factors.

4.4. INITIATION COMPANY

Our respondents were asked to state in whose company they used their first cocaine. As could be expected from the findings from Amsterdam in 1987 and 1991, early experimentation with cocaine generally occurs in the company of one friend or more.[12] Four of our respondents reported being with a brother or sister at initiation. Our qualitative material clarified that in these particular cases, the siblings were members of the same social group of the respondent's close friends. As such, a brother or sister could be added to the category of friends.[13] Colleagues and others clearly play a very minor role in initiation, as percentages are even lower than those of the 1987 and 1991 Amsterdam samples.[14]

Table 4.4.a   Initiation into cocaine use with... in the 1987 Amsterdam I sample and the 1997 Antwerp
sample [15]

Company	Amsterdam I 1987		Antwerp 1997	
	N	%	N	%
With group of friends	83	51.9	48	43.2
With one friend	57	35.6	48	43.2
With colleagues	11	6.9	4	3.6
Nobody (alone)	1	0.6	5	4.5
With others [♠]	8	5.0	2	1.8
With brother/sister [♠]	-	-	4	3.6
Total	**160**	**100.0**	**111**	**100.0**

The specific data on initiation company for cocaine (and for other drugs) that are available from other major community cocaine studies,[16] yield a consistent tendency. Erickson *et al.* report that virtually all participants in the first Toronto study (1983) *'were with friends when cocaine was offered, and most accepted the initial invitation. All of them had other prior drug-taking experiences and were curious to see what all the fuss was about.'* (Erickson, 1994: 105)[17].Waldorf *et al.* report that *'the first use of cocaine, as in beginning use of cigarettes, alcohol or any illicit drug, is nearby always initiated by friends as a part of some social situation. It is a rare case indeed in which one's first use of cocaine is occasioned by a stranger. (...) Typically, a friend offers another friend a line of cocaine at a party, a dinner, or some other get-together.(...) These initiates are usually intimates whom the giver knows well, trusts, and wishes to treat or favor.'* (Waldorf *et al.*, 1991: 17-18)[18] [19]

4.5. LOCATION OF FIRST COCAINE USE

As shown in table 4.5.a, the main location of initiation in the Antwerp sample, was the home of a friend or one's own home. Locations such as 'car', 'outside on the street', 'school', 'nightclub' and 'work' were not very important for initiation. Parties seem to play a minor role in initiation for the Antwerp respondents (2.7%).

Table 4.5.a   Location of first cocaine use in the 1997 Antwerp sample

Antwerp (1997)		
Location	N	%
Friend's home	51	45.9
At home	16	14.4
Disco	15	13.5
Bar/café	10	9.0
Abroad	8	7.2
At a party	3	2.7
At school	3	2.7
At work	2	1.8
Car	1	0.9
Outside on the street	1	0.9
Elsewhere	1	0.9
Total	**111**	**99.9**

Among our Antwerp users, 25 respondents reported 'discotheques' (13.5% of the total sample) or 'bars' (9.0%) as places of initiation. This is almost twice as much as the findings in the 1987 Amsterdam sample. This is partially explained by the fact that unlike Cohen we actively recruited respondents through participant observations in the Antwerp nightlife scene (including discotheques). Yet, the difference might also reflect different climates or lifestyles in the Netherlands and Belgium.

Eight of our respondents (7.2%) reported having used cocaine for the first time 'in another country'. It must be remarked that only one person was initiated in the Netherlands, which in a way contradicts the popular belief about the Netherlands as a 'drugs paradise'. Three respondents used their first cocaine while traveling through South American countries, and 4 others were initiated in other countries: with a friend in Bombay (India), with a friend in Paris (France), with an acquaintance in the United States, and with a stranger in a discotheque in Spain).

The data from other major community studies of cocaine confirm the findings of the present study.[20] Merlo *et al.* describe the typical setting for first use of cocaine as *'tendentially unplanned, which almost always occurs in company with close friends and/or partner or during parties (taking place in a house), or in special conditions of privacy, calm and empathy in one's own friendship circuit.'* (Merlo *et al.*, 1992: 67; see also Mugford, 1994: 100-101). Waldorf *et al.* (1991: 22) report that *'cocaine was offered by a trusted friend in a setting that both found comfortable (typically a private space in which no one who might be offended was present.'*

4.6. FIRST ROUTE OF INGESTION

We asked our respondents which route of ingestion they had chosen on the first occasion. We showed a card that mentioned snorting (intranasal), injecting (intravenous), eating, rubbing on genitals, freebasing and smoking (in a cigarette). In our sample, snorting was the most frequent first route of ingestion (84.7%).[21] Eating, freebasing, smoking and application to genitals are extremely rare as a first route of ingestion (see table 4.6.a). Two of our Antwerp users reported having used cocaine for the first time the way 'it was usually done in those South American countries': chewing coca leaves, or drinking coca-tea. Three respondents reported a combination of routes of ingestion at initiation: snorting and injecting (1), snorting and eating (1) and snorting and freebasing (1).

Comparison with other European and American cities is feasible when all data are re-coded into 'snorting', 'injecting', 'basing' and 'other'. In all samples, an overwhelming majority of respondents first used cocaine intranasally. Average percentages based on eight community samples for each of the routes of ingestion, show the following. The average proportion of respondents first trying cocaine intranasally is 86.6%. The overall proportion of respondents having injected cocaine at initiation is 3.8%,[22] and the proportion of respondents having freebased is 2.5%. In short, the data on route of ingestion at initiation from the Antwerp sample do not differ markedly from those from other community studies.

Table 4.6.a   Route of ingestion at initiation in the 1997 Antwerp sample

Antwerp (1997)		
Route of ingestion	N	%
Snorting	94	84.7
Injecting	6	5.4
Smoking	3	2.7
Snorting plus other method	3	2.7
(Free-)basing	3	2.7
Other methods	2	1.8
Eating	-	-
Total	**111**	**100.0**

4.7. WAYS OF OBTAINING FIRST COCAINE

From his 1987 and 1991 data, Cohen (1995: 39) concluded that only a minority of his respondents had been actively seeking cocaine, versus a large majority simply 'finding' cocaine in their social environments. Most were offered their first cocaine without asking for it. We find the same tendency among our Antwerp users, although less clearly delineated (see Table 4.7.a). One respondent *literally* found cocaine in her environment, when she saw a man throw away a packet on the street as the police arrested him, and picked it up...

Nineteen respondents (17.1% of the total sample) actively asked for it, and 17 respondents (15.3%) actually bought their first cocaine. This active drug-seeking behavior can be seen as an indication for the fact that drug use is not (solely) explainable in terms of personal or social inadequacy and peer pressure. The active role of the individual drug user needs to be underlined: it is not true that all drug users are 'forced' or talked into drug use by ('bad') peers. We established above that in this context the interaction between individuals and their peers should be explained as a confirmation of 'peer preference' or 'peer clustering', rather than as a consequence of 'peer pressure'...23 Consider this 30-year-old cocaine user's description of his circle of friends:

People who want to learn something, who want to have new experiences... It was not specifically about drugs, it was always about going one step further, just to have new experiences. In that kind of environment I was introduced to drugs, and I always felt good there. [...] A very intellectual, emotional environment... [...] So it was like: okay, there is this substance, and we need to know it, what it is all about and how it works... people tell us about it, but we would like to try it ourselves... [...] We were all... we were all tuned in to the same thing, so everybody helped everybody. No one talked anyone else into trying it; everybody wanted to try it, and so it was like: 'I got coke there and then.' 'Aha, and how did it go? And can you get some more?' And: 'Now I managed to get this or that...' So, there was no... like a power over the group by some individuals or something. [L/0/01]

Table 4.7.a   Ways of obtaining first cocaine, in three samples

Way of obtaining	Amsterdam I 1987		Amsterdam II 1991		Antwerp 1997	
	N	%	N	%	N	%
Offered (without asking)	137	85.6	87	80.6	74	66.7
Asking for it	13	8.1	9	8.3	19	17.1
Buying	10	6.3	12	11.1	17	15.3
Finding it accidentally	-	-	-	-	1	0.9
Total	**160**	**100.0**	**108**	**100.0**	**111**	**100.0**

It can be argued that asking respondents about the way that they obtained their first cocaine is a poor way of measuring the influence of peers ('peer pressure' versus 'peer preference'). Retrospective reports of ways of obtaining first cocaine (being offered, having asked for it, or actively sought to buy it) may be not accurate enough for a clear understanding of the processes of initiation. During the second (unstructured) interviews we asked respondents whether they ever had felt being 'pushed' towards illicit drug use. Eighty-three respondents (74.8% of the total sample) answered negatively. Twenty-eight respondents (25.2% of the total sample) reported having felt 'pushed'.24 Only 5 respondents, however, referred to encounters with obtrusive individuals during their initiation phase:

Yes, once, with that coke, the first time. I said: 'No, it's for you, you wanted to have it...' and then he talked me into it, like: 'Come on, join me in the toilet', and he made two lines, and he said: 'Come on, here, I did it, so snort it'; it was more like that. But otherwise, no, never actually. Yes, in a bar it happens, when you order a glass of water, those funny faces... [R/0/04]

I got the first few grams for free, right, from a dealer. So it's not like pushing, I could have said no, right? I had never done it, and I could have said no, but I was eager to know what it was, it had always fascinated me, since I was a child; it's a bit like the underworld, the things that are not allowed, the secret things... [H/1/28]

In short, less than 5% of the total sample report having felt 'pushed' at the time. Almost all respondents report that trying out cocaine was their own (often conscious)

choice, although they also acknowledge that friends (or intimates, or 'peers') play an important role in the onset and the continuation of cocaine use.

There are few specific data on the way of obtaining first cocaine in samples from other European and American cities. Mugford (1994: 100) reports that first experiences with cocaine usually occurred through chance circumstances. For the majority it was simply a case that while either visiting friends or in a party situation they had been offered some cocaine and decided to try it. Ditton and Hammersley (1996) report that 71% of the Scottish sample (1989-90) were offered their first cocaine, while a considerable proportion (21%) bought it themselves. Merlo *et al.* (1992) report that for 82% of the Turin sample (1990-91) the 'first snort is offered by friends'. From the Barcelona sample (1990-91), 73.9% initially received cocaine as a gift, whereas 12.4% bought their first cocaine (Diaz *et al.*, 1992). In their first Toronto study (1983) Erickson *et al.* (1994: 105) state that *'little coaxing had been required for that first snort. (...) It seems that it was not so much if they were going to try it but when the opportunity would present itself.'* And finally, Waldorf *et al.* (1991) report that almost none sought out cocaine on their own the first time. It was offered by a trusted friend. The other community studies offer no specific data.

4.8. DOSAGE AT INITIATION

Based on Siegel's estimates of the dosage of an average recreational user at 100 mg of street cocaine, Cohen (1989: 39) defined an average line of cocaine as 25 mg. Although we have reason to believe that this definition is an underestimation[25], we have maintained Cohen's basic assumption throughout this report for reasons of comparability. Table 4.8.a presents our findings on dosage at initiation and those of Amsterdam, all based on the same definition of an average line of cocaine as ca 25 mg.

Table 4.8.a.   Comparison of dosage at initiation in three samples (Cohen's definition)   [♦]

Dosage	Amsterdam I 1987		Amsterdam II 1991		Antwerp 1997	
	N	%	N	%	N	%
1-99 mg	104	65.0	77	71.3	63	56.8
100-249 mg	39	24.4	20	18.5	24	21.6
250-499 mg	7	4.4	7	6.5	10	9.0
>500 mg	6	3.8	3	2.8	8	7.2
no answer	*4*	*2.5*	*1*	*0.9*	*6*	*5.4*
Total	160	100.0	108	100.0	111	100.0
Mean	104 mg		94 mg		146.7 mg	

The average dose at initiation is 146.7 mg, i.e. 6 lines according to Cohen's definition (or 3 lines according to our definition).[26] Whichever definition is used, the average dose at initiation is slightly higher for the Antwerp sample than for both Amsterdam samples. Some observations can help explain this phenomenon:

-   This mean dose at initiation is elevated probably because a small number of respondents reported a very high dose at initiation (500 mg (n=3); 625 mg (n=1); 750 mg (n=1); 1,000 mg (n=1); and 1,250 mg (n=2). Excluding these eight 'outliers' or extreme values, the average dose at initiation in our sample lowers to 93 mg.

- Three respondents reported that they freebased at initiation, and their average dose at initiation is 611 mg! Six respondents injected, but their average dose was only 89 mg. This is consistent with the fact that freebasing as a route of ingestion is associated by most respondents with higher doses and a higher frequency of intake (the *binge-pattern*).[27]

Comparison with other major community studies on cocaine use is seriously hampered by the difficulties associated with defining the precise dosage used on the first occasion. Merlo *et al.* (1992) acknowledge the difficulties associated with defining the dose used at the first occasion. In their Turin sample (1990-91) the most common answer was *'A little, less than one gram.'*[28] Only a few other major community studies on cocaine use present data on the doses used at initiation.[29] Diaz *et al.* (1992: 138) report: *'Early use is generally limited to one or two lines, meaning that they start with just a small amount that can only be well defined in just a few cases.'*[30] Reporting on the San Francisco sample (1986-88) Waldorf *et al.* (1991: 19) comment that *'in most instances the initiates took one or two lines on the first occasion and declined second offers because they were not impressed with the initial effects'*.

4.9. CIRCUMSTANCES OF INITIATION

In the last decades there has been little or no research in initiation into cocaine use, and there is a lack of information on which to base prevention and harm reduction interventions. Identifying the circumstances surrounding initiation into drug use and the influence it has on subsequent behavior may be important in understanding interactions between drug, set and setting factors. Moreover, these insights may allow current harm reduction strategies to target specifically those at greatest risk, and new approaches to the young, beginning cocaine user could be devised. We therefore asked our respondents about the circumstances surrounding their initiation into cocaine use.

4.9.1. Experience with cocaine before first use

We asked our respondents whether they had ever seen anybody else use cocaine before they first tried it themselves. More than half of the sample (62 respondents, or 55.9%) report never having seen another person use cocaine, versus 49 respondents (44.1%) who had witnessed cocaine use by others on one or more occasions. It must be noted that among those who report never having seen cocaine being used, three respondents add they had seen other people snorting speed (which looks the same) and nine respondents explain they had seen cocaine use on television or in motion pictures.

Of those having witnessed cocaine use before their own first use, 6 respondents indicate that this was immediately before they first used it. The most common scenario was one in which the idea of using cocaine was the person's own, but the actual event was unplanned. The reasons for trying cocaine were curiosity, especially because they had already experienced the effects of other drugs, and a desire to experience the cocaine 'high':

It was an acquaintance of an acquaintance. It was, I happened to come in there, and that guy was snorting. And he said: 'You feel like it?' And I said: 'Yes, of course. I want to try that.' 'Are you sure?' I said: 'Of course.' Before that, I had never seen anyone use it. I knew it existed, but suddenly you're part of it, then it started, and I came to know more and more people who were snorting as well. [E/1/03]

However, 43 respondents (38.7% of the total sample) report having witnessed other people using cocaine long before they first used it. In other words, at initiation being offered cocaine does not necessarily coincide with trying it for the first time. There is often a considerable time gap between the first observation of cocaine (use) and the first use. Use of cocaine is typically observed in friends or acquaintances in a social situation: at a party, at a friend's home, in a bar or discotheque, etc. Parties, in a wide sense, are key locations for observation of cocaine use and initiation into it. The initiation context usually contains friendship relations: school friends or work colleagues, friends in the bars, brothers or sisters, friends of friends (acquaintances) and partners.

The month before I used it, I had seen it regularly with friends. That is why I started to think about it. Normally, it would not have come to my mind to enquire about it or to get involved with it. But I just saw it and yes, that's why I thought about it, like: what is it like and why? And that's why I did it. [M/1/03]

Another typical scenario is accidentally observing a stranger being caught in the act in the lavatory of a bar or discotheque. The stereotype of the drug dealer or stranger actively recruiting new cocaine users to expand his market - the drug pusher - did not feature in our sample. Waldorf *et al.* (1991: 17) come to a similar conclusion: *'It is a rare case indeed in which one's first use of cocaine is occasioned by a stranger. This only stands to reason, for the practice of sniffing a white powder up one's nose, even if it were not a heavily stigmatized drug, is utterly foreign to most people'.* We strongly suspect that initial resistance to experimental use of other drugs (such as MDMA, sedatives and hypnotics), even if occasioned by strangers, is much lower because of people's familiarity with taking pills and medicines and because the use of legal drugs (medicines) by significant others serves as a model.

We also wanted to investigate the influence of observing 'examples' on subsequent behavior. Our qualitative data indicate that in general it is the person him or herself who is the active player in the initiation event (see e.g. Schaler, 2000; Coggans & McKellar, 1994). Curiosity about cocaine and association with people who use it, bring the uninitiated in a situation where cocaine is being used, but despite the unplanned nature of the event, the majority of our respondents report it as having been their idea:

They were people I knew, while we were going out. I joined this group, they were always snorting coke in the car, but I was somewhat suspicious. But once, I had been taking too much speed, and I said: 'Now you're gonna give me a line of coke.' And they said: 'Okay, it's up to you eh, here you are.' In the X. [i.e. a discotheque, TD] people used to make lines on the table tops... [G/1/03]

Another possible indicator of the influence of observing 'examples' on subsequent own behavior, is the relation between the route of ingestion observed in other users and the route of ingestion at first use. Of the forty-four respondents who specified the route of ingestion they observed in others before they tried cocaine for the first time, 42 reported having seen other people snort. Eight respondents saw other people inject cocaine, 5 respondents saw other people freebase, and 1 person saw other people swallowing cocaine (eating).

We checked whether there was a clear link between the route of ingestion observed in other before own cocaine use and the route of ingestion at initiation. It appeared that two out of eight respondents who witnessed others inject cocaine, became regular intravenous users themselves. Both had been injecting heroin before they started injecting cocaine as well. One respondent had injected cocaine only once, and the other 5 respondents had never tried cocaine intravenously. As far as freebasing is concerned, all 5 respondents who witnessed other people do it, became more or less regular freebasers themselves.

These findings do not indicate causal relations between observing others and becoming initiated. A striking similarity between all these respondents having witnessed the more direct modes of ingestion (injecting and freebasing), however, is that the people they observed were mostly friends or intimates (brother, partners). Whereas accidental observation of strangers having 'a snort' of cocaine at a party or in a discotheque may occur, chances of watching unknown persons inject or freebase are relatively rare. Clearly, freebasing and injecting is more confined to a closed circle of intimates and friends. Furthermore, our qualitative data on both methods of administration suggest that respondents frequently see them as more embedded in 'rituals' and 'private' circles.

4.9.2. Knowledge available before first use

We also asked our respondents whether they possessed any information on cocaine before they first tried the substance (see also Zinberg, 1984: 112). Their accounts clearly illustrate that initiates often had established expectations of the drug. Typically, cocaine using friends or intimates had told them about its positive effects, while parents and official sources of information (the media, the authorities, the police, medical practitioners and the school) had warned them about the negative aspects. Nine respondents claim never having received negative information on cocaine use.

4.9.2.1. Dissuading information

The majority of the Antwerp sample (102 respondents or 91.9%) report having been warned about the negative aspects of drug use in general and cocaine use in particular, usually referring to its addictive potentiality. Respondents were taught that cocaine is a hard drug (like heroin), that a single use is enough to get hooked for life, that it is dangerous, that it changes your personality or otherwise makes you do crazy things (e.g. hallucinate or jump out of the window), etc. These warnings are pervaded with adjectives such as 'addictive', 'dangerous', 'bad' (evil), 'diabolic', 'illegal' (thus punishable), and above all 'unhealthy' (e.g. for the nasal septum, for the liver, for the brain).

It is striking that the sources of information are as a rule described in a general way. Dissuading information comes from the media (television), the authorities, the police, the teachers, preventive campaigns, etc. Respondents often state that 'everybody' tried to discourage them. However, we also found that 'the official line' was mostly discounted by these respondents. Official warnings are perceived as exaggerated, one-sided and faulty:

It was constantly like: it's bad, bad for your health, it was bad for everything, right? That is what they always told me. I knew that, it had been drummed into me. Everybody says so: the school, the parents, the media... [Q/0/01]

I had heard and read a lot about it. Yes, on TV and stuff, and junkies who become insane, and parents who become depressed, and junkies who use once and never get off it. That's one of those myths and false information. [H/0/27]

Obviously, negative information. But okay, in fact it was wrong information from the press and so on, from people who actually don't know anything about it. I find that information very unscientific, and so it is not relevant to me. [R/0/01]

Our data support the finding of Waldorf *et al.* (1991: 22) that what their subjects took as extreme anti-drug warnings did not match with their personal experience. Although they had heard about the dangers of cocaine, they tended to discount these warnings once they experienced the drug personally. The disparity between official warnings and personal experiences seems to inoculate users against such warnings, leading many to throw out the proverbial baby with the bathwater. Instead of keeping our respondents away from cocaine, warnings were ignored even before the first use of cocaine. Once initial personal experience further discredits these 'stories', many neophyte users are even more inclined to further use.

A few respondents report having received negative or dissuading information from friends or other cocaine users. In some cases these warnings were equally discounted, sometimes even before respondents experienced the drug firsthand. These cautions are ignored because the sources of information are perceived as unreliable (strangers, non-users and/or problem drug users) or ambiguous (users who discourage use).

These guys did it themselves, and they said: 'Hey, you shouldn't do that'. But no one can fool you at that moment. You will do it anyway. If it's on your mind, you'll do it anyway. And there's always someone present who will say: 'No, you shouldn't do it', but they do it themselves, you know. [...] It's like that book by Christiane F., that's real bullshit. It was advertisement, eh, it was an advertising pamphlet to use drugs... [H/0/01]

They say: 'Stay off it.' These are people you don't know so well, but who you get in touch with because, yes, because it is available in certain circles, and because you have to go there. These people have problems with it, and they say: 'Stay off it, never do it.' But it's only problematic users who say that. [R/0/06]

Others, however, remember receiving warnings about cocaine use from friends, and not ignoring them. These respondents perceive their sources of information as reliable and accurate:

A distant friend of mine, the publican of the pub I used to go to, said that you never really get off it, that you would always feel like doing it. You might get off it, but you will always feel a desire to do it. [G/0/01]

4.9.2.2. Encouraging information

About one in five respondents was unable to remember whether he/she had ever received positive or encouraging information about cocaine before first using it. Eight respondents (7.2% of the total sample) declared that they never had heard anything positive about cocaine before their actual initiation. Almost three-quarters of the sample (81 respondents, or 73.0%) report having picked up encouraging information about the substance or its effects.

Respondents had been told that cocaine keeps you going on all night, that it is nice, that it makes you feel great, that it makes you party, that it makes sex more fun and improves sexual performance (gives you a hard-on), that it is better than 'speed' (amphetamines), that it is more subtle than other drugs, that it makes you feel able to cope with anything, that it helps you to lose weight, that it is special, that is has been used for ages by the Indians, that it stimulates creativity, that it is not as dangerous as 'they' say, that it makes you self-confident (towards the other sex), that it sets you free, etc...

> *But yes, I did not know many advantages of it. I knew it existed, that it was illegal, that it was not allowed and so on, but when my sister said: 'We do it regularly', I was like: oh well, it can't be bad then.* [I/1/02]

In short, people are encouraged to use through other (experienced) users' stories about the pleasant effects. Accounts of nice experiences with cocaine give an implicit (and very often explicit) message that 'you should try it once'. Nevertheless, several respondents indicate that positive information was not communicated through explicit, verbal behavior. Many recall having felt encouraged to try cocaine because they had directly observed its 'positive' effects in other people:

> *By seeing a fellow musician use it, and by playing together with him and seeing that he was playing very well. We sat together, and he took a line, and then we played together, and afterwards we went out to eat something, to drink, and everything was okay. So it had to be okay then.* [H/0/02]

> *Those youngsters never said how fantastic it was. I just watched them, and I saw their reaction, and I saw they liked it. Friends too, I saw that they were having fun with it, that it was fantastic. Your best information is watching those people... the way, in fact, they change a little in their behavior, in their thinking, their doing, and the way they feel, that was for me the most important positive information.* [H/1/28]

Without exception, all positive information came from a broad category of 'friends' or 'intimates': friends in bars or discotheques, school friends, friends from the neighborhood, youth centers, acquaintances, housemates, partners, brothers or sisters, relatives, fellow musicians, etc. Thus, whether it is communicated explicitly and verbally, or observed through non-verbal behavior, positive or encouraging information always comes from 'friends' or 'peers'.

Like in other European and American cities, we found that the main motive for trying out cocaine can be described as 'curiosity'. Most of our respondents already had experience with other drugs (see above, § 4.3), so it was not a giant step for them to indulge their curiosity about a new kind of high. Furthermore, stories about pleasurable experiences and observations of other users made our respondents eager to 'know what it is all about'. Although many of them did not actively seek out cocaine on their own the first time, most respondents look back upon their initiation as something they chose to do.

4.9.2.3. False information about cocaine

We asked our respondents whether they had received (read, heard, saw,...) false information about cocaine. Eighty-seven respondents (78.4% of the sample) answered affirmatively, 24 respondents (21.6%) said they had never received false information about cocaine. Some of the answers summarized in table 4.9.a were categorized as follows: cocaine makes you horny, it stimulates sexual feelings (4), cocaine makes you aggressive (2), cocaine makes you relaxed (1), coke makes you self-confident (1), cocaine makes you euphoric (1), cocaine makes you hallucinate (1) [effects of cocaine]; cocaine users inject (2), they are zombies (1), cocaine detoxification is horrible (1) [junkie stories]; cocaine is very expensive (1), it is only for rich people, yuppies (1) [elitist character of cocaine]; this is cocaine of good quality, this is 90% pure cocaine (4), cocaine is usually adulterated with heroin (1) [quality of cocaine]; if you use once, you are lost (17), cocaine is a demon drug (5), cocaine is a hard drug (4), cocaine is toxic (1), cocaine is addictive (20) [addictive].

We see that general statements about the addictive characteristics of cocaine (such as 'once you try it, you are hooked for life') are renounced as false information by 42.3% of our respondents. A smaller group of respondents did not specifically refer to the addictive potentiality of cocaine, but strongly disapprove of all kinds of incomplete or biased ideas (11.7%). Others condemn the oversimplification underlying the idea that all drugs and any type of drug use have the common denominator of 'bad' (10.8%).

Table 4.9.a   False information about cocaine, in the 1997 Antwerp sample [*]

Antwerp (1997)		
False information about	**N**	**%**
Addictive characteristics of cocaine	47	42.3
Incomplete/biased/partial/over-simplified information	13	11.7
All drugs are bad (a common denominator)	12	10.8
Effects of cocaine	10	9.0
Cocaine users are bad people/criminals	9	8.1
Cocaine is **not** addictive	5	4.5
Quality of cocaine	5	4.5
Junkie stories (injecting, zombie, detoxification)	4	3.6
Cocaine does not harm your body	2	1.8
Stepping stone theory (soft drugs lead to hard drugs)	2	1.8
Elitist character of cocaine	2	1.8

[*] More than one answer was possible

Others report having received false information about drug users. They do not believe that all drug users are bad people, that cocaine makes you a criminal (8.1%). Nor do the typical junkie stories about injecting, withdrawal symptoms and zombie-like users tally with every user's reality (3.6%). According to 2 respondents it is not true that cocaine is an expensive or a rich men's drug (1.8%). Furthermore, 10 respondents (9.0%) stated that certain effects, such as aggressivity, anxiety, self-confidence and sexual stimulation, have been falsely ascribed to cocaine. Five people reported having received false information about the quality of (specific doses) of cocaine. Finally, it is important to see that some stated that they had been confronted with ideas such as 'cocaine is *not* addictive' (4.5%) and 'cocaine does not harm your body' (1.8%), which subsequently appeared to be untrue information to them.

Where do all these false ideas come from? Table 4.9.b shows that the sources of false information most often mentioned are: the newsmedia (35.1%) and non-users or the vernacular (19.8%). All kinds of 'official agencies' such as the government, the school, the police, the prevention agents, and the medical world are mentioned by 33 respondents (29.7%). On the other hand, false information is also passed on by members of the drug subculture(s), especially by cocaine using friends (14.4%) and less markedly by dealers (2.7%). In the residual category 'other' we have included answers like fictional media (Hollywood-films, books,...)(2), junkies and pushers (1), and drug movement (1).

Table 4.9.b   Sources of false information; in the 1997 Antwerp sample [*]

Antwerp (1997)		
Source	N	%
Newsmedia (non-fiction)	39	35.1
Non-users / vernacular	22	19.8
Friends (users)	16	14.4
Police	10	9.0
Parents	10	9.0
School	7	6.3
The authorities	7	6.3
Prevention agents	7	6.3
Dealers	3	2.7
Treatment agents/ the medical world	2	1.8
Other	4	3.6

[*] More than one answer was possible

It is quite obvious that certain false information can be linked to certain sources of information. Cross-tabulating both variables shows that distortions about the quality of cocaine are very likely to be started by dealers, while false information about specific effects or the non-addictiveness of cocaine usually come from cocaine using friends. The 'false' ideas about the elitist character of cocaine reported by 2 respondents in table 4.9.a were ascribed to films and books in table 4.9.b. And most importantly, most false information about the addictive characteristics of cocaine and incomplete or oversimplified information were ascribed to the newsmedia and all kinds of official agencies.

We must bear in mind that the 'false' label is a matter of subjective appreciation by our respondents. What may seem false ideas and notions to one person, may seem accurate descriptions to another, and vice versa. But the simple observation that an important proportion of our sample, after all very experienced cocaine users, reported mainly receiving false information or at least incomplete, biased, partial or oversimplified information from the media and the official agencies, raises questions about the validity of official preventive and repressive efforts. We do not believe that mere product information (usually stressing the adverse effects and disadvantages) is effective. As long as the pleasurable effects and advantages of cocaine remain underexposed or even kept under wraps, experienced and even experimental users will never be able to identify with official ideas and imagery. If official sources (parents included) prove to be wrong during the initial drug experiences, they may be definitively dismissed.

I was a punk, so I was not susceptible to any kind of official messages, and prevention stuff. Because for example, they told me: 'It's good to brush your teeth'. I said: 'No, because

there's no future'. [...] Now I don't think like that anymore, but then as a punk I did...
[F/0/01]

From my parents, obviously, but they just don't know what they are talking about. Yes, be-
cause of their ignorance. They did not know coke, they were just talking about drugs in gen-
eral. Like; these are junkies, it's another world, and all that stuff that goes with it. [K/1/03]

4.10. BECOMING A COCAINE USER

Based on the literature, we described the social learning process of the use of (il)licit drugs in Chapter 1. The process by which one learns to use a drug varies. Most individuals acquire it gradually during the course of their drug-using careers. Also in Chapter 1, we referred to Becker's (1973) classical essay *'Becoming a marihuana user'* , in which he describes the social learning process in three stages: learning the technique, learning to perceive the effects, and learning to enjoy the effects. During the second interview, we asked our respondents how they had learned to use cocaine, and whether they had had any guidance or supervision.

4.10.1. Learning the technique

The first step in the sequence of events that must occur if the person is to become a cocaine user is that he/she must learn the proper technique (snorting, freebasing, injecting, etc.). Respondents may learn that technique through instruction but, as Becker indicates, new users are often ashamed to admit ignorance and have to learn through the indirect means of observation and imitation.

Yes, it happened, when they tell what happens when you use it, how you feel. So they create
an image of what you will feel, right? And how you should use all that stuff, which ways, be-
cause you also shoot coke. Yes, you are informed about all those things, as to the technique,
you pick up the information. Yet, for shooting up, I wouldn't know how to do it. [P/0/01]

Most respondents who have experience with various routes of administration agree that injecting and freebasing require far more technical skill than snorting cocaine. However, even the relatively 'easy' technique of snorting a line of cocaine calls for some elementary skill, as the following illustrates:

I watched carefully and he demonstrated it all very clearly, the cutting, well okay, it's not a
big fuss, just cutting... He didn't say: 'Watch it, I'm doing this and this and this', but he
said: 'I'm going to cut it', he had a razor that cut on both sides, and it was on a glass table,
very fine, and he said it was very important to cut it very fine, and he put the lines properly
with his razor, and then we snorted it. [...] We were with three or four people, and as I was
new, they quickly saw I was new, well, new, I mean, I knew how it was done in the movies,
[...]They showed me, for example for cutting, how to do it best, and also for dividing the
lines, the lines are always done with elegant gestures, like eh... and also the quantity. I
asked them: 'Isn't that too little? How fine do you have to crush it?' As to that grinding, I
know that guy told me the first time:'You have to crush it real fine, very fine, don't be too
hasty, because you'd have big lumps, and then you lose half of it'. [P/0/03]

Typically, freebasing in the Antwerp sample is performed in two ways: basing (on a glass) or chasing (on an aluminum foil). Both techniques are described in detail in

Chapter 7.[31] Both methods require know-how about the process of making freebase cocaine (from cocaine hydrochloride) and about the technique of using (smoking) it.

> *It was nice for me too to see first how you should chase perfectly, before you do it yourself; whether you need ammonia to make a base, but those are technical aspects, and so primarily training on technical issues. But in fact, I did not really hear anyone say: you shouldn't do this or you should do that...; a guru, or whatever you call it, no... engineers yes* [he laughs] *, to tell you how it works best, how you can get the most out of the substance.* [E/0/01]

The following illustrates initiation into injecting cocaine, and the difficulties of learning the technique.

> *It took me a long time before I could shoot myself, I had to practice a lot before I could... and now I can do it like an expert. [...] In the beginning I always asked somebody: 'Can you fix me a shot, I have my own coke, but can you fix me a shot?' After a while, people started to be annoyed and said: 'Shoot it yourself'. And so I started to learn it. At first I never found the veins, it's true, trial and error, but after one month I got it, you know, after a month it was prick, and the needle was in. But at first, I missed the vein many times* [he laughs] *, but I also, in the beginning, I chased it for a while, smoked it, and that was something I could do right from the start. I saw others do it, I imitated it and I could do it.* [F/0/01]

4.10.2. Learning to perceive the effects

Secondly, the user must be able to discern the effects of the drug. Most respondents report having read books or articles about various drugs and their general effects.[32] Some respondents refer to references to drug use in song lyrics (The Grateful Dead, The Rolling Stones, J.J. Cale, etc.) or in motion pictures (Scarface, Trainspotting, etc.). As could be expected from the previous paragraphs, however, friends and intimates are the most important sources of information about the effects of cocaine. The user may ask more experienced users or provoke their comments. Or he/she can pick up some concrete referents of the term 'high' and apply these notions to his/her own experience.

> *So this older person explained a lot to me, about what cocaine is, and what XTC is, and I have a friend who had used a lot as well, and I always asked him: what's this, what does it do? Because he had used a lot himself, and he always explained it to me. That it is addictive, when you use it this way it is surely addictive; when you use it that way it is not physically addictive, but you can have this and that effect if you use it too often. So basically, he explained well, I think. [...] They have told me that it is very addictive if you base it or inject it, and you shouldn't do that...* [I/1/09]

> *It was very nice, because I was really waiting for it, like: 'what is it going to do', and because everybody there knew: 'Ah, it's her first time', while I was older than most other people. It was a very nice night, because I went to other people asking all the time: 'Hey, is it normal that I feel like that', and they said: 'Oh yes, that's normal, this is this and that is that'.* [I/1/12]

Waldorf *et al.* (1991) report that many initiates in their sample had a definite image and expectations of cocaine. With their high expectations (cocaine as a glamorous party drug), they were usually somewhat disappointed by the subtle qualities of the effects. Moreover, although some users did recognize the effects during initiation, this recognition was not typical when first use was intranasal. Our respondents report very similar experiences:

> *But those first times, I'm telling you, it didn't have any effect. You just don't know it, you don't know how you're supposed to feel, you understand? [...] It was the same with a joint eh, the first time you don't feel anything of it* [she laughs] ... [H/1/07]

> *The effects, yes, what you ought to feel, at first it is very uncomfortable, you don't know what to expect... no, in the beginning I found it disappointing... but in the long run it becomes a habit, a recognition of... the more you really recognize that feeling, the more you feel it.... it takes a while and other people help you with it too.* [I/1/01]

4.10.3. Learning to enjoy the effects

The user has to learn to enjoy the effects he/she has just experienced. Drug-induced sensations are not automatically or necessarily pleasurable. The taste for such experience is socially acquired. The beginner thus learns to redefine the sensations as pleasurable, and this redefinition occurs typically in interaction with more experienced users. They may reassure him as to the temporary character of the unpleasant sensations, and teach him how to avoid any severely uncomfortable symptoms while retaining the pleasant ones (Zinberg, 1982: 22).

Between 1972 and 1979, Zinberg (1984) interviewed 249 users of marihuana, opiates and psychedelics. His description of rituals, sanctions and control mechanisms regarding these drugs is a classic in the field. He argued that, because of the illicit status of psychedelics (such as LSD), the average user cannot be certain of the content of his purchase. Therefore, he can only guess the proper dosage. The risk of a *bad trip*, which is always present, is to some degree increased by the lack of quality control of the drug. Most rituals and social sanctions related to psychedelics deal with making the specific drug experience as safe as possible for the user (Zinberg, 1984: 144-148). Because of the power of psychedelic drugs to dislocate perception, it was recognized in the early 1960s that a beginner might not know what was happening to him and therefore might need guidance. The custom of having a guide was quickly translated into the social sanctions that someone tripping for the first time should always have an experienced user present. The guru or guide would soothe the anxiety by telling the user: "It's OK. It is what is supposed to happen. Let it happen. Go with the flow." Twenty years after Zinberg's research, our users reaffirm his observations. When asked about guidance in their becoming a cocaine user, many refer to the social rituals around LSD:

> *They say that you have to be careful when taking a trip, that you should never trip alone. That there should always be someone with you, to make sure you don't get stuck in that trip, or that you should make someone trip properly.* [C/0/01]

> *The first time I injected, I was with a French guy... he was perfect for that role, and he put on some music, he prepared a bed, a real nice way, you knew you were in good hands, with LSD too, that when something happened which made you think: hey, what's that?, that the other could say: yes, isn't it beautiful? Just that, those positive words... that's very important.* [D/0/02]

Unlike the intensive experience of psychedelics, the cocaine high is of shorter duration and does not usually involve hallucinations. Because of the different pharmacological qualities, most rituals and social sanctions related to cocaine deal with chemistry and frequency of use rather than with the presence of a guru, like with LSD and the like. However, many Antwerp users indicate that it was important to have others present who can be trusted and who can be relied upon to help them cope with adverse or unforeseen effects (see also: Mugford, 1994: 101):

> *In fact, it is important, when you experiment with drugs, that you have a point of reference, a person you trust, I recommend that to everyone. Of course, if someone is about to try something for the first time, I always say: make sure you're together with someone you trust, someone you can count on, just that you feel good, that you don't do it in an environment where you feel tense anyhow, but to be with someone you feel good with. And then little can go wrong.* [R/0/07]

> *In the beginning when I was experimenting with coke, there was a person in our group who had been doing it for a long time, and he told us: 'Look, now you have done this, are you aware, are you aware that this and that... so you should not exaggerate with it, make sure you do this and that, and when you feel you can't cope with it or you become aggressive, stop in time'. There was this guy who always took care when a new person entered the group and tried it, who cared about it and gave us explanations. And at first he said: 'Hey, take half an XTC because it can be too much', or: 'be careful, you shouldn't take so much, or you should do it like that, and that's in fact the whole ritual, and that's why it is fun'...* [Z/1/04]

The rules or sanctions passed on from the (experienced) user to the neophyte contain a lot of information: on the adequate dosage, the preferable route of ingestion, where to obtain good quality cocaine, safe places to use, good times to use, 'good' people to use with, how to avoid trouble, etc.

> *Now I know more about what is okay and what is not. I don't base it anymore. I must admit, in the beginning I had problems once, but not anymore, because you know: there's my limit. I can handle this, I can't handle that. [...] My brother also told me: 'Start with a little and don't exaggerate'. I did exaggerate a few times, but okay, I took the consequences and I didn't want those anymore. Because it was no fun anymore, so... [...] If I saw that someone is doing it too frequently, I'd say for example: 'You don't need more, really, you're okay like that, and you will stay awake another few hours anyway...' I do that and I find it important. I found it important for me that someone could tell me: see, this and that and that you can feel. And for me that person was my brother.* [V/1/01]

From these initiation stories from our Antwerp respondents it becomes clear that the circumstances surrounding beginning use are very important. Where one is initiated, with whom and what guidance one receives are crucial factors in the genesis and development of informal control mechanisms. The learning or internalization of adequate use patterns varies from individual to individual, and from social group to social group. The informal learning process an individual goes through to become a cocaine user, is not only determined by the power of the drug (its pharmacology) and the personality of the user (his/her set), but also by the social setting. For example, a user initiated in the 1960s may have received different guidance from that of a user initiated in the 1990s. A man born and bred in South America may have learned to use cocaine in quite a different way than a man living in Antwerp. Initiation in the company of users who inject daily may have a different influence from initiation in the company of casual snorters.

Some final observations can be made. Some respondents emphasize that they did not receive any guidance from other users. They state that they learned to use cocaine on their own. For some, these statements probably reflect a lived experience of isolation and distrust towards other users. For most others, these reports illustrate that the development of sanctions and rituals is usually unconscious: i.e. the user believes he is only doing things the way he has to do them to be safe, or the way he likes to do them because that is how he is.

> *No, everybody has his own, everybody will experience it in his own way. You can read 300,000 books about it, and it may turn out completely different. It's an experiment you experience and live on your own. [...] No, I wonder whether you can learn to handle something, or whether people can teach you how to use it? I don't think so.* [L/1/03]

> *It started with literature. But no real gurus, you know. I mean, I quickly found out that I just wanted to try it all and then... Anyway, I do not accept anything from other people. I want to try it myself. What other people say about it will probably play a role in the beginning, when you know nothing about it, and with your first experiences and so... But you only really get to know it when you use it yourself... When you know how you should use it and when you have used it in various situations and so.* [R/0/06]

It is beyond doubt that the most important source of precepts and practices for control is the peer using group. Virtually all our respondents had been assisted by other experienced users in constructing appropriate rituals and sanctions out of the folklore and practices circulating in their drug-using subculture. However, this knowledge transfer is not always flawless. Users may need to adapt informal control mechanisms to their personal preferences and demands. Others may learn that guidance at their initiation into cocaine was unexistent, or that other users were obtrusive rather than instructive. And finally, respondents indicate that their initiators were not as experienced as they had assumed, and that the knowledge being transferred was incomplete:

> *That time I burnt my palate, I remember thinking afterwards: 'They should at least have told me that this could happen' but then again, they probably had never had it themselves, so how could they have told me? But they kept going on, so I used with them. Yes, they were doing it, so I thought: 'It won't hurt'. [...] It's also because I experienced more side effects that I would tell other people.* [R/1/05]

4.11. CONCLUSION

The data on mean *age at initiation* from the Antwerp sample are quite consistent with findings from other major community studies of cocaine users. The mean age at which our respondents consumed their first cocaine is 20 years. More than two in three respondents of the Antwerp sample are 18 years or older at initiation. The majority of respondents first use cocaine before they were 25 years old. Proportions of respondents who started using cocaine before they were 20 years old, of respondents who started using cocaine between 21 and 25 (31.5%) and of respondents who started using at the age of 31 years or older (3.6%) are comparable to those found in other studies. The Antwerp sample is only different from other studies in that the proportion of respondents who first used cocaine before they were 21 years old (61.3%) is markedly higher, and the proportion of respondents who first used cocaine between 26 and 30 years old (3.6%) is markedly lower.

Cocaine is rarely one of the first illicit drugs youngsters experiment with. More than 90% of the Antwerp sample report having experimented with three to six other *types of drugs before using cocaine* for the first time. Almost all the Antwerp respondents were seasoned drug users, first of alcohol and tobacco and later marijuana. More than half of them have used LSD and amphetamines, while one in four has used MDMA before trying cocaine. Our data are fairly consistent with findings from other European and American cities: the vast majority of respondents from other samples did not, metaphorically speaking, lose their virginity on cocaine. Most users start with alcohol and/or tobacco, then move on to cannabis and later to other (illicit) drugs. Thus, licit drug use generally precedes the onset of illicit use in normal population samples. Cocaine and heroin are usually the drugs into which initiation comes last. Another conclusion is that most users experiment with a wide variety of drugs. The population(s) under study are essentially multi-drug user ones.

Although it still is an implicit assumption taken for granted by the general public and by many policy makers, both American and European scientists have since long renounced the pharmacological variant of the 'stepping stone' theory. Explanations for this data on sequences of drug use must be based on social factors (setting) rather than on pharmacological or drug-related factors.

Early experimentation with cocaine generally occurs in the *company* of a friend, a group of friends or other 'intimates'. When specific data on initiation company for cocaine (and for other drugs) are available from other major community cocaine studies, they yield a consistent tendency. The first use of cocaine, as in beginning use of cigarettes, alcohol or any illicit drug, is nearby always initiated by trusted friends as a part of some social situation and rarely by a stranger. As to the *location,* initiation typically occurs at a friend's home or one's own home. The data from community samples of cocaine users from other cities confirm the findings of the present study. The typical setting for first use of cocaine is tendentially unplanned, and almost always occurs in the company of close friends and/or partner, or during parties (in a home), or in special conditions of privacy, calm and empathy in one's own circle of friends.

Both in the Antwerp sample and in all other community samples, an overwhelming majority of respondents first used cocaine intranasally (in the present study: 84.7%). Eating, freebasing, smoking and application to genitals are extremely rare in all three samples as a *first route of ingestion.*

Only a minority of the Antwerp respondents appeared to have been actively seeking cocaine, versus a large majority simply 'finding' cocaine in their social circle. Most were offered their first cocaine spontaneously. Drug use is not (solely) explainable in terms of personal or social inadequacy and peer pressure. The active role of the individual drug user needs to be stressed: it is not true that all drug users are 'forced' or talked into drug use by ('bad') peers. Although it can be argued that retrospective reports of *ways of obtaining first cocaine* (being offered, having asked for it, or actively sought to buy it) may not be accurate enough for a clear understanding of the process of initiation, we also find that fewer than 5% of the total sample report feelings of 'being pushed' into cocaine. Almost all respondents report that trying out cocaine was their own (often conscious) choice, although they also acknowledge that friends (or intimates or 'peers') play an important role in the onset and continuation of cocaine use. It seems that it was not so much *if* they were going to try it, but *when* the opportunity would present itself.

Based on Cohen's definition (1989) of an average line of cocaine as approximately 25 mg, we have estimated the *average dose at initiation* among our respondents at 146.7 mg, or 6 lines. Comparison with other major community studies on cocaine use is seriously hampered by the difficulties associated with defining the precise dosage used on the first occasion.

Regarding the *circumstances surrounding initiation* into drug use, we find that more than half of the sample (62 respondents, or 55.9%) report never having seen anyone else use cocaine. Forty-three respondents (38.7% of the total sample) report having witnessed other people using cocaine long before they first used it themselves. Use of cocaine is nearly always observed in friends or acquaintances as a part of some social situation (at a party, at a friend's home, in a bar or discotheque, etc) and in a circle of friends (school friends or work colleagues, friends at the bar, brothers or sisters, friends of friends (acquaintances) and partners). The stereotype of the drug dealer or stranger actively recruiting new cocaine users to expand his market - the drug pusher - is not a feature of our sample. Cocaine use is not transmitted mysteriously from deviant strangers to virginal citizens. It spreads between ordinary people who know each other.

Our qualitative data indicate that in general it is the initiate him or herself who is the active player in the initiation event. Like other major community cocaine studies, we found that curiosity about cocaine and association with people who use it lead to the uninitiated being present when cocaine is being used. But despite the unplanned nature of the event, the majority of our respondents report it as having been their idea – they were not simply passive participants. The stories about pleasurable experiences and the observations of other users made our respondents eager to 'know what it is all about'. Although many of them did not actively seek out cocaine on their own the first time, most respondents look back upon their initiation as something they chose to do.

Initiates often have an fixed image and expectations of the drug. Typically, cocaine using friends or intimates have told them about its positive effects, while parents and *official sources of information* (the media, the authorities, the police, medical practitioners and the school) have warned them about the negative aspects. Four in five Antwerp respondents had received *false information* about cocaine. Most of them refer to general statements about the addictive characteristics of cocaine (such as 'once you try it, you are hooked for life'). Others refer to all kinds of incomplete or biased ideas, the oversimplification underlying the idea that all drugs and any type of drug use must be placed under the common denominator of 'bad', or the typical junkie stories about injecting, withdrawal symptoms, criminal behavior and zombie-like users. Most of this false information is ascribed to the newsmedia, official agencies (such as the government, the school, the police, the prevention agencies and the medical world), the public discourse or non-users in general. On the other hand, false information is also passed on by members of the drug subculture(s), especially by cocaine using friends, and in a much less marked way by dealers. Distortions about the quality of cocaine are very likely to be started by dealers, while false information about specific effects or the non-addictiveness of cocaine usually comes from cocaine using friends.

The fact that most experienced cocaine users reported receiving mainly false, or at least incomplete, biased, or over-simplified information from the media and the official agencies, leads to questions about the validity of official preventive and repressive efforts. 'The official line' is mostly discounted by the respondents. Official warnings are perceived as exaggerated, one-sided and faulty, which leads many to throw out the proverbial baby with the bathwater. Official sources (including parents) will be dismissed, as long as preventive efforts ignore the pleasurable effects and advantages of illicit drugs to the user and overexpose the adverse effects and disadvantages of drugs.

Finally, we described the *social learning process* of the use of cocaine in three stages (following Becker). The first step in the sequence of events that must occur if the person is to become a cocaine user, is that he/she must learn the proper technique (snorting, freebasing, injecting, etc.). Respondents can learn that technique by direct instruction but, as Becker indicates, new users are often too ashamed to admit ignorance and must learn through the indirect means of observation and imitation.

Secondly, the user must be able to discern the effects of the drug. Most respondents report having read books or articles about various drugs and their general effects. Yet, friends and intimates are the most important sources of information about the effects of cocaine. With their high expectations (cocaine as a glamorous party drug), many initiates are usually somewhat disappointed by the subtle qualities of the effects. Moreover, although some users do recognize the effects the first time, this recognition is not typical when first use is intranasal.

Third, the user has to learn to enjoy the effects he/she has just experienced. Experienced users may reassure the beginner as to the temporary character of the unpleasant sensations, and teach him/her how to avoid any severely uncomfortable symptoms, while retaining the pleasant ones. Most rituals and social sanctions related to cocaine initiation involve chemistry and frequency of use, rather than the presence of a guru, like LSD and the like. However, many Antwerp users indicate that it was important to have others present who could be trusted and who could be relied upon in case of adverse or unforeseen effects.

The rules or sanctions passed on from the experienced user to the neophyte contain a lot of information: on the adequate dosage, the preferable route of ingestion, where to obtain good quality cocaine, which safe places to use, good times to use, 'good' people to use with, how to avoid trouble, etc. All the reports of the Antwerp respondents show that, without doubt, the most important *source of precepts and practices for control* during initiation is the peer using group. Virtually all our respondents had been assisted by other experienced users in constructing appropriate rituals and sanctions out of the folklore and practices circulating in their drug-using subculture. However, this process of knowledge transfer is not always flawless. Users may need to adapt informal control mechanisms to their own personal preferences and demands, or the knowledge being transferred may be incomplete.

NOTES

1   For the comparative data in this Chapter, see: COHEN, P. (1989), *Cocaine use in Amsterdam in non-deviant subcultures*, 37-40. Amsterdam: Instituut voor Sociale Geografie. COHEN, P. and SAS, A. (1995), *Cocaine use in Amsterdam II. Initiation and patterns of use after 1986*, 37-39. Amsterdam: Instituut voor Sociale Geografie.

2   For the comparative data in this Chapter, see: ERICKSON, P.G. *et al.* (1994), *The Steel Drug. Cocaine and crack in perspective*, 99-100 and 105-106. New York: Lexington Books. WALDORF,

D., REINARMAN, C. and MURPHY, S. (1991), *Cocaine changes. The experience of using and quitting*, 17-28. Philadelphia: Temple University Press. DITTON, J. and HAMMERSLEY, R. (1996), *A very greedy drug. Cocaine in context*, 31-35. Amsterdam: Harwood Academic Publishers. MERLO, G., BORAZZO, F., MOREGGIA, U. and TERZI, M.G. (1992), *Network of powder. Research report on the cocaine use in Turin*, 64-69. Ufficio Coordinamento degli interventi per le Tossicodipendenze. DIAZ, A., BARRUTI, M. and DONCEL, C. (1992), *The lines of success? A study on the nature and extent of cocaine use in Barcelona*, 117-123 and 135-147. Barcelona: Ajuntament de Barcelona. BIELEMAN, B. and DE BIE, E. (1992), *In grote lijnen. Een onderzoek naar aard en omvang van cocaïnegebruik in Rotterdam*, 53-55. Groningen: Intraval.

3   The difference between our findings and those of Cohen is not extraordinary, in the context of other research. Chitwood reports a mean age at initiation for his Miami subjects of 19.2 years, which is almost 1 year younger than our sample (Chitwood, 1985: 114). Cohen (1989) also refers to a survey by Kandel *et al.* (1985: 77), which shows a mean age at initiation of 21 years for a New York sample of young adults. In other major community studies of cocaine users, mean age at initiation was 22.2 years (Toronto, 1983), 21.6 years (Australia, 1986-87), 22.7 years (Toronto, 1989-90), 20.83 (Turin, 1990-91), 20.8 years (Barcelona, 1990-91) and over 20 years (Rotterdam, 1990-91). For exact references, see note 1 and 2.

4   Age of first use does not help to predict intensity and consequences of alcohol and drug use in young adulthood (between ages 20 and 30). In other words, early onset of either licit or illicit use is not necessarily associated with individuals being less likely to moderate their alcohol use and/or mature out of illicit drug use by age 30. LABOUVIE, E., BATES, M. and PANDINA, R. (1997), Age of first use: its reliability and predictive utility, *Journal of Studies on Alcohol* 58, 638-643.

5   Comparison with other major community studies of cocaine users is possible if all data are re-coded into four categories: 20 years or younger, 21 to 25 years, 26 to 30 years, and 31 years or older. In all samples, the majority of respondents first used cocaine before they were 25 years old. In all samples (with the exception of Turin, 1990-91, and Scotland, 1989-90) the category of respondents who started using cocaine before they were 20 years old is the largest. Comparison of the average percentages based on the nine community samples for each of the age categories, shows the following: the proportion of respondents who first used cocaine before they were 21 in the Antwerp sample (61.3%) is markedly higher compared to the overall average (49.1%). The proportion of respondents who first used cocaine between 26 and 30 in the Antwerp sample (3.6%) is markedly lower compared to the overall average (11.1%). The proportions of respondents who started using cocaine between 21 and 25 (31.5%) and of respondents who started using at the age of 31 years or older (3.6%) are comparable to the average proportions calculated on the nine studies (respectively 33.6% and 5.9%). For exact references, see note 1 and 2.

6   Throughout our fieldwork it became clear that it was much easier to find experienced MDMA users (and in particular under twenty years old) than experienced cocaine users. This could be considered an indication that drug use fashions (especially in nightlife) changed for those under twenty. But then again, the difficulty to find experienced cocaine users could also be the result of a discrepancy between subculturally defined 'secrecy rules' over different drugs. For example, 'ecstasy' and 'speed' may be seen as more instrumental or appropriate in an youth lifestyle than cocaine, and therefore more likely to be talked about.

7   Two thirds of the Turin sample (1990-91) had already used at least two different psychoactive substances, mostly cannabis (89%) and LSD (40%). Heroin was used by 37% before cocaine, which is much higher compared to our findings (15.9%). On the other hand, markedly more Antwerp users had experimented with amphetamines before trying cocaine (57.9%) than in this Turin sample (25%). MERLO, G., BORAZZO, F., MOREGGIA, U. and TERZI, M.G. (1992), *op. cit.*, 64-69.

8   Diaz *et al.* (1992: 117-123) report average ages upon initiation into the different drugs (Barcelona, 1990-91) that are again quite similar to our data: cocaine and heroin are the drugs into which initiation comes last, with cannabis at the extreme opposite of the age ranking. They too report that the first contact with illegal drugs is rarely if ever with cocaine. Respondents indicate relative early initiation for over the counter drugs and volatile substances (solvents). The differ-

ence with our findings is probably due to underreporting in our sample. For exact references, see note 1 and 2.

9   No exact data on the sequence of different drugs could be retrieved for the Scottish and the Rotterdam sample.

10   It would be rash to derive a 'typical initiation age' from such data. Studies on the reliability of retrospectively recalled ages of onset of use lack absolute agreement, which results primarily from a systematic tendency of most individuals to shift their estimates of age of onset upwards as they get older. While not accurate enough for precise dating, retrospective reports of age of onset nevertheless may be accurate enough to reconstruct the sequencing of events relative to each other. LABOUVIE, E., BATES, M. and PANDINA, R. (1997), *loc. cit.*, 638-643. HENRY, B., MOFFITT, T.E., CASPI, A., LANGLEY, J: and SILVA, P.A. (1994), On the "remembrance of things past": a longitudinal evaluation of the retrospective method, *Psychological Assessments* 6, 92-101. BAILEY, S.L., FLEWELLING, R.L. and RACHAL, J.V. (1992), The characterization of inconsistencies in self-reports of alcohol and marijuana use in a longitudinal study of adolescents, *Journal of Studies on Alcohol* 53, 636-647.

11   The fact that most users begin as they do has led to the development of the stepping stone theory or domino theory. This theory states that using 'soft' drugs like nicotine, alcohol and cannabis leads inexorably to taking 'hard' drugs like LSD, MDMA, heroin and cocaine. Lenson's (1995: 160) comment on the stepping stone theory summarizes the critique of many, if not most scientists nowadays: *'The best rationale for this theory is gained by reading backwards from the "hard" drugs, since most smack-, blow- and acidheads have used marijuana, and most marijuana smokers have drunk alcohol or smoked cigarettes. Of course this is a case of post hoc, ergo propter hoc. Run forward, the model is less persuasive. There are many drinkers who never try cannabis, and many pot smokers who never try any "hard" drugs. [...] But the hypothesis is valuable for the conduct of the drug war, since it suggests rapid and irreversible escalation [...]. This theory is easily adapted to the new therapeutic regime. "Drug addiction" is now understood as a "progressive disease" that moves through its list of substances in the same way that a malady produces one symptom after another during its course. "Drugs" are once again undifferentiated. This adds a strange emphasis to the hypothesis: the notion that a users doesn't want one drug or another, but seeks "drugs" in some general way, as if all highs were the same, as if the addict were really addicted to the condition of addiction itself. So the problem is getting high. The existence of a vast variety of drugs on which to get high has provided plenty of counters to be moved up and down into some semblance of order, stacked hierarchically from bad to badder to baddest. Getting high, no matter on what, when, or in what circumstances, is now regarded as a disorder. And the progression of the illness is demarcated by the users' successive drugs of choice.'* LENSON, D. (1995), *On drugs*, 160. Minneapolis/London: University of Minnesota Press.

12   A notable difference between the 1991 Amsterdam sample and the 1997 Antwerp sample on the one hand, and the 1987 Amsterdam sample on the other, is that only 1 respondent of the latter sample reported having been alone at first use, while this was the case for about 5% of the former samples (in 1991 and 1997). Unfortunately, the numbers are too low to establish whether this indicates a systematic change. For exact references, see note 1 and 2.

13   The relevance of these details will become more clear in Chapters 16, 17, 18 and 19 (the influence of parents, working colleagues, partner and friends on the respondent's cocaine use).

14   It should be kept in mind that anyone who has been 'initiated' by a colleague is most likely to see that person as a 'friend'.

15   The exact figures on initiation company in the A'dam II sample (1991) are not incorporated in Table 4.3.a, because they were not (fully) published in the report of Cohen & Sas (1995).

16   There are no specific data on the initiation company at first use of cocaine from the Scottish sample (1989-90) and from the Rotterdam sample (1990-91).

17   In their second study (Toronto, 1989-90) 69% were introduced to cocaine by a friend, 12% by a co-worker or associate, 8 % by his/her partner, and 4% by a relative (Erickson, 1994: 169).

18   The data on initiation from the Australian sample (1986-87), and the Turin sample and the Barcelona sample (1990-91) confirm that cocaine is usually tried for the first time at parties or in private settings, and amongst friends. For exact references, see note 1 and 2.

19   For similar findings, see also: CROFTS, N., LOUIE, R., ROSENTHAL, D. and JOLLEY, D. (1996), The first hit: circumstances surrounding initiation into injecting, 91 *Addiction* 8, 1187-1196.

20   The main locations of initiation in the second Toronto study (1989-90) were a friend's or acquaintance's home (41%), the respondent's home (7%), a bar or a club (7%) and at work (7%). In the Scottish sample (1989-90), 34% first consumed cocaine in a friend's house, 16% in their own house, and 21% at a party. Although all participants of the Scottish study (1989-90) had used cocaine in Scotland at least once, a substantial minority had first tried it in other locations in the United Kingdom (20%), such as London, or in other countries (14%), such as the United States. The data from the Barcelona sample (1990-91) also bear a strong resemblance to the findings of the present study. There are no specific data on the location of initiation available from the first Toronto study (1983) and from the Rotterdam study (1990-91). For exact references, see note 1 and 2.

21   Cohen (1989) and Cohen and Sas (1995) found even higher percentages in the Amsterdam samples of 1987 and 1991.

22   Initiation into injecting is usually done by a significant other person: a friend, a brother or sister, an acquaintance, a partner or lover, etc. and often by older people. Although our data on initiation into injection are limited, they show a marked consistency with other studies. For example, see: CROFTS, N., LOUIE, R., ROSENTHAL, D. and JOLLEY, D. (1996), *loc. cit.*, 1187-1196.

23   See Chapter 1, p. 43-44.

24   The accounts of feelings of 'being pushed' by other people will be discussed in Chapter 9 (p. 224-225), Chapter 17 (p. 367-368) and Chapter 19 (p. 395-396). Only reports about obtrusive behavior during initiation are presented here.

25   In the next chapter we will extensively explain this. See Chapter 5, p. 125-127.

26   See Chapter 5, p. 125-127.

27   See also Chapter 5, p. 149.

28   However, their quantitative data suggest much higher doses at initiation compared to the Antwerp and Amsterdam samples: 65.4% of the Turin sample used less than half a gram at the first occasion, 28.4% used between 0.5 and 1 gram, and 6.1% used more than 1 gram (Merlo *et al.*, 1992: 69).

29   No data are available from the Toronto studies (1983 and 1989-90), the Scottish sample (1989-90) and the Rotterdam sample (1990-91).

30   The Barcelona sample (1990-91) contained some cases of a larger quantity, usually among those who would later use the drug more heavily and regularly, and among those who were already regular heroin users when trying cocaine (Diaz *et al.*, 1992: 138).

31   See Chapter 7, p. 182-184.

32   For example, several respondents referred to books such as: HERMANN, K. and RIECK, H. (1980), *Christiane F. Verslag van een junkie*. Dutch edition. Amsterdam: H.J.W. Becht. SABBAG, R. (1976), *Snowblind. A brief career in the cocaine trade*. New York: Avon Books. HELLINGA, G. and PLOMP, H. (1996), *Uit je bol. Over XTC, paddestoelen, wiet en andere middelen*. Amsterdam: Ooievaar. MILLER, J. and KORAL, R. (1995), *White rabbit. A psychedelic reader*. San Francisco: Chronicle Books.

CHAPTER 5

LEVEL OF USE OVER TIME

5.1. INTRODUCTION

One of the conditions for a rational discussion of drug use is that the concept of 'use' is defined clearly, and where possible quantified. Cohen (1989: 41) distinguished four career stages for measuring cocaine use: initiation, first year of regular use, period of heaviest use (top period), and last three months. By multiplying dose by frequency of use per week for each respondent, he computed the level of use in three periods (excluding initiation). Levels of use were defined as *low* (less than 0.5 gram per week), *medium* (between 0.5 and 2.5 gram per week) and *high* (more than 2.5 gram per week). In this chapter the use of cocaine in the Antwerp sample will be described with exactly the same variables as in the Amsterdam studies: dose (§5.2), frequency of ingestion per week (§5.3), level of use (§5.4), distribution of occasions of use during a week and patterns or changes of use during the user career (§5.5).

5.2. AVERAGE COCAINE DOSAGE OVER TIME

5.2.1. Operationalizing 'dosage'

We have reason to believe that Cohen's basic assumption of an average line of cocaine being approx. 25 mg is wrong. For his analysis, Cohen (1989: 39-40) followed Siegel who estimated the dose of an average recreational cocaine user to be 100 mg of street cocaine, or four lines of 25 mg (Siegel, 1983; Siegel, 1985a). Although we maintained Cohen's definition, we also asked our respondents *how many lines of cocaine they extracted on average from 1 gram of cocaine*. Eighty-two respondents (73.8%) replied to this question. The average number of lines is 15.18 (SD 6.84). The minimum answer is 2, the maximum 35 (i.e. even fewer than 40 lines in 1 gram, which was Cohen's assumption). From the fact that the median is 15, it follows that Cohen's definition (also used by Chitwood and Morningstar, 1985) is an underestimation. According to our respondents, a more accurate definition of an average line of cocaine would be 66.66 mg.

Using a different definition, e.g. one line of cocaine is around 50 mg, which is closer to what our respondents reported, might have had important consequences for the classification of the data on 'dosage'. In table 5.2.a we reproduce our data from table 4.8.a (see Chapter 4) and we have recomputed them according to this new definition (1 line = 50 mg). The consequences of this shift of definition are clear: mean dose at initiation would now be 293.5 mg (almost 0.3 gram), which is twice as high as according to Cohen's definition (146.7 mg).

Table 5.2.a   Dosage at initiation in the 1997 Antwerp sample, according to our definition and according to Cohen's definition

Dosage	Antwerp (definition Cohen)		Antwerp (definition Decorte)	
	N	%	N	%
1-99 mg	63	56.8	18	16.2
100-249 mg	24	21.6	53	47.7
250-499 mg	10	9.0	16	14.4
>500 mg	8	7.2	18	16.2
No answer	*6*	*5.4*	*6*	*5.4*
Total	111	100.0	111	100.0
Mean	146.7 mg		293.5 mg	

As 'amount of use per occasion' is a key element in the definition of 'level of use' in the Amsterdam studies, we wanted to see whether the different definition of an average line of cocaine (25 mg or 50 mg) changes the data on 'level of use' significantly. In table 5.2.b we present two ways of classifying the data from the Antwerp sample: 1) according to the basic assumption that an average line of cocaine = around 25 mg (Cohen); and 2) according to the basic assumption that an average line of cocaine = around 50 mg (Decorte).

Table 5.2.b   Two ways of classifying the 1997 Antwerp sample (according to Cohen and to Decorte) into levels of cocaine use, in %

Level of use	Antwerp (1997)					
	First year (N=110)		Top period (N=111)		Last 3 months (N=111)	
	Decorte	Cohen	Decorte	Cohen	Decorte	Cohen
Low	67.3	70.0	16.2	21.6	62.2	64.9
Medium	25.5	22.7	29.7	28.8	13.5	10.8
High	7.3	7.3	54.1	49.5	5.4	5.4
None	-	-	-	-	18.9	18.9
Total	100.0	100.0	100.0	100.0	100.0	100.0

Comparison of these two ways of classifying the Antwerp sample into levels of use shows no marked differences. Looking at the first year of regular use, only 3 respondents (2.7%) are classified differently (into medium or low level of use). Looking at the top period, we see that the proportion of high level users is somewhat smaller according to Cohen's way of classification, while the proportion of low level users would be somewhat smaller according to our way of classification. And finally, looking at the last three months prior to the interview, again only 3 respondents (2.7%) are classified differently (into medium or low level of use).[1]

Using a different definition (e.g. one line of cocaine is around 50 mg, which is closer to what our respondents reported) might have had an impact for the classification of the data on 'dosage'. *For the sake of comparability, we will maintain Cohen's definitions of 'dose per occasion of use' and 'level of use', based on the basic assumption that an average line of cocaine is approx. 25 mg.*

Moreover, this problem of operationalization would not have been solved if we had stuck to our own finding that an average line of cocaine is about 50 mg. Accurate measurement of a typical 'dose' or 'line' of cocaine is very difficult for a number of reasons. First, there is no such thing as a standard line in reality: witness the fact that the answers ranged from 2 to 35 lines extracted from 1 gram. Every user makes his/her own lines, and while some like it short, others like it long. Second, even the same individual may go from short lines of cocaine at one point in his/her career to longer lines at another, or conversely.

> *Yes, I have learned to reduce the quantity I use. At first, they were lines like other people were snorting... But I learned to reduce that... that it was not necessary to take so much... That you could have the same effects with a smaller line.* [H/0/02]

Third, the typical dose may vary according to set and setting factors. Quite comparable to the smoker who may smoke more when he/she feels depressed or nervous or when he/she is in the company of chain smokers, or to the alcohol consumer who may drink more beer when he/she has something to celebrate or when an old friend pays him a surprise visit, the dose of cocaine may differ from one occasion to another. Thus, the length and width of a 'typical' line of cocaine may depend on the user's mood and on how long ago he/she last used the drug, on the user's company and the activities during use.

Fourth, it is because of the illicit status of cocaine that the average user cannot be certain what is in the substance he/she purchases. What he/she presumes to be cocaine with 90% purity may be adulterated with other substances. It therefore remains unsure whether differences found between 'typical' doses of cocaine in the Antwerp and other samples reflect differences in real cocaine intake. In other words, the net amount of cocaine hydrochloride absorbed may be constant, even though the gross dose on a typical occasion is different from one person to another.

Finally, the most accurate way to measure an individual's dose at a certain period would be to let him/her indicate the average length of his/her lines (and even their width), and the number of lines consumed on a typical occasion. After measuring the weight of these lines (e.g. of 3 cm, 5 cm, 10 cm, etc.), one would be able to calculate quite accurate the mean dose consumed by this individual. An even better method would be to give respondents a gram of cocaine and let them make their 'standard' lines, but this would be expensive and raise ethical questions...

In short, accurate measurement of a typical 'dose' or 'line' of cocaine is very difficult for a number of reasons. Therefore, and for the sake of comparability, we will maintain Cohen's definitions of 'dose per occasion of use' and 'level of use', based on the basic assumption that an average line of cocaine is approx. 25 mg.

5.2.2. Development of average cocaine dosage over time

We asked our respondents how much cocaine they normally used in a day during three distinct periods: the first year of regular use, the period of heaviest use and the three months preceding the interview. Respondents could answer in grams or milligrams. If they did not know precisely, they were allowed to state their consumption in 'lines' of cocaine. We explicitly told them that our standard definition of such a line was around 25 mg (or 40 lines in 1 gram).

Table 5.2.c shows that the average dose per occasion rises from 146.7 mg at initiation to 1,331.8 mg at the period of heaviest use.[2] The average dose of cocaine consumed per occasion of use during the first year of use was less than 0.5 gram for over half of the participants. This proportion decreases to 27.9% during the period of heaviest use, and then rises again to 45.9% during the last 3 months.

Table 5.2.c   Use of cocaine in mg per occasion at four measuring points in the 1997 Antwerp sample, in %; mean dose per period

	Antwerp (1997) (definition Cohen)				
Dose	First time N=105	First year N=109	Top period N=111	Last 3 months N=111	Last 3 months excl.non-users N=90
0 mg	-	-	-	18.9	-
1-99 mg	60.0	29.4	5.4	21.6	25.8
100-249 mg	22.9	22.9	12.6	18.9	23.6
250-499mg	9.5	10.1	9.9	5.4	6.7
>500 mg	7.6	34.9	45.0	30.6	38.2
>2,000 mg		2.8	27.0	4.5	5.6
Total	100.0	100.0	100.0	100.0	100.0
Mean =	146.7mg	423.9mg	1,331.8mg	390.7mg	486.75 mg

High-quantity consumption was relatively rare. None of the Antwerp respondents reported more than 3 grams on any occasion of use.[3] The proportion of respondents taking 2 grams or more grew from 2.8% (during the initial year) to 27% (during the period of heaviest use). By the last three months, only 4.4 percent of the sample were using 2 grams or more, and 18.9 percent had not used at all. The majority of those still using during the last three months used less than 1 gram per occasion (the mean dose among those still using was 486.75 mg, the median was 250 mg).

We verified how many respondents used more than 2 gram per occasion during the period of heaviest use (n=30): 13 of them mainly freebased their cocaine at that period, 10 mainly injected, and 7 snorted. Of the 5 respondents reporting more than 2 grams per occasion of use during the last three months, 4 mainly freebased (and 1 snorted).

Our data generally confirm that quantities used vary according to the route of ingestion, although we find few statistically significant differences. Average doses of those who *inject* are usually higher (although not statistically significant).[4] The average dose of those who are *registered* (i.e. convicted for a felony and/or having been in contact with a drug treatment agency) is consistently higher than the average dose of non-registered respondents (although not statistically significant).

As to *freebasing*, we find statistically significant differences in average doses per occasion, both for the initial year of use and for the period of heaviest use. The average dose per occasion of those who freebased during the initial year of use is 1,083.3 mg versus 405.3 mg for those who did not freebase (t=2.46; df=107; p=0.015). Average dose per occasion of those who freebased during the period of heaviest use is 2,027.9 mg versus 1,118.9 mg for those who did not (t=3.106; df=109; p=0.002).

The proportion of respondents who stopped using (during the last three months) in our sample was 18.9%, versus 26.9% in the 1987 Amsterdam sample.[5] Nevertheless, in both samples respondents report an average use below the level of the first year of regular use. Excluding ex-users, we find an average use of 487.3 mg per occasion with the remaining 90 respondents of our sample, versus 188 mg in the Amsterdam I sample.

5.2.3. Tentative comparison of dose levels in other European and American studies

By standardizing the dose at initiation at 100, we can compare the 1987 and 1991 Amsterdam samples and the 1997 Antwerp sample for each period (see figure 5.2.a). In most other major community cocaine studies (Toronto, 1989-90; Scotland, 1989-90; Turin, 1990-91; Rotterdam, 1990-91; and Barcelona, 1990-91) amount and frequency of use were presented for the first year of use, the period of heaviest use, and the three months prior to the interview. In general, in the first year of use, amounts of cocaine used were higher than in the three months prior to interview, but lower than during their 'heaviest' period of use.

Figure 5.2.a   Development of average cocaine dosage over time in three samples, with average dosage at initiation standardized at 100

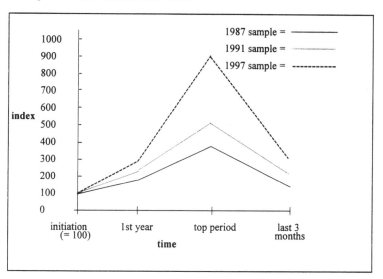

That a similar up-top-down pattern is found in all samples comes as no surprise, because respondents were asked for dosage at initiation, in the period of heaviest use, and in the last three months. Yet, if most cocaine use careers were characterized by a steadily increasing intake over time, the pattern found here would rather be slowly more (and the period of heaviest use would coincide with the period of three months prior to the interview) than escalation and then reduction (up-top-down).[6]

To interpret these data, a comparison with other studies would be very useful. However, thorough comparison is seriously hampered by a number of factors.

First, as can be seen from the tables 5.2.d to 5.2.g, the dose levels in the various studies are categorized differently. For example, the Scottish sample (1989-90) only shows which proportions of the sample used less or more than 100 mg at a typical occasion (Ditton & Hammersley, 1996: 36). For the Barcelona, Rotterdam and Turin samples (1990-91), the typical amounts used at different periods were calculated 'per month' and not 'per occasion of use' (Bieleman *et al.*, 1993: 72).

Second, Erickson *et al.* report that some users found it hard to estimate the quantity of cocaine they typically consumed per occasion. Among all the Toronto respondents (1983), 12 percent were unable to estimate the number of lines, or hits, taken, and 44 percent were unable to estimate the number of grams consumed (Erickson *et al.*, 1994: 96). The chances are that some participants in the other studies had similar difficulties in estimating doses (whether expressed in grams, lines or hits). Above all, as we have shown above, individual definitions of a typical 'line' are highly variable. It remains impossible to recompute data from other studies unless a standard definition of one 'line' is accepted. Assumptions can never be validated, which is another reason for regarding the comparison with extreme caution.

Third, although most other cocaine studies were based on some variation of snowball sampling, the community-based samples were not created in exactly the same way. Apart from small differences in methods of sampling, there are clear differences between the groups respondents were recruited from. Some samples are purposely made multi-ethnic, others are almost exclusively white. Some samples contain respondents recruited from treatment settings (Miami), from the sex industry (Rotterdam), from the nightlife scene (Antwerp), etc. As Cohen (1989: 43) pointed out correctly, the concept of a 'normal' dose may vary considerably between these different (subcultural) groups.

Fourth, quantities used may vary with the quality of cocaine available. We present some data on the quality of cocaine in Antwerp in chapter 13, but these give only a notion of what respondents are talking about.[7] We know nothing about the quality of cocaine during a user career, and we know little about quality differences between community samples studied in other cities and countries.

Fifth, quantities used certainly vary with the route of ingestion. It is generally accepted that freebasing as well as injecting usually imply higher 'typical' doses' than snorting. Thus, comparability is difficult when proportions of users who have intravenous use or freebasing as their sole method or as a frequent method, differ from one sample to another. For example, life time and last month prevalence of both injecting and freebasing as routes of ingestion were considerably higher in the Antwerp sample (1997) than in both Amsterdam samples (1987 and 1991).[8]

In his 1987 survey Cohen (1989: 41-44) made a tentative comparison of dose levels of his own sample with a Toronto sample and a Miami sample. In Table 5.2.d we present our data added to Cohen's table. Tables 5.2.e to 5.2.g present our own attempt to bring data from different community cocaine studies together in a comparative overview.

In table 5.2.d, the most important observation is that the Toronto and Amsterdam I Obviously, tables 5.2.e to 5.2.g pose comparability problems because dose levels are categorized in a different way in these six community samples. Still, this is the nearest we can get to a comparison of the distribution of user quantities. In general, the samples give similar pictures for the three different periods (first year of use, period of heaviest use, and three months prior to the interview). For each of these periods, dose levels seem lower in the Amsterdam I sample, the Scotland sample and the Amsterdam II sample. Dose levels appear to be higher in the Toronto sample, the Turin sample and the Antwerp sample.

Table 5.2.d Tentative comparison of dose levels in Antwerp (1997), Amsterdam (1987), Toronto (1983) and Miami (1983), in % [♠]

Dosage	Antwerp (1997) last 3 months ex users excl. N=89		Amsterdam I (1987) last 3 months ex users excl. N=117		Toronto (1983) 'typically taken' N=111		Miami (1983) last 3 months treatm.+non treatm. N=170	
1-99mg	25.8}		35.9 }		39.6 }		}	
100-249 mg	23.6}	56.1	37.6 }	91.6	36.9 }	85.5	}	47
250-499 mg	6.7}		18.1 }		9.0 }		}	
> 500 mg		43.8		8.5		2.7		53
No answer		-		-		*11.7*		*0*
Total		99.9		100.1		99.9		100

Table 5.2.e Tentative comparison of dose levels in first year of use in Antwerp (1997), Amsterdam I (1987), Amsterdam II (1991), Turin (1990-91), Scotland (1989-90) and Toronto (1989-90), in % [♠]

dose levels in first year of use						
	A'dam I 1987	Toronto 1989-90	Scotland 1989-90	Turin 1990-91	A'dam II 1991	Antwerp 1997
1-99 mg	42.5	}	49	}	31	29.4
100-249 mg	30.6	} 35	}	} 28	38	22.9
250-500 mg	15.7	15	}	}	16	10.1
500-750 mg	}	19	}	}52	}	}
750-1,000 mg	}	1	} 51	}	}	} 34.9
1,000-2,000 mg	} 11.2	17	}	}	} 15	}
2,000-3,000 mg	}	6	}	} 19	}	}
3,000-5,000 mg	}	}	}	}	}	} 2.8
> 5,000 mg	}	} 7	}	-	}	}

Table 5.2.f Tentative comparison of dose levels in heaviest period of use in Antwerp (1997), Amsterdam I (1987), Amsterdam II (1991), Turin (1990-91), Scotland (1989-90) and Toronto (1989-90), in % [♠]

Dose levels in heaviest period of use						
	A'dam I 1987	Toronto 1989-90	Scotland 1989-90	Turin 1990-91	A'dam II 1991	Antwerp 1997
1-99 mg	12.7	}	35	}	15	5.4
100-249 mg	39.8	}16	}	} 15.5	26	12.6
250-500 mg	20.9	15	}	}	33	9.9
500-750 mg	}	10	}	}44	}	}
750-1,000 mg	}	5	} 65	}	}	} 45.0
1,000-2,000 mg	} 26.6	20	}	}	} 25	}
2,000-3,000 mg	}	9	}	} 35	}	}
3,000-5,000 mg	}	}	}	}	}	} 27.0
> 5,000 mg	}	}23	}	5.5	}	}

Table 5.2.g Tentative comparison of dose levels in three months prior to interview in Antwerp (1997), Amsterdam I (1987), Amsterdam II (1991), Turin (1990-91), Scotland (1989-90) and Toronto (1989-90), in % [♠]

	dose levels in three months prior to interview					
	A'dam I 1987	Toronto 1989-90	Scotland 1989-90	Turin 1990-91	A'dam II 1991	Antwerp 1997
0 mg	26.9	}36	68	}	26	18.9
1-99 mg	26.2	}	}	} 26.7	22	21.6
100-249 mg	27.3	20	}	}	27	18.9
250-500 mg	13.0	10	}	}	15	5.4
500-750 mg	}	11	}	}50	}	}
750-1,000 mg	}	1	}32	}	}	}30.6
1,000-2,000 mg	} 6.2	14	}	}21.1	}10	}
2,000-3,000 mg	}	}	}	}	}	}
3,000-5,000 mg	}	}3	}	2.2	}	}4.5

Although comparison of dose levels in different studies is seriously hampered by different categorizations of dose levels, recruitment differences, difficulties in estimating the quantity of cocaine consumed per occasion, cocaine quality differences between community samples, etc. a major explanatory factor is the prevalence of specific routes of ingestion in these samples. Both freebasing and injecting are clearly associated with higher doses. Indeed, for the Antwerp and the Turin samples, the higher doses can be explained by a higher proportion of respondents ever having been in contact with treatment agencies, and a higher proportion of freebasers/injectors. However, these factors do not seem to offer an explantion for the higher dose levels in the Toronto sample.

In short, our findings on the variation of average cocaine dosage over time seem consistent with most other major community cocaine studies. A similar pattern of slow, gradual escalation is found in most samples. Waldorf *et al.* found the same and suggested that this pattern of slow, gradual escalation had to do partly with the general availability of the drug and with an individual's access to sellers or personal contacts who would supply. *'For example, many of the older San Francisco respondents, who began experimenting with cocaine in the late 1960s and early 1970s when it was much less available, used very infrequently during the early years of their cocaine careers. This was less true for those who began their use in the late 1970s and early 1980s when cocaine was much more widely available.'* (Waldorf *et al.*, 1991: 24). Generally, when cocaine became more available, most users tended to use larger amounts and use more often. Waldorf *et al.* cited two other factors as contributing to escalating use: a slow increase in tolerance for the drug, and the seductive and insidious nature of the drug itself.

But escalation of use is far from inevitable.[9] First, when respondents are asked for dosage at initiation and in the period of heaviest use, one naturally finds an increase over time. Second, average dosage during the three months prior to the interview shows that about one in five respondents quit using and that among respondents who continue to use the average dose per occasion drops to 487.3 mg. Typically, cocaine use may escalate, but it does not do so endlessly. If most cocaine use careers were characterized by a steadily increasing intake of cocaine over time, the pattern found here would rather be slowly more (and the period of heaviest use would coincide with the period of three months prior to the interview) than escalation and then reduction (up-top-down).[10]

Although comparison of dose levels in different studies is seriously hampered by different categorizations of dose levels,[11] recruitment differences,[12] difficulties in estimating the quantity of cocaine consumed per occasion (see e.g. Erickson, 1994: 96), cocaine quality differences between community samples,[13] etc. a major explanatory factor is the prevalence of specific routes of ingestion in these samples. It is generally accepted that freebasing as well as injecting usually imply higher 'typical' doses' than snorting. Thus, comparability is difficult when proportions of users who have intravenous use or freebasing as their sole method or as a frequent method, differ from one sample to another. For example, life time and last month prevalence of both injecting and freebasing as routes of ingestion were considerably higher in the Antwerp sample (1997) than in both Amsterdam samples (1987 and 1991).[14]

5.3. FREQUENCY OF INGESTION

5.3.1. Frequency of ingestion at three periods

Our respondents were asked how often they would use a typical dose in their first year of regular use, their period of heaviest use, and the three months preceding the interview. They were shown a card with the following options: (1) daily; (2) not daily, but more often than once a week; (3) once a week; (4) less often than once a week, but at least once a month; and (5) less often than once a month. Considering frequency in the same way as we considered dose per occasion, we find the following frequency distributions. See table 5.3.a.

Daily use shows a spectacular rise from first year (3.6%) to the top period (45.0%), and then drops to zero for the last three months. This means that almost half of our sample were frequent users during their top period, but that none of them subsequently continued this pattern. We investigate the reasons for this in chapter 12 and 13.[15] More than 60% of our respondents used less frequently than once a week during the first year. After a drop during the period of heaviest use, almost 65% of the sample used less frequently than once a week during the three months prior to the interview. Almost 1 in 5 respondents did *not* use these last three months.

Table 5.3.a Frequency of ingestion of a typical dose at three temporal measuring points, in the 1997 Antwerp sample, in %

	Antwerp (1997)	N=111	
Frequency	**First year**	**Top period**	**Last 3 months**
Daily	3.6	45.0	-
> 1 p.w.	21.6	26.1	13.5
1 p.w.	13.5	12.6	2.7
> 1 p.m.	25.2	14.4	27.0
< 1 p.m.	36.0	1.8	37.8
None	-	-	18.9
Total	**100.0**	**100.0**	**100.0**

Compared with the Amsterdam samples, frequencies of use of our Antwerp sample are higher for the first year and for the period of heaviest use. During the three months prior to the interview, almost none of the respondents subsequently continued this increased frequency. Compared to both Amsterdam samples, frequencies of use in the Antwerp sample are lower for the 3 months prior to interview.[16]

5.3.2. Frequency of ingestion and level of use

Like in the Amsterdam study, we examined frequency of use at the three temporal measuring points of four different groups. These groups are: 1) those who used at a high level during the top period; 2) those who used at a medium level during top period; 3) those who used on a low level during top period; and 4) those who had stopped using (see for a definition of each level of use, paragraph 5.4).

Table 5.3.b Frequency of ingestion for 'high level' users (during period of heaviest use) at three measuring points, in two samples, in %

Frequency	Amsterdam I (1987) (N=33)			Antwerp (1997) (N=55)		
	First year	Top period	Last 3 months	First year	Top period	Last 3 months
Daily	3.0	93.9	6.1	3.6	70.9	-
> 1 p.w.	33.3	6.1	21.2	34.5	27.3	18.2
1 p.w.	12.1	-	3.0	21.8	1.8	3.6
> 1 p.m.	33.3	-	18.2	16.4	-	23.6
< 1 p.m.	18.2	-	24.2	23.6	-	30.9
None	-	-	27.3	-	-	23.6
Total	**99.9**	**100.0**	**100.0**	**99.9**	**100.0**	**99.9**

Table 5.3.c Frequency of ingestion for 'medium level' users (during period of heaviest use) at three measuring points, in two samples, in %

Frequency	Amsterdam I (1987) (N=49)			Antwerp (1997) (N=32)		
	First year	Top period	Last 3 months	First year	Top period	Last 3 months
Daily	2.0	44.9	-	3.1	28.1	-
> 1 p.w.	22.4	49.0	22.4	12.5	31.3	9.4
1 p.w.	12.2	6.1	8.2	6.3	21.9	3.1
> 1 p.m.	34.7	-	16.3	40.6	18.8	25.0
< 1 p.m.	28.6	-	26.5	37.5	-	50.0
None	-	-	26.5	-	-	12.5
Total	**99.9**	**100.0**	**99.9**	**100.0**	**100.1**	**100.0**

Table 5.3.d Frequency of ingestion for 'low level' users (during period of heaviest use) at three measuring points, in two samples, in %

Frequency	Amsterdam I (1987) (N=77)			Antwerp (1997) (N=24)		
	First year	Top period	Last 3 months	First year	Top period	Last 3 months
Daily	-	1.3	-	4.2	8.3	-
> 1 p.w.	5.2	32.5	2.6	4.2	16.7	8.3
1 p.w.	5.2	19.5	3.9	4.2	25.0	-
> 1 p.m.	31.2	29.9	19.5	25.0	41.7	37.5
< 1 p.m.	58.4	16.9	49.4	62.4	8.3	37.5
None	-	-	24.7	-	-	16.7
Total	**100.0**	**100.1**	**100.1**	**100.0**	**100.0**	**100.0**

Table 5.3.e Frequency of ingestion for current non-users (during period of heaviest use) at three measuring points, in two samples, in %

Frequency	Amsterdam I (1987) (N=44)			Antwerp (1997) (N=21)		
	First year	Top period	Last 3 months	First year	Top period	Last 3 months
Daily	-	36.4	-	4.8	61.9	-
> 1 p.w.	15.9	31.8	-	33.3	23.8	-
1 p.w.	6.8	15.9	-	9.5	4.8	-
> 1 p.m.	43.2	11.4	-	19.0	9.5	-
< 1 p.m.	34.1	4.5	-	33.3	-	-
None	-	-	100.0	-	-	100.0
Total	**100.0**	**100.0**	**100.0**	**99.9**	**100.0**	**100.0**

From tables 5.3.b, 5.3.c, 5.3.d and 5.3.e, we can make the following observations. Note that each of these tables refers to each group's period of heaviest use (the top period). No notable difference in the propensity to stop using cocaine[17] between the groups of low level, medium level and high level users (during the period of heaviest use) was found in Amsterdam. In the Antwerp sample, we find 23.6% ex-users among high level users, 12.5% among medium level users and 16.7% among low level users. These differences are not statistically significant.

Like in Amsterdam, we find a difference regarding the prevalence of daily use; from 70.9% daily use in the high level group, through 28.1% in the medium level group, prevalence of daily ingestion drops to 8.3% in the low level group. Cohen's (1989: 46) findings on this point were even more marked: from 94% daily users in the high level group to 1.3% in the low level group. Of course, as level of use was computed with frequency of ingestion, it is logical that the prevalence of daily users increases with level of use. But we also found 9 people who used daily while maintaining a medium level of use and 2 persons who used daily while maintaining a low level of use.

Concerning frequency of ingestion during the three months before the interview, a lot of similarities between high level and medium level users (during period of heaviest use) were observed among the cocaine users in Amsterdam. The only difference was the persistence of a small proportion of daily use in the high level group during their top period. As already stated, we did not find such a persistence of daily use in any of our groups. It is odd that we find more similarities between the low level and the medium level group than between the medium level and the high level group. Both low and medium level groups show similar proportions of 'more than once a week users' (around 9%), of 'less than once a week users' (around 75%), and of 'non users' (around 15%).

Of those who were abstinent during the time of the interview, more than 85% had been using more often than once a week during the period of heaviest use. And more than one third of them had been using more often than once a week during the first year of regular use. This means that frequent use of cocaine during certain (top) periods of use does not exclude later abstinence at all.

However, most of these current non-users may eventually have abstained from their cocaine use with the help of treatment facilities. After checking the 21 respondents who were abstinent at the time of the interview (see table 5.3.e), we found that 18 of them (85.7%) never had any contact with treatment organizations. These data clearly illustrate that frequent users can become abstinent without any professional help.

5.3.3. International comparison with other community studies

In table 5.3.f, we have added our data to the comparative table Cohen presented in his 1987 Amsterdam report (1989: 48). Our findings are very similar to his. The proportion of daily users was considerably larger in the Miami sample, because many of these respondents made contact with treatment institutions.[18] This table also shows that if we study samples of cocaine users not recruited through treatment institutions and the like, the proportion of daily use is almost negligible, and the proportion of occasional use (< once per month) is spectacularly larger.

Table 5.3.f   Frequency of cocaine use in the 1987 Amsterdam I sample, in the 1997 Antwerp sample in the last three months (prior to interview), and in the 1980-81 Miami sample in last three months (prior to treatment), in % [♠]

Frequency	Amsterdam I (1987) N=116 [*]	Miami N=170 [**]	Antwerp (1997) N=90 [*]
Daily	1.7	31	-
>1 p.w.	17.2	27	16.7
1 p.w.	6.9	10	3.3
> 1 p.m.	25.0	18	33.3
< 1 p.m.	49.1	14	46.7
Total	**100.0**	**100.0**	**100.0**

[*]   non users excluded
[**] treatment + non treatment

Although a different classification was used, the data from the Barcelona, Turin and Rotterdam samples (1990-91) can be compared with the Antwerp and the Amsterdam samples to a certain extent.[19] Data on frequency of ingestion at three temporal measuring points in these six samples are presented in table 5.3.g. Comparison is somehow hampered because of the following differences in categorizations:

- In the studies of Amsterdam I (1987), Amsterdam II (1991) and Antwerp (1997), the initial period covers the first 12 months of use, whereas in the studies of Barcelona, Turin and Rotterdam (1990-91) the initial period covers the first 6 months of use.
- In the tables of Amsterdam I (1987), Amsterdam II (1991) and Antwerp (1997), the categories 'more than once a week' and 'once a week' were summarized in one category 'weekly'.
- In the tables of Amsterdam I (1987), Amsterdam II (1991) and Antwerp (1997), the categories 'less than once a month' and 'none' were summarized in one category 'less than once a month'.
- In the tables of Barcelona, Turin and Rotterdam (1990-91) the third period (in the third column) covers the last six months of use. This period thus represents 'present' use of those being interviewed, or the 'last' period of use in the case of ex-users. In the tables of Amsterdam I (1987), Amsterdam II (1991) and Antwerp (1997), the third period (in the third column) covers the last three months prior to the interview. About one in five respondents were non-users during that period.
- The Table 'Average' was made by computing the average of each cell from the six tables above.

Table 5.3.g   Frequency of ingestion of a typical dose in six community samples, in %

Amsterdam I (1987) N=160			
Frequency	First year	Top period	Last 3 months
Daily	1.2	33.7	1.2
> 1 p.w.	25.7	43.7	17.5
> 1 p.m.	32.5	14.4	18.1
< 1 p.m.	40.6	8.1	63.1
No answer	-	-	-
Total	100.0	99.9	99.9

Barcelona (1990-91) N=153			
Frequency	First 6 months	Top period	Present or last
Daily	11.1	49.7	17.6
Weekly	12.4	27.5	23.5
> 1 p.m.	11.1	9.2	24.2
< 1 p.m.	64.7	13.1	34.0
No answer	0.7	0.7	0.7
Total	100.0	100.0	100.0

Amsterdam II (1991) N=108			
Frequency	First year	Top period	Last 3 months
Daily	1.8	20.4	5.5
> 1 p.w.	26.0	49.1	17.6
> 1 p.m.	21.3	26.8	22.2
< 1 p.m.	50.0	3.7	54.6
No answer	1.8	-	-
Total	100.0	100.0	99.9

Turijn (1990-91) N=100			
Frequency	First 6 months	Top period	Present or last
Daily	11	38.8	15.3
Weekly	32	34.7	29.6
> 1 p.m.	46	23.5	42.9
< 1 p.m.	10	3	12.2
No answer	1	2	2
Total	100	100	100

Antwerp (1997) N=111			
Frequency	First year	Top period	Last 3 months
Daily	3.6	45.0	-
> 1 p.w.	35.1	38.7	16.2
> 1 p.m.	25.2	14.4	27.0
< 1 p.m.	36.0	1.8	56.7
No answer	-	-	-
Total	100.0	100.0	100.0

Rotterdam (1990-91) N=110			
Frequency	First 6 months	Top period	Present or last
Daily	22.7	53.6	37.3
Weekly	29.1	28.2	21.8
> 1 p.m.	27.3	12.7	27.3
< 1 p.m.	19.1	5.5	13.6
No answer	1.8	-	-
Total	100.0	100.0	100.0

Average			
Frequency	First 6 months	Top period	Present or last
Daily	8.7	40.2	12.8
Weekly	26.8	37.0	21.1
> 1 p.m.	27.5	16.8	26.9
< 1 p.m.	37.0	6.0	39.2
Total	100.0	100.0	100.0

Regarding the initial year, we can see that the proportion of daily users in the Antwerp sample (3.6%) is among the lowest of the six samples. In the Barcelona, Turin and Rotterdam samples these proportions are markedly higher. The proportion of respondents using once a week or more (but not daily) in the Antwerp sample (35.1%) is among the highest of the six samples. Regarding the proportion of respondents using less frequently than once a month, there are very large differences between the samples: from 64.7% in the Barcelona sample, to 36.0% in the Antwerp sample, to 10% in the Turin sample.

Regarding the period of heaviest use, we find that the proportions of respondents using daily and using once a week or more (but not daily) in the Antwerp sample are higher than the average percentages for all six samples. The proportions of respondents using more than once a month and using less than once a month in the Antwerp sample are smaller than the average percentages for all six samples. Regarding the proportions of respondents using daily, there are considerable differences between the samples: from 53.6% in the Rotterdam sample to 20.4% in the Amsterdam sample. Both are Dutch samples (i.e. from a similar national context), but the Amsterdam respondents had been recruited from non-deviant subcultures, whereas the Rotterdam respondents had been partly recruited from the hard drug scene (or street scene).

In short, comparison with other studies shows that if cocaine users are recruited through treatment institutions and the like (as in Miami) or in deviant subcultures or street scenes (as in Rotterdam), the proportion of daily use is consistently higher, and the proportion of occasional use (less than once per month) is typically lower. As to the Antwerp sample, we find that the proportion of daily users during the initial year is lower and the proportion of daily users during the period of heaviest use is higher than in most other samples.

5.4. LEVEL OF USE

5.4.1. Definition of levels of use

In discussing the use of cocaine, or of any other drug, it is imperative to define not only frequency, but also level of use, i.e. a combination of frequency, dose and possibly route of ingestion. Cohen (1989: 50) chose to define 'level of use' by multiplying 'amount of use per occasion' and 'frequency of ingestion per week', as it appeared that these were the only two discriminating variables. He decided to treat route of ingestion as a completely different variable, and not to give intravenous use ('IV use') a role in the definition of level of use.[20] To make reliable comparisons with the Amsterdam findings, we chose to maintain Cohen's definition of level of use:[21]

- *Low = less than 0.5 gram per week*
  (vs Chitwood less than 1 gram per week mainly intranasal)

- *Medium = between 0.5 and 2.5 gram per week*
  (vs Chitwood 1-7 gram per week mainly intranasal or less than 1 gram)

- *High = over 2.5 gram per week*
  (vs Chitwood over 7 grams a week mainly intravenous)

5.4.2. Levels of cocaine use over time

In table 5.4.a, we compare the levels of cocaine use at the initial year, in the period of heaviest use and in the three months prior to interview. The following similarities and differences between the three samples can be observed. In all three samples, levels of use tend to be low for a majority of the respondents during the initial year and during the last three months.

The proportion of high level users is higher in our Antwerp sample than in both Amsterdam samples, in all three periods. The proportion of current non-users in the three months prior to the interview in our Antwerp sample (18.9%) is smaller than in both Dutch samples (27.5% in the Amsterdam I sample and 25.9% in the Amsterdam II sample).

Figure 5.4.b   Levels of cocaine use over time, in %, in the 1997 Antwerp sample

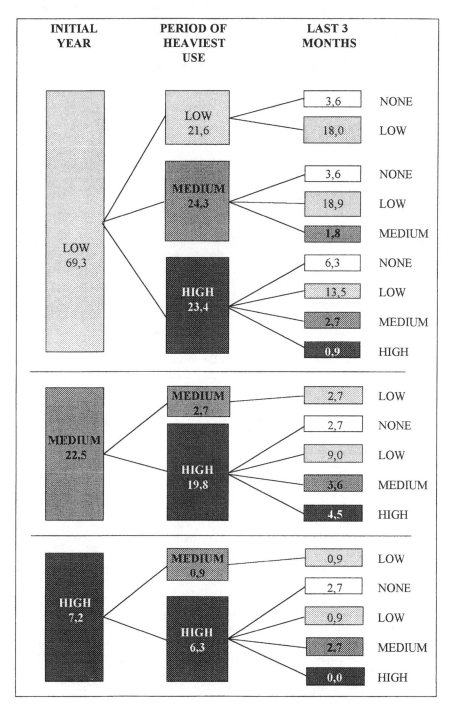

In both Amsterdam samples, proportions of respondents gradually decrease as level of use increases, during the period of heaviest use. The inverse tendency is observed in the Antwerp sample: the proportion of high level users is higher than the proportion of medium level users, while the proportion of low level users is even lower.

Table 5.4.a Levels of cocaine use in three periods, in three samples, in % (Cohen's definition)

Level of use	Amsterdam I (N=160) 1987			Amsterdam II (N=108) 1991			Antwerp (N=111) 1997		
	Period			Period			Period		
	Initial year	Heaviest use	Last 3 months	Initial year	Heaviest use	Last 3 months	Initial year	Heaviest use	Last 3 months
None	-	-	27.5	-	-	25.9	-	-	18.9
Low	89.4	48.1	64.4	82.4	52.8	60.2	69.4	21.6	64.9
Medium	8.1	30.6	6.3	13.9	30.6	9.2	22.5	28.8	10.8
High	2.5	20.6	1.9	1.8	15.7	3.7	7.2	49.5	5.4
No answ.	-	*0.6*	-	*1.8*	*0.9*	*0.9*	*0.9*	-	-
Total	**100.0**	**99.9**	**100.1**	**99.9**	**100.0**	**99.9**	**100.0**	**100.0**	**100.0**

Figure 5.4.b illustrates a way of presenting cocaine use over time, adopted from Chitwood (1985).[22] It shows that 18.0% of the Antwerp respondents *never exceed a low level of use*. It is thus possible for a proportion of cocaine users to maintain a low level of use, although higher proportions were found in the Amsterdam I sample (34.8%) and the Amsterdam II sample (38.9%). Including the ex-users who never exceed a low level, this proportion rises to 21.6% in our sample, but again in both Amsterdam samples these proportions are higher (48.7% and 51.9%).

Half of all users (49.5%) reach a high use level in their period of heaviest cocaine use, but only 5.4% had stayed at that level in the three months prior to interview. Our findings at this point are even more marked than those of both Amsterdam samples. *All these data indicate that cocaine use does not escalate infinitely* (see also Cohen, 1989: 51; and Waldorf *et al.*, 1991: 23-28). Of those people using more than 2.5 gram per week in their top period (55 respondents), 23.6% evolved to non use, 47.3% to a low level of use, and 16.4% to a medium level of use.

It is only for a very small number of respondents that the cocaine career is characterized by a continuosly increasing intake. One respondent beginning at a low level had progressed to use at a high level in the three months prior to interview (versus none in the Amsterdam I sample and 2 respondents in the Amsterdam II sample). Of those beginning at a medium level, one fifth (20%) progressed to a high level the three months prior to the interview (compared to 7.7% in the 1987 Amsterdam sample and 6.7% in the 1991 Amsterdam sample). These respondents report that their period of heaviest use and the three months prior to the interview coincided. It remains unsure whether these participants would have reduced their use or would have continued to increase their use, had we interviewed them again at a later stage.

In both the 1991 and 1987 samples, use level during top period is not necessarily connected with abstinence during the three months prior to interview. When Cohen aggregated from both samples those who had ever used at a high level during their top period of use, he found that 26% of them reported abstinence at the time of interview. Respondents using at a medium level during their top period yielded 28% of the abstainers, while those using at a low level during their top period yielded 27% of the abstainers. In our Antwerp sample we found 23.6% abstainers at the time of interview among those who had used at a high level during their top period, 12.9% abstainers among those who had used at a medium level, and 16.7% abstainers among those who had used at a low level during their top period.

Thus the fact of ever having used cocaine at a high level does not reduce the probability of finding somebody abstinent, compared to having used at a low level during the top period. The Antwerp sample shows an even slightly higher probability of abstinence for those who used at a high level during their top period. *Both the findings from Antwerp and from Amsterdam indicate that among people who have used cocaine regularly abstinence occurs independently of the use levels during the periods of heaviest use* (Cohen & Sas, 1995: 48).

Among the 77 Antwerp respondents reporting a low level of use during the initial year, about one third (33.7%, n=26) developed a high level of use during their top period (versus 8% of the 1991 Amsterdam sample). Of the 25 Antwerp respondents who used at a medium level during their first year, a much larger proportion (88%, n=22) eventually used cocaine at a high level (versus 44% of the 1991 Amsterdam sample). A similar proportion of the 8 Antwerp respondents who used at a high level during their first year of regular use remained at this level of use during their top period (87.5%, n=7) (versus 100% of the 1991 Amsterdam sample).

Again, both the Belgian and Dutch data lead to a similar conclusion: *if high level or near high level use occurs during the early stages of a user career, the odds are that high level use will continue* (Cohen & Sas, 1995: 48). In other words, although abstinence at the time of the interview is not connected with the level of use during users' top period, high level use at the time of the interview might be related to early high levels of use. Without wanting to equal high level use with problematic use, the question arises whether there are indications for more problematic use among users who started at a high level of use from the onset, and continued to use at this level during their career.

5.4.3. Level of use and length of cocaine use career

Of course there may be a certain relation between levels of use over time and the length of the cocaine user career. Is it that those who never exceed a low level of use also have a very short use career? We found that the average duration of cocaine use with those 18 respondents who never exceed the low level, is 3.75 years, with a range of 1 to 11 years.[23] In table 5.4.c we compute the average length of cocaine using careers by subtracting the age at first year of regular use from the age at the time of the interview. The letters L, M, H and O stand for Low, Medium, High and Zero Use. So LLO means Low in first year, Low in top period, Zero use at last three months, etc... Unfortunately, we failed to ask respondents who had not used cocaine during the last three months, when they last used. We could not exactly assess the length of these respondents' cocaine using career, but we approximated this by supposing their last occasion was not longer than one year before, like Cohen did (Cohen, 1989: 52, footnote 1). In table 5.4.c these respondents' estimates are accompanied by a question mark.

Table 5.4.c   Average length of cocaine using career by level of use index, in years, in the 1987 Amsterdam I sample and in the 1997 Antwerp sample

Users index	Amsterdam I (1987)		Antwerp (1997)	
	N	Average length of career	N	Average length of career
LLO	20	6.6 ?	4	12.25?
LLL	52	5.5	18	3.75
LMO	12	5.2 ?	4	8.5?
LML	28	5.7	20	5.8
LMM	2	2.5	2	2.0
LHO	8	8.3 ?	7	5.4?
LHL	10	8.8	15	9.0
LHM	3	4.0	3	6.2
LHH	-	-	1	1.0
MMO	1	2.0 ?	-	-
MML	2	9.5	3	5.8
MMM	1	6.0	-	-
MHO	1	13.0 ?	3	6.0?
MHL	5	8.0	10	9.1
MHM	2	2.0	4	4.9
MHH	1	13.0	5	8.3
HML	-	-	1	4.0
HHO	-	-	3	3.2?
HHL	1	14.0	1	5.0
HHM	-	-	3	6.0
HHH	2	5.5	-	-
Total	**151**	**6.2**	**107**	**6.4**
Total*	109	6.0	86	6.26
* rows with "?" excluded				

The 43 people who at some moment in their career used at a high level *and* are still using, have an average career length of 7.8 years, with a range of 1 to 18 years (compared to 7.6 years, with a range of 1 to 17 years for the 1987 Amsterdam sample). On average, careers of the latter category are more than twice as long as the average for users who never exceeded the low level. Cohen (1989: 52) concluded that the users who always remained at low level use did not do so as an artifact of short careers. However, our data do not confirm his suggestion. They show that continuous low level users actually have a shorter cocaine use career than those who used at a high level at some moment.

This analysis shows the importance of keeping in mind that data on drug users only refer to one moment in a dynamic development of use patterns. In other words, a drug user may be using at a high level at one moment in time, and at a low level (or even be abstinent) at another. An individual can be using a substance in a controlled way, but at a certain moment he or she can lose control over it, leading to a period of abuse or compulsive use, and later on he/she can regain power over the drug. Over a long-term period drug use patterns are ever-changing trajectories followed by individuals who have never definitely gained control over their substance, nor permanently lost control over it. Moreover, whether the balance of 'control' and 'abuse' tips to either side clearly does not solely depend on pharmacological characteristics of the drug, but also on an variety of set and setting variables (see chapters 14 and 15).[24] And finally, the availability of financial means is an important factor for continuation of cocaine use or for temporary abstinence (see Chapter 12).[25]

5.5. AGE AND TIME INTERVALS BETWEEN STAGES OF USE

In this paragraph we discuss the age and the time intervals between different stages of use (initiation, second use, first year of regular use, first year of heaviest use, time of the interview). The data from the 1987 Amsterdam I sample, the 1991 Amsterdam II sample and the 1997 Antwerp sample on average time intervals between initiation (first use) and first year of regular use, average time intervals between first year of regular use and first year of heaviest use, the average age of respondents at these different stages in their cocaine using career, and average duration of the period of heaviest use are presented together.

In an attempt to describe an average course of cocaine use careers in these three samples, we have tried to summarize all these data from three samples in one comprehensive figure. From figure 5.5.a the following observations can be made:

Figure 5.5.a   Time intervals and ages between stages of use, and average duration of period of heaviest use, in three samples

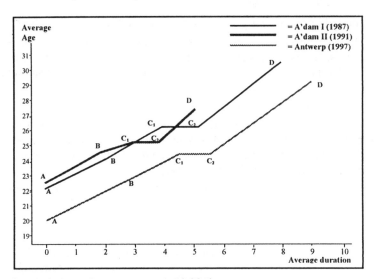

Legenda: A = average age at initiation
             B = average age at first regular use
             C_1 = average age in first year of heaviest use
             $C_1 - C_2$ = average duration of period of heaviest use
             D = average age at interview

(1) average age at initiation (A):

The mean age at which the Antwerp respondents consumed their first cocaine was 20.0 years. Average age of initiation into cocaine use was 22.0 years in the Amsterdam I sample (1987) and 22.4 years in the Amsterdam II sample (1991).[26]

143

(2) average age at first regular use (B)

The mean age in the first year of regular use was 22.8 years for the Antwerp respondents, 24.1 years in the Amsterdam I sample (1987) and 24.4 years in the Amsterdam II sample (1991). Clearly, mean age at first regular use in the Antwerp sample is lower than in both Amsterdam samples, indicating that in general our respondents started using cocaine at an earlier age.

(3) time interval between initiation and first year of regular use (A – B)

The Antwerp respondents progressed quite slowly from initiation to regular use. On average it took the Antwerp users 2.8 years before starting to use regularly, versus 2.0 years in the 1987 Amsterdam sample and 1.8 years in the 1991 Amsterdam sample.

(4) average age in the first year of heaviest use (C_1)

The mean age in the first year of heaviest use was 24.7 years in the Antwerp sample, 26.4 years in the Amsterdam I sample (1987) and 25.2 years in the Amsterdam II sample (1991).

(5) time interval between first year of regular use and first year of heaviest use (B–C_1)

The 1987 Amsterdam sample and the 1997 Antwerp sample show many similarities. In both samples it took respondents on average 1.9 years to progress from first regular use to the period of heaviest use. In the Amsterdam II sample (1991) it took respondents on average 1.1 years.

(6) average duration of period of heaviest use (C_1–C_2)

The average duration of period of heaviest use in the Amsterdam I sample (1987) and in the Antwerp sample (1997) is very similar: 14 months (or about 1.2 years) and 13.5 months (or approx. 1.1 years). The duration of the top period is 5 months shorter in the Amsterdam II sample (1991).

(7) The average period between initiation and top period is 4.9 years, which is higher than what was found in the 1987 Amsterdam I sample: 4.2 years.

In short, Figure 5.5.a shows that the average course of a cocaine use career in the Amsterdam I sample (1987) and in the Antwerp sample (1997) is quite similar. Time intervals between different stages of use do not differ markedly, although the Antwerp users progress somewhat slower from one stage to the next. The most marked differences between both samples are the mean ages at different stages. At each stage in their career, the Antwerp cocaine users are consistently younger than the participants of both Amsterdam samples.

Compared to both the Amsterdam I sample (1987) and the Antwerp sample (1997), the average course of a cocaine use career of the Amsterdam II sample (1991) shows significant differences. The data regarding time intervals and ages at different stages of use may have been influenced by the length of respondents' use careers, and should be interpreted cautiously. First, the interviewees of the 1991 sample were younger (M=27.4) at the time of the interview than those in the 1987 sample (M=30.4) and the 1997 sample (M=29.2). Second, in 1991 Cohen interviewed subjects an average of 5 years after initiation compared to 7.6 years after initiation in 1987. The Antwerp respondents were interviewed an average of 6.4 years after initiation. Thus, for both variables our sample can be situated between both Amsterdam samples.

Cohen and Sas assumed that the respondents in the 1991 sample might have had less developed patterns of use: *'They may have continued using cocaine and experienced higher levels of use during later periods. As a result, were we to interview them again they might report longer periods from regular use to top period and might more closely resemble respondents in the 1987 sample.'* (Cohen & Sas, 1995: 50). To investigate this possibility further, Cohen recomputed the 1987 data for those respondents who reported first regular use 7 years or less prior to the interview. He wanted to correct for the longer use-career of the 1987 sample, making them more comparable to the 1991 sample. The same recomputations were performed for the Antwerp sample. The results are the following (see Figure 5.5.b).

Figure 5.5.b   Time intervals and ages between stages of use, and average duration of period of heaviest use, corrected for length of career in the Antwerp sample (1997), and the Amsterdam II sample (1991)

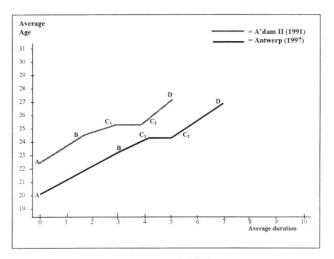

Legenda: A = average age at initiation
B = average age at first regular use
C_1 = average age in the first year of heaviest use
$C_1 - C_2$ = average duration of period of heaviest use
D = average age at interview

Regarding the time interval from first regular use to top period, the effect of length of career is clearly visible. When the 1987 Amsterdam I data and the 1997 Antwerp data are corrected for length of career, average time from regular use to top period for respondents in the Amsterdam I sample decreases from 1.9 to 0.9 years and for the Antwerp respondents from 1.9 years to 1.2 years. This drop is less spectacular than for the 1987 Amsterdam sample, but it is consistent with our finding that overall average length of career is longer in our sample (see table 5.4.c).

Because subjects in the 1991 sample had shorter careers on average, we cannot be certain about having captured the users' highest use period; for some respondents their top period may follow rather than precede their selection for the study. To compensate for this, Cohen controlled for length of career for the 1987 sample, as he did for time intervals between stages of the users' career. Controlled for length of career, average duration of top period for the 1987 Amsterdam sample drops from 14 to 10 months, and for our 1997 Antwerp sample from 13.5 to 9.5 months. Figure B shows the average course of cocaine use careers in the Antwerp (1997) sample after correction for length of career and the average course of cocaine use careers in the Amsterdam II sample (1991).

The figure shows that the average course of cocaine users from the Amsterdam II sample is similar to that of the respondents who report first regular use 7 years or less prior to the interview in the Antwerp sample. Cohen and Sas (1995: 50) interpreted the results of this recomputation as a confirmation of similarities in the development of use patterns over time in his two Amsterdam samples. Again, the logical conclusions are that the Antwerp users progress somewhat slower from one stage to the next and that the Antwerp cocaine users are consistently younger than those of the Amsterdam sample at each stage in their career.

5.6. OTHER FEATURES OF USE PATTERNS

Our respondents were asked the same questions about use patterns as those in the Amsterdam sample, taken from Morningstar and Chitwood's questionnaire (Chitwood & Morningstar, 1985: 449-459). These questions related to development of use over time, partitioning of a typical week during the last month in use and non-use days, and speed of use at a typical occasion of cocaine consumption.

5.6.1. Patterns of use

The development of use over time was represented as simple graphic shapes, clarified by a short text. A card showing Figure 5.6.a was shown to the respondents. Respondents were asked (in all three samples) which of the patterns best conformed to their career. Each of the graphical patterns was also described verbally.

Figure 5.6.a   Theoretical patterns of development in cocaine use

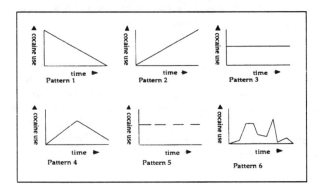

The distribution of these different modes of development of use in the Antwerp sample is shown in table 5.6.b together with comparable data from the Amsterdam community samples. Responses in all three samples were similar, in that they show that many modes of development can occur. The following observations can be made.

The two development patterns most mentioned were 'up-top-down' and 'varying'. The pattern 'up-top-down' (pattern 4) was the pattern of use most frequently found in both the Amsterdam samples. In the Antwerp and Scotland samples it was the second most frequently reported pattern. The pattern 'varying' (pattern 6) was the pattern of use most frequently mentioned in the Antwerp sample (one in two participants) and the Scotland sample, and the pattern second most mentioned in both the Amsterdam samples. This pattern often refers to situations characterized by periods of non-use and by periods of use of variable length produced with varying degrees of regularity and intensity.

In the Amsterdam I sample, the Scotland sample and the Antwerp sample, the 'slowly more' pattern, a mode that reflects an implicit theory of cocaine gradually producing dependency, is reported by a very small minority (approx. 5% or less). In the Amsterdam II sample, a proportion of approx. 11% was found. According to Cohen and Sas (1995: 53) this was due to the fact that more respondents of the Amsterdam II sample were still in the process of developing their cocaine use careers.

Table 5.6.b   Frequency of development patterns, in four samples

Development pattern	Amsterdam I 1987		Scotland 1989-90		Amsterdam II 1991		Antwerp 1997	
	N	%	N	%	N	%	N	%
1 first much-slowly less	8	5.0	19	14.3	10	9.1	3	2.7
2 slowly more	5	3.1	7	5.3	12	11.1	4	3.6
3 stable	21	13.1	21	15.8	17	15.7	5	4.5
4 up-top-down	63	39.4	29	21.8	38	35.1	29	26.1
5 intermittent	10	6.3	-	-	7	6.9	14	12.6
6 varying	53	33.1	57	42.8	24	22.1	56	50.5
Total	**160**	**100.0**	**133**	**100.0**	**108**	**100.1**	**111**	**100.0**

Table 5.6.b also shows that pattern 3 ('stable') is mentioned significantly less frequently by the Antwerp sample (4.5%) than in all other samples. It remains unclear whether the prevalence of this pattern is a reflection of (un)stable availability of cocaine in different countries or cities.

The fifth pattern ('intermittent') is reported almost twice as often in our sample (12.6%) as in the two Dutch samples (6.3% and 6.9%). This is consistent with our finding that more respondents from the Antwerp sample report periodic abstinences (see Chapter 12).[27]

Furthermore, these data are consistent with those from other European cities such as Barcelona, Turin and Rotterdam (Diaz *et al.*, 1992: 178-179; Merlo *et al.*, 1992: 75; Bieleman *et al.*, 1993: 67 and 208). The two development patterns most mentioned were 'up-top-down' and 'varying'. The 'slowly more' pattern is reported by a very small minority (approx. 5% or less). The most eye-catching finding here is the significantly larger proportion found in the Rotterdam sample (33.6%). The authors explain this through the large proportion of frequent heroin users in that sample

(Bieleman *et al.*, 1993: 67-68). Among the seven samples we find a marked difference in the prevalence of this intermittent pattern (from zero in the Scottish sample to 28.3% in the Turin sample).

The first three patterns are marked by a linear progression (steady increase, steady decrease or stable), while the last three patterns (peak, intermittent or varying) are more irregular. In table 5.6.c percentages of table 5.6.b are recomputed into two categories: continuous versus discontinuous patterns of use.

Table 5.6.c Continuous versus discontinuous patterns of use, in four samples

Patterns of use	Amsterdam I	Amsterdam II	Antwerp	Scotland
Continuous	21.2	35.9	10.8	35.4
Discontinuous	78.8	64.1	89.2	64.6
Total	**100.0**	**100.0**	**100.0**	**100.0**

In all samples, the proportion of respondents reporting a discontinuous pattern of use is larger than the proportion of those reporting a continuous one. In the Antwerp sample almost 90% report irregular patterns (half of our respondents report the 'varying' pattern, indicating a development marked by constant variation in amounts and frequencies of use and another 38.7% choose the fourth or the fifth pattern). This clearly shows that respondents experience their cocaine use career as a dynamic, often irregular, pattern, subject to many changes (caused by a variety of drug, set and setting factors).

5.6.2. Partitioning of week

We asked respondents how their cocaine use was spread over a typical week during the four weeks prior to interview (see table 5.6.d).[28] More than half of our respondents (54.0%) had not used cocaine during this period, which is considerably more than in Cohen's Amsterdam samples (39.4% and 34.3%). Although the number of observations is small, we find very similar proportions of respondents who report a preference for weekends (mostly or only), i.e. about 38%. These data are consistent with the findings about the importance of going out, partying and meeting friends as setting factors (chapter 14).[29] Only 6.3% of the Antwerp sample said their cocaine use was evenly spread, or even more frequent on weekdays, versus 18.75% and 29.6% in the Amsterdam samples (Cohen & Sas, 1995: 53).

Table 5.6.d   Partitioning of week (during last four weeks) in days of use, in three samples

	Amsterdam I 1987		Amsterdam II 1991		Antwerp 1997	
Partitioning of week	**N**	**%**	**N**	**%**	**N**	**%**
Only/mostly weekends	61	38.1	39	36.1	44	39.7
Evenly spread/more often weekdays	30	18.75	32	29.6	7	6.3
Never (no cocaine used)	63	39.4	37	34.3	60	54.0
No answer	*6*	*3.75*	-	-	-	-
Total	**160**	**100.0**	**108**	**100.0**	**111**	**100.0**

5.6.3. Speed of use at a typical occasion

In 1987 Cohen (1989: 57) designed a question to determine the proportion of users who could be described as 'bingers'. Binge use is described as a *'continuous period of repeated dosing, usually at least once every 15 to 30 minutes, during which users consume substantial amounts of cocaine. During binges users may assume some of the behavioral characteristics of compulsive users'* (Siegel, 1985a: 210).

Table 5.6.e   Speed of use at a typical occasion, in three samples

Speed of use at occasion	Amsterdam I 1987		Amsterdam II 1991		Antwerp 1997	
	N	%	N	%	N	%
A little-stop-a little etc	105	65.5	72	66.7	69	62.2
A little-stop	32	20.1	15	13.9	10	9.0
Everything in one binge	22	13.8	20	18.5	32	28.8
No answer	*1*	*0.6*	*1*	*0.9*	*0*	*-*
Total	**160**	**100.0**	**108**	**100.0**	**111**	**100.0**

Table 5.6.f   The prevalence of the binge pattern for 'snorters' and for 'basers/injectors', during last three months and during top period, in the 1997 Antwerp sample.

Route of ingestion (last 3 months)	Antwerp (1997) speed of use at a typical occasion			
	A little-stop-a little...	A little-stop.	Binge	Total
Snorting	51 (77.3%)	4 (6.1%)	11 (16.6%)	**66 (100.0%)**
Basing/injecting	7 (29.2%)	3 (12.5%)	14 (58.3%)	**24 (100.0%)**
Total	**58**	**7**	**25**	**90**

(χ2= 18.258; df=2; p<0.000)

Route of ingestion (top period)	Antwerp (1997) speed of use at a typical occasion			
	A little-stop-a little...	A little-stop.	Binge	Total
Snorting	47 (73.4%)	5 (7.8%)	12 (18.8%)	**64 (100.0%)**
Basing/injecting	21 (45.6%)	5 (10.9%)	20 (43.5%)	**46 (100.0%)**
Total	**68**	**10**	**32**	**110**

(χ2=9.243; df=2; p=0.01)

From the 1987 to the 1991 Amsterdam sample, Cohen and Sas (1995: 54) found a slight increase in the binge pattern. In our Antwerp sample we found a percentage of 28.8% for this way of use (see table 5.6.e).[30]

This important difference in the prevalence of the 'binge-pattern' is clearly related with the main route of ingestion applied by our respondents. In chapter 6 we will show that life time and last month prevalence of injecting and freebasing are higher in our Antwerp sample than in the Amsterdam samples.[31] In table 5.5.f. we cross-tabulated speed of use at a typical occasion with the main route of ingestion during the three months prior to interview. We compared 'snorters' with 'basers/injectors'.

These cross-tabulations show a statistically significant difference between the prevalence of the binge-pattern and the route of ingestion (p<0.001). We did the same with the main route of ingestion during the period of heaviest use, and we found a less marked, but still statistically significant, difference (p<0.025).

5.7. CONCLUSION

The core concepts discussed in this chapter were dose, frequency of use, level of use, average course of cocaine use and patterns of use. For measuring cocaine use we distinguished four career stages : initiation, first year of regular use, period of heaviest use, and three months prior to the interview.

We argued that accurate measurement of a typical 'dose' of cocaine is very difficult for a number of reasons. For the sake of comparability we employed Cohen's definitions of 'dose per occasion of use' and 'level of use', based on the assumption that an average line of cocaine is approx. 25 mg. Our findings regarding development of *average cocaine dosage over time* confirm those of most other major community cocaine studies: a similar pattern of slow, gradual escalation is found in most samples and is explained through a variety of factors: increased availability of cocaine, increased accessibility, a slow increase in tolerance for the drug, the seductive nature of cocaine, etc. The most important factor associated with higher doses, however, is the prevalence of more direct routes of ingestion, such as freebasing and injecting. Nevertheless, cocaine use does not escalate infinitely. During the three months prior to the interview one in five respondents had quit using and among respondents who continued to use the average dose per occasion dropped significantly.

As to *frequencies of use*, our data suggest that if cocaine users are recruited through treatment institutions and the like (like in Miami) or in deviant subcultures or 'street scenes (like in Rotterdam), the proportion of daily use is consistently higher, and that of occasional use is typically lower. Compared to most other samples the proportion of daily users during the initial year in the Antwerp sample is low and the proportion of daily users during the period of heaviest use is high. In particular, daily use in the Antwerp sample increases with the level of use and shows a spectacular rise from the first year to the top period.

However, almost none of our subjects subsequently continued this increased frequency during the three months prior to the interview. One in five did not use and their frequency of daily use dropped to zero. Indeed, frequent use of cocaine during certain (top) periods of use does not exclude later abstinence or decreased frequency of use at all. The propensity to stop using cocaine does not change with the level of use (during period of heaviest use). Furthermore, most of the current non-users eventually abstained from their cocaine use without the help of treatment facilities. Even frequent users can quit without any professional help.

By multiplying dose by frequency of use per week for each respondent, we computed *the level of use*. Three levels of use were distinguished: *Low* (= less than 0.5 gram per week), *Medium* (= between 0.5 and 2.5 gram per week) and *High* (= over 2.5 gram per week). Levels of use tend to be low for a majority of the respondents in all three samples during the initial year and during the last three months. About one in five of the Antwerp respondents *never exceeded a low level of use*. Thus it proves possible for a proportion of cocaine users to maintain a low level of use.

The proportion of high level users is higher in our Antwerp sample than in both Amsterdam samples, in all three periods, whereas the proportion of current non-users in the three months prior to the interview in our Antwerp sample is smaller than in both Dutch samples. About half of all users reach a high use level in their period of heaviest cocaine use, but only 5% had stayed at that level in the three months prior to interview. Our findings on this point are even more marked than those of Cohen for both his Dutch samples. *All these data indicate that cocaine use does not escalate infinitely.*

Both the Antwerp and the Amsterdam findings indicate that among people who have used cocaine regularly, abstinence occurs independently of actual use levels during the periods of highest use. Conversely, the data from all samples suggest that if high level or near high level use occurs during the early stages of a user career, the odds are that high level use will continue. In other words, although abstinence at time of the interview is not connected with the level of use during users' top period, high level use at the time of the interview may be related to early high levels of use. This might be an indication that problematic use is found more among users who started at a high level of use from the onset, and continued to use at this level during their career.

Our analysis shows that data on drug users only reflect one moment in a dynamic development of use patterns. Drug use patterns are ever-changing trajectories followed by individuals who have never definitely gained control over their substance, nor permanently lost control over it.

Many different *patterns of use* can occur, but the two development modes most mentioned are 'up-top-down' and 'varying'. Half of our respondents reported the 'varying' pattern, indicating a development marked by constant variation in amounts and frequencies of use. The 'slowly more' pattern, a mode that reflects an implicit theory of cocaine gradually producing dependency, is reported by a very small minority in most samples. Only in the Rotterdam sample was a significantly larger proportion found, probably because of the large proportion of frequent heroin users in that sample.

In all samples the majority of respondents report a discontinuous pattern of use. In the Antwerp sample almost 90% report irregular patterns (up-top-down, intermittent, or varying) and 10% report continuous patterns (steady increase or decrease, or stable). This clearly shows that respondents experience their cocaine use career as a dynamic, often irregular pattern, subject to many changes caused by a variety of drug, set and setting factors.

More than half of our respondents had not used cocaine during the four weeks prior to interview. Most respondents report a preference for weekends, which is consistent with the findings about the importance of going out, partying and meeting friends as setting factors. Fewer than one in three of the Antwerp respondents can be described as 'bingers', i.e. continuous use of repeated dosing. This 'binge-pattern' is clearly related with freebasing and injecting as route of ingestion.

NOTES

[1] We do not reproduce other relevant tables here, but one can imagine the impact of a change in definition of an average line of cocaine on table 5.2.c ('Use of cocaine in mg per occasion at four measuring points, in %') or table 5.4.a ('Levels of cocaine use in three periods').

[2] This is a ninefold increase. In his 1987 sample, Cohen (1989: 42) found the same tendency, with average dose rising fourfold from initiation to top period. See paragraph 5.2.3.

[3] In the 1991 Amsterdam sample, consistently higher average dose levels were found than in 1987: 240 mg during the first year of regular use; 530 mg during the top period and 250 mg during the

4
three months prior to interview (Cohen & Sas, 1995: 41). Still, these average dose levels are consistently lower than those in the Antwerp sample. See also paragraph 5.2.3.

Those who injected their cocaine during the initial year (N=8) report an average dose at a typical occasion of 906.25 mg. Those who did not inject during the initial year (N=103) report an average dose at a typical occasion of 385.72 mg. The difference is not statistically significant. Those who injected their cocaine during the period of heaviest use (N=8) report an average dose at a typical occasion of 2,125 mg. Those who did not inject during their top period (N=103) report an average dose at a typical occasion of 1,270.2 mg. The difference is not statistically significant.

5
A respondent is considered to have 'stopped' using cocaine if he/she has not used any cocaine during the last three months and perceived him- or herself as an ex-user (or 'quitter').

6
See Chapter 5.

7
See Chapter 10.

8
See Chapter 6.

9
Waldorf *et al.* (1991: 24) found that about as many of the San Francisco respondents maintained stable use patterns as escalated.

10
See also §5.6.1, p. 146.

11
For example, compare DITTON, J. and HAMMERSLEY, R. (1996), *A very greedy drug. Cocaine in context*, 36. Amsterdam: Harwood Academic Publishers, and BIELEMAN, B., DIAZ, A, MERLO, G. and KAPLAN, C. (1993) (eds.), *Lines across Europe. Nature and extent of cocaine use in Barcelona, Rotterdam and Turin*, 72. Amsterdam: Swets & Zeitlinger.

12
Although most other cocaine studies were based on some variation of snowball sampling, the community-based samples were not created in exactly the same way. Apart from small differences in methods of sampling, there are clear differences between the groups respondents were recruited from. Some samples are purposely made multi-ethnic, others are almost exclusively white. Some samples contain respondents recruited from treatment settings (Miami), from the sex industry (Rotterdam), from the nightlife scene (Antwerp), etc. As Cohen (1989: 43) pointed out correctly, the concept of a 'normal' dose may vary considerably between these different (subcultural) groups.

13
Quantities used may vary with the quality of cocaine available. We present some data on the quality of cocaine in Antwerp in chapter 10, but these give only a notion of what respondents are talking about (See Chapter 10, p. 233-236). We know nothing about the quality of cocaine during a user career, and we know little about quality differences between community samples studied in other cities and countries.

14
See Chapter 6, p. 155-158.

15
See Chapter 12, p. 267-275 and 278-279, and Chapter 13, p. 289-304.

16
When we look at the previous 3 months, the proportion of respondents who use less frequently than once a week (>1 per month + <1 per month) is larger in the Antwerp sample (64.8%) than in both Amsterdam samples (55.6% and 50.9%). Conversely, the percentage of those who did *not* use the last 3 months is smaller for the Antwerp sample (18.9%) than for both Dutch samples (25.6% and 25.9%). (Cohen, 1989: 46; Cohen & Sas, 1995: 44).

17
A respondent is considered to have 'stopped' using cocaine if he/she has not used any cocaine during the last three months and perceives him- or herself as an ex-user (or 'quitter').

18
The data from the Miami sample are copied from Cohen's report (Cohen, 1989: 48). Cohen cites two publications by Chitwood: CHITWOOD, D. (1985), Patterns and consequences of cocaine use. In: KOZEL, N. and ADAMS, E. (eds.), *Cocaine use in America: epidemiologic and clinical perspectives*. Rockville: NIDA. CHITWOOD, D. and MORNINGSTAR, P. (1985), *loc. cit.*, 449-459.

19
Comparison with the Toronto study (1983) was not possible because the frequency of use was measured completely different. See: ERICKSON, P.G. *et al.* (1994), *op. cit.*, 96-101. Comparison with the Scotland study (1989-90) was not possible because exact data on frequency of use were not published. See: DITTON, J. and HAMMERSLEY, R. (1996), *op. cit.*, 59-60.

20
Originally, Cohen and his colleagues had wanted to adopt the same cut-off points between low, medium and high level use as Chitwood did, but their respondents in their sample hardly ever

reached a level as high as that defined by Chitwood (1985). Cited in: COHEN, P. (1989), *op. cit.*, 49.

[21] See also §5.2.1, p. 125-126, on the operationalization of the concept of 'dosage'. For the sake of comparability we maintained Cohen's definitions of 'dose per occasion of use' and 'level of use', based on the basic assumption that an average line of cocaine = approx. 25 mg.

[22] Cohen produced comparable figures showing levels of cocaine use over time for the 1987 Amsterdam sample (Cohen, 1989: 51), the 1991 Amsterdam sample (Cohen, 1995: 47) and the Miami sample studied by Chitwood (Cohen, 1989: 58).

[23] Compared to Cohen's data (1989: 52) from his 1987 Amsterdam sample (5.5 years. with a range of 1-15 years), and to the average duration of cocaine using careers in our total sample (6.4 years), this may seem short, but whether 3.75 years must be interpreted as a very short career, is a highly subjective matter.

[24] See Chapter 14, p. 317-322 and chapter 15, p. 336-338.

[25] See Chapter 12, p. 268 and 274.

[26] See also Chapter 4, p. 99-100.

[27] See Chapter 12, p. 266-267.

[28] No comparable data were found in other major community studies of cocaine users.

[29] See Chapter 14, p. 312-315 and 317-322.

[30] No comparable data are found in other major community studies of cocaine users.

[31] See Chapter 6, p. 155-158.

CHAPTER 6

ROUTES OF INGESTION

6.1. INTRODUCTION

In this chapter we explore different routes of ingestion of cocaine.[1] Life time prevalence and last month prevalence of six routes of ingestion are discussed: snorting, injecting, eating, freebasing, smoking and application on genitals (§6.2). In §6.3 we differentiate for three periods of use: the first year of regular use, the period of heaviest
use and the three months prior to the interview. In §6.4 we present the advantages and
disadvantages ascribed to snorting, injecting and freebasing by our respondents. These
opinions can be interpreted as the equivalent of rules of use. Therefore, special attention is given to those opinions that are *not* based on the respondents' own experience.
Finally, most users have experience with more than one route of ingestion. The factors
influencing the choice of route of ingestion are discussed in §6.5.

International comparison with other European and American cities is difficult because of different data sets.[2] Wherever possible, we present comparable data from
these community studies.

6.2. PREVALENCE OF DIFFERENT ROUTES OF INGESTION

Here we present the relative frequencies of six routes of ingestion, both in terms of life
time prevalence ('*Did you ever...*') and in terms of last month prevalence. The six
routes of ingestion we questioned our respondents about were: eating, rubbing on
genitals, smoking, snorting or intranasal use (i.n.), injecting or intravenous use (i.v.),
and freebasing.

6.2.1. Life time prevalence

Intranasal use is the dominant route of ingestion in our population. It ranks number one
both in terms of life time prevalence and of last month prevalence, like for the respondents in the Amsterdam studies. But compared to both Dutch samples, *life time prevalences* of other routes of administration in our sample were considerably higher (see
table 6.2.a): 72.1 % of the Antwerp respondents had freebased, compared to 18.1 % of
the 1987 Amsterdam sample and 30 % of the 1991 Amsterdam sample; 24.3 % of our
respondents had used cocaine intravenously, compared to 6.2 % of the Amsterdam

sample in 1987, and 5 % of the Amsterdam sample in 1991. Clearly, no single route of ingestion can be said to be unpopular with the Antwerp users.[3]

Table 6.2.a Life time prevalence and frequency of different routes of ingestion, in %, in three samples

Amsterdam I (1987)						
Frequency	**i.n.** N=159	**Smoking** N=158	**Freebase** N=160	**Eating** N=160	**Genitals** N=159	**i.v.** N=160
Always	73.6	0.6	-	1.9	-	0.6
Mostly	21.4	1.2	0.6	-	-	1.2
Sometimes	2.8	7.5	0.6	1.2	1.9	1.2
Rarely	2.8	60.0	16.9	13.7	11.9	3.1
Total ever	100.0	69.3	18.1	16.9	13.8	6.2
Never	-	29.3	81.9	83.1	85.6	93.8
No answer	*0.6*	*1.2*	-	-	*0.6*	-
Total	**100.0**	**99.8**	**100.0**	**100.0**	**100.0**	**100.0**

Amsterdam II (1991)						
Frequency	**i.n.** N=108	**Smoking** N=108	**Freebase** N=108	**Eating** N=108	**Genitals** N=108	**i.v.** N=108
Always	75.0	1.9	4.6	1.8	-	0.9
Mostly	16.7	4.6	2.8	-	-	0.9
Sometimes	2.8	4.6	1.8	-	-	-
Rarely	3.7	50.0	20.4	11.1	10.2	2.8
Total ever	98.2	61.1	29.6	12.9	10.2	4.6
Never	1.8	38.9	70.4	87.0	89.6	94.4
No answer	-	-	-	-	-	*0.9*
Total	**100.0**	**100.0**	**100.0**	**99.9**	**100.0**	**99.9**

Antwerp (1997)						
Frequency	**i.n.** N=111	**Smoking** N=111	**Freebase** N=111	**Eating** N=111	**Genitals** N=111	**i.v.** N=111
Always	39.6	0.9	-	-	-	7.2
Mostly	26.1	5.4	12.6	0.9	-	6.3
Sometimes	16.2	18.0	15.3	0.9	1.8	3.6
Rarely	17.1	64.8	44.1	18.9	25.2	7.2
Total ever	99.0	89.3	72.1	20.7	27.0	24.3
Never	0.9	10.7	27.9	79.3	73.0	75.7
No answer	-	-	-	-	-	-
Total	**99.9**	**100.0**	**100.0**	**100.0**	**100.0**	**100.0**

The majority of those users, who practised smoking, freebasing, eating or application on genitals, only did this *rarely* or *sometimes*. Conversely, a considerable proportion of those Antwerp users who snorted or injected their cocaine, did this *always* or *mostly*.

We merged the categories 'always', 'mostly' and 'sometimes' from table 6.2.a and checked whether the group of injecting users belonged to specific chains of our snowballs. It appeared that 14 of these 19 respondents (73.7%) were part of chain H, and 3 of chain F (15.8%). Clearly, this is a bias caused by our snowball sampling technique *without* randomized sequences. Chapters 3 and 12 make it clear that the respondents of snowball chain H more often report difficulties with cutting back and/or periodic abstinence, they tend to be less skilled, they report more contacts with treatment agencies, more convictions for a felony, more intravenous use of cocaine, etc. [4]

Most authors of other community cocaine studies do not report on life time prevalence. Erickson *et al.* report on the 'usual' method of administration of their respondents (Toronto, 1983): 93% of their sample usually snort cocaine, 5% usually inject it and 2% normally smoke it. No regular freebasers are identified (Erickson *et al.*, 1994: 96). For the Rotterdam sample (1990-91), Bieleman and de Bie (1992: 33) report that 74.5% 'usually' snort, 21.0% 'usually' inject and 28.2% 'usually' freebase (basing and/or chasing). We do have data on life time prevalence from two other community samples: Australia (1986-87), Scotland (1989-90) and Toronto (1989-90).[5] These data from different samples reveal that the overwhelming majority of cocaine users snort cocaine. In all samples, fewer than one in four participants have life time experience with intravenous use of cocaine. The proportion of cocaine users having life time experience with injecting is highest in the Antwerp sample (24.3%). This does not mean, however, that these users continue to inject throughout their using career (see below).

The most intriguing aspect of the comparison between these community samples is undoubtedly the major difference in life time prevalence of freebasing.[6] It is as if in some countries (or cities) the practice of freebasing has not spread as fast as in others. This may be due to differences in marketing (distribution of ready-made crack) or to development in users' folklore (the manufacture of freebase by users themselves). Apart from geographical differences between different samples, variation in figures on freebasing may also reflect a temporal evolution. With the exception of the American samples (Toronto), data on freebasing in European studies show a gradual increase over time (Scotland, Amsterdam, Antwerp).

6.2.2. Last month prevalence

If we examine *last month prevalence* of different routes of ingestion, we find that the picture changes (see table 6.2.b). Prevalence of smoking and snorting is about the same as for both the Amsterdam samples.[7] Again, freebasing and injecting seem to be more prominent routes of ingestion compared to the Dutch samples. It seems to us that the phenomenon of freebasing cocaine has markedly increased during the last decade, both in the Netherlands and in Belgium. We examine this route of ingestion in more detail in the next chapter.[8]

Last month prevalence of eating and application on genitals is almost negligible, which might indicate that our Antwerp users merely experiment with these routes, but do not prefer them as a dominant way of administering cocaine.

Table 6.2.b   Last month prevalence and frequency of different routes of ingestion, in %, in three samples

Amsterdam I (1987)					
Frequency	**i.n.** N=160	**Smoking** N=160	**Freebase** N=160	**Eating** N=160	**Genitals** N=160	**i.v.** N=160
Always	40.6	0.6	-	1.3	-	-
Mostly	5.0	0.6	1.3	-	-	-
Sometimes	1.3	3.8	-	-	-	0.6
Rarely	3.1	9.4	1.3	0.6	0.6	0.6
Total ever	50.0	14.4	2.5	1.9	0.6	1.2
Never	41.9	74.4	86.9	87.5	89.4	88.8
No answer	*8.1*	*11.2*	*10.6*	*10.6*	*10.0*	*10.0*
Total	**100.0**	**100.0**	**100.0**	**100.0**	**100.0**	**100.0**

Amsterdam II (1991)						
Frequency	**i.n.** **N=108**	**Smoking** **N=108**	**Freebase** **N=108**	**Eating** **N=108**	**Genitals** **N=108**	**i.v.** **N=108**
Always	48.1	1.8	0.9	0.9	-	0.9
Mostly	4.6	1.8	-	-	-	-
Sometimes	-	1.8	0.9	-	-	-
Rarely	-	8.3	1.8	1.8	-	0.9
Total ever	52.8	13.9	3.7	2.8	-	1.8
Never	43.5	83.3	93.5	96.3	99.1	96.4
No answer	*3.7*	*2.8*	*2.8*	*0.9*	*0.9*	*1.8*
Total	**100.0**	**100.0**	**100.0**	**100.0**	**100.0**	**100.0**

Antwerp (1997)						
Frequency	**i.n.** **N=111**	**Smoking** **N=111**	**Freebase** **N=111**	**Eating** **N=111**	**Genitals** **N=111**	**i.v.** **N=111**
Always	40.5	0.9	6.3	-	0.9	4.5
Mostly	2.7	0.9	0.9	-	-	1.8
Sometimes	2.7	3.6	5.4	-	-	-
Rarely	7.2	7.2	4.5	0.9	-	0.9
Total ever	53.2	12.6	17.1	0.9	0.9	7.2
Never	46.8	87.4	82.9	99.1	99.1	92.8
No answer	*-*	*-*	*-*	*-*	*-*	*-*
Total	**100.0**	**100.0**	**100.0**	**100.0**	**100.0**	**100.0**

It is very important to note that of those 8 respondents who injected cocaine at least once during the month prior to the interview, 6 (75%) were part of the chain H of our snowball (see figure 2.6.a).[9] The other two respondents were part of chains F and D. It follows that the high prevalence on injecting in our sample is probably an artifact of our sampling method. This does not hold for the high prevalence of freebasing, because these respondents belonged to various chains (C, E, G, H, I, L, O, Q, R and W).

6.3. ROUTE OF INGESTION IN THE THREE PERIODS OF USE

Respondents were shown a card with six different routes of ingestion: snorting, injecting, eating, rubbing on genitals, freebasing and smoking. They were asked to indicate the main route of administering they practised during the initial year of use, the period of heaviest use and the last three months (see table 6.3.a).

Table 6.3.a Main route of ingestion at three measuring points, in %, in the 1997 Antwerp sample [*]

Antwerp			
Route of ingestion	**First year** **N=111**	**Top period** **N=111**	**Last 3 months** **N=90**
Snorting	89.2	57.7	73.3
Injecting	7.2	18.0	10.0
Eating	-	-	-
Freebasing	2.7	23.4	16.7
Smoking	0.9	0.9	-
Rubbing on genitals	-	-	-
Total	**100.0**	**100.0**	**100.0**

[*] These figures are not comparable with those of the Amsterdam samples, because our respondents reported only one answer (probably due to interviewer bias).

Eating and rubbing on genitals were not mentioned at all, and smoking only rarely. Some of our respondents remarked they did not know cocaine could be eaten or applied on genitals, an observation that was also made in the Amsterdam I study (Cohen, 1989: 65). During the period of heaviest use, about 40 % of our respondents mainly engaged in injecting or freebasing, i.e. the more direct modes of ingestion. During the initial year this percentage is less than 10 %; during the last three months it is 26.7 %.

Comparison of our data on snorting, injecting and freebasing during the first year of use (initial period), the period of heaviest use (top period) and the three months prior to the interview (recent period) with the Turin, Barcelona and Rotterdam samples (1990-91) is possible to a certain extent (Diaz *et al.*, 1992: 175-176; Merlo *et al.*, 1992: 76; Bieleman & de Bie, 1992: 177-178). Although a perfect comparison cannot be made because in some samples the respondents combining two or more routes of ingestion (e.g. smoking and basing, or snorting and injecting, etc.) are categorized separately, the data on the 'main' route of ingestion are interesting. We find that in all four samples and in all three periods snorting is practised by an overwhelming majority of the respondents. For all three periods of use, the proportion of snorters is the lowest in the Rotterdam sample, which is probably because the respondents were recruited from 'deviant' or 'marginal' settings.

In all four studies, the proportion of injecting respondents is relatively small (the highest proportion is 22.4% during the period of heaviest use in the Turin sample). We find an overall increase of the prevalence of injecting during the period of heaviest use, while it drops during the most recent period (the three months prior to interview). Again, the most striking finding from this comparison is the higher prevalence of freebasing as a route of ingestion in the Antwerp sample, especially during the period of heaviest use and the most recent period.

6.4. ADVANTAGES AND DISADVANTAGES OF THE VARIOUS ROUTES OF INGESTION

Of the three most familiar routes of ingestion (snorting, injecting and freebasing) all 111 respondents were asked to list advantages and disadvantages. In tables 6.4.a through 6.4.f, we present all reported advantages and disadvantages. The reader must keep in mind that comparing our data to the Amsterdam samples was difficult and could be deceptive, because of inevitable small coding differences. Therefore, after each table more detailed information on some answer categories is presented. Categorizations of answers that might have been coded otherwise in the Amsterdam study, are marked with an ' ♠ '.

6.4.1. Advantages and disadvantages of snorting

As 110 of our respondents (99%) have snorted cocaine (cf. table 6.2.a), our sample can provide information about the advantages and disadvantages of this route of ingestion from their own experience (see tables 6.4.a and 6.4.b).

In this table, the advantages of snorting are categorized as follows: snorting gives a more direct effect, a faster effect, the cocaine effect lasts longer, it gives the best effect, a more constant effect, the effect is not too strong, snorting gives a better effect [efficient, better effect][10]; there is no risk for contagion, no risk for an overdose, it is less harmful for health [not as bad for health]; snorting is more sociable, makes it easier to share with friends [sociable, sharing]; snorting can be done anywhere, people do not notice it, it is easy to hide for the police [discrete, inconspicuous].

Table 6.4.a   Advantages of snorting, in three samples, in % [♠][*]

Advantages of snorting	A'dam I 1987 %	A'dam II 1991 %	Antwerp 1997 N	%
Easy to use	36.9	62.0	45	40.5
Efficient, better effect [♠]	31.9	51.8	49	44.1
Not as bad for health [♠]	15.6	20.4	10	9.0
Dosage easy to measure	5.6	9.3	3	2.7
Allows regulation of use	2.5	-	17	15.3
Like my friends	2.5	8.3	-	-
Clean	2.5	4.6	6	5.4
Pleasant ritual	-	7.4	8	7.2
Economical	-	-	17	15.3
Discrete, inconspicuous	-	-	43	38.7
Sociable, sharing	-	-	9	8.1
Numbing effect	-	-	5	4.5
Pleasant taste	-	-	4	3.6
Better for going out	-	-	6	5.4
Other [♠]	22.5	2.8	-	-
Don't know/no answer	*10.6*	*-*	*5*	*4.5*
Total no. of advantages mentioned	156	180	222	
Total no. of resp. mentioning adv.	143	108	106	
Average no. of adv. per respondent	1.1	1.7	2.1	

[*] Percentages do not add up to 100, because more answers were possible

In the table below, some disadvantages of snorting are categorized as follows: quality of cocaine is unstable, cocaine is adulterated [adulterated]; you may accidentally drop the powder on the ground or in a toilet, you need a razor blade, it needs to be cut, it can become moisty when going out [impractical]; snorting is bad for your lungs, for your heart, for your skin, for your brains, your teeth start falling out, it's bad for your health [bad for health].

From both tables some observations can be made. First of all, our cocaine users report several disadvantages that are not real side effects of cocaine use, or at least normally not attributed to the use of this drug by scientific research. For example, several respondents claim that snorting cocaine is unhealthy for the lungs or even the skin (table 6.4.b). Others believe that by snorting, the white powder directly hits the brain, or that teeth crumble quite soon after using cocaine, irrespective of the frequency and the amount of use. Two respondents even find it disadvantageous that part of the cocaine they snort gets stuck in the mucous membrane, and therefore part of the drug is inevitably lost (while in fact, snorting cocaine implies the absorption of cocaine by the mucous membrane!).

We believe that this shows that at least some cocaine users, despite their 'experience' with the drug, are badly informed about the possible (adverse) effects and its pharmacological action on the body. Some of these fallacies are probably the result of persistent myths within user groups; others must be the remnants of non-users' values and/or prejudices, which regard cocaine as a very addictive, hard-drug with immediate and extremely dangerous adverse effects (e.g. on the brain, teeth, skin,...).

Table 6.4.b   Disadvantages of snorting, in three samples, in % [♠][*]

Disadvantages of snorting	A'dam I 1987 %	A'dam II 1991 %	Antwerp 1997 N	Antwerp 1997 %
Nose problems	68.8	84.3	79	71.1
Throat problems	6.3	19.4	6	5.4
Dry mouth	3.1	1.8	1	0.9
Effect not optimal	0.6	7.4	9	8.1
Adulterated	-	3.7	6	5.4
Conspicuous	-	-	15	13.5
Adverse mental effects	-	-	12	10.8
Stomach problems	-	-	5	4.5
Impractical	-	-	6	5.4
Bad for health	-	-	18	16.2
Effect too short	-	-	4	3.6
Impossible when having a cold	-	-	2	1.8
Seems harmless, but isn't	-	-	2	1.8
Part is lost via mucous membrane	-	-	2	1.8
Higher chance of being caught	-	-	2	1.8
Unpleasant taste	-	-	2	1.8
Unhygienic (toilets)	-	-	3	2.7
Other [♠]	21.3	28.7	-	-
Don't know/no answer	*15.7*	-	*4*	*3.6*
Total no. of disadv. mentioned	160	157	174	
Total no. of resp. mentioning disadv.	135	108	107	
Average no. of disadv. per resp.	1.2	1.5	1.6	

[*] Percentages do not add up to 100, because more answers were possible

It is also interesting to note that for snorting, a total of 222 advantages were given versus 174 disadvantages (tables 6.4.a and 6.4.b). The average number of advantages per respondent (2.1) was also higher than that of disadvantages per respondent (1.6).

Finally, it is fascinating to observe that several aspects are advantageous for some respondents, disadvantageous to others. Some believe that snorting is bad for their health, but others do not. Some respondents praise the beneficial effects of snorting cocaine, others dismiss this route of ingestion because its effect is not optimal, or too short. Forty-three of our respondents regard snorting as a discrete technique, while 15 think of it as a conspicuous route of administration. And finally, what some call an unpleasant taste, can be a true delicacy for others...

6.4.2. Advantages and disadvantages of injecting

All 111 respondents were asked to list advantages and disadvantages of injecting as a route of ingestion. It must be kept in mind that 24.3% of the Antwerp sample reported having injected cocaine.

In table 6.4.c, some advantages of injecting are categorized as follows: injecting gives the best effect, gives a complete bodily experience, gives a better, faster effect [effect better], faster; injecting gives no taste, injecting makes it possible to test it in advance [other]. In table 6.4.d, some disadvantages of injecting are categorized as follows: the effect is too direct, you get a 'junky' stigma, you get involved in a different (unpleasant) coke scene [other]; you cannot inject anywhere, you can only inject at home [conspicuous].

Table 6.4.c   Advantages of injecting, in three samples, in % [♠][*]

	A'dam I 1987	A'dam II 1991	Antwerp 1997	
Advantages of injecting	%	%	N	%
Effect better, faster	33.8	75.0	82	73.9
Economical	2.5	8.3	6	5.4
Pure	0.6	2.8	3	2.7
Less harmful for health	-	-	2	1.8
Nose not damaged	-	-	2	1.8
Kick of needle	-	-	3	2.7
Effect lasts longer	-	-	7	6.3
Other [♠]	5.6	1.8	2	1.8
Don't know/no answer	*61.8*	*25.0*	*27*	*24.3*
Total no. of adv. mentioned	68	95	107	
Total no. of resp. mentioning adv.	61	81	84	
Average no. Of adv. per resp.	1.1	1.2	1.3	

[*] Percentages do not add up to 100, because more answers were possible

The total number of reported disadvantages (247) is higher than the total number of advantages (107). Equally, the average number of disadvantages per respondent (2.3) is higher than that of advantages per respondent (1.3).

Table 6.4.d   Disadvantages of injecting, in three samples, in % [♠][*]

	A'dam I 1987	A'dam II 1991	Antwerp 1997	
Disadvantages of injecting	%	%	N	%
Unhealthy	40.6	62.0	33	29.7
Scary	25.6	32.4	30	27.0
Addictive	16.9	24.1	44	39.6
Like 'junky' behavior	12.5	25.0	13	11.7
Impractical	10.0	13.9	13	11.7
Asocial	4.4	9.3	4	3.6
Difficult to measure dosage	2.5	7.4	4	3.6
Painful	0.6	6.5	4	3.6
Risk of contagion (i.a. AIDS)	-	-	23	20.7
Makes you worked up	-	-	3	2.7
Conspicuous scars	-	-	18	16.2
Risk of OD	-	-	12	10.8
Stepping stone to heroin	-	-	5	4.5
Adverse effects afterwards	-	-	11	9.9
Difficult technique	-	-	9	8.1
Uneconomical	-	-	6	5.4
Effect too short	-	-	5	4.5
Conspicuous	-	-	3	2.7
Makes you use more	-	-	3	2.7
Other [♠]	-	8.3	4	3.6
Don't know/no answer	*27.5*	*0.9*	*4*	*3.6*
Total no. of diasadv. Mentioned	181	204	247	
Total no. of resp. mentioning disadv.	116	107	107	
Average no. of disadv. per resp.	1.6	1.9	2.3	

[*] Percentages do not add up to 100, because more answers were possible

Again we find that some aspects are interpreted both as advantages and as disadvantages by different users: injecting is both an economical and an uneconomical route of ingestion; the effect is too short and it lasts longer...

6.4.3. Advantages and disadvantages of freebasing [11]

In Table 6.4.e some advantages of freebasing are categorized as follows: freebasing does not leave scars, when freebasing you remain at ease, you do not have to go out [other].

Table 6.4.e   Advantages of freebasing, in three samples, in % [♠][*]

Advantages of freebasing	A'dam I 1987 %	A'dam II 1991 %	Antwerp 1997 N	Antwerp 1997 %
More intense	28.8	40.7	29	26.1
Less adulterated	9.4	23.1	17	15.3
Better effect, more pleasure	3.7	25.9	46	41.4
More sociable	-	-	19	17.1
Smokeable	-	-	3	2.7
Less harmful for health	-	-	5	4.5
Better sex afterwards	-	-	3	2.7
Pleasant taste	-	-	5	4.5
Effect lasts longer	-	-	5	4.5
Nice ritual	-	8.3	5	4.5
Economical	-	-	3	2.7
Other [♠]	8.8	5.6	3	2.7
Don't know/no answer	*56.8*	*30.6*	*25*	*22.5*
Total no. of adv. mentioned	82	112	143	
Total no. of resp. mentioning adv.	69	75	86	
Average no. of adv. per resp.	1.2	1.5	1.7	

[*] Percentages do not add up to 100, because more answers were possible

In table 6.4.f, some disadvantages of freebasing are categorized as follows: freebasing can give throat problems, makes you very thirsty, you can be nauseous, there is a risk of an overdose, freebasing gives you little wounds inside your mouth [other adverse physical effects]; when freebasing, you are forced to share, a line of cocaine after having freebased does not give any effect [other]; freebasing might result in an unpleasant situation, in a fight or an argument, it is asocial, unsociable [asocial, unsociable].

From tables 6.4.e and 6.4.f we can derive the same conclusions for freebasing as we did for injecting. The total number of disadvantages mentioned (209) is higher than the total number of advantages (143), and the average number of disadvantages per respondent (2.0) is higher than that of advantages per respondent (1.7).

We also find the same ambiguous evaluation of certain aspects of this technique of ingestion: economical versus uneconomical; more sociable versus unsociable/asocial; pleasant taste versus unpleasant taste/smell; effect too short versus longer effect.

Table 6.4.f   Disadvantages of freebasing, in three samples, in % [♠][*]

Disadvantages of freebasing	A'dam I 1987 %	A'dam II 1991 %	Antwerp 1997 N	Antwerp 1997 %
Unhealthy, 'junky'like, dangerous	25.0	25.0	20	18.0
Addictive	15.0	25.9	43	38.7
Uneconomical	10.0	18.5	26	23.4
Complicated	6.9	25.0	21	18.9
Difficult to measure dosage	5.6	0.9	3	2.7
Makes you crazy	5.0	7.4	2	1.8
Effect too strong	3.1	3.7	6	5.4
Effect too short	-	-	12	10.8
Adverse mental effects	-	-	16	14.4
Bad for your lungs	-	-	22	19.8
Asocial, unsociable	-	-	11	9.9
Possible at home only	-	-	13	11.7
Other physical adverse effects	-	-	6	5.4
Can't do it myself	-	-	3	2.7
Unpleasant smell/taste	-	-	3	2.7
Other [♠]	-	12.0	2	1.8
Don't know/no answer	*42.8*	*25.0*	*8*	*7.2*
Total no. of disadv. Mentioned	119	128	209	
Total no. of resp. mentioning disadv.	92	81	103	
Average no. of disadv. Per resp.	1.3	1.6	2.0	

[*] Percentages do not add up to 100, because more answers were possible

6.4.4. Perceptions of routes of ingestion and rules of use

If we collate tables 6.4.c, 6.4.d, 6.4.e and 6.4.f we find that 84 respondents report advantages and 107 respondents report disadvantages of injecting, while only 27 have actually tried this route of ingestion (cf. table 6.2.a.). Less markedly, the number of people reporting advantages and disadvantages of freebasing is larger than the number of those who have actually tried it. Some respondents obviously do not speak from their own experience.[12]

Although in both Amsterdam samples life time prevalence of injecting and freebasing was lower, similar figures were found (cf. table 6.2.a). Cohen concluded that the predominance of disadvantages over advantages for those routes of ingestion could not be based on his respondents' own experience, but rather on negative connotations of intravenous or freebasing user groups. *'[These] opinions can be interpreted as the equivalent of certain rules of use. From this perspective, rules of use might be the balance (or net outcome) of perceived advantages and disadvantages, irrespective of the factual correctness of these perceptions. Probably, the perceived net merit of each route of ingestion is a construction, made out of a mix of perceived effects of the drug on self or significant others, and social conventions about specific routes of ingestion. In this case social conventions could very well be related to the status of user groups that are especially associated with injecting and freebasing.'* (Cohen, 1989: 66)

These routes of ingestion are associated with asocial and dangerous behavior, probably 'junky' type drug use. Injecting is seen as the worst, still according to Cohen. To check this, we divided our sample into two subsamples: those who reported having freebased, and those who did not. From tables 6.4.e and 6.4.f we took the (dis)advantages most mentioned, and we checked for differences between our 2 sub-samples. We applied the same computations to those who had 'ever' injected ('injectors') and those who had 'never' injected ('non-injectors'), and the most frequent (dis)advantages of injecting as a technique of ingestion. The results are shown in tables 6.4.g and 6.4.h.

Table 6.4.g Advantages (+) and disadvantages (-) mentioned by injectors and non-injectors in the 1997 Antwerp sample

	Antwerp					
	'Ever' injected N=27		'Never' injected N=84		Total sample N=111	
	N	%	N	%	N	%
Better effect (+)	21	77.8	56	66.7	77	73.9
Addictive (-)	8	29.6	36	42.8	44	39.6
Scary (-)	1	3.7	29	34.5	30	27.0
Unhealthy (-)	10	37.0	23	27.4	33	29.7

Table 6.4.h Advantages (+) and disadvantages (-) mentioned by freebasers and non-freebasers in the 1997 Antwerp sample

	Antwerp					
	'Ever' freebased N=80		'Never' freebased N=31		Total sample N=111	
	N	%	N	%	N	%
Intense (+)	22	27.5	7	22.6	29	26.1
Better effect (+)	39	48.7	7	22.6	46	41.4
Addictive (-)	33	41.3	10	32.3	43	38.7
Uneconomical (-)	21	26.3	5	16.1	26	23.4
Unhealthy for lungs (-)	17	21.3	5	16.1	22	19.8

Cohen was obviously right about the associations of injecting with 'junky' type characteristics (such as 'addictive' and 'scary'). These disadvantages were mentioned far more by those who had never injected than by those who had tried this technique.[13] The advantage 'better effect' was mentioned more by those who had injected (77.8%), but even 66.7% of those who had never injected indicated the intense effect as an advantage. Our qualitative material yielded more information about how to interpret the ambiguous perception of this route of ingestion:

> *[...] it was very very good, [...] but my decision to mainly snort would be because I did not want to become a complete junky, because I knew it was too dangerous for me, and I had very little power over myself. I knew I would be fucked if I started injecting. It scared me basically.'* [S/0/01]

As to the technique of freebasing, negative connotations (such as 'addictive', 'unhealthy' and 'uneconomical') and positive connotations (such as 'intense' and 'better effect') are more frequently mentioned by those who have tried this route of ingestion. Therefore it is based on their own experience. The perceived net merit of freebasing is clearly not so negative as with injecting.

6.5. CHOICE OF ROUTE OF INGESTION

Respondents who reported having used cocaine in more than one way, were asked what their choice of route of ingestion depended on. Eighty-three respondents replied to this question. In this paragraph the most frequent factors that may influence the choice of the route, are listed and illustrated with some quotations. But drug users do not only experiment with products. They often try out different routes of ingestion as well. Some users experiment with various methods, combine two or more routes of ingestion at the same occasion, or alternate periods of snorting, freebasing, etc... Some users go from one route of ingestion to another alternately, until they find their preferred method. Moreover, as techniques have to be learnt from other users, some users get the occasion to learn how to freebase or to inject, while others do not.

Twenty-nine respondents (26.1% of the total sample) reported that their choice of route of ingestion depended on *setting-factors and/or the activities engaged in while using cocaine.* Most of them referred to freebasing and snorting: the latter usually took place when going out, in a discotheque, in (the toilet of) a bar, at a party, etc.; the former is almost exclusively practised at home, in an easy atmosphere, with some (close) friends. Others say that freebasing is only done when there is plenty of time for it (because of the extensive preparations, see Chapter 7) and when the user feels like doing all 'that work'. Many respondents also refer to the 'easy' or 'quiet' effect freebasing has, which is associated with a cosy sitting room, rather than with a noisy discotheque.

Another 29 respondents (26.1% of the total sample) declare that their choice of method is often influenced by *other users and/or the company they are in.* One respondent claimed that her boy-friend always chose the route of ingestion, without respecting her opinion. Most other respondents' answers do not imply direct 'pressure' from other users. They report that other users 'simply talked them into' other routes of ingestion, that they were 'persuaded' by other users' stories. Many others state that they just joined in with their friends, motivated by feelings of 'respect', 'solidarity' and 'fellowship':

> *It depends on the other person too, I think. If the other person prepares it to snort or to base, or... I mean, it was the same for all kinds of drugs: if that person takes it this way or that way, I'd do it the same way.* [H/1/25]

> *I like snorting. Those few times I based it, that was because I was with people who didn't do otherwise, and they said: join us. But here I would never think of doing it like that. I find snorting much more pleasant.* [I/1/02]

Conversely, a specific route of ingestion can also be eliminated by the presence of certain other people. Users are clearly not prone to use cocaine with anyone as long as they can ingest their drug: there are certain categories of people in the company of whom respondents do not want to use:[14]

> *When they are well-known friends, and you know just everything about each other, then you can start basing, because you are more occupied with yourself at that moment, on your trip. Whereas snorting, that's more something to socialize... to talk, to waffle [she laughs]. And with basing, you rather draw in your horns, so I'd rather do that with my husband or with people I really know well.* [L/1/03]

A factor that is closely related to the company one is using in, is the *ownership of the cocaine* that is being used. Three respondents (2.7% of the total sample) mention that it is often the owner who decides in which way the cocaine will be used:

> *When I went basing or smoking, it was more with other people and with their coke. Never with mine.* [I/1/16]

Sixteen respondents (14.4% of the total sample) mentioned *the quantity of cocaine available*. Again, most of these respondents refer to freebasing: one of the preconditions for freebasing cocaine seems to be the availability of a large quantity of street cocaine. This factor is closely related to the quality of street cocaine, because a considerable part can get lost during the preparatory process of freebase cocaine (which involves the use of ammonia).

> *When I wanna base, I prefer to have very good quality and to have a lot. Because if I go to buy in the town, and it's a little packet like that, and it costs a lot, and if I clean it, and there's not much left.... So I inject it.* [H/1/03]

Six of these respondents referred to the smoking of cocaine hydrochloride (street cocaine) in a cigarette or joint. This route of ingestion is usually considered as an expensive method, a waste of the product, and less effective than other methods such as snorting, freebasing or injecting. Therefore, it is only done when cocaine supplies are abundant or when the amount of cocaine is too small to snort, freebase or inject ('the leftovers'):[15]

> *Every time I had sent five people to him to buy coke, I got a free gram from him. I mean, if you smoke a joint of coke then, it doesn't matter. It doesn't matter. When I only have 1 gram, I won't smoke a joint of it.* [G/1/02]

> *When I smoked it in a cigarette, usually it would be after a line, when I was with some people, after a line, and some one would leave a piece of it, everybody leaves a piece sometimes, you scrape it together and put it in a cigarette, that would be the way it was done.* [S/0/01]

Two respondents also referred to the available quantity of cocaine as a decisive factor in the choice between 'chasing the dragon' (from an aluminum foil) and 'freebasing' (from a glass):

> *When I don't have a lot of coke, I'll chase. When there is plenty of it, I'll base.* [I/1/17]

Yet, all this does not mean that the choice between different routes of ingestion mainly depends on factors beyond the individual's power. Seven respondents (6.3% of the total sample) report that their *personal preference for a specific route* is usually decisive:

> *I prefer to snort. They know that: I prefer it on a mirror. The others can do whatever they want.* [E/1/03]

Six other respondents said they preferred *not* to use certain routes of ingestion because of *adverse effects associated with these methods*. Four of them had injected or freebased cocaine in the past, but decided to snort because of the physical and psychological problems they had experienced with the former methods. The other two respondents reported to chose eating or smoking as an alternative for snorting, when they had experienced problems with their nose (clogged or irritated, possibly as a result of snorting).

Six respondents (5.4%) mentioned the *quality of the cocaine available*. All these accounts refer to freebasing, which is seen as a way of checking the purity of the product being used.[16] Through the processing of freebase cocaine most adulterants are removed from the street cocaine. This is noteworthy because it shows that some users prefer a more 'dangerous' or 'addictive' route of ingestion because they believe it guarantees higher quality/purity.

> *When I don't know what I got. Because you depend on the person who sells it to you. That's my biggest fear: that I can't recognize it. And coke, it's just a white powder and you can't see it. So I always base it then.* [H/0/02]

> *When I was sure that it was good quality, then I thought snorting was okay, especially for going out. When the quality was bad, I based it.* [Z/1/04]

The following statement by a respondent provides more insight in this mechanism: apart from informal rules that might help to minimize the harmful and adverse effects of cocaine use, the choice of a route of ingestion is often determined by the concern of maximizing the positive and pleasurable effects. The more expensive the drug and the lower its quality, the more users might be inclined to chose 'stronger' routes of ingestion (such as freebasing) in order to maximize the 'flash' or pleasure...

> *When you don't have a lot of money and you only have a little coke, then you have to get as much as you can out of it, right?* [H/1/04]

Four respondents reported *set-factors* (their emotional state) as decisive in the choice of a route of ingestion:

> *It also depended on how much respect I had for myself at that moment. When I didn't have any respect, I would probably shoot it or base it. [...] And if you are a bit sweeter to your own body, then you smoke it or snort it.* [I/1/01]

Four others indicated that they had experimented with freebasing and injecting cocaine, but decided not to use these routes of ingestion any longer. Here, the effect of 'horror' stories about other users and warnings by fellow users clearly deterred them. This shows how cocaine users can help to control or curb the use of their friends...

Finally, other factors were: the risk of police attention (by two injecting respondents), the available budget (2 respondents), the kind of cocaine available: street cocaine or freebase cocaine (2 respondents), and the lack of injecting material (1 respondent).

6.6. FLOW BETWEEN ROUTES

How constant is an individual's route of cocaine administration? Is the initial cocaine snorter or chaser merely a cocaine user who has not yet injected but is inevitably bound to do so? And is the cocaine injector bound to continue as an injector for the entire duration of his/her cocaine career? Or may some of the non-injecting routes of cocaine use be stable routes? Strang *et al.* (1997) have examined the flow between different main routes among heroin users from a treatment and a non-treatment sample. Their paper served as a model for the analysis in this paragraph.

For this analysis the main route of ingestion in each of the three periods has been used (see §6.3), and possible overlap of several routes of ingestion has not been taken into account.

6.6.1. Transitions from first year of regular use to period of heaviest use

Figure 6.6.a shows the transitions between routes of ingestion from first year of regular use to period of heaviest use. Seventy-three respondents (or 65.8% of the total sample) kept a stable route of ingestion (mostly snorting).

Figure 6.6.a   Transitions between routes of ingestion in the 1997 Antwerp sample, from first year of regular use to period of heaviest use (total transitions: N = 38)

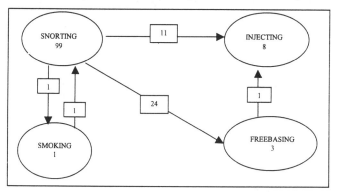

Conversely, 34.2% of the respondents reported a transition of route of ingestion. Most changes were to basing (63.2% of the total number of transitions) and, to a lesser extent, to injecting (31.6% of the total number of transitions). Of the respondents who snorted during their first year of regular use, 63.6% kept snorting during their period of heaviest use, while 24.2% changed to freebasing, and 11.1% to injecting.

6.6.2. Transitions from period of heaviest use to time of interview

Figure 6.6.b shows the transitions between routes of ingestion from period of heaviest use to time of interview (i.e. the three months prior to interview). Again, a considerable majority (68 respondents, or 61.3% of the total sample) kept a stable route of ingestion (again mostly snorting).

Conversely, 38.7% of the respondents reported a transition of route of ingestion. Almost half of them (21 respondents, or 48.8% of the total number of transitions) stopped using altogether. Of those who had been mainly snorting during their period of heaviest use, 75% continued doing so at the time of interview, while 21.9% quit using. Of those who had been mainly injecting during their period of heaviest use, 45% continued doing so at the time of interview, while 40% changed to other routes of ingestion (mostly snorting). Of those who had been mainly freebasing during their period of heaviest use, 42.3% continued doing so at the time of interview, while 46.2% changed to snorting.

Figure 6.6.b   Transitions between routes of ingestion in the 1997 Antwerp sample, from period of heaviest use to time of interview (total transitions: N = 43)

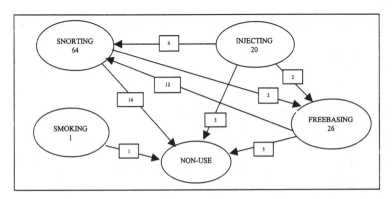

From period to heaviest use to the three months prior to interview, most changes were to non-use (48.8% of the total number of transitions) and to snorting (41.9% of the total number of transitions).

6.6.3. Flow between routes in the treatment sub-sample

We checked the flow between routes of ingestion in the respondents who had been in contact with treatment agencies for drug-related problems.

Of the 8 respondents who used cocaine intravenously during their first year of regular use, 5 reported having been in treatment. Of the 3 respondents who mainly freebased during the first year of regular use, 1 reported having been in treatment for drug-related problems. And of the 99 respondents who mostly snorted cocaine during the first year of regular use, only 16 ended up in treatment (16.2%).

In the period of heaviest use, 12 of the 20 respondents using intravenously report contact with treatment. Of the 26 respondents mainly freebasing during their period of heaviest use, only 4 report contact with a drug treatment center. Six of the 64 respondents mainly snorting during top period, report contact with a treatment agency.

There are interesting flow patterns. For example, of the 5 respondents reporting a flow pattern of 'snorting-injecting-injecting', 4 report contact with treatment agencies. All 3 respondents reporting a flow pattern of 'injecting-injecting-injecting' have been in treatment. From the 3 respondents reporting a flow pattern of 'injecting-injecting-stopped' 2 sought treatment... Conversely, from the 48 respondents reporting a constant pattern of snorting ('snorting-snorting-snorting'), only 4 report ever having been in contact with a treatment center.

In short, intravenous cocaine use shows a clear link with treatment contact: those who start injecting cocaine (at any point in their drug use career) are more likely to have contact with treatment agencies (at any point in their career).

6.7. CONCLUSION

Intranasal use (snorting) is the dominant route of ingestion in the Antwerp sample, like in most other European or American community samples of cocaine users. In all samples, fewer than one in four participants has life time experience with intravenous use of cocaine. The proportion of cocaine users having life time experience with injecting is highest in the Antwerp sample. Yet, this is probably an artifact of our snowball sampling technique, as we find that most regular injectors belong to two snowball chains (F and H).

The most striking outcome of the international comparison is the major difference in prevalence of freebasing (both life time prevalence and prevalence at three periods of use). Whether these differences between community samples are attributable to geographical variations in market fluctuations or to temporal evolutions (especially in the European samples) is unclear.

Of the three best known routes of ingestion (snorting, injecting and freebasing) respondents were asked to list advantages and disadvantages. We found that at least some cocaine users, despite their 'experience' with the drug, are badly informed about the possible (adverse) effects and the actual pharmacological action of cocaine on the body. For all three methods, we found that several aspects are advantageous for some respondents, and disadvantageous to others at the same time.

For injecting and, less markedly, for freebasing, we found that the number of people giving advantages and disadvantages of these methods is larger than the number of people who have actually tried it. The same phenomenon was observed in both the Amsterdam samples. Cohen (1989) concluded that the predominance of disadvantages over advantages for those routes of ingestion could not be based on his respondents' own experience, but on negative connotations that intravenous or freebasing user groups have. Our analysis confirmed these associations of injecting with 'junky' type characteristics (such as 'addictive' and 'scary') by users who have never injected themselves. As to the technique of freebasing, we found that our respondents' accounts were to a large extent based on own experience. Clearly, the perceived net merit of this route of ingestion is not as negative as with injecting.

Finally, respondents who reported having used various routes of ingesting cocaine, indicated some of the determinant set and setting factors in their choice of a route of ingestion: the activities engaged in while using cocaine; the other users and/or the company one is in; the quantity of cocaine available; personal preference for a specific route; adverse effects associated with a method; the quality of cocaine available; the emotional state one is in; who owns the cocaine...

Finally, we have examined the flow between different main routes among respondents. Almost half of the sample (46.8%) kept a stable route of ingestion, usually snorting. Among the respondents reporting a transition of route from first year of regular use to period of heaviest use, most changes were to basing and to a lesser extent to injecting. Among the respondents reporting a transition of route from period of heaviest use to the last three months prior to interview, most changes were to non-use and to snorting.

In short, the initial cocaine snorter or chaser is not merely a cocaine user who has not yet injected but is inevitably bound to do so. And the cocaine injector is not bound to continue as an injector for the entire duration of his/her cocaine career. Some of the non-injecting routes of cocaine use may be stable routes. However, analysis of those respondents reporting having been in contact with drug treatment agencies indicates that those who start injecting cocaine (at any point in their drug use career) are more likely to have contact with treatment agencies (at any point in their career). Again, this suggests that official registration figures of drug use are mainly based on 'worst case scenarios', i.e. uncontrolled or problematic users.

NOTES

1   The route by which a drug is administered impacts on its bioavailability, its psychopharmacological potency and in turn its dependence liability. Each route of drug use is also associated with its own specific complications distinct from its pharmacological effects. See also: STRANG, J., BEARN, J., FARRELL, M., FINCH, E., GOSSOP, M., GRIFFITHS, P., MARSDEN, J. and WOLFF, K. (1998), Route of drug use and its implications for drug effect, risk of dependence and health consequences, 17 *Drug and Alcohol Review*, 197-211. GOSSOP, M., GRIFFITHS, P., POWIS, B. and STRANG, J., (1994), Cocaine: patterns of use, route of administration, and severity of dependence, 164 *British Journal of Psychiatry*, 660-664.

2   Some authors only report on the 'usual' method of ingestion of their respondents (Toronto, 1983 and 1989-90). Waldorf *et al.* only present qualitative data on routes of ingestion (San Francisco, 1986-88).WALDORF, D., REINARMAN, C. and MURPHY, S. (1991), *Cocaine changes. The experience of using and quitting*, 30-31 (injecting) and 103-139 (freebasing) Philadelphia: Temple University Press. For two samples (Toronto, 1989-90 and Scotland, 1989-90) we were able to calculate life time prevalence of the most important routes of ingestion. Finally, the Turin, Barcelona and Rotterdam (1990-91) reports contain detailed figures on routes of ingestion in three periods of use.

3   The fact that life time prevalence of freebasing and injecting is considerably higher in the Antwerp sample than in the Amsterdam samples cannot be attributed to the fact that our respondents are older (and thus more experienced). The mean age in the Antwerp sample did not differ significantly from mean ages in the Dutch samples (cf. Chapter 3, note 8 and also p. 79-80). However, the mean age at initiation in cocaine for the Antwerp sample was lower than for the other samples (see Chapter 4, note 5 and also p. 99-100). A possible explanation might be that the Antwerp users started experimentation with cocaine at an earlier stage, and thus were more likely to experiment with freebasing and injecting. But then again, the average length of cocaine using career was only slightly longer for the Antwerp respondents (6.4 years) compared to the Amsterdam subjects (6.2 years) (see Chapter 5, p. 141-142).

4   See Chapter 3, p. 82, 86-88, 95 and 97. See Chapter 12, p. 275-277.

5   DITTON, J. and HAMMERSLEY, R. (1996), *A very greedy drug. Cocaine in context*, 60. Amsterdam: Harwood Academic Publishers. ERICKSON, P.G. *et al.* (1994), *op. cit.*, 167-168.

6   Note that although they do not report on the life time prevalence of various methods of ingestion in the Turin sample (1990-91), Merlo *et al.* (1992: 76) state that 'basing' and 'chasing the dragon' are completely absent in their sample.

7   The data on last month prevalence (table 6.2.b) include the respondents who report not having used any cocaine during the last four weeks (in the Antwerp sample 43 respondents). Thus, the

category of 'never' contains some respondents who did not use the last month (irrespective of their usual route of ingestion). See also Chapter 5.

8   See Chapter 7, p. 175.

9   See Figure 2.6.a in Chapter 2, p. 68.

10 If respondents reported advantages of snorting such as 'more direct', 'faster', 'longer', 'the best', 'more constant', etc. we did not ask them with which other routes of ingestion they compared when saying these things. We suspect these perceptions of the 'efficient, better effect' of snorting are strongly related to persistent judgments about other routes of ingestion (such as freebasing and injecting).

11 For a detailed description of the technique of freebasing, see Chapter 7, p. 182-185.

12 For another example of opinions that are not based on own experience, see the results presented on the experience of our respondents with 'crack' in Antwerp. Chapter 7, p. 187-193.

13 These data illustrate how non-injecting users perceive injecting users to be 'dangerous' and 'scary'. This process of *stereotyping* can be misleading in that it does not represent individual variability and it can be dangerous in that it may become entrenched in society and could serve to fuel rather than combat present drug use.See for example: FINNIGAN, F. (1996), How non-heroin users perceive heroin users and how heroin users perceive themselves, 4 *Addiction Research* 1, 25-32.

14 See Chapter 14, p. 315-316, and Chapter 15, p. 333-336.

15 This is consistent with the findings presented above (the low prevalence of smoking cocaine), see p. 156-159.

16 See also Chapter 10, p. 237-241 on quality control by respondents.

CHAPTER 7

FREEBASING
IN THE ANTWERP SAMPLE

7.1. INTRODUCTION

In Chapter 6 we explored six different routes of ingestion of cocaine: snorting, injecting, eating, freebasing, smoking and application on genitals. We discussed life time prevalence and last month prevalence of each of these routes, we differentiated for three periods of use, and we presented the advantages and disadvantages ascribed to snorting, injecting and freebasing by our respondents. It was shown that freebasing was a more prominent route of ingestion in the 1997 Antwerp sample compared to the 1987 and 1991 Amsterdam samples.[1]

This chapter presents more detailed data about freebasing cocaine in the Antwerp sample. None of the other European and American cocaine studies have devoted specific attention to this topic. First, the conceptual confusion among users (not unlike that among researchers) is illustrated by the Antwerp freebasers' vocabulary in §7.2. The processes of making and using freebase cocaine are described subsequently (§7.3). Paragraph 7.4 presents the experiences of the Antwerp respondents with freebasing. The differences between 'crack' and 'freebase' as perceived by our respondents, and their experience with what they call 'crack', are discussed in §7.5.

The reader will not find many references to community studies of cocaine users in other European and American cities, because the descriptions of freebasing in these studies were usually not very elaborated.

7.2. USERS' VOCABULARY ABOUT FREEBASING

Those respondents who had freebased cocaine, were asked what names they usually give to the *product* being freebased and to *the technique* of using it.

7.2.1. The product

All the respondents (N=80) report using the term 'base', 'freebase' or 'coke-base' to indicate the *product*. Another term frequently heard is 'cleaned coke' (= *'gecleande coke', 'gekuiste coke'*). This term refers to the preparation of freebase cocaine with ammonia (see next paragraph). This term also suggests indirectly that freebase cocaine is a purer form of cocaine than street cocaine (cocaine hydrochloride). Clearly, the users' freebasing terminology is rather limited. Yet, some respondents indicate that the term 'crack' is sometimes used among users in Antwerp, but they all add promptly that 'crack' is different from 'base', and consequently the former term is being used inadequately:

> *They call that basing, but they also call it: making your own crack. I mean, I don't know what other users say, but I think, when you buy coke, and you put it in a spoonful of ammonia, and you purify it, you're actually making base, you're actually making crack, in my opinion. And they call it crack here in Antwerp, but I don't think there's any crack in Antwerp. To me, what they call crack in Antwerp, is just base made out of coke.* [F/0/01]

7.2.2. The technique

As to *route of ingestion*, the vocabulary of freebasers seems to be more elaborate. Obviously, for all respondents 'freebasing' (= *'basen'*) is the common term for the technique of using freebase cocaine.[2] Another term frequently heard is 'to hang to the little glass' (= *'aan het glaske hangen'*), referring to the most common technique of freebasing in Antwerp: on a glass (see §7.3). Some respondents also report using other expressions: 'Do you want me to make a little pipe for you?' (K/1/03), 'to do a (little) glass' or 'to do some glass' (Q/0/01).

For the technique of using freebase cocaine (or 'cleaned cocaine'), the terms 'freebasing' (= *'basen'*), 'smoking' (= *'roken'* of *'smoren'*) and 'chasing the dragon' (= *'chinezen'*) are used interchangeably. Theoretically, each of these terms describes a specific technique of drug administration (Grund & Blanken, 1993: 5-15). The descriptive term *'chasing'* refers to trying to inhale the curling fumes of heroin vapor with a tube as the heated liquid drug flows along a piece of foil. When heated, heroin melts and vaporizes. The vapors are then inhaled. *'Basing'* cocaine requires preparation of freebase cocaine (as described in the next paragraph) and refers to inhalation of the vaporized product through a pipe. All kinds of self-constructed or commercial pipes are used for this. Specially prepared water glasses are observed most. The vaporized substance is drawn into the chamber of the pipe and taken into the lungs in one or two inhalations. The descriptive term *'smoking'* refers to the inhalation of smoke, when burning a substance (such as tobacco or cannabis).

However, both our field notes and our qualitative interviews indicate that respondents give these three terms various meanings. These are summarized in Figure 7.2.a.

Figure 7.2.a.   Users' vocabulary on freebasing (as a method), in Antwerp (1997)

Term	Meaning
'CHASING THE DRAGON' (= In Dutch: *'chinezen'*)	1) = inhaling the fumes of heroin from an aluminum foil 2) = inhaling the fumes of freebase cocaine from an aluminum foil
'FREEBASING' (= In Dutch: *'basen'*)	1) = inhaling the fumes of freebase cocaine from an aluminum foil 2) = smoking freebase cocaine from a pipe or a glass 3) = using freebase cocaine (irrespective of the method)
'SMOKING' (= In Dutch: *'roken', 'smoren'*)	1) = smoking a tobacco cigarette 2) = smoking a joint (cannabis) 3) = smoking a cocaine cigarette 4) = 'freebasing' or 'chasing the dragon'

First, certain similarities between practices have led to the double use of the term 'chasing'. Traditionally, 'chasing' (= *'chinezen'*) was being used to refer to the inhalation of heroin vapors from an aluminum foil. More recently, 'chasing' freebase cocaine, i.e. melting and vaporizing it and then inhaling the fumes ('the dragon') through a tube from an aluminum foil, has been observed.

> *You put it on aluminum paper, and then you suck it with a pipe, an aluminum paper roll. In that aluminum paper there is a crease. You put the lump on it, with a lighter underneath, it becomes a drop, and you inhale the vapor that is set free, you suck it. You hold a lighter under it, and you follow the drop, because it goes from one end to the other and back, and you inhale that smoke.* [C/1/08]

Second, although the descriptive term '(free-)basing' refers to the administration of freebase cocaine fumes through a pipe (or glass), some respondents also use it to refer to the technique of 'chasing' (from an aluminum foil). Others use the term '(free)basing' for any use of freebase cocaine, irrespective of the technique (inhalation from a foil, or inhalation through a pipe).

Third, the term 'smoking' (= *'smoren'* of *'roken'*) suggests that the substance be burned. For example, tobacco is burned in a cigarette, cannabis is burned in a 'joint', and sometimes cocaine hydrochloride is put in a tobacco cigarette and then burned. But many of our respondents used the term 'smoking' to refer to the technique of chasing or basing freebase cocaine. However, as explained above, the drug is actually not smoked when it is based or chased. It melts and vaporizes.

And finally, to make conceptual confusion complete, two respondents reported using the term 'chasing' (= *'chinezen'*)[3] to indicate the technique with the glass, and 'basing' to indicate the technique with the aluminum foil. Despite this conceptual confusion surrounding the phenomenon of freebasing, most users seem to make a rigid distinction between 'chasing the dragon' and 'freebasing'. As a plausible way of clarifying the issue, we borrow these user' definitions:

> *Chasing, that is smoking from an aluminum paper, and basing, that's smoking with a pipe or from a glass.* [D/0/01]

> *The method on aluminum paper, that's 'chasing'. There is a difference. With coke, when they say: we're going to 'base', you still don't know what they mean, because here they say 'chasing' when talking about basing coke, but chasing always makes you think of heroin, because chasing is following a drop on an aluminum paper. And 'basing', that's the trick with the glass. But yes, many people are just confused about it. So when they say basing, it's usually on an aluminum paper or from a glass.* [H/0/11]

7.3. PREPARING AND USING FREEBASE COCAINE

Eighty respondents report having freebased cocaine. They were asked who usually prepares the cocaine before basing it ('the cook'), how this is done ('the recipe'), and how they use it ('the dinner set').

7.3.1. The 'cook': who makes it?

In table 7.3.a we present the answers to the question who usually prepares the freebase cocaine. Exactly half of the respondents having freebased report that it is prepared by someone else (50%); 19 respondents (23.75%) prefer to prepare the freebase themselves, and another 11 users say that either other people or they themselves usually prepare the product (13.75%).

Table 7.3.a.   Who (usually) prepares the freebase cocaine, in Antwerp (1997) [*]

Antwerp (1997)		
Who prepares	**N**	**%**
Other people	40	50.0
Me	19	23.75
Other people or me	11	13.75
At first others, now me	8	10.0
Ready made	1	1.25
No answer	*1*	*1.25*
Total	**80**	**100.0**

[*] Based only on those respondents who report ever having freebased (N=80)

When asked why respondents have other people preparing the freebase for them, several idiosyncratic reasons were given.[4] Yet, most of these referred to the skill and ability of others in the technical procedure of processing freebase, or conversely, to their own lack of skills (although they would like to be able to do it). Other people prepare it, because 'I'm not good at it', 'I waste too much', 'I'm too shaky to do it', 'I don't know how to do it', 'I'm too sloppy',etc.

Remarkably, some report that they do not want to learn the skills, either because they are 'not interested' in the technique, or because they consciously want to avoid the knowledge necessary to be able to make freebase cocaine themselves, as a kind of self-protection:

I don't dare to do it, and I don't really want to know how to do it, because I would do it too much... [H/1/24]

When asked why people prefer to prepare the freebase cocaine themselves, similar categories of reasons were reported. Users prefer to do it themselves, because 'I'm an expert', 'Other people may waste some of it', 'My girlfriend always burns it', 'I don't trust the others',etc. One respondent said her boy friend did not want to teach her the technique of preparing freebase because he was afraid that she would want to do it too often (a method of protection). In their description of similar practices in the Dutch drug scene, Grund and Blanken (1993: 9) suggest that home-made freebase cocaine is preferable to the users as it gives them more control over the product.

Clearly, the most important informal rule in deciding who prepares the freebase product, is the (lack of) experience and technical skills of the users present. If there are several people with the necessary skills, the decision depends on who insists to do the 'cooking'. Yet, some respondents also indicate that there are some other informal rules (although of less importance). One user reported that it is usually the owner of the cocaine (the one who bought it) who is allowed to prepare it. Another person says:

I usually did it myself, or anybody who wanted to... [...] But mostly... in fact, usually the same person prepares it, you know. [C/0/09]

The etiquette of who prepares the freebase cocaine (and for example also the order in which freebase is used within a group of users) might be worth a study in itself (see for example on the etiquette of needle sharing: Crisp *et al.*, 1997).[5] We have identified some factors that determine who will be the 'cook', but these were found in an ad hoc manner while researching the technical procedure of processing freebase.

Furthermore, eight respondents (10%) state that at first somebody else prepared the freebase cocaine, but eventually they learned to do it themselves:

At first I couldn't prepare it, I just left it to others. But when you're involved, you have to be able to do it as well. I tried it a few times myself, but it went wrong a couple of times. So then I started to look carefully how it was done. [C/0/03]

Becker (1973) describes this process of social learning in his classical essay *'Becoming a marihuana user'*.[6] The first step in the sequence of events if the person is to become a freebaser is that he or she must learn the proper technique. For some this includes not only the smoking technique itself (see §7.3.3.), but also the technique of making the freebase cocaine out of street cocaine or cocaine hydrochloride (see §7.3.2.). As the quotations above illustrate, some respondents have acquired the latter technique by direct teaching, while others have learnt through observation and imitation (trial and error).

The fact that users are left to their own devices and to those of other 'experienced' users to learn and test tools and techniques, also illustrates the fact that there is no central clearing-house for information about the specific knowledge and equipment for preparing freebase cocaine. Personal experiences are exchanged casually in informal networks. Therefore, this information (which also contains elements of informal control mechanisms, e.g. how to use and prepare safely, how to minimize adverse effects, how to maximize pleasurable effects,etc.) may contain non-rational and wrong information. In the next paragraph, this problematic phenomenon will be explored further.

Interestingly, several respondents admit that they really like the procedure of making freebase cocaine. Most of them explicitly refer to the processing of freebase as a *ritual*:

I did it myself because it's part of the kick, actually. [I/1/01]

I do it myself, I even like doing it. It's a whole act, a ritual. [L/0/01]

We explicitly asked our respondents whether their freebase cocaine was already prepared by dealers. Only one respondent reports that his freebase cocaine is prepared in advance (see table 7.3.a): he buys his freebase cocaine in Brussels. Clearly, freebase cocaine is almost exclusively prepared by the users themselves, and it is not sold ready-made by dealers in Antwerp. Of course, the reader should keep in mind that these data may be subject to unexpected changes on the black cocaine market. Future research should monitor these practices, as it cannot be excluded that freebase cocaine becomes available in small, ready-made quantities processed by dealers, like in the United States (and also in the Netherlands: 'cooked cocaine').

7.3.2. The 'recipe': how is it made?

Respondents who had used freebase cocaine (N=80) were also asked to describe in detail how it is made. Nineteen of them (23.75%) did not answer this question, because they couldn't remember ('too long ago') or because they had not paid attention to how it was done (by others). All other respondents (about three quarters of those who had freebased cocaine) gave a similar account of the process of 'cleaning coke'. Despite the numerous variations among respondents in technique as well as in personal style, tools and personal preferences, we were able to 'reconstruct' a general 'recipe' for the manufacture of freebase cocaine in several steps:

1. Put cocaine hydrochloride in a spoon (or half a tin);
2. add ammonia (until cocaine is submerged);
3. heat the spoon with a cigarette lighter, candle, an electric stove or gas stove;
4. stir or dip with a (cold) knife until cocaine contracts;
5. absorb ammonia with a tissue (or toilet paper, coffee filter);
6a. rinse the rock of freebase cocaine with water, then dry it;
    or
6b. boil the rock of freebase cocaine with water, then absorb the water with a tissue;
7. break the rock into lumps.

Regarding this reconstruction of processing freebase cocaine, the following observations can be made: whatever the precise 'recipe', to obtain a smokable form of cocaine, the hydrochloride-part must be removed by treating it with an alkaline substance (Siegel, 1982). What remains is the alkaloid, the so-called cocaine freebase. The method as described by our Antwerp respondents bears most resemblance to two methods Siegel describes: the Ammonia Method and the Spoon Method.

We also asked our respondents how much time they usually needed to prepare freebase cocaine. Answers ranged from 'just a minute' to 'less than half an hour'. Most respondents reported a time span between 10 and 15 minutes. Apparently, the speed of processing freebase cocaine is influenced by several factors, such as the quantity of cocaine hydrochloride to be 'cleaned' (standard quantity is between 1 and 5 grams), the ritual significance to the user, the frequency of practicing this process (hence the experience of the user), the availability of the tools needed (ammonia, cigarette lighter, tissue), the mood of the user (whether or not he/she is relaxed, paranoid, etc.), and the intensity of the craving while preparing freebase cocaine.[7]

> *It depends on the moment. It depends on how much time you need, and how much you feel like cleaning it.* [J/0/01]

> *In fact, it depends on how strong your desire is. Now it's done in ten minutes, a quarter of an hour, and then it takes you twenty minutes or half an hour.* [H/1/28]

Although all respondents who described the processing of freebase cocaine referred to the 'recipe' with ammonia (see above), 12 respondents (15% of those having freebased) also explicitly refer to a similar method with sodium bicarbonate (or bicarbonate soda or 'baking soda'). According to Siegel (1982), this Baking Soda Method is the most popular street extraction method. That is clearly not the case for our subsample of

Antwerp freebasers. Only three respondents were able to describe the Baking Soda Method in detail. In their accounts the only important difference is that water is added together with the baking soda. The others only knew this method from hearsay or had witnessed it only once or twice.

Most of these respondents acknowledge that the Baking Soda Method is far healthier than the Ammonia Method, because the user does not have the bad taste and the burning feeling in his/her throat and lungs. Yet, they also report not using the Baking Soda Method because it's too complicated, too difficult, or because it takes too much time:

> *The first time I had it with me, here in Antwerp, with four people. One guy had already done that, and he had to explain: it was like ¼ sodium bicarbonate and then some coke, it was mathematics really. But with ammonia it's much easier... [...] With sodium bicarbonate it's something completely different, the chemical combination occurs much faster, and then you see those crystals, it's hard to see, so it's a little more complicated with sodium bicarbonate for most people.* [H/0/01]

It is remarkable that two respondents who were able to describe the Baking Soda Method in detail, were both older users (more than 30 years old) and they both indicated that the Baking Soda Method used to be a more popular method. Although it is difficult to check, both experienced users suggest there is a link between the transition from the Baking Soda Method to the Ammonia Method and the steady decrease of the quality of cocaine on the black market:

> *In the beginning, we used to have very good coke, you could boil it in a test tube. It wasn't with ammonia, it was with sodium bicarbonate. But you needed very good coke for that. Why? Because it cleans much better. But if you did have bad quality, there was nothing left. [...] I know for example, in Germany that is the way to prepare coke. Here, in Belgium, in Antwerp, at this moment, all the people I know do it with the spoon and with ammonia.* [H/0/05]

Both the Ammonia Method and the Baking Soda Method are well known in the Dutch drug scene. Kools and van den Boomen (1997: 12-13), and Grund and Blanken (1993: 9) describe both methods in detail (see also: Grund, 1993: 61). Because both methods show very close resemblance to the methods used by our Antwerp freebasers, photo-reports of both methods are presented here.[8] In most other community studies of cocaine users in European and American cities no specific attention was devoted to the procedure of processing smokable freebase cocaine. Only Diaz *et al.* (1992: 174-175) offer a short but very similar decription of the ammonia method.

Of all respondents who gave a relatively detailed description of the processing of freebase cocaine, about two thirds reported skipping the sixth step (= rinse the rock of freebase cocaine with water, or boil the rock in water). Explanations given for this omission are quite diverse and sometimes non-rational: 'If I take out the ammonia by absorbing it with a tissue, it is okay. I don't have to clean it with water', 'If I clean it with water, I will lose more of my cocaine', 'Rinsing with water decreases the quality of the cocaine crystals'. Others blame themselves for their own weakness: 'I'm not patient enough', 'When my feelings of craving are too strong, I forget it'. Despite their negligence, most of these people acknowledge that cleaning the rock of cocaine is useful to extract the ammonia leftovers ('I know I ought to do this, but...'). Another respondent claimed to use yet another technique to get rid of the ammonia:

> *So with a lighter you go over it... in fact, not on the underside of the aluminum foil, but over the product itself, and briefly on the underside, you see it crackle, and then the best part is left. I do that to take out the ammonia.* [L/1/03]

Finally, even respondents who claim not to skip the cleaning of the cocaine with water, report that many others deliberately skip this step:

> *There are many people who only clean it with ammonia. You can also clean it with bicarbonate. They do not clean it with water because they lose too much to do it again with water. Because it can make you lose another 10%.* [E/0/02]

Still, ammonia is highly poisonous. Because of its bad smell immediate poisoning is not the problem, but long term use can result in irritation of the airways, breathlessness, infections and asthma attacks. Thus, properly cleaning the base coke with water is necessary to prevent permanent physical damage. Consider this account of a male freebaser:

> *The most negative climax I have ever experienced, it was half a year ago, I had an ammonia poisoning, my lungs were burnt, and I was on a respirator for a day or two. I was completely out of this world too. [...] It had been two months or one month and a half since I had done it, and the desire had become so urgent, I had to hurry to fix a meeting with that guy, rush home, and then, it had to be done swiftly, no one was supposed to see it, and I took out the ammonia in a bad way, I didn't dry it properly, and by the third hit I didn't get any air anymore. I passed out for a while. Luckily, someone who lived in the house called the doctor, I managed to wake that guy with my last breath, to get him to my room.* [Q/0/01]

Grund (1993: 98) has pointed out that the social learning process surrounding illegal drugs develops in a long process of casual information exchanges in informal networks (see also Zinberg, 1982: 19). Neophytes are informed by drug using peers, and the information passed on is usually based on personal experience, rather than on objective information. Therefore, it should not come as a surprise that some users have acquired (maybe through trial and error) their own experimental tools or techniques. Compared to the stereotypical 'recipe' as presented above, these techniques can be considered *atypical*:

> *You throw a gram or half a gram of coke into some water. I did it in a little bottle, and that coke completely dissolved in the water, then I added a drop of ammonia, and then something happened. It became white as milk, then I poured some ether in it, shook it, so the coke that is dissolved in the water is separated by the drop of ammonia, and is dissolved in ether. [..] When you leave the bottle for while, it becomes transparent like water again. [...] And the ether, when you hold the bottle under the light, you can see the ether floating on the water. Then you take a little pipette, and you suck the ether from the water with that pipette [...] . And then you put the ether on another glass, the ether evaporates and you get some coke on the glass. [...] And then you scrape it off with a knife, and when you weigh it, about 15% has remained in the water. It's no loss, because it's dirt that was in your coke.* [H/0/02]

THE AMMONIA METHOD

1. Add ammonia

2. Heat briefly

3. Take out lump with knife

4. Pour off remaining ammonia

5. Heat briefly again

6. Take out lump

7. Dry lump with tissue paper

THE BAKING SODA METHOD

1. Divide cocaine into two parts

2. Add one part of baking soda

3. Add enough water

4. Heat briefly

5. **Take little rock (or lump) out with a knife**

6. **Pour off the water**

7. **Heat briefly again**

8. **Take out little rock (lump)**

7.3.3. The 'dinner set': how is it used?

Respondents who had freebased cocaine were asked to describe in detail how they usually used the product. Again we were able to 'reconstruct' the processes of using freebase cocaine. In general, two major techniques of using freebase cocaine can be distilled from the respondents' accounts: (1) *'chasing'* (or the Aluminum Foil Method) commonly referred to as 'chasing the dragon' *('chinezen'*; see also §7.2); and (2) *'basing'* (or the Glass Method), commonly referred to as 'freebasing' *('basen')*. Both methods of using freebase cocaine are generally known among the Antwerp freebasers.[9] Yet, our qualitative data clearly show that basing is far more popular among our experienced freebasers than chasing.

Grund (1993: 62-65) offers some explanations for the fact that cocaine is more often based than chased. He states that cocaine is harder to chase for a number of reasons. When heated, the cocaine base becomes liquid and colorless and therefore it is harder to follow the cocaine drop over the foil with the tube-shaped pipe (see below). Furthermore, when heated less cautiously, the liquid cocaine base has a very low cohesion and behaves very capriciously on the foil (in contrast with heroin). And finally, basing is a more direct and efficient smoking mode, producing a *rush*, comparable with, and according to some authors even more rapid and intense than injecting. *'Chasing is also efficient, but a much more moderate way of ingestion. When a certain amount of cocaine base is chased, it may take five to ten runs of the drug along the foil, depending on the (heating) technique. Each run accompanied by inhalation of the vaporized product through the tube. When the same amount of cocaine is based, the vaporized substance is ingested in one or two inhalations.'* (Grund, 1993: 64)

7.3.3.1. Chasing ('Chinezen') from an aluminum foil

The user prepares an aluminum foil by cutting it to an appropriate format (16 cm X 7 cm, according to one respondent). Some users burn this aluminum foil 'to remove the toxic substances incorporated in the foil'. The aluminum foil is first smoothed flat, then folded in two. The little rock of freebase cocaine is put on it. To inhale, a pipe (or pipette) is used, or anything that works as a tube. A cigarette lighter or any other fire source is held under the aluminum foil, causing the hard rock of freebase cocaine to melt and form a drop. By cautiously moving the foil, the user makes the drop slide on it, meanwhile following the fumes of the heated cocaine with the pipe in his/her mouth and sucking to inhale.

Some users make their own pipe by wrapping aluminum foil around a pencil, and taping it together. After the drop of freebase cocaine has completely evaporated, this self-made tube can be cut: inhalation of the fumes through the tube results in small sediments. Some users scrape these sedimentary deposits off the foil and put them on another foil, in order to heat them again and inhale the fumes.

7.3.3.2. Basing ('basen') with a glass

Despite the fact that this technique can also be applied by using a water pipe, a special base pipe or any kind of pipe, the overwhelming majority of our Antwerp freebasers reported using a small glass, hence our choice of terminology (the 'glass method'). Some users reported using a bottle or a Coca Cola can instead of a glass.

The user needs a glass (e.g. a large beer glass), which is usually half filled with water. An aluminum foil is put over the glass, and tightened with a rubber band (or elastic band). At one side of the glass little holes are made with a pencil, a pin or a needle (a square centimeter of tiny holes, according to one user) in the aluminum foil. At the opposite side of the glass a large hole is made in the foil, which will serve to suck out the fumes. A cigarette is lit, and left burning in an ashtray. Then the ashes are put on the little holes in the aluminum foil. Sometimes these ashes are crushed a little before the rock(s) of freebase cocaine are put on them. The user takes the glass in one hand, and a lighter in the other. As he/she burns the rock cocaine, he/she sucks the fumes through the large hole in the aluminum foil.

As to the reconstruction of this method of using freebase cocaine (the Glass Method), some observations can be made. Our qualitative data yield indications of social learning regarding the technique of (free-)basing (on a glass), similar to the ones we found regarding the technique of processing freebase. The following illustrates how users can receive information from other users without understanding exactly the rationale behind it:

> *You take a needle or a pair of compasses, you make little holes in that aluminum foil, you put some cigarette ash on top. They told me it had to be cigarette ash, not ash from rolled cigarettes, I don't know why, actually, but I just do it.* [R/0/06]

Again, two people report that they refuse to learn the technique with the glass, in order to avoid the knowledge necessary to use freebase cocaine themselves, as a method of self-protection:

> *Respondent: The others do that for me. I only have to inhale* [she laughs] .
> *Interviewer: You don't know how they prepare the glass?*
> *Respondent: No, and actually, I don't wanna know that. I always think: the less you know, the better for you* [she laughs] *. It's the same for shooting, I never wanted to know how much water you have to put in it, because if I would want to try it... It's just to protect myself.* [H/1/25]

Although most freebasers report using water to fill the glass, some of them have experimented occasionally with alcohol (whisky, wine, rum, etc.).[10] Because of the strong effects associated with this combination, it is usually dismissed by these users as 'experiments':

> *What you can do as well, I didn't do that often, but instead of water we sometimes used cognac or whisky. Then you get a different special effect, you didn't just become high from the coke, but also from the alcohol. It's a very serious combination. But we didn't do that often, because it kinda hits you hard.* [H/0/05]

Several freebasers from our Antwerp sample stress the ritual importance of basing. Not only do they report about the excitement and pleasure they experienced when preparing the glass construction, but they also stressed the sociable character of freebasing due to the passing on of the glass (or the aluminum foil):

> *First I prepare my bottle, because I don't base with a glass pipe or with a glass [...] . It's a real trifling work to put it together, but it's just... yes, working on it gives a kick in its own. And when it's all gone, you can't find a trace of it the next day, because I destroy it and I throw it away. So when I do it the next time, I have to make it again... because it's a kind of ritual to manufacture it.* [Q/0/01]

Some of the freebasers we interviewed gave elaborate and very detailed descriptions of the ways they performed these drug-using rituals. Apart from their idiosyncratic character,[11] what struck us most was their detailed elaboration of tools or techniques, as opposed to the apparent lack of rational knowledge about the functionality and meanings of these devices. Users often have quite specific knowledge and equipment, while many of them cannot explain why they act as they do. Consider the following –sometimes contradictory- quotes about the function of water in the glass:

> *Well, it's better not to add any water, but you do so to take out the ash.* [H/0/05]

> *There's a little water in it, it's not necessary, you know, but that's the way they do it.* [H/0/10]

> *You put some water in the glass for the ash, right? It's just to hold the ash, to make sure you don't get ash in your mouth.* [H/0/11]

> *When you add less water, you have to suck harder, it circulates, and when you add a lot of water, it goes in much faster.* [H/1/04]

Interestingly, many respondents add to their description of the use of freebase cocaine that the product initially makes a crackling sound when it is heated. The freebase cocaine is said to 'crackle', 'rustle', 'sputter', 'simmer', 'sizzle' etc. Explanations given for this phenomenon are: 'the coke is humid' (1 respondent) and 'there is too much ammonia in it' (3 respondents). One respondent states: 'it crackles a little, hence the name crack', which is an explanation often found in drug literature: one more indication that there are few differences between 'crack' and 'freebase'.

Comparison of our findings with those from other European and American community studies is hampered because most of them do not devote much attention to these practices. The reports on the Toronto sample, on the Amsterdam samples and on the Rotterdam sample contain no detailed information on the technique of freebasing. Diaz *et al.* (1992: 174-175) offer short but very similar descriptions of chasing and basing in the Barcelona sample. Merlo *et al.* (1992: 76) report that basing and chasing the dragon is completely absent in the Turin sample. Waldorf *et al.* (1991: 112) offer some 'basics' of the quite specific knowledge and equipment necessary for getting a 'real good hit': one must have a good fire (i.e. steady heat at the correct temperature), one should not put too large a chunk of the ball into the pipe (for this can be wasteful and impede proper burning), one needs close coordination between the person operating the flame and the person holding the pipe (if people work together), etc.

7.4. EXPERIENCES WITH FREEBASING

7.4.1. Buying freebase cocaine

Table 7.3.a shows only one respondent reporting that his freebase cocaine is prepared in advance. An important conclusion we drew was that freebase cocaine is prepared almost exclusively by the users themselves, and it is not sold ready-made by dealers in Antwerp. To gain some insight in the world of freebasing, we explicitly asked those respondents who had freebased cocaine whether it was possible to buy ready-to-use freebase cocaine in Antwerp or Belgium.

Forty-one of these respondents (53.3%) were unable to answer this question. Twenty-three respondents (29.8%) answered it in the negative and 13 (16.9%) in the affirmative. Yet, the stories about ready-made freebase cocaine deserve a closer look. Some of these respondents refer to experiences abroad (the Netherlands, Germany, etc.) rather than to the Antwerp scene. Others founded their opinion on hearsay from others users: although they never bought ready-made freebase cocaine, they heard vague and unconfirmed stories about places (streets, deal houses, etc.) where it could be bought.

In fact, only a small number of respondents know from their own experience that ready-made freebase cocaine is being sold in Antwerp. Two respondents claim they usually bought ready-made 'cleaned coke'. Others had been offered prepared freebase cocaine at one or two occasions.

> *Not that much. I once knew one female dealer who sold it, yes. Three thousand francs for one cleaned gram.* [H/0/11]

> *Not on the street, but house dealers did that. They sell a gram, I mean, 0.8 or 0.9 that is cleaned. But it doesn't occur that often, you know.* [H/1/17]

Several respondents indicate that selling ready-made freebase cocaine is not widespread, because it is against the dealers' interest. In fact, it depends on the quality of the cocaine: the more adulterated it is, the less a dealer will want to 'clean' it with ammonia, because he will lose too much weight. In other words, selling freebase cocaine is only be profitable if the original street cocaine has a (very) high purity, or if prices for this 'cleaned' cocaine are considerable higher compared to street cocaine. This line of reasoning is confirmed by some respondents' accounts about the prices of freebase coke ('3,000 francs for a gram' [H/0/10]; '500 francs for two tenths' [H/1/04]; '15,000 francs for a gram' [R/0/01]; '5,000-6,000 francs' [Z/0/02]).

7.4.2 Using freebase cocaine

Finally, at the end of the questionnaire on freebasing as a route of ingestion, respondents were asked to make any other remarks about (their experiences with) this particular method. Seventy-seven respondents did, and we found that for twenty-five respondents freebasing is a very dangerous or addictive route of ingesting cocaine. They all feel that they can't stop until all the freebase is gone:

So you really notice that you are looking for it: didn't we drop something on the ground, go take that napkin again, aren't there some little crumbs left on it... [B/1/01]

It's better to snort coke than to base coke, because with basing, there's no limit. You can go on forever. You cannot get enough of it. [...] Basing, it's a game without frontiers. [C/0/13]

Interestingly, to some respondents the first 'hit' is the best:

The first hit is the best [he laughs] *. [...] And for the rest of the night you try to equal that. And sometimes you come up to that peak again. I've had it once, just once, that I had to say: stop! Now I had enough. That's really unique, it doesn't happen often with coke. You'd have to take quite a lot...* [H/0/29]

Yet, 17 respondents also state that freebasing is a particularly pleasant activity. Many of them declare that it is 'the best possible way of using cocaine'. Nine people refer to its very strong effect ('the hard hit' or the 'flash'):

It hits you harder. A line is softer, it has a longer action, while basing is an up, and then finito. Just full speed ahead, and when it's over, you immediately make another one. [L/0/02]

The 'hit' from freebasing cocaine is so strong, that many 'normal' activities such as working, visiting people, administrative formalities, shopping, or even going out become impossible. According to some respondents, the intensity of the effect explains why freebasing is almost exclusively done at home and during leisure hours.[12] Moreover, six respondents refer to the 'calming', 'soft', 'serene' effect of freebasing. Preferably, this 'glorious' feeling is experienced in the reassuring environment of a home, in the company of friends, rather than in the fast and hectic nightlife (cafes, discotheques etc.).

Some respondents also produce 'positive' characteristics of freebasing that appear rather idiosyncratic: one respondent explains how he used to be an intravenous cocaine user, but switched to freebasing because he was tired of 'sticking a needle in my arm' and because he could not find his veins anymore. Another respondent argued that the advantage of using freebase cocaine is its relatively high purity compared to street cocaine (hydrochloride). It must be noted here that the common expression 'cleaning cocaine' clearly suggests that freebase cocaine is of a higher purity than cocaine hydrochloride.

Whether or not freebasing cocaine is a highly sociable activity is somewhat controversial. Four respondents argue that freebasing is a 'social thing', because the glass ('basing') or the aluminum foil ('chasing') is passed from one person to another and because people talk a lot while using it. Two other respondents disagree and state that the 'greedy feeling' caused by the drug alters the sociable atmosphere into an egoistic activity:

Using should be fun, something you can do in-between, and not when everybody is sitting at the table, and the aluminum foil is going around, and everybody is breathing down each other's neck [shows a greedy face] *... And also, once you start basing, you start being attached to the drug, because it is passed from person to person, while when you take a line, it is in between the conversations, that's nice.* [L/1/03]

Apart from its addictive potential, respondents report several further negative effects of freebasing cocaine. The aspects most mentioned were the high quantities of cocaine needed (6 respondents), 'I didn't feel much' (5 respondents), the high cost of freebasing (4 respondents), the short action (4 respondents), other adverse effects (2 respondents), and the feeling of craving when you stop using it (1 respondent). One respondent calls it a 'waste of cocaine'.

> *With freebasing, much more coke is done. First, you boil it so you lose a lot of dirt, so there's less left, and then you want a good flash of course, so you suck more and you use more, it's finished much faster.* [H/0/05]

Above, we illustrated how people practice some kind of self-control or self-protection by consciously avoiding to acquire knowledge about certain tools or techniques. When asked whether they wanted to tell us anything more about freebasing, six respondents spontaneously told us about similar self-protecting measures regarding this route of ingestion. Their reasoning seems to be: the less I know about it, the smaller the risk of doing it too often (and become addicted).

> *I don't want to learn the technique of basing myself, because then I can't do it myself. Also because I felt that you can get addicted to basing much faster than to lines. And if I don't know how, I won't do it, right?* [G/0/01]

7.5. EXPERIENCES WITH CRACK

In an attempt to clear the conceptual confusion that characterizes the users' vocabulary, all 111 respondents were asked about the differences between 'crack', 'freebase' and 'cooked cocaine'. The latter term is a typically Dutch term (*'gekookte coke'*), commonly used by users and researchers in the Netherlands (Grund, 1993: 207-217; Kruyer, 1997: 4-9; Grund *et al.*, 1991). We wanted to check whether this term might have been imported in the Belgian users' vocabulary. Only four respondents had ever heard this term before and claimed to know what it meant. Two people answered 'cocaine ready to inject' and 'another term for crack'. The two other stated that 'cooked cocaine' (*'gekookte coke'*) was a Dutch term for ready-made freebase cocaine sold by dealers, which must be the most plausible explanation.

To the question whether they knew the difference between 'crack' and 'freebase', almost all respondents reacted by mentioning (perceived) characteristics of 'crack'. For a definition of freebase cocaine, most of them referred to answers at other occasions (see above, the qualitative data on users' vocabulary, how freebase cocaine is processed, the technique etc.). Generally, respondents shortly explained 'freebase' as 'the technique with ammonia', 'the glass method', 'cleaning cocaine yourself', or 'the aluminum foil method'. These expressions were explained earlier, but we will summarize the main characteristics of 'crack', that differentiate it from 'freebase' according to our respondents.

A first important finding is that 34 respondents (30.6% of the total sample) do not know the differences between 'crack' and 'freebase' (if there are any at all). Seventeen respondents (15.3% of the total sample) state that 'crack' and 'freebase' are (almost) identical products. In these both groups we checked for differences between those respondents who reported having freebased and those reporting that they never had. We found similar proportions of ever-basers and never-basers among those who could not tell any differences between 'crack' and 'freebase'. But we did find a considerable difference among those respondents who said there was no difference between 'crack' and 'freebase': only one respondent had never freebased, versus 12 respondents who had at least freebased once.

Table 7.5.a. Perceived characteristics of 'crack' (as different from 'freebase') in the 1997 Antwerp sample, in % of respondents who state there is a difference (N=60) [*]

Antwerp (N=111)		
Compared to freebase, crack...	N	%
Is extremely (or more) addictive	20	33.3%
Contains more rubbish (chemical solution)	15	25.0%
Is more cut with heroin (smack)	8	13.3%
Is a residue of cocaine (waste)	6	10.0%
Is ready-made	5	8.3%
Has a stronger effect	4	6.7%
Is crystallized coke	4	6.7%
Is more cut with speed / has a more speedy effect	2	3.3%
Is only found in the U.S.	2	3.3%
Is something boiled	1	1.7%
Is coke cut with addictive substances	1	1.7%
Has a faster effect	1	1.7%
Is cheaper	1	1.7%

[*] More than one answer per respondents was possible

Sixty respondents (54.0% of the total sample) state there is a clear difference between 'freebase' and 'crack'. Table 7.5.a. presents the perceived characteristics of 'crack' as different from 'freebase', according to the respondents. It is striking that most characteristics attributed to 'crack' are rather vague. According to our respondents, 'crack' is extremely addictive ('to use it once is enough to get hooked', 33.3%), it is chemical rubbish (25.0%), it is cut with heroin (13.3%), it is waste left over from the cocaine production process (9.4%). Some respondents refer to the crack phenomenon the way it is sometimes portrayed in the media: cheap,[13] ready-made and a typically American phenomenon. Others refer to the chemical production process of 'crack': something boiled, 'crystallized coke', etc.

Yet, other respondents think it is typically adulterated with other drugs, such as heroin, speed, or other 'addictive substances'. And finally, some respondents define crack as different from freebase cocaine, because of its effects: 'stronger than freebase', 'faster effect than freebase'.

From all this, it is clear that there is great controversy among users about whether there is a difference between 'freebase' and 'crack'. Some do not know the exact differences, others simply do not see any differences. Even those respondents who claim that there are clear dissimilarities, do not agree. In fact, some of the perceived typical characteristics of 'crack' (or its processing) bear close resemblance to 'freebase' (or its processing) as it is described by some Antwerp respondents (more addictive than snorting cocaine, chemically prepared, with ammonia, ether or baking soda, etc.).

There is scant evidence that a product called 'crack' is being used in the Antwerp nightlife, and that is significantly different from freebase cocaine. Our analysis of qualitative data shows that users' knowledge about 'crack' is often partial, biased and sometimes even irrational and wrong. Our respondents' definitions of 'crack' and 'freebase' revealed a striking conceptual confusion. Whenever possible, we tried to bring up this topic during the second interview by asking respondents whether it was possible to buy 'crack' in Belgium or Antwerp, whether they had ever used crack themselves, and whether they knew anyone who had used crack. Although it turned out to be impossible to discuss these items with all respondents, the results can teach us even more about users' knowledge and 'experience' with 'crack'.

According to thirty-six respondents (32.4% of the total sample) 'crack' is not sold in Antwerp or Belgium. An equal proportion, 36 respondents, say it is possible to obtain 'crack' in Belgium. Only two of them could give an indication of the price of 'crack' in Belgium (500 to 700 francs for a gram). Given the conceptual confusion about 'crack' and 'freebase cocaine', it is useful to have a closer look at the respondents who answered this question in the affirmative.

Ten respondents stated that it was possible to buy 'crack' in Brussels (and not in Antwerp): most of them had heard this, one of them had actually bought 'crack', and one respondent had been accosted by a street dealer. Three of these respondents also added that most crack sellers in Brussels are black ('Nigerians' according to one of them). Two other respondents referred to a discotheque (not in Antwerp), and another one referred to Genk (in the province of Limburg).

Ten other respondents acknowledged that it was possible to buy 'crack' in Antwerp, but they could not give any details. They just 'knew' or had 'heard' at some point in time that crack was being sold in Antwerp or Belgium. Two respondents had heard 'horror stories', one about an overdose caused by crack, the other about two mental patients who had escaped from a psychiatric clinic and taken crack. Three other respondents said they had heard about crack in Belgium through the media (newspaper articles, magazines, etc.). Four people reported that at one or more occasions they had been offered 'crack' by a dealer (usual or casual):

> *I wouldn't pay much attention to that, I've heard dealers in Antwerp say: crack this and crack that, but I attach little credit to those stories.* [H/0/27]

Some statements tell us more about the respondents' perception of certain places or environments than about their own lived experiences.[14] Reference is made to some 'natural' congregation sites of illicit drug use or areas with heightened drug activity. If crack is to be found in Antwerp at all, that is where it should be, according to these respondents:

> *Crack belongs to another circuit. More in the neighborhood of the* Coninckspleintje [i.e. a square in the inner city, a well-known drug-copping zone, TD] , *I think you can get it there. I think if you know the right people. But in my circle of friends it is not really popular.* [R/0/01]

Finally, two respondents had been told about crack in Antwerp by their own friends. Both statements reveal the apparent similarities between 'crack' and 'freebase', thus raising the question again whether there is a difference at all?

> *Yes, they once gave something they said was crack. But I didn't experience any difference. So what people here call basing and crack, are the same.* [H/0/29]

To the question whether they had ever used crack themselves, five respondents answered in the affirmative (4.5% of the total sample). They all acknowledged that their subjective experiences of 'using crack' and 'using freebase cocaine' had been similar. Indeed, there are no clear indications that these users actually used a significantly different substance. Their slightly different perceptions might as well have been caused by quality differences between various freebase cocaine samples, by different set and setting factors, or other intermediary influences. Moreover, the conceptual confusion around 'crack' and 'freebase' may cause misunderstandings among users and dealers, among users, and among respondents and researcher.

> *Sometimes I had the feeling we got crack instead of coke. It's so strong, this urge to have more and so, that you start thinking: this is more crack than coke.* [H/0/08]

> *Pfff, those times I used it I was already 'out', so basically you can't establish any longer whether there is a difference. [...] I think it is stronger, it hits your lungs harder. But I wouldn't say there is a difference.* [L/1/03]

Thirty-one respondents (27.9% of the total sample) report not knowing anyone who has ever used 'crack'. Sixteen respondents, 14.4% of the total sample and about half as many as those who do not know a crack user, state that they know other people who have used 'crack'. Again, a closer look at the statements of these respondents may prove useful. Who are these so-called 'crack users' our respondents refer to? Two of them talk about a friend who had made a trip to the United States and tried crack there. Seven respondents base their statement on hearsay about other users, either unknown to them, or acquaintances. These 'stories' are not based on their own direct observation.[15]

> *Yes, but I mostly discarded those as wild stories, and by the way, these stories are not so 'wild'. [...] There have been very 'wild' stories about crack, in 1991-1993, such as: oh, there's crack in Belgium and this and that. It's possible, but the question is: what is crack, right? When I clean coke, and I get me some plastic vials, and I put it in them, do I have crack?* [H/0/27]

Similarly, the quotations above illustrate that the knowledge about other people's crack use is usually based on hearsay and vague stories about unknown or barely known people. These tales seem to be based on travelers' stories, bragging and hyperbole, and on incorrect information (from the media, other people, official sources). Moreover, the conceptual confusion surrounding 'crack', 'freebase', 'chinezen', 'basen' and 'roken' (=smoking) makes tangle of fact and fiction all the more inextricable.

Thus, on the one hand an important part of our sample declare never having heard about crack sales in Antwerp or Belgium, not having used crack, not knowing any people that have used it. On the other hand, several of 'stories' about crack circulate among certain groups of users. We found no significant differences for variables such as sex, age, professional category, ever having freebased or not, snowball chain, etc. between those respondents who have never heard of crack and those who have heard stories about crack. Although future research may prove us wrong, it is our hunch that there is no distinctive 'crack phenomenon' in the Antwerp nightlife scene. To us, 'crack' and 'freebase' refer to similar realities, and much of the existing entanglement (especially among users) is based on a confusing terminology.

7.6. 'CRACK' IN CONTEXT

Waldorf *et al.* (1991: 111) state that *'much of what a user feels is the product of his or her psychological makeup and expectations (set) and the situational and cultural context (setting) in which the drug is used. Highs are thus usually not merely physiological reflexes induced by the pharmacological properties of the drug, but to a significant degree they are learned by users in an interpretive process involving both their personal character and the cultural context.'*

That cultural context consists partly of the 'stories' about the diabolical drug named 'crack', engendered by extensive exposure to American sources and misperceptions of the threat posed by crack. When crack appeared, it was presented to the public as extremely dangerous because its quick and intense high made it so powerfully addictive that serious health and financial consequences were inevitable. Both the general public and the media linked crack use to crime, asserting that its extraordinary addictiveness led users to do 'anything' for another hit. Crack was portrayed as a menace and its users were associated with low status, disadvantaged and ethnic minority group members in the United States.

However, several studies suggest that crack may not be as overwhelmingly reinforcing as one might guess from examining the minority of users whose problems land them in jail or treatment (e.g. Waldorf *et al.*, 1991). For example, the media legends about crack cocaine imply that crack cocaine smokers have much less control over their behavior than cocaine users. If a large number of drug users can decide, deliberatley, to take a dangerous drug like crack cocaine, but cautiously to avoid problems, this debunks the idea that crack cocaine is spontaneously 'addictive', and that its use drains users of any responsibility for their actions. Consequently, most community studies of cocaine and crack users have seriously questioned media depictions of cocaine as inevitably addicting or as curable only through treatment by professionals (e.g. Erickson *et al.*, 1994: 84 and 177-187; Ditton & Hammersley, 1996: 68-70 and 119-121).

Through the mass media (newspapers, books, magazines, radio and television) these images of cocaine are diffused into the public awareness. All the newspapers carrying the cocaine and crack-stories are widely available, and we can expect both the public in general and the cocaine users in particular to be influenced by them. The mass media play an important, albeit covert, role in the definition of acceptable and deviant forms of behavior. Other authors have illustrated the largely negative image of cocaine that pervades the news media (Ditton & Hammersley, 1996: 1-7 and 11-15; Erickson *et al.*, 1994: 25-38). Frequent exposure to such portrayals is likely to have an impact.

Since these negative images exceed the real problem level, the community is left with a misperception of the nature of (crack) cocaine and its users. Furthermore, attitudes and beliefs unfavorable to its use will be strengthened in the general public.

As to the cocaine and crack users themselves, they too will be influenced by the 'crack' and 'cocaine' stories diffused by the popular media. Our data suggest that the exaggerated horrors of crack cocaine have deterred the Antwerp users to a certain extent. Fewer than 5% of the total sample have ever used 'crack'. Although most participants cannot explain the exact differences between 'crack' and 'freebase', they typically describe crack as something more addictive and dangerous, containing more chemicals and more dirt. From their point of view, this drug is perceived as too risky and too dangerous to use.

The question thus arises: why did a considerable proportion of the Antwerp sample experiment with 'freebase cocaine' and continue to use it? In our view, the following may explain this strange contradiction. Official evidence of cocaine use is patchy, and that of crack-cocaine non-existent. Most Antwerp freebasers began using this mode of ingestion before word of the dangers of 'freebase' spread through the user folklore. In fact, we believe that most users have remained unaware of the similarities between 'crack' and 'freebase'. For them, 'crack' has not yet arrived on the Belgian drug scene, and 'freebase' is something different...

Another explanation for the spreading of 'freebasing', while many remained convinced that 'crack' is to be avoided, is that many Antwerp respondents *believe* it is possible to be a controlled freebaser, that freebasing is not necessarily addicting. They have at least the rudiments of a vocabulary with which to conceive and articulate normative expectations of controlled use (Waldorf *et al.*, 1991: 277).

And third, almost all freebasers had been snorting cocaine for some time before they began smoking it in freebase form. Thus, the step to this new mode of ingestion was a small one down a well-worn path, rather than a giant one down a road never taken before (Waldorf *et al.*, 1991: 109).

Finally, several authors have shown that users elsewhere believe the cocaine they smoke is different in important ways from 'crack' cocaine. For example, Steve Koester, an ethnographer who has studied cocaine smokers in Denver, reports that Denver smokers rarely use the term 'crack', often are insulted by the suggestion that they smoke crack, and believe crack is more dangerous than the cocaine they smoke (personal communication, cited by Ouellet *et al.*, 1997: 223).[16]

Two research teams working independently (one in Chicago, Illinois and one in Anchorage, Alaska) studied cocaine smokers and suggested that some – perhaps many - cocaine smokers concluded that the cocaine they smoked did not cause as much harm as that reported in widely disseminated stories about crack and thus must be a different substance (Ouellet *et al.*, 1997). These authors hypothesized that, given these harsh accounts of crack use, many smokers may have experienced cognitive dissonance from having self-images more robust than those associated with crack users. *'As a consequence, cocaine smokers have found some relief from the psychological strain caused by this discordance between self-image and behavior by defining their smoking of cocaine as something other than crack use. Finally, the denial of crack use –both within peer groups of cocaine smokers and by individuals in interactions with non-smokers-may have served to deflect the considerable stigmatization associated with being a crack user.'* (Ouellet *et al.*, 1997: 232)

Whether those using different terms for the same substance and ascribing important differences to each term are correct, is not so relevant here. The more important issue is that people are likely to act on such understandings. If people believe 'freebase' is less harmful than 'crack' and that the freebase they manufacture is 'freebase', not 'crack', then it seems plausible that they will be more willing to try the drug, recommend it to others, and facilitate use by others.

It also seems plausible that the perceptual differences embedded in the terms used to identify smokable cocaine are likely to affect a person's experience in using the drug and readiness to identify use as a problem (Ouellet *et al.*, 1997: 232). An intriguing issue is the possible effect of instructing these users about the similarity between 'crack' and 'freebase'. What would happen if we told them that 'freebasing' could be as risky as smoking 'crack', and that in fact, there are few differences? Some users might be deterred from further using freebase cocaine, because they realise that in fact they are using a form of 'crack'. Other users, however, may be confirmed in their views that all official warnings should be discounted. When their personal experience with 'crack' (or 'freebase') tells them it is not inevitably addicting, in contrast with the horror stories from official sources, they might throw away the proverbial baby with the bathwater.

7.7. CONCLUSION

In this chapter we described the vocabulary of freebase ('base', 'freebase', cleaned coke') and the technique of using it ('chasing the dragon', 'freebasing', 'smoking'). We found that these terms are often used interchangeably, which causes a conceptual confusion among users, between drug experts, and between researcher and respondents. Furthermore, we showed that freebase cocaine is almost exclusively prepared by the users themselves, and not bought ready-made from dealers. In fact, apart from vague hearsay, only a few respondents can tell from their own experience that prepared, cleaned cocaine is sold in Antwerp. According to most respondents, selling freebase cocaine would only be profitable if the original street cocaine was of high purity or if prices for this 'cleaned coke' were very high.

The decision who actually prepares the freebase cocaine usually depends on the skill of the users present. The technique of making base coke requires relatively great precision, and must be learnt through direct observation and imitation from peer users. The most popular method of 'cleaning cocaine' is the Ammonia Method (almost identical to the ammonia methods described in Dutch drug literature), although some users have acquired their own experimental tools and techniques. Remarkably, two thirds of the respondents reported to omit the phase of rinsing the rock of freebase cocaine with water, to expulse the ammonia. Yet, ammonia fumes can cause permanent damage to the user's health.

We specified the two main methods of using freebase cocaine: inhalation of cocaine fumes from an aluminum foil ('chasing the dragon') and smoking freebase cocaine with a glass ('basing'). Especially the latter method often appeared to be a highly ritualized and elaborate technique, although many respondents lack rational knowledge about the functionality and significance of these devices. When asked to make further remarks about (their experiences with) freebasing, many indicated that it is a dangerous or addictive route of ingestion (difficult to stop). We described several other positive and negative experiences with freebasing.

It was also shown that there is great controversy among users about whether there is a difference between 'freebase' and 'crack'. Some users (15.3% of the sample) believe both products are more or less identical substances; but more than half of the respondents (54.0%) state there is a difference. Whatever may be the case, it is clear that users' knowledge about 'crack' is often based on hearsay and (horror) stories, and thus partial, biased and possibly incorrect. In our opinion, the indications produced in this chapter suggest that there is no distinct 'crack' product in Antwerp. 'Crack' and 'freebase' refer to similar products.

Much of what a user feels is the result of his or her psychological make-up and expectations (set) and the situational and cultural context (setting) in which the drug is used. Part of that cultural context are the 'stories' about the diabolical drug named 'crack'. However, several studies suggest that crack may not be as overwhelmingly reinforcing as one might guess from examining the minority of users whose problems land them in jail or treatment. Yet, through the mass media these images of cocaine are diffused into the public awareness, and we can expect both the public in general and the cocaine users in particular to be influenced by them. Not only will attitudes and beliefs unfavorable to its use will be strengthened in the general public, the exaggerated horrors of crack cocaine may have deterred the Antwerp cocaine users themselves.

The question is, why did a considerable proportion of the Antwerp sample experiment with 'freebase cocaine' and continue to use it? We believe that most users have remained unaware of the similarities between 'crack' and 'freebase' . Furthermore, many Antwerp respondents *believe* it is possible to be a controlled freebaser, they *believe* that freebasing is not necessarily addicting, and that it can and should be used in a controlled fashion.

NOTES

[1] Two thirds of the Antwerp respondents (72.1%) had freebased (lifetime prevalence), almost one fifth of the sample (17.1%) had freebased their cocaine at least once during the month prior to the interview (Chapter 6, p. 156 and p. 158). Freebasing was the main route of ingestion during the period of heaviest use for 23.4% of our respondents. And finally, we also found that the perceived net merit of freebasing was clearly larger than of injecting. See Chapter 6, p. 161-165.

[2] Most respondents point out that 'freebasing' refers to a technique which requires preparation with ammonia, which will be described more in detail in the next paragraph. Again, respondents stress that 'freebasing' as a technique has nothing to do with 'crack', which they consider quite different from freebase cocaine.

[3] 'Chasing' is an abbreviation of 'chasing the dragon'. See: GRUND, J.P. and BLANKEN, P. (1993), *op. cit.*, 5-15. GOSSOP, M., GRIFFITHS, P. and STRANG, J. (1988), Chasing the dragon: characteristics of heroin chasers. *British Journal of Addiction* 83, 1159-1162.

[4] 'Idiosyncrasy' = a way of thinking or behaving that is peculiar to a person; personal mannerism (adjective: idiosyncratic). Zinberg repeatedly argued that the lack of culturally based learning about controlled drug use meant that informal control mechanisms tend to be idiosyncratic (Zinberg, 1984: 80).

[5] Crisp *et al.* (1997) have described in detail the variety of factors that determine the order in which intravenous drug users use shared equipment (needle and syringe): ownership of the needle and syringe, assertiveness, paying for or obtaining the drug, gender, perceived or actual serostatus, being injected by someone else, injecting in one's own home, withdrawal, wanting a sharp needle, age, number of years injecting, the nature of the relationship, and who went first last time. CRISP, B.R., BARBER, J.G. and GILBERTSON, R. (1997), The etiquette of needlesharing, 24 *Contemporary Drug Problems*, 273-291.

[6] See also Chapter 1, p. 42, and Chapter 4, p. 114-118.

[7] See also Chapter 13, p. 289 and the following.

[8] With special thanks to Adrie Mouthaan, photographer of *Mainline*, Amsterdam.

9   See also the descriptions offered by Grund and Blanken. GRUND, J.P. and BLANKEN, P. (1993), *op. cit.*, 5-15.

10   For combinations of cocaine and alcohol, see also Chapter 8, p. 201-202 and 206.

11   See note 4 of this Chapter.

12   See also Chapter 6, p. 166-168, on the factors influencing the choice of the route of ingestion.

13   As stated in the general Introduction, price analyses have shown that crack is not, in fact, cheaper per pure unit than powder cocaine. But they are qualitatively different, and in that light, it may be more accurate to say that crack gained a market share in the United States not because it was cheaper than powder and 'just as good', but because crack was not more expensive and preferred by some users. CAULKINS, J.P. (1997), Is crack cheaper than (powder) cocaine?, 92 *Addiction* 11, 1437-1443.

14   This is another illustration of the process of stereotyping. These accounts tell us more about how our respondents perceive 'crack users' and some 'copping areas'. See: FINNIGAN, F. (1996), How non-heroin users perceive heroin users and how heroin users perceive themselves, 4 *Addiction Research* 1, 25-32.

15 Another respondent did see someone else using crack, but from her description no clear differences with the use of freebase cocaine emerge.

16   Cited in: OUELLET, L.J., CAGLE, H.H. and FISHER, D.G. (1997) , "Crack" versus "rock" cocaine: the importance of local nomenclature in drug research and education, 24 *Contemporary Drug Problems*, 219-238.

CHAPTER 8

COMBINATION OF COCAINE
WITH OTHER DRUGS

8.1. INTRODUCTION

This chapter investigates the use of other drugs apart from cocaine by members of the Antwerp sample (§8.2) and their use of cocaine in combination with other drugs (§8.3). In §8.4 special attention is given to the prevalence of polydrug use in our sample. Finally, we present some quantitative (§8.5) and qualitative data (§8.6) on suitable and unsuitable combinations of cocaine with other drugs, according to our respondents.

8.2. OTHER DRUGS

Before showing the combinations of drug use by our respondents, a survey of the raw prevalence of other drugs used by the sample is given. First, the data from the Antwerp sample are presented in comparison with the two Amsterdam samples (§8.2.1). Then, they are compared with data from other major community studies of cocaine users (§8.2.2).

8.2.1. Data from the Antwerp and the Amsterdam samples

Respondents were asked to report life time prevalence and last two weeks prevalence of alcohol, tobacco, sedatives, hypnotics, cannabis (marihuana and hashish), LSD, solvents, amphetamines ('speed'), MDMA ('ecstasy') and opiates. In the 1987 Amsterdam I study, amphetamines and MDMA were not included.

Alcohol, tobacco, cannabis and MDMA are the four drugs used most often (see table 8.2.a). Life time prevalence of cannabis (!) and alcohol is 100 %, and of tobacco and MDMA it is 95.5 %. Life time prevalence of LSD and amphetamines is also very high (about 85%) compared to both Amsterdam samples. It is striking to see that our Antwerp respondents have a higher life time prevalence for all drugs, including solvents, hypnotics and sedatives.

One possible explanation for this is that the respondents of the Antwerp sample are more experienced drug users than the Amsterdam respondents. Although the mean age of our sample did not differ markedly from that of other community samples, the mean age at initiation for cocaine was somewhat lower compared to the Amsterdam sample,[1] and average length of their cocaine using career was somewhat longer.[2] It is plausible that the Antwerp respondents on average started experimenting with other drugs at an earlier age, that they have longer use careers for other types of drugs as well, and have thus built up more experience with other drugs (and with combinations with cocaine).

Table 8.2.a   Life time prevalence and last two weeks prevalence of other drugs, in % of total sample, in three samples

Life time prevalence	Amsterdam I 1987 (N=160)	Amsterdam II 1991 (N=108)	Antwerp 1997 (N=111)
Tobacco	96.2	98	95.5
Cannabis	91.2	94	100.0
Alcohol	89.7	97	100.0
LSD	36.9	41	85.6
Opiates	36.2	41	63.1
Hypnotics	25.6	27	52.3
Sedatives	24.5	31	57.7
Solvents	6.3	13	26.1
MDMA	-	63	95.5
Amphetamine	-	57	84.7

Last two weeks prevalence	Amsterdam I 1987 (N=160)	Amsterdam II 1991 (N=108)	Antwerp 1997 (N=111)
Tobacco	80.0	90	91.0
Cannabis	53.7	54	82.0
Alcohol	83.7	90	90.1
LSD	0.6	6	9.0
Opiates	1.9	5	17.1
Hypnotics	2.5	6	17.1
Sedatives	0.6	8	19.8
Solvents	-	2	0.9
MDMA	-	19	23.4
Amphetamine	-	10	33.4

For the last two weeks prevalence, alcohol and tobacco rank first. Last two weeks prevalence of cannabis (82.0%) is considerably higher than that of both Amsterdam samples (53.7% in 1987 and 54% in 1991). As the use of cannabis is tolerated in the Netherlands, while it is subject to a repressive policy in Belgium, this is a striking result. The same holds for amphetamines, sedatives, hypnotics and opiates, and in a less marked way for MDMA. Only for LSD and solvents, last month prevalence is low. In short, the Antwerp respondents clearly claim to have more experience with most types of drugs than the participants from both Amsterdam samples.

8.2.2. Data from other European and American cocaine studies

Unfortunately international comparison of (simple) data on life time prevalence and last period prevalence is seriously hampered by a number of methodological differences. First, many community studies do not present quantitative data on the use of legal drugs (alcohol and tobacco). Second, the studies in Turin, Rotterdam and Barcelona (all in 1990-91) only present data on the use of other drugs by participants prior to their first use of cocaine. Life time prevalence of these drugs cannot be calculated because the data do not take into account experiences with other drugs after initiation into cocaine. Third, most studies do not include the use of solvents (or inhalants) and MDMA ('ecstasy'). Fourth, there are some differences in definitions of drug types between some studies. For example, both the Toronto studies use categories such as 'heroin' and 'narcotics other than heroin', while other studies use 'opiates'. Waldorf *et al.* (1991: 292) present specific data on the use of 'Quaaludes' and 'Valium', whereas most studies present data on 'sedatives' and 'hypnotics', or 'tranquilizers' and 'barbiturates'. And fifth, comparison of our data on last two weeks prevalence of other drug use with other studies is impossible. Waldorf *et al.* (1991: 292) coded their answers for seven different frequencies, ranging from never to more than one thousand times (in a life time). Other studies asked for prevalence in the last year and the last month, but not in the last two weeks (Toronto, 1983 and 1989-90). Still other studies studied prevalence during the last three months (Scotland, 1989-90).

However, the following observations can be made from the comparison of the data on life time prevalence in all these community samples:

• When the use of legal drugs is included in the questionnaire, life time prevalence of alcohol and tobacco always proves to be among the highest of all types of drugs.
• Life time prevalence of cannabis is very high in all samples (94% or higher), except for the Turin sample (89%) and the Amsterdam II sample (91.2%).
• Life time prevalence of LSD is over 80% in most samples. It is strange to find that in the Turin sample (1990-91) and in both Amsterdam samples (1987 and 1991) life time prevalence of LSD is only half as high, i.e. around 40%.
• In all samples life time prevalences of solvents (or inhalants), opiates (heroin, opium, etc.), sedatives (or tranquilizers) and hypnotics (or barbiturates) are lower than life time prevalences of other illegal drugs, such as amphetamines, MDMA, LSD and cannabis.

In short, the data of the present study are consistent with the data from other European and American studies of cocaine users in that they reflect a similar hierarchy of types of drugs experienced by the respondents: alcohol, tobacco, cannabis and MDMA are the four drugs most often used. Life time prevalences of solvents, opiates, sedatives and hypnotics are lower than life time prevalences of other illegal substances. However, compared to most other community studies the Antwerp respondents clearly claim to have more experience with most types of drugs.

8.3. COMBINATION OF COCAINE WITH OTHER DRUGS

The data from the Antwerp sample are presented separately in paragraph 8.3.1, and then compared with data from other major community studies of cocaine users (§8.3.2).

8.3.1. Data from the Antwerp sample

Table 8.3.a shows that alcohol, tobacco and cannabis are also used most often in combination with cocaine. In the 1991 Amsterdam sample, MDMA was important: in the total prevalence of *combined use* it ranked fourth, after cannabis.

Table 8.3.a   The use of cocaine plus another drug, in %, in the 1997 Antwerp sample

| | | Antwerp (1997) | | | | | |
| | | | Ever | | | | |
Cocaine plus	N	Often	Regularly	Rarely	Subtotal	Never	Total
Alcohol	111	69.4	10.8	9.0	89.2	10.8	100.0
Tobacco	111	89.2	3.6	0.9	93.7	6.3	100.0
Sedatives	111	14.4	12.6	8.1	35.1	64.9	100.0
Hypnotics	111	11.7	13.5	6.3	31.5	68.5	100.0
Cannabis	111	56.7	23.4	8.1	88.2	11.7	99.9
LSD	111	0.9	2.7	14.4	18.0	82.0	100.0
Solvents	111	-	-	-	-	100.0	100.0
Opiates	111	14.4	7.2	13.5	35.1	64.9	100.0
MDMA	111	11.7	16.2	21.6	49.5	50.5	100.0

In our 1997 Antwerp sample we find the same ranking for the total prevalence of combined use: (1) tobacco (93.7%); (2) alcohol (89.2%); (3) cannabis (88.2%) and (4) MDMA (49.5%). The total prevalence of combined use of cocaine with sedatives, hypnotics and opiates is also very important in the Antwerp sample. It is striking, though, that this matches with higher life time prevalences and last month prevalences for each of these drugs compared to the Amsterdam samples (cf. table 8.2.a). Finally, combined use of cocaine and solvents was *not* reported by our respondents. Combined use of cocaine and LSD was reported by some respondents, but usually qualified as *rarely*. Merging the 'often' and 'regularly' categories from table 8.3.a yields the following (see table 8.3.b).

Table 8.3.b.   Often or regularly used drugs in combination with cocaine in the 1997 Antwerp sample

Cocaine in combination with	Antwerp (1997) N=111	
	N	%
Alcohol	89	80.2
Tobacco	103	92.8
Sedatives	30	27.0
Hypnotics	28	25.2
Cannabis	89	80.2
LSD	4	3.6
Opiates	24	21.6
Amphetamines	29	26.1
MDMA	31	27.9
Solvents	-	-

The difference between combined use of cocaine and MDMA, and combined use of sedatives, hypnotics, amphetamines and opiates has now become smaller: roughly, about one quarter of our respondents often or regularly combine cocaine with one of these drugs.

The results of cross-tabulations of the use of combinations of cocaine plus another drug with level of cocaine use, as measured during the period of heaviest use, are shown in Table 8.3.c: our high level users of cocaine (during the period of heaviest use) show a markedly higher use of sedatives (45.5% vs. 27.0%), hypnotics (40.0% vs. 25.2%) and opiates (30.9% vs. 21.6%) compared to the total sample. Their use of MDMA (30.9% vs. 27.9%) and amphetamines (30.9% vs. 26.1%) is only slightly higher than is the case for the total sample. Although cell numbers in the 1997 Antwerp sample are too low to test for statistical significance, we dare say that high level use is related to a higher combinational use of sedational drugs (and less markedly, of MDMA and amphetamines).[3]

Table 8.3.c   Often or regularly used drugs, in combination with cocaine, differentiated for level of cocaine use during period of heaviest use, in the 1997 Antwerp sample

Cocaine plus	Antwerp (1997)			
	Total N=111	Low N=24	Medium N=32	High N=55
Alcohol	80.2	75.0	84.4	80.0
Sedatives	27.0	4.2	12.5	45.5
Hypnotics	25.2	-	18.7	40.0
Cannabis	80.2	87.5	84.4	74.5
LSD	3.6	8.3	-	3.6
Opiates	21.6	8.3	15.6	30.9
Amphetamines	26.1	8.3	15.6	30.9
MDMA	27.9	8.3	15.6	30.9

The interrelationship between a high level of use and the combined use of cocaine and sedatives/hypnotics can be explained by looking at data presented elsewhere. First, many of the disadvantages that our respondents mentioned (see chapter 6) concern adverse effects when the cocaine's action ends. In § 8.6 we will show that some respondents take sedational drugs as a kind of self-medication for negative after-effects such as insomnia, restlessness, depression, and unpleasant physical effects (to 'come down' after the use of cocaine).[4] Furthermore, the use of sedatives/hypnotics helps some people to offset feelings of craving for (more) cocaine. Second, chapter 14 presents our findings regarding the influence of set-factors.[5] As to the combined use of cocaine and other drugs, respondents who were using at a high level during period of heaviest use and who report combining cocaine and sedatives/hypnotics often or regularly, also report more often negative feelings (depression, boredom, frustration, anger) that generate an appetite for cocaine (59.2% of all feelings mentioned). Respondents who were using at a high level during their top period and who report combining cocaine and MDMA/amphetamines often or regularly, report much fewer negative feelings that generate an appetite for cocaine (36.8% of all feelings mentioned).

In short, high level use and higher combinational use of cocaine and sedatives/hypnotics may be linked with 'escapist' motives for using cocaine (negative feelings), whereas high level use and higher combinational use of cocaine and XTC or speed may be linked with socializing motives for using cocaine (positive feelings such as joy, love, etc.).[6]

8.3.2. Data from other European and American cocaine studies

For reasons explained above, exact comparison of our data on the combined use of cocaine with other drugs with other community samples of cocaine users is impossible. Although both quantitative and qualitative data from other studies contain manifold indications that cocaine is often used in combination with other drugs, we will only summarize the main findings of authors who have explicitly presented some data on the combined use of cocaine with other drugs: the Amsterdam I sample (1987), the first Toronto sample (1983), the Barcelona sample, the Turin sample and the Rotterdam sample (all three 1990-91).

In the 1987 Amsterdam I sample alcohol, tobacco and cannabis were the three most often used drugs (apart from cocaine) and they were also used most often in combination with cocaine. All other drugs were insignificant in this respect (Cohen, 1989: 68). In the 1991 Amsterdam II sample, MDMA was important: in the total prevalence of *combined use* it ranked fourth, after cannabis (Cohen & Sas, 1995: 65). In our 1997 Antwerp sample we find a virtually identical ranking for the total prevalence of combined use. Diaz *et al.* (1992) report that only 15% of the Barcelona respondents assert that they use cocaine by itself, whereas most of them (64.1%) combine cocaine with other drugs (such as cannabis, amphetamines, tranquillizers, hallucinogens and others –except opiates) and a further 11.8% use cocaine and, amongst other drugs, mainly heroin.

Erickson *et al.* (1994: 101) find that 52% of the participants in the first Toronto study (1983) reported concurrent use of *cocaine and alcohol*, i.e. use within a couple hours of each other. Diaz *et al.* argue that cocaine forms part of a multi-drug use pattern and the role of alcohol in this is significant, above all when the cocaine is being used for social purposes or as part of the relationship with friends. *'In such situations, addictional alcohol use comes about due to the use of cocaine. That is to say that cocaine is used in order to drink more ("the night lasts longer", the negative effects of alcohol disappear, etc.). [...] Cocaine and alcohol emerge as being complementary drugs, [...] it becomes difficult to distinguish between the effects of the one and the other. [...] Cocaine consequently becomes "useful" in order to drink more alcohol as it eliminates the latter's effects. The use of cocaine also makes it possible to increase one's alcohol intake and thus enjoy "the party" longer. [...] Going to parties thus represents an appropriate setting for the consumption of alcohol and other drugs. According to some of the interviewees, a party or friends' gathering without alcohol mainly, but also other drugs such as cocaine and cannabis, would be "unthinkable".'* (Diaz *et al.*, 1992: 188-189). Bieleman and de Bie (1992: 38-39) indicate that the combined use of alcohol and cocaine is frequently mentioned in both the international and the Dutch drug literature. Descriptions of the combined use of both substances by many of their respondents from the Rotterdam sample are very similar to those reported by Diaz (see above).

Erickson *et al.* (1994: 101) report that 39% of the participants in the first Toronto study (1983) reported concurrent use of *cocaine and cannabis*, that is, they usually consumed cannabis within a couple hours of using cocaine. Diaz *et al.* (1992: 190) argue that cannabis is often used for relaxing after heavy use of cocaine and alcohol. In certain cases, cannabis is used to eliminate those negative effects of cocaine (anxiety, etc.) that are sometimes attributed to the substances used for adulteration.

According to the authors of the Barcelona study, cocaine is seldom mixed *with LSD or ecstasy*, although such combinations have their devotees. More often the use of cocaine mixed with some of these substances is valued negatively. Diaz *et al.* conclude that *'beyond the most usual combinations where there is a certain consensus, other combinations and the appraisals of them depend too much on individual factors and it is therefore difficult to make generalizations.'* (Diaz *et al.*, 1992: 190). Bieleman and de Bie (1992: 47-48) too indicate that cocaine and MDMA are rarely combined.

In the Turin sample (1990-91) 40% combined the use of *cocaine with heroin*. Only 12% exclusively used cocaine; 39.4% used cocaine combined with cannabis derivatives and only 8% used also other drugs (to the exclusion of heroin) besides cocaine and cannabis (Merlo *et al.*, 1992: 76-79). Diaz *et al.* (1992: 191) report that the heroin addicts in their Barcelona sample occasionally combine cocaine with heroin ('speed-balls') to perk themselves up. At times they may use cocaine on its own for the same reason or in order to 'normalize' their capacity for performing certain activities. Some ex-heroin addicts may have replaced heroin with cocaine as their main drug, but at times they may use heroin to eliminate the anxiety caused by the use of cocaine.

And finally, Merlo *et al.* (1992: 76-79) attempted to construct a typology of ways of using based on the role of cocaine in combination with the other substances:

(1) *Subsidiary (or functional) role of cocaine*: cocaine is used in close connection with other substances. Use is tendentially of circular type [alcohol/hashish – cocaine – alcohol/hashish], like a spiral where each substance is used in relation to the effects of the previous one, in order to either counterbalance its unwanted aspects or in-crease its potentiality.

(2) *Marginal role of cocaine*: cocaine is a surplus. It plays a positive role, but it is not indispensable in the interviewees' pattern of use of substances. Cocaine is often confined to a marginal role because of its exorbitant cost.

(3) *Cocaine as main drug*: cocaine is the most important substance, the favourite one because of its effects and sensations ('Coke is something more compared to all the other substances').

8.4. POLY-DRUG USE

In the 1987 Amsterdam I sample, high level users (during period of heaviest use) dis-tinguished themselves as poly-drug users, in that many of them reported a life time prevalence of more drugs. They also scored higher on life time prevalence of the use of three or more drugs. In the Amsterdam I survey, respondents were asked to report on their life time prevalence and last two weeks prevalence of alcohol, tobacco, cannabis, LSD, opiates, hypnotics, sedatives and solvents. In the 1991 Amsterdam survey, Cohen and Sas added MDMA to this list. We asked our respondents to report on amphetamines as well.

Table 8.4.a presents the findings from Amsterdam and from Antwerp in a commen-surable way, i.e. we left out the answers regarding our respondents' use of ampheta-mines and MDMA. We find some major differences between the Antwerp and the Am-sterdam sample: none of the Antwerp respondents report a life time prevalence of 0 drugs (other than cocaine, alcohol and tobacco), versus 6.9% of the Amsterdam I sam-ple. Similarly, only 9.9% of our respondents report a last two weeks prevalence of 0 drugs, versus 45.0% of the Amsterdam sample.

While the high-level users in Amsterdam scored higher in life time prevalence of three or more drugs, we did not find such consistent figures.[7] On the other hand, we did find differences between low, medium and high levels of use for the prevalence of certain kinds of drugs. High-level users show a considerable higher prevalence of the use of amphetamines, LSD and sedatives, although not statistically significant. High level users show a statistically significant higher prevalence of the use of opiates ($\chi2=6.809$; df=2; p<0.05) and of hypnotics ($\chi2=12.489$; df=2; p< 0.005) than medium and low level users.

Table 8.4.a   Life time prevalence and last two weeks prevalence of other drugs than cocaine, alcohol, tobacco, amphetamines and MDMA, per level of use in period of heaviest use, in the 1997 Antwerp sample and the 1987 Amsterdam I sample, in %

	Amsterdam I (1987)						
	Life time prevalence					Last 2 weeks	
No. of	Low	Medium	High	Total		Total	
drugs	N=77	N=49	N=33	N	%	N	%
0 drug	6.5	10.2	3.0	11	6.9	72	45.0
1 drug	40.3	42.9	15.2	57	35.6	83	51.9
2 drugs	22.1	16.3	15.2	31	19.4	3	1.8
3 drugs	14.3	16.3	24.2	27	16.9	2	1.2
4 drugs	9.1	8.2	21.2	18	11.3	-	-
5 drugs	7.8	6.1	18.2	15	9.4	-	-
6 drugs	-	-	3.0	1	0.6	-	-
Total	100.0	100.0	100.0	160	100.1	160	99.9

	Antwerp (1997)						
	Life time prevalence					Last 2 weeks	
No. of	Low	Medium	High	Total		total	
drugs	N=24	N=32	N=55	N	%	N	%
0 drug	-	-	-	-	-	11	9.9
1 drug	4.2	15.6	1.8	7	6.3	56	50.5
2 drugs	41.7	9.4	10.8	19	17.1	30	27.0
3 drugs	20.8	28.1	14.5	22	19.8	10	9.0
4 drugs	12.5	15.6	16.4	17	15.3	4	3.6
5 drugs	16.7	3.1	41.8	28	25.2	-	-
6 drugs	4.2	28.1	14.5	18	16.2	-	-
7 drugs	-	-	-	-	-	-	-
8 drugs	-	-	-	-	-	-	-
Total	100.1	99.9	99.9	111	99.9	111	100.0

We can legitimately conclude that our Antwerp sample reports more poly-drug use than the Amsterdam sample. This becomes even more obvious when we also add the replies on life time prevalence and last two weeks prevalence of amphetamines and MDMA (see table 8.4.b). Life time prevalences of zero, one or two drugs (other than cocaine, alcohol and tobacco) are quite rare in our sample, and a life time prevalence of 7 drugs is reported by 27.0%; a life time prevalence of 8 drugs by 11.7% of our respondents.

Table 8.4.b.   Life time prevalence and last two weeks prevalence of other drugs than cocaine, alcohol and tobacco, per level of use in top period, in the 1997 Antwerp sample, in %

	Antwerp (1997)						
	Life time prevalence					Last 2 weeks	
No. of	Low	Medium	High	Total		total	
drugs	N=24	N=32	N=55	N	%	N	%
0 drug	-	-	-	-	-	6	5.4
1 drug	-	3.1	-	1	0.9	42	37.8
2 drugs	4.2	-	1.8	2	1.8	24	21.6
3 drugs	8.3	15.6	1.8	8	7.2	24	21.6
4 drugs	37.5	6.3	12.7	18	16.2	13	11.7
5 drugs	16.7	31.2	14.5	22	19.8	1	0.9
6 drugs	12.5	12.5	18.2	17	15.3	1	0.9
7 drugs	16.7	12.5	40.0	30	27.0	-	-
8 drugs	4.2	18.7	10.9	13	11.7	-	-
Total	100.1	99.9	99.9	111	99.9	111	100.0

Again, we do not find a significant relation between level of use and life time prevalence of three or more drugs.[8] It is as if poly-drug use is not related to level of cocaine use, but to other (set and setting) factors... This does not mean that our respondents are *permanent* poly-drug users. The data support the hypothesis that the Antwerp respondents have experience with many types of drugs, i.e. they are 'multi-drug users'. These data do not prove that the respondents use all these types of drugs on the same occasion.

In table 8.4.c, we examine last two weeks prevalences of other drugs in the Antwerp sample and the Amsterdam I sample. In the second column we exclude amphetamines and MDMA from our figures. In the third column we also exclude cannabis. Comparison with the Amsterdam figures shows that the differences in last two weeks prevalence of other drugs can be largely explained by the fact that we asked for two more drugs, and by the nearly omnipresence of cannabis in our sample.

Table 8.4.c. Comparison of last two weeks prevalence of other drugs in the 1997 Antwerp sample and the 1987 Amsterdam I sample, in %

No. of drugs	Amsterdam I		Antwerp [♦]		Antwerp [♥]	
	Last two weeks prevalence					
	N	%	N	%	N	%
0 drug	72	45.0	11	9.9	62	55.9
1 drug	83	51.9	56	50.5	31	27.9
2 drugs	3	1.8	30	27.0	14	12.6
3 drugs	2	1.2	10	9.0	4	3.6
4 drugs	-	-	4	3.6	-	-
5 drugs	-	-	-	-	-	-
Total	**160**	**99.9**	**111**	**100.0**	**111**	**100.0**

[♦] MDMA and amphetamines excluded
[♥] MDMA, amphetamines and cannabis excluded

This clearly shows that our sample have a lot of experience with all kinds of drugs. It is especially noteworthy that the use of cannabis is completely 'normalized' in our sample. We strongly suspect this to be true for a much broader population. First, all epidemiological data available in Belgium show that cannabis is the most often mentioned illicit substance by people who report having used (or are still using) illegal drugs (Van Daele & Casselman, 1997; Van Daele *et al.*, 1996; Wydoodt & Noels, 1996: 95; Wydoodt & Booms, 1997: 108). Second, most population surveys focus on schoolgoing youth, thus excluding drop-outs, recent graduates and adults. Cautious attempts to extrapolate from these fragmentary population surveys to the total population have led to estimations of the total number of cannabis users at around 100,000 (Van Scharen, 1997: 12). In his book on the cannabis policy in Belgium, Van Scharen (1997) quotes several drug experts who assert the 'normalized' status of cannabis in a broad spectrum of subcultures.

Finally, it would be wrong to conclude that our respondents are permanently taking 'drug cocktails' (i.e. combining several types of drugs on the same occasion). Our figures merely show that these users have experimented with several drugs (and probably used some of them on a regular basis). But the qualitative material in the next paragraph shows that respondents have clear ideas (and informal rules) about which drugs can be combined, and which substances should not!

8.5. SUITABLE AND UNSUITABLE COMBINATIONS OF SUBSTANCES

We asked our respondents which combinations of cocaine and other drugs they perceived as advantageous (this paragraph) and why (paragraph 8.6). Table 8.5.a shows the combinations that are perceived as advantageous. The category 'other' contains two answers: 'with 2C-B'[9] and 'with poppers'[10]. The category 'hypnotics/sedatives' includes substances like Rohypnol®, Valium®... [11] The top three combinations are [cocaine + alcohol], [cocaine + cannabis], and [cocaine + opiates (mostly heroin)]. The former two are not only perceived as advantageous, they are in fact often or regularly used together (see Table 8.3.b).

Table 8.5.a   Advantageous combinations of cocaine with other drugs, in %, in the 1997 Antwerp sample [*]

Cocaine with	Antwerp (N=111)	
	N	%
Alcohol	49	44.1
Cannabis	44	39.6
Opiates	24	21.6
Amphetamines	16	14.4
MDMA	15	13.5
Hypnotics/sedatives	10	9.0
Tobacco	5	4.5
LSD	4	3.6
Other	2	1.8
No answer	*17*	*15.3*

[*] More than one answer was possible

As to the latter combination, it should be noted that these users do not regularly combine cocaine and heroin. As we illustrate below with qualitative data, some of our respondents experienced 'merits' of this combination, but they have concluded that it is 'too good'.

> *I didn't do snowballs often, you know, a blessing perhaps. That was after I said: I'm gonna quit. That's so strong that you get hooked to it very easily and very fast, in my view.* [H/0/26]

So it is for reasons of self-protection that these people do not repeat the experiment. Moreover, our findings in table 8.3.b already illustrated that only 21.6% of our sample often or regularly combine the use of cocaine and opiates.

The least mentioned combinations are [cocaine + LSD] and [cocaine + tobacco]. Table 8.3.b shows the former combination is actually only rarely used. But although [cocaine + tobacco] is only mentioned by 5 respondents as an advantageous combination, it is actually used often or regularly by 92.8% of our sample. Explanations given by most respondents seldom refer to any advantages, but rather to their physical dependence on nicotine or the habituation to tobacco:

> *I do notice that I want to smoke more the first half hour. To me, those cigarettes taste better, it's like a cigarette after dinner or after having sex, these are the cigarettes I really enjoy, their taste.* [E/0/01]

> *There's no advantage to the coke-cigarettes combination. It's a sheer habit, I think. You smoke more, but it's like when you drink alcohol, then you smoke more too.* [X/0/01]

Of course, we also asked our respondents which combinations of cocaine and other drugs they perceived as disadvantageous (see table 8.5.b). Here, the residual category 'other' contains two answers: 'with coffee' and 'with fruit juice'. The top three of disadvantageous combinations were [cocaine + alcohol], [cocaine + MDMA], and [cocaine + opiates]. If we compare these data with table 8.3.b, we find that although [cocaine + alcohol] is the disadvantageous combination most mentioned, it is used often or regularly by 80.2% of our sample. On the other hand, MDMA, amphetamines and opiates are perceived as not suitable for combination with cocaine, and they are in fact used often or regularly by one fifth to one quarter of our sample.

Table 8.5.b   Disadvantageous combinations of cocaine with other drugs, in %, in the 1997 Antwerp sample [*]

Antwerp (N=111)		
Cocaine with	N	%
Alcohol	25	22.5
MDMA	20	18.0
Opiates	17	15.3
Amphetamines	16	14.4
LSD	12	10.8
Cannabis	10	9.0
Tobacco	5	4.5
Hypnotics/sedatives	4	3.6
Other	2	1.8
No answer	*42*	*37.8*

[*] More than one answer was possible

In chapter 6 we showed that the number of respondents giving (dis)advantages of injecting was larger than that of those who actually had tried this route of ingestion.[12] With reference to suitable and unsuitable combinations of drugs, we can observe the same phenomenon: the number of respondents giving (un)suitable combinations of cocaine with other drugs is larger than that of those who actually tried these specific combinations.[13] Again some respondents clearly do not speak from their own experience.[14] The analysis of the reasons why certain combinations of cocaine with other substances are perceived as advantageous or disadvantageous will shed more light on this issue (see §8.6).

Finally, it must be noted that both [cocaine + alcohol] and [cocaine + opiates] rank in the top three of advantageous and of disadvantageous combinations. This may seem contradictory at first sight, but we have argued above that the [cocaine + alcohol] combination is functional in an outgoing lifestyle because it extends the 'party' and is therefore advantageous to many users. However, it is often perceived as disadvantageous at the same time by the same users: cocaine and alcohol prompt the user to take more of both substances, which results in a 'double' hangover the next day (i.e. headache, nausea, diarrhea, etc.). Furthermore, some respondents see [alcohol + cocaine] as a dangerous combination because they believe it is associated with total 'loss of control' over oneself, it may cause heart palpitations and, possibly, an overdose (cardiac arrest). On the other hand, [cocaine + opiates] may seem advantageous to some (heroin using) respondents because of its intense and pleasant effects, while it may seem disadvantageous to others for the same reason: too intense and/or too pleasant.

8.6. RULES OF (COMBINED) USE

In chapter 6 we interpreted the opinions of respondents as the equivalent of certain rules.[15] Cohen (1989: 66) argued that from this perspective, rules of use might be the balance of perceived advantages and disadvantages, irrespective of the factual correctness of these perceptions. As to the (un)suitable combination of cocaine with other drugs, we can distill some rules of (combined) use as constructions made out of a mix of perceived effects of the drug and of social conventions about specific combinations.

We identified about nine categories of rules, which are illustrated below with some qualitative data: (1) Rules for continuation; (2) Rules for 'coming down'; (3) Rules for maximization of positive effects; (4) Rules for management of finances; (5) Rules for minimizing adverse effects while using; (6) Specific taboos; (7) General taboos; (8) Rules for minimizing the risk of an overdose; and (9) Rules reflecting a learning process.

This typology is an ideal-typical construction by the author and some of these categories may in fact overlap.[16] Furthermore, any one who attempts to construct this type of typology of informal control mechanisms is walking on thin ice. The accounts of respondents on suitable and unsuitable combinations may be interspersed with myths, factual experiences and retrospective rationalizations, etc. and it may be difficult to assess the scientific status of reports of perceived effects... At least, the interviewees' accounts reflect a kind of folk model of drug effects, i.e. an idea of how specific (combinations of) drugs are perceived by users and how this user-folkore might influence individual drug use patterns.

8.6.1. Rules for continuation

Many of the respondents' statements about suitable and unsuitable combinations of cocaine and other substances refer to mechanisms aiming at the prolongation of the festive atmosphere. According to these people, combinations such as cocaine and MDMA, cocaine and speed, and cocaine and alcohol are highly instrumental in an outgoing lifestyle. Rather than the use of cocaine alone, these combinations help to extend the user's stamina (endurance) and sociability, and the party atmosphere in general.

> *Because coke makes the effect of XTC last longer, sometimes, and because it makes you not fall down completely, or withdraw into a corner. So you can party even more.* [I/1/12]

> *Coke and speed: you feel good and it lasts longer with speed. Compared to just coke: I used to take two lines: one of coke and one of speed. It's better and it lasts longer.* [Z/0/01]

> *If you just drink alcohol, you get drunk in the end, until you drop with exhaustion. But with coke, you feel good, you're not drunk at once, so you can talk more, you can keep going on all night, you can...* [C/0/05]

8.6.2. Rules for 'coming down'

Many of the disadvantages that our respondents mentioned (see chapter 6) concern adverse effects when the cocaine's action ends. As a kind of self-medication for negative after-effects such as insomnia, restlessness, depression, and unpleasant physical effects, some people take other substances to 'come down' after the use of cocaine. For this purpose, the combined use of cocaine and 'downers' (cannabis, heroine, sedatives, hypnotics or alcohol) appears to be the rule. Furthermore, this combination helps some people to offset feelings of craving for (more) cocaine.

The alcohol slightly dampens the desire for more, and I use hash to really ease up and to be able to sleep. [Q/0/01]

With heroin because it gives you a smooth landing, that's an advantage. The same if you take a sedative to... be not too worked up. Also with hash or weed, right? [H/0/01]

And then, at the end of the night, a smoke [i.e. cannabis, TD] *will bring you right down, as a downer, as a kind of sleeping pill, that kinda brings you down, and you're not so high, so you can go home and you can fall asleep.* [S/0/01]

I'm only after the orgasm, that feeling to be one with the universe, so to speak. But then I have a period of being restless, and sometimes also feelings of anxiety, and then that downer [heroin or Valium] can calm me down. [F/0/01]

People can experience adverse effects *while* they are using cocaine. We decided to distinguish arbitrary separate categories of rules for minimizing adverse effects during the 'high' of cocaine (see below, §8.6.5) and for minimizing adverse effects *after* using cocaine (when 'coming down').

8.6.3. Rules for maximisation of positive effects

A major reason why two or more drugs are combined is of course the exploration of pleasurable experiences. Combinations such as cocaine and cannabis, cocaine and heroin, cocaine and LSD, cocaine and MDMA, and cocaine and alcohol are despised by some people, but praised by others. For the latter, these drugs perfectly fit together, because they reinforce positive effects like euphoria, clear thinking, relaxed feeling, etc... Two respondents called it 'candy-flipping': the combined use of two drugs that are both pleasurable:

Coke and heroin are two extremes, and you are somewhere in between. Not really assertive, but being able to talk, kinda dreamy anyway, the combination of both. [L/0/01]

"Candyflipping" is a term we use when we take LSD and XTC together: the combination of two trips, which you both like, yes, it can't be bad. I think it also holds for coke and LSD, and coke and weed. It all becomes trip-like then, and I like it very much. I think it gives you a better perspective on things. Some people are surprised when I say things like that. I also think these things help you to get to know yourself, especially with coke. You feel very distant from things, and yes, sometimes you're surprised about yourself, how it all works inside your head, and what you do with yourself. It's great. [R/1/02]

With XTC, because they are a perfect match. Because XTC usually gives me a kind of peace, even if I'm dancing like a fool, or whatever, and coke doesn't have that, so I'm also clear, but more 'in action', and that combination is exactly in between, it's perfect. [R/0/04]

Coke and alcohol, it enhances that feeling, because alcohol makes you more sociable, you talk more too, it sometimes makes it easier to have fun too. [I/1/09]

I find it fun to take a line and then smoke some weed, and then again a line. To reach a wavy effect, that it alternates. You can reach a kind of constant with that, which you direct yourself, so you can perfectly flow along with everything. [H/0/30]

8.6.4. Rules for management of finances [17]

Some respondents state that they combine the use of cocaine and amphetamines, or cocaine and MDMA for financial reasons. According to them, 'speed' and MDMA prolong the action of cocaine, and therefore a smaller dose or quantity of cocaine is sufficient to reach the desired effects:

Every now and then, I combine cocaine with XTC, simply because... it makes the effects of cocaine last longer. And it's not that expensive. [C/0/12]

So, first speed and then coke. I like that best, financially, it's also more economical. [I/1/16]

8.6.5. Rules for minimizing adverse effects while using

Analogous with the minimization of adverse effects *after* the use of cocaine (see §8.6.2), the so-called 'coming down from coke', people can also experience adverse effects *while* using a drug. Apparently, using some other drug can counteract these negative feelings or effects. Some people use cocaine to soften the intoxicating effect of alcohol, to dim the agitation of speed or hallucinogens, etc. And conversely, cannabis or alcohol is sometimes used to dampen the stimulating effects of cocaine.

On the one hand, coke curbs the psychedelic action of certain drugs too. Which makes it interesting for certain people. [...] Actually, coke has a stabilizing and comforting action, together with that euphoric component. So, it is actually a very good drug to, yes, use drugs in a reasonably normal way, so to prolong certain effects and to bring down the flash a little, so to stabilize everything so you can use it longer. [R/0/01]

If you are really drunk and you take a line of coke, then you feel somewhat more sober. If you are really out because of pills or trips, and you feel kinda bad, you take a line of coke and you feel somewhat better. As with speed, if you've taken too much speed, coke will calm you down. [G/1/03]

For example, when I take an XTC, and it starts acting too hard, I take a line of coke, and I'm perfectly controlled again. Coke is more a regulator, so to speak: when you are too drunk or when you are too far out, it brings you back into balance. [C/0/09]

In general, hash or weed calms the coke, so it stagnates your drug, and that's how you determine your rhythm. If I become restless or something, I will not take another line, I will smoke a joint, to be at ease. That's how you can determine how you feel. If you know it, you know how to use it... [C/0/06]

8.6.6. Specific taboos

A lot of our respondents have informal rules about certain combinations of cocaine and other drugs. These rules mostly take the form of a taboo: 'these two drugs must not be used together'. Reasons for these taboos vary endlessly, but their rationale is often that certain combinations are not done because they are too intense, too pleasurable, and therefore too dangerous, too tempting. The example usually given is that of cocaine and heroin.

> *Coke and heroin... I think, if you start doing that too much, you will want to go on. I think if you do that too much, you will want to shoot it up, you will want to know what the needle does.* [Y/0/01)

> *Coke and heroin... I mean, if you start to like that, you're on the wrong track.* [B/1/01]

We also found indications of taboos on other combinations (cocaine + cannabis; cocaine + MDMA; cocaine + LSD; cocaine + amphetamines). Reasons for these restrictions are usually inspired by the subjective perception that 'uppers' and 'downers' are not to be combined because 1) one drug neutralizes the action of another; or 2) these combinations are supposed to give strong adverse effects:

> *Using hash and coke, that is completely contradictory. If I smoked a joint and then take coke, I really wouldn't feel good, it would be terrible. It would be quite frightening.* [K/0/01]

> *I think you can't for example combine coke with XTC because each dissolves the other. You can't mix them, because then you don't feel either anymore.* [I/1/14]

> *Coke and LSD are two opposite things: LSD opens and coke closes. So you will get in a paranoid condition.* [H/0/22]

8.6.7. General taboos

Some respondents refuse to combine the use of cocaine with any other drug (although they admit having used other drugs at other occasions). Their philosophy seems to be twofold: 1) one can only get to the bottom of a drug's mysteries if it is used in its pure form, excluding every interaction with effects of other drugs; and 2) combined use of drugs is more harmful than the use of a single drug.

> *I think coke in itself is better. It all comes into your body, and you shouldn't mix too much, to my opinion, it's not good.* [H/1/07]

> *I think that, if you use something, you should use it in a pure form. That's why I'm also opposed to the use of cannabis with tobacco, because it is bullshit too, so to speak. These are principles.* [H/0/27]

8.6.8. Rules for minimizing the risk of an overdose

According to some respondents, combinations such as cocaine and alcohol, cocaine and speed, and cocaine and LSD are not done because they increase the risk of an overdose.

> *Normally, drugs and alcohol don't go together too well, do they? It's either the one or the other, right? If you combine them, that might be the deciding factor. Your heart will pump more, and the risk of getting a cardiac arrest is higher.* [C/0/06]

*Combining with speed or so, that is crazy. People who do that don't know what they're do-
ing. It's too strong, your heart can't handle that. Or with LSD or XTC, that's not okay. Two
stimulants together is not good. [L/0/02]*

8.6.9. Rules that reflect a learning process from bad experiences

People often experiment with several combinations of substances. Afterwards, they
make a balance and avoid those combinations that proved to be disadvantageous. Some
of our respondents had bad experiences (unpleasant physical feelings, aggressive feelings) with the combined use of cocaine and speed, cocaine and MDMA, and cocaine
and alcohol, and decided not to use these any longer.

When things like that happen to me, I just don't do that anymore, you know [she thinks] .
Coke and speed gives you a bad feeling. Not a nice feeling. [H/\/18]

*I've tried coke and XTC once, just out of curiosity, and then I thought: no, that's not for me.
I became completely dizzy, and I started shaking and stuff. Then I thought: no. I was glad to
be home really, to be alone for a moment. I won't do that anymore. [I/0/13]*

*With alcohol, I'm afraid that I'll be completely bound up in it, that I will lose control over
myself. I really don't know what I'm doing then. So it's better not to. I don't drink anymore,
right, I quit drinking, so I don't think that combination is... It's not in that controllable zone
anymore, so that's why I will not mix opposites... [I/1/04]*

8.7. CONCLUSION

In this chapter we have investigated the use of other drugs apart from cocaine and the
use of cocaine in combination with other drugs by our Antwerp sample. We have presented some qualitative data on combinations of cocaine with other drugs that are regarded as (un)suitable by our respondents.

Despite a number of methodological difficulties, the comparison of data on life time
prevalence in several European and American community studies of cocaine users
shows that the data of the present study are consistent with those of other studies in
that they reflect a similar hierarchy of types of drugs. Alcohol, tobacco, cannabis and
MDMA are the four drugs most often used. Life time prevalences of solvents, opiates,
sedatives and hypnotics are lower than life time prevalences of other illegal substances.
However, compared to most other cities the Antwerp respondents claim to have more
experience with most types of drugs.

The data from the Antwerp sample and from other community samples of cocaine
users indicate that only a minority use cocaine by itself, whereas most combine the use
of cocaine with other drugs. Clearly, cocaine is not an isolated drug used by a separate
group or subculture of individuals who are exclusively dedicated to one drug. Cocaine
is embedded in various drug using subcultures, where different types of people use it
together with many other substances and where it may have various functions. In short,
there is no such thing as 'the' cocaine scene or 'the' cocaine user.

Alcohol, tobacco and cannabis are the drugs most often used in combination with
cocaine, irrespective of level of use. Most authors assert that the role of alcohol in particular is significant, above all when the cocaine is being used for social purposes or as

part of the relationship with friends. Cocaine and alcohol emerge as complementary drugs. Cannabis is often used for relaxing after heavy use of cocaine and alcohol. According to most authors cocaine and MDMA are rarely combined. However, we find that MDMA is important: in total prevalence of *combined use* it ranks fourth after cannabis. About one quarter of our respondents often or regularly combine cocaine with MDMA, irrespective of their level of use.

Conversely, our data and those of other community studies indicate that the combined use of cocaine with opiates, sedatives and hypnotics is related to a high level of use during period of heaviest use. Although total prevalences of combined use of cocaine with sedatives, hypnotics and opiates are important in the Antwerp sample, other authors have associated this phenomenon with levels of use and with (former) heroin addiction. Finally, combined use of cocaine and solvents was *not* reported by our respondents. Combined use of cocaine and LSD was reported by some respondents, but for most of these it was rare. Other studies come to similar conclusions: cocaine is not often mixed with LSD, although such a combination has its devotees.

From the analysis of poly-drug use (i.e. reporting a life time prevalence of more than one drug), it is clear that our sample has a lot of experience with all kinds of drugs. It is especially noteworthy that the use of cannabis is completely 'normalized' in our sample. Data from other studies suggest this to be the case for a much broader population. Finally, it would be wrong to conclude that our respondents are continuously taking 'drug cocktails' (i.e. combining several types of drugs on the same occasion). Our figures merely show that these users have experimented with several drugs (and probably used some of them on a regular basis).

Our qualitative material shows that respondents have clear ideas (and informal rules) about which drugs can be combined, and which substances must not be combined. The top three advantageous combinations are [cocaine + alcohol], [cocaine + cannabis], and [cocaine + opiates (mostly heroin)]. The top three disadvantageous combinations are [cocaine + alcohol], [cocaine + MDMA], and [cocaine + opiates]. The respondents' accounts reflect a kind of folk model of drug effects and drug combinations, which can influence individual drug use patterns.

Like with routes of ingestion, we observe that the number of respondents giving (un)suitable combinations of cocaine with other drugs is larger than the number of people who actually tried these specific combinations. Clearly, some respondents do not speak from their own experience. Opinions of respondents can be interpreted as the equivalent of certain rules. Fom this perspective, rules of use might be the balance of perceived advantages and disadvantages, irrespective of the factual correctness of these perceptions. As to the (un)suitable combination of cocaine with other drugs, we have distilled some rules of (combined) use, as constructions made out of a mix of perceived effects of the drug and social conventions about specific combinations. We roughly identified nine categories of rules: (1) Rules for continuation; (2) Rules for 'coming down'; (3) Rules for maximization of positive effects; (4) Rules for management of finances; (5) Rules for minimizing adverse effects while using; (6) Specific taboos; (7) General taboos; (8) Rules for minimizing the risk of an overdose; and (9) Rules reflecting a learning process.

NOTES

1   See Chapter 4, p. 99-100.

2   See Chapter 5, p. 141-142.

3   Cohen's findings (1989: 69) were virtually identical in this respect. We could add some data on the combined use of cocaine with MDMA and amphetamines.

4   See p. 208-209.

5   See Chapter 14, p. 310-312 and 317-322.

6   This difference could not be tested statistically because numbers were too small.

7   High-level users are only distinguished in the categories of having used 4 drugs, while medium-level users clearly report more frequently a life time prevalence of 1 drug, 3 drugs and 6 drugs. Low-level users in our sample are distinguished in the category of having used 2 drugs.

8   High-level users are distinguished in the categories of '6 drugs' or '7 drugs', while low-level users report more frequently a life time prevalence of '4 drugs', and medium-level users report more frequently a life time prevalence of '3 drugs', '5 drugs' and '8 drugs'.

9   '2C-B' is a designer drug that is often associated with the use of MDMA ('XTC'). The official name is 4-bromo-2,5-dimethoxyphenethylamine, but it became popular in the United States under names such as 'Nexus', 'Spectrum', 'Zenith' and 'Bromo'. 2C-B can be snorted, but it is usually taken in the form of pills. Its effects have been described as a cross between the effects of LSD and MDMA, but nothing like a combination of the two. It is mildly psychedelic, much less mind-expanding or dissociative than mushrooms or LSD, but much less directed than MDMA. The effects last 4 to 8 hours. (Sources: EVENEPOEL, T. (1996), 2C-B duikt op in Vlaanderen, *Nieuwsbrief Verslaving*, nr. 96/6, 7-8. And: http://www.erowid.org/entheogens/2cb).

10   'Poppers' (also known as Amyl Nitrate; Butyl Nitrate; n-Nitrate; Amys or Rush) are yellowish liquids which evaporate at room temperature. The liquids smell sweet and fruity. When first used as a medicine, amyl nitrate came in a small glass capsule encased in cotton wool. As it was crushed between the fingers it made a popping noise –giving the nitrites one of their present-day street names. Most nitrites sold these days are in small screw top bottles, under brand names such as 'Liquid Gold', 'Ram' and 'Thrust'. They are commonly sold in sex shops. Sniffing 'poppers' makes the user light headed. Users may get the feeling of blood rushing to the head, a heat flush and increased sensual awareness. These effects may last less than one minute and are unlikely to last more than two. Some side effects include headaches, nausea, coughing and dizziness. (Source: http://area51.upsu.plym.ac.uk/infoserv/drugs/graphical).

11   The 'opiates' category contains one respondent who reported the combined use of Valtran® (an opiate) with cocaine.

12   See Chapter 6, §6.4.2 (p. 161) and §6.4.4. (p. 164-165).

13   Some examples: of the 12 respondents who had never combined cocaine and alcohol, 3 mentioned this combination as disadvantageous. Of the 64 respondents who had never combined cocaine and amphetamines, 8 mentioned this combination as disadvantageous. Of the 56 respondents who had never combined cocaine and MDMA, 6 mentioned this combination as disadvantageous. Of the 72 respondents who had never combined cocaine and opiates, 7 mentioned this combination as disadvantageous, etc.

14   These data may also reflect existing stereotypes about other users. See: FINNIGAN, F. (1996), How non-heroin users perceive heroin users and how heroin users perceive themselves, 4 *Addiction Research* 1, 25-32.

15   See Chapter 6, §6.4.4, p. 164-165.

16   We were also confronted with an endless range of idiosyncratic reasons for using certain combinations. It is precisely because of the lack of opportunity for culturally based learning about controlled drug use in general (and the controlled use of combinations of drugs) that informal rules tend to be idiosyncratic (Zinberg, 1984: 80).

17   These rules for management of finances can also be seen as rules for continuation (see §8.6.1, p. 208). Through the prolongation of the effects from cocaine, they reduce the cost of the drug experience.

CHAPTER 9

BUYING COCAINE

9.1. INTRODUCTION

Any illegal drug is used within the context of supply and demand. This chapter presents mainly qualitative data on buying cocaine (some data on selling cocaine are discussed in Chapter 13). Starting from the (subjective) experiences of users who buy their cocaine, the following issues are discussed: price variations (§9.2), sources and location of cocaine purchase (§9.3) and user lore (i.e. knowledge) on (types of) cocaine (§9.4). Qualitative data on the reliability of dealers (as perceived by respondents), and on the experience of being ripped off, are presented in paragraphs 9.5 and 9.6.

9.2. PRICES

We asked our respondents how much they had to pay per gram of cocaine during the last four weeks preceding the interview, or how much they would have had to pay. Only 44 of our respondents had actually bought some cocaine during the last four weeks, but 107 people knew the current average price of cocaine. Three Antwerp respondents did not know average price, and 1 stated that she had never had to pay for her cocaine. In Figure 9.2.a, we show the replies of the 107 respondents who knew the current average price of 1 gram of cocaine.

One respondent reported paying an average 300 BEF (BEF) for 1 gram of cocaine, but he was clearly talking about average cocaine price in Mexico, his home country. As this answer was irrelevant to the Belgian situation, we decided to exclude it. The remaining sub-sample of 106 respondents yields an average price of exactly 2,300 BEF for 1 gram of cocaine. The range was between 1,000 and 4,500 BEF. Standard deviation was 502.7, so we can conclude that most cocaine prices fluctuate between 1,800 and 2,800 BEF (at the time of our fieldwork: August 1996 – April 1997).

To find out why some people pay either markedly less or more than the average prices, we checked the respondents who reported an average price of 1 gram of cocaine of 1,500 BEF or less, and those who reported an average price of 3,500 BEF or more. Apart from the Mexican respondent described above, we found that 1 respondent paid on average 1,000 BEF per gram: he used to be a professional dealer, importing cocaine to Belgium by dozens of kilos. One respondent usually buys his cocaine in Rotterdam (the Netherlands), where he has a regular dealer. Because he buys in large amounts (approx. 10 gs), he pays 1,400 BEF per gram. One respondent usually paid 1,500 BEF:

he used to be a sailor, and also reported having often sold cocaine. And finally, a fourth respondent who has often sold cocaine usually paid 1,350 BEF per gram.

Figure 9.2.a   Current price (in BEF) of 1 gram of cocaine in Antwerp (1997), in percentage of sub-sample that knew the price (N=107)

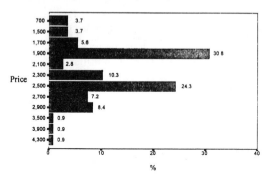

At the other extreme, we find 1 respondent who usually pays 3,500 BEF, 1 that usually pays 4,000 BEF, and 1 reporting an average price of 4,500 BEF per gram. Neither the semi-structured interviews nor the open interviews yielded any contextual information on why these respondents paid such high prices for their cocaine. One of them mainly bought his cocaine in the Netherlands, and one of them mainly bought hers via friends.

In the 1987 Amsterdam I study, an average price of 1 gram cocaine of 180 NLG (Dutch guilders) was found (Cohen, 1989: 72). In the 1991 Amsterdam II study, the average price of a gram of cocaine had dropped from 180 to 140 NLG in the four years since 1987 (Cohen & Sas, 1995: 67). To make our findings and those of Amsterdam perfectly comparable, we retrieved Cohen's rough data of 1987 and 1991, and recomputed them following a 2-step procedure:

1) The rough data of the Amsterdam I sub-sample who knew price (N=102) were corrected for average exchange rate in 1987 (1 NLG = 18.35 BEF);

2) These data were corrected for the average inflation rate from February 1987 (date of the Amsterdam interviews) to June 1997 (date of our interviews), which was approx. 2.33%.[1]

The same procedure was applied to the rough data of the 1991 Amsterdam II sub-sample who knew price (N=98), using the average exchange rate of 1991 (1 NLG = 18.30 BEF) and the average inflation rate from January 1991 to June 1997 (approx. 2.34%).

For 1 gram of cocaine, we found an average price of 3,374.4 BEF in the Amsterdam I sample (1987); an average price of 2,974.2 BEF in the Amsterdam II sample (1991); and as mentioned above, an average price of 2,300 BEF in the Antwerp sample (1997).

What do these data tell us? Many of a nation's anti-drug efforts have been directed at increasing the price of illicit drugs by intercepting drugs at the nation's borders and by disrupting drug markets within its borders. Price data can be an adequate means to evaluate interventions, to analyze alternative policies, and to give early notice of changes in supply and/or consumption patterns. Unfortunately, price data of illicit drugs have not been effectively collected, reported, and analyzed (Caulkins, 1994a).

Furthermore, prices vary over time, between cities, and even within a single city at one time. There is even variability across purchases made by a single user (Caulkins, 1994b). Transactions vary in quantity and quality (principally purity). Recently, several efforts to construct price series have concurred in their treatment of some aspects of the price data (e.g. using a log-linear adjustment for *transaction size*), but have adjusted differently for purity (e.g. quantity is all that matters versus the expected purity hypothesis) (Rhodes *et al.*, 1994; Farell *et al.*, 1996; Caulkins, 1994a).

To complete our data on the average price of cocaine, further research into purchase patterns, prices (at different market levels), various sizes of transactions, actual purity and expected purity (by consumers) is needed. We can, however, draw some conclusions.

Price per gram at different market levels can differ dramatically. Consumers pay more per unit than retailers do to wholesalers, and retailers pay more per unit than wholesalers do to importers. This is logical because, just like for licit products, expenses are incurred moving the cocaine from the wholesale to the retail level. The mark-ups are typically more pronounced for illicit drugs because the distribution risks are greater. The average price of 2,300 BEF for one gram of cocaine should be interpreted as a retail price, because most of our respondents were mere consumers. Those few respondents reporting a lower price of cocaine were usually involved in cocaine selling networks. Furthermore, the price of cocaine mentioned by our respondents typically refers to a 'packet' of cocaine, which usually contains less than 1 gram (0.9 or 0.8 g according to some respondents)[2] and which is typically adulterated.[3]

When comparing our data with those of Amsterdam, we find that the average price of cocaine has steadily decreased over the last decade. This conclusion is consistent with that of Farrell *et al.* (1996). Between 1983 and 1993, they found a general decline in prices of cocaine (and heroin) in European countries, particularly in retail prices. After adjusting retail prices in US dollars per gram for inflation to 1983 prices, Farrell *et al.* find the following price series for Belgium: 120 US$ in 1983, 108 US$ in 1984, 140 US$ in 1985, 73 US$ in 1986, 119 US$ in 1987, 102 US$ in 1988, 56 US$ in 1989, 66 US$ in 1991, 48 US$ in 1992, and 67 US$ in 1993. Adjusted for inflation to 1983 prices in US dollars, we find an average price of 44 US$ in our sample (in 1997).[4] Basic laws of supply and demand suggest that the fall in prices in Belgium and elsewhere across Europe is either due to a decrease in demand or to an increase in supply. Few would claim that demand for drugs in Europe decreased in the late 1980s and early 1990s. The falling prices are therefore almost certainly a consequence of increased supply.

According to the official figures from 1994 and 1995 the average price of cocaine of one gram of street cocaine is approx. 2,750 BEF (and ranges between 1,500 and 4,000 BEF). Our data confirm the price range (we find prices between 1,000 and 4,500 BEF), but the average price of cocaine according to our respondents (2,300 BEF) is clearly lower than the average price according to the official figures. It might be that criminal justice agencies tend to overestimate the impact of their actions on trafficking by publicizing the 'street value' of their large seizures – figures which are decidedly more dramatic than the corresponding wholesale value (Maguire & Flanagan, 1992). The impact of seizures should be assessed in replacement value, rather than in street value (Reuter, 1988).

9.3. SOURCES AND LOCATION OF PURCHASE

We investigated where our respondents normally bought cocaine: from a single dealer, from several dealers, or from friends (see Table 9.3.a). We encountered a great deal of suspicion when asking questions about sources and locations of purchase. Many respondents initially were anxious to know why we needed this information. Although the non-response rate was low, the figures should be interpreted cautiously. Some respondents might have deliberately lied or answered vaguely, for fear of being caught.

The main sources of cocaine in our sample were friends (37.8%) and regular dealers (35.1%). The findings from Amsterdam are almost identical to ours, but 8 persons from our sample specified that they bought their cocaine from a friend who was also a dealer. If we had included these 8 respondents in the category of 'regular dealer', this category would have been the main source in our sample (42.3%), and friends would rank second (30.6%), whereas in the Amsterdam samples the balance was the reverse.

Table 9.3.a   Main source of cocaine, in three samples

Source	Amsterdam I 1987		Amsterdam II 1991		Antwerp 1997	
	N	%	N	%	N	%
Friends	69	45.4	46	43.4	42	37.8
Regular dealer	47	30.9	33	31.1	39	35.1
Different dealers	27	17.8	11	10.4	25	22.5
No buying	-	-	14	13.2	4	3.6
Other	9	5.9	2	1.9	1	0.9
Total	**152**	**100.0**	**106**	**100.0**	**111**	**99.9**

We find that 22.5% of our respondents bought their cocaine from various dealers: this is slightly more than in the 1987 sample, and twice the proportion found in the 1991 sample. Four respondents stated they never paid for their cocaine, and one respondent imported cocaine by dozens of kgs (and obviously did not want to reveal his source of purchase).

Cohen (1989: 74) suggested that the dominance of friends or a single dealer in the purchase of cocaine was reflected by the very low percentage of respondents who checked the quality when buying (18% in his 1987 sample). Our sample revealed a much higher percentage of respondents testing their cocaine (41.4%).[5] This might be an indication that, although most respondents rely on friends or a regular dealer for the quality of their cocaine, this quality is highly unpredictable and/or subject to rapid changes. This explains why several testing methods (some of which are not very efficient) are used, even if the cocaine is bought from a 'reliable' source.

We investigated the location of cocaine purchase (Table 9.3.b).[6] The percentage of respondents who mainly bought their cocaine in a discotheque in our sample (2.7%), was even lower than that in both Amsterdam samples. This runs counter to the recent witch hunt by some Belgian police forces against the so-called 'disco drug tourism'. According to the advocates of such repressive police raids, hundreds of Dutch party goers come down to Belgian discotheques, because of the wider availability and better quality of drugs.[7] Our data show that Antwerp cocaine users do not buy their cocaine in discotheques, but prefer other locations.

Eighteen percent of our sample mainly bought their cocaine in a café/bar, which is more than in both Amsterdam samples. The proportion of users buying their cocaine at the dealer's home is similar in all three samples: 37.8% of our Antwerp respondents, 37.0% of the 1991 Amsterdam respondents and 45.0% of the 1987 Amsterdam respondents. We chose not to include all other answers in a residual category, but prefered to supply more detailed information on other locations of purchase: 18% of our respondents usually phoned a dealer and waited for him (or one of his runners) to deliver the order at home; 13.5% did not know a dealer personally and had to rely on friends to buy cocaine; 10.8% regularly traveled abroad (the Netherlands) to buy their cocaine;[8] 9.0% of our sample bought their cocaine mainly on the street (more specifically, two squares in the city of Antwerp that are 'known' as copping areas); and finally, 6.3% of our respondents usually contacted their dealer in advance, while the actual deal was done on a pre-arranged spot (this could be practically anywhere, even in another town).

Table 9.3.b   Location of purchase of cocaine, in three samples [*]

Location of purchase	A'dam I 1987		A'dam II 1991		Antwerp 1997	
	N	%	N	%	N	%
Dealer's home	72	45.0	40	37.0	42	37.8
Bar/café	13	8.1	13	12.0	20	18.0
Home delivery	-	-	-	-	20	18.0
Friends	-	-	-	-	15	13.5
Abroad	-	-	-	-	12	10.8
On the street	-	-	-	-	10	9.0
A pre-arranged place	-	-	-	-	7	6.3
'Coffeeshop'	-	-	2	1.8	-	-
Discotheque	19	11.9	4	3.7	3	2.7
Other [♠]	46	28.7	35	32.4	-	-
No answer	*10*	*6.2*	*14*	*13.0*	*2*	*1.8*

[*] More than 1 answer was possible

Sometimes cocaine is offered for free. Only one person of our sample reported never getting any cocaine free (see Table 9.3.c). For 88.2% of our respondents, friends were the main source. Almost 10% occasionally received cocaine as a present from their regular dealers, and 6.3% from various dealers. These figures are very similar to those in the 1987 Amsterdam I sample.

Table 9.3.c   Getting cocaine for free, in the 1997 Antwerp sample [*]

Antwerp		
Cocaine as a present	N	%
Friends	98	88.2
Regular dealer	11	9.9
Various dealers	7	6.3
Employer	1	0.9
Never	1	0.9
No answer	*1*	*0.9*

[*] More than 1 answer was possible

9.4. USER LORE ON (TYPES OF) COCAINE [9]

Early in our fieldwork in the Antwerp nightlife scene, a key informant told us about the existence of different 'types' of cocaine. It is generally known that there are several varieties of cannabis plants and various types of MDMA pills, but the existence of different types of cocaine came as a surprise. Therefore our respondents were asked during the second (open) interview about different types of cocaine. Although there is a considerable consensus among respondents on this issue, we prefer not to draw any conclusions about the veracity of their statements, i.e. whether their accounts correspond with biological and economic realities. To verify these stories, the present study would have to include interviews with coca farmers and/or reliable cocaine traders. From an ethnographic point of view, the coherence of these stories and the question whether and how they reflect the construction of a user lore on 'types' of cocaine are more important.

Table 9.4.a shows the 'types' of cocaine mentioned by the Antwerp respondents.[10] All res-pondents who claimed to have heard about different 'types' of cocaine answered in binary oppositions. In other words, all the types these participants mentioned referred to opposite types of cocaine, e.g. there is 'rock' cocaine and 'powdery' coke. Within these differences, one 'type' usually refers to good quality (left column) and the other to bad quality cocaine (right column).

Table 9.4.a   User lore of 'types' of cocaine, in the 1997 Antwerp sample

Good quality	Bad quality
<pure coke>	<adulterated or cut coke>
<white coke>	<yellowish coke> or <brownish coke>
<crystal coke>	<ordinary coke>
<Colombian coke>	<Peruvian coke> or <Venezuelan coke>
<rock> or <hard coke>	<powdery coke> or <soft coke>
<flakes> or <flamingo>	<powdery coke>
<sticky coke> or <moist coke>	<dry coke>
<natural coke>	<chemical coke> or <synthetic coke>
<glittering coke>	<dull coke>
<odourless coke>	<coke with a nasty smell>

Causal explanations by respondents for the differences between 'types' of cocaine may refer to the country of origin (there are several varieties of the coca plant) or to the country of production (the production process differs from one country to another), but mostly to the dealers. Thus, irrespective of the objective value of this typology of cocaine, its binary construction reflects the existence of user lore on cocaine. This knowledge on 'good' and 'bad' quality of cocaine helps the user to decide whether or not he/she will buy this or that 'cocaine' from a particular dealer. As such, user lore on (types of) cocaine and its quality can be an informal control mechanism.

Naturally, the effectiveness of this informal control may be hampered by several factors. First, it remains unsure whether these stories really reflect differences in quality and 'types' of cocaine. Second, the passing of this user lore on cocaine quality from one user, or generation of users, to another is complex. Some respondents report never having heard about different 'types' or 'qualities' of cocaine, other report contradictory stories (for some users <white coke> is synonym for pure, non-adulterated cocaine, whereas for others the white color is a full proof of adulteration). In short, there is a user lore on 'quality' of cocaine, but it is unevenly spread among users and it may be incomplete and, in some cases, false.

9.5. RELIABILITY OF DEALERS

Controlled users do not just look for dope, they look for a dealer in whom they have confidence (Zinberg, 1984: 164). Table 9.3.a showed that 35.1% of our respondents bought their cocaine from a regular dealer and 22.5% from various dealers. To form a picture of cocaine dealers we discussed this with our respondents during the second interview. Again, we encountered a great deal of suspicion, and 22 respondents preferred not to answer. It is clear, however, that almost all respondents take it for granted that the cocaine they buy is adulterated. Pure cocaine (i.e. 95% pure or more) cannot be found in this country, so they say. All respondents believe adulteration is an inevitable part of the illicit cocaine trade. This is confirmed by the accounts of respondents who sell (or have sold) cocaine themselves (see Chapter 10).[11]

Like with the construction of users' lore on 'types' of cocaine, a model of 'types' of cocaine dealers can be deduced from the stories and general descriptions of dealers by our respondents. For example, interviewees often distinguish between <sellers who are users themselves> and <sellers who are not using cocaine themselves>. Another frequently made distinction is that between <selling cocaine as an extra income> and <selling cocaine as a main occupation>. Although the respondents' accounts contained many idiosyncratic features (see also Zinberg, 1984: 80), two major types of 'dealers' could be derived from these stories. The first type is often referred to as <young>, <yuppie-like>, <dealing for the easy money>, <pushy> or <obtrusive>, <unreliable> or <incorrect>, and <with an extended run of customers>. The second type is often described as <old(er)>, <selling like a commercial merchant>, <unobtrusive>, <honest>, <settled> and <with a restricted number of customers>.

Respondents were asked whether they perceived the dealer(s) they knew as reliable. Although we did not define the concept of 'reliability' to the interviewees, we noticed that it was usually interpreted by the respondents in a narrow sense. For them, a 'reliable' seller is a person who sells cocaine of reasonable or good *quality* (not adulterated) and who is honest about the *quantity* he/she supplies (i.e. when one buys 1 g of cocaine, one gets the full gram).

> *When I ask for a gram, I must have a gram. They shouldn't give me 0.7 or 0.8, or they shouldn't mix it with speed or ground glass, they should just give what I asked. The quality, yes, they usually can't do anything about it, it comes a long way, you know, but they should give you what you asked for, or else I don't buy from them. [C/0/09]*

Of the 89 respondents who replied to this question, 37 perceived the dealer(s) they knew as 'reliable' (41.6%) while another 27 perceived the dealer(s) they knew as not reliable at all (30.4%). Twenty-three respondents claimed to know both reliable and unreliable dealers (25.8%), and 2 interviewees did not know (2.2%).

> *Those who really sell it to earn their living can sometimes end up in bad situations and then they become unreliable. Unreliable means to me: mixing their stuff which used to be so good and so pure, but which becomes less pure, although they keep saying it's good stuff. But when you know, you notice it. They would rip off their best friend, because they can't*

cope with it any longer, because they have landed in trouble themselves and so. And there are people who are really reliable, who I got a lot from even without paying for it. Just guys who were doing well in business, who didn't have to rip anyone off. [C/0/06]

'Unreliable dealers' are usually characterized by respondents as follows: strangers (e.g. in a discotheque); very young people; people who also sell heroin; people who earn their living selling cocaine; sellers who use cocaine themselves or who are addicted to it; dealers who operate on the street; people who are also involved in other types of crime (prostitution, burglary, con games, etc.); certain nationalities (black people, Jews, Moroccans, Belgians, etc.);... *'Reliable dealers'* are mostly described as: regular dealers; personal friends of the respondent or people he/she regularly uses cocaine with; older people; people who are not dependent on selling cocaine for their living; sellers who do not use it themselves; house-dealers; certain nationalities (Chileans, Dutch, etc.);...

They are very reliable, I've been going there for eight, nine, ten years. I trust them a 100%. They're friends of mine as well. These are people I've known for years. [H/1/14]

9.6. 'BEING RIPPED OFF'

We asked participants whether they had ever been 'ripped off' when buying cocaine. Of the 89 respondents who answered this question, 64 report having been ripped off at least once (71.9%). In general, rip-offs or swindle games can take three forms: (1) the buyer receives cocaine, but in too small a quantity (e.g. 0.8 or 0.7 instead of a full gram) or of poor quality; (2) the buyer receives some substance which turns out to be something else (e.g. brown sand, white powdered sugar, etc.); (3) the buyer does not get anything for his money, because the seller or a go-between runs off with the money.

We met this guy in the street, we were looking for something, and we thought: this guy might help us, and he comes over to the car, and BEFore we even asked, he said: 'You want some coke, or smack?' And we said: 'A couple of grams.' He said: 'Just give me the money, I'll go get it just around the corner.' And we said: 'No, fuck off!' And he said: 'Well, I can't get it then.' But the next thing I know, my mate said: 'Here's the money.' I said: 'No, don't do that.' And we never saw the guy again of course. I wouldn't have done that. If I had been with someone else, I would want to see it first. I want to see the quantity, and maybe just have a taste... [S/0/01]

The circumstances in which respondents have been swindled are consistent with the characteristics of 'unreliable' dealers described above. Several respondents have been ripped off by strangers in a discotheque.

When you buy something in a discotheque, you're most likely to be ripped off... They crush a pill or something like that... Especially when you don't know these people... [C/1/08]

Sometimes you get real bad quality which rather gives you a down effect, I mean, which makes you fall asleep instead of waking you up. Or when you get much too little. Like those little bags you open and half of the coke is wrapped up wrongly. That you lose half of it when you open it. That's mostly the case when you buy while going out. When you buy in the nightlife scene, you usually buy shit, in fact. [I/1/16]

Most interviewees tell stories about being ripped off when they wanted to buy cocaine from a dealer in the street. In this type of situation, the client has no opportunity to check the quantity and/or the quality of the product. Buying and selling cocaine are illegal activities and thus tend to be hidden from the public and from the police. Especially when buyer and seller do not know each other, the exchange of money and/or drugs usually takes place in an atmosphere of mutual distrust. Furthermore, street dealers often try to take advantage of the hasty and nervous character of the transaction. In some cases respondents partly blame themselves for being ripped off, because they were too impatient or nervous (because of craving):[12]

> *Well, on the street, you know. Buying from someone you don't know and pfff... you can't control it properly on the spot. They are little balls wrapped up in plastic. Those dealers put that in their mouth all day, and when they are arrested they can swallow them, you know. Yes, there was some coke in it, but it was a minimum, you could hardly feel anything.* [L/0/02]

> *Yes, in a discotheque, and we felt like doing some at that moment. So you call that guy, and he wasn't there at that moment, or he was already in bed or something. And that moment, we really felt like it, and we said: 'Okay, let's try that other guy, I know another guy', and we went there. And yes, we were ripped off.* [I/0/05]

'Being ripped off' is often associated with the initial phase of cocaine use. Many respondents suggest that it is typical for young, inexperienced or experimental users.

> *Yes, in the beginning, when you're just new, you're always ripped off. You buy something and it is adulterated or it is less than what you asked for. In the beginning it always occurs, but the people I buy it from now, I've been buying from them seven years. No trouble at all anymore.* [Z/0/01]

Over the years users learn the tricks of the trade, and these become part of user lore. Negative experiences, such as being cheated by a dealer, lead to informal rules regarding the purchase of cocaine. Some of these social sanctions and rituals relate to the definition of 'reliable' and 'unreliable' dealers. Being ripped off sometimes leads respondents to accept informal rules such as: 'never buy from a stranger', 'never buy from a street dealer', 'never buy from junkies', 'try to find a dealer who is not involved in other types of crime', 'try to find a regular dealer', etc. Respondents also report that other users have dissuaded them from buying from a particular person or in a particular place. Others develop *informal rules* regarding the act of purchasing cocaine itself:

> *First of all, never go alone. Always go by two when you buy something: one who stays with the dealer and one who checks it, you open it or you put your finger in it. And the first time I go to buy something from someone, I check it on the spot whether it's good stuff. [...] Usually it's like: when we are allowed to taste it, it is good stuff. When they tell you: you can't taste it, then... Then we just don't buy it.* [G/0/01]

> *I never just give money. I check everything on the spot.* [H/0/10]

> *When I have been ripped off, I never return. No, they can only fuck with me once. When I know it, maybe I might go there again to ask some, but then I'd have to see first what he gives me, and I learned one good lesson about coke: never buy powder.* [H/0/11]

Nevertheless, clients are usually in no position to take action against the swindler. Buying cocaine is an illegal act, so the buyer cannot appeal to the law. The only thing the 'customer' can do is to raise his/her voice in protest against the seller. Some cheated respondents report satisfactory arrangements after intense complaining:

> *When it's always from the same person, you can say: last time you gave us real shit. If you're gonna give us the same shit again, don't bother... we don't give that much money for that, I mean, they take it into account. If you didn't say anything, they'd keep doing it like that, I think. But not those I know personally. They are really... with them I can always be sure it's 'stuff'.* [V/1/01]

In most cases, however, rip-offs do not have happy endings. The customer is usually unable to retrace the seller (e.g. in a discotheque, or on the street). And if he/she finds the swindler, discussions often turn to arguments, and often end up in physical violence.

> *Well, once I had snorted a line in a discotheque, and eh, there was a boy, and I wanted to buy a pill, an XTC-pill, and he ripped me off. He had given me an aspirin, I mean, some kind of... And I had paid him seven or eight hundred francs, and I was really... I have been looking for him throughout the disco, I thought: I'll find him, and he's gonna give me back my money. And I found him, he was against a wall at the entrance, I just went up to him, and I just beat him up. I was furious, I thought he was not supposed to do such thing, I found it ridiculous.* [H/1/04]

Most respondents have not been personally involved in violent incidents with dealers or other users, but many report having witnessed aggression or violence between the dealer and other customers or between two or more dealers.

> *Clients who become rather aggressive, you know, who are getting sick or don't feel well, and they're not allowed to consume at the dealer's place or so, and they have to wait, but they want to do it anyway, and they want to do it in the hallway, and then there is a fight between those two. Or because the dealer ripped off that person or so... that there is a fight or... that the dealer threw the other out, you know. But I've seen more aggression among users. That one guy freaks out, and that there is a fight in a bar, and that one wants to get his gun... starts fighting...* [H/1/28]

Other respondents have not directly witnessed verbal or physical aggression, but they perceive the dealer(s) they know as 'aggressive' because they carry arms (guns, knives or electric shock weapons). Two respondents state that they see the dealer(s) they know as violent because of their machismo: these dealer(s) often tell stories about violent acts or brag about their own aggressive behavior towards other dealers. The term 'aggression' is often interpreted as a synonym for 'pushing': dealer(s) are perceived as aggressive when they tend to 'push' clients into buying more cocaine or more regularly.

> *Those guys who come up to you and ask: hey, don't you want to buy some, don't you want to buy something, very pushy, and those who start annoying you when you haven't bought from them for a while.* [C/0/09]

Two female respondents report sexual aggression by dealers. In these cases dealers proposed to supply free cocaine in exchange for sexual favors. Fortunately, both these respondents were able to avoid trouble, but they have learnt from these experiences not to visit a dealer alone. In general, aggressive behavior is often associated with 'un-reliable' dealers and strangers (e.g. in a discotheque) or foreigners (certain nationali-ties), addicted dealers or sellers who earn their living selling cocaine, etc. Stories about verbal and/or physical violence usually feature 'street dealers', such as those selling cocaine in the generally known drug copping areas in the inner city of Ant-werp.[13] Many respondents have learnt from their own experience or from users' sto-ries that it is better to buy cocaine from a regular dealer with whom a relationship based on (mutual) trust can be developed. In order to secure good quality (and quan-tity) cocaine, it is better to have a trusting relationship with a seller:

> *It all adds up to this: there is a bunch of aggressive pushers there, who rip you off again and again, but you're an imbecile if you keep on seeing these people. You should look for a dealer who you think is okay. Unless you buy sporadically, then it gets difficult, when you just want to do it a few times a year, then you have to look, because you don't know the right person. I know them by now, but when you want to get it fast, yes, on the street [...] . But that's a different level. That's where most heavy junkies come looking for their daily dose, you know, because they can't do anything with a fixed dealer, because they can't stay, or because they steal from him once, they can't keep a dealer.* [H/0/29]

> *I mean, when you cut your drugs, you know that, that's asking for trouble. Other dealers can get a bad name through it, and they will take care that he is eliminated, and it can be done quite roughly. I do think those are exceptions, you can't keep on doing that, you can do that when you always have different clients, for example when you sell it on the street to passers-by, or whatever; but when you have fixed customers, you can't do that, or you lose your custom, it's like a shop. You make sure you have good quality. You can't keep on fooling someone, you can do it once, but not twice, I mean, if you're dealing with an intelli-gent person.* [U/0/01]

One respondent associates aggression with police pressure: the more police activity in the area, the more nervous (and aggressive) some dealers become. Whether or not this conforms with reality remains unclear, but even if police activity is not intensified, some dealers may play it smart by suggesting that police pressure is forcing them to act hastily and nervously, thus facilitating rip-offs and aggression.

> *There are aggressive ones and there are less aggressive ones, it's like with other people, but especially when there is more police, they are much more aggressive. The more illegal-ity, I mean the more pressure there is, the more aggressive they are. Yes, you can notice it because for example they are acting very busy with the money, and you're not allowed to test the stuff or taste it, you can't tell them: I wanna see it first, no, you have to trust them.* [F/0/01]

9.7. CONCLUSION

Cocaine prices in Antwerp fluctuate between 1,800 and 2,800 BEF for 1 g and the av-erage price is around 2,300 BEF. The reader must bear in mind that our data reflect the prices during our fieldwork phase (August 1996 – April 1997). After recomputing the Amsterdam data, we find that the average price of cocaine has steadily decreased over the last decade: from an average price of 3,374.4 BEF in the Amsterdam I sample (1987) for 1 g to 2,974.2 BEF in the Amsterdam II sample (1991) to 2,300 BEF in the Antwerp sample. This finding is consistent with those in other studies, which report a general decline in prices of cocaine (and heroin) in European countries, particularly retail prices. Although in many countries the anti-drug efforts are directed toward increasing the price of illicit drugs by intercepting drugs at the borders and by disrupting drug markets at home, the basic laws of supply and demand make the fall in cocaine prices in Europe almost certainly a consequence of increased supply. Price data can be an adequate means to evaluate interventions but more systematic research into purchase patterns, prices (at different market levels), various sizes of transactions, actual purity and expected purity (by consumers) are needed.

The main sources of cocaine in our sample are friends (37.8%) and regular dealers (35.1%), like in the Amsterdam samples. About one in five buy their cocaine from various dealers. Although most respondents rely on friends or a regular dealer for the quality of their cocaine, this quality is highly unpredictable and/or subject to rapid changes. This explains why several testing methods (some of them not very efficient) are used, even when cocaine is bought from a 'reliable' source. The proportion of users buying their cocaine at the dealer's home is similar in all three samples: around 40 %. About one in five respondents mainly buy their cocaine in a café/bar, and one in five usually phone a dealer, and wait for him (or one of his runners) to deliver the order at home. Around 10% of the Antwerp sample have to rely on friends to buy cocaine; similar proportions regularly travel abroad (the Netherlands) to buy their cocaine or buy their cocaine mainly on the street. When cocaine is offered for free, this is virtually always by friends.

Respondents often refer to different 'types' of cocaine. Based on the binary oppositions or dual concepts found in their stories we have tried to reconstruct user lore on 'good' and 'bad' quality of cocaine. This knowledge of 'good' and 'bad' cocaine helps the user to decide whether or not to buy a particular product from a particular dealer. User lore on (types of) cocaine and its quality can be perceived as an *informal control mechanism*. The effectiveness of this informal control, however, may be hampered by several factors, it is unevenly spread among users and it may be incomplete (and in some individual cases even false).

Most users distinguish between 'fair' and 'rip-off' dealers. Around two in five respondents perceive the dealer(s) they know as 'reliable', i.e. a person who sells cocaine of reasonable or good *quality* (not adulterated) and who is honest about the *quantity*. One in three perceive the dealer(s) they know as not reliable at all, and one in four respondents claim to know both reliable and unreliable dealers. Unreliable dealers are mostly strangers, very young people, people who also sell heroin, people who earn their living selling cocaine, sellers who use cocaine themselves or who are addicted to it, dealers who operate on the street. People who are also involved in other types of crime, people of certain nationalities, etc. 'Reliable dealers' are mostly described as: regular dealers, personal friends of the respondent or people he/she regularly uses cocaine with, older people, people who are not dependent on selling cocaine for their living, sellers who do not use it themselves, house-dealers...

More than two in three respondents report having been ripped off at least once. Rip-offs or swindle games can take three forms: (1) the buyer receives cocaine, but in too small a quantity or of poor quality; (2) the buyer receives some cocaine-like substance which turns out to be something else; (3) the buyer does not get anything for his money, because the seller or a go-between runs off with the money. Respondents are ripped off typically in situations where they have no opportunity to check the quantity and/or the quality of the product (e.g. buying from a stranger in a discotheque or in the street). Especially when buyer and seller do not know each other, the exchange of money and/or drugs takes usually place in an atmosphere of mutual distrust and calculated actions. Furthermore, street dealers often try to take advantage of the hasty and nervous character of the transaction to rip off their clients.

The experience of 'being ripped off' is often associated with the initial phase of cocaine use. Negative experiences, such as being cheated by a dealer, lead to *informal rules* regarding the purchase of cocaine such as: 'never buy from a stranger', 'never buy from a street dealer', 'never buy from junkies', 'try to find a dealer who is not involved in other types of crime', 'try to find a regular dealer', etc. Nevertheless, clients are usually unable to take action against the swindler. All the 'customer' can do is to raise his/her voice in protest. But most rip-offs do not have happy endings. Usually, the customer is unable to retrace the seller and if he/she finds him, discussions often turn to arguments, and arguments may end up in physical violence. More police activity may facilitate rip-offs and aggression, because dealers become nervous and are forced to act hastily, or because dealers feign to be chased (even if there are no police around). Aggressive behavior is often associated with 'unreliable' dealers and strangers (e.g. in a discotheque) or foreigners (certain nationalities), addicted dealers or sellers who earn their living selling cocaine, 'street dealers', etc. Many respondents have learnt from their own experiences or from other users' stories that it is better to buy cocaine from a regular dealer with whom a relationship based on (mutual) trust can be developed.

NOTES

1. Special thanks to Ms. Veerle Schelfaut from the Department of Economics and Statistics at a major Belgian bank (*Stafafdeling Economie en Statistiek, Kredietbank*). and Mr. Vincent Decaluwé (Crédit Lyonnais Belgium) who provided the average exchange rates and inflation rates. These rates were based on the Bloomberg index.

2. See Chapter 10, p. 236.

3. See Chapter 10, p. 233-236.

4. Source for adjustment: Ms. Veerle Schelfaut (Department of Economics and Statistics at a major Belgian bank - *Stafafdeling Economie en Statistiek, Kredietbank*).

5. See Chapter 10, p. 237-240.

6. Cohen was especially eager to learn about the role of Dutch 'coffeeshops', where selling cannabis is tolerated. His findings in his 1987 and 1991 Amsterdam samples (Cohen, 1989: 74; Cohen & Sas, 1995: 67-68) showed that coffeeshop owners were apparently able to enforce one of the conditions under which the cannabis system is tolerated, i.e. no cocaine or heroin sales on the premises. 'Coffeeshops' were not mentioned by our Antwerp respondents.

7. See for example internal police reports such as: BALTHAU, M. (1996a), *(Mega)dancings*. Brussels: Gendarmerie (internal police report). BALTHAU, M. (1996b), *Horecadan*. Brussels: gendarmerie (internal police report). Both cited in: LAMOT, I. (1997), *België, de buren en drugs. Drugstoerisme onder de loep genomen*. Leuven: licentiate's thesis.

8. Of the 12 respondents who report travelling to the Netherlands to buy their cocaine, most specify that they buy cocaine at a dealer's home. However, we maintained a separate answer category [abroad] because we could not specify the exact location of purchase for all these respondents.

9. The term *'lore'* means: learning or knowledge, especially handed down from past times, or possessed by a class of people (Oxford Advanced Learner's Dictionary of Current English).

10   Apart from these binary oppositions, some respondents referred to types of cocaine related to route of ingestion. They talked about <raw coke> or <snorting coke> which probably refers to street cocaine or cocaine hydrochloride, <base coke>, referring to freebase cocaine or smokable cocaine, and to <shooting coke>, which is cocaine ready to inject. We suspect the latter form of cocaine is just another street name for cocaine hydrochloride, although none of the respondents confirmed this. Furthermore, two respondents talked about <Pipi Delgado> and <Colombian Pet>, which they claimed were typical brands of cocaine in South American countries.

11   In some cases, the practice of adulteration may be the result of a self-fulfilling prophecy. Some dealers report that they started to adulterate cocaine because they had heard from others that all cocaine is cut and that every dealer adds adulterants to the substance before selling it.

12   See also Chapter 7, p. 180, and Chapter 13, p. 289-304 (on the effect of nervousness).

13   For example, around the *Conincksplein* and the *Statiestraat*.

CHAPTER 10

QUALITY OF COCAINE

10.1. INTRODUCTION

The previous chapter illustrated the user lore on (types of) cocaine. The distinction of 'good' and 'bad' quality cocaine helps the user to decide whether or not to buy cocaine from this or another dealer. Furthermore, the previous chapter discussed how our respondents perceived the reliability of cocaine dealers. Both in the Amsterdam sample and in the Antwerp sample, we found that most respondents take it for granted that the cocaine they buy or use is adulterated (Cohen, 1989: 107). In this chapter we present our data on the quality of cocaine.[*] Paragraph 10.2 discusses the opinions of our Antwerp respondents with respect to adulterants in the cocaine they use. Then we analyze the effects of amphetamines (or 'speed') in cocaine, as perceived by our respondents (§10.3). In §10.4, the results of an examination for impurities and the cocaine hydrochloride percentage in 30 Antwerp samples are shown. And finally, we give an account of testing methods used by our Antwerp respondents and illustrate them with qualitative data in §10.5. Wherever possible, we present comparable data from other European and American cities.

10.2. ADULTERANTS

Almost all respondents in the Rotterdam sample report that their cocaine was adulterated (Bieleman & de Bie, 1994: 20). In the 1987 Amsterdam sample 74.4% of the respondents thought that their cocaine was 'always' or 'regularly' adulterated.[1] Similarly, 74% of the participants in the 1991 Amsterdam study thought their cocaine was always, often or regularly cut. In the present study this proportion is even slightly higher than 80 % (see table 10.2.a.).

Table 10.2.a   Frequency of prevalence of adulterants in cocaine according to respondents, in the 1987 Amsterdaml sample and the 1997 Antwerp sample

	Amsterdam I (1987)		Antwerp (1997)	
Frequency	N	%	N	%
Always	82	51.3	73	65.8
Often / regularly	37	23.1	16	14.4
Sometimes	20	12.5	5	4.5
Hardly ever	7	4.4	9	8.1
Never	5	3.1	4	3.6
No answer	*9*	*5.6*	*4*	*3.6*
Total	160	100.0	111	100.0

We also asked our respondents which adulterants they thought were used. The adulterant most mentioned was 'speed' (amphetamines): it was reported by almost one third of our respondents. That is very similar to what was found in the 1991 Amsterdam sample (31%) (Cohen & Sas, 1995: 66), but considerably less than the finding for the 1987 Amsterdam sample (45.6%). Bieleman and de Bie (1992: 50) present qualitative data from a Rotterdam sample (1990-91) that are very consistent with the former studies. The 'adulterants' most mentioned by the participants from their Rotterdam sample were: 'speed', baby laxatives, calcium, abrasive, lime, caffeine, lidocaine, washing powder, ground glass, cleaning powder, etc. (Bieleman & de Bie, 1994: 20). It is striking that in all these samples 'speed' is the most important adulterant according to the experienced cocaine users (Cohen, 1989: 107).

Table 10.2.b   Adulterants used for cocaine according to respondents, in the 1987 Amsterdam I sample and in the 1997 Antwerp sample [*] [♠]

Supposed adulterant	Amsterdam I 1987		Antwerp 1997	
	N	%	N	%
Amphetamines	73	45.6	35	31.5
Mannitol	26	16.3	8	7.2
Laxatives	24	15.0	2	1.8
Ground glass	12	7.5	11	9.9
Cleaning powder	9	5.6	1	0.9
Washing powder	8	5.0	5	4.5
Talcum powder	8	5.0	8	7.2
Novocaine/procaine [♣]	8	5.0	2	1.8
Lidocaine	7	4.4	2	1.8
Milk powder	7	4.4	12	10.8
Lime	7	4.4	-	-
Salts	7	4.4	1	0.9
Sugars	7	4.4	10	9.0
Caffeine	5	3.1	2	1.8
Ascorbic acid (vitamin C)	4	2.5	-	-
Opiates	3	1.9	5	4.5
Aspirin	3	1.9	4	3.6
Pervitine	2	1.3	-	-
Ether [♥]	2	1.3	2	1.8
Flour	2	1.3	10	9.0
Synthetic coke	-	-	2	1.8
Crack	-	-	1	0.9
Crushed pills/medicines	-	-	7	6.3
Some anaesthetic used by dentists	-	-	6	5.4
Something from the pharmacist	-	-	4	3.6
Strychnine	-	-	5	4.5
Dirt (anything)	40	25.0	5	4.5
Other [♠]	9	5.6	7	5.4
None	5	3.1	4	3.6
No answer	*13*	*8.1*	*37*	*36.9*

[*]   More than 1 answer was possible
[♣]   Novocaine is an often used commercial name for procain[2]
[♥]   Strictly spoken, ether can be used to trim cocaine, but it cannot be used as an adulterant.[3]

The comparison of all supposed adulterants reported by both the Antwerp and the Amsterdam sample (table 10.2.b) reveals some interesting differences. After 'speed', the adulterants most frequently mentioned by the Antwerp respondents were: 'milk powder' (10.8%), 'ground glass' from strip lights or neon tubes (9.9%), 'sugar' and 'flour' (both 9.0%), 'talcum powder' and 'mannitol'[4] (both 7.2%), 'crushed pills/medicines' (6.3%) and 'some anaesthetic used by dentists' (5.4%). For the 1987 Amsterdam sample quite a different hierarchy was found: 'mannitol' was mentioned twice as often

(16.3%), while the other adulterants listed above were mentioned less often (Cohen, 1989: 107). The Amsterdam users also mentioned 'laxatives' considerably more often (15% versus 1.8% in Antwerp).

In the 'other' category, we gathered some vague or rare answers such as 'chalk', 'something crystalline', 'disinfectant', 'something odorless and colorless', 'any kind of whitish substance that can be crushed'...

Some of the adulterants (lime, novocaine, pervitine[5] and ascorbic acid[6]) mentioned by the Amsterdam respondents were not mentioned by the Antwerp respondents. Vice versa, the Antwerp users mentioned some adulterants (such as crack, strychnine, and synthetic cocaine) that were not reported by the Amsterdam sample. Three of these categories were: 'crushed pills/medicines' (6.3%), 'an anaesthetic used by the dentist' (5.4%) and 'something from the pharmacist' (3.6%). These categories taken together make up an important category of answers, referring to relatively easily obtainable drugs via legal pharmaceutical or medical channels.

The 'no answer' category is considerably larger for the Antwerp sample (36.9%) than for the Amsterdam sample (8.1%). This suggests that one third of our respondents (and probably even more) do not have the slightest idea of the proportion and the nature of impurities in their cocaine. This is made more obvious by the findings in the following paragraphs.

It is striking that respondents give so many divergent answers relating to the adulterants that are used to cut the cocaine they use or buy. In our opinion these answers reflect a common view among cocaine users in particular and illicit drug users in general, i.e. illicit street drugs are routinely adulterated or diluted with dangerous substances. Furthermore, this is a view commonly held by those involved in the treatment of drug users, the policing of drug users and the research of drug use and related issues. Items in the media dealing with drugs, their effects and their dangers almost always (especially after a drug-related death) insinuate that one of the reasons street drugs are unsafe is that they contain dangerous impurities inserted by the dealer. Both the general public and most illicit drug users take their views of drugs and their risks from the mass media, where the (hidden) message of adulteration of illicit drugs is: "Remember, it could be cut with anything, so it's like playing Russian roulette with your life" (Coomber, 1997d).

The adulteration of street drugs with other (sometimes dangerous) substances is thus in normative discursive terms relatively uncontested. It is an assumption that gains the status of a 'fact'. Within an area that is littered with contested meanings and stereotypes, it is an assumption that elicits little discussion or opposition. Both our data and other recent research, however, suggest that adulteration with dangerous or poisonous substances is not common, if indeed it occurs at all – as opposed to the relatively common practice of adulteration of drugs with relatively innocuous substances (such as glucose, caffeine and paracetamol).

10.3. AMPHETAMINE ('SPEED') IN COCAINE

As already indicated, amphetamine ('speed') was the adulterant most often mentioned. After we had given respondents the opportunity to mention any adulterant they knew, we asked them -like Cohen did- if they were able to sense the presence of amphetamines in cocaine. Of all respondents 88.3 % answered in the affirmative (84% in the 1987 Amsterdam sample). In table 10.3.a we present the effects of cocaine, according to respondents, when it is adulterated with amphetamine. Most of these effects are perceived *after* consumption of cocaine, like in the 1987 Amsterdam sample.

Some of our Antwerp users, however, also reported that the 'appearance' of the product (7.2 %) and its 'strong smell' (12.6%) were indications for the presence of amphetamine in cocaine. These 'effects' are perceived *before* consumption of the drug. If a sample of cocaine is adulterated with amphetamines, the user probably perceives a distinct smell. Especially when it is 'fresh', amphetamine has a typical smell which is much stronger than the typical smell of cocaine. However, contrary to what many users believe, amphetamine is hardly ever found in cocaine samples (see §10.4).

The appearance of the cocaine product may indicate the presence of amphetamine: cocaine has a whitish color, while amphetamine is typically yellowish or ecru. However, color and appearance differ according to the humidity and the purity of the products, and both can easily be combined in solution and reconstituted by evaporation. Some of the most sophisticated connoisseurs can be fooled by the result.

Table 10.3.a　　Effects of amphetamine in cocaine according to respondents, in the 1987 Amsterdam I sample and in the 1997 Antwerp sample [*] [♦]

Experiences	Amsterdam I 1987		Antwerp 1997	
	N	%	N	%
Pressure on throat	10	6.3	-	-
Higher pulse rate	18	11.3	11	9.9
Raised motor activity	4	2.5	8	7.2
Different taste	16	10.0	17	15.3
Unpleasant in nose	27	16.9	24	21.6
Different	13	8.1	5	4.5
Teeth grinding	22	13.8	10	9.0
Agitation	57	35.6	25	22.5
Insomnia	20	12.5	9	8.1
Feeling shaky	7	4.4	5	4.5
Prolonged action of cocaine	10	6.3	-	-
Shortened action of cocaine	3	1.9	-	-
Headaches	4	2.5	2	1.8
Sweating	4	2.5	1	0.9
Action of cocaine less subtle	16	10.0	6	5.4
Unpleasant long lasting effect	4	2.5	4	3.6
Other physiological reactions	11	6.9	22	19.8
Other mental reactions	4	2.5	19	17.1
Strong smell	-	-	14	12.6
The appearance of the product	-	-	8	7.2
Other [♦]	10	6.3	7	6.3
No answer	*24*	*15.0*	*14*	*12.6*

[*] More than 1 answer was possible

We used the same coding system as in the Amsterdam study, which included answers like diarrhea, bad feeling in gums, cramps, a burning feeling, feeling sick or queasy, a tense stomach, no or less freeze, pain in neck in an 'other physiological effects' category. The 'other mental effects' category contains: more talkative, highly preoccupied, a feeling of distance towards people, anxiety, less euphoric. The category 'other' contains answers that refer to the outcome of tests, the different effect on genitals, the time between consumption and the onset of effects, etc. Almost all of these effects are perceived as unpleasant:

But I found it terribly bad, it made me extremely nervous, I couldn't smile anymore, a contorted face, so... [C/0/02]

Like nowadays, when I go to a discotheque I want to go to bed at ten or eleven o'clock and sleep, but when there's speed you just can't. And the next day you can't eat, and you feel bad and... And when you take it, you become very aggressive and stuff, yes, you're really disgusting, I think. [G/0/01]

If we compare the top five of the rank order of reported amphetamine effects in the 1987 Amsterdam sample and the 1997 Antwerp sample, 'agitation' and 'unpleasant in nose' rank first and second in both samples. But while in the Amsterdam sample 'teeth grinding', 'insomnia' and 'higher pulse rate' rank third to fifth, Antwerp users reported more 'other physiological reactions', 'other mental reactions' and 'different taste'. While the Amsterdam users reported a prolonging or shortening effect of amphetamine on the action of cocaine, we did not find these 'effects' in our sample. Neither did any of our respondents mention 'pressure on throat' as an effect of speed in cocaine.

With Cohen we assume that most of the reported negative effects of 'speed' in cocaine were cocaine effects, or effects of cocaine in combination with another drug (Cohen, 1989: 108).[7] Indeed, effects like insomnia, higher pulse rate, headaches, talkativeness, diarrhea, teeth grinding, sweating, nose problems and restlessness were also mentioned by some of our respondents as effects of cocaine (see chapter 11).[8]

10.4. PURITY OF COCAINE

In the 1987 Amsterdam survey respondents were asked whether they had cocaine available in their homes, and if so, whether they were willing to sell a sample of about 50 mg for 50 NLG (Dutch guilders). There was a written agreement with the Chief of Police and the Public Prosecutor in Amsterdam that no effort would be undertaken at any time to demand any data from this research and that interviewers carrying a sample of cocaine bought for analysis from a respondent would not be prosecuted in case they were arrested.[9] Cohen (1989: 108) managed to buy 45 cocaine samples from respondents. After laboratory analysis, he found that only 39 of them contained cocaine. None of them contained any amphetamines. The average purity of the samples containing cocaine was 65.1% cocaine hydrochloride. No dangerous adulterants were found.[10]

After intensive efforts to reach a similar agreement with the Public prosecutor in Antwerp and with the Ministry of Public Health, we realized that the Belgian authorities were not willing to cooperate in this part of the study. So we decided to work out an alternative. We asked our respondents to give us a sample of around 50 mg, which we sent to the same laboratory where Cohen had had his samples analyzed. We did not offer any financial or other compensation, which is probably why none of our respondents tried to deliberately cheat us. Eventually, out of 111 respondents in our survey, 26 respondents gave a sample of approx. 50 mg; two respondents gave two samples (from different dealers). These samples were sealed in plastic containers and brought to the laboratory under an anonymous envelope.

The samples were investigated for impurities and for content of cocaine hydrochloride with two methods: IR-spectrometry and solution in dichloromethane.[11] As can be seen from table 10.4.a, none of the Antwerp cocaine samples contained less than 20% cocaine hydrochloride and more than 80% contained more than 60% cocaine hydro-chloride. The purity of the Antwerp samples ranged from 28.68 % to 91.9 %. The average purity was 73.9 %. Thus, the average purity in 1991 in Amsterdam and in 1997 in Antwerp was about ten percent higher than in the 1987 Amsterdam sample.

Table 10.4.a   Purity in percentages of cocaine hydrochloride in 39 samples from Amsterdam (1987), 23 samples from Amsterdam (1991), 26 samples from Rotterdam (1993) and 30 samples from Antwerp (1997)

% cocaine hydrochloride	Amsterdam I 1987		Amsterdam II 1991		Rotterdam 1993		Antwerp 1997	
	N	%	N	%	N	%	N	%
1-19%	3	7.7	-	-	-	-	-	-
20-39%	2	5.1	-	-	2	7.7	4	13.3
40-59%	8	20.5	6	26.1	3	11.5	1	3.3
60-79%	14	35.9	8	34.8	10	38.5	13	43.3
>80%	12	30.8	9	39.1	11	42.3	12	40.0
Total	39	100.0	23	100.0	26	100.0	30	100.0
Mean	65.1%		74%		74%		73.9%	

Bieleman and de Bie (1994: 17-19) obtained 26 samples of cocaine hydrochloride and 9 samples of freebase cocaine from their Rotterdam respondents. The average purity of the cocaine hydrochloride samples was approx. 74%. The range of purity percentage was almost identical to the one found in the present study: from 29% to 92%.[12] In the follow-up study to the 1987 Amsterdam sample, Cohen and Sas (1993: 81) analyzed another nine cocaine samples. One sample appeared to contain only gastric soda. The average purity of the remaining eight samples was 87%, with a range between 74% and 96%.

Respondents who sent a cocaine sample to the laboratory expected the following adulterant(s) to be found: no idea (24), amphetamine (3), mannitol (1), chalk (1), anaesthetic used by dentists (1), a kind of stimulant (1). Again, the hypothesis that most users do not have the faintest idea of the quality of their cocaine is confirmed. After laboratory testing the samples, we found that, except for one respondent, those who did believe certain adulterants would be found in their sample, all proved to be wrong. Similarly, these data clearly show that most respondents who estimated the purity of the sample they had supplied, proved to be wrong: the respondent with a cocaine sample of which the purity proved to be 91.9% perceived the quality to be 'rather good', just like the respondent whose sample proved to be 45.41% pure. Cohen's conclusion that respondent judgement on purity of cocaine is poor is thus confirmed by our results (Cohen, 1989: 110).

Adulterations found through IR-spectrometry were: mannitol (4), lidocaine (3), glucose (2), caffeine (1) and starch (1). An insolvable rest in dichloromethane was found in 10 samples (33.3%), which indicates the presence of mannitol, glucose, starch etc. For 18 samples, no adulterants could be identified.

More importantly, none of the Antwerp cocaine samples contained any amphetamines, contrary to what many users believe.[13] Other studies have reached similar conclusions. None of the cocaine samples obtained from the 1987 Amsterdam sample contained any amphetamines (Cohen, 1989: 108-110). Bieleman and de Bie (1994: 20) found adulterants in 20 of the 26 cocaine hydrochloride samples. The adulterants most often detected were mannitol and inositol,[14] and caffeine. Only one sample contained a very small quantity of amphetamines. Again, these data suggest that cocaine users often underestimate the stimulant effects of cocaine itself (such as agitation, higher pulse rate, raised motor activity, shakiness, insomnia, etc.) and that they wrongly attribute negative effects of cocaine to supposed adulterants (such as amphetamines).

Third, analysis of cocaine samples by the Belgian National Institute for Criminalistics and Criminology (N.I.C.C.) shows similar findings.[15] From 1995 to 1998 a total of 757 cocaine samples were analysed, and only 1 sample was found to contain amphetamines. None of the samples contained dangerous 'cuts' such as ground glass, washing powder, cleaning powder, strychnine, etc. The adulterants most often detected were lidocaine, coffeïne, novocaine/procaine, paracetamol and benzocaine. The average purity of the 289 powder cocaine samples[16] analyzed by the N.I.C.C. in 1997 and 1998 was 75.3%, which is very close to our finding. Purity ranged from 4.6% to virtually 100%.[17]

Fourth, Coomber (1997a) attempted to make comparative sense of the diverse forensic literature relating to the purity and constituents of illicit drugs. What emerged was a picture of illicit drug adulteration/dilution that differed significantly from popular perceptions. Coomber concluded that, although adulteration is a common practice, forensic evidence does not reveal adulteration with *dangerous* substances such as brick dust, rat poison, ground lightbulb glass, washing powder, and the like. When adulterants are found, they are substances such as glucose and other sugars, caffeine, paracetamol, etc.[18]

Moreover, when substances are used to adulterate or dilute, forensic analysis reveals rational, strategic, and at times market-sensitive activity rather than haphazard, unpredictable, and belligerent activity desperate to increase profit at any cost. The evidence suggests that the adulteration is purposeful and controlled rather than reckless. Coomber enumerates some reasons for this and much of our qualitative data confirms his arguments:

(1) it is not good commercial practice to poison your customers – you will soon run out of customers, and dealers may fear reprisals (Coomber, 1997c);

> *I was ripped off, yes, it's normal, right? You enter a discotheque, you buy coke in a roundabout way, then you're bound to be conned. Why? Because you don't know a good dealer. But with a dealer you know well.... It's the same as when I go to the grocer's, to buy potatoes, or to buy apples, or bananas... When you come there every day, you can say: Hey no, not those, those are more than a week old, I need fresh ones. It's the same with a dealer, when you go to a good dealer, he won't pull that one on you. Because he earns his living with you. [B/0/02]*

(2) It is often easier and even cheaper to use readily available substances that are relatively harmless (sugars, paracetamol, caffeine, mannitol...) than to grind down a lightbulb or a brick or to get access to and use rat poison, etc.;

(3) Substances such as washing powder, lightbulb glass and brick dust are not soluble in water and would easily be 'sussed' (discovered) by customers. For a description of some testing methods used by the Antwerp respondents, see §10.5;

(4) Eighty-one per cent of the dealers interviewed by Coomber (1997c) declared that they would not adulterate (either at all or with dangerous substances) because of concern for the users' health. In addition, a number of dealers stressed that they felt they had a reputation for quality merchandise and did not want to jeopardize that reputation.

> *I never cut it. I always sold my stuff the way I got it. I never cut it. And let me tell you one thing: when my 'stuff' wasn't the way I wanted it when I got it, when I bought it, I didn't sell it. I just beeped that person and I had to have other stuff, or else I didn't sell it. And those guys said: okay, no problem.* [H/0/23]

Both the drug user and the drug commentators of varying persuasions may 'invest' in the idea of dangerous adulteration. For drug users, beliefs about certain dangerous aspects of drug use, such as the possibility of dangerous contaminants in their drugs, may also add to the 'glamour' of drug use itself. To those in favor of drug prohibition, dangerous adulteration (among other dangers to the individual and to society) is indicative of why drug use and trade must be prevented. For those committed to certain harm-reduction approaches it represents a rationale for the provision of clean, consistent drugs to enhance the users' safety. We agree with Coomber: *'The idea of dangerous adulteration/dilution is a myth that is essentially reliant upon a number of other drug myths for its origin and perpetuation. Without the myth of the evil drug dealer, which itself is partially reliant upon the image of the depraved drug fiend, which in turn is partially reliant on the unreasonable exaggeration of the degenerative powers of drugs such as heroin* [and cocaine, td], *the rationale for its existence would be difficult to maintain. [...] While dangerous adulteration/dilution is uncontested it gives greater credence to those who choose to believe and perpetuate the other myths.'* (Coomber, 1997d).

The 15 respondents who reported selling (or having sold) cocaine on a regular basis were asked whether they had added other substances to the cocaine before selling it. Five respondents stress the fact that they never adulterated the cocaine they bought to enhance profits. Yet, two in three regular sellers admit they consciously adulterated the cocaine they sold. The following stories by regular dealers illustrate the process of adulteration and the enormous profits that are generated through the selling of illicit substances:

> *Respondent: I'd cut it with milk sugar. Or flour, eh corn flour, whatever I found. Yes, I heard that some people put ground glass in it, very finely ground glass, and then they say it's crystal coke.*
> *Interviewer: And in what proportions did you cut it?*
> *Respondent: Oh, well.* [he thinks] *I did three grams of milk sugar in twenty grams. In fifty grams of coke I did ten grams of milk sugar or so.*
> *Interviewer: And how much profit did you make in doing so?*
> *Respondent: I paid 1,700 francs per gram. And I sold it for 2,500 francs. But when you mix it with three grams of milk sugar, and you weigh 0.8, I think, that's not a full gram. 0.8 including the paper. So you had per five so-called 'grams', an extra gram, for 2,500 francs pure profit. On twenty grams you could make six grams pure profit.*
> *Interviewer: And in what quantities did you buy it then?*
> *Respondent: Twenty or fifty grams.*
> *Interviewer: And how long did it take you to sell those?*

Respondent: Once I did it in one day. Once, I went to get twenty grams on Friday, I came dealing, in a flash, and those twenty grams were gone, and I could leave again, to get an-other twenty grams. Fifty gram in one weekend, and it was all gone. [C/0/01]

10.5. QUALITY CONTROL BY RESPONDENTS

Given the uncertainty about purity and quality of the substance (which is a conse-quence of its illegal status), and given the unreliability of at least some sources of drugs, it may come as no surprise that users have acquired techniques to test the drugs they buy and use. For the 1987 sample of non-deviant cocaine users, Cohen (1989: 110) concluded that his respondents' testing methods were poor. In table 10.5.a we present our own findings. We see that 58.6% of our respondents do not test their co-caine at all (versus 81.9% of the Amsterdam respondents). Our respondents report nine different testing methods: visual and tactile examination, tasting, snorting, four differ-ent kitchen tests (water glass test, bleach test, solvent test, flame test), adding a test solution, and the melting point test.[19]

Table 10.5.a   Method of testing cocaine before buying, in the 1997 Antwerp sample [*]

Antwerp (1997)		
Method	N	%
Cleaning with ammonia	21	18.9
Tasting (waiting for 'freeze')	15	13.5
Visual and tactile examination	12	10.8
Snorting	6	5.4
Add test solution	4	3.6
Water glass test	4	3.6
Burning (flame test)	1	0.9
Bleach test	1	0.9
Melting point test	1	0.9
None	65	58.6

[*] More than 1 answer was possible

The testing method most mentioned by the Antwerp sample was *'cleaning with am-monia'* (18.9%). We must be cautious when interpreting this figure, because the pro-cess of 'cleaning' cocaine with ammonia is also a popular way of preparing freebase cocaine. The manufacture of freebase cocaine usually includes the following steps: (1) put cocaine hydrochloride in a spoon, (2) add ammonia (until cocaine is submerged), (3) heat the spoon with a cigarette lighter, candle, etc..., (4) stir or dip with a cold knife until cocaine contracts, (5) absorb the ammonia with a tissue, (6) rinse the rock or freebase cocaine with water, then dry it, and (7) break the rock into lumps.[20]

It is important to note that this 'recipe' to obtain a smokable form of cocaine (freeba-se cocaine) is also seen by our respondents as an effective method for testing the qua-lity of cocaine.[21] By observing how much of the substance floats on the surface of the ammonia, users believe they are able to make estimates of the quality of their cocaine. However, not all the adulterants will be separated from the cocaine by this process, and remnants of highly poisonous ammonia can result in irritation of the airways, bre-athlessness, infections and asthma attacks. As many of our respondents report to skip the cleaning of the cocaine with water, it is clear that the 'cleaning' of cocaine with ammonia does not always result in a purer form of cocaine, contrary to what many users believe.

Another frequently reported method was *'waiting for freeze'* (13.5% of the respondents). One of the two main pharmacological actions of cocaine is its local anesthetic action (the other being a stimulation of the central nervous system). Cocaine exerts its local anaesthetic actions ('numbing or freezing') by blocking the conduction of sensory impulses within nerve cells (Washton, 1989: 11). This effect is most pronounced when the drug is applied to the skin or to mucous membranes. When cocaine is snorted, it temporarily numbs the user's nasal and throat passages because of its local anaesthetic actions, an effect known to all experienced users. Consequently, most users think that an immediate 'freeze' after putting some cocaine on the gums is a proof of high quality.

However, most synthetic variants of cocaine such as lidocaine, xylocaine and novocaine (used routinely in dental procedures), and procaine and tetracaine also produce this local anaesthetic effect (but no euphoric effects). Thus, to increase their profits some dealers may add these cheaper anesthetics to reduce its purity while retaining the drug's anticipated effects. Analysis of 30 cocaine samples from the Antwerp respondents showed the presence of lidocaine in 3 samples. Consequently, the idea that an immediate 'freeze' after tasting cocaine is a proof of high purity may be erroneous, and 'waiting for a freeze' may not be such a reliable method of testing the quality of cocaine.

One would expect that the first thing a cocaine purchaser will do is look at the product and examine its appearance.[22] However, only 8 respondents report that they examined the appearance of cocaine by looking at it (*visual examination*), and 4 respondents reported they rubbed the cocaine between their fingers (*tactile examination*):

> *You can feel it, if you take coke between your fingers, you ought to have a little ball, if it sticks to your pores, then it's usually adulterated. Coke is greasier, it's a paste. So with coke, you should be able to roll little balls between your fingers.* [I/0/11]

The truth is that a user cannot tell much from visual or tactile examination. Most cuts blend very well with cocaine, especially if the product contains a lot of duff (cocaine that has been crushed to powder through handling). To make matters more difficult, cocaine suppliers can combine the cocaine and the adulterant in solution and reconstitute it by evaporation. The result is what appears to be beautiful solid chunks of rock cocaine or –if the evaporation technique is different – perfect flakes. Except for cases where the adulterant looks radically different from cocaine there is little that can be distinguished with the naked eye. The quotations below show very clearly that examining the appearance of the product is an ambivalent way of checking for quality: some respondents claim that high quality cocaine looks like fine powder, while others claim that it should stick together in lumps...

> *You open it and you see what it looks like. Are they flakes or lumps? Usually, the adulterant is a powder, and for most adulterants they have to chop their coke finely, so you cannot see the difference anylonger.* [H/0/21]

Or by seeing if it is powder all right. When it contains lumps, then you know: yes, they've put something in it. [H/0/29]

No, but you do check whether you get lumps or powder. When it's powder, you can assume it's rubbish. When it's a lump, it's probably, usually good coke. [H/1/17]

Another thing a purchaser can do is *snort* some of the product to see if the high is a good coke high (reported by six respondents, or 5,4% of the Antwerp sample). If a line or two does not fully stimulate as would be expected of this much cocaine, it has obviously been cut with some inert substance or with a non-stimulating anesthetic cut. However, we have shown earlier that cocaine users often underestimate the stimulant effects of cocaine itself (such as agitation, higher pulse rate, raised motor activity, shakiness, insomnia, etc.) and that they wrongly attribute negative effects of cocaine to supposed adulterants (such as amphetamines).

Four respondents (3,6% of the sample) report *adding a test solution*. The mixture then gradually turns into a specific color (green, red, blue), or a coloured precipitate occurs. There are test solutions (such as potassium permanganate) that can help the user to estimate the purity of their sample of cocaine.[23] Furthermore, specific test solutions can be prepared to determine the presence of a specific adulterant in a sample of cocaine.[24] Finally, some test solutions can only be used to test for presence of cocaine, and not to estimate the purity of the sample (Gottlieb, 1975). It goes without saying that most users lack sufficient knowledge about the preparation of chemical test solutions. Those few respondents who report using test solutions, did not prepare these themselves, but they bought them ready-made. Furthermore, users lack the expertise to interpret the results of these tests: most of them only know that 'if it turns blue, there's cocaine in it'.

Another quality test is the *water glass test* (reported by 4 respondents). When a pinch of cocaine is dropped on the surface of a glass of water, the particles will sink to the bottom leaving transparent trailers behind them. It is a popular believe that only cocaine will do this and that this is a sure test for purity. But procaine hydrochloride will do exactly the same thing. Substances which are insoluble or poorly soluble in water will not sink to the bottom of the glass, but will remain on the water's surface (Gottlieb, 1975).

Respondent: Or by boiling it, then you know what is left. You can drop it in a glass of water, and see what floats. Coke becomes a kind of milky line.
Interviewer: How do you recuperate the coke then?
Respondent: [laughs] It's fucked up, but you just do it with a little bit of coke, just to check. [H/0/29]

Only one respondent mentioned the *bleach test* (or 'solvent test'). When a tablespoonful of liquid bleach is added to a glass of water, cocaine hydrochloride can be distinguished from procaine hydrochloride. The particles and trailers of procaine hydrochloride will turn brick-red or orange, whereas those of cocaine will not. The water glass test combined with the bleach test is also quite good for making rough estimates of the percentage of cuts by observing the approximate proportions of product that remain on the surface.

So you take a glass of domestic bleach, you put a little coke in it, one tenth, and then, if you put that in it from the top, it will drop in strings, and then it goes up again. The slower it goes down, the better your coke. Most of the coke goes down right away, and stays down. And after that you can take it out, make it evaporate, and then you can weigh how much is left of it. [H/0/22]

Another respondent described the *flame test* ('burning'). When pure cocaine hydrochloride is placed on a piece of aluminum foil and a flame is held underneath it, the cocaine will melt and vaporize leaving almost no residue on the foil. If a flame is held to the vapors, these will ignite. A popular fallacy is that none of the common cuts will do this. Mannitol, for instance, will do exactly the same thing. Still, this is a useful test. Some cuts evaporate with thick fumes and distinctive odors. Lactose, dextrose and sucrose carmelize and give off a sweet odor. Some cuts leave characteristic residues or go through observable transformations while melting and evaporating. Other cuts do not melt, vaporize, or decompose at all (Gottlieb, 1975).[25]

And finally, one respondent mentions the *melting point test*. Simply expressed, it involves gradually heating the substance until it melts or decomposes, and noting at what exact temperature this occurs. Pure cocaine hydrochloride should melt somewhere between 192 and 197 degrees Celsius. If it contains a cut, its melting point may deviate widely. Sometimes the cut may be observed melting out at a lower temperature if it has a vastly lower melting point than that of cocaine. This is a most exacting test, but it requires special equipment (such as an high quality aluminium block with a thermometer sensor, or a glass capillary tube that can be immersed in a silicon oil bath with a thermometer) and sufficient knowledge about the melting points of both cocaine and the most common adulterants.

In conclusion, the Antwerp users reported a slightly more varied range of testing techniques than the Amsterdam respondents. But it is questionable whether these testing methods are as reliable (and healthy) as some users believe (Gottlieb, 1975). If the 'cleaning' process of cocaine with ammonia is done carelessly, the remaining ammonia can cause serious damage to the bronchial tubes. Most users think that an immediate 'freeze' after putting some cocaine on the gums is a proof of high quality. But they ignore that most synthetic variants of cocaine (such as lidocaine and novocaine) also produce this local anaesthetic effect (but no euphoric effects). Reliable testing of the quality is not only technically difficult and time consuming (Cohen, 1989: 110), but as cocaine is expensive and sometimes scarce, users are not always prepared to sacrifice a part of the precious powder to test its quality.

Surely, rubbing between fingers, tasting and examining the appearance are less expensive but these methods are poor testing methods (see e.g. Bieleman & de Bie, 1992: 49). They may prove useful to protect the consumer from buying pure sugar or milk powder, but they are ineffective to detect more 'subtle' adulterants such as lidocaine or novocaine. In the previous chapter it was argued that a distinction between 'good' and 'bad' quality cocaine helps the user to decide whether or not to buy this or that 'cocaine' from a dealer.[26] As such, user lore on (types of) cocaine and its quality can be perceived as an informal control mechanism. The effectiveness of this informal control, however, may be hampered by the fact that it is unevenly spread among users and may be incomplete (and in some individual cases false). The contradictory stories told by respondents illustrate this. For example, for some users <white coke> is synonym for pure, non-adulterated cocaine, whereas for others the white color is proof of adulteration. Another example are the contradictory stories cited above on the appearance of cocaine (what good quality looks like).

Finally, apart from these testing methods, most respondents have reasonable confidence in their dealers or supplying friends. If these sources become unreliable for quality, users start looking for other, more trustworthy supply channels.[27]

10.6. CONCLUSION

Most Antwerp respondents think that their cocaine is 'always' or 'regularly' adulterated. Consistent with other cocaine studies, we find that 'speed' is the most important adulterant according to experienced cocaine users. It is mentioned by almost one third of our respondents. Other adulterants frequently mentioned by the Antwerp respondents are milk powder, ground lightbulb glass, sugars, flour, talcum powder and mannitol. The fact that respondents give so many divergent answers to the question which adulterants are used to cut the cocaine they use or buy, reflects the common view among users that illicit street drugs are routinely adulterated or diluted with dangerous substances.

Thirty cocaine samples from the Antwerp respondents were examined for impurities and for content of cocaine hydrochloride with IR-spectrometry and solution in dichloromethane. Adulterations found were mannitol, lidocaine, glucose, caffeine and starch. In 18 samples no adulterants could be identified. The purity of the Antwerp samples ranges from 28.68 % to 91.9 %. The average purity is 73.9 % (similar to the average purity in 1991 in Amsterdam and about ten percent higher than in the 1987 Amsterdam sample).

More than 88% of the Antwerp respondents state they were able to sense the presence of amphetamines in cocaine. Apart from the 'appearance' of the product and its 'strong smell' (both 'effects' perceived *before* consumption of the drug), the effects most mentioned *after* consumption of cocaine were 'agitation', 'unpleasant in nose', 'other physiological reactions', 'other mental reactions' and 'different taste'. Almost all of these effects mentioned by our respondents are perceived as unpleasant. However, none of the Antwerp cocaine samples contained any amphetamines. We assume that most of the reported negative effects of 'speed' in cocaine are cocaine effects, or effects of cocaine in combination with another drug. Indeed, effects like insomnia, higher pulse rate, headaches, talkativeness, diarrhea, teeth grinding, sweating, nose problems, and restlessness are also mentioned by some of our respondents as effects of cocaine.

Most users do not have the faintest idea of the quality of their cocaine. Moreover, laboratory tests of the cocaine samples shows that those respondents who expected certain adulterants to be found in their sample, all proved to be wrong. Cohen's conclusion (1989: 110) that respondent judgement on purity of cocaine is poor is thus confirmed by our results. Yet, the adulteration of street drugs with other (sometimes dangerous) substances is relatively uncontested. It is an assumption that gains the status of a 'fact'. Both our data and those from other recent studies, however, suggest that adulteration with dangerous or poisonous substances (such as brick dust, rat poison, ground lightbulb glass, washing powder and the like) is not common, if indeed it occurs at all – as opposed to the practice of adulteration with relatively innocuous substances (such as glucose, caffeine and paracetamol).

Moreover, contrary to the official discourse, the evidence suggests that adulteration is purposefull and controlled rather than reckless. We have argued that the idea of dangerous adulteration/dilution is a myth that essentially relies on a number of other drug myths for its origin and perpetuation. Without the myth of the evil drug dealer, which itself derives from the image of the depraved drug fiend, which in turn derives from the unreasonable exaggeration of the degenerate powers of drugs, the rationale for its existence would be difficult to maintain.

Finally, we have shown that more than half of the Antwerp users do not test their cocaine at all. The testing methods most mentioned by the Antwerp sample were 'making a solution' (i.e. the solvent test, or bleach test) and 'waiting for freeze' (after snorting). Other methods such as 'the water glass test', 'examining the appearance of the product', 'rubbing between fingers', 'burning' (i.e. the flame test) were described.

Whether these testing methods are as reliable (and healthy) as some users believe, remains questionable. Reliable testing of the quality is technically difficult and time consuming, and as cocaine is expensive and sometimes scarce, users are not always prepared to sacrifice a part of the precious powder to test its quality. Surely, rubbing between fingers, tasting and examining the appearance are less expensive means for a quality test, but these methods are poor testing methods. It was argued in a previous chapter that knowledge of 'good' and 'bad' quality of cocaine helps the user to decide whether or not to buy 'cocaine' from a dealer and, as such, can be perceived as an informal control mechanism. The contradictory stories on the appearance of cocaine (how good quality should look) illustrate that the effectiveness of this informal control may be hampered by the fact that it is unevenly spread among users and may be incomplete (and in some individual cases false).

NOTES

(*) We wish to thank Dr. Crista Van Haeren, senior assistant at the Department of Drugs and Toxicology, National Institute for Criminalistics and Criminology (*Nationaal Instituut voor Criminalistiek en Criminologie*), Brussels (Belgium), for her valuable comments on this chapter.

[1] In his 1987 report Cohen presents data that indicate a proportion of 74.4% of respondents who think their cocaine is always, often or regularly adulterated (Cohen, 1989: 106). In 1991, Cohen reported a proportion of 67% for the same sample (Cohen & Sas, 1995: 66). We have maintained the percentage from the first publication, as we assumed the percentage given in the second publication was an error.

[2] Personal communication from Dr. Crista Van Haeren (N.I.C.C., Brussels).

[3] Personal communication from Dr. Crista Van Haeren.(N.I.C.C., Brussels)

[4] According to Washton, mannitol is a relatively safe commercial filler used in the manufacture of various pills (WASHTON, A. (1989), *Cocaine addiction. Treatment, recovery and relapse prevention*, 20. New York: W.W. Norton & Company). According to a Dutch dictionary, mannitol is a sugar alcohol that is used, amongst others, to manufacture synthetic materials, electrolytic condensers, etc. and in medicine for renal (or kidney) function tests and as a sweetener for diabetics. (in Dutch: *'een suikeralcohol o.a. gebruikt voor vervaardiging van kunststoffen, elektrolytische condensatoren, in de geneeskunde o.a. voor nierfunctieproeven en als zoetmiddel bij suikerziekte (synoniem: mannasuiker) '*).

5 Pervitine is a methylamphetamine-like substance with stimulating effects. It was already used in medicine around 1900. It has also been used during the war to make soldiers more aggressive.

6 Ascorbic acid = vitamin C.

7 This was also confirmed by Dr. Crista Van Haeren (personal communication).

8 See Chapter 11, p. 256-260.

9 COHEN, P. (1989), *op. cit.*, 108 (footnote 1).

10 In his 1991 survey Cohen repeated this practice and bought 22 cocaine samples. The average purity in 1991 was about 10 percent higher (74%) compared to 1987 (65%). Purity under 46 percent was not found in 1991. These 22 samples were not tested for adulterants. COHEN, P. and SAS, A. (1995), *op. cit.*, 66.

11 Both methods are not 100% accurate (personal communication from Dr. Crista Van Haeren). Solution in dicholoromethane can detect adulteration with sugars, but other organic molecules that are easily soluble in dichloromethane (such as lidocaine) may not be detected. Very small concentrates of adulterants (e.g. 5%) will not be detected with IR-spectrometry. It must also be noted that not *all types* of adulterants are found through a regular analysis, because not all types of substances are looked for.

12 The average purity of the 9 samples of freebase cocaine was around 91%. One sample contained 54% freebase cocaine, the other eight samples had a purity of more than 92%. The high purity of freebase cocaine is explained by the fact that a number of adulterants (such as mannitol) are separated from the cocaine hydrochloride when ammonia or ether is added (for the process of making freebase cocaine, see Chapter 7, p. 179-182). BIELEMAN, B. and DE BIE, E. (1994), *op. cit.*, 18 and 32.

13 Dr. R. Jellema, pharmacologist at the Central Police Laboratory that carried out the cocaine sample analysis, believes that amphetamines are rarely found in cocaine, as is the case for other 'dangerous' products such as strychnine, ground glass, washing powder etc. In spite of persistent stories in user subcultures, 'dangerous adulteration' is a myth. According to Jellema, most cocaine is adulterated with mannitol, lidocaine or caffeine. Personal communication from Dr. R. Jellema. See also: SIJMONS, R., 'De politieapotheker', *Vrij Nederland*, June, 14th 1997, 44.

14 Muscle sugar *('Spiersuiker'* in Dutch, i.e. *'zoete zelfstandigheid die o.a. in de spieren voorkomt. Syn. Glycogeen*).

15 Data provided by Dr. Crista Van Haeren (N.I.C.C., Brussels).

16 In 1997 and 1998 a total of 314 cocaine samples were analyzed by the N.I.C.C., but we excluded the samples in which cocaine was impregnated in other materials (as camouflage), such as alcoholic beverages, cosmetics, foods, clothes, cardboard boxes, polymere, etc.

17 Although forensic evidence does not reveal adulteration with *dangerous* substances, the data from the N.I.C.C. indicate that adulteration is a common practice. Additional information about the cocaine samples is mostly missing, but we were able to identify 40 cocaine samples (from 1997 and 1998) as 'street samples' (i.e. samples taken from individual users) and 41 samples 'just arrived on the Belgian drug scene' (i.e. samples taken from a large seizure). The street samples had an average purity of 58.8% while the 'large shipment cocaine' had an average purity of 79.1%.

18 Washton distinguishes two general types of adulterants (or 'cuts'): (1) *active cuts* – those which mimic specific pharmacologic effects of cocaine, e.g. lidocaine, procaine, and CNS stimulants (including amphetamines) – and (2) *inactive cuts* – those which usually have no pharmacologic action but are similar in appearance to cocaine, e.g. mannitol, lactose, sugars, flour, talcum powder, etc. WASHTON, A. (1989), *op. cit.*, 19.

19 Most testing methods discussed here were also described by Bieleman and de Bie in their Rotterdam study in 1990-91 (Bieleman and De Bie, 1992). Methods such as the water test, visual and tactile examination were not reported by the 1987 Amsterdam sample, while the flame test ('burning') was only mentioned by one Antwerp respondent, versus six Amsterdam respondents (Cohen, 1989).

[20] See Chapter 7, p. 179-182.

[21] Bieleman and de Bie (1992) made very similar observations.

[22] The N.I.C.C. data on cocaine samples contain some limited information about the appearance of the drug. Cocaine samples could be classified according to the following categories: 'powder', 'block', 'lumps', 'flakes', 'little ball' (i.e. a very small amount of cocaine wrapped in sticky tape in the form of a little ball with). The average purity varied markedly between these different categories of 'appearance': 'little balls' = 65.2%; 'powder' = 74.8%; 'lumps' = 77.9%; 'block' = 78.5%; and 'flakes' = 90.2%.

[23] For example: dissolve 100 mg of the sample of cocaine in 5 ml of water, add three drops of dilute sulfuric acid, stir, add one drop of permanganate test solution (prepared by dissolving 100 mg of potassium permanganate in 10 ml of water). If the cocaine hydrochloride sample is fairly pure, the mixture will have a pink tint that will gradually fade, but not entirely disappear during the next 30 minutes. If it does not take on this pink tint, or if the tint disappears before 30 minutes have elapsed, the sample is probably not very pure.

[24] For example, to test a cocaine sample for the presence of lactose, add five ml of 5% sodium hydroxide solution to five ml of a 1/20 solution of the material and gently warm it. If it is lactose, it will turn yellow, then reddish brown. To test for lidociaine, dissolve 100 mg of the substance in 1 ml of ethanol or methanol. Add 10 drops of 10% cobalt chloride solution, and shake well for two minutes. If it is freebase lidocaine, a bluish-green precipitate will form. To test for quinine, dissolve 5 mg of the substance in 5 ml of hot ethanol, add two drops of bromine test solution and one ml of ammonia test solution, shake well, and let it stand for a few minutes. If it is quinine, it will gradually turn green.

[25] This burning technique (or flame test) is not to be confused with the melting point test, which is a more exacting procedure.

[26] See Chapter 9, p. 220.

[27] See Chapter 9, p. 221-225.

CHAPTER 11

ADVANTAGES, DISADVANTAGES AND (ADVERSE) EFFECTS OF COCAINE

11.1. INTRODUCTION

This chapter deals with the advantages and disadvantages of cocaine, as perceived by our respondents (§11.2) and with the prevalence of (adverse) effects of cocaine (§11.3). While the latter paragraph is based on our sample's responses to a structured list of effects found in the literature, the former primarily focuses on the spontaneously reported appealing and unappealing aspects of cocaine as subjectively experienced by respondents. [1]

This chapter wants to offer a description of the effects of cocaine from the perspective of the cocaine users themselves (the insider's view).[2] The analytic descriptions of cocaine effects (positive and negative) may be closer to the way the drug is seen and responded to within the socio-cultural context of our respondents than to the portrait painted by some health professionals, law enforcement agencies, politicians and media reports.

11.2. ADVANTAGES AND DISADVANTAGES OF COCAINE

This paragraph deals with the advantages (§11.2.1) and disadvantages (§11.2.2) of cocaine, as perceived by our respondents. It focuses on the spontaneously reported appealing and unappealing aspects of cocaine as subjectively experienced by respondents. In open-ended questions we asked respondents to mention advantages (or appealing aspects) and disadvantages (or unappealing aspects) to a maximum of five each, just as Cohen (1989) did in Amsterdam. Both advantages and disadvantages were then put in order of importance by the respondents. This allowed us to analyze not only which advantages and disadvantages were mentioned most frequently, but also whether there was any agreement as to their relative importance. Respondents were completely free to use their own words. Respondents were also asked whether either dose or circumstances of use, or both, influenced the advantages and disadvantages of cocaine as mentioned by them. If so, they were invited to explain this.

11.2.1. Users' perceptions of advantages of cocaine

The advantages or appealing aspects of cocaine were categorized by Cohen (1989: 82) as follows: cocaine gives excitement [excitement], makes partying better, more festive, easier [partying better], gives feelings of being high, relaxed, beautiful [high, relaxed], gives self confidence [self-confidence], makes the user clear-headed, better concentrated, more creative [more creative], it enables the user to drink longer [drinking longer], it improves the quality of love making [better sex], it facilitates communication, relationships, and lessens shyness [communication], it gives energy, the user needs less sleep and is tired less easily [more energetic]. A small residual category referred to other advantages [other].

Although small coding differences are inevitable, the Antwerp respondents have mentioned four appealing aspects that were not reported by the Amsterdam respondents (although these might have been included in the residual category 'other'). Therefore, we added some other categories: cocaine has a nice taste, gives a pleasant feeling of numbness, gives nice physical effects such as pleasant stimuli [physical effects], the use of cocaine goes together with a typical group atmosphere, a group alliance [group alliance], it gives fewer adverse effects in comparison to other drugs, is easier to hide, bears fewer risks, has a shorter period of action [advantages to other drugs], the ritual character of the preparation acts and of the consumption itself [ritual]. Answers that referred to the kick of doing something illegal were included in the [excitement] category.

Table 11.2.a   Number of times each advantage of cocaine is mentioned, and rank order given, in the 1997 Antwerp sample [*]

Advantage of cocaine	Antwerp (1997)	N=111					Rank total	Rank subtotal
	Rank order					Total		
	1	2	3	4	5			
Communication	21	21	14	5	2	63	1	2
High, relaxed	43	12	6	-	-	61	2	1
More energetic	8	13	8	6	1	36	3	3
Self-confidence	6	12	5	4	1	28	4	4
Physical effects	1	14	7	1	1	24	5	6
More creative	10	5	5	1	2	23	6	5
Better sex	4	5	7	6	1	23	7	8
Group alliance	3	10	4	1	2	20	8	7
Other drugs	3	2	5	5	3	18	9	9
Drink longer	2	2	6	3	3	16	10	13
Partying better	3	2	4	3	1	13	11	10
Excitement	3	1	3	2	2	11	12	12
Ritual	1	4	-	2	1	8	13	11
Other	-	-	-	-	-	11	-	-
Total	**111**	**104**	**78**	**41**	**21**	**355**	**-**	**-**

[*] More than one answer was possible

Table 11.2.a shows the total number of times each of these advantages was mentioned by the Antwerp respondents, and how often each advantage was given rank one, rank two etc. through rank five. We looked into two ways of establishing a hierarchy of advantages of cocaine. One is based on the total number of times an advantage is mentioned (in table 11.2.a under 'rank total'), the other on the total number of times an advantage receives rank one or two ('rank subtotal'). The following features of table 11.2.a are most striking.

Respondents gave an average of 3.2 advantages.[3] More importantly, the average number of advantages per interviewee was higher than the average number of disadvantages, as we will show below.[4]

The three advantages that rank first, second and third, keep their top three ranks in the number of times they are perceived as one or two, relative to other advantages mentioned by the same respondent. It follows that the most important advantages of cocaine as perceived by our Antwerp sample are: 'communication', 'high, relaxed' and 'more energetic'. Some other perceived advantages change ranks, depending on which way we compute them. The 'physical effects' and 'more creative' advantages switch ranks, only when their frequency of being mentioned as number one or two is considered. The same holds for 'better sex' and 'group alliance'. Finally, 'drink longer', 'partying better' and 'ritual' exchange ranks.

The advantages most of all mentioned, including the three most important ones, are instrumental in a socializing life style.[5] According to Cohen (1989: 83) , 'more creative' plays a role for a particular type of user for whom cocaine is more instrumental in intellectual or artistic activities. We checked whether there was a relation between profession and the frequency of reporting 'more creative' as an advantage of cocaine, and we found that only 5 of the 20 respondents having an art-related profession reported 'creative' as an advantage of cocaine. Of those who did report 'creative', 6 worked in hotels/bars/restaurants, 3 were unemployed, 2 worked in the social sector, etc. However, whether respondents have an art-related profession does not say anything about their intellectual or artistic activities outside their occupational life.

The fact that our respondents also report that cocaine has certain appealing aspects compared to other drugs, is not only consistent with our finding that our users have a lot of experience with different drugs,[6] but it could also be an indication for rational motives for the choice of a certain drug. According to some respondents, using cocaine is less conspicuous, it gives fewer adverse effects, it has a shorter period of action, etc. than other drugs, and it is *thus less likely to interfere with daily activities*.[7]

A remarkable difference between our sample and the Amsterdam samples is that 'excitement' is ranked considerably lower by the Antwerp respondents, independent of the way we compute the ranks. Moreover, the 'excitement' advantage dropped from rank no. 6 in the 1987 Amsterdam sample, to no. 9 in the 1991 Amsterdam sample, to no. 12 in the 1997 Antwerp sample. It led Cohen to assume that using cocaine has become a 'normalized' activity (Cohen & Sas, 1995: 83). Using cocaine in the seventies was a novel and strange activity, and its reported popularity among various celebrities glamorized its use. Cocaine was perceived as a special drug (like caviar), it was 'in vogue' and 'the chic thing to do', but now it no longer gives (so much) excitement. Surely, it might be true for the Belgian sample too that the use of cocaine has been gradually 'normalized' within certain user groups, because of its increased availability, its lower price for relatively high quality, etc. But participant observations in the Antwerp nightlife left us with the impression that - in the Belgian repressive climate - cocaine is still surrounded with an aura of *illegality*, creating a feeling of excitement to non-users. Furthermore, it still has a semblance of *exclusivity*, thus creating a feeling of excitement to non-users or users of other (cheaper) drugs such as cannabis or amphetamines.

The devaluation of the 'excitement' advantage over the years in the three samples might be due to the fact that feelings of excitement are more important to younger or inexperienced users. Indeed, although the mean age in the Antwerp sample did not differ significantly from the mean age in the Amsterdam samples,[8] we find several indications that the Antwerp respondents are more experienced than their Amsterdam counterparts. On average, the Antwerp participants started to experiment with cocaine at a younger age,[9] most of them were using it regularly at a younger age,[10] there is a higher proportion of high level users during the period of heaviest use,[11] and in general the Antwerp interviewees experimented with several types of drugs.[12]

Furthermore, we compared the Antwerp respondents who mentioned 'excitement' as an advantage of cocaine with the rest of the sample. Although not statistically significant, we can observe a similar tendency: those who mention 'excitement' tend to have started cocaine use more recently (after 1988), to have less experience with other types of drugs, to be low or medium level users, and to have been using cocaine for a shorter time... In short, 'excitement' as an advantage of cocaine may well be related to the (age and) experience of the user.

> *Of course, the first time was... you're so nervous that it makes you excited anyhow, that you have that energy of being nervous, and the fact itself of doing it, and the fear and all that stuff. Eh, now it's like, when you have been using for a while, that you can perfectly say: 'Look, that's what is going to happen'. You're already on that wavelength, you know what is going to happen, you already adapt yourself to it, you resign yourself to, you automatically become calm because you know what is going to happen.* [H/0/30]

According to 12.6% of our respondents, *dose* has no influence on the mentioned advantages (versus 29% in the 1987 Amsterdam sample). Another 84.7% felt that dose does have an influence on the advantages (versus 68% in the 1987 Amsterdam sample), and 2.7% did not answer this question (see table 11.2.b). This was mostly explained in terms of an optimum or minimum dose, or advantages becoming stronger as dosage increased. Almost half of our Antwerp respondents (44.1%) stressed the importance of the optimum dose.

Table 11.2.b   Relation of dose to advantages of cocaine use, in the 1997 Antwerp sample [*]

Relation to dose	Antwerp (1997) N=111	
	N	%
Optimum dose	49	44.1
Stronger	18	16.2
Minimum dose	17	15.3
Quality	9	8.1
Tolerance	9	8.1
To be repeated	6	5.4
Varies	6	5.4
Longer	3	2.7
Other	1	0.9
No answer/no influence	*17*	*15.3*

[*] More than one answer was possible

Although not mentioned by the Amsterdam I respondents, our users also reported 'quality' and 'tolerance' as important dose-related factors influencing advantages. For a good understanding of the relation of dose to the advantages of cocaine, here are some illustrative statements from our respondents:

My measure is always the same. If you have been doing it for such a long time, you should now: there's the limit, and if you cross it, your heart will start aching, and you will feel like this and that, you know the complete range of feelings, so you never use too much. Up to there, to that maximum, but if you cross the limit the advantages are gone. [W/0/01]

The most important thing is that you shouldn't use all the time, because then the fun is soon over. If you want to enjoy going out, drinking, having sex, it means you shouldn't be using all the time, of course. So, in a way, you need to have that self-discipline not to do that, to enjoy until the effects wear off, and then you can have another blast, and then you can carry on. [...] You must be able to enjoy the effect itself, and not just want more and more. Because that is the biggest problem with cocaine: you always need more. No, you really have to enjoy it. [H/0/10]

For the first two shots in an evening you don't need so much. Later you need to take more to get the same result, and in the end you can take as much as you want, it'll only be a faint version of the initial feeling. [H/1/15]

When asked whether *circumstances* influence the perceived advantages of cocaine, 11.7% denied and 87.4% agreed versus 30% and 68% of the Amsterdam 1987 sample (see Table 11.2.c). The most frequent explanations for the influence of circumstances were in terms of social relations within a group: 59.5% of the Antwerp respondents stated advantages of cocaine were experienced more in a 'pleasant' or 'safe' environment, and when the respondent was 'not alone'. Smaller proportions of the Antwerp sample experience the appealing aspects mostly at home (13.5%), when they are relaxed (9.9%) and when they are in the 'right mood' (9.0%).

Table 11.2.c   Relation of circumstances to advantages of cocaine use, in the 1997 Antwerp sample [*]

Relation to circumstances	Antwerp (1997) N=111	
	N	%
Pleasant	46	41.4
Safe	16	14.4
Better at home	15	13.5
Relaxed	11	9.9
Right mood	10	9.0
Good music	9	8.1
Parties	6	5.4
Varies	5	4.5
Other	5	4.5
Not alone	3	2.7
Better alone	3	2.7
Continuation	-	-
No answer/no influence	*14*	*12.6*

[*] More than one answer was possible

Six respondents of the 1987 Amsterdam sample mentioned some task or job ([continuation] in table 11.2.c) as a positive circumstance for the advantages of cocaine to appear. None of our respondents mentioned this. On the other hand, 9 of our Antwerp users stated that good music was a condition for advantages, versus none of the 1987 Amsterdam sample. Our respondents probably associate cocaine use more with going out (discotheques, bars with good music) or socializing with friends at home, rather than with working (i.e. continuation).

As will be shown below, individual preferences can have an important influence on the setting of drug use: while some people like to use cocaine at parties (5.4%), others prefer to consume it at home (13.5%).[13] Some (although not many) people prefer being alone, while others love to share the experience of using... Again, the best way to make these quantitative data understandable, is to let our respondents speak for themselves:

> *You have a kind of feeling that you are completely detached from the world. That's what I mean by relaxing. And that can be enervating when you are going out. Because people come to you and say: jeezes, what's up, you pull a long face, don't you have fun? Yes, actually, you feel fantastic, but you don't want any contact with anybody, you want to be on your own, and you can enjoy that more at home than when you go out.* [B/1/01]

> *I prefer not to use at home. Because I get the feeling: they will burst into the house, or they will do this or that. I prefer being somewhere else...* [H/0/10]

> *When you do it with a person you feel at ease with, it's more fun than with people you don't know very well.* [Z/0/01]

> *You're already high, and if you go to a party where they play house music or so. I'm not a house freak but at that moment, I can dance to it, you're kinda like one with that beat, you're in a kind of trance, and it amplifies that, I think.* [H/1/28]

11.2.2. Users' perceptions of disadvantages of cocaine

In the same way as we asked our respondents about advantages of cocaine, we asked them about unappealing aspects or disadvantages. The sum total of all disadvantages mentioned by our Antwerp users, was 330. This means that each respondent perceived about 3.0 disadvantages versus 3.2 advantages.[14] In other words, the balance of perceived advantages and disadvantages per respondent tips to the side of advantages. This may state the obvious, but classical ideas on addiction often suggest that drug users continue to use a substance because they cannot behave otherwise and because the pharmacological action of the drug creates a 'need' that has to be fulfilled despite obvious disadvantages. It is often forgotten that any (illicit) drug use is highly functional. Users may benefit from it (or at least perceive advantages in the use of these substances).

Table 11.2.d presents the results of the Antwerp sample. We see the number of times a particular disadvantage was mentioned by the total sample, and how often a disadvantage received ranking one, two, etc. through five. In our 'other' category, we included answers like: guilt feelings afterwards (2), hard to obtain (3), neglecting engagements (3), negative effects on social relations (5), on work (2), on your life in general (1), short action of cocaine (3), the greedy effect (2), etc.

The most important disadvantage reported by our sample is the financial cost of cocaine, (as was the case for the 1987 Amsterdam sample).[15] For the rest of his analysis, Cohen (1989: 86) discarded this disadvantage because it might be an artifact of the present legal situation and not a characteristic of the drug. We agree with him, but it deserves special attention that the financial consequence of the use of cocaine is perceived by interviewees as a more important disadvantage than any physical or psychological adverse effect.[16]

Table 11.2.d   Number of times each disadvantage of cocaine is mentioned, and rank order given, in the 1997 Antwerp sample [*]

| Disadvantages of cocaine | Antwerp (1997)   N=111 | | | | | | Rank total | Rank subtot. [♣] |
| | Rankorder | | | | | Total | | |
	1	2	3	4	5			
Expensive	20	25	13	4	-	62	1	1
Unpleasant physical effects	11	8	11	3	2	35	2	2
Unhealthy	8	8	3	4	1	24	4	3
Psychological dependence	12	2	8	2	1	25	3	4
Makes one egocentric, introverted	6	6	2	-	3	17	5	5
Creates bad physical condition	3	4	1	1	-	9	11	11
Takes much time to recuperate	1	3	-	-	-	4	18	15
Aggressivity, irritability	-	3	1	1	-	5	17	18
Depression	6	1	2	2	-	11	8	9
Induces too much drinking	1	1	-	1	-	3	20	20
Insomnia	2	3	1	2	-	8	12	13
Negative feelings	1	1	-	-	1	3	21	21
Unpleasant/criminal environm.	-	1	1	-	1	3	22	22
Induces too much smoking	-	-	2	-	1	3	23	24
Adulterated, low quality	5	2	1	2	-	10	10	10
Physical dependence	-	1	-	-	-	1	24	23
Makes one superficial	1	2	-	-	1	4	19	17
Megalomania	3	2	-	1	1	7	14	12
Makes one speedy, exaggerating	3	1	3	1	-	8	13	14
Makes one insensitive, cold	2	-	2	2	-	6	15	19
Takes away appetite for food	1	2	-	2	-	5	16	16
Paranoia	6	3	3	1	-	13	7	7
Illegal character/stigma	3	5	2	-	1	11	9	8
Difficult to stop	6	5	3	-	1	15	6	6
Other	-	-	-	-	-	38	-	-
Total	101	89	59	29	14	330	-	-

[*] More than one answer possible   [♣] Based on first two ranks

Because so many different unappealing aspects were mentioned, Cohen (1989: 86) reduced the list to three categories (apart from the 'expensive' disadvantage):

(1) *Disadvantages relating to physical effects* (Cohen included: unpleasant physical effects, bad for health, creates bad physical condition and creates physical dependence);

(2) *Disadvantages relating to psychological effects* (Cohen included: psychological dependence, makes one egocentric, makes one aggressive, makes one depressed, makes one feel negative, makes one agitated ('speedy'), gives one megalomaniac feelings, makes one superficial, makes one insensitive, gives one paranoiac feelings; we have added: negative effect on personality, makes one feel fake, and difficult to stop);

(3) And a residual category, *other* (Cohen included: takes time to recuperate, induces too much smoking or drinking, insomnia, unpleasant/criminal environment, low quality, takes away appetite for food; we have added: illegal character/stigma).

Disadvantages that relate to physical effects are mentioned 69 times (20.9% of all disadvantages). Two of these four are in the top 10: 'unpleasant physical effects' and 'bad for health'. Disadvantages that relate to psychological effects are mentioned 114 times (34.5%) of all advantages. Four of these ten are in the top 10: 'creates psychological dependence', 'makes egocentric, introverted', 'makes feel depressed' and 'gives paranoiac feelings'.

Table 11.2.e   Relation of dose to disadvantages, in the 1997 Antwerp sample [*]

Relation to dose	Antwerp (1997) N=111	
	N	**%**
Stronger	38	34.2
Less when moderate	20	18.0
Not when moderate	16	14.4
Quality	9	8.1
Specific dose	1	0.9
Incidental	1	0.9
Other	2	1.8
No answer	*27*	*24.3*

[*] More than one answer was possible

When asked whether *dose* played a role in the occurrence of stated disadvantages, 75.7% of our respondents agreed (versus 81.9% of the Amsterdam sample). 13.5% disagreed and 10.8% did not answer. Thirty-eight respondents claimed that disadvantages increased gradually as the dose increased (see table 11.2.e). As we have seen for the issue of a possible relation between dose and advantages, again 8.1% of our respondents stated that the quality of their cocaine was an important condition for the (non-)appearance of disadvantages. Some typical statements were:

> *The more you use, the more worked up you can be, the more money you spend on it, the more you become asocial and cool in a large group, the more fake effects you have... For me, it's the excessive use that can be disadvantageous to all these aspects.* [H/0/27]

> *If I have a drink and I become sick, it's because I've taken too much. That doesn't happen when I take a little. If I take a lot, it's a fact that I will have pressures on my chest, and I feel bad, it's not pleasant. I don't have that if I take a few lines.* [H/1/20]

> *Particularly the quality, I think. When the quality was less, I always used more. Probably to have the same dose, but that is one of the disadvantages: what kind of dirt do you get with it. Especially with coke it is hard to estimate. There have been moments I felt like I had sinusitis, and then I knew it wasn't pure stuff.* [E/0/01]

> *It's very personal, it's like with alcohol. Somebody else can drink a bottle of whisky, and I might fall asleep after two glasses. Everyone has his own measure. I know for myself: I can go that far, and I also know: if I do another line, it'll be too much. And yet, sometimes I do take another line, just to check: am I right?* [W/0/01]

When we add up 'not when moderate', 'less when moderate' and 'stronger', more than 65% in the Antwerp sample (as well as in the 1987 Amsterdam sample) mentioned one of these three. With some imagination, a general rule of use could be deduced from these findings: *when used moderately, advantages of cocaine will remain stronger than disadvantages. If you do not use moderately, the balance will tip to the side of disadvantages.* It is obvious that a governing rule so often heard from users, and so vague and subjective, leaves much space for a highly personal interpretation of the term 'moderate'... The data presented in Chapter 14 and in Chapter 15 provide more insight in the users' views on moderate (or controlled) use and the set and setting factors that are related with the idea of 'moderate' use.[17]

Forty respondents, or 36.0% of the Antwerp sample, stated that *circumstances* had no impact on the disadvantages of cocaine use (versus 56.6% of the 1987 Amsterdam

sample). Sixty-four respondents, or 57.7%, confirmed a relation between circumstances and unappealing aspects. Circumstances such as the presence of friends (or
non-users or irritating people), the atmosphere (whether there are arguments or discussions, or not), the (joyful or depressive) mood of the other users, the location (at home
or not), etc. play an important role (see table 11.2.f). Some typical answers may illuminate these findings:

*If you're going out with some friends, and after that you go home together, and you sit there
together for a while, I have less trouble the next day, compared to when I'm home alone, far
from everybody.* [I/1/12]

*When you are with friends, and there have been some arguments, you feel even worse after
that. Compared to when you had fun all night long in a discotheque...* [C/0/04]

*If it was based at home with that friend, depression came up more quickly, because that guy
was quite a depressive person, and you drag each other along.* [Y/0/01]

*As soon as I feel uncomfortable somewhere, those disadvantages increase rapidly. If I'm not
at ease, I will use faster, and use more, which in turn has a financial impact. So now I try
not to use anywhere... One person who starts enervating you is enough to fuck it all up. So I
prefer at home.* [H/0/05]

*Yes, if you are among friends, it's not that bad. And among people who are not addicted to
it. If you are with people who are really pushing you, without you realizing what you are
doing, it is not an advantage.* [H/0/10]

*It depends on the experience of the people you're doing it with. The more experienced the
others are, the more you use too. Because you do it together, and the craving increases
when you are with several people.* [R/0/01]

Table 11.2.f   Relation of circumstances to disadvantages, in the 1997 Antwerp sample [*]

Relation to circumstances	Antwerp (1997) N=111	
	N	%
Friends or not	12	10.8
Not safe	11	9.9
Discussions/arguments	10	9.0
Not at home	7	6.3
Heavy use of others	7	6.3
Many people	6	5.4
Irritating company	5	4.5
At home	4	3.6
Lonely	4	3.6
Mood other users	3	2.7
Non users around	3	2.7
Combined with alcohol	2	1.8
Busy	2	1.8
Other	5	4.5
No answer	*47*	*42.3*

[*] More than one answer was possible

As Cohen and Sas (1995: 83-85) suggested rightly, these outcomes do not refer to the
prevalence of these phenomena themselves, but only to their perception as being disadvantageous. And vice versa, the mere prevalence of an effect does not give a useful
insight in the value of this effect for a particular aggregate of respondents.[18]

11.2.3. Relationship between dose, circumstances and (dis)advantages

Table 11.2.g shows the proportions of respondents who affirm a relationship between: a) dose and disadvantages; b) dose and advantages; c) circumstances of use and disadvantages; and d) circumstances of use and advantages.

In the 1987 Amsterdam sample and the 1997 Antwerp sample, both advantages and disadvantages are perceived as related to *dose*. In the Amsterdam study, however, the relationship was more marked for the disadvantages, while we found a more marked relationship between dose and advantages. In both samples advantages and disadvantages were perceived as related to *circumstances*, and this relationship was more marked for the advantages. Table 11.2.g also shows that for *advantages or appealing aspects*, both dose and circumstances play a more or less equal role in both samples. But while in our sample, the proportion of respondents affirming a relation between advantages and dose/circumstances is approx. 85%, a proportion of about 68% was found in Amsterdam. For the occurrence of *disadvantages or unappealing aspects*, dose is clearly the most important factor in both samples, although the difference regarding circumstances is more marked in the 1987 Amsterdam sample. These findings are consistent with our findings elsewhere: in the next paragraph it is shown that the probability of the occurrence of several adverse effects is related to dose and frequency of use.[19]

Table 11.2.g   Proportions of respondents who affirm a relation between dose and or circumstances with advantages and/or disadvantages, in percentages, in the 1987 Amsterdam I sample and the 1997 Antwerp sample

Relation to...	Amsterdam I (1987) Influenced by		Antwerp (1997) Influenced by	
	Dose	Circumstances	Dose	Circumstances
Advantages	68.1	67.5	84.7	87.4
Disadvantages	81.9	41.3	75.7	57.7

11.2.4. International comparison with other cocaine studies

The data of the present study are consistent with most other community studies of cocaine users. The most commonly reported advantages or appealing aspects of cocaine are related to its stimulating action (energetic feeling, excitement, self-confidence) and to a socializing lifestyle (relaxation, sociability). Clearly, cocaine provides a wide range of positive effects to those who use it in moderation: more energy, a certain intellectual focus, enhanced sensations, and increased sociability and social intimacy (e.g. Mugford, 1994; Ditton & Hammersley, 1996; Erickson *et al.*, 1994; Waldorf *et al.*, 1991; Diaz *et al.*, 1992). Social, sexual, or recreational activities and work can be enlivened, and many respondents used the drug not only in pleasurable but also in productive ways. Erickson *et al.* (1994: 103-113) devote a separate chapter to the subjective 'appeal' of cocaine. Some respondents of their Toronto sample (1983) acknowledged that the 'champagne of drugs' label was part of the attraction of cocaine. The stimulating properties of the drug were mentioned by many in conjunction with the notion of a controlled high that did not interfere with normal activities.

The high financial cost of cocaine is the most often reported disadvantage. Despite some differences in rank order, respondents from all samples report disadvantages related to physical effects (fatigue, hangover and insomnia), disadvantages related to

psychological effects (anxiety, depression, paranoia, irritability and aggression), cocaine-related sexual problems (impotence, feeling insensitive, feeling too sensitive),
negative social consequences (isolation, selfishness, insensitivity to others) and financial, workplace and relational problems (Diaz *et al.*, 1992: 207-208; Waldorf *et al.*,
1991: 159-186; Ditton & Hammersley, 1996: 54-55; Erickson *et al.*, 1994: 119-120). It
must be stressed that intention to continue using was not related to cost nor to any of
the other unappealing aspects. Users are prepared accept the unappealing aspects of
cocaine, which were outweighed by its appealing factors (Erickson *et al.*, 1994: 103-
113).

Whether dose or circumstances of use, or both, have an influence on appealing and
unappealing aspects of cocaine use, is rarely specifically discussed. Most studies, however, suggest that the appearance of disadvantages at the expense of the disappearance
of advantages is generated by an increased use of cocaine (Diaz *et al.*, 1992: 207-208;
Waldorf *et al.*, 1991: 223). These studies thus seem to support our finding that dose
(i.e. the frequency or the quantity of cocaine use) has an influence on the occurrence of
advantages and disadvantages. Similarly, most community studies do not report overtly
on the relation between appealing and unappealing aspects and the circumstances of
use. Yet, most authors suggest that there is a link because people can find cocaine useful or pleasurable in a larger number of activity spheres. Depending on the various
functions cocaine use can have for these people (festive-social, performance at work,
escapism, sexual, etc.), circumstances of use may have a serious impact on advantages
and disadvantages.

It is important to note that most studies on cocaine use focus on the prevalence of
adverse effects or on cocaine-related problems, and tend to neglect the spontaneously
reported appealing aspects of cocaine as subjectively experienced by respondents. The
positive effects or advantages of cocaine are usually minimized whereas descriptions
of the negative effects, disadvantages or unappealing aspects of cocaine are universal.
A typical example is the Turin study (1990-91), where the discussion of the effects of
cocaine is limited to disadvantages, health problems and negative effects on the users'
financial situation (Merlo *et al.*, 1992: 69-70 and 90). Positive experiences and sensations are only acknowledged during the initial phase of experimentation. This suggests
that the use of illicit drugs only yields positive experiences or advantages in the beginning of a user's career and that eventually the balance always tips to the side of the
negative effects or disadvantages. Appealing aspects are presented as highly subjective
and temporary, and unappealing aspects as inevitable and more 'objective'. 'When the
honeymoon is over', problems start to appear for most users.[20]

Waldorf *et al.* (1991) observe that in many ways the pharmacology of cocaine encourages increasing use. The pharmacological qualities of cocaine make people find
cocaine useful or pleasurable in a growing number of activity spheres. Similarly, Ditton *et al.* (1996: 121) state that - taking into account the very qualities of the cocaine
high - it is not surprising that a minority of the people who initially like cocaine, subsequently come to find it difficult to manage without it. However, this does not mean
that positive effects and advantages can only appear during initial use (Diaz *et al.*,
1992: 198-209; Ditton *et al.* (1996: 47-51) recognize that the effects of cocaine are
poorly treated in the scientific literature, not least because most authors start from the
notion that cocaine is 'bad', and can have but negative effects.

11.3. (ADVERSE) EFFECTS OF COCAINE AND THEIR RELATION TO LEVEL OF USE

Our respondents were asked to report the life time prevalence of 91 symptoms, divided into three lists. We replicated the three extensive check-lists of effects (totaling 91 items), from Morningstar and Chitwood (1983) -list 1 and 2- and Spotts and Shontz (1980) -list 3. The discussion in this paragraph is limited to the question whether the probability of adverse effects of cocaine increases with level of use.[21] As was explained in chapter 5, the level of use is a construct, based on frequency of use multiplied by dose per occasion.[22] This means the level of use consists of a certain amount of cocaine per time period (here, per week). In this paragraph we focus only on the period of heaviest use. To find out whether a certain effect is level-of-use-related, we use the life time prevalence of certain cocaine-related effects. If Cohen's hypothesis (1989: 94) that certain effects are level-of-use-related holds, the probability that a certain effect will be reported increases if we take as a point of measurement the level of use during the period of a respondent's heaviest use.

In tables 11.3.a through 11.3.c we show the effects of cocaine use, and the percentage of respondents who report having experienced each effect (under 'total'). We also show the percentages in which low, medium and high level users during their top period reported their experience of each effect. This way we can assess whether a rising level of use increases the probability of experiencing each effect. Three preliminary observations should be made on the following tables:

(1) They only contain what cocaine users subjectively consider to be symptoms related to cocaine use. The objective validity of their perceptions is unknown. Thus some of the symptoms could be over- or underestimated, or both. Nevertheless, the subjective validity of these self-reports makes them an interesting indication for the users' knowledge of the effects of cocaine.

(2) We are aware that giving the respondents long lists of effects and then asking them if they have experienced them as a consequence of cocaine use is sensitive to bias. Respondents may have inadequately attributed some effects to cocaine, or may have interpreted the description (e.g. of 'delirium tremens' or 'serious accidents') differently.

(3) One of the fundamental problems of measuring drug effects with this research technique is that the absence of a control group precludes assessing the non-cocaine-related prevalence of certain effects (such as 'nose bleeding' or 'urge to carry weapons').

(4) These structured lists of effects obviously must be interpreted very cautiously, because *simple occurrence of a drug effect, be it negative or positive, does not say very much about its significance for users.* For example, effects such as 'depression', 'insomnia', 'lack of appetite' and 'megalomania' are reported by many respondents as an effect of cocaine use, but they are clearly not perceived as important disadvantages by our sample. Other effects, such as 'self-confidence', 'energetic feeling' and several unpleasant physical effects are related to cocaine and and many of our users also see these as significant effects, as they were highly ranked as (dis-)advantages of cocaine in paragraph 11.2.

We found a prevalence of 100% for three effects: 'energetic feeling' and 'self-confidence' only for low level users (table 11.3.b) and 'euphoria' for medium level users (table 11.3.c). [23]

Table 11.3.a   Probability of occurrence of cocaine effects (list 1), for level of use in top period and for total sample, in %, in the 1997 Antwerp sample

Effects of cocaine (list 1)	Level of use top period			Total N=111	χ2 sign.
	Low N=24	Medium N=32	High N=55		
Lack of appetite	70.8	62.5	74.5	70.3	~
Runny nose	62.5	59.4	56.4	58.6	~
Insomnia	33.3	56.25	61.8	54.1	~
Restlessness	29.2	34.4	58.2	45.0	~
No orgasm	29.2	53.1	47.3	45.0	~
Anxiety	25.0	28.1	45.4	36.0	~
Nose/bronchial problem	16.7	21.9	38.2	28.8	~
Phys. Unfit>1month	4.2	6.25	41.8	23.4	~
Impotence [♦]	15.4	37.5	42.4	22.5	~
Depression>1month	4.2	9.4	34.5	20.7	~
Lack of sexual interest	4.2	18.7	25.4	18.9	~
Nose infections	12.5	12.5	23.6	18.0	~
Infections	8.3	3.1	30.9	18.0	~
High blood pressure	8.3	18.7	18.2	16.2	~
Nose problems	4.2	6.25	21.8	13.5	~
Delirium tremens	8.3	6.25	20.0	13.5	~
Haemorrhages	-	9.4	21.8	13.5	~
Overdose of some drug	-	9.4	21.8	13.5	~
Skin infections	4.2	-	16.4	9.0	~
Streetfight injuries	-	6.25	12.7	8.1	~
Liver disease	-	-	14.5	7.2	~
Serious accident/injury	4.2	6.25	5.4	5.4	~
Kidney diseases	-	-	10.9	5.4	~
Small operations	-	-	5.4	2.7	~
Pneumonia	-	-	5.4	2.7	~
Heart diseases	-	3.1	1.8	1.8	~
Ulcer	-	-	3.6	1.8	~
Gynaecol. Problems [♥]	-	-	-	-	~
Veneral diseases	-	-	-	-	~
Diabetes	-	-	-	-	~

* p<0.10   [♦] Only for men (Antwerpen: N= 13; 24; 33; 70)
~ = is not appl.   [♥] Only for women (Antwerpen: N= 11; 8; 22; 41)

If we lower our threshold for 'universal' prevalence of effects to 75%, we see in list 1 (table 11.3.a) that none of these (mainly physical) effects is reported with a prevalence of 75% or more in our sample. A summary of tables 11.3.a through 11.3.c shows that in our sample (as was the case in both Amsterdam samples) the number of negative effects reported by 75% or more of the respondents increases with level of use:

(a) We find a 75% or higher prevalence for 8 positive and 8 negative effects for the low-level users of our Antwerp sample.[24]

(b) For the medium-level users, we find a slightly negative balance in the Antwerp sample: 10 positive and 12 negative effects.[25]

(c) The high-level users in our Antwerp sample have a prevalence of 75% (and over) for 10 positive and 19 negative effects.[26]

Thus, a level of use higher than 2.5 grams a week definitely alters the balance between positive and negative effects. For low-level users the balance is overwhelmingly positive, for medium-level users it is in equilibrium, and for high-level users it turns rather negative.

Table 11.3.b   Probability of occurrence of cocaine effects (list 2), per level of use in top period and for total sample, in %, in the 1997 Antwerp sample

Effects of cocaine (list 2)	Low N=24	Medium N=32	High N=55	Total N=111	χ2 sign.
Energetic feeling	100.0	96.8	98.2	98.2	~
Restless/nervous	87.5	93.8	96.4	93.7	~
Dry mouth	91.7	90.6	94.5	92.8	~
Increased heartrate	82.6	96.9	94.5	92.7?	~
Think faster	91.7	93.8	90.9	91.9	~
Clear thinking	91.7	90.6	90.9	91.0	~
Self-confidence	100.0	96.8	83.6	90.9	~
Lack of appetite	87.5	78.1	98.2	90.1	~
Forget worries	83.3	90.6	83.6	85.6	~
Sweating	66.7	81.3	92.7	83.8	***
Insomnia	79.2	84.4	81.8	82.0	ns
Mind wanders	58.3	81.3	76.4	73.9	ns
Teeth grinding	66.7	71.9	76.4	73.0	ns
Feeling cold/distant	66.7	71.9	76.4	72.9	ns
Megalomania	62.5	75.0	74.5	72.1	ns
Tremor	50.0	68.8	78.2	69.4	**
Difficult orgasms	45.8	81.3	70.8	68.5	***
Meaningless tasks	45.8	71.9	72.7	66.7	*
Feeling detached	70.8	65.6	61.8	64.9	ns
Overly suspicious	41.7	59.4	76.4	64.0	***
Nosebleeding	66.7	71.9	50.9	60.4	ns
Depression	25.0	53.1	67.3	54.0	*****
Headaches	45.8	53.1	56.4	53.2	ns
Change in breathing	41.7	46.9	61.8	53.1	ns
Anxiety	37.5	53.1	58.2	52.3	ns
Visual distortions	29.2	40.6	53.7	44.5	ns
Dizziness	29.2	43.8	45.5	41.4	ns
Nausea	25.0	37.5	48.1	40.0?	ns
Convulsions	29.2	18.8	54.5	38.7	*****
Menstr.cycle changes [♥]	27.3	25.0	45.4	36.6	~
Mystic experiences	29.2	31.3	40.0	35.1	ns
Hallucinations	12.5	12.5	36.4	24.3	***
Skin bugs	4.2	12.5	21.8	15.3	~
Unconsciousness	-	6.3	5.5	4.5	~

* p<0.10   ** p<0.05   *** p<0.025   ****p<0.01   *****p<0.005   ******p<0.001
ns=non significant   ~ = not applicable   [♥] Only for women (Antwerpen: N= 11; 8; 22; 41)

Finally, we tested for statistical significance the relation between level of use (at top period) and the occurrence of cocaine effects, wherever possible. Again, there are a lot of minor and major differences between the three samples, and examining them in detail would be too time-consuming. Suffice it to say that statistically significant relations were found in all three samples for 'weight loss' (p<0.001 in all three samples), 'overly suspicious' (at least p<0.05), 'tremor' (at least p<0.05), 'depressions' (at least p<0.005) and 'sweating' (at least p<0.025).

The relationship between levels of use and the prevalence of the different effects is problematic: some effects that were related to level of use during period of heaviest use in one sample were not in another sample, and vice versa.[27] Cohen indicated that the instruments we use for measuring cocaine effects are still far from perfect. *'This may be due to bias in sampling (...), interviewer effects, wording of the cocaine effect questions, changes in fashions about route of ingestion, differences in functional percep-*

tions of cocaine, etc. Another unknown source of bias can be caused by the use of combinations of drugs.' (Cohen & Sas, 1995: 88-89).

Table 11.3.c   Probability of occurrence of cocaine effects (list 3), per level of use in top period and for total sample, in %, in the 1997 Antwerp sample

| Effects of cocaine (list 3) | Antwerp (1997) | | | | |
| | Level of use top | | | | |
	Low N=24	Medium N=32	High N=55	Total N=111	χ2 sign.
Talkative	95.8	96.9	90.9	93.7	~
Euphoria	95.8	100.0	85.2	91.8?	~
Local stupefaction	87.5	90.6	87.0	88.2?	~
Sense of perfectness	95.8	81.3	83.6	85.6	~
Dilation of pupils	79.2	86.7	87.0	85.2?	~
Prolonged sex	70.8	81.3	87.3	82.0	ns
Sexual stimulation	70.8	81.3	78.2	77.5	ns
Feeling indifferent	79.2	75.0	74.5	75.6	ns
Weight loss	50.0	56.3	89.1	71.2	******
Diarrhoea	70.8	71.9	67.3	69.4	ns
Urinate more often	58.3	59.4	76.4	67.6	ns
Indifference to pain	50.0	62.5	70.9	64.0	ns
Lack of ambition	45.8	50.0	75.9	61.8?	***
Better orgasms	50.0	62.5	58.2	57.7	ns
Yawning	50.0	56.3	60.0	56.8	ns
Tightness in chest	33.3	53.1	54.5	49.5?	ns
Ringing in the ear	41.7	28.1	60.0	46.8	***
Visual flashes	29.2	41.9	43.6	40.0	ns
Panic, being scared	20.8	25.0	40.0	31.5	ns
Allergies	25.0	18.8	32.7	27.0	ns
Violence	8.3	18.8	32.7	23.4	**
Imaginary enemy	8.3	3.1	27.3	16.2	****
Spontaneous orgasm	4.2	12.5	20.0	14.4?	~
Urge to carry weapon	4.2	-	16.4	9.0	~
Convulsions	-	-	3.7	1.8	~

* p<0.10   ** p<0.05   *** p<0.025   ****p<0.01   *****p<0.005   ******p<0.001
ns=non significant   ~ = not applicable

We also asked our respondents for effects that were not included in the three checklists of 91 effects. Their replies are interesting, not only because they reflect what users perceive as important or impressive, but also because they are descriptions of effects in the respondents' own words (and not pre-determined in a questionnaire). As such they complement the previous paragraphs.

Twenty-two respondents reported effects not included in the checklists. Still, eleven of them actually referred in their own words to effects that were in the list, such as restlessness, feeling detached, depressions, talkativeness, mystic experience, overly suspicious, sweating etc. Others referred to idiosyncratic effects such as: three-dimensional sound effects; a timeless feeling ('the here and now are important'); increased tendency to dream, to daydream, to fantasize; being absorbed in your own world; a desire for being alone; an upset stomach; cold legs or shaking knees; a better sense for music; a long period of sobering up; etc.

The following quotations illustrate some other effects reported by respondents: restlessness, paranoia, a feeling of exclusivity (closely related to the kick of doing something illegal), increased susceptibility to diseases.

It often happens that I start looking for something, little things, and then I don't find them, yes probably because it even isn't there. What I mean with looking, for example [...] I can't find my lighter. Well, I can spend one hour and a half looking for it, I'll turn everything upside down to find it, while maybe my friend forgot it at her job or at a friend's. [H/0/05]

A sense of exclusivity. That you felt exclusive in some way. You have the impression you were doing something other people didn't do, and it gave a satisfaction in some way, that you thought:: I'm doing something here which is not allowed. We are doing hard drugs here. Because they call it hard drugs it was something you wanted to do one way or another, it was fascinating in a way. It may sound silly for an old guy like me, but I continued doing it for a long time, first because it was not allowed! [K/0/01]

When I was using a lot, I started looking on the floor, hoping you would find something great. There were little lumps everywhere that had fallen off, supposedly, and sometimes I put some breadcrumbs on the glass, so it was really scary [she laughs] . [K/1/03]

This list needs another item: the flu. When you use something, you have the flu the next day. And it's not a coincidence, I know it now through all those years, [...] you are more vulnerable for microbes or whatever, and the next day I'm sick. [W/0/01]

11.4. CONCLUSION

Most studies on cocaine use focus on the prevalence of adverse effects or cocaine-related problems, but tend to neglect the spontaneously reported appealing and unappealing aspects of cocaine as subjectively experienced by respondents. The positive effects or advantages or appealing aspects of cocaine are minimized whereas descriptions of the negative effects or disadvantages or unappealing aspects of cocaine are universal. This leads to suggest that the use of illicit drugs yields positive experiences or advantages in the beginning of a user's career only and that eventually the balance always tips to the side of the negative effects or disadvantages. This chapter has presented data on the advantages and disadvantages of cocaine (§11.2), and on the prevalence of (adverse) effects of cocaine (§11.3). The data presented here do not refer to the prevalence of these phenomena themselves, but only to their perception by our respondents. And vice versa, the mere prevalence of an effect does not give a useful insight in its value for a particular aggregate of respondents.

The Antwerp data indicate that the balance of perceived advantages and disadvantages per respondent tips to the side of advantages. In most community samples of cocaine users, there is agreement on the relative importance of advantages such as 'more energetic', 'high, relaxed' and 'communication', and less markedly also on 'more creative' and 'self-confidence'. Advantages most frequently mentioned are instrumental in a socializing life style. The observation that cocaine use is highly functional and that users may benefit from it (or at least perceive advantages in its use), runs counter to the classical theories of addiction that suggest that drug users continue to use a substance because they cannot behave otherwise and because the pharmacological action of the drug creates a 'need' that has to be met, despite obvious disadvantages.

Our data and those from some major community samples of cocaine users (Scotland, San Francisco, Toronto) show that cocaine provides a wide range of positive effects to those who use it in moderation: more energy, an intellectual focus, enhanced sensations, and increased sociability and social intimacy. Social, sexual, or recreational activities and work can be enlivened, and many respondents used the drug not only in pleasurable but also in productive ways. Moreover, compared to other drugs, cocaine is less likely to interfere with daily activities. Typically, interviewees perceive the financial consequence of their cocaine use as a more important disadvantage than any physical or psychological adverse effect they report. Participants from different samples, like most of the Antwerp respondents, are prepared to live with the unappealing aspects of cocaine, which are outweighed by its appealing factors.

According to most respondents, *circumstances* such as the user's mood, the user's individual preferences, the presence of friends (or non-users or irritating people), the atmosphere (whether there are arguments or discussions, or not), the (joyful or depressive) mood of the other users, the location (at home or not), etc. play an important role in the presence of (dis-)advantages. Similarly, (dis-)advantages are perceived by our respondents (as well as Cohen's respondents in 1987) as related to *dose*. The general rule of use deduced from these findings is that when used moderately, advantages of cocaine will remain more important than disadvantages. If you do not use moderately, the balance will tip to the side of disadvantages. Furthermore, the Antwerp interviewees also reported 'quality' and 'tolerance' as important dose-related factors influencing advantages.

Naturally, the pharmacology of cocaine encourages increasing use. The pharmacological qualities of cocaine help users to find cocaine useful or pleasurable in a larger number of activity spheres. Depending on the various functions cocaine use can possibly have for these people (festive-social, performance at work, escapism, sexual, etc.) circumstances of use may have a serious impact on advantages and disadvantages. Moreover, the presence of disadvantages at the expense of the absence of advantages is generated by an increase in cocaine use (i.e. the frequency or the quantity of cocaine use). Indeed, both in the Antwerp sample and in the Amsterdam samples, the number of negative effects increases with level of use. A level of use higher than 2.5 grams a week definitively alters the balance between positive and negative effects. For low-level users the balance is overwhelmingly positive, for medium-level users it is in equilibrium, and for high-level users it becomes negative.

Many (adverse) effects mentioned in the cocaine literature occur in our sample of cocaine users. However, it appears that simple occurrence of a drug effect, be it negative or positive, does not say very much about its significance to users. Some effects which might be looked upon as negative are hardly if ever perceived as such by users. For example, we find that a considerable proportion of our respondents experienced depression, insomnia, megalomania, lack of appetite as an effect of cocaine use, while only smaller numbers of respondents report them as a disadvantage of cocaine. Some other effects, such as talkativeness, unpleasant physical effects, energetic feeling and self-confidence, are often reported as cocaine effects and are also seen as significant by users.

Usually, health professionals, law enforcement agencies, politicians and media reports take the position that in the long run, illicit substances can only have adverse effects and disadvantages, and that prohibition and abstinence are essential. Contrary to this official discourse, our respondents' accounts show that well-known adverse effects are often experienced as minor discomforts, and that level of use (including dose and frequency of use), set and setting factors all have an important impact on the balance of positive and negative experiences with cocaine. Above all, the data presented here illustrate the importance of acknowledging the fact that cocaine and other drugs can and do have clear advantages and positive effects for the user (i.e. drug use is always functional to the user).

NOTES

[1]   In this chapter the terms 'advantages' and 'appealing aspects', and 'disadvantages' and 'unappealing aspects' are used interchangeably.

[2]   See Introduction, p. 3.

[3]   Similarly, Cohen's respondents in Amsterdam (Cohen & Sas, 1995: 83) gave about three advantages of cocaine use (an average of 2.9 advantages in 1987 and 3.1 advantages in 1991).

[4]   See p. 250.

[5]   For similar conclusions, see: MUGFORD, S.K. (1994), Recreational cocaine use in three Australian cities, 2 *Addiction Research* 1, 103.

[6]   See Chapter 8, p. 197.

[7]   See Chapter 14, p. 307 and 320-322.

[8]   See Chapter 3, p. 79-80.

[9]   See Chapter 4, p. 99-100.

[10]   See Chapter 5, p. 143-146.

[11]   See Chapter 5, p. 139-140.

[12]   See Chapter 8, p. 197-198.

[13]   See Chapter 14, p. 314.

[14]   In 1987, Cohen found an average of 2.5 disadvantages per respondent versus 2.9 advantages (Cohen, 1989: 85); in 1991, he found 2.7 disadvantages per respondent versus 3.1 advantages (Cohen & Sas, 1995: 83).

[15]   We checked whether the group of respondents reporting 'expensive' as a disadvantage of cocaine showed any specific characteristics, but we found no significant differences for level of use during top period, average net income, application of financial limits on the monthly purchase of cocaine, or mean price paid for cocaine.

[16]   Remarkably, three of our respondents replied they could not think of any disadvantage of cocaine use. After checking for length of cocaine use career, two of them had already been using for 7 years, and the third person had a 5-year career.

[17]   See Chapter 14, p. 310-315 and Chapter 15, p. 328-333.

[18]   See below, p. 256.

[19]   See p. 256-260.

[20]   Similarly, Bieleman and de Bie's (1992: 34-35) classical description of the effects of cocaine, pays no attention to the advantages and disadvantages experienced by the participants in their Rotterdam study (1990-91).

[21]   In his 1987 report Cohen (1989: 97-99) calculated the probability of occurrence of each effect when the effect is correlated with dose and frequency of weekly ingestion during top period. In this way he showed that the probability of certain effects changes with frequency of use, that the probability of other effects changes with dose, and that still other effects only show a change of probability of occurrence with the more complicated construct of level of use. The reader will not find comparable analyses here for two reasons. First of all, Cohen's study has clearly shown that measurement, analysis and comparison of cocaine effects is a very complicated matter. Specific cocaine research would have to be designed to deal with this complexity. Secondly, a detailed analysis of the occurrence of (sets of) effects is time-consuming and probably would lead us too far away from our hypotheses. Be it sufficient to concur with Cohen's conclusion: 'Simply

speaking of 'the' effects of cocaine seems to be too much of a reduction of the realities of cocaine use'. (Cohen, 1989: 105).

[22] See Chapter 5, p. 138.

[23] Cohen found a prevalence of 100% for 'energetic feeling' and 'lack of appetite' for high level users in his 1987 sample (Cohen, 1989: 96), and 'dry mouth' and 'increased heartbeat' for high level users in his 1991 sample (Cohen & Sas, 1995: 90).

[24] In the 1987 Amsterdam I sample, Cohen (1989: 94) found 75% or more prevalence for 9 positive and 3 negative effects for the low-level users. In his 1991 sample, he found the same prevalence for 7 positive and 1 negative effects for the low-level users (Cohen & Sas, 1995: 89-91).

[25] Cohen (1989: 94) found a still overwhelmingly positive balance in his Amsterdam I sample (9 positive and 4 negative effects with a prevalence of 75% or more), but in his Amsterdam II sample (Cohen & Sas, 1995: 89-91), the balance is slightly negative for medium-level users (9 positive and 10 negative effects).

[26] The high-level users in Cohen's Amsterdam I sample have a prevalence of 75% (and over) for 9 positive and 14 negative effects (Cohen, 1989: 94). The high-level users in Cohen's Amsterdam II sample have a prevalence of 75% (and over) for 7 positive and 11 negative effects (Cohen & Sas, 1995: 89-91).

[27] In his 1991 report, Cohen did check whether the route of ingestion contributed to bias, but apparently this variable in the relationship between the prevalence of effects and its level of use-relatedness did not matter... (Cohen & Sas, 1995: 91-95).

CHAPTER 12

ABSTINENCE, CUTTING BACK AND QUITTING COCAINE USE

12.1. INTRODUCTION

As stated in the general introduction we assume a critical attitude to the idea that pharmacology is destiny ('pharmacocentrism').[1] Based on the worst case scenarios, this paradigm suggests that a drug such as cocaine has the same effect on every user under different sets of conditions: physiological disturbances, health problems, and eventually, dependence and/or addiction. Similarly, it is the layman's opinion that one line of cocaine inevitably leads to another, relentlessly in ever increasing doses.

But does one line of cocaine inevitably lead to another? Do drug users take their drug relentlessly, in ever increasing doses? Are the adverse effects and disadvantages described in the previous chapter inevitable?

In §12.2 data on respondents who report periods of abstinence (of one month and sometimes much longer) are presented. Cocaine users also seem to be able to cut back (i.e. to reduce dosage or frequency, without becoming abstinent or quitting) for a variety of motives (§12.3). For some, introducing periods of abstinence or spontaneously cutting back on their cocaine use, may prove to be difficult. These problems are discussed in §12.4. And although it sometimes requires conscious efforts, some people decide to quit cocaine use definitively (§12.4).[2][3]

12.2. TEMPORARY ABSTINENCE

12.2.1. Periods of abstinence

We asked our respondents whether they had ever stopped using cocaine for a month or longer.[4] The possible answer categories we used for this item (once, twice, three times, four times, five times or more than five times) were slightly different from those used in the Amsterdam questionnaire (1-2 times, 3-5 times, 6-10 times, more than 10 times), but comparison remains possible.

A very large proportion of our respondents reported having stopped for more than one month (86.5% against 7.2% who never had) and 5.4% who did not reply. Our data show only small differences (see table 12.2.a) with the findings in Amsterdam in 1987 and 1991. Within the group of users who had had at least one such abstinence period, the Belgian respondents had it slightly more frequently than those of the two Dutch samples. Nearly 60% of our total sample reported more than 5 abstinence periods of one month or longer.

Table 12.2.a   Number of times people stopped using cocaine 1 month or longer, in three samples

	Amsterdam I 1987		Amsterdam II 1991		Antwerp 1997	
Frequency	N	%	N	%	N	%
0 times	20	12.5	18	16.7	8	7.2
1 or 2 times	29	18.1	20	18.5	11	9.9
3 - 5 times	28	17.5	19	17.6	20	18.0
> 5 times	81	50.6	49	45.4	66	59.5
No answer	*2*	*1.2*	*2*	*1.8*	*6*	*5.4*
Total	**160**	**99.9**	**108**	**100.0**	**111**	**100.0**

As to the proportion of those who never stopped, Cohen and Sas (1995: 54) attributed the distinction between both Amsterdam samples to the different duration of the users' careers in both samples. Whether valid or not, our data are consistent with their hypothesis: the proportion of non-stoppers is smaller than in both Dutch samples, while the average length of career is greater.[5] Furthermore, we find a statistically significant difference in the average length of career between those who had abstained temporarily (9.5 years) and those who had never abstained temporarily (4.4 years) (t-test: 5.165; df: 13.011; p<0.000). All this indicates that the longer the career of cocaine use, the more the user tends to have abstained temporarily at least once.

Table 12.2.b   Duration of longest period of abstinence among respondents who reported periods of abstinence of one month or longer, in three samples

	Amsterdam I 1987		Amsterdam II 1991		Antwerp 1997	
Longest period	N	%	N	%	N	%
1 month	7	5.0	10	11.2	1	1.0
2-3 months	27	19.3	25	28.1	24	23.5
4-6 months	34	24.3	27	30.3	24	23.5
7-12 months	34	24.3	21	23.6	26	25.5
13-24 months	22	15.7	4	4.5	14	13.7
25-60 months	12	8.7	1	1.1	10	9.8
>60 months	1	0.7	-	-	3	2.9
No answer	*3*	*2.1*	*1*	*1.1*	*-*	*-*
Total	**140**	**100.1**	**89**	**99.9**	**102**	**99.9**
Mean	**12 months**		**7 months**		**15 months**	

In the 1987 Amsterdam I sample, a minor relation between the number of times people stop using cocaine and their level of use during the period of heaviest use was found (Cohen, 1989: 59-60). Medium level users stopped less often than high level users, and low level users stopped most often. In our sample we also found a relation between both variables, although not statistically significant. High level users stopped less often than medium level users, while low level users stopped most often. In fact, all low level users (during top period) had at least stopped using cocaine once for a month or longer. These Dutch and Belgian findings might seem to differ at first sight, but they are both consistent with our findings elsewhere. We also found a relation of level of use (at top period) with the average net income and the proportion of fully employed respondents. In both samples, the group with the highest level of employment (and consequently with the highest average net income) reports the fewest periods of abstinence.

We asked those who had ever stopped using cocaine for one month or longer about the length of the longest period of abstinence. As shown in table 12.2.b, 26.4% of the 1997 Antwerp sample had periods of abstinence lasting a year or longer. This is very similar to the 1987 Amsterdam sample (25.1%), but there is a large difference with the 1991 Amsterdam sample (5%).

The average duration of abstinence was 15 months in our Antwerp sample, compared to 12 months in the 1987 Amsterdam I sample and 7 months in the 1991 Amsterdam II sample. One might think that this large difference is caused by a higher proportion of our sample who reported a period of abstinence of 2 years or even longer. However, even after correcting for length of career (as earlier in chapter 5), we see that the difference remains -although it is smaller. Table 12.2.c shows that the longest period of abstinence for our sample is reduced from an average of 15 to 12 months, while this average dropped from 12 to 10 months for the 1987 Amsterdam sample.

Table 12.2.c   Duration of longest period of abstinence among respondents who reported periods of abstinence of one month or longer in the 1991 Amsterdam II sample, and in the 1987 Amsterdam I and 1997 Antwerp samples (*both corrected for length of career)

Longest period	Amsterdam I 1987 *		Amsterdam II 1991		Antwerp 1997 *	
	N	%	N	%	N	%
1 month	4	4.4	10	11.2	-	-
2-3 months	23	25.6	25	28.1	20	28.6
4-6 months	25	27.8	27	30.3	17	24.3
7-12 months	21	23.3	21	23.6	19	27.1
13-24 months	11	12.2	4	4.5	9	12.9
25-60 months	4	4.4	1	1.1	4	5.7
>60 months	-	-	-	-	1	1.4
No answer	*2*	*2.2*	*1*	*1.1*	-	-
Total	**90**	**99.9**	**89**	**99.9**	**70**	**100.0**
Mean	**10 months**		**7 months**		**12 months**	

We find that the proportions of those who had stopped for maximum 1 month are reduced from 1% to zero in the Antwerp sample, and from 5% to 4.4% in the 1987 sample, compared to 11% in the 1991 Amsterdam II sample. And at the other extreme we find also major differences: a greater number of abstinence periods of 1 year or more in the 1987 sample (16.6%) and the 1997 sample (20%), compared to the 1991 Amsterdam II sample (5.6%). These are still sizable differences compared to those obtained without correcting for length of user's career.

12.2.2. Reasons for (periodic) abstinence [6]

We also asked respondents in an open-ended question to explain *why* they occasionally abstained from cocaine for periods of one month or longer. The reasons for periodic abstinence were quite numerous. It should be remarked that tables 12.2.f and 12.2.g (and the explication in the text) are based on the *main reasons* for abstinence. This was done for the sake of comparability with the Dutch data. As respondents were allowed to give more than one answer, it remains unclear why Cohen only included the main reasons given by respondents. It would have been more logical in our opinion to analyze these answers as multiple response sets. After establishing that Cohen's restriction did not change the hierarchy of reported reasons too drastically, we decided to copy his mode of operation. However, to provide a complete picture, we will first present our figures based on multiple responses.

Table 12.2.d   Total number of reasons for periodic abstinence from using cocaine (n(1), %(1): normal abstinence; n(2), %(2): longest abstinence), in the 1997 Antwerp sample (percentages are calculated on total number of reasons). [♠] [♦]

Antwerp (1997)				
Reason	**N (1)**	**% (1)**	**N (2)**	**% (2)**
1. to maximize positive effects	2	1.1	-	-
2. to evade problems	12	6.6	7	5.3
3. leads to too much drinking [♣]	-	-	-	-
4. fear of dependence	5	2.7	5	3.8
5. negative mental effects	11	6.0	5	3.8
6. negative physical effects	10	5.5	2	1.5
7. no desire for cocaine	27	14.7	17	13.0
8. to be away from coke scene	4	2.2	4	3.0
9. not enough pleasure	4	2.2	2	1.5
10. illness [♣]	-	-	-	-
11. other interests/activities	10	5.5	1	0.8
Subtotal	**85**	**46.4**	**45**	**34.3**
12. pregnancy	2	1.1	6	4.6
13. no environment for coke use	10	5.5	4	3.0
14. coke unobtainable	21	11.5	10	7.6
15. no money	31	16.9	11	8.4
16. friends do not use cocaine	10	5.5	8	6.1
17. partner raised objections	1	0.5	10	7.6
18. work/study	9	4.9	6	4.6
19. lower quality of cocaine	2	1.1	2	1.5
20. traveling	4	2.2	5	3.8
21. prison/treatment [♥]	5	2.7	9	6.9
Subtotal	**95**	**51.9**	**71**	**54.2**
22. other reasons	-	-	-	-
23. no specific reasons	3	1.6	15	11.5
Total	**183**	**99.9**	**131**	**100.0**

[♠] These percentages add up to 100 because they are calculated on the total number of reasons given by respondents, and not on the total number of respondents.

[♦] More than one answer per respondent was possible.

[♣] Although these answers were not given by the Antwerp respondents, we include them in this table because they were mentioned by some of the Amsterdam respondents.

[♥] 'Prison' and 'treatment' are merged into one category because both answers refer to a stay in a closed, residential setting.

Reasons for the *longest abstinence* were not distributed in the same way as those for shorter periods of abstinence (one month and longer). In table 12.2.d we will contrast these distributions. Under 'n(1)' and '%(1)' all the reasons for the normal periods of abstinence (i.e. any period of one month or more) are given; under 'n(2)' and '%(2)' the reasons for the longest period. The first eleven reasons are related to subjective internal effects of various types. The next ten reasons are related to external motivations.

'No desire for cocaine', 'no money', 'negative mental effects', 'coke unobtainable' and 'other interests/activities' are mentioned far more often as reasons for a normal abstinence period, than for the longest abstinence. As for 'no desire for cocaine', the opposite was found in the 1987 Amsterdam I sample: it was mentioned twice as often as the reason for the longest abstinence. As for financial reasons ('no money'), Cohen found a similar tendency as in our sample.

'Partner raised objections' is more often mentioned as a reason for the longest abstinence (10 times), as for other occasions of abstinence of a month or longer (once).

In the 1987 Amsterdam sample negative effects of some sort (reasons 2 through 6) account less for the period of longest abstinence than for shorter periods of abstinence. We found a similar tendency: negative effects were mentioned 38 times as a reason for normal periods of abstinence, versus 19 times for the longest periodic abstinence.

For both the normal abstinence periods and the longest abstinence, external reasons are mentioned more often (approx. 50%) than internal reasons. The number of internal reasons mentioned drops from 85 for the normal abstinence periods to 45 for the longest abstinence.

Fifteen people (15) explicitly stated they had *no specific reasons* for the longest period of abstinence. This was caused by an interviewer-effect, and this answer should be interpreted as a reference to the reasons respondents already cited for their normal abstinence periods.[7]

In table 12.2.e, we present the *main* reasons for *normal abstinence periods* given by respondents. Comparison of the three samples now becomes possible, and we can make the following observations. In all three samples, external reasons for 'normal' abstinence periods are mentioned somewhat more often than internal reasons.

The two most frequent reasons in the 1987 and the 1997 sample are 'no money' (both approx. 25%) and 'no desire for cocaine' (both around 14%). The latter reason is much more substantial in the 1991 Amsterdam II sample (24.7%), while the former reason is mentioned considerably less often as main reason (7.9%).

Three new reasons appear in our sample: 'other interests', 'lower quality of cocaine' and 'prison/treatment'. These were not mentioned by the Dutch respondents (which for the 'prison/treatment' category is logical as Cohen excluded respondents from so-called deviant subcultures: junkies, full-time prostitutes and criminals). On the other hand, none of our respondents mentioned 'leads to too much drinking' and 'illness', while some Dutch respondents did.

The fact that cocaine was temporarily unobtainable was mentioned more often by respondents of the 1991 and 1997 samples. This might reflect *either* fluctuations in the supply of cocaine over the years, *or* changes in the respondents' information on where and how to obtain cocaine, *or* both. Cell counts are too low to permit valid statements about this. Yet, some quotes from the qualitative interviews may illustrate this issue:

In the summer holidays, it was because I was in another town then, just because I couldn't get any coke, or because the quality was useless. [G/0/01]

First, that it's not available with the supplier. And second, every now and then when we... you know, that particular period when we had a gram a few subsequent times, we had agreed not to purchase any for the next few weeks or months. Just not to make it a habit. [I/0/03]

Because it wasn't available, I didn't look for it anymore, if there wasn't anything available with the friends, then I didn't use any. In other words, it just didn't occur. When I go out, and someone has some, and he gives me a line, I will take a line of course. If it's free, it's free. But I personally don't go out looking for it. [L/0/01]

I just don't have direct contacts. Anyway, the availability is low, and I'm not really interested in it, as well. It doesn't give me a kick or so. Until recently there was no regularity in my use: it is once this night, and then none for a month, and then again once, and then again none for three months, depending on what is offered. [R/0/06]

'No environment for coke use' is significantly more often mentioned by the Amsterdam II respondents, compared to the 1987 and 1997 samples.

Reasons 2 through 6, all describing negative effects of cocaine, made up 11.1% of all main reasons in the 1991 Amsterdam II sample, 17.5% in our 1997 Antwerp sample, and 25% in the 1987 Amsterdam I sample.

Table 12.2.e   Main reasons for abstinence periods of one month or longer (normal abstinence), in the 1987 Amsterdam I sample (N=140), the 1991 Amsterdam II sample (N=89), and the 1997 Antwerp sample (N=103). [⊙] [♦] [♠]

Reason	Amsterdam I 1987 N	Amsterdam I 1987 %	Amsterdam II 1991 N	Amsterdam II 1991 %	Antwerp 1997 N	Antwerp 1997 %
1. to maximize positive effects	3	2.1	-	-	2	1.9
2. to evade problems	10	7.1	-	-	4	3.9
3. leads to too much drinking	1	0.7	2	2.2	-	-
4. fear of dependence	6	4.3	5	5.6	3	2.9
5. negative mental effects	7	5.0	1	1.1	7	6.8
6. negative physical effects	11	7.9	2	2.2	4	3.9
7. no desire for cocaine	18	12.9	22	24.7	15	14.6
8. to be away from coke scene	4	2.9	-	-	2	1.9
9. not enough pleasure	1	0.7	3	3.4	2	1.9
10. illness	1	0.7	-	-	-	-
11. other interests/activities	-	-	-	-	5	4.8
Subtotal	**62**	**44.3**	**35**	**39.2**	**44**	**42.7**

Reason	Amsterdam I 1987 N	Amsterdam I 1987 %	Amsterdam II 1991 N	Amsterdam II 1991 %	Antwerp 1997 N	Antwerp 1997 %
12. pregnancy	2	1.4	1	1.1	2	1.9
13. no environment for coke use	6	4.3	14	15.7	3	2.9
14. coke unobtainable [♣]	5	3.6	12	13.5	10	9.7
15. no money	36	25.7	7	7.9	26	25.2
16. friends do not use cocaine	16	11.4	1	1.1	5	4.8
17. partner raised objections	1	0.7	-	-	-	-
18. work/study	-	-	5	5.6	5	4.8
19. lower quality of cocaine [•]	-	-	-	-	-	-
20. traveling	-	-	8	9.0	1	1.0
21. prison/treatment [♥]	-	-	-	-	4	3.9
Subtotal	**66**	**47.1**	**48**	**53.9**	**56**	**54.4**

Reason	Amsterdam I 1987 N	Amsterdam I 1987 %	Amsterdam II 1991 N	Amsterdam II 1991 %	Antwerp 1997 N	Antwerp 1997 %
22. other reasons	12	8.6	6	6.7	-	-
23. no specific reasons	-	-	-	-	3	2.9
Total	**140**	**100.0**	**89**	**99.9**	**103**	**100.0**

[⊙]   These percentages add up to 100 because they are calculated on the total number of reasons given by respondents, and not on the total number of respondents.

[♦]   More than one answer per respondent was possible.

[♥]   'Prison' and 'treatment' are merged into one category because both answers refer to a stay in a closed, residential setting.

[♣]   'Coke unobtainable' refers to situations in which the respondents is not able to obtain cocaine owing to circumstances beyond his/her control (e.g. usual dealer is arrested or other regular supply channels ran dry…).

[•]   'Lower quality of cocaine' is included in this table because it was mentioned by some respondents as one of the reasons for periodical abstinence (although not the main one).

We have already pointed at a considerable difference between the three samples related to the length of the longest abstinence period (see above, table 12.2.b). After correcting for length of career, we found an average of 12 months for our Antwerp sample, compared to 10 months for the 1987 sample and 7 months for the 1991 sample (see above, table 12.2.c). To find an explanation for the clear differences in length of the longest period of abstinence in the three samples, we analyzed the main reasons given by respondents for this longest period of abstinence (see table 12.2.f).[8]

Table 12.2.f   Main reasons for the longest abstinence period in the 1991 Amsterdam II sample (N=89), and in the 1987 Amsterdam II sample (N=86, corrected for length of career) and the 1997 Antwerp sample (N=70, corrected for length of career) [۞] [♦] [♠]

Reason	Amsterdam I 1987		Amsterdam II 1991		Antwerp 1997	
	N	%	N	%	N	%
1. to maximize positive effects [♣]	-	-	-	-	-	-
2. to evade problems	3	3.5	1	1.1	2	2.8
3. leads to too much drinking [♣]	-	-	-	-	-	-
4. fear of dependence	3	3.5	6	6.7	5	7.1
5. negative mental effects	2	2.3	3	3.4	-	-
6. negative physical effects	4	4.6	3	3.4	-	-
7. no desire for cocaine	24	27.9	15	16.9	5	7.1
8. to be away from coke scene	1	1.2	-	-	-	-
9. not enough pleasure	1	1.2	3	3.4	2	2.8
10. illness	-	-	2	2.2	-	-
11. other interests/activities	-	-	-	-	1	1.4
Subtotal	**38**	**44.2**	**33**	**37.1**	**15**	**21.4**
	Amsterdam I 1987		Amsterdam II 1991		Antwerp 1997	
12. pregnancy	-	-	1	1.1	5	7.1
13. no environment for coke use	14	16.3	13	14.6	1	1.4
14. coke unobtainable	2	2.3	9	10.1	5	7.1
15. no money	11	12.8	4	4.5	9	12.9
16. friends do not use cocaine	6	7.0	1	1.1	3	4.3
17. partner raised objections	2	2.3	1	1.1	6	8.6
18. work/study	4	4.6	3	3.4	4	5.7
19. lower quality of cocaine [♣]	-	-	-	-	-	-
20. traveling	-	-	15	16.9	2	2.8
21. prison/treatment [♥]	-	-	-	-	5	7.1
Subtotal	**39**	**45.3**	**47**	**52.8**	**40**	**57.1**
	Amsterdam I 1987		Amsterdam II 1991		Antwerp 1997	
22. other reasons	9	10.5	9	10.1	-	-
23. no specific reason	-	-	-	-	15	21.4
Total	**86**	**100.0**	**89**	**100.0**	**70**	**99.9**

[۞] These percentages add up to 100 because they are calculated on the total number of reasons given by respondents, and not on the total number of respondents.
[♦] More than one answer per respondent was possible.
[♥] 'Prison' and 'treatment' are merged into one category because both answers refer to a stay in a closed, residential setting.
[♣] 'To maximize positive effects', 'Creates too much drinking' and 'quality of cocaine lower' are included in this table because they were mentioned by some respondents as one of the reasons for periodical abstinence (although not the main one).

In all three samples, 'no desire for cocaine' and the combination of 'no money/coke unobtainable' were the main reasons given specifically for the longest period of abstinence. Again, external reasons are mentioned more often than internal reasons, in all three samples.

'Partner raised objections' and 'pregnancy' were slightly more important for the Antwerp sample than for the Amsterdam samples, while 'no environment for coke use' was mentioned considerably less often by the Belgian respondents, compared to the Dutch respondents.

'To be away from coke scene' only appears as a main reason for the longest abstinence in the 1987 Amsterdam I sample; 'illness' only appears in the 1991 Amsterdam II sample; and 'prison/treatment' is only mentioned by respondents from the 1997 Antwerp sample. Again, the former finding can be explained by Cohen's sample exclusion criteria (no respondents from so-called deviant subcultures, such as criminals and junkies).

Reasons such as 'to maximize positive effects', 'leads to too much drinking' and 'lower quality of cocaine' are not mentioned in any of the samples for the longest period of abstinence.

Negative effects (reasons 2 through 6) played a similar role in all three samples, accounting for 9.9% of the reasons for the longest abstinence in our sample (even 11.3% if we included previous answers of those who report 'no specific reason', see above), compared to 14.6% in the 1991 Amsterdam II sample and 13.9% in the 1987 Amsterdam I sample.

In conclusion, analysis of the main reasons mentioned for the longest abstinence period offers no explanation for the differences in length of the longest period of abstinence between the three samples. Rather, the differences found seem to relate to differences in sampling method and/or idiosyncratic features of the respondents under study.

12.2.3. Comparison with other European and American cocaine studies

Most other authors of major community studies of cocaine users are aware that abstinence phases of variable lengths and for different reasons occur frequently during use periods. Beyond this awareness, however, in interviews it is difficult to obtain details about the number and the length of such abstinence periods with any acceptable degree of accuracy. Second, differences in data collection (and coding) hamper a thorough comparison of data from different studies.

Both the Toronto samples (1983 and 1989-90), the San Francisco sample (1986-88) and the Scottish sample (1989-90) give no detailed data on periodical abstinence. Apart from indirect references to periodical abstinence during use periods, we found further specific information on this issue in two community studies of cocaine users: Turin and Barcelona (both carried out in 1990-91). Merlo *et al.* (1992: 81-83) and Diaz *et al.* (1992: 153-156) explicitly report on periods of non-use. Unfortunately, both studies focus their attention on periods of abstinence of over 1 year during use (while the present study deals with abstinence periods of one month or longer). Both samples show extreme differences: while only 8 of the Barcelona respondents (5%) declared having had any abstinence period of over 1 year during use, 90 respondents of the Turin sample (90%) had had such a period of non-use! An explanation for these data is not offered by the authors.[9] Diaz *et al.* (1992: 154) add, however, that references to 'abstinence periods' (meaning non-use periods of less than 1 year but longer than the periods of 'non-use' as specified by the interviewees' frequency patterns) are very frequent.

As to the reasons for the short or long abstinence intervals in the cocaine use careers of the Turin and Barcelona respondents, we find indications that are very consistent with our data. Merlo *et al.* (1992: 154-155) report that 'money, market and decision' are the most frequent words used by the interviewees when describing these interruptions of use. Respondents usually abstain for a while when they run out of money, when their supply of cocaine dries up, or when cocaine is too expensive (i.e. external reasons). Apart from those factors, the decision to interrupt can be related to fear of serious physical problems or the feeling of losing control over the substance (i.e. internal reasons). Diaz *et al.* (1992: 154-155) state that abstinence periods often occur when the relationship with the group with whom drugs are used or from whom cocaine is obtained comes to an end, especially where festive-recreational use is involved. Other reasons mentioned are lack of money, going on holiday, or nothing specific at all. For the category of compulsive users, these authors conclude that they *'sustain a high rate of use, nearly always increasing, without any abstinence periods until they start to have serious problems. The emergence of these usually leads them to asking for treatment and to giving the drug up altogether.'*

12.3. CUTTING BACK ON COCAINE USE

Participants were also asked whether they ever cut back their cocaine use, i.e. reduced the *dosage* taken per occasion or the *frequency* of consumption, without stopping completely. 'Cutting back' is thus defined as different from 'quitting' (i.e. considering oneself as having stopped completely, and reporting non-use for the last three months) and 'periodical abstinence' (i.e. to stop using cocaine for at least one month or longer, and to consider oneself as not having given up cocaine completely).

When asked whether they had ever cut back on their cocaine use, either in frequency or in dosage, 71 respondents (64.0%) of our sample answered in the affirmative, compared to 69.4% of the 1987 Amsterdam I sample and 57% of the 1991 Amsterdam II sample (see table 12.3.a).[10]

Table 12.3.a   Number of times users cut back on cocaine use, in the 1997 Antwerp sample

Antwerp		
Frequency	**N**	**%**
0 times	40	36.0
1 -2 times	13	11.7
3 - 5 times	7	6.3
> 5 times	36	32.4
Don't know	*15*	*13.5*
Total	**111**	**100.0**

In table 12.3.b, we again included only the *main* reason respondents reported for cutting back on their cocaine use, as Cohen did. We do not reproduce our data for *all reported reasons* (when more than one answer per respondent is possible), but it is remarkable that 'no money' was mentioned by thirty-one respondents as one of the reasons for cutting back; 16 people reported 'negative mental effects', 14 people reported 'negative physical effects' and 12 people work/study reasons... The following observations can be derived from table 12.3.b:

In 1987 negative effects of cocaine (reasons 2 through 6) accounted for 22.5% of the reductions in use, compared to 22% in 1991. In our 1997 Antwerp sample, these reasons account for 26.7%.

A striking difference is that 8% of the main reasons mentioned by respondents in the 1991 Amsterdam II sample were 'no money', compared to 31.5% in the 1987 Amsterdam I sample and 38.0% in the 1997 Antwerp sample.

The combination of 'no desire' and 'not enough pleasure' accounted for 30% of the reasons for cutting back in 1991, but only for 12.6% in the 1987 Amsterdam I sample and 9.9% in the 1997 Antwerp sample.

In both the 1987 Amsterdam I sample and the 1997 Antwerp sample, external reasons are mentioned somewhat more often than internal ones. The difference between totals of internal and external reasons is more marked, but the residual category of 'other reasons' is much smaller.

Table 12.3.b Main reasons for cutting back on cocaine use, in the 1987 Amsterdam I sample and in the 1997 Antwerp sample [♦] [✪] [♠]

Reason	Amsterdam I 1987		Antwerp 1997	
	N	%	N	%
1. to maximize positive effects	2	1.8	-	-
2. to evade problems	5	4.5	5	7.0
3. leads to too much drinking [♣]	-	-	-	-
4. fear of dependence	4	3.6	2	2.8
5. negative mental effects	5	4.5	8	11.3
6. negative physical effects	11	9.9	4	5.6
7. no desire for cocaine	13	11.7	7	9.9
8. to be away from coke scene	1	0.9	1	1.4
9. not enough pleasure	1	0.9	-	-
10. illness	1	0.9	-	-
Subtotal	**43**	**38.7**	**27**	**38.0**
	Amsterdam I 1987		**Antwerp 1997**	
11. pregnancy	1	0.9	1	1.4
12. no environment for coke use	2	1.8	1	1.4
13. coke unobtainable	2	1.8	3	4.2
14. no money	35	31.5	27	38.0
15. friends do not use cocaine	8	7.2	2	2.8
16. partner raised objections	1	0.9	3	4.2
17. lower quality of cocaine	1	0.9	-	-
18. work/study	4	3.6	6	8.5
19. advice from friends [♣]	-	-	-	-
Subtotal	**54**	**48.6**	**43**	**60.6**
	Amsterdam I 1987		**Antwerp 1997**	
19. other reasons	13	11.7	1	1.4
No answer	*1*	*0.9*	-	-
Total	**111**	**99.9**	**71**	**100.0**

[✪] These percentages add up to 100 because they are calculated on the total number of reasons given by respondents, and not on the total number of respondents.

[♦] More than one answer per respondent was possible.

[♣] 'Leads to too much drinking' and 'advice from friends' are included in this table because they were mentioned by some respondents as one of the reasons for cutting back (although not the main one).

In his 1991 report, Cohen put these data about 'reasons' into perspective by suggesting that they might be '*particularly sensitive to qualitative differences related to the interviewer(s), the nature of the interactions with subjects and subjects' desire to justify their behavior.*' (Cohen & Sas, 1995: 57-58). But at least some of the differences illustrate some genuine differences between the samples. The fact that 'prison/treatment' is mentioned as a (main) reason for abstinence in our sample and not in the Amsterdam samples is consistent with the higher proportion of respondents having been in treatment or having been convicted for a felony (chapter 3). As we stated above, it is probably also a reflection of a difference in sample acceptability criteria (Cohen excluded participants from so-called deviant subcultures). The fact that 'pregnancy' as a reason was mentioned more often by members of our sample, compared to the 1991 Amsterdam II sample, is consistent with our finding that 17.1% of our sample had children living at home, versus only 4.6% of the 1991 Amsterdam II sample (we do not have any data from the Amsterdam I sample). Similarly, proportions of respondents who have a steady partner and/or live together with a partner are larger in our Antwerp sample than in both the Amsterdam samples, which might explain why 'partner raised objections' is cited more often as a main reason for abstinence periods and for cutting back by our respondents.

12.4. PROBLEMS WITH ABSTINENCE OR CUTTING BACK

In the previous paragraphs, we made reference to some respondents who experienced problems with cutting back on their cocaine use or with being abstinent for one month or longer. In this paragraph some qualitative data from the Antwerp sample are presented (12.4.1) and compared with other major community samples of cocaine users (12.4.2).

12.4.1. Data from the Antwerp sample

Twenty-one respondents (18.9% of the total sample) reported some kind of difficulty with these periods of abstinence. Twenty-six respondents (23.4% of the total sample) reported difficulties with cutting back on their cocaine use. A small group of 14 respondents answered in the affirmative on both items.

Thirteen of the 26 respondents (50.0%) reporting difficulties with cutting back, 10 of the 21 respondents (47.6%) reporting difficulties with periodic abstinences, and 8 of the 14 respondents (57.1%) reporting difficulties on both variables, *belonged to chain H*.[11] The snowball sampling technique without randomized sequences indeed produced some biases.[12] For example, the respondents that belong to snowball chain H not only report difficulties more often with cutting back and/or periodic abstinence, they also tend to be less skilled, they report more contacts with treatment agencies, more convictions for a felony, more intravenous use of cocaine, etc.

In the 1987 Amsterdam survey, 23 persons of the 111 respondents who had ever cut back on their cocaine use (20.7%) found it difficult to do so. Respondents illustrated these 'problems' with stories about craving, unpleasant mental or physical effects, cocaine use by friends, possible isolation from friends, and some idiosyncratic reasons. Cohen and Sas did not report on this item in the 1991 Amsterdam survey. In our sample, we found a lot of qualitative material referring to difficulties, which for the majority of these respondents seem of minor importance (and relatively easy to overcome).

First of all, most respondents who have ever experienced difficulties with cutting back on their cocaine use or abstaining temporarily, stress the fact that these 'problems' manifest themselves *at the beginning of this period*.[13] After a few days or weeks, most of the discomforts fade away:

After a certain period, you don't find it so hard to cope. Psychologically, I feel stronger after having quit cocaine for two months than after two weeks. If I meet these guys after two weeks, it's like: okay, I quit using for two weeks, there is no problem anyway, I do not exaggerate, so let's go. But if you've quit for two months, you say: why did I quit using for two months now? I spend less money, I sleep better. Then you say: you guys go ahead, but not me. [C/0/06]

Difficulties experienced while abstaining or cutting back are craving, restlessness, feeling depressed or miserable, feeling irritable, bad-tempered, insomnia, etc. Feelings of craving after periodically abstaining from cocaine sometimes are expressed through dreaming of cocaine (see Chapter 13).[14] All respondents claim that these feelings of discomfort are of *a psychological, rather than of a physical nature*:[15]

Let's say, in the beginning, a sort of feeling of missing it. You feel a bit bored, stressed, you think about it, you feel like it, and after that, you're okay. It's really something psychological. [C/0/12]

You always get some kind of withdrawal symptoms, a little, and also mainly mentally, because it keeps calling for you. It's a very unreliable girlfriend, she's always there, but you cannot trust her an inch... [I/1/04]

The respondents who have experienced difficulties often report that informal support from friends or partner is very helpful with overcoming these discomforts.[16] Without emotional support from peers, difficulties are subjectively experienced as more severe.

No, not really, it's not harder than when you'd say: today I'm not drinking anymore. But that's very personal, and I do have a strong character in this. I have a tough time for a while, but I usually kept my promise if I wanted to stop for a while [...] It also depends on your mood, and if you have somebody who loves you, it is easier. If you're on your own, it's harder. If your friends support you and they too have the courage to temper or to say: all right, now we are exaggerating, then it's not that hard. But of course, you shouldn't go out and look for it. [P/0/06]

On the other hand, while cutting back on cocaine use or even temporarily abstaining may not be so difficult in itself, it can be hampered if friends or significant others continue to use (at the same level). In that case, 'problems' are often overcome avoidance behavior: respondents make conscious efforts to avoid certain places, parties, people, etc...

You see, it's not just coke, it's a life-style as well, these are people who stay up late, who drop in at each other's house at midnight or 01 a.m. as if it is nothing. It's a whole way of life surrounding it, so the only real way to quit is to say: from now on I put on my answering machine at midnight, I cut myself off, even from the possibility that it comes in... At that moment you have to change everything, you have to review your whole life-style. But it is mainly a way of life during weekends. I now go for a walk in the weekend, I go out to drink something only one night, I used to go out every day... [H/1/19]

A similar strategy to overcome these difficulties is to look for new interests, new (leisure) activities.

So when you temper, you don't use, there you are: what do I have to do? Actually, you're bored. You have no alternative for that coke, so it's hard. Of course, it bothers you, and that is in my opinion the only reason why I got through: because I have an alternative, because other things fascinate me. [H/0/05]

We need to keep in mind that only 33 respondents reported difficulties with temporary abstinence and/or cutting back (including 14 respondents who answered in the affirmative on both variables). We find some marked differences between these thirty-three respondents reporting difficulties and those reporting no difficulties. Of the 33 respondents reporting difficulties with temporary abstinence *or* cutting back on cocaine use, fifteen belong to snowball chain H, two respondents belong to chain F, and 3 to chain Z. It is shown elsewhere that these snowball chain are different from other snowball chains, in that they probably recruited respondents in subcultures of more problematical use.[17] Similarly, of the 14 respondents reporting difficulties with temporary abstinence *and* cutting back on cocaine use, 8 belong to snowball chain H.

We find a clear correlation between level of use during the period of heaviest use and whether or not respondents report difficulties with temporary abstinence or cutting back. For example, 75.8% of those reporting difficulties were using at a high level during their top period versus 38.5% of those reporting no difficulties. Of those reporting difficulties none were using at a low level during their top period versus 30.8% of those reporting no difficulties. (χ^2=17.006; df: 2; p<0.000).

While most qualify these 'problems' as minor discomforts, some of them experienced major difficulties. It is striking that these people often report escapist motives for using cocaine (and other drugs). These people are not recreational users, they show characteristics of compulsive use:

Yes, you can't temper, you can't leave it there. Maybe in the beginning, if you go get something, you can wait. Maybe you can wait for an hour or so, but in the end you can't wait for 5 minutes. Then it's like: shooting up, take your flash, and prepare another one, until it's all gone. [H/1/15]

When you freebase it, you are... yes, you really want to push away your feelings, you want to stun them, because you don't want to be confronted with reality, because you can't cope with it anymore. Like that. [N/0/01]

Furthermore, these quotations illustrate that there is also a relation between the route of ingestion and 'problems' when abstaining or cutting back. Most respondents reporting difficulties referred to injecting and/or freebasing of cocaine (and/or heroin).

12.4.2. Comparison with other European and American cocaine studies

As stated above, only few other major community studies of cocaine users have reported explicitly on cutting back and abstinence, let alone the problems associated with these phenomena. Only the reports on the Turin sample and on the Barcelona sample (both in 1990-91) explicitly present specific information on this issue.

Merlo *et al.* (1992: 81-83) describe three large categories of 'sensations' that are connected with abstinence intervals: (1) *'nostalgia'* (e.g. a weak hope that at the party where you've been invited somebody will offer you some coke); (2) *'longing'*, which differs from 'nostalgia' in that it implies some activity aiming at the satisfaction of the longing (e.g. *'It's a bit the same as with orgasm: after some time that you've been without it, you burst of the wish to have it again.'* - Q052); and (3) *'craving'*, the classic state of yearning for the substance, a pressing need that must be satisfied (e.g. *'With heroin I could save some for the following morning; with coke you can't stop, you always finish the whole dose.'* - Q028). The authors state that the growing wish, up to craving, seems more connected with the route of ingestion, than with the dose of use. All the interviewees from the Turin sample who answered in terms of 'craving' had been using cocaine intravenously. Diaz *et al.* (1992: 155-156) report similar craving or anxiety when abstaining from cocaine among former heroin addicts in the Barcelona sample, whose preference later turned to the intravenous use of cocaine.

12.5. QUITTING COCAINE

We also asked a set of questions regarding the respondents' attempts to stop using cocaine alltogether.[18] The data from the Antwerp sample are presented in §12.5.1. Subsequently, they are compared to those from other major community studies of cocaine users (§12.5.2).

12.5.1. Data from the Antwerp sample

Thirty-two respondents (29.7% of our total sample) reported to have quit cocaine. We call these respondents 'quitters'. Note that to consider oneself as having quit cocaine use does not necessarily mean the respondent has been completely abstinent during the three months prior to the interview (cf. chapter 5). Similarly, it is striking that certain people consider themselves as having 'quit' cocaine use, although they do not exclude using cocaine again. We also found that many of the respondents who answered 'no' to the question whether they had ever tried to quit cocaine definitively, argued that nobody can be certain: 'Never say never again'.

> *I definitely quit using cocaine, eh. I say: if it presents itself by coincidence, and there is an opportunity and the right ambiance, okay, it can happen. I'm not saying it kills you. But I'll say: I don't need it. But I don't know if it will present itself within a month, or some years, or within ten years, and if I feel like it, I will do it. For the moment, I really don't feel like it.* [H/0/22]

We will come back to this issue when comparing our data with those of the San Francisco sample (1986-88), described by Waldorf *et al.* (1991).

When asked whether it was a conscious decision to quit cocaine, 25 of the respondents (78.1%) answered in the affirmative, while 6 people (18.8%) reported to have quit cocaine without consciously reflecting about it (1 respondent did not answer this question).

Seventeen of the 32 'quitters' (53.1%) stated they had quit suddenly, from one day to the next. Fifteen of them (46.9%) reported that quitting cocaine was a long-term process with 'relapses' and renewed efforts. When asked whether they were more concerned about their physical health at the time they decided to quit cocaine, 22 respondents (68.8%) said yes, and 10 (31.3%) said no.

Reasons for quitting cocaine are diverse. Some respondents quit because their partner raised objections about their cocaine use. Others quit because their partner started to use cocaine too or because he/she started to show symptoms of compulsive drug use.

One night I had coke, and my girlfriend didn't, and she asked me if she could have mine, but I didn't want that. I made her choose between me and that cocaine, and she chose the coke. And then I seriously thought about that, and I said: I have to stop now, or I will become like her. My family, my work, it will all suffer from it. So I quit, and I never touched it again. [X/0/01]

Others decide to stop using cocaine because it interferes with their job or their study performance. For example, a photographic model quit because it started to affect her looks. Several women quit because they became pregnant, or 'for the sake of my children', i.e. arguments that are often used for quitting smoking too. This respondent had several reasons:

First of all, because I regret it the next day, that you put a lot of money in it. And secondly, I always drink more then. And thirdly, yeah, I'm sometimes worried whether I could get fertility problems from it, you know, I didn't read this or something, but... I'm 24 years old, I would like to start a relationship soon, more focussed on the future. [C/0/09]

Some respondents quit because of adverse effects such as aggression, paranoia, self-centredness, anxiety... or because of some specific bad experience ('bad trips' or the experience of having an 'overdose')[19].

Because I got frightened. Because once, I had used too much, and I fainted, so actually I got frightened. I don't want it anymore. [H/1/13]

Others quit because of the low quality of cocaine or simply because cocaine has become unobtainable in their environment (arrest of the usual dealer, disappearance of cocaine supplying friends, etc...). Some stop using cocaine because of a lack of desire, or because cocaine no longer yields sufficient pleasure:

I was in a toilet, and I was looking for a place to cut it somewhat with that razor, and there was no other possibility than to put it on the seat, the lavatory seat, and I thought: 'This is the last thing I would do, that I would have to snort my coke from the lavatory seat, goddamn'. But I said: 'I'm not gonna let that happen to myself'. I said: 'Com'on, now it's over, no more stupid coke.' [H/0/02]

It wasn't like: I will try to quit. I just quit, and that was it. Because I didn't like it anymore. Sometimes you see people react, people that use coke, and suddenly they think they know everything, think everything, and that doesn't fit my pattern. I would like to know everything, but I doubt too much to believe in that. Yes, I started to put things in perspective, and then you quit. [K/0/01]

Other reasons for quitting cocaine are financial problems ('coke is too expensive'), 'problems' with law enforcement or other official agencies... Some respondents acknowledge the influence of other cocaine using friends as a decisive factor to quit cocaine:[20]

Because I want to make sure that I can stay away from it, that I don't go too far. I think now is not too late, that's why. It's better to stop in time. As a matter a fact, that's the only rea-

son, and also because of my friends, who are not opposed to it, but still, they say I'm going too far, I should be careful what I'm doing. They do it every now and then, but only seldom, compared to me. [T/0/01]

We presented the respondents who had tried to quit cocaine, with a structured questionnaire about strategies and actions for quitting, borrowed from Waldorf, Reinarman and Murphy (1991: 212): see table 12.5.a. All methods were applied by at least some of the respondents. The methods most often mentioned were: 'looking for new interests, hobbies' (59.4%); 'stop going to specific places where coke was being used', 'make conscious efforts to avoid coke-using friends' and 'change eating habits' (all three 56.3%).

Table 12.5.a   Methods for quitting cocaine, reported by those who ever tried to quit, in the 1997 Antwerp sample (N=32)

Antwerp (1997)			
Method	Yes	No	No answer
1. Move to another city or country	40.6	59.4	-
2. Move to another neighborhood	34.4	65.6	-
3. Take a long vacation (to be away)	31.3	68.8	-
4. Get out of town	40.6	59.4	-
5. Make conscious efforts to avoid coke-using friends	56.3	43.8	-
6. Stop going to specific places where coke is being used	56.3	40.6	3.1
7. Seek new, non-drug-using friends	50.0	46.9	3.1
8. Seek new interests, new hobbies	59.4	37.5	3.1
9. Get involved in sports	34.4	62.5	3.1
10. Change your eating habits	56.3	43.8	-
11. Start a new program of physical conditioning (fitness, etc.)	31.3	68.8	-
12. Start taking vitamins	46.9	53.1	-

The least popular methods were 'taking a long vacation' and 'starting a new program of physical conditioning' (both 31.3%). All strategies and actions could be reorganized in three main categories: 1) avoidance of cocaine and cocaine users or *geographic moves* (strategies 1 through 6); 2) *social actions* and *new interests* towards more conventional goals (strategies 7 and 8); and 3) general attention for physical condition, or *health efforts* (strategies 9 through 12).

Table 12.5.b   Help from others with quitting, reported by those who ever tried to quit, in the 1997 Antwerp sample (N=32)

Antwerp (1997)		
Help from	Yes	No
1. Financial help, welfare (OP. CIT.M.W.)	18.8	81.3
2. Help for physical health	40.6	59.4
3. Help for mental health	43.8	56.3
4. Legal help	9.4	90.6
5. Family or child care	9.4	90.6
6. Telephone aid	3.1	96.9
7. Family members	50.0	50.0
8. Spouse or partner	43.8	56.3
9. Friends	46.9	53.1
10. Employer	3.1	96.9
11. Other	6.3	93.8

Table 12.5.b summarizes another list of actions, again taken from Waldorf, Reinarman and Murphy (1991: 212). These actions relate to appealing for help from others while quitting, and can be divided into two main categories: *formal assistance* (action 1

through 6) and *informal assistance* (action 7 through 10). The kinds of help most often mentioned were 'family members' (50%), 'friends' (46.9%) and 'help for mental health' and 'partner' (43.8%). The kinds of help least often mentioned were 'telephone aid' and 'employer'.

We examined which respondents sought for informal assistance, formal assistance, or both, and which respondents did not seek any assistance at all. Of the 32 respondents who had tried to quit cocaine, 5 people did not look for any assistance (15.6%). Twenty-six respondents sought informal assistance (81.3%), and 14 respondents sought both formal and informal assistance (43.8%). Naturally, the 15 respondents who had sought formal assistance (46.9%), also report having been in contact with drug treatment agencies (see chapter 1).

In the residual category 'other', we have included replies from two respondents: one claimed that the owner of a discotheque had helped him a lot when trying to quit; the other reported the help of a 'shelter' (a refuge).

Twelve respondents (37.5% of those who had tried to quit) never used again after their first attempt to quit. Another 6 respondents (18.8%) 'relapsed' 1 to 5 days: 4 of them used less than 1 gram on those occasions, one of them used between 1 and 2 grams, and another respondent used more than 2 grams after deciding to quit.

At the moment of the interview, 15 of the 32 respondents reporting that they had tried to quit (45.5%), had succeeded in doing so. The other 17 (53.1%) were still using at the time of the interview (8 were using at a low level, another 8 at a medium level and 1 other at a high level during the three months prior to the interview).

In chapter 5 we mentioned that 19.8% of the total sample) reported that they had not used any cocaine during the three months prior to the interview.[21] Only 16 of these 22 non-users at the time of the interview reported ever having tried to quit cocaine definitively. The 6 other non-users reported never having tried to quit cocaine, indicating that their non use at the time of the interview was only temporary, and probably caused by accidental set and setting factors...

No relationship between levels of use and success at quitting was found in the 1991 Amsterdam sample.. As shown in table 12.5.c, Cohen and Sas (1995: 58) found that quitting is just as probable for those with high levels of use during their highest use period as for those with medium or low levels.

Table 12.5.c   Cross tabulation of level of use during period of heaviest cocaine use, and success of the attempts to quit cocaine use of respondents in the 1991 Amsterdam II sample (N=38) and the 1997 Antwerp sample (N=32) who indicate they tried to quit.

| Level of use during top period of cocaine use | Amsterdam II | | | Antwerp | | |
| | Quitted cocaine use | | | Quitted cocaine use | | |
	Yes	No	Total	Yes	No	Total
Low	6	8	14	2	1	3
Medium	4	6	10	1	-	1
High	5	9	14	9	19	28
Total	15	23	38	12	20	32

In our Antwerp sample, 32.1% of the 28 high level users (during top period) who attempted to quit, did so successfully, against 66.7% of the 3 low level users. As cell numbers are too low to make any valid generalizations, we cannot contradict Cohen's hypothesis (1995: 58), that *'for cocaine users who want to quit, factors other than the (...) prior levels of use determine the probability of success.'*

Finally, we asked respondents who had tried to quit, whether they had smoked more cigarettes, drunk more alcohol or used more other drugs while attempting to quit. Sixteen (50.0%) reported having drunk more alcohol, while 15 respondents had not (46.9%). Thirteen 'quitters' (40.6%) reported having used more other drugs -mainly cannabis; the 18 others (56.3%) had not. Twelve quitters (37.5%) reported having smoked more cigarettes while quitting cocaine, versus 18 (56.3%) who had not. We found that the proportions of respondents answering in the affirmative overlapped: 5 respondents had consumed more alcohol, more tobacco and other drugs while quitting. Eight respondents scored on two out of these three variables.

12.5.2. Comparison with other European and American cocaine studies

Although it is not studied systematically, some information on quitting cocaine use is found in other major community studies. Waldorf *et al.* (1991: 189-244) devote two entire chapters to quitting cocaine, and Shaffer and Jones (1989) have written a classic study on the process of quitting cocaine. Most authors focus on three major aspects of quitting: (1) the reasons or motives for stopping; (2) the different styles for quitting; and (3) the (coping) techniques and strategies used or actions taken for quitting and staying quit. For each of these aspects, our data are consistent with their findings.

(1) Our respondents reported the following reasons for quitting: a partner made problems about their cocaine use, a partner started to use cocaine too or too much, it interfered with their job or their study performance, they were pregnant, adverse effects or specific bad experiences, cocaine became unobtainable, or its quality became worse, or it did not yield enough pleasure anymore, financial problems, problems with law enforcement, or the influence of friends. Erickson *et al.* (1994: 110-111) report that certain unappealing aspects of cocaine, such as 'coming down', the high financial cost, effects associated with the technique, the potential for addiction, the negative social consequences (such as being labeled a user and becoming self-centered and insensitive to others) and unfavorable psychological and physical effects, may play a role in the decision either to continue or cease using the drug.[22] This Toronto study (1983) and other studies have shown that neither a perceived certainty nor a perceived severity of legal sanctions is related to cessation of use (Erickson *et al.*, 1994: 151). Our qualitative data confirm that the effects of fear of legal consequences are either negligible or much less important than extralegal factors. Ditton and Hammersley (1996: 42-43) describe reasons such as 'boredom with cocaine' and 'natural maturation' as causes for cessation.

(2) Shaffer and Jones (1989: 129-130) describe two quitting styles among natural recoverers: those who quit 'cold turkey' (suddenly and completely) and those who 'taper' their usage. The quitters among the Antwerp sample included both these polar types and others who fell in between or tried both methods in different combinations until they succeeded. Some users tapered naturally over several years without ever actively quitting; they did not think about it. Shaffer and Jones (1989: 127-129) also postulate two types of quitters: those who experience existential crises, or 'rock bottom quitters', and those who set about finding activities to take the place of cocaine use, or 'structure builders'. Several of our respondents clearly resemble either of these cessation types. Finally, Waldorf *et al.* (1991: 241) reach similar conclusions as both Shaffer and Jones and the present study, which leads them to note:

'*First, most of the treatment and recovery literature regards this tapering style of cessation as a cruel delusion or a form of "denial", while [our study...] suggests otherwise. Second, most treatment programs insist that patients quit "cold turkey", and most treatment professionals assume that withdrawal sickness always occurs. Neither was the case for most of our quitters.*'

We have also indicated that some 'quitters' in the Antwerp sample did not exclude that they would ever use cocaine again. Waldorf *et al.* (1991: 287) also met such 'quitters' in their San Francisco sample (1986-88): quitters who did not believe that they would never use cocaine again once they had stopped heavily using or abusing the drug. Most believed that they could use cocaine on occasion and not return to heavy use, and they generally lived by those standards. Although they did not hold abstinence values, they typically neither bought cocaine nor sought it out. Ditton and Hammersley (1996: 42-43) report on a similar phenomenon in the Scottish sample (1989-90). They call it '*a sort of user limbo which does not lie easily with the idea that cocaine is "addictive"*'.

(3) As stated above, we found that all the strategies and actions for quitting listed by Waldorf, Reinarman and Murphy were applied by at least some of the Antwerp 'quitters'. Compared to the San Francisco study, however, the Antwerp respondents report more geographic moves to avoid cocaine and fewer social actions and health efforts. Furthermore, we find that more Antwerp respondents report seeking informal and formal assistance compared to their San Francisco counterparts (Waldorf *et al.*, 1991: 208-210).[23] The most marked differences are: 40.6% of the Antwerp 'quitters' versus 7.2% of the San Francisco 'quitters' that sought help for mental health; 43.8% of the Antwerp 'quitters' that sought help for physical health, versus 13.2% of the San Francisco 'quitters'; and 43.8% of the Antwerp 'quitters' versus 14.2% of the San Francisco 'quitters' that required help from a spouse or partner. These differences may be due to different definitions of 'quitters' in both samples,[24] differences in treatment facilities and health care systems, and cultural differences.

Ditton and Hammersley (1996: 15) report that some respondents of their Scottish sample used cocaine very heavily for a period of time, but most lowered or stopped this heavy use on their own. A similar conclusion can be drawn for the Antwerp sample. Many of the strategies and actions for quitting described by the Antwerp respondents, were also listed by Shaffer and Jones (1989: 131-138). Our data confirm their descriptions of (coping) techniques such as avoidance, development of new lifestyle patterns and self-development.

12.6. CONCLUSION

A very large proportion of our respondents reported having stopped for more than one month (86.5%). Almost 60% of our total sample reported more than 5 abstinence periods of one month or longer. Our data are consistent with those of the 1987 Amsterdam I sample. The group with the highest professional level (and consequently with the highest income) report the fewest periods of abstinence. The average duration of the longest period of abstinence was 15 months in our Antwerp sample, compared to 12 months in the 1987 Amsterdam I sample and 7 months in the 1991 Amsterdam II sample. To explain the differences in length of the longest period of abstinence in the three samples, no indications could be found in the main reasons mentioned for the longest abstinence period. The differences related to differences in sampling method and/or to idiosyncratic features of the respondents under study.

Reasons for periodic abstinence were quite numerous. The two reasons most mentioned were 'no money' (an external reason) and 'no desire for cocaine' (an internal reason). Apart from the fact that reasons for the *longest abstinence* were not distributed in the same way as the reasons for shorter periods of abstinence of one month and longer, external reasons were mentioned more often (approx. 50%) than internal reasons.

Apart from the recognition that abstinence phases of variable lengths and for different reasons occur frequently during use periods, few detailed information on abstinence periods can be found in other major community studies of cocaine users. We found specific information on this issue in two community studies of cocaine users. As to the reasons for the short or long abstinence intervals in the cocaine use careers of the Turin and Barcelona respondents, the indications are highly consistent with our data. Respondents usually abstain for a while when they run out of money, when their supply of cocaine dries up, or when cocaine is too expensive. Furthermore, the decision to abstain can be connected to fear of serious physical problems or to the feeling of losing control over the substance.

Seventy-one respondents (64.0% of our sample) reported ever having cut back on their cocaine use (i.e. reduced the *dosage* taken per occasion or the *frequency* of consumption, without stopping completely), which is similar to both Amsterdam samples. The high financial cost was by far the most frequent main reason for cutting back, and to a lesser extent negative mental effects, no desire for cocaine, and work/study.

Some respondents had experienced problems with cutting back on their cocaine use or with being abstinent for one month or longer. Many of them belonged to snowball chain H, indicating some bias produced by the snowball sampling technique (the respondents who belong to snowball chain H also tend to be less skilled, they report more contacts with treatment agencies, more convictions for a felony, more intravenous use of cocaine, etc.).

Most respondents who have experienced difficulties with cutting back on their cocaine use or abstaining temporarily, stress the fact that these 'problems' manifested themselves at the beginning of this period. Difficulties while abstaining or cutting back are craving, restlessness, feeling depressed or miserable, feeling irritable, bad-tempered, insomnia, etc. All respondents claim that these feelings of discomfort are of a psychological, rather than of a physical nature. Informal support from friends or a partner is very helpful with overcoming these discomforts. Without emotional support from peers, difficulties are subjectively experienced as more severe. On the other hand, cutting back or even temporarily abstaining can be hampered if friends or significant others continue to use (at the same level). In that case, 'problems' are often overcome by avoidance behavior or by looking for new interests, new (leisure) activities. Only a few respondents had experienced major difficulties. They often report escapist motives for using cocaine (and other drugs) and show some characteristics of compulsive use. Furthermore, most respondents reporting difficulties referred to injecting and/or free-basing of cocaine.

Few other major community studies of cocaine users have reported explicitly on the problems associated with cutting back and abstinence. The growing wish (from 'nostalgia' and 'longing' up to 'craving') connected with abstinence intervals seems related to the route of ingestion rather than to the dose. Craving has been associated with intravenous use and former heroin addiction.

Thirty-two respondents (29.7% of our total sample) reported having quit cocaine. Some 'quitters' in the Antwerp sample did not believe that they would never use cocaine again once they had stopped heavily using or abusing the drug. Most believed that they could use cocaine on occasion and not return to heavy use, and they generally lived by those standards. Although they did not hold abstinence values, they typically neither bought cocaine nor sought it out.

The quitters in the Antwerp sample included both respondents who quit 'cold turkey' (quitting suddenly and completely) and respondents who 'tapered' their usage. Others tapered naturally over several years without ever actively quitting; they didn't think about it. Furthermore, we found examples of two types of quitters: those who experience existential crises, or 'rock bottom quitters', and those who set about finding activities to take the place of cocaine use, or 'structure builders'.

Consistent with other studies, reasons for quitting cocaine mentioned by the Antwerp respondents are diverse: their partner raised objections about their cocaine use; their partner started to use cocaine too or he/she started to show characteristics of compulsive drug use; it interfered with their job or their study performance; they became pregnant; adverse effects such as aggression, paranoia, self-centredness, anxiety... or some specific bad experiences; the low quality of cocaine or simply because cocaine had become unobtainable in their environment; a lack of desire; cocaine did no longer yield sufficient pleasure; financial problems ('coke is too expensive'), 'problems' with law enforcement or other official agencies; or the influence of other cocaine using friends. Our qualitative data too confirm the finding that the effects of fear of legal consequences are either negligible or much less important than extralegal factors.

Respondents who had tried to quit cocaine were presented with a structured question about strategies and actions for quitting. All methods were applied by at least some of the respondents. The methods most often mentioned were: 'look for new interests, hobbies'; 'stop going to specific places where coke was being used', 'make conscious efforts to avoid coke-using friends' and 'change eating habits'. The least popular methods were 'take a long vacation' and 'start a new program of physical conditioning' (both 31.3%). Most of the strategies and actions for quitting described by the Antwerp respondents can be categorized into avoidance strategies, development of new lifestyle patterns and self-development (Shaffer and Jones, 1989), or into geographic moves to avoid cocaine, social actions, and health efforts (Waldorf *et al.*, 1991).

Furthermore, the Antwerp respondents also report seeking help while quitting. The kinds of help most often mentioned were 'family members' (50%), 'friends' (46.9%) and 'help for mental health' and 'partner' (43.8%). The kinds of help least often mentioned were 'telephone aid' and 'employer'. Of those 32 respondents who had tried to quit cocaine, however, only 15 sought formal assistance (46.9%).

These conclusions contradict the inevitability (of the repercussions) of cocaine use: one line of cocaine does not inevitably lead to another, relentlessly in ever increasing doses. Cocaine does not inevitably lead to dependence and/or addiction. Pharmacology is not destiny. For a variety of internal and external reasons, users seem to be able to abstain periodically from cocaine use or cut back on their use. The difficulties, if any, they encounter in doing so are not insurmountable. By cutting back their cocaine use or introducing periods of abstinence, cocaine users can sustain a controlled use pattern, i.e. avoid any dysfunction in the roles and responsibilities of daily life. However, there is nothing necessarily permanent about a pattern of controlled use. But while it is not difficult to lose control, it is not impossible to find it again either, or to quit altogether (even without formal treatment).

NOTES

[1] See Introduction, p. 3-4.

[2] See also Chapter 1, p. 27 to 36, on cessation of drug use.

[3] It must be kept in mind that the precise nature of the causal relations between the use of cocaine and its availability on the market is very hard to assess. Consequently, this chapter will only present rough data on the interrelationship between the availability of cocaine to users and the prevalence of temporary abstinence, cutting back and/or quitting cocaine use. In our opinion, this shortcoming could have been corrected only in a legally approved model of cocaine supply (where availability and purchasing behavior of cocaine users can be monitored).

[4] 'Periodical abstinence' is defined as: 'to stop using cocaine for at least one month or longer, without the intention to quit cocaine once and for all'.

[5] For data on the average length of career in these samples, see Chapter 5, p. 141-142.

[6] Twenty-one respondents (18.9% of the total sample) reported some kind of difficulty with these periods of abstinence. We will deal with this in a separate paragraph below (see § 12.4, p. 275-277).

[7] We checked which main reasons the 15 respondents gave for normal abstinence periods. If they all referred to these reasons when they answered 'no *specific* reason' for their longest period of abstinence, would it cause any changes in the distribution of frequencies in the right column of table 12.2.e (and also in table 12.2.f below)? We found this was not the case, because 4 of these 15 people reported 'no desire for cocaine' as the *main* reason for normal periods of abstinence; 3 of them cited 'cocaine unobtainable'; 2 of them 'no money', etc.

[8] Again, if we were to consider the answer 'no specific reason' for the longest period of abstinence (by 15 respondents) as a referral to the answers about main reasons for normal periods of abstinence, it would not change the distribution of frequencies in this table...

[9] We did not find any information on non-use periods in the Rotterdam study (1990-91), or in the comparative publication on the three city studies of Barcelona, Rotterdam and Turin (BIELEMAN, B., DIAZ, A, MERLO, G. and KAPLAN, C. (1993) (eds.), *Lines across Europe. Nature and extent of cocaine use in Barcelona, Rotterdam and Turin*, 79-104. Amsterdam: Swets & Zeitlinger.).

[10] Twenty-six respondents (23.4% of the total sample) reported some kind of difficulty with cutting back on their cocaine use. We will deal with this in a separate paragraph below (§ 12.4, see p. 275).

[11] The other respondents belonged to chains C, D, F, G, I, M, P, S, U, and Z.

[12] See Chapter 3, p. 82 and 86-88; Chapter 6, p. 156 and 158.

[13] Out of the 33 respondents who had ever experienced difficulties with cutting back on their cocaine use or abstaining temporarily, 18 respondents mentioned this.

[14] See Chapter 13, p. 295-296.

[15] It must be kept in mind that the perception as 'psychological' by respondents of the problems they experience while abstaining or cutting back is not necessarily a proof of the 'psychological' nature of these phenomena. Popular and scientific definitions of what draws the distinction between 'psychological' and 'physical' phenomena may be quite different.

[16] Out of the 33 respondents who had ever experienced difficulties with cutting back on their cocaine use or abstaining temporarily, 14 respondents mentioned this.

[17] See Chapter 3, p. 82 and 86-88; Chapter 6, p. 156 and 158.

[18] Quitting cocaine is defined as: to consider oneself as having stopped completely and reporting non-use for the last three months.

[19] See also Chapter 19, p. 409-413.

[20] See also Chapter 19, p. 397-405.

[21] See Chapter 5, p. 128.

[22] In a study of a non-clinical sample from the State of New Jersey (USA) White and Bates conclude that differential associations (friends' use) and punishments (negative consequences) are most strongly related to cessation from cocaine use. WHITE, H.R. and BATES, M.E. (1995), Cessation from cocaine use, 90 *Addiction*, 947-957.

[23] In addition, Waldorf *et al.* (1991: 159) discovered very few statistically significant differences between those who quit (N=106) and those who continued to use (N=122). Indeed, some of the heavier users seemed to be able to quit with far fewer problems than some of the lighter users, and some of the heavier users were able to quit without any treatment assistance, whereas some of the lighter users were not.

[24] To be included as 'quitters' in the San Francisco sample, respondents had to be cocaine-free or to have drastically reduced their use to less than four single occasions in the twelve months prior to the interview (Waldorf *et al.*, 1991: 287). To be included as 'quitters' in the Antwerp sample, however, respondents had to perceive themselves as having quit their cocaine use.

CHAPTER 13

CRAVING

13.1. INTRODUCTION

Cohen (1992) states that the desire for a drug ('craving' in scientific literature labeled) is commonly seen as an inevitable physical or pharmacological effect of that drug. The implication of 'craving' is that the person in question does not simply want, but in some sense has to have, something (Davies, 1992: 49-52). The desire may be so strong that many, if not most, people are unable to resist and continue taking the drug, in spite of negative or even life threatening consequences. As a consequence, the drug is assumed to exert power over a user who often becomes its victim. Classic examples are the ex-heroin user who is irresistibly drawn to the old copping areas, and the laboratory experiments with rats and monkeys. Everybody knows there are 'desires' for tobacco, coffee and alcohol, but apparently these desires are considered less victimizing than those for illegal drugs, such as cocaine.

However, several authors are aware of difficulties with the concept of 'craving', especially where this is postulated as an independent entity (Gossop, 1990; West & Kranzler, 1990). In fact, the evidence for the existence of craving is basically that people say they feel it, when asked the appropriate question. Craving cannot be inferred from merely observing behaviour. Yet, the word craving refers to the fact that sometimes people feel a strong desire to use, or use more of, their preferred drug, but it gives the impression of an autonomous force whose power cannot be resisted. This chapter examines this mysterious desire for cocaine with two kinds of indicators. In §13.2, we summarize some objective measures of desire elaborated in previous chapters. In §13.3 we present our data on the subjective experience of craving by our respondents. And finally, we present both quantitative and qualitative material on the kind of (illegal) activities our respondents engaged in in order to obtain (money to buy) their cocaine (§13.4).

13.2. OBJECTIVE MEASURES OF DESIRE

In his paper 'Desires for cocaine', Cohen (1992) interpreted simple behavioral variables as indications of desire for a drug: frequency of use during a week, evolution of levels of use, length of period of heaviest use, and periods of abstinence.

In chapter 5 we showed that the proportion of respondents reporting daily use rises spectacularly from the first year (3.6%) to the period of heaviest use (45.0%) and then drops to zero for the three months prior to interview.[1] This means that almost half of our sample were frequent users during their top period, but none of them subsequently continued this pattern.

The group who used 2.5 grams of cocaine or more per week during their period of heaviest use (the high level users, N=55) is interesting in this respect. 70.9% of them used cocaine daily, and 27.3% of them used more than once a week. According to the literature these users were highly probable to continue their use, and to experience a strong desire for cocaine. However, we found that only 5 of these 55 respondents maintained cocaine consumption at the high level they had at period of heaviest use;[2] 23.6% evolved to non-use, 47.3% evolved to a low level of use and 16.4% to a medium level of use.

In Chapter 5 we showed that these periods of heaviest use are limited in time.[3] Our respondents reported an average duration of top period of consumption of 13.5 months (after correcting for length of career this dropped to 9.5 months). 86.4% reported a duration of the top period of consumption of 2 years or less. All these data suggest that if any desire developed at all during a period of heaviest use, such a desire is not strong enough to compel consumers to maintain a cocaine consumption of 2.5 grams per week.

Finally, if a large number of respondents did not have periods of abstinence, this might be interpreted as a strong desire for cocaine. In chapter 12 we showed that 86.5% of our respondents reported to have stopped for more than one month.[4] The average duration of the longest period of abstinence among those who reported periodic abstinence was 15 months, and even after correcting for length of career, this was 12 months.[5] Having a strong desire for cocaine clearly does not prevent users from abstaining periodically, even for long periods of time.

13.3. SUBJECTIVE MEASURES OF DESIRE

13.3.1. *Quantitative data*

In chapter 11 we dealt with the advantages and disadvantages of cocaine perceived by our respondents. The average number of disadvantages was 3.0 versus 3.2 advantages per respondent. Twenty-five respondents mentioned 'creates psychological dependence' as a disadvantage (22.5% of the total sample) and only 1 respondent mentioned 'creates physical dependence' (0.9% of the total sample).[6]

To analyse *periods of abstinence*, we also asked our respondents in an open-ended question to explain why they had occasionally abstained from cocaine. Since 86.5% of our sample reported periods of abstinence,[7] the reasons were quite numerous. Like in the Amsterdam studies, we distinguished between reasons for any period of abstinence and reasons for the longest periods of abstinence. For this chapter, the reasons that relate to desire are the most relevant (see table 13.3.a).

'No desire for cocaine' was the reason for the longest period of abstinence mentioned most often (17), followed by 'no money' (11) and 'coke unobtainable' and 'partner made problems' (both 10). For normal abstinence periods, the reason most mentioned was 'no money' (31), followed by 'no desire for cocaine' (27) and 'coke unobtainable' (21).

Table 13.3.a   Number of respondents who give reasons for abstinence related to desire, in the 1997 Antwerp sample

	Antwerp (1997)	
Reason	Normal abstinence	Longest abstinence
No desire for cocaine	27	17
Fear of dependence	5	5

Similarly, 'no money' was the main reason for *cutting back* mentioned most often (27 times), 7 respondents cut back mainly because of no desire for cocaine and 2 respondents because of fear of dependence. As similar tendencies were found in the 1987 Amsterdam I sample, we can conclude that 'desire of cocaine', the fear of losing control, is not a significant regulator of cocaine consumption.

Furthermore, we also examined the subjective experience of desire (or craving) itself. Cohen (1989: 121) used the Dutch word for 'longing' (*'verlangen'*) in his questionnaire (and so did we) to avoid the possible moral connotation of the words 'craving' and 'dependence'. Of all our respondents, 93.7 % reported having experienced a craving for cocaine. This is significantly more than the 76% of the Amsterdam I sample who had experienced a craving. We also calculated after how many years of cocaine use this phenomenon first emerged (see table 13.3.b).

Table 13.3.b   Age and number of cocaine use years at onset of first craving in %, in the 1987 Amsterdam I sample and in the 1997 Antwerp sample

	Amsterdam I (1987)	Antwerp (1997)
Age at 1st craving	% (N=122)	% (N=104)
≤20yrs	23.0	39.4
20-25	31.1	34.6
26-30	21.3	13.6
≥30yrs	15.6	10.6
No answer	*9.0*	*1.8*
Total	100.0	100.0

	Amsterdam I (1987)	Antwerp (1997)
Length of cocaine use at 1st craving	%	%
<1year	32.0	27.9
1-2 years	23.0	28.8
3-5 years	16.4	26.0
>5years	18.0	12.5
No answer	*10.7*	*4.8*
Total	100.0	100.0

Of those respondents having experienced craving, 74% did so before the age of 26. This is more than the findings for the 1987 Amsterdam sample, but our 'no answer' category was considerably smaller. Distribution of percentages for the length of cocaine use at first craving shows smaller differences with the Amsterdam sample: in both samples, more than half of the respondents experienced craving after less than 3 years of cocaine use.

The 104 respondents who reported craving were asked if they had this feeling when cocaine was available, when it was not available or both. The distribution presented in tables 13.3.c through 13.3.e shows no significant differences with the Amsterdam findings.

Table 13.3.c Current craving for cocaine when it is available and when it is not available, in the 1987 Amsterdam I sample and in the 1997 Antwerp sample [♠]

	Amsterdam I (1987) N=117		Antwerp (1997) N=104 [*]	
Craving for cocaine	**When not available**		**When not available**	
	Yes	No	Yes	No
When available yes	67	42	55	42
no (=never)	2	6	1	6

	Antwerp [*]		
	When not available		**Total**
	Yes	No	
When available never	1	6	7
Seldom	2	3	5
every now and then	12	7	19
often	10	7	17
(almost) always	31	25	56
Total	56	48	104

[*] Based on the number of respondents who report ever having experienced craving (N=104)

Six persons who reported having experience with cocaine craving, do no longer have it, neither when cocaine is available nor when cocaine is not available (see table 13.3.c). Just like in the 1987 Amsterdam I sample, we did not find a difference in reported craving between users and ex-users (at the time of the interview).

In Amsterdam a significant relation between level of use during top period and the probability of reporting craving was found. This meant that high-level users in his sample had a higher probability of experiencing craving than low-level users ($\chi 2$, p<.025). In our sample we found the same tendency: 83.3% of the low-level users, 93.7% of the medium-level users, and 98.2% of the high-level users reported having experienced craving. Unfortunately, cell numbers were too low to test for $\chi 2$ statistical significance. However, if we collapse medium and high-level users to make a 2x2 table, we can do the Fisher's Exact test (an alternative test for chi-square). Thus, we find a significant relation between level of use during top period and the probability of reporting craving (Fisher's Exact test: p=0.038).

Our interview protocol allowed craving for cocaine *when it is available* to be reported for different frequencies of occurrence (see table 13.3.d). In the 1987 Amsterdam I sample Cohen (1989: 123) found that craving for cocaine when it was available, is significantly more frequent with females than with males ($\chi 2$, p<0.025). Again we find a similar tendency: all 41 women reported craving when cocaine is available, against 63 of the 70 men (90%). After collapsing the rows in table 13.3.d into two rows 'never' and 'ever', we find a statistically significant difference between men and women (Fisher's Exact test: p=0.045).[8] However, if we summate the 'often' and '(almost) always' categories in table 13.3.d, we find that the proportion of women (68.3%) is even slightly smaller than of men (70.0%).

Looking at craving for cocaine *when it is not available*, again a significant difference between men and women was found in Amsterdam (p=0.1). In our Antwerp sample we did not find a statistical significant difference: half of both men and women reported a 'longing' when cocaine was not available (see table 13.3.e).

Table 13.3.d   Craving for cocaine when it is available, in the 1987 Amsterdam I sample and in the 1997 Antwerp sample [♠]

	Amsterdam I (1987)					
	Total		Men		Women	
Frequency	N	%	N	%	N	%
Never	10	6.3	9	9.4	1	1.6
Seldom	41	25.6	28	29.2	13	20.0
Approx. 25%	10	6.3	5	5.2	5	7.8
Approx. 50%	13	8.1	5	5.2	8	13.0
Approx. 75%	13	8.1	3	3.1	10	16.0
(Almost) always	45	28.1	26	27.1	19	30.0
No answer	*28*	*17.5*	*20*	*20.8*	*8*	*13.0*
Total	**160**	**100.0**	**96**	**100.0**	**64**	**101.4**

	Antwerp (1997)					
	Total		Men		Women	
Frequency	N	%	N	%	N	%
Never	7	6.3	7	10.0	-	-
Seldom	5	4.5	3	4.3	2	4.9
Every now and then	22	19.8	11	15.7	11	26.8
Often	18	16.2	14	20.0	4	9.8
(Almost) always	59	53.2	35	50.0	24	58.5
Total	**111**	**100.0**	**70**	**100.0**	**41**	**100.0**

Table 13.3.e   Craving for cocaine when it is not available, in the 1987 Amsterdam I sample and in the 1997 Antwerp sample

	Amsterdam I (1987)					
Desire	Total		Men		Women	
	N	%	N	%	N	%
Yes	70	44.0	36	37.5	34	53.1
No	61	38.0	41	42.7	20	31.3
No answer	*29*	*18.0*	*19*	*19.8*	*10*	*15.6*
Total	**160**	**100.0**	**96**	**100.0**	**64**	**100.0**

	Antwerp (1997)					
Desire	Total		Men		Women	
	N	%	N	%	N	%
Yes	56	50.3	35	50.0	21	51.2
No	55	49.5	35	50.0	20	48.8
Total	**111**	**100.0**	**70**	**100.0**	**41**	**100.0**

Over half of our respondents reported that cocaine had been an 'obsession' at some time in their career (table 13.3.f). This is significantly more than in both the Amsterdam samples (36.3% in 1987, 40% in 1991). Exactly 50% of our male and 56.1% of the female respondents stated that cocaine had been an obsession. This difference is not statistically significant. Cohen (1989: 123) did not find a difference between men and women on this variable either.

These data clearly show that evidence for the existence of 'craving' (or desire, longing) is found in subjective indicators (experiences told by respondents), rather than in objective measurements (behavioral indicators). Many of our respondents (even more than in the Amsterdam samples) reported having experienced a certain longing for cocaine, or even a temporary obsession for it. Throughout our fieldwork and our open interviews we found several indications for the existence of a desire or longing for cocaine.

Table 13.3.f   Prevalence of cocaine 'ever' having been an obsession, in the 1987 Amsterdam I sample and in the 1997 Antwerp sample

Amsterdam I (1987)						
Obsession	Total		Men		Women	
	N	%	N	%	N	%
Yes	58	36.3	38	39.6	20	31.3
No	87	54.4	48	50.0	39	60.9
No answer	*15*	*9.4*	*10*	*10.4*	*5*	*7.8*
Total	**160**	**100.0**	**96**	**100.0**	**64**	**100.0**

Amsterdam II (1991)						
Obsession	Total		Men		Women	
	N	%	N	%	N	%
Yes	36	40	18	36	18	44
No	55	60	32	64	23	56
Total	**91**	**100**	**50**	**100**	**41**	**100**

Antwerp (1997)						
Obsession	Total		Men		Women	
	N	%	N	%	N	%
Yes	58	52.2	35	50.0	23	56.1
No	53	47.7	35	50.0	18	43.9
Total	**111**	**100.0**	**70**	**100.0**	**41**	**100.0**

Whether this experience is rooted in pharmacological properties of the drug, individual personality traits (set factors), social learning processes (setting factors), or a combination of these three, does not really matter here. The crucial point is that, in spite of the subjective experience of a certain desire for cocaine, people are able to resist it, and to exert control over the drug (and not the other way round). This longing for cocaine might be no more overwhelming or victimizing than the occasional longing for a pint of beer, a T-bone steak with French fries on the side (I am a Belgian), or for sex... Our findings (and those from Amsterdam) about the (non-)persistence of daily use, the dynamic evolution of levels of use, the relatively short periods of heaviest use, and the considerably long periods of abstinence show that a (strong) desire does not prevent users from stopping using cocaine, cutting back on their use, or in other words: regulating their cocaine consumption.[9] How can this apparent contradiction be explained?

In Chapter 11 we analyzed 90 cocaine effects.[10] As for effects that were reported by at least 75 percent of the users, the number of negative effect increases with level of use. Both in the Antwerp sample and in the Amsterdam sample, data are consistent: a level of use higher than a certain level (e.g. 2.5 g a week) definitively alters the balance between positive and negative effects. Adverse effects occur more frequently as level of use increases and so compel most such users either to abstain, or to return to a more pleasurable level of use. Most users manage to do so.[11]

A second explanation can be found in the informal control mechanisms most users apply. In Chapter 14 we showed that they have clear ideas about (un)suitable situations and circumstances for cocaine use, about emotional states that maximize positive effects of cocaine, etc.[12] In chapter 11 we related perceived (dis-)advantages of cocaine with dose and circumstances, proving that many cocaine users gain through experience a broad knowledge about doses and circumstances that stimulate or hamper a pleasurable cocaine experience.[13] And finally, in chapter 14, we listed 49 rules of use and 53 rules of advice to novice users.[14] Furthermore, 63.1% of users report that they know 'risky' users of cocaine, indicating their recognition that some forms of cocaine use have negative consequences.[15] These informal control devices (especially the category of 'general rules') may be vague and stereotypical, but they do operate as a system of control, through which users can regulate their use, in spite of a subjective craving...[16]

To conclude, our data confirm the subjective experience of 'desire for cocaine'. Although respondents may report these 'desires' as strong, a number of objective and subjective measures indicate that these desires can be controlled in the sense that high levels of use are not maintained indefinitely. It remains unclear, however, whether this longing or liking is a pharmacological effect of the drug. As Cohen (1992) suggested, such desires may be complicated social learning or a mixture of pharmacological and social learning effects.

13.3.2. *Qualitative data*

During the second (biographical) interview, the subjective experience of desire (or craving) was not a separate issue. Some respondents, however, spontaneously referred to feelings of longing or desire for cocaine. Their accounts yielded qualitative data that complement the quantitative data presented above.[17]

> *When there is coke in the house, I always feel like it, and it's like, yes, mmm but then again I look at it as a glass of wine or something... In fact, it sure isn't powerlessness, but yes, that feeling of desire, feeling like it, it's very strong and it... it's the same with other drugs, for example with XTC or with alcohol as well in a way, but it's the strongest with coke: the desire for more...* [R/0/01]

> *There was a time I knew I had a big desire for it, really, when I was somewhere, I was thinking: 'I wish I had coke', and, when they didn't have it, that I was thinking: 'How am I supposed to go out, how can I get through the night...' and you really went from bar to bar looking for someone you know who is selling.* [I/1/09]

A first observation is that almost all respondents acknowledge having experienced desire for cocaine. While some interviewees feel like having some cocaine every now and then, they are certainly not confronted with a constant urge to use it:

> *I definitely quit using coke. I'm telling you: when it comes up coincidentally, and there is an opportunity, and there is an ambiance, okay, it happens. I'm not saying it kills you. But I don't have to have it. But I don't know whether it comes up within a few months, or within a year, or within ten years, and when I feel like having it, I will do it. For the time being, I really don't feel like it.* [H/0/22]

> *No, I'm never dying for cocaine, it's just when I feel like doing it, on a particular night, at a particular moment, then I will do that. So with me, it's never a situation that I end up in a situation in which I say: 'I got to have my coke or it won't be fun', that will never happen.* [P/0/04]

Second, feelings of desire or craving may fade as the user drifts out of cocaine use. Other participants indicate more frequent and more intense experiences of craving which make it hard to abstain temporarily or cut down. All these respondents have been high-level users, injecting or freebasing cocaine, they tell stories of intense craving, e.g. *dreaming* about cocaine:

These were always dreams, I can remember very well, especially when I used to take it every day and I had to stop suddenly, these were mostly dreams like: I want it but I can't get it. So for example I would dream that I was sitting with you at a table, you would be preparing a base for me, you want to give it to me, the dog comes in here and blows everything away with its tail, that kind of situations, like: I want to take it, but I can't. Or dreaming about a needle that looked as white as a sheet, and oh, it was presented so tastefully, and the moment I wanted to shoot it, somebody thumped my arm, and the needle was gone. I've seen some creepy movies in my dreams [he laughs]. [H/0/11]

Several other respondents, however, state that the craving –although 'real' and sometimes quite intense – does not inevitably lead to actual use of cocaine. When a user feels like using cocaine, he or she may choose to abstain (see also: Dudish-Poulsen & Hatsukami, 1997: 1-9). Thus, craving for the substance is not absolutely imperative:

Maybe a week after or a few days after, you have that urge to take it again, but when you don't know anyone at that moment, or it doesn't suit you, every now and then I have it, you know, like: I feel like it but I just won't make any effort for it [she laughs]. [I/1/17]
When I can't get it easily, then I say this: 'Let it be, boy, come on, not today, next week, okay? That's as good to me, we just go out and have some beers.' [C/0/06]

Indeed, the desire or longing is clearly not the result of simple pharmacological effects of an illicit drug. It is often triggered by specific set and setting factors, such as the presence of certain friends, specific moods of the user (and his/her company), etc.

When I feel bad and some friends come in and they offer me some, then I will feel like doing it. [P/0/02]

I must say honestly, now, I feel more like using coke, to be honest, just to feel good for a moment, to forget those problems... I mean: I really doubt myself, I really wonder whether I am really abnormal, whether I'm really a good-for-nothing, whether I'm really no good for anything, [...] whether I really am a dumb blonde, whether I am a puppy, I'm starting to believe all those things, and... Then I really feel like being out for a while. [H/1/28]

Another setting factor that stimulates a desire for cocaine is *talking about it*. This was explicitly mentioned by two respondents during the first semi-structured interviewed when they described specific emotional states that generate an appetite for cocaine (see Chapter 14).[18] Other participants spontaneously reported feelings of craving when the conversation among friends turned to cocaine. Several respondents indicated that the questions (or some of them) asked during the interviews aroused a desire for cocaine in them.

You don't push each other, but by talking about it with some people, you start feeling like it. And then you want to do more of it, it's true. [...] For example: last week Tuesday, after we talked about it the whole night [i.e. after the first interview, TD], *I did take a line. I really felt like doing it at that moment.* [R/0/08]

I always prepare it. First you put your spoon, the coke... you see, when I'm telling this, I start feeling like it [he laughs],*... you add the ammonia, you boil it, pull out the ammonia, add water.* [H/0/11]

A final and important indicator of the subjective experience of craving is the observation that almost all interviewees agree on the fact that the capacity to resist desire is a central characteristic of a controlled user.[19] Being able to abstain from cocaine when confronted with craving is what ultimately separates the user from 'addiction' or 'abuse' or 'uncontrolled use':

> *When you say 'Hey, I've got something in the house, do you feel like it?', that they refuse it, that they say: 'No, not for me today. I don't need it today.'* [C/0/02]

13.4. EXTRA SOURCES OF INCOME TO SPEND ON COCAINE

We asked the complete set of questions first used by Morningstar and Chitwood (and also used in Amsterdam), to find out what kind of activities people engage in to buy or use cocaine (see table 13.4.a). These activities comprise both ways of procuring income as well as general social activities (like tolerating the presence of unpleasant people, just to obtain some cocaine). We hoped to find out how often cocaine users would engage in behaviors that are illegal or menial.

Table 13.4.a   Special activities to obtain (money to buy) cocaine, in %, in three samples [*]

Activity ever engaged in	Amsterdam I 1987 N=160		Amsterdam II 1991 N=108		Antwerp 1997 N=111	
	N	%	N	%	N	%
1. Theft (face-to-face)	-	-	1	0.9	10	9.0
2. Car theft	1	0.6	1	0.9	6	5.4
3. Car-breaking	-	-	3	2.8	8	7.2
4. Stealing from friends	5	3.1	-	-	14	12.6
5. Shoplifting	6	3.7	4	3.7	16	14.4
6. Burglary	9	5.6	3	2.8	14	12.6
7. Forging checks	10	6.2	6	5.5	8	7.2
8. Running con games	9	5.6	4	3.7	22	19.8
9. Prostitution	4	2.5	5	4.6	8	7.2
10. Trading sexual favors	8	5.0	2	1.8	15	13.5
11. Stealing cocaine	5	3.1	7	6.5	22	19.8
12. Selling cocaine	37	23.1	24	22.2	57	51.3
13. Taking an extra job	11	6.9	9	8.3	16	14.4
14. Selling personal possession	13	8.1	9	8.3	37	33.3
15. Borrowing money	14	8.7	19	17.6	13	11.7
16. Tolerating the presence of unpleasant persons	52	32.5	48	44.4	64	57.7

[*]More than one answer was possible

In the 1987 Amsterdam I sample, two activities (face-to-face theft and car breaking), and in the 1991 Amsterdam II sample one activity (stealing from friends) had a zero prevalence. In our Antwerp sample, none of the activities had zero prevalence. Moreover, all activities (criminal or not) were reported more often by our respondents compared to both Dutch samples (Cohen, 1989: 123-124; Cohen & Sas, 1995: 97-99). We found only one exception: 'borrowing money' was reported by 17.6% of the Amsterdam II sample, versus 11.7% of the 1997 Antwerp sample.

Almost 60% of our respondents reported tolerating the presence of unpleasant persons in order to obtain cocaine. This is almost twice as many compared to the Amsterdam I sample, and significantly more than in the Amsterdam II sample. Nevertheless, it was the 'activity' mentioned most often in all three samples. Qualitative material gives us some hints to interpret these figures:

I also thought, I mean, that man who was really interested in me, he used that as a means to buy people, and I found that not attractive at all. He felt himself quite interesting because I am 'someone' and I have some coke with me, and so I must be very welcome.' [K/1/03]

Yes, for example, an uncontrolled user, when he offers you something, he will push you more to take it, compared to someone who uses it in a controlled way. Someone who is an uncontrolled user, yes I'm telling you, those are people who become another person when they are under the influence of coke, and because I'm not like that, I find that very disturbing. [P/0/05]

In all three samples, selling cocaine was the second most prevalent activity, reported by about 23% in both Amsterdam samples. Half of our respondents (51.3%) have at some time during their cocaine use career engaged in selling cocaine, twice as many as Cohen's findings in both Amsterdam samples. This does not mean half of our respondents are professional dealers, who gain a substantial part of their income from selling drugs. Most of these respondents explained 'selling cocaine' this way:

I didn't really deal it. It was mostly for friends, for 2 or 3 intimate friends, real good friends who gave their money to me when I bought it, and I gave it to them, but I never sold to all and sundry. [H/0/16]

When somebody asked me: can't you get this or that for me? To do him a favor, I would, but not to deal coke, I didn't like the atmosphere around those people. [...] But selling, it just meant passing a few grams, or ten grams, to another person, like: I'll supply you ten grams, and then you take care of it, you make sure those people get it, because I didn't want anybody at my front door. [Z/0/02]

Most interviewees merely drifted into small-scale dealing because other users asked them to procure cocaine and/or because selling small quantities of cocaine helped to reduce the cost of their own use.[20] These cocaine sellers clearly differ from the popular stereotype of drug dealers as the very embodiment of evil: rapacious, greedy, violent, indifferent to the human toll their transactions exact. In accordance with the conclusions Waldorf *et al.* (1991: 74-102) made, we find that drug sellers are often not very different from the users we talked to. Typically, they were just people buying from and selling to friends, usually in relatively small quantities, and often with little profit.[21]

There are many motives for selling cocaine, and most of our respondents who to some extent became involved in selling had more than one reason for doing so. In contrast to common stereotypes, few of the dealers we interviewed were in it solely for the money or just to feed their own habits. Distribution often takes the form of a group of friends who pool funds to buy a larger amount of the drug in order to get lower prices (Waldorf *et al.*, 1991: 76-77). Some of them, such as both sellers quoted above, do not even consider themselves sellers; they are simply using their connection to assist their friends in getting better quality cocaine at a lower price.[22]

Despite the enormous profit margins, selling illicit substances can be a risky business for several reasons. Seven respondents report that the decision to start selling cocaine had a serious impact on their own pattern of cocaine use. They learned the hard way that having a permanent supply of cocaine around the house may be difficult to control:

In the end, I didn't control my cocaine use anymore. Because, you see, you're a seller, you start testing it. The trick is: selling and not using it, you know. But I did it wrong: I sold it, but I used it as well, you know. For example, every time I got my stuff, I started to test it, but you always take a little more, and you're gone. That is, yes... Some people come, they ask to buy some, yes, test a little bit, and you test it with them. You start smoking with them. In 1986, 1987 I didn't control it. The reason: because I sold it, right? Why did I sell it? Because it brought in a lot of money. I earned a lot of money with it. I'm honest: a lot of money. But I invested everything in my apartment, not the furniture, but a new cover, new electricity. I invested all my money well. I lived a good life. [H/0/23]

Unlike other users, sellers have cocaine available to them almost all the time, and at wholesale prices. Those who cut their product can often snort for free. Also Waldorf *et al.* (1991: 100) found that the escalation of their own cocaine use was the occupational hazard most frequently mentioned and they concluded: *'Given the reinforcing qualities of the high and the tendency to find more and more uses for cocaine, this presents a clear risk of escalation and abuse.'*

Stealing cocaine was mentioned by 19.8% of our respondents. Again, this is considerably more than in both Amsterdam samples (3.1% in 1987, and 6.5% in 1991). We do not know how to interpret these findings, because we did not ask for further details. Nor did our qualitative material yield any information on this 'stealing' of cocaine. As most respondents were not engaged in organized distribution networks, this theft of cocaine must probably be interpreted as stealing from friends, accidentally and opportunistically.

Activities that relate to prostitution are reported by 8 Antwerp respondents (6 men and 2 women); trading sexual favors was reported by 15 people (10 men and 5 women). Six respondents (4 men and 2 women) answered affirmatively on both variables.

As for criminal activities (activity 1 through 8), the most frequently reported illegal activities were: running con games (19.8%), shoplifting (14.4%), stealing from friends and burglary (both 12.6%). In both Amsterdam samples, 'forging checks' ranks first.

At first we were struck by the level of 'criminal activity' of our sample, which was incontestably higher than in both the Amsterdam studies. So, we took a closer look at the respondents who reported criminal activities:

Table 13.4.b   Number of criminal activities respondents engaged in, in the 1997 Antwerp sample

Antwerp (1997) N=111		
Number of criminal activities	N	%
No criminal activity	81	73.0
1 criminal activity	9	8.1
2 criminal activities	3	2.7
3 criminal activities	6	5.4
4 criminal activities	5	4.5
5 criminal activities	2	1.8
6 criminal activities	3	2.7
7 criminal activities	2	1.8
Total	111	100.0

(1) We computed for each respondent how many criminal activities he or she had ever engaged in. The results are shown in table 13.4.b. It is clear that all these crimes were committed by a small group of 30 respondents (including 20 male and 10 female).

Eighty-one respondents (73.0%) of our sample had never engaged in any of the criminal activities to obtain (money for) cocaine.

Nine respondents reported having engaged in only 1 criminal activity (including 5 who engaged in running con games, 2 in shoplifting, 1 stealing from friends or family, and 1 forging checks). Frequencies of these crimes were 4 times 'once' and 4 times 'sometimes'. Although one must be cautious with interpreting these figures, we believe that these respondents engaged in these activities when the occasion presented itself (opportunistic crime).

Twelve people (10.8% of our total sample) reported having engaged in 4 or more criminal activities; they are thus responsible for 65.3% of all the affirmative answers (62 of the 95 positive answers). Eleven of them reported having engaged in running con games, 10 in burglary, 10 in shoplifting, 9 in stealing from friends, 7 in car-breaking, 6 in car theft, and so on... For these people, the frequencies of illegal activities are also much higher ('often' and 'almost always').

We found that 14 of these 30 respondents belonged to snowball chain H; 4 to chain I; 3 to chain F; 1 to chain C, D, G, J, O, P, S, U and Y. The 12 respondents who reported having engaged in 4 or more different criminal activities, included 7 belonging to chain H, 3 to chain F, and 1 to chain I and J. 'Criminal' respondents were obviously mainly recruited in chains H, F and J. This is very logical in view of the key informants through which these chains had been initiated (see chapter 2).[23] Furthermore, snowball chains F and H differ markedly from the other snowball chains in that they contain higher proportions of registered respondents, regular injectors, and respondents reporting difficulties with abstaining or cutting back on their cocaine use.[24]

(2) Table 13.4.c shows more detailed information on the frequency of activities to obtain (money to buy) cocaine. In the residual category 'other' we included answers such as: swindling with cash dispensers (1), begging (2), selling other drugs (1), buying cocaine on credit (2), swapping for other drugs (2), taking money from one's savings account (2), and 'doing business' (1).

Table 13.4.c   Number of respondents engaging in each special activity to obtain (money to buy) cocaine, in the 1997 Antwerp sample (N=111)

Activity	Antwerp				
	Never	Once	Sometimes	Often	(Almost) always
1. Theft (face-to-face)	101	3	4	2	1
2. Car theft	105	5	-	1	-
3. Car-breaking [♣]	103	4	1	2	-
4. Stealing from friends [♣]	97	5	5	3	-
5. Shoplifting	95	1	9	5	1
6. Burglary	97	6	6	2	-
7. Forging checks	103	1	4	3	-
8. Running con games [♣]	89	8	10	2	1
9. Prostitution	103	2	6	-	-
10. Trading sexual favors	96	10	4	1	-
11. Stealing cocaine	89	10	9	2	1
12. Selling cocaine	54	16	20	15	6
13. Taking an extra job	95	5	8	2	1
14. Selling personal possession	74	9	15	11	2
15. Borrowing money	98	5	3	4	1
16. Tolerating the presence of unpleasant persons	47	19	35	9	1
17. Other	.	3	3	5	.

[♣] No answer: 1%

Fifteen respondents reported having engaged 'often' and 6 respondents reported having engaged '(almost) always' in selling cocaine.

Of the criminal activities (activity 1 through 8), the category 'once' has a total of 33 affirmative answers, which is 34.7% of all affirmative answers for criminal activities. Thus one third of all crimes reported are committed only 'once', indicating opportunistic and accidental criminal behavior. In other words, these respondents used illegal means for the satisfaction of their needs only once, in a way that is comparable to rare and impulsive petty crimes committed in department stores, when the occasion presents itself...

As the categories of 'often' and '(almost) always' remain empty for 'engaging in prostitution', we conclude that our sample does not include any fulltime prostitutes.

We checked whether there was a correlation between illegal activity and level of use during period of heaviest use. We found that 25 of the 30 respondents who reported engagement in at least one illegal activity, were using at a high level during their top period. Five of them were using at a medium level and none at a low level. If we consider only those 12 respondents who reported 4 different illegal activities or more, all of them were using at a high level during their period of heaviest use.

All 30 'criminal respondents' reported ever having experienced craving. Sixteen of them reported having experienced craving when cocaine was not available, while 28 of them reported having experienced craving when cocaine was available.

As to a possible relation between illegal activity and route of ingestion during period of heaviest use, 14 of the 30 criminal respondents were mainly injecting during their top period, 8 were mainly freebasing and 8 were mainly snorting during period of heaviest use. If we only take into consideration the 12 respondents reporting at least 4 different illegal activities, we see that 8 of them were mainly injecting cocaine at their top period, and 3 were mainly freebasing. We even find that 4 of them mainly injected from the first year of regular use, and 6 of them were still injecting during the three months prior to interview.[25]

13.5. CONCLUSION

Most people see the desire for a drug (in the scientific literature labeled as 'craving') as an inevitable physical or pharmacological effect of the drug. The desire may be so strong that many, if not most people are unable to resist and continue drug taking, even when negative or life threatening consequences become apparent. As a consequence the drug is assumed to exert power over a user.

On the one hand, more than 90% of the Antwerp respondents reported having experienced a certain longing for cocaine (i.e. markedly more than in the Amsterdam samples). Three in four respondents who had experienced craving, had done so before the age of 26. More than half of the respondents experienced craving after less than 3 years of cocaine use. A significant relation was found between level of use during top period and the probability of reporting craving. In other words, high-level users have a higher probability of experiencing craving than low-level users. Like in the 1987 Amsterdam sample, we found that craving for cocaine when it was available, is found more often in females than in males. Finally, over half of our respondents reported that cocaine had been an 'obsession' at some time in their career.

On the other hand, both our quantitative and qualitative data indicate the following. Our findings (and those in Amsterdam) about the (non-)persistence of daily use, the dynamic evolution of levels of use, the relatively short periods of heaviest use, and considerably long periods of abstinence, show that whether or not there is a (strong) desire, it clearly does not prevent users from stopping using cocaine, cutting back on their use, or in other words: regulating their cocaine consumption. Some interviewees feel like having some cocaine every now and then, but they are certainly not confronted with a constant urge to use. Furthermore, the desire or craving may fade as the user drifts out of cocaine use.

There is a relation between high levels of use, direct routes of ingestion such as injecting or freebasing, problems with temporary abstinence or cutting down, and frequent and more intense experiences of craving. But several respondents state that the craving –although 'real' and sometimes quite intense – does not inevitably lead to use of cocaine. For them, the craving for a substance is not so absolutely imperative. Feelings of desire or longing are simply not the result of pharmacological effects of an illicit drug. They are often triggered by specific set and setting factors, such as the presence of certain friends, specific moods of the user (and his/her company), conversations about cocaine, etc. Almost all interviewees agree that the ability to resist desire is a central characteristic of a controlled user. Being able to abstain from cocaine when confronted with craving is what the user separates from 'addiction' or 'abuse' or 'uncontrolled use'.

Third, it is sometimes suggested that the desire for a drug may be so strong that many, if not most, people are unable to resist, even if they have to engage in criminal activities to buy or use cocaine. We found that in both the Antwerp and the Amsterdam samples the activities most frequently mentioned were tolerating the presence of unpleasant persons to obtain cocaine and selling cocaine (usually to friends). Most of the respondents who report selling cocaine at some time during their cocaine use career in order to obtain money for cocaine, differ from the popular stereotype of drug dealers as the very embodiment of evil. Distribution often takes the form of a group of friends who pool funds to buy a larger amount of the drug in order to get lower prices. Selling illicit substances can be a risky business for several reasons, but an important occupational risk is the impact on one's own pattern of cocaine use.

All activities (criminal or not) were reported more often by the Antwerp respondents compared to both Dutch samples. Additional analysis revealed that three in four respondents had never engaged in any of the criminal activities to obtain (money for) cocaine. One third of all crimes reported had been committed only 'once', indicating opportunistic and accidental criminal behavior. Most of these crimes had been committed by a small group of 12 respondents, who were were mainly recruited from snowball chains with higher proportions of registered respondents, regular injectors, and respondents reporting difficulties with abstaining or cutting back. Furthermore, these 'criminal' respondents show higher frequencies illegal activities, they were all using at a high level during their top period, they reported having experienced craving, and they tended to inject or freebase during their period of heaviest use.

To conclude, our data confirm the subjective experience of 'desire for cocaine'. It remains unclear whether this feeling of longing is rooted in the pharmacological properties of the drug. As Cohen suggested, such desires may be complicated social learning effects or a mixture of pharmacological effects, set or setting factors, and social learning effects. Although respondents may describe these 'desires' as strong, a number of objective and subjective measures indicate that these desires can be controlled in the sense that high levels of use are usually not maintained indefinitely. In spite of the subjective experience of a certain desire for cocaine, people are able to resist, and to exert power over the drug.

Two explanatory factors were discussed for this apparent contradiction: (1) a high level of use (e.g. 2.5 g a week) definitely alters the balance between positive and negative effects. Adverse effects occur more frequently as level of use increases and so compel most users either to abstain or to return to a more pleasurable level of use. Most users manage to do so; and (2) most users apply informal control mechanisms (rules about (un)suitable situations and circumstances for cocaine use, about emotional states that maximize positive effects of cocaine, suitable emotions before use are, appropriate dose, etc.). Through all these informal control devices users can regulate their use, despite their subjective feelings of craving...

NOTES

1 See Chapter 5, p. 133-135.
2 See Chapter 5, p. 138.
3 See Chapter 5, p. 140 and 143-146.
4 See Chapter 12, p. 265.
5 See Chapter 12, p. 266-267.
6 See Chapter 11, p. 250-252.
7 See Chapter 12, p. 267-272.
8 Chi-square test would be invalid because two cells of the 2x2 table have an expected count of less than 5. The Fisher's Exact test is an alternative for chi-square, especially for small samples. See: SIRKIN, R.M. (1995), *Statistics for the social sciences*, 363-367. Thousand Oaks: Sage Publications.
9 Similarly, Dudish-Poulsen and Hatsukami designed a study to explore the relationship between craving and cocaine-seeking behavior with the use of both subjective and behavioral measures. Their results suggested that while craving for cocaine can successfully be manipulated by both external and internal cocaine-related stimuli in a laboratory setting, craving alone may be neither necessary nor sufficient to drive cocaine-seeking behavior. DUDISH-POULSEN, S.A. and HATSUKAMI, D.K. (1997), Dissociation between subjective and behavioral responses after cocaine stimuli presentations, 47 *Drug and Alcohol Dependence* 1, 1-9.
10 See Chapter 11, p. 256-260.
11 See Chapter 12, p. 265-275.
12 See Chapter 14, p. 310-317.
13 See Chapter 11, p. 248-249 and 252-253.
14 See Chapter 14, p. 305-309.
15 See Chapter 3, p. 92-93.
16 It must be noted that the informal control mechanisms described here are not always efficient. See for example Chapter 7, p. 180-190.
17 The Flemish/Dutch term most common among respondents to describe feelings of desire is '*goesting*'. '*Goesting hebben in coke*' is the most frequently used expression for feeling like using cocaine.
18 See Chapter 14, p. 325 (note 8) and 314.

19 See also Chapter 15, p. 330.

20 For similar conclusions, see: MUGFORD, S.K. (1994), Recreational cocaine use in three Australian cities, 2 *Addiction Research* 1, 103. *'Another feature of the supply of cocaine was the lack of a clear cut separation between buyers and sellers. Twenty-one respondents (29%) had sold cocaine at some time. Typically, they bought a quantity larger than their immediate wants, and sold the remaining portions, usually in non-profit transactions with friends.'*

21 Similarly, eleven respondents spontaneously reported having sold other drugs (such as cannabis, MDMA or amphetamines) at one period in their lives. Apart from a few exceptional instances, these interviewees never sold other illicit substances (such as amphetamines, MDMA or cocaine). For two of them selling cannabis was a main source of income for a while. The others claim to have started selling cannabis for two main reasons: 1) they became aware of a demand for cannabis among their friends and acquaintances; and 2) they had relatively easy access to the substance (either because they knew sources or because they had grown cannabis themselves). Four respondents reported having sold other products, such as MDMA, amphetamines or 'poppers'. Three of them explained that they were mainly dealing to party goers in the Antwerp nightlife scene (in discotheques, bars, cafés, etc...). The fourth interviewee sometimes sold amphetamines ('speed') to his fellow workers, hotel and catering staff in Antwerp.

22 Waldorf *et al.* (1991: 94-95) also report motives for selling cocaine that have to do with sociability, prestige and social standing. Our qualitative interviews did not yield any valuable data on this topic.

23 See Chapter 2, p. 69-70.

24 See Chapter 3, p. 86 and 88; Chapter 6, p. 158; and Chapter 12, p. 277.

25 We did not find a statistically significant relation between 'criminal activity' and 'net income'. The average net income of the 30 criminally active respondents is only slightly lower than the average net income of the total sample. The only (non-significant) difference we find is that 36.7% of the criminally active respondents have a net income of 30,000 Belgian francs or less, compared to 29.7% of the total sample.

CHAPTER 14

RITUALS AND RULES FOR COCAINE USE

14.1. INTRODUCTION

In chapter 1 we argued that understanding the drug experience requires more than knowledge of the pharmacology of the drug. Norman Zinberg's investigations on the physical and social setting of drug use have shown that a person's emotional and social situation has a significant impact on drug use. Set and setting may determine not only the choice of drug itself, but also the effects of use. In this Chapter we want to check whether our respondents have rules, routines, and rituals that help them limit (or 'tame') their cocaine use, and whether they stick to them.

Rules of use were a separate and overt item in our questionnaire. Paragraph 14.2 focuses on our respondents' answers to these direct questions. As one of the methods to learn about personal rules of cocaine use, we analyze what advice our subjects would now give to novice users (§14.3).[1] Paragraphs 14.4 and 14.5 present emotional states (sets)[2] and situations (settings) that were reported by our respondents as (un)suitable for cocaine use. In paragraph 14.6 we discuss frequencies of categories of persons with whom respondents would definitely not use cocaine. In paragraph 14.7 we compare our data on limits on monthly cocaine purchase with those of the Amsterdam sample. Finally, we illustrate with qualitative data the set and setting factors that either facilitate or hamper respect for the personal rules of use (§14.8).

14.2. RULES FOR CONTROLING COCAINE USE

Many respondents recognize situations, feelings or persons that play a role in the use or non-use of cocaine. These principles of use can be regarded as part of the *control system* that is active when people consume drugs (see e.g. Zinberg, 1984: 152). *Control mechanisms* or rules of use were a separate and overt item in our questionnaire. We simply asked respondents if they had any rules to control cocaine use, and if so, what they were. We wanted to know whether situations, feelings or persons could be recognized or amalgamated in these rules.

Bearing in mind the difficulties that Cohen and his interviewers (1989: 79) experienced to persuade respondents to cooperate on this item, we interviewed them as assertively as possible.[3] This resulted in a much smaller 'no answer' category. Both in the 1987 and in the 1991 Amsterdam studies, about one third of the respondents did not answer the question concerning governing rules applied to their use. In our Antwerp sample only 10 % of our respondents could not or did not answer this question (see tables 14.2.a and 14.2.b).

Table 14.2.a   Rules applied to control cocaine use, in three samples [*]

Rule	Amsterdam I 1987 N	Amsterdam I 1987 %	Amsterdam II 1991 N	Amsterdam II 1991 %	Antwerp 1997 N	Antwerp 1997 %
1. Not earlier	33	20.6	26	24	18	16.2
2. Next day	29	18.1	16	15	17	15.3
3. Work/study	28	17.5	9	8	41	36.9
4. Amount	10	6.3	7	6	11	9.9
5. Dinner	10	6.3	4	4	4	3.6
6. Persons	7	4.4	4	4	16	14.4
7. Alcohol	5	3.1	6	6	6	5.4
8. Depressive	5	3.1	2	2	7	6.3
9. Time period	4	2.5	5	5	15	13.5
10. Account	4	2.5	5	5	10	9.0
11. Not alone	3	1.9	1	1	10	9.0
12. Week	3	1.9	6	6	8	7.2
13. Effect	1	0.6	2	2	9	8.1
14. Sleep	1	0.6	1	1	7	6.3
15. Habit	1	0.6	6	6	2	1.8
16. Own cocaine	1	0.6	-	-	-	-
17. Do not buy	1	0.6	2	2	5	4.5
18. Strangers	1	0.6	-	-	2	1.8
19. Quality	1	0.6	-	-	3	2.7
20. $ limits	1	0.6	1	1	8	7.2
21. Not with sex	1	0.6	-	-	-	-
22. Only when going out	-	-	3	3	4	3.6
23. Only special occasions	-	-	5	5	-	-
24. Only use for fun	-	-	4	4	-	-
Other [♠]	3	1.9	13	12	-	-
No answer/no rules	*51*	*31.9*	*32*	*30*	*11*	*9.9*

[*] More than one answer was possible
[♠] Coding differences are possible

The following categories of rules of use were used in the Amsterdam study (Cohen, 1989: 79). Abbreviations for table 14.2.a are in square brackets: [*not alone*], not earlier than a certain time of the day [*not earlier*], if you have the next day available for resting or sleeping [*next day*], no more than a certain amount [*amount*], not when working, doing sports or studying [*work/study*], not or only rarely on weekdays [*week*], not before dinner [*dinner*], not more often than N times per time period [*time period*], when using cocaine check alcohol intake [*alcohol*], stop if feeling certain effects [*effect*], take into account how situation relates to cocaine use [*account*], not with certain persons [*persons*], not when feeling depressed [*depressive*], not before going to sleep [*sleep*], not always accept cocaine when offered [*habit*], only own cocaine [*own cocaine*], never buy cocaine [*do not buy*], not with sex [*sex*], do not accept from strangers [*strangers*], only good quality cocaine [*quality*], limits on purchase [*$limits*], [*not with sex*], [*only when going out*], [*only special occasions*], and [*only for fun*].

Table 14.2.b lists all other rules of use our Antwerp respondents reported. We used some abbreviations: not in combination with other drugs [*combination*], not when important things have to be done, when formalities have to be taken care of, when you need to appear in public places, or have to contact official agencies [*formalities*], not when you have to meet parents or other family members [*family*], only when it was pre-arranged [*pre-arranged*].

Table 14.2.b   Rules applied to control cocaine use (continued), in the 1997 Antwerp sample [*]

Antwerp					
Rule (continued)	**N**	**%**		**N**	**%**
25. Never inject	11	9.9	38. Not without alcohol	2	1.8
26. Secrecy	10	9.0	39. Not when sick	1	0.9
27. Family	9	8.1	40. Always alone	1	0.9
28. Only with specific persons	8	7.2	41. Always per 2 fixes	1	0.9
29. Never offer non-users	8	7.2	42. Not when very happy	1	0.9
30. Never bother other people	5	4.5	43. Never freebase	1	0.9
31. Not when driving a car	4	3.6	44. Never like it too much	1	0.9
32. Formalities	4	3.6	45. Not as condition for fun	1	0.9
33. Combination	4	3.6	46. Pre-arranged	1	0.9
34. Avoid coke scene	4	3.6	47. Respect free will	1	0.9
35. Always at home	3	2.7	48. Never keep a stock	1	0.9
36. Only when at ease	3	2.7	49. Never hide for friends	1	0.9
37. Not on holiday	3	2.7			

[*] More than one answer was possible

Our respondents answered in their own words, which makes a detailed comparison with the Amsterdam sample difficult (coding differences were inevitable). Nevertheless we found very similar mechanisms governing cocaine use: users often manage to keep their cocaine use from interfering with activities that take priority (see also: Waldorf et al., 1991: 267). Most of the informal rules listed above serve as boundary protection mechanisms. They keep users from going over the edge, or allow many of them to climb back. Informal rules of use help to prevent disruption of everyday life in which users have invested (jobs, homes, families, communities and identities). In spite of cocaine's reinforcing power, these informal control mechanisms may help to maintain or restore the user's balance, i.e. they serve as boundary protectors. As long as everyday life is a distinct and a paramount reality at the fringes of which drug use takes place, the user succeeds in maintaining control over his/her cocaine use.

Because so many rules were mentioned, we reduced them to 14 categories of rules.[4] The number of specific rules included (tables 14.2.a and 14.2.b) are between brackets. The total numbers and percentages of each category of rules are also indicated. We found that our respondents recognized rules relating to:

1. The setting, situations and priorities   (n=90; **81.0%**)
   (No. 2,3,5,10,22, 23, 31, 32, 35, 37)
2. Company of use, persons   (n=36; **32.4%**)
   (No. 6,11, 28, 40,49)
3. Time period   (n=27; **24.3%**)
   (No. 1, 12, 46)
4. General rules   (n=24; **21.6%**)
   (No. 13, 14, 24, 34, 41, 44, 45, 47)
5. Relations with non-users   (n=22; **19.8%**)
   (No. 27, 29, 30)
6. Frequency of use   (n=15; **13.5%**)
   (No. 9)
7. Set, feelings   (n=12; **10.8%**)
   (No. 8, 21, 36, 39, 42)
8. Combinations with other drugs   (n=12; **10.8%**)
   (No. 7, 33, 38)
9. Route of ingestion   (n=12; **10.8%**)
   (No. 25, 43)
10. Amount used, dose   (n=11; **9.9%**)
    (No. 4)
11. Avoiding police attention   (n=10; **9.0%**)
    (No. 26)
12. Buying cocaine   (n=8; **7.2%**)
    (No. 17, 18, 48)
13. Financial consequences   (n=8; **7.2%**)
    (No. 20)
14. Quality of cocaine   (n=3; **2.7%**)
    (No. 19)

In table 14.2.c, rules given for cocaine use ('yes' vs. 'no') are crosstabulated with level of use at the time of interview. We did not find a statistically significant relationship in the Antwerp sample.[5]

Table 14.2.c Rules given for cocaine use against level of use at time of interview for combined 1987 and 1991 Amsterdam sample (N=267) versus 1997 Antwerp sample (N=111)

	Amsterdam I and II (N=267)					
	Do you have rules for cocaine use?					
	Yes		No		Total	
Level of use	N	%	N	%	N	%
None	48	26	24	28	72	27
Low	119	65	49	58	168	63
Medium	13	7	7	8	20	7
High	2	1	5	6	7	3
Total	182	100	85	100	267	100

	Antwerp (N=111)					
	Do you have rules for cocaine use?					
	Yes		No		Total	
Level of use	N	%	N	%	N	%
None	16	16.0	5	45.5	21	18.9
Low	68	68.0	4	36.4	72	64.9
Medium	11	11.0	1	9.1	12	10.8
High	5	5.0	1	9.1	6	5.4
Total	100	100.0	11	100.1	111	100.0

14.3. ADVICE TO NOVICE USERS

We asked our respondents what advice they would give to novice users. Our data on this item are not comparable to the Amsterdam data. The Amsterdam respondents were asked what advice they would give about mode of ingestion, dose, circumstances fit to use cocaine, combination of cocaine with other drugs, buying cocaine, disadvantages of cocaine, and methods of countering these (Cohen, 1989: 115-117). We just asked them a general, open-ended question. Nevertheless, we can see from table 14.3.a that our respondents spontaneously reported advice on all the above mentioned categories.

We argued above that respondents often fail to recognize the implicit guidelines or rules they apply to the amount, the route of ingestion, sets and settings of use, financial limits, etc. (Zinberg, 1984: 167-168). Responses to questions about advice to novice users may provide indirect access to regulatory rules (see also Cohen & Sas, 1995: 74; Zinberg, 1984: 141). If such 'advice' is guided by the structuring principles of use, the respondents' advice to novice users illustrates the informal control mechanisms that help drug users to limit their use, to prevent ill effects and enhance positive effects, and to avoid legal, medical and psychological problems.

In short, our respondents would advise novice users not to use at all in the first place, but if they choose to continue, they should be careful, not use too often (certainly not daily), they should be aware of the advantages and disadvantages, make sure they have good quality cocaine, watch their expenses, do not inject, and use only when feeling well.

Table 14.3.a   Advice for novice users of cocaine, in the 1997 Antwerp sample [*]

Antwerp (1997)					
Advice	N	%	(continued)	N	%
1. Do not use at all	26	23.4	29. Use as pleasure	3	2.7
2. Be careful	21	18.9	30. Make sure you are not caught	3	2.7
3. Not (too) often	20	18.0	31. Do not snort	2	1.8
4. I'd explain adv. and disadv.	20	18.0	32. No supply around	2	1.8
5. Watch expenses	13	11.7	33. Do not buy in public places	2	1.8
6. Do not use daily	10	9.0	34. Do not buy at all	2	1.8
7. Make sure cocaine is good quality	10	9.0	35. If problems, take drug treatment	2	1.8
8. Do not shoot	9	8.1	36. If problems, come to me	2	1.8
9. Feeling well	9	8.1	37. If getting dangerous, stop	2	1.8
10. In company/not alone	8	7.2	38. Do not use cocaine from strangers	2	1.8
11. Do not base	7	6.3	39. Keep distance from coke-scene	2	1.8
12. Buy from reliable persons	6	5.4	40. Freebase it	1	0.9
13. Take breaks	6	5.4	41. Hygienic	1	0.9
14. Do not abuse	6	5.4	42. Do not combine with other drug	1	0.9
15. Use with reliable people	5	4.5	43. Respect sleep	1	0.9
16. Realize when exaggerating	5	4.5	44. Not if unintelligent	1	0.9
17. Little	4	3.6	45. Clean properly	1	0.9
18. Use only when you want	4	3.6	46. Do not start too young	1	0.9
19. Only special occasions	4	3.6	47. Do not fixate on use	1	0.9
20. Only weekends	4	3.6	48. Smoke it	1	0.9
21. Be aware of your use	4	3.6	49. Do not bother other people	1	0.9
22. Snort it	3	2.7	50. Read about it	1	0.9
23. Get advice first	3	2.7	51. Do not like it too much	1	0.9
24. Going out	3	2.7	52. Not in the morning	1	0.9
25. Reflect about use regularly	3	2.7	53. Say no every now and then	1	0.9
26. Not if lacking self-confidence	3	2.7	*No answer*	4	3.6
27. Not combining with work	3	2.7			
28. Stay yourself	3	2.7			

[*] More than one answer was possible

In the previous paragraph we reduced the huge amount of governing rules reported by our respondents to 14 categories.[6] We have copied this procedure for the 53 different rules of advice listed in table 14.3.a. We now have a completely different hierarchy of topics compared to the 14 categories in the previous paragraph (see below). The Antwerp respondents report rules of advice on the following topics: the frequency of use; the appropriate route of ingestion; the setting, situations and priorities; the company of use; financial consequences; the set; buying cocaine; the dosage; the quality of cocaine; time period; avoiding police attention; relations with non-users; combinations with other drugs; and some general rules of use.

1. general rules   (n=107; 96.4%)
   (no. 1, 2, 4, 14, 16, 21, 23, 25, 28, 29,
   35, 36, 37, 43, 44, 46, 47 50, 51, 53)

2. frequency of use   (n=30; 27.0%)
   (no. 3, 6)

3. route of ingestion   (n=25; 22.5%)
   (no. 8, 11, 22, 31, 40, 41, 45, 48)

4. the setting, situations and priorities   (n=16; 14.4%)
   (no. 18, 19, 24, 27, 39)

5. company of use, persons   (n=15; 13.5%)
   (no. 10, 15, 38)

6. financial consequences   (n=13; 11.7%)
   (no. 5)

7. set, feelings   (n=12; 10.8%)
   (no. 9, 26)

8. buying cocaine   (n=12; 10.8%)
   (no. 12, 32, 33, 34)

9. amount used, dose   (n=10; 9.0%)
   (no. 13, 17)

10. quality of cocaine   (n=10; 9.0%)
    (no. 7)

11. time period   (n=5; 4.5%)
    (no. 20, 52)

12. avoiding police attention   (n=3; 2.7%)
    (no. 30)

13. relations with non-users   (n=1; 0.9%)
    (no. 49)

14. combinations with other drugs   (n=1; 0.9%)
    (no. 42)

14.4. EMOTIONAL STATES IN WHICH COCAINE USE OCCURS

To know more about the *set* and *setting* factors relating to our Antwerp sample of cocaine users we gave respondents the chance to first describe *feelings or emotional states* (§14.4) and then *situations* (§14.5) in which they had used cocaine during the previous three months. When respondents had not used cocaine in that period, they could answer the question for the period in which they previously used. We additionally asked frequency of occurrence of both emotional states and situations, and we also tried to find out if the occurrence of the situation or emotional state mentioned created an appetite for cocaine.[7]

In the Amsterdam study, answers were reduced to the following categories (between square brackets are the abbreviations used in table 14.4.a): [*excitement*], feelings of joy, exuberance, festive mood [*joy*], being in love, or sexually excited [*in love*], energetic, ambitious [*energetic*], insecure, shy [*shy*], tired, flat [*tired*], melancholic, depressed [*depressive*], frustrated, restless [*frustrated*], [*bored*], wanting to be detached, to forget, to explode [*explode*]. We added two new categories: [*aggressive/anger*], [*anxious*].

Table 14.4.a shows that the two emotional states that generate the appetite for cocaine use most often mentioned in our Antwerp sample were joy (68.7%) and depression (27.7%). The high ranking of joy by respondents is equivalent with the findings in both the Amsterdam samples, but the high ranking of depression is not: Cohen only found a high frequency of depression in his 1991 sample (Cohen & Sas, 1995: 72). But then again, in our sample, joy is more 'often' reported, while depression is more 'sometimes' or 'rarely' reported as an 'appetizer' for cocaine. Furthermore, it is strange that 'being tired' is only mentioned by 6 Antwerp respondents (7.2%), while it was more frequently reported by the Amsterdam respondents of 1987 (22.1%) and 1991 (25%). A very small minority of our respondents also mentioned feelings of aggression and anxiety as emotional states that generate an appetite for cocaine.[8]

Table 14.4.a   Emotional states in which appetite for cocaine use can be generated often, sometimes or rarely, in three samples, in % of total number of respondents who reported emotional states [*] [♦]

Amsterdam I - 1987 (N=104)							
			Frequency of occurrence				
	Total		Often		Sometimes		Rarely	
Emotion	N	%*	N	%*	N	%*	N	%*
Joy	48	46.1	24	23.1	17	16.3	5	4.8
Tired	23	22.1	7	6.7	11	10.6	5	4.8
In love	20	19.2	7	6.7	10	9.6	2	1.9
Explode	14	13.5	5	4.8	7	6.7	1	0.9
Depressive	12	11.5	3	2.9	3	2.9	5	4.8
Shy	8	7.7	5	4.8	3	2.9	-	-
Excitement	8	7.7	3	2.9	4	3.8	1	0.9
Energetic	10	9.6	3	2.9	3	2.9	2	1.9
Bored	5	4.8	1	0.9	3	2.9	1	0.9
Frustrated	4	3.8	-	-	3	2.9	1	0.9
Other	42	40.4	6	5.8	18	17.3	7	6.7

[*] More than one answer was possible

Amsterdam II - 1991 (N=87)								
			Frequency of occurrence					
	Total		Often		Sometimes		Rarely	
Emotion	N	%*	N	%*	N	%*	N	%*
Joy	31	36	8	9	14	16	9	10
Tired	22	25	7	8	11	13	4	5
In love	12	14	5	6	5	6	2	2
Explode	10	11	3	3	4	5	2	2
Depressive	22	25	8	9	7	8	7	8
Shy	9	10	4	5	2	2	3	3
Excitement	7	8	4	5	1	1	2	2
Energetic	2	2	-	-	-	-	2	2
Bored	3	3	1	1	-	-	2	2
Frustrated	4	5	-	-	4	5	-	-
Feeling good	18	21	7	8	9	10	2	2
Other	13	15	6	7	5	6	2	2

[*] More than one answer was possible

Antwerp - 1997 (N=83)								
			Frequency of occurrence					
	Total		Often		Sometimes		Rarely	
Emotion	N	%*	N	%*	N	%*	N	%*
Joy	57	68.7	36	43.4	16	19.3	5	6.0
Tired	6	7.2	4	4.8	1	1.2	1	1.2
In love	6	7.2	3	3.6	2	2.4	1	1.2
Explode	3	3.6	1	1.2	1	1.2	1	1.2
Depressive	23	27.7	6	7.2	9	10.8	8	9.6
Shy	3	3.6	2	2.4	1	1.2	-	-
Excitement	2	2.4	-	-	1	1.2	1	1.2
Energetic	3	3.6	1	1.2	2	2.4	-	-
Bored	7	8.4	2	2.4	3	3.6	2	2.4
Frustrated	7	8.4	3	3.6	1	1.2	3	3.6
Aggressive/anger	4	4.8	2	2.4	2	2.4	-	-
Anxious	2	2.4	-	-	1	1.2	1	1.2
Other	2	2.4	1	1.2	1	1.2	-	-

[*] More than one answer was possible

Feelings or emotional states that are *unsuitable* for cocaine use are shown in table 14.4.b. In the residual category of 'other', we included the following answers: no desire (4), sober (1).

Feeling depressive is mentioned by 72.7% of our respondents who reported emotional states. That is even more than in the Amsterdam samples. Of the 56 respondents stating that 'depression' is an emotional state *unsuitable* for cocaine use, 9 reported at the same time that depression could generate an appetite for cocaine. So, while as a set factor, depression can generate an appetite for cocaine, it is seen as incompatible with cocaine use by a majority of our respondents.

This finding is consistent with the conclusion that many experienced cocaine users have a simple, implicit theory about how to use cocaine (and/or other drugs) without falling into the trap of abuse: never when you feel bad, only when you feel good:

When things look bad, you must stay off drugs, so when you feel down, you have to stay off drugs, because you would only sink deeper, so it's only when you feel good that you take something, if not, you don't touch it. [I/1/10]

You lose control from the moment you need coke every night or every day. First of all: because you don't feel good or something, I mean, sometimes you have those periods that people use because they don't feel good, or because they're in a tough period. And I think you have to be very careful then, because you might start using very fast. [I/1/16]

Table 14.4.b   Emotional states in which cocaine is not used, in % of total number of respondents who reported emotional states, in three samples [*] [♠]

Emotion	Amsterdam I (1987) N=98		Amsterdam II (1991) N=74		Antwerp (1997) N=77	
	N	%*	N	%*	N	%*
Depressive	47	48.0	43	58	56	72.7
Not well	13	13.3	11	15	11	14.3
Frustrated	9	9.2	9	12	6	7.8
Energetic	7	7.1	13	18	1	1.3
Erotic	8	8.2	1	1	-	-
In love	3	3.1	1	1	1	1.3
Anger	3	3.1	-	-	7	9.1
Anxiety	2	2.0	-	-	2	2.6
Bored	1	1.0	-	-	-	-
Shy	-	-	6	8	-	-
Tired	-	-	-	-	4	5.2
Very happy	-	-	-	-	6	7.8
Stressed/nervous	-	-	-	-	5	6.5
Other	21	21.4	13	18	5	6.5

[*] More than one answer was possible

From tables 14.4.a and 14.4.b we computed the total of negative emotional states (tired, explode, shy, depressive, bored, frustrated, aggressive, anxious) and the total of positive emotional states (joy, in love, excitement, energetic, feeling good). We found that our Antwerp respondents reported a total of positive emotional states of 68 (55.3%) and a total of negative emotional states of 55 (44.7%). If asked which set factors were unsuitable for cocaine use, our users reported a total of positive emotional states of 18 (19.4%) and a total of negative emotional states of 75 (80.6%). This means that illicit substances are not solely taken for escapist motives (to avoid negative feelings), as is generally believed. Many respondents prefer not to take cocaine when feeling bad. Contrary to the official discourse of the media, politicians and many scnientists, it seems that most of our respondents did not use cocaine and other drugs to help them manage preexisting psychological problems.9

14.5. SITUATIONS FOR COCAINE USE

The Amsterdam data revealed the following categories of situations for cocaine use (abbreviations used in the tables are in square brackets): going out to dance or meet people (cafe, bar, disco) [*going out*], going to a private party [*party*], meeting friends at home [*friends*], around dinner (before, during or just after) [*dinner*], alone at home [*home*], going to the theatre, a concert [*theatre*], in erotic or sexual situations [*sex*], wanting to continue (working, playing, partying, love making) [*continuation*], after an accomplishment, self-gratification [*self-gratification*]. Our data revealed two other categories: outdoor, open air, in nature [*outdoor*], [*public places*]. In our residual category 'other' we have included 5 answers: school (2), with dealer (2) and holidays (1).

The figures of the Antwerp sample are quite complementary to those of Amsterdam: in all three samples, the most suitable situations for cocaine use are those in which people enjoy each other's company: going out, partying and gatherings (reunions, meetings) with friends (see table 14.5.a). Similarly, smaller categories such as 'dinner', 'sex', 'theatre' and even 'outdoor' refer to social situations in which respondents do not use cocaine on their own... 'Continuation' and 'alone at home', two situations in which people act more individually, are less frequent, but still clearly present (as Cohen also found in his 1987 sample). Sexual situations are mentioned by a minority of all three samples, which runs counter to cocaine's reputation as an aphrodisiac.

Table 14.5.a   Situations in which cocaine use occurs often, sometimes or rarely; and causal relationship between situation and appetite for cocaine, in % of total number of respondents who reported situations, in three samples [*] [♦]

	Amsterdam I (1987) N=143										
			Frequency of occurrence								
	Total *		Often		Sometimes		Rarely		Causes appetite	
Situation	N	%*	N	%*	N	%*	N	%*	N	%*
Going out	76	53.1	43	30.1	22	15.4	11	7.7	53	37.1
Party	74	51.7	29	20.3	30	21.0	15	10.5	52	36.4
Friends	48	33.6	25	17.5	20	14.0	5	3.5	30	21.0
Continue	26	18.2	7	4.9	15	10.5	4	2.8	15	10.5
Alone at home	22	15.4	14	9.8	6	4.2	2	1.4	10	7.0
Dinner	9	6.3	4	2.8	3	2.1	2	1.4	2	1.4
Sex	9	6.3	2	1.4	5	3.5	2	1.4	4	2.8
Theatre	7	4.9	2	1.4	4	2.8	1	0.7	3	2.1
Self-gratification	5	3.5	-	-	3		2	1.4	5	3.5
Other	40	28.0	13	9.1	17	11.9	7	4.9	21	14.7

	Amsterdam II (1991) N=107										
			Frequency of occurrence								
	Total *		Often		Sometimes		Rarely		Causes appetite	
Situation	N	%*	N	%*	N	%*	N	%*	N	%*
Going out	78	73	35	33	26	24	17	16	53	50
Party	55	51	23	21	19	18	12	11	35	33
Friends	48	45	17	16	16	15	13	12	17	16
Continue	10	9	3	3	4	4	3	3	7	7
Alone at home	8	7	3	3	2	2	2	2	2	2
Dinner	-	-	-	-	-	-	-	-	-	-
Sex	4	4	-	-	1	1	3	3	1	1
Theatre	2	2	1	1	-	-	1	1	1	1
Self-gratification	9	8	4	4	2	2	3	3	3	3
Other	23	21	12	11	3	3	7	7	12	11

	Antwerp (1997) N=111										
			frequency of occurrence								
	Total *		Often		Sometimes		Rarely		Causes appetite	
Situation	N	%*	N	%*	N	%*	N	%*	N	%*
Going out	70	63.0	33	29.7	20	18.0	17	15.3	38	34.2
Party	33	29.7	9	8.1	17	15.3	7	6.3	22	19.8
Friends	81	72.9	40	36.0	21	18.9	20	18.0	37	33.3
Continue	21	18.9	8	7.2	6	5.4	7	6.3	8	7.2
Alone at home	17	15.3	6	5.4	4	3.6	7	6.3	5	4.5
Dinner	3	2.7	3	2.7	-	-	-	-	3	2.7
Sex	1	0.9	1	0.9	-	-	-	-	1	0.9
Theatre	9	8.1	5	4.5	1	0.9	3	2.7	7	6.3
Self-gratification	2	1.8	-	-	1	0.9	1	0.9	2	1.8
Outdoor	4	3.6	-	-	2	1.8	2	1.8	1	0.9
Public places	5	4.5	4	3.6	-	-	1	0.9	1	0.9
Other	5	4.5	3	2.7	-	-	2	1.8	4	3.6

[*] More than one answer was possible

In both his Amsterdam samples, Cohen (Cohen, 1989: 76; Cohen & Sas, 1995: 70) found that going out, partying and friends rank first, second and third. In the Antwerp sample, this ranking is turned upside down: gatherings with friends ranks first (72.9%), going out second (63.0%) and partying third, mentioned by less than one third of all respondents who reported situations (29.7%). Our ethnographic data suggest that this difference is not as important as it may seem. Throughout our fieldwork we discovered that the words 'party' and 'partying' (in Dutch: 'feestje' and 'feesten') can have a very particular meaning. Not only do almost all of our respondents use these words to indicate a private party, i.e. a gathering of many people in a particular place, to celebrate a special occasion, to drink and to dance, etc. but the term 'partying' is quite often used to indicate the mere consumption of cocaine, independent of the place and the company. Throwing a party in this sense could mean using cocaine alone at home, *or* with some friends, *or* at a private party.

It is noteworthy that for all situations mentioned, the proportion of respondents who actually experienced an appetite for cocaine in these situations is always -and in some cases even considerably- smaller. For example, 72.9% of our respondents mentioned gatherings with 'friends', but only 33.3% stated that this situation caused an appetite for cocaine. 15.3% of our respondents mentioned 'alone at home', but only half of them (7.2%) declared that this solitary situation triggered an appetite for cocaine. Setting factors alone rarely determine whether illicit drugs are used or not (and how). Illicit drugs use generally occurs in the company of other people (see also next paragraph) and set factors also play an important role.

In the previous paragraph, we mentioned two respondents for whom the mere fact of talking about cocaine use and cocaine effects can generate an appetite. Several respondents mentioned this on other occasions during the interviews (see Chapter 13).[10]

Table 14.5.b shows situations in which cocaine use is *not* suitable according to our respondents. Small coding differences are possible. In the residual category 'other' in table 14..b. we have included answers like: theatre/concert (2), public places (2), if I'm being pushed (2), if I have to hide my use (2), if I want to be quiet (2), on a toilet (1), after several days of use (1).

Table 14.5.b   Situations in which cocaine is not used, in % of total number of respondents, in three samples [*] [♠]

Situation	Amsterdam I 1987 N=160		Amsterdam II 1991 N=108		Antwerp 1997 N=111	
	N	%*	N	%*	N	%*
Work/study	66	41.3	47	44	52	46.8
Before achievement	57	35.6	25	23	19	17.1
Daily life	37	23.1	13	12	10	9.0
With non users	32	20.0	40	37	16	14.4
Just before dinner/bedtime	9	5.6	5	5	1	0.9
At home	6	3.8	7	6	8	7.2
Car driving	5	3.1	6	6	3	2.7
Certain hours of day/night	4	2.5	2	2	5	4.5
Sex	3	1.9	4	4	2	1.8
Important business next day	-	-	8	7	-	-
When parents present	-	-	-	-	26	23.4
When children around	-	-	-	-	12	10.8
During pregnancy	-	-	-	-	3	2.7
After other drug	-	-	-	-	5	4.5
On holiday	-	-	-	-	4	3.6
Serious conversation	-	-	-	-	3	2.7
Tense/nervous situation	-	-	-	-	4	3.6
Funeral	-	-	-	-	6	5.4
Going out	-	-	-	-	4	3.6
More than 3 or 4 people present	-	-	-	-	6	5.4
Other	-	-	20	19	12	10.8
No answer	*1*	*0.6*	-	-	*16*	*14.4*

[*] Percentages of total number of respondents (more than one answer was possible).

Our data not only indicate that setting is an important aspect for cocaine users, but they also confirm the existence of implicit rules of use. Irrespective of whether respondents always respect these rules, these answers show that at least a proportion of our respondents act according to governing principles such as 'not when I have to work', 'not when I have to see my parents', 'never when I'm pregnant', etc. The category 'after other drug' suggests informal ruling related to the combination of cocaine with other drugs (see paragraph 14.2, and also chapter 8).[11]

Like in both the Amsterdam samples, we found that cocaine use is negatively associated with work or study (46.8%), achievement (17.1%) and the presence of non-users (14.4%). Our data also revealed two specific categories of non-users with whom cocaine use is not appropriate (see Chapter 16): *parents* (23.4%), probably because of fear of stigmatization or apprehension, and *children* (10.8%), probably because of a sense of responsibility towards youngsters.[12]

Some situations mentioned by our respondents, such as 'tense, nervous situations' and 'funeral' may be more related to emotional states (see paragraph 14.4.) rather than to settings, but detailed questioning of these respondents revealed that their answers related to the emotional states of others, rather than to their own personal feelings.

14.6. PERSONS WITH WHOM COCAINE IS NOT USED

In Chapter 4 we found that early experimentation with cocaine generally occurs in the company of a friend or friends.[13] In paragraph 14.2 we showed that some respondents reported informal rules relating to the company of use (see table 14.2.a), while table 14.5.a showed that 17 of our respondents mentioned 'alone at home' as a situation in which cocaine use occurs often, sometimes or rarely. Of our respondents 64.0% appeared to use cocaine occasionally when alone, versus 36.0% who never did (versus 59.4% and 39.4% in the 1987 Amsterdam sample).

Table 14.6.a shows frequencies of categories of persons with whom respondents would definitely *not* use cocaine. These figures demonstrate that our respondents are not prone to using cocaine with any one. They do have informal rules about the company of use. These rules can serve different goals (sometimes at the same time).

Some users do not want to use with non-using significant others because these persons could be angry or disappointed (e.g. parents or non-using friends). Other reasons for not using when certain people are present (and thus for concealing the drug use) are because these persons could inform the police, or the employer (for the user's protection). Most users will never use when their own children or those of others are around, because these persons are not mature enough to be confronted with drugs (for protection of others).

Other categories of persons, such as compulsive users or junkies, are avoided in order to maximize the positive effects of cocaine use and to minimize the risk of adverse effects. Association with junkies might not only lead to increased use and potential addiction but also to the risk of arrest (see also Zinberg, 1984: 130-131 and 154-155). Most respondents are scared of becoming dependent on cocaine, like the compulsive users they have seen ('counterexamples', see also next chapter). The user's constant fear of associating with junkies implies a sanction against uncontrolled use.

Table 14.6.a   Category of persons with whom respondents would definitely not use cocaine, in % of total number of respondents who report persons, in three samples [*] [♦]

No cocaine with	Amsterdam I (1987) N=113		Amsterdam II (1991) N=94		Antwerp (1997) N=98	
	N	%*	N	%*	N	%*
Partner	32	28.3	6	6	6	6.1
Family member	26	23.0	53	56	32	32.6
Strangers	17	15.0	25	27	2	2.0
Non-users	17	15.0	39	41	30	30.6
Colleagues	8	7.1	10	11	7	7.1
Heavy users	7	6.2	5	5	16	16.3
Junkies	5	4.4	2	2	9	9.2
Children	1	0.9	-	-	5	5.1
Users I do not trust/like	-	-	-	-	32	32.6
Users who ruin my pleasure	-	-	7	7	21	21.4
Other	32	28.3	13	14	13	13.3

[*] More than one answer was possible

14.7. FINANCIAL LIMITS ON COCAINE PURCHASES

When our respondents were asked overtly for informal rules, 8 persons mentioned purchasing limits (see table 14.2.a). When asked explicitly about this, 61.3% stated they had limits to the amount of cocaine they bought per month. This is more than Cohen's findings in both his Amsterdam samples (Cohen, 1989: 79; Cohen & Sas, 1995: 74).

Table 14.7.a   Financial limits on cocaine purchases and level of use during top period, in three samples

Amsterdam I (1987)							
	Total		Level of use of top period				
			Low		Medium		High
Financial limit	N	%	N	%	N	%	N	%
Yes	80	50.3	43	55.8	23	46.9	14	42.4
No	57	35.8	22	28.6	18	36.7	17	51.5
No answer	*22*	*13.8*	*12*	*15.6*	*8*	*16.3*	*2*	*6.1*
Total	159	100.0	77	100.0	49	100.0	33	100.0

Amsterdam II (1991)							
	Total		Level of use of top period				
			Low		Medium		High
Financial limit	N	%	N	%	N	%	N	%
Yes	58	54	34	60	20	61	4	24
No	48	44	22	39	13	39	12	71
No answer	*2*	*2*	*1*	*2*	*-*	*-*	*1*	*6*
Total	108	100	57	100	33	100	17	100

Antwerp (1997)							
	Total		Level of use of top period				
			Low		Medium		High
Financial limit	N	%	N	%	N	%	N	%
Yes	68	61.3	19	79.2	23	71.9	26	47.3
No	43	38.7	5	20.8	9	28.1	29	52.7
No answer	*-*	*-*	*-*	*-*	*-*	*-*	*-*	*-*
Total	111	100.0	24	100.0	32	100.0	55	100.0

In the 1987 Amsterdam sample no significant relationship between having or not having a financial limit (per month) and level of use in the top period was found. With the

1991 sample Cohen and Sas (1995: 74) were able to show that those who used at a high level during their period of heaviest use report significantly less often than medium or low top level users that they apply some financial limits ($\chi 2$=6.98; DF=2; p<0.05). In our sample, we found a similar statistical significant relationship ($\chi 2$= 9.296; DF=2; p=0.01) (see table 14.7.a).

Within the group of Antwerp respondents who report a financial limit on cocaine purchase per month, this limit correlates significantly with level of use during the three months prior to the interview (Pearson's R= 0.291; p=0.027),[14] but not with level of use during period of heaviest use.[15] See table 14.7.b. [16]

Table 14.7.b   Level of financial limit on purchase of cocaine (per month) and level of use during top period, in the 1997 Antwerp sample

	Antwerp (1997)							
			Level of use top period					
	Total		Low		Medium		High	
Limit	N	%	N	%	N	%	N	%
< 2,000 BEF	13	22.4	6	37.5	3	15.0	4	18.2
2,000 - 3,999 BEF	20	34.5	4	25.0	7	35.0	9	40.9
4,000 - 5,999 BEF	12	20.7	3	18.7	5	25.0	4	18.2
6,000 - 7,999 BEF	5	8.6	2	12.5	2	10.0	1	4.5
8,000 - 9,999 BEF	1	1.7	-	-	1	5.0	-	-
10,000 - 11,999 BEF	3	5.2	1	6.2	2	10.0	-	-
12,000 - 13,999 BEF	1	1.7	-	-	-	-	1	4.5
14,000 - 19,999 BEF	3	5.2	-	-	-	-	3	13.6
Total	58	100.0	16	99.9	20	100.0	22	99.9

Within the group of the Antwerp respondents who report a financial limit on cocaine purchase per month (N=58), the average limit is 4,034.5 BEF. Nine respondents of this subsample, however, report a financial limit on cocaine purchase of zero ('I do not spend any money on cocaine'): they are non-users during the three months prior to the interview. Excluding these non-users from the subsample, the average limit on cocaine purchase per month is 4,775.5 BEF. If the average price of cocaine is 2,300 BEF,[17] the average limit on cocaine purchase per month is approximately 2 grams per month.[18]

14.8. THE INFLUENCE OF SET AND SETTING FACTORS ON (DIS-)RESPECT FOR RULES

The existence of informal control mechanisms does not necessarily imply that they are always effective.[19] People may have conscious or unconscious rules about when and where to use cocaine, they might 'plan' to use only with particular people and only when they are in the 'right mood', but things may turn out differently. At least as important as the recognition of informal rules is the way in which the illicit drug user handles conflicts between these rules and interfering set and setting factors. In other words, does the cocaine user who tells us he/she has certain rules respect these informal control mechanisms unconditionally?

The Antwerp respondents were asked in which circumstances they find it hard to respect their rules or principles regarding cocaine use, whether they violate them when confronted with such circumstances. And finally, participants were asked in which circumstances they find it easier to respect their own principles.

14.8.1. Interfering set and setting factors

The factors that can interfere with informal rules of use most mentioned are: 'when it is offered for free (by friends)' (11 times), 'when I am with intimate friends' (10 times), 'when I am in an extremely pleasant environment' (9 times), 'when others continue to use' (7 times), 'when I have been using all night long' (7 times), and 'when it is around or when it is right under my nose)' (6 times). All interfering factors reported by the Antwerp respondents are listed below. It is (more) difficult to respect my own principles...

When cocaine is scarce and rare to obtain
When I am in an extremely pleasant environment
When I am selling it
When it is around (when it is right under my nose)
In unforeseen situations
In very erotic or sexual situations
When I didn't use it for a long time
When I am with intimate friends
When I have a lot of money
When I am too tired
When we talk about it
When I feel bad
After an argument or a fight
When I am in a situation where nobody knows me
When my partner is not around
When I have been using it all night long
When I feel insecure or not self-confident
When I have used too many lines
When I feel bored

When I have a strong desire for cocaine (craving)
On very special occasions
When it is offered for free (by friends)
When I have been drinking alcohol
When I am coming down from heroin
When I am with users who have no rules of use
When it is easy to obtain
When I sell it, and I have to taste it
When it is in the house
When I am alone
When I am emotionally unstable
When others continue to use
When I am on a holiday
When I am pushed by others
When I have to work after going out
When the quality of cocaine is bad
When I do not have to leave the house
When I am in a rebellious mood

...

Some clear conclusions can be drawn from these interfering factors. First of all, respondents may find it harder to respect their informal rules or principles of use in the case of *increased availability*, i.e. when cocaine is more easily accessible or offered freely.

> *Then I sin. When it's in the house, I have a weak character. It's better not to have it at home. I quit dealing, because of that...* [H/0/11]

> *You're more likely to violate your rules when there are more opportunities to use it. And, when you have it available, you're more likely to violate some rules you had complied with before.* [P/0/02]

Second, the effectiveness of informal control mechanisms is often linked with the *user's inner life*. The participants report that respect for informal rules is usually hampered by negative emotional states such as tiredness, loneliness, depression, boredom, insecurity, emotional instability, etc.

> *Sometimes I have those moments that I'm thinking: 'Oh, we'll see on Monday'. Happy moments. That you feel so good, that it is so much fun, that you think: 'Pfff, get lost everybody'. [...] Sometimes when I am quite clear-minded, I think: 'Oh, you don't really need it now, S. [i.e. her own name, TD]. It will remain pleasant, even without taking more. And you will feel better tomorrow as well.'* [V/1/01]

I think it has to do with stable and unstable situations. When you do not feel so good, you're more inclined to satisfy your direct needs. In stable periods I don't have any problem with that at all. [H/0/27]

Third, the application of informal rules is also influenced by *the social character of occasions of use*. Respondents find it hard to respect their principles of use when intimate friends are involved, when they are in an extremely pleasant environment (with friends), when it is offered by friends, when friends talk about it... The presence of particular persons may stimulate respondents to use more or more frequently than they initially intended to, e.g. when the others continue to use, when the user feels pushed, when the respondent is with users who have no rules of use, etc. Conversely, the absence of certain significant others is sometimes perceived as a lack of social control. For example, some respondents report disrespecting their own rules of use when their partner is not around, when they are in a situation where nobody knows them, when they are alone, etc.

That rule of 'not during the day' can become difficult when I have been going out all night, and when other people continue during the next day, then it's hard to say:'No, I don't follow.' And 'not too much', that can be hard too, in the same kind of situations. When it is very nice, and when it is very tempting to stay and to hold that nice feeling. [I/1/12]

Fourth, some interfering factors may be related with *the pharmacological actions of cocaine itself or of other drugs*. Three respondents report violating their own rules of use because they felt a strong desire for cocaine (craving). Seven interviewees report having trouble respecting their principles when they are already high on cocaine or when they have been using all night long. A small number report becoming weak when they have consumed alcohol or when the effects of other drugs (such a heroin) start to wear off.

There are times I do it, but mostly I can... I can be hard for myself in that respect. It depends on how much alcohol I have been drinking. [C/0/04]

14.8.2. Supporting set and setting factors

The factors that support respect for informal control mechanisms most mentioned are: 'when I have to work' (6 times), 'when I feel emotionally stable' (5 times) and 'when it is not offered' (3 times). The supporting factors mentioned by the Antwerp respondents are:

When I am not going out
When I am in a methadone program
When I am not too tired
When I have to work
When I have a steady partner / children
As I become older and have more responsibilities
When everything works out fine
When the one who offers it looks miserable or sad
During the day
When it is not offered
When my partner is not present

When there are people around who know me
When I feel very good
When I have smoked some cannabis
When I have an important appointment
When I have planned my cocaine use in advance
When I feel emotionally stable
When I am at home
When I have used recently
When the people who offer it are not friends
When I am alone
After some negative experiences with cocaine

When my life is well-regulated
When the weather is nice
After a negative experience with violating my rules
When I really do not feel like it (no desire)
When I do not drink alcohol
When I see my partner has taken too much cocaine
When I have violated my principle once
When I am with people who have no (drug-related) problems

When I am with non-users
When I feel secure and self-confident
When I have to perform music
When my partner does not use
When I have lots of things to do
When my partner is with me

Again, some clear categories of set and setting factors can be distinguished. The most important cluster of factors is the social setting. Especially when the user is faced with *specific responsibilities* – such as a job or a performance, a family, important appointments, at home, during the day, when life is well-regulated, etc. - he/she finds it easier to respect his/her own principles of use.

> *Some moments you are stronger in life about everything, and you say: 'Now I won't do it' [...] and sometimes I could do that. Because I had a well-organized life, I had a job, I had responsibilities on that job, so I couldn't just drop it, and that stopped me. Like: I can't afford losing that job. I'm always a bit like: I must do this and do that...* [H/1/15]

> *In periods that you're working, you have more healthy ethics about drugs anyway. As to your relationships, it has an enormous impact on it, because, [...] When you're alone, you have other limits compared to when you're together. And when you live with a sober person, it is different compared to when you both use.* [H/0/10]

> *When you have a family, you know, when you have something, I'd say. When I am completely on my own, I don't have a wife, no daughter, like it is now, no parents I often see, yes, then you react differently, then you live at night, and not during the day, right? So, when you have some job or something, then you have to stick to some rules, right?* [H/0/11]

Furthermore, the *company in which the user finds himself/herself* plays an important part in the decision to respect informal rules. For example, respect for one's own rules of behavior is supported when the user is among people who know him/her, when he/she is with other users who have no (drug-related) problems, when the user is with non-users, etc. Others report it is easier to refuse freely offered cocaine when the person offering it looks miserable or depressed, when the person offering it is not a trusted friend, when it looks like the person who offers it has already used too much, etc...

> *It depends on who's present, what kind of people. When they are people I'm very close with, maybe yes, when they are people I'm not so close with, I don't. Then I can stick to those rules more easily.* [I/1/04]

Second, the effectiveness of informal control mechanisms is linked with *the user's inner life*. The participants report that respect for informal rules is usually supported by positive emotional states such as feeling good, feeling not too tired, feeling emotionally stable, self-confident, when everything works out fine, etc.

> *Yes, when you really feel good. When I have just gone out with friends, and you made a lot of fun, and you know you go out again later on, and you come home, and there's some coke, then I could say: 'No, never mind, it is going to spoil my fun. I feel better now, so never mind.'* [H/0/05]

Third, some accounts indicate that 'craving' for cocaine may not be a constant inter-fering factor. Two respondents report having no difficulty to respect their own rules of use because they felt no desire for cocaine at all. Another interviewee reports having no trouble respecting her principles when she had used recently.

> *Usually, it's in a situation where it's been a long time, that I jump at it more easily, and I consequently not respect my appointments. When it's only, when I used a lot only one week ago, and when I have something like: no, not again! Because when I did it again then, I would relapse. Then I can just say: 'No, I've had enough. I've had it.'* [H/1/32]

Six respondents refer to a *learning process* regarding informal rules of use. They state that negative experiences (after violating their own principles) helps them to respect these informal rules on next occasions of use.

> *When I look at the first period of use, that was the moment I realized I was violating a rule, that I realized I had to quit. [...] You catch yourself in it: oh, now I'm going too far. Yes, a few times, because I realized: now I have to quit. I mean, when I caught myself violating them, I quit.* [Z/0/02]

> *Yes, you are with friends, and you say beforehand: I won't take anything, because you have to go to work the next day, and then you feel like it anyway. Then it occurs that I say: come on. But then I regret it the next day, then I think: 'I wish I hadn't done it.' [...] So from my experience, I know I shouldn't do it, because I feel bad afterwards. That's learning how to handle drugs.* [Z/0/03]

> *Once, I had to go to a family party the next day, but the day before it was so pleasant, and you get some, okay, just one line. But the day after I didn't go to that family party and I re-gret it. But you always have to experience it first, before you regret it, right? Then I said: 'Never again.' Whenever I have a party the next day, like on a Sunday or something, a bar-becue party or a family party, then I won't do it the day before, or the night before. No, be-cause you're just sitting there 'crashing', right?* [I/1/14]

Some respondents report that it is easier to respect their informal rules or principles of use in the case of *limited availability*, i.e. when cocaine is not offered or not easily ac-cessible.

14.8.3. Respect or disrespect for rules?

The set and setting factors that may have an impact on the user's informal control mechanisms are quite numerous. The key question is whether or not the user can stick to his/her informal rules when confronted with interfering circumstances. It is impossi-ble to present quantitative data on the number of respondents who usually respect their informal rules of use and those who typically do not. Most respondents acknowledge having violated their own principles of cocaine use on one or more occasions, but at the same time, they state they have respected these rules on other occasions.

> *I dare to sin, every now and then, but rarely. I try not to... I've trained myself in saying no at those moments. And it works.* [H/1/32]

Only a few respondents declare that they never disrespect any of their rules of behavior regarding cocaine ('I never sin') and only a few indicate that they always violate their own informal rules when certain set or setting factors interfere with them ('I have no backbone, I have no character'). Yet, an overwhelming majority state that they can at times resist temptation and respect their own principles of use, and at other times they violate these rules and 'let themselves go'.

> *It does happen once in a while. When it is already there, when I know that certain friends are planning to do things, and they have coke. Or when I'm calling someone, and it's already been taken care of. When it is before, I'd rather say no, but when I know they already have it, then I feel like doing it, it's like: shit, oh no. I'm letting myself go again.* [H/1/32]

These are some of the answers to the question whether they respected their informal rules when confronted with interfering set and/or setting factors. Some stories show that respondents often violate their informal rules of use when they are confronted with multiple interfering factors. One single set or setting factor does not necessarily constitute a temptation. In other words, respondents often calculate pros and cons of a given situation and when they 'decide' to break their own principles it may be due to a combination of different interfering set and setting factors.

> *Yes, when it is a real cool party, where you have been drinking somewhat, and there is a great atmosphere with coke at that moment, then I find it hard sometimes to say: 'I won't do it.' But it must be really fun. Then I might sin against it.* [K/1/02]

> *Yes, in a period when you... feel like doing other things. When you sort of want to violate the rules explicitly, just to violate them. When I feel like that, I would dare to do it on my job, and not to give a damn about my principles, but it's... gosh, it has hardly ever occurred. [...] Yes, in a period when I take my job very seriously, it's the opposite. Like: I have to finish a report urgently, I have to do this and that, and it's quite important, I would surely say: no. I wouldn't even think of it.* [R/0/01]

Many respondents report shame and regret after having violated their own informal rules or principles of use. In our view, feeling bad about rule breaking behavior can be an indication of the internalization of these rules, norms or values about cocaine use. Remorse illustrates the strength of social rituals and social sanctions and the important role they play in self-regulation of illicit drug use. These feelings of regret indirectly reinforce the existing informal rules of use and often support rule-awareness and rule-abidance.

> *I'll sin then, but the next day I'll regret it, for sure. But I won't be able to say no, I guess.* [L/0/02]

> *It has happened that I did not respect my rule, but I really regret that, because the next day I am unsure when I'm on stage.* [H/1/20]

14.9. CONCLUSION

To understand the drug experience we have to consider more factors than simply the pharmacology of the drug. A person's emotional and social situation has a significant impact on drug use as well. In this chapter we have shown that many respondents are able to develop, and stick to, rules, routines, and rituals that help them limit their cocaine use to specific times, places, occasions, amounts, or spheres of activity. These can be considered part of the *informal control mechanisms* that are active when people consume drugs.

When asked overtly about rules of use, only 10 % of our respondents did not answer this question (versus one third of the respondents from both Amsterdam samples). In none of the Amsterdam and the Antwerp samples, a statistically significant relationship was found between level of use at time of interview and reporting rules of use. We found that our respondents recognized rules relating to the setting and situations of use, the activities that should take priority, the persons (not) to use with, the maximum number of times one should use cocaine in a given time period, relationships with non-users, frequency of use, appropriate feelings when using, suitable and unsuitable combinations of cocaine with other drugs, route of ingestion, appropriate dose, how to avoid police attention, where and how to buy cocaine, how to manage financial consequences of cocaine use, how to control the quality of cocaine, etc.

Similarly, the Antwerp respondents report rules of advice on the same topics. As respondents tend not to recognize the implicit guidelines or rules they apply to their use, their replies to questions about advice to novice users may provide indirect access to regulatory rules. If such 'advice' is guided by the structuring principles of use, the respondents' advice to novice users illustrates the informal control mechanisms that help them to limit their use, to prevent ill effects, to enhance positive effects, and to stay out of legal, medical and psychological trouble.

The emotional state most frequently mentioned to generate a longing (desire) or appetite for cocaine is joy (68.7%). Depression is reported by fewer than one in three respondents. Most of them claim depression is 'sometimes' or 'rarely' an 'appetizer' for cocaine. When asked about feelings or emotional states that are *unsuitable* for cocaine use, 72.7% of our respondents refer to feeling depressive. Clearly, as a set factor, depression can generate an appetite for cocaine, but at the same time, it is regarded as incompatible with cocaine use by a majority of our respondents. Many experienced cocaine users have an implicit theory about how to use cocaine (and/or other drugs) without falling into the trap of abuse: never when you feel bad, only when you feel good. Furthermore, our data indicate that illicit substances are not solely taken for escapist motives (to avoid negative feelings), as is generally believed. Contrary to the official discourse, many respondents prefer not to take cocaine when feeling bad.

For the respondents of the Antwerp sample and both Amsterdam samples, the most suitable situations for cocaine use are those in which people enjoy each other's company. In all three samples, going out, partying and gatherings with friends rank in the top three. Similarly, smaller categories such as 'dinner', 'sex', 'theatre' and even 'outdoor' refer to social situations in which respondents do not use cocaine on their own... Like community studies in other European and American cities, we find that cocaine use is negatively associated with work or study, achievement and the presence of non-users, especially parents and children. The data do not only indicate that setting is an important aspect for cocaine users, but they also confirm the existence of implicit rules of use. Irrespective of whether respondents are always able to respect these rules, the answers show that at least a proportion of our respondents act according to principles that determine which situations are unsuitable for cocaine use and which are not. Drug users try and make sure that their cocaine use does not interfere with other activities that have priority.

One in three respondents have never used cocaine when alone, while two in three do so occasionally. However, our data demonstrate that the respondents are not prone to using cocaine with no matter who. The most frequent categories of persons with whom respondents would definitely *not* use cocaine were: family members, non-users, users they don't trust/like, heavy users, etc. Clearly, these respondents have informal rules about the company of use that can serve different goals: (1) to conceal drug use from non users (because these persons could be angry, or disappointed, or inform the police or the employer (for the user's protection), or because these persons need to be protected ; (2) To maximize positive effects of cocaine use; (3) To minimize the risk of adverse effects, of becoming dependent on cocaine, of using too much (for the user's protection).

More than three in five Antwerp respondents (more than in both Amsterdam samples) stated they put limits to the amount of cocaine they bought per month. In general, the level of financial limits in the Antwerp sample tends to be somewhat higher than in the Amsterdam I sample. Like in the 1991 Amsterdam II sample, we find that those who used at a high level during their period of heaviest use report financial limits significantly less often than medium or low-level users. Within the group of Antwerp respondents who report a financial limit on cocaine purchase per month, this limit correlates significantly with level of use during the three months prior to the interview, but not with level of use during period of heaviest use. After exclusion of the current non-users from the subsample of the Antwerp respondents who report a financial limit on cocaine purchase per month, the average limit on cocaine purchase per month is 4,775.5 BEF, i.e. approximately 2 grams per month.

In short, many respondents recognize situations, feelings or persons that play a role in the use or non-use of cocaine. Most of the informal rules listed above serve as *boundary protection mechanisms*. They help to prevent disruption of everyday life in which users have invested (jobs, homes, families, communities and identities) and help to maintain or restore the user's balance. As long as everyday life is still a distinct and a paramount reality at the fringes of which drug use takes place, the user maintains control over his/her cocaine use. *The existence of informal control mechanisms does not, however, necessarily imply that they are always effective.* At least as important as the question of whether an illicit drug user recognizes informal rules is the way in which the user handles conflicts between these rules and interfering set and setting factors.

The set and setting factors that can interfere with informal rules of use most mentioned are: increased availability (i.e. when cocaine is more easily accessible or offered freely), the inner life of the user (i.e. negative emotional states such as tiredness, loneliness, depression, boredom, insecurity, etc.), the social character of the occasions of use (i.e. the presence or absence of significant others), the pharmacological actions of cocaine itself or of other drugs.

The factors that support respect for informal control mechanisms most mentioned are: specific responsibilities (a job, a performance, a family, important appointments, etc.), the company in which the user finds him/herself (trusted friends versus strangers, problematic users, or non-users), the user's inner life (i.e. positive emotional states such as feeling good, feeling not too tired, feeling emotionally stable, self-confident, etc.), the absence of 'craving', limited availability, etc. Some respondents refer to a learning process regarding informal rules of use: negative experiences after violating their own principles may help them to respect these informal rules on next occasions of use.

The key question is whether or not the user can stick to his/her informal rules when confronted with interfering circumstances. An overwhelming majority of the participants state that while they are sometimes able to resist temptations and respect their own principles of use, on other occasions they violate these rules and 'let themselves go'. Typically, one single set or setting factor does not necessarily constitute a tempting situation. Respondents often calculate pros and cons of a given situation and when they 'decide' to break their own principles it is often because of a combination of different interfering set and setting factors. In our opinion, the fact that many respondents report feelings of shame and regret after having violated their own informal rules or principles of use, illustrates the strength of social rituals and social sanctions and their important role in the self-regulation of illicit drug use. Feelings of remorse may indicate the internalization of rules, norms or values about cocaine use, reinforce the existing informal rules of use, and often support rule-awareness and rule-abidance.

NOTES

1   Unlike Cohen, we did not differentiate this question into separate topics like advice about mode of ingestion, dose, circumstances to use cocaine, combination of cocaine with other drugs, buying cocaine, disadvantages of cocaine, and methods of countering the latter.

2   We are aware of the fact that the term 'set' refers to more than the emotional states or feelings the user experiences. In Zinberg's classical work, the term 'set' referred not only to the person's attitude at the time of use, but also to his or her personality structure and genetic (physical and psychological) predisposition (See: ZINBERG, N. (1984), *Drug, set, and setting. The basis for controlled intoxicant use*, 5. New Haven: Yale University Press). Throughout this chapter, the term 'set' is used in a narrow sense, referring to 'emotional states' or 'feelings' only.

3   Cohen (1989: 79) found a large 'no answer' category, which he attributed to interviewer bias. He observed that 'to persuade respondents to answer this question sometimes needed more assertive questioning than some interviewers were willing to adopt.

4   This classification is a result of the lengthy and complex procedure of coding and recoding of the qualitative data using the QSR NUD*IST software. By processes of 'system closure' (the results of enquiry were put back into the system as more data to enquire about), we eventually created these 14 categories that could be linked to central themes in this book (see other chapters and paragraphs).

5   More than 20% of the expected frequencies have an expected count of less than five. After collapsing the 'none' and 'low' levels into one row, and the 'medium' and 'high' levels into one row, we obtain a 2x2 table. Chi-square test is still invalid, but we can do a Fisher's Exact test (an alternative test for chi-square in small samples). This test does not yield a statistically significant relationship between level of use and the presence of informal rules. A similar test for the crosstabulation of level of use during period of heaviest use and given rules does not yield a statistically significant relationship.

6   See p. 307.

7   We were confronted with the same difficulty described by Cohen (1989: 78): it is easier to mention settings than sets (we found an average of 2.26 situations per respondents and 1.14 emotional states per respondent). We have to bear in mind that respondents recognized considerably more rules related to situations than to feelings.

8   When asked for emotional states that can generate an appetite for cocaine, two respondents stated that the mere fact of talking about cocaine use and cocaine effects can generate an appetite. This

was heard a number of times during the interviews, and because we consider these statements to refer to setting factors rather than to an emotional state, they are discussed in the next paragraph.

9   Consider for example this statement from the former Belgian Minister of Internal Affairs, Mr. Louis Tobback, in 1993 (at a national drug conference): *'The trouble with that whole discussion is that it threatens to turn out in 'trivializing' the fact which fills me with dread, namely that young people flee to the world of intoxications because they fail to find other solutions.'* [our translation] In Dutch: 'Het probleem dat ik heb met heel dat debat is dat het op een banalisering dreigt uit te draaien van wat ik een verschrikking vind, nl. dat jonge mensen vluchten in de wereld van de roes omdat ze geen andere oplossingen meer vinden.' See: DE RUYVER, B. and DE LEENHEER, A. (1994), *Drugbeleid 2000. Gestion des drogues en 2000,* 475. Antwerpen/Brussel: Maklu/Bruylant.

10   See Chapter 13, p. 296.

11   See Chapter 8, p. 208-212.

12   See Chapter 16, p. 345-359.

13   See Chapter 4, p. 102-103.

14   The average financial limit for cocaine purchase per month of low-level-users during the last three months is 4,430.2 BEF (after exclusion of current non-users). The average financial limit of medium and high-level users during the last three months is 7,250.0 BEF (Belgian francs).

15   The average financial limit of cocaine purchase per month of low-level users during period of heaviest use is 3,730.8 BEF (after exclusion of current non-users). The average financial limit of medium and high-level users during the period of heaviest use is 5,152.8 BEF.

16   Within the group of respondents of the 1987 Amsterdam I sample (Cohen, 1989: 80-81) who report a financial limit on cocaine purchase per month, this limit correlated significantly with level of use during top period (Pearson's R= 0.48; p<0.0001).

17   See Chapter 9, p. 215.

18   Comparison with the Amsterdam I sample (Cohen, 1989: 80-81) shows that the level of financial limits in the Antwerp sample tends to be somewhat higher. More than half of the Amsterdam respondents have a limit of less than 100 NLG, versus 22.4% of the Antwerp respondents who report a limit lower than 2,000 BEF. The differences between both samples are most marked for the low-level users (the respondents of the Antwerp sample tend to report higher financial limits than those of the Amsterdam I sample) and for the high-level users (the highest financial limit reported by Antwerp respondents was 15,000 BEF – more or less the equivalent of 750 NLG, while two Amsterdam respondents reported financial limits higher than 20,000 BEF, i.e. more than 1,000 NLG).

19   See also Chapter 1, p. 41 and the following.

CHAPTER 15

THE CONCEPTS OF 'CONTROLLED' AND 'UNCONTROLLED' USE

15.1. INTRODUCTION

In Chapter 3 some data on networks of cocaine users were presented.[1] Respondents were asked how many other users they knew personally and how many of these were 'risky' users (i.e. apparently using cocaine in an uncontrolled, or problematic or hazardous way). Unsurprisingly, all Antwerp respondents know other cocaine users. More interesting is the fact that 63.1% of the Antwerp sample reports knowing risky users of cocaine. When leaving out the respondents claiming to know more than 100 other cocaine users, we find an average number of 25 other users known to respondents, and an average of 4 'risky' users per respondent.

Clearly, the Antwerp interviewees acknowledge that some forms of cocaine use have negative consequences and others are relatively safe. In this Chapter qualitative data are presented to illustrate the users' concepts of 'controlled' and 'uncontrolled' use, or 'risky use' and 'safe use', or 'use' and 'abuse'. First, a catalogue of indicators for controlled and uncontrolled use is constructed (§15.2). Then, the process of confirmation of boundaries and informal rules through counter-examples is illustrated (§15.3). Subsequently, Becker's ideas (1973: 41-58) on the role of social learning in illicit drug use are tested again: how do people become 'controlled' users (§15.4)? Finally, respondents were asked about their preferred official drug policy relating to cocaine (§15.5).

15.2. INDICATORS OF 'CONTROLLED' AND 'UNCONTROLLED' USE

15.2.1. Respondents' self-image

Participants were asked whether they perceived themselves as 'controlled' or 'uncontrolled' users of cocaine. Of the 107 respondents who participated in the second interview, 11 saw themselves as 'uncontrolled' users (10.3%), 83 perceived themselves as 'controlled' users (77.6%) and 4 interviewees declare both 'controlled' and 'uncontrolled' aspects in their use pattern (3.7%). Nine respondents did not answer this question.

Sometimes I feel that I have no control anymore and then I have to fight hard to get myself back on my feet again. Sometimes I'm in my bed at night and I am really yearning to base coke again. That I really can't sleep. [...] And from the moment I get the chance to buy it or to get it, I do it. [G/0/01]

I had no control anymore afterwards. I took drugs to be off the earth, to have no contact with the world anymore... [H/0/29]

Table 15.2.a shows the comparison of the total sample with the subsample of 15 respondents who perceive themselves as 'uncontrolled users' or who perceive at least some 'uncontrolled' aspects in their cocaine use pattern.

Table 15.2.a   Comparison of the subsample of respondents who perceive themselves as 'uncontrolled' users (N=15) with the total sample (N=111) (Antwerp, 1997)

Variable	Antwerp (1997)	
	% of subsample of 'uncontrolled' users (N=15)	% of total sample (N=111)
Gender	86.7% male	63.1% male
Snowball chain	46.7% belong to chain H 20.0% belong to chain F	28.8% belong to chain H 2.7% belong to chain F
Registered respondents	73.3%	49.5%
Treated respondents	60.0%	19.8%
Convicted respondents	60.0%	41.4%
Level of use (top period)	73.3% high-level users	49.5% high-level users
Level of use (last 3 months)	20.0% high-level users	5.4% high-level users
Route of ingestion (top period)	46.7% injectors 40.0% freebasers	18.0% injectors 23.4% freebasers
Route of ingestion (last 3 months)	20.0% injectors 26.7% freebasers	10.0% injectors 16.7% freebasers
Combination of cocaine and heroin	66.7% have used this combination at least once	35.1% have used this combination at least once
Life time prevalence heroin	80.0%	63.1%
Last 2 weeks prevalence heroin	46.7%	17.1%

The subsample of respondents who perceive themselves as 'uncontrolled' users differs markedly from the total sample in that the proportion of male respondents is higher, and that the proportions of treated, convicted and registered respondents tend to be higher. Furthermore, we find higher proportions of high-level users, intravenous users and freebasers during the period of heaviest use and the last three months in the subsample. Those who perceive themselves as 'uncontrolled users', have higher life time prevalence and last two weeks prevalence of opiate use as well as life time prevalence of combined use of opiates and cocaine.

15.2.2. Indicators of 'controlled' use

Typically, at one point or another during the second interview, the conversation turned to the topic of 'controlled use of cocaine'. In a few cases the interviewer directed the conversation towards this item. Eventually, 102 respondents replied in their own words to questions such as: how do you know whether someone controls his/her cocaine consumption? How does a (controlled) user contrast with an uncontrolled user (or abuser)? Table 15.2.b shows a catalogue of the major indicators of 'controlled' use, as perceived by the Antwerp respondents.

Table 15.2.b Most important indicators of 'controlled' use according to the 1997 Antwerp sample (N=102) [*]

Indicator	N	%
Periodical abstinence	18	17.6
Being able to refuse cocaine when it is offered	16	15.7
Small doses	15	14.7
Low frequency of use	15	14.7
Not making active efforts to look for it	13	12.7
Other activities ('normal life') take priority over cocaine	11	10.8
Job/study takes priority over cocaine	10	9.8
No negative reasons for using cocaine	10	9.8
Being able to resist craving	9	8.8
No need/desire for cocaine	7	6.9
Using only during weekends	7	6.9
Being able to keep off cocaine when it is in the house	7	6.9
Being able to have fun without cocaine	6	5.9
Not going to bed late	5	4.9
No health problems	4	3.9
Use is limited to specific settings, places, company	3	2.9
Respect for own rules of use	3	2.9
Being able to quit cocaine use	3	2.9
Good eating habits	3	2.9
Being able to talk about topics other than drug use (or cocaine)	3	2.9

[*] More than one answer per respondent was possible

Other indicators mentioned by respondents were having opportunities in life (low social and economic vulnerability), looking good and well-dressed, sociability (communicative and not distant), not living during the night only, appropriate self-knowledge (introspective abilities), not in treatment, being rich (having enough money), having a steady relationship, being aware also of the negative sides of cocaine use, route of ingestion (snorting), using only on special occasions, feeling no physical urge to use, personality unchanged, not bragging about one's cocaine use, being able to talk about it without feeling a desire for cocaine, not lying about one's use, no feelings of paranoia, paying attention to quality of cocaine...

We illustrate the indicators of 'controlled use' most mentioned with some respondents' accounts. Eighteen interviewees (17.6% of the 102 respondents who replied to this question) declared that *periodical abstinence* is an important indicator of 'controlled use'.

> *There are people who, for example, only take coke during the weekend, or just Thursday, Friday, Saturday, and after that nothing, but they had to do that every week, I don't call that controlled users. Someone who uses in a controlled way, in my opinion, must be able to say: 'Now I quit for half a year, and it doesn't bother me.'* [F/0/02]

> *To control something means that when you decide like: I quit for a while, that you just do it, and when it turns out you can't stick to your words, yes, well you can't call that control, of course.* [H/0/10]

These data confirm our findings on temporary abstinence in Chapter 12.2 Indeed, we found that 86.5% of our respondents reported to have stopped for more than one month. Motivations for periodic abstinence were both internal and external, but together with the data presented here, our data illustrate the process through which cocaine users regulate their cocaine intake. By temporarily abstaining (or cutting back) respondents try to maintain a pattern of controlled use. The fact that many respondents believe temporary abstinence is an important indicator for controlled use, illustrates their awareness of informal control mechanisms.

Sixteen respondents (15.7% of those who replied) say that a controlled user is able to *refuse cocaine when it is offered*, while an uncontrolled user is not. Again, the data presented here are consistent with other findings of the present study. In Chapter 13 it was shown that most respondents report having experienced craving for cocaine.[3] We argued that notwithstanding a certain desire for the drug, respondents are able to resist and to exert power over the drug. Here we find that many respondents acknowledge the importance of resisting craving when cocaine is offered, as an indicator of 'controlled use'.

> *I think you are a controlled user when you can refuse it when the opportunity is there, and say: 'I don't need that now, I want to do that when I feel like it.'* [P/0/02]

> *That's my clue: that I can say no. Even if it's there. That it doesn't have power over me.* [I/1/04]

Fifteen participants (14.7% of the 102 respondents who replied) believe that patterns of controlled use are characterized by *small doses*, and another 15 respondents (14.7%) say controlled users can be identified by their *low frequency of use*:

> *Controlled use means to me to use cocaine moderately. That you don't exaggerate, that you don't use one or two gram in one evening. That is not controlled, you might feel okay for a while, but after that you fall down three times as deep. When you can keep the frequency low, I think you control it.* [P/0/06]

> *The criterion is: I snort with little lines... you become so stiff when you take too much, eh, when you are sitting there so stiff, then you don't have it under control, in my opinion. As with the talkativeness, when you dose it well, it doesn't bother you, then you can function perfectly.* [C/0/09]

These data illustrate the importance of the dose and the frequency of use, just like we showed in Chapters 5 and 11.[4] These data also confirm indirectly the importance of level of use (which we defined as *dose x frequency*) as a factor for describing patterns of controlled and uncontrolled use.

According to thirteen respondents (12.7%) a controlled user tends to *make fewer active efforts to obtain cocaine* than an uncontrolled user. These accounts illustrate that cocaine use is often unplanned:

> *The fact that I'm not bad tempered because there is no coke around. I mean, the fact that I just don't need it. That I can appreciate it and find it amusing, but that I am not anxiously looking for it or so.* [I/0/07]

> *It doesn't rule my life, let me put it this way. I don't think about it every day, I'm not constantly thinking: how can I get a gram, where do I find it, right? If it is available, okay, then it's available, so what, that's the way it is. There are many people who make phone calls, who go walk around looking for it.* [H/1/28]

For eleven respondents (10.8%) an important indicator for controlled use is that the user makes sure that *other activities take priority over his/her cocaine use*. Another ten respondents (9.8%) state that a controlled user will not let cocaine take priority over his/her job (or study). These data are consistent with our findings on informal rules of use (Chapter 14): users try to make sure that their cocaine use does not interfere with other activities.[5] Both the informal rules listed in Chapter 14 and the indicators listed here serve as boundary protection mechanisms.

> *I think that when a person wants to do particular things and he/she can't do them anymore because he/she takes too much dope, he/she doesn't control it. [...] When you're not in control, then you let yourself go at a moment you're not supposed to let yourself go.* [M/0/02]

> *That I just quit, even before it's too late, before I get into financial problems, before I spoil my studies, before I spoil my job. That when I feel I'm going too far, that I just quit with it, before there is any trouble in other spheres of life: my living situation, my job, my studies.* [H/1/18]

Similarly, many respondents have a single, implicit theory about how to use cocaine without falling into the trap of abuse: although negative feelings can generate an appetite for cocaine, they are seen as incompatible with cocaine use.[6] Positive emotional states are seen as more suitable for cocaine use. Indeed, ten interviewees (9.8%) report that *positive reasons for using cocaine* characterize patterns of controlled use, while negative reasons for using are typical for uncontrolled use.

> *Eh, the reason I take it? It always has to do with: I feel nice already, and let's throw ourselves into it. If I took it to* [she thinks] *feel better, I think I would be doing it wrong.* [V/1/01]

> *That I only use it when I feel like doing it myself, that I never let it tempt me, like: 'Fuck, I don't feel good', or I get out of my bed and I say: 'Hey, I don't like this day, hup, I take a line of coke or something.' That doesn't happen.* [R/0/06]

15.2.3. Indicators of 'uncontrolled' use

Table 15.2.c shows a catalogue of the most important indicators of 'uncontrolled' use, as perceived by the Antwerp respondents.[7] The indicators of 'uncontrolled' use most mentioned are illustrated with the qualitative interviews. Fourteen respondents (13.7% of the 102 who replied to this question) believe that uncontrolled users are *unable to stop using* (the *binge* pattern).[8] It is remarkable that many respondents refer to this binge pattern when talking about freebasing.

> *They all base too, and when it's gone, they start looking for lumps on the carpet, anything. Or they see white lumps everywhere or so, and I think that's' the best proof they don't control it anymore. When you say: it's over, then it's over, when it's gone, it's gone. You can't conjure anymore but these people want to call and say: 'Can you bring us some more and some more'...* [I/0/05]

Another 14 respondents (13.7%) declare that *too large doses* and overt signs of 'over'-dosing are typical signs of uncontrolled cocaine use. This confirms the impact of accurate dosing on advantages and disadvantages of cocaine.[9] Of the following accounts, the first illustrates the informal social control among users through comments, and the second refers to similarities between 'overdosing' of cocaine and that of other drugs.

I know two guys, and they are totally uncontrolled, they use two or three grams every week-
end. So I think: Jeezes, how can you do that. And I tell them too, I told it this weekend. I
said: 'Can't you see what you're doing, you're going too far.' [I/1/02]

Yes, like with alcohol... drunks who get pissed... so overdosing... the overdosing... getting
pissed... it shows a weakness in character... and with shit too... [i.e. cannabis, TD] there are
people who keep smoking pipes and more pipes, and more joints and stuff... it is actually
quite useless to do that... [H/0/02]

Table 15.2.c   Most important indicators of 'uncontrolled' use according to the 1997 Antwerp sample
(N=102) [*]

Indicator	N	%
Binge pattern of use (unable to stop using)	14	13.7
Too large doses (and overt signs of 'over'-dosing)	14	13.7
Spending too much money on cocaine (financial problems)	13	12.7
Lying about one's cocaine use	12	11.8
High frequency of use	10	9.8
Making active efforts to find cocaine	10	9.8
Constantly talking about cocaine	10	9.8
Route of ingestion (freebasing, injecting cocaine)	9	8.8
Looking bad	9	8.8
Cocaine takes priority over other activities	9	8.8
Negative effects of cocaine use (being nervous, tense...)	8	7.8
Negative reasons for use	8	7.8
Aggression	7	6.9
Paranoia	7	6.9
Conspicuous behavior (towards non-users or the police)	7	6.9
Not being able to function without cocaine	6	5.9
Always high on cocaine (never approachable)	5	4.9
Engaging in criminal activities	5	4.9
Not being able to keep off cocaine when it is in the house	5	4.9
Not being able to have fun without cocaine	4	3.9
Need for / desire for cocaine	4	3.9
Craving caused by cues	4	3.9
Changes in personality (becoming cold, hard)	4	3.9
Use on weekdays	3	2.9
Unable to refuse cocaine when it is offered	3	2.9
Unable to quit or to abstain temporarily	3	2.9
Bad eating habits	3	2.9

[*] More than one answer per respondent was possible

The financial consequences of regular cocaine use can play an important role in informal regulation. In Chapter 12 we showed that lack of financial means can be an important reason for temporary abstinence or cutting back.[10] In Chapter 11 we argued
that the high prices are often perceived as an important disadvantage of cocaine.[11]
Furthermore, many respondents maintain financial limits on their cocaine purchase.[12]
Thirteen interviewees (12.7%) state that uncontrolled users typically spend more
money on cocaine than they can afford, and consequently get *financial problems*:

I think, [...] when you get into financial trouble just to get it... I have that too, that when I'm
short of money, I just don't do it. [P/0/03]

I think that when you spend a lot of money to it, so that you can't pay for the rest, the bills
and stuff, so that you get into financial trouble, emotionally, that tells me they have problems
with it. [H/1/28]

Lying about the extent of one's cocaine use is considered an important indicator of un-controlled use by 12 respondents (or 11.8%). This is further discussed in subsequent chapters.

> *That he did it secretely, in the end he did everything quite secretely. At first he didn't, but in the end he did. And just the fact that he was hiding it, and that he said: 'I didn't use' while you very well noticed he had used. [...] I'm not going to do it secretely for people who know me well. Because to me, that is already a step in the wrong direction, when I start hiding things or so, or when I start lying when they ask 'Did you use?'. Because then you start ly-ing to yourself... so-called white lies, that is already a sign to me that things go wrong.* [R/0/08]

Ten respondents (9.8% of the repliers) find that uncontrolled use is characterized by a *high frequency of use*:

> *And yes, when you have to disappear every quarter of an hour for ten minutes to the toilets, then... That's how you can see whether people are using it in a controlled or uncontrolled way. Because you always see when people go away, or when you are at some people's house, how much they use... Everybody keeps an eye on it as well, like: oh, he's gone for ten minutes now, then you know why.* [I/1/16]

Another ten participants (9.8% of the repliers) believe that uncontrolled users tend to make more *active efforts to obtain cocaine* than controlled users:

> *But there are people who go look for stuff in the course of the night and who really make ef-forts and then... When I see them put on their coats again or make another phone call, then I prefer to disappear.* [M/1/03]

Finally, ten interviewees (9.8% of the repliers) state that uncontrolled users tend to *talk about cocaine incessantly.*

> *Primarily that you can't have a meaningful conversation with them anymore, with these people, or that they can't talk about anything else anymore but drugs, particularly that is a symptom. From their conversations, the way they show little interest in things that are not related to cocaine, I think that in particular.* [I/1/01]

15.3. COUNTEREXAMPLES

Respondents were also asked whether they knew users who served as counterexamples for their own use. When the interviewer was asked what he meant by 'counterexam-ples', he would reformulate the question as follows: 'Do you know any users of whom you think: I would never want to use cocaine like that person?' Sixty-two respondents (57.9% of the total sample) reported knowing users with whom they did not want to identify themselves.

> *Probably when I look in the mirror at myself, that's probably the best example. But it's a kind of defense, I suppose, when you look at yourself sometimes, and you think, and you see the real truth in there, and that's probably the best example. But I also know some other guys... yes, in particular, in the past, there were a couple of friends who were really bad us-ers, I've seen them go really depressed on it, because of it. And I've seen a couple of really*

good friends who got really fucked up with it, and who went into manic depression-like and eventually had to leave, and I helped them to get out of the country. There were a lot of people I've seen, that I said: I don't want to end up like that. [S/0/01]

Most of these counter-examples are found among friends and acquaintances: 47 respondents (43.9% of the total sample) reported having a friend or acquaintance who served as a counterexample. It is striking that nine respondents (8.4% of the total sample) declare that their own behavior in the past serves as a counterexample. These interviewees refer to a period in their own life when they used too much, too frequently, or when they injected or lost control over their cocaine use:

For me, it's not like: 'Oh no, that's not the way I want...' because me too, I have been in a very heavy phase, and I just think of myself then. I'll never get as far as then, I was stupid, okay, and... Now, for me, that victory is so great to me, inside, I'll never give up that feeling in my life, because it's really nice, that you say: yes, you can cope with the world, and people make a fuss about little things and you are much more stable in life now. [H/1/04]

No, because I can't say that... yes, I can say: that's how I would never want to do it again, but I did it all myself, you know, I did it in the worst possible forms, I've injected in public, I did it all, so I can't say about someone else: I would never want to do it that way, because... I can say: that's how I would never want to do it again. [F/0/01]

Look, we're thinking about somebody else, but basically we're not a whit better... actually, in the beginning I didn't know that basing, for example, could be so addictive... I couldn't imagine that someone spent all his money on it... I just didn't get it... and in fact, I only started to realize that it was possible the moment I was using seriously myself... I couldn't imagine that until I experienced it myself... but now I have something like: yes, I never want to be like that again. [H/0/05]

Six respondents report knowing junkies whose lifestyle in general and illicit drug use in particular serve as a counterexample (see also Zinberg, 1984: 131 and 155). Three respondents indicate an ex-partner as counterexample, 2 respondents a relative, and 1 a colleague.

An interesting issue is which aspects of the counterexample's cocaine use puts the respondents off. In other words, why is the other user seen as counterexample for the respondent's own use? The other user's deterring characteristics most mentioned by our respondents are the following.

Fourteen respondents (13.1% of the total sample) declare that *overdosing* (too large doses) is a typical feature of the counterexamples they know: they use too much, too frequently. Consequently, they experience *negative physical effects* such as nose problems, stomach problems, weight loss, exhaustion, etc.

Yes, like that colleague, he did let it go too far, that guy was using quite a lot, and one night he collapsed in a discotheque, and they brought him to hospital, and yes, perforation of the stomach, so it was a hemorrhage, but yes, he would rather take a pill or a joint than eat a sandwich. Yes, it frightened me, those stories make you think. [H/0/21]

Sometimes he's playing records in the bar, and suddenly he's on the floor, as he hasn't slept for five days or so, from exhaustion... yes, I don't want that... and also, yes, people who use it to become aggressive or so, I don't want to demean myself, or identify with those people. [C/0/09]

Twelve respondents (11.2% of the total sample) point at the *activities undertaken to obtain (money to buy) cocaine*. Cocaine users who engage in selling cocaine (4), in other criminal acts such as shoplifting and car-breaking (4), prostitution (3), and/or in selling personal things (1) are seen as examples of problematic use patterns:

> *That they sell it, with all those risks that are associated with it, no, I would never dare. I know that those who are in jail for drugs, that they are scrutinized thoroughly, and they are allowed less than an ordinary prisoner, it really is true, it really made me think, you know! I'm really saying: I never want to be arrested for drugs.* [I/1/14]

> *Now they try to deal pills. They failed to buy one or two thousand pills from some big dealers and they were ripped off for one hundred thousand francs. They had pooled money with friends, and yes, he was quite depressed after that, and he started to use more drugs because of that and trying to borrow money from everybody to buy drugs and...* [G/0/01]

Another twelve respondents (11.2% of the total sample) indicate that *negative mental effects* such as aggression (6), greed (2), depression (1), apathy (1), arrogance (1), distance (1) are characteristic for the counterexamples they know.

> *They became completely apathetic and my brother became aggressive. I didn't recognize my brother or my old friends. These were people I had known since they were little 12-year-old kids. And really, they had changed so much.* [V/1/01]

> *There are people who use coke, that I say: hey guys, when you're doing it like that, give it up. They become aggressive, they become greedy all the time. Eh X.* [i.e. a friend of hers, and a participant in the present study, TD] *is such a person. When he takes coke, it's like: greed, greed, greed, and he doesn't care about anything anymore, he's constantly focused on himself, and that's how I would not want to become, brrr, it makes me shake with horror.* [H/1/17]

Intravenous drug use is often associated with 'junky' type characteristics (such as 'addictive' and 'scary').[13] Obviously, injecting deters most respondents: 5 respondents report other users' injecting behavior as a counterexample, and 6 respondents declare that 'junkies' serve as counterexamples for their own pattern of use (see also: Finnigan, 1996).

> *They really lived in a dunghill, eh... they didn't have a roof over their head, they never worked, they went out to steal, and also when they were using needles, it was really really filthy.* [I/1/01]

Finally, other characteristics of the respondents' counter-examples were: people who have children and continue to use cocaine, people who let their cocaine use affect their professional life, people whose life is entirely focused on cocaine use, people who spend too much money on cocaine, yuppies and moviestars, people who use it to enhance their self-confidence, people who use cocaine to buy friendship, love or sex, people who push other users to use more, people who are addicted to cocaine, etc.

To conclude, problematic or extreme cocaine use patterns of friends, acquaintances, partners, relatives and others can serve as counterexamples. These examples of how not to use cocaine help the user to draw the line between use and abuse. Like in the process of modeling and imitation of significant others, users tend to observe other cocaine use patterns and lifestyles, and decide *not* to follow counterexamples. Boundaries

335

of appropriate cocaine use are set and informal rules to help the user not to cross these limits are deduced from these observations. The user's fear of becoming like these 'counterexamples' implies a sanction against uncontrolled use (Zinberg, 1984: 155)

15.4. BECOMING A 'CONTROLLED' USER OF COCAINE

During the qualitative interviews, respondents were prompted to describe the evolution of their cocaine use. They were asked to talk about their first use, their latest occasion of use, and the most important changes they perceived between the first and the last occasion. Table 15.4.a shows these changes in their pattern of use. The residual category [other] contains the following replies: after I had problems, I quit using; my pattern of use over time varied; my cocaine use has become less conspicuous; I see no evolution at all; I gained more introspection through my cocaine use.

A large number of respondents find that the most important change between their first and their last occasion of cocaine use is a sense of increased mastery and control over the product. Over the years they have gained better knowledge about the product and its (adverse) effects, about the influence of set and setting factors on their cocaine experience, about the potential sources of supply, about the quality cocaine, about other cocaine users, and about other types of drugs (such as MDMA, amphetamines and opiates).

Table 15.4.a   Most important changes between first and last occasion of cocaine use, according to the 1997 Antwerp respondents (N=107) [*]

Antwerp (1997)		
Most important change	N	%
1. Better knowledge of the product	21	19.6
2. Less kick (less curiosity)	18	16.8
3. More control, after a period of loss of control	16	14.9
4. More control over cocaine (more conscious)	15	14.0
5. More tolerance for the drug (larger doses)	14	13.1
6. Transition to another route of ingestion	9	8.4
7. More experience with negative/dangerous aspects of cocaine	9	8.4
8. Better knowledge of set and setting effects	7	6.5
9. Better mastery of the technique of using	6	5.6
10. Less pleasure	6	5.6
11. Other activities became more important	5	4.7
12. More pleasure	5	4.7
13. Better knowledge of potential sources of supply	5	4.7
14. Better knowledge of quality differences	5	4.7
15. Better knowledge drug users' circles	4	3.7
16. More able to put cocaine into perspective	3	2.8
17. Less interest in cocaine	3	2.8
18. More dependent	3	2.8
19. Better knowledge of all types of drugs	3	2.8
20. Quality of cocaine deteriorated	3	2.8
21. Other	5	4.7

[*] More than one answer per respondent was possible

That you have learned it. That I now know what it is. How it's like with that high and so, what it is good for, what it isn't good for, in what circumstances I prefer to use it and eh... What is good stuff, what is bad stuff. But mostly that I've got it, that I understand it and those effects. It really took a long time, let's say you need at least ten times to understand why people find it nice and so. And now I really see that. [R/0/06]

That you start to reflect about it, you think about it twice now, and before, you didn't. Now you do, now you look at it, you look with your eyes wide open at what you are doing, you see, thinking about it, you see, before you didn't. Like, what am I actually doing, and why am I doing it...? [N/0/01]

That I am a more responsible user, I know what I'm doing, I reflect it to myself: how far can I go with it? That I am dealing with it more responsibly... [H/1/18]

Through increased knowledge, the user is able to 'tame' cocaine, to grasp its essence (i.e. its appealing and unappealing aspects, its merits and pitfalls) and he/she gets an increased feeling of mastery and control (see e.g. Diaz *et al.*, 1992: 204). Three respondents see the transition of freebasing/injecting to snorting as a major change for the better in their pattern of use. Sometimes the user had to experience one or more periods of loss of control over the substance (rock-bottom), or he/she learned about its negative or dangerous aspects, but in the end he/she is better able to put cocaine into perspective, to use the substance more consciously and to avoid that cocaine takes priority over other activities (such as job, family life, etc.). Some declare that using cocaine has become more pleasure.

When I take a line, it always gives me a good feeling, I can't deny that, and it's not that it would affect me less than three or four years ago. But... now I have it under control and I can really do without it, that's the difference. I had a period that unless I had it every weekend, my night was worthless. And now I can go out without it, and I really don't need it. So that's the change. Now it can happen, that I'm offered some in the weekend, and that I say no. Four years ago that would have been impossible. And now it really... isn't a must anymore. [Z/1/04]

That I started with very little and then went to a high peak and then... went down again. And now I'm quite stable. Also because you know those high peaks, you know how far you can go, and yes. [...] Now it is more quiet, it's always in a relaxed, pleasant company. [I/1/04]

Then I thought it was quite exciting and so. And now, I rather look at it as dangerous and expensive. I'm more apprehensive. [H/1/32]

Well, in any case I... I can now better... there was a period that I had less control over it, I mean, less control: that I used too much in my opinion. That at a given moment I said: stop, I'm not going to do that anymore. But now I know perfectly: I'm going to do this or I'm going to do that... [C/0/02]

We have argued that the main motive for trying cocaine is curiosity, an aspiration to experience the 'high'.[14] Although many did not actively seek out cocaine on their own the first time, most look back upon their initiation as something they chose to do. Obviously, the initial hunger for new drug experiences is appeased, and many respondents report a decrease in excitement as the major evolution in their use. Typically, they no longer experience the kick of the unknown, the extraordinary, the forbidden fruit, and some even completely lose interest in cocaine.

Yes, well the first time I didn't really know what I started with, and it was more something like, yes, this is exceptional and this is expensive and I just get it and it really is something for special occasions, while now I think: I know it all right and it doesn't have to be such a special occasion... [I/1/12]

In the end that feeling isn't so special anymore, it's just feeling nice'like. I know I felt very special in the beginning, it's like that: your heart starts to beat, and everything becomes warm and it's so nice. And you don't have that anymore in the end, it is a nice feeling, but else there is nothing special about it anymore. [I/1/16]

Not all users, however, describe the evolution between the first and last occasion of cocaine use in positive terms. Fourteen respondents report the emergence of (physical or psychological) tolerance for the drug, and consequently a steady increase of the dose taken. Three participants state they have become more dependent on the drug, and another six declare that using cocaine is less pleasurable than it used to be. Six respondents see the transition from snorting to a more direct route of ingestion (freebasing or injecting) as the major evolution in their use.

The first time it was fun, and the last time it was disgusting. In the end I got a disgust for it. First of all, you get diarrhea, you can't eat anymore, it's rather bad for the body. True, it is great to use it once, for the kick, to have a great fuck. But it's not life, life is not taking coke, there are many things in life that are nicer than coke. [B/0/02]

That it is very nice in the beginning, but that it doesn't stay nice. What happened, is it my thinking, is it me or the coke who does it, or is it both, it probably is both, right? But I used to relax on coke, and I can't do that anymore: I want a lot, too much, and I can't keep myself calm. I don't know why, but I can't enjoy it anymore. [H/1/15]

The effect has changed as well. It just changes, after a while your body digests it better or the body knows more what it is, I don't know, but... yes, it's completely different. [L/0/02]

In Chapter 4 we referred to Becker's classical essay *'Becoming a marihuana user'* (1973), which describes the process of social learning in three stages: learning the technique, learning to perceive the effects, and learning to enjoy the effects. The data above show that the process of 'becoming a cocaine user' does not end when the user has learned to enjoy the effects caused by the drug. Some time may be required to gain mastery of the proper technique (snorting, freebasing, or injecting) and sufficient knowledge about the beneficial effects of cocaine, but the social learning process continues throughout the entire using career. The user continuously learns from his/her own experience and that of others and the process of 'becoming a *controlled* cocaine user' is nearing completion as knowledge about the product extends.

15.5. PREFERENCE FOR A DRUG POLICY RELATING TO COCAINE

We asked respondents a question about the national cocaine policy that they would prefer. We gave them the same choice between policies as Cohen (1989: 118) did in Amsterdam: 1) similar to that already effective in Belgium and the Netherlands for alcohol (*'legalisering'*); 2) similar to the policy of tolerance towards cannabis as it is effective in the Netherlands (*'gedoogbeleid'*); or 3) similar to a zero-tolerance policy like for cocaine and heroin, as it is effective nowadays in Belgium (*'repressie'*).

From table 15.5.a we can see that there are marked similarities between the Antwerp sample and the Amsterdam samples, in spite of the clear differences in drug policy of both countries. A majority of our respondents prefer a cocaine policy that is more liberal and tolerant than the one we have now. One third of our sample opted to maintain the current repressive policy (like for heroin). None of the Antwerp respondents thought the policy should get tougher.

Table 15.5.a   Preferred cocaine policy, in three samples

Policy preference	Amsterdam I 1987		Amsterdam II 1991		Antwerp 1997	
	N	%	N	%	N	%
Like alcohol	37	23.1	20	18.5	30	27.0
Between alcohol and cannabis	5	3.1	1	0.9	4	3.6
Like cannabis (Netherlands)	39	24.4	34	31.5	27	24.3
Between cannabis and heroin	7	4.4	22	20.4	9	8.1
Like heroin	64	40.0	25	23.1	37	33.3
More repressive than heroin	-	-	3	2.8	-	-
Do not know/no answer	*8*	*5.0*	*3*	*2.8*	*4*	*3.6*
Total	**160**	**100.0**	**108**	**100.0**	**111**	**100.0**

In table 15.5.b we present the motives behind the preferred cocaine policy option. Respondents were asked to explain their views on cocaine policy in their own words (open-ended question). For the answer category 'no criminal setting'[♣], we split the answers into two figures: the first bears on arguments like 'users will not be chased by police, will not be prosecuted, will not end up in prison'; the second refers to arguments like 'cocaine will not be distributed by criminals, by organized crime'.

Motives for complete legalization (like alcohol) and for a quasi-legalization (like cannabis in the Netherlands) were quite similar in our sample: cocaine should be removed from its criminal context; cocaine is just as (non) dangerous as cannabis or alcohol; users themselves, not the State are responsible for their drug use; users would be able to exert better control over the quality of cocaine; people would be less easily 'seduced' by a forbidden fruit (less appeal). The latter motive was mentioned by the Antwerp respondents, but not by the Amsterdam users (unless Cohen included these answers in his residual category 'other'). Other unique answers were: there would be no taboo around the use of cocaine; consequently, this would offer better treatment perspectives; drug use is ineradicable anyway (so we must learn to live with it); and in the long run, the consumption of drugs would not increase.

The 'no criminal setting' motive is mentioned markedly more often by the Belgian respondents compared to the Dutch respondents. This might reflect a difference in current drug policies in both countries, or more accurately: a difference in the subjective perception of these policies by the respondents.

The motives for treating cocaine like heroin (and cocaine nowadays) most mentioned in our sample were: the hazards of cocaine; the fear that overall cocaine use would increase, especially among youngsters; and cocaine's danger of habit formation. The fear that more (young) people would start using cocaine was not mentioned by the Dutch respondents, as were arguments like 'it would not change anything for me personally, I can get it anyway' and 'the high price is a helpful restraint on my personal use'.[15]

Finally, it is striking that many motives behind preferred cocaine policies (whatever these may be) are usually inspired by a kind of general concern about drug use in society and about drug use by others, rather than by perceived personal profit. These respondents motivate their choice of a certain policy by saying that other people would be less or more seduced to use cocaine, that other people should get better treatment, that drug use by others would or would not increase, etc. This proves that our respondents rather than ego-centered, asocial and narrow-focused on their own drug use, and their own profits, are concerned about others' ability to control use.

Table 15.5.b   Motives behind preferred cocaine policy option, in the 1987 Amsterdam I sample and the 1997 Antwerp sample [*] [♠]

	Amsterdam I N=148	Antwerp N=98
Motives for policy like alcohol	N	N
No criminal setting	6	11 + 6 [♣]
Same risks	11	12
Own responsibility	8	9
Quality control	-	9
Less appeal	-	4
Better treatment possibilities	-	3
Drug use is ineradicable	-	2
Removes taboo	-	2
Price moderation	4	1
Other	10	2
Total	**39**	**61**
Motives for policy like cannabis	N	N
No criminal setting	10	14 + 5 [♣]
Same risks	8	6
Less appeal	-	6
Own responsibility	3	4
Quality control	3	4
Drug use is ineradicable	-	3
Price moderation	4	2
Better treatment possibilities	-	2
Drug use will not increase	-	2
Removes taboo	-	1
Other	18	10
Total	**46**	**59**
Like alcohol and like cannabis summated	N	N
No criminal setting	16	36
Same risks	19	18
Own responsibility	11	13
Quality control	3	13
Less appeal	-	10
Drug use is ineradicable	-	5
Better treatment possibilities	-	5
Removes taboo	-	3
Price moderation	8	3
Drug use will not increase	-	2
Other	28	12
Total	**85**	**120**
Motives for policy like heroin	N	N
Too dangerous	19	17
If not, drug use would increase	-	16
Like addictive	27	6
High price puts check on use	-	4
Should remain exclusive	3	4
Difficult to handle	6	3
I can get it anyway	-	3
Other	8	3
Total	**63**	**56**

[*]   More than one answer was possible
[♣]   The first figure bears on arguments like 'users will not be chased by police, will not be prosecuted, will not end up in prison'; the second refers to arguments like 'cocaine will not be distributed by criminals, by organized crime'.

This was also observed by other authors (Erickson, 1989: 175-188; Cohen, 1989: 119) and explained by referring to a kind of general principle: *'Many were of the opinion that while they themselves were able to control their use of these drugs, they were not confident that other people would be so successful in this regard.'* (Mugford & Cohen, 1989: 47). This *tendency to be 'tougher' for others*, is also reflected in the statistically significant over-representation of ex-users opting for cocaine to be treated like heroin in the 1987 Amsterdam sample (Cohen, 1989: 119). The proportion of ex-users among the respondents opting for cocaine to be treated like heroin in the Antwerp sample (27.8%) is higher than the proportion of ex-users in the total sample (18.9%), but the difference is not statistically significant.[16] The fact that one third of the respondents are in favor of a repressive cocaine policy, despite the fact they were able to use moderately, to lace periods of abstinence, or to quit cocaine use, also surprised Cohen. We found no statistically significant differences between the subsample of respondents in favor of a repressive policy (like heroin) and the total sample. Yet, we find the following marked differences:[17] the subsample of respondents in favor of a repressive policy tends to contain more female respondents, more high-level users and more injectors/freebasers during period of heaviest use, and more ex-users. These respondents also tend to report more craving when cocaine is around, more obsession with cocaine (at any point in time), and more problems with temporary abstinence or quitting.

Although most differences found are not statistically significant, our data and the data from the Amsterdam samples indicate that the participants regard present policies as less negative for themselves than for the 'others'. *Most (ex-)users of cocaine perceive themselves as better able to control use than the others, probably because they have learned to cope with the dangers of cocaine and with the discomforts caused by the official policy, but at the same time they attribute a smaller capacity for controlling cocaine use to others* (see also Cohen, 1989: 119; Cohen & Sas, 1995: 79). Indeed, the Antwerp respondents in favor of a repressive policy tend to report more problems (craving, obsession, problems with temporary abstinence). Although they themselves are aware of the 'dangers' of cocaine, have sophisticated opinions about cocaine and cocaine policy (both the pros and cons), and exhibit patterns of moderated and controlled use, they feel others have to be stopped before it is too late.

15.6. CONCLUSION

Some forms of cocaine use have negative consequences and other forms are relatively safe. Eighty-three respondents (77.6% of the total sample) perceive themselves as 'controlled' users (77.6%) 11 see themselves as 'uncontrolled' users (10.3%), and 4 interviewees find both 'controlled' and 'uncontrolled' aspects in their use pattern (3.7%). The subsample of respondents who perceive themselves as 'uncontrolled users' differs markedly from the total sample in that it contains higher proportions of male respondents, of treated, convicted and registered respondents, of high-level users, intravenous users and freebasers during the period of heaviest use and the last three months in the subsample. Among those who perceive themselves as 'uncontrolled users', life time prevalence and last two weeks prevalence of opiate use as well as life time prevalence of combined use of opiates and cocaine are higher.

The following indicators of *'controlled' use* were reported most frequently by the Antwerp respondents: periodical abstinence, refusing cocaine when it is offered (in other words: resisting craving), small doses and/or low frequency of use (and consequently, low level of use), fewer active efforts to obtain cocaine, other activities taking priority over cocaine use, positive reasons for using cocaine. The most important indicators of *'uncontrolled' use* perceived by the Antwerp respondents were: being unable to stop using (the *binge* pattern), too large doses and overt signs of 'over'-dosing, financial problems, lying about one's cocaine use, a high frequency of use, active efforts to obtain cocaine, and talking about cocaine incessantly.

These indicators of controlled and uncontrolled use serve as boundary protection mechanisms: they keep users from going over the edge with cocaine, or allow them to climb back. These mechanisms help to prevent disruption of everyday life in which users have invested. Furthermore, counterexamples help the user to draw the line between use and abuse, to set boundaries of appropriate cocaine use, and to develop informal rules to prevent crossing these limits.

Indeed, friends, acquaintances, partners, relatives, and others can serve as examples of how not to use cocaine. Respondents report having been deterred by other patterns of use for various reasons: because these people use too much, too frequently, and consequently experience *negative physical effects* (such as nose problems, stomach problems, weight loss, exhaustion, etc.); because they engage in illegal activities or behavior looked down upon (such as prostitution); because of negative mental effects (such as aggression, greed, depression, apathy, arrogance, etc.); because they use cocaine intravenously or possess other 'junky'-like characteristics; etc. Some respondents declare that their own behavior in the past serves as a counterexample. They refer to a period in their own life when they used too much, too frequently, or when they injected or lost control over their cocaine use.

When asked about the changes between the first and the last occasion of cocaine use, most respondents report *a sense of increased mastery and control over the product*. Obviously, the initial hunger (curiosity) for new drug experiences has disappeared and several respondents report the emergence of (physical or psychological) tolerance for the drug, a steady increase of the dose taken, a feeling of having become more dependent on the drug, and a transition from snorting to a more direct route of ingestion (freebasing or injecting). However, *over the years most respondents have gained better knowledge* about the product, its (adverse) effects, the influence of set and setting factors, potential sources of supply, good and bad quality cocaine, other cocaine users, other types of drugs, etc. Many users have to go through a period of loss of control over the substance, or to learn about the negative and dangerous aspects, but in the end they are able to use the substance more consciously and prevent cocaine from taking priority over other activities (such as job, family life, etc.).

The data presented in this chapter indicate that Becker's description (1973) of the process of social learning in three stages (learning the technique, learning to perceive the effects, and learning to enjoy the effects) can be expanded. The process of 'becoming a cocaine user' does not end when the user has learned to master the proper technique (snorting, freebasing, or injecting) and to enjoy the effects caused by the drug. The analysis of subjective indicators of 'controlled' and 'uncontrolled' use, of counterexamples, of perceived changed in cocaine use patterns, and the informal rules developed through the years, shows that the drug user continuously learns from his/her own experience and that of others and the process of 'becoming a *controlled* cocaine user' is nearing completion as knowledge about the product extends.

The process of social learning, i.e. becoming a controlled cocaine user, is further illustrated in the next four chapters. They discuss the impact of family members, partners, fellow workers and friends on the respondent's use and conversely, how the respondent's cocaine use affects those around him/her.

Finally, respondents were asked about their preferred official drug policy relating to cocaine. A majority of the respondents prefer a more liberal and tolerant cocaine policy, because cocaine would be removed from its criminal context; cocaine is just as (non) dangerous as cannabis or alcohol; users themselves not the State are responsible for their drug use; users would be able to exert more control over the quality of cocaine; people would be less easily 'seduced' by a forbidden fruit (less appeal); there would be no taboo on the use of cocaine; etc. One third of our sample opted to maintain the current repressive policy (like for heroin). The motives for such a policy most mentioned in our sample were: the hazards of cocaine; the fear of an overall increase in use, especially among youngsters; and the risk of habit formation.

Many motives behind their preferred cocaine policies (whatever these may be) are usually inspired by a kind of general concern about drug use in society and about drug use by others, rather than by perceived personal profit. *Many respondents are of the opinion that while they themselves are able to control their use, they are not confident that other people would be so successful.* This tendency to be 'tougher' for others, is also reflected by the over-representation of ex-users opting for cocaine to be treated like heroin in both samples. *Respondents consider present policies less negative for themselves than for 'others', probably because they have learned to cope with the dangers of cocaine and with the discomforts caused by the official policy, but at the same time they attribute a weaker capacity for controlling cocaine use to others.* Indeed, the Antwerp respondents in favor of a repressive policy tend to report more problems (craving, obsession, difficulties with temporary abstinence).

NOTES

1   See Chapter 3, p. 92-93.
2   See Chapter 12, p. 265-272.
3   See Chapter 13, p. 289-290.
4   See Chapter 5, p. 125-137 and Chapter 11, p. 248 and 252.
5   See Chapter 14, p. 307.
6   See Chapter 14, p. 310-312.
7   Other indicators mentioned by respondents were: insufficient job performance, pushy towards other users, more combined use of cocaine with other drugs, avoiding responsibilities for family members, selling drugs, prostitution, living during the night only, unrealistic self-image, isolation from friends, using during the day, overdosing, being in treatment, being unreliable to other friends, anxiety, suicide attempts...
8   See Chapter 5, p. 149.
9   See Chapter 11, p. 248, 252 and 254-255.
10 See Chapter 12, p. 267-271.
11 See Chapter 11, p. 250.
12 See Chapter 14, p. 316-317.

13 See Chapter 6, p. 161-162 and 164.

14 See Chapter 4, p. 110-111.

15 The addictive potential of cocaine was mentioned far less often by our respondents, compared to the Amsterdam I sample (Cohen, 1989: 119). This is consistent with our findings in Chapter 11, where 'creates physical dependence' as a disadvantage of cocaine ranked higher in both Dutch samples (although we did not find a difference regarding the disadvantage of 'creates psychological dependence'). See Chapter 11, p. 250-253.

16 In their follow-up study of 64 cocaine users from the Amsterdam I sample, Cohen and Sas (1993: 43) found that non-users tended to prefer a more restrictive cocaine policy, although the difference was not statistically significant.

17 We find no differences for level of use during the first year of use, life time prevalence of intravenous use, life time prevalence of opiate use, last two weeks prevalence of opiate use, life time prevalence of combined use of cocaine and opiates, prevalence of craving when cocaine is not around, having a financial limit of cocaine purchase, proportion of registered respondents, having been convicted, reporting informal rules, etc.

CHAPTER 16

COCAINE USERS AND THEIR FAMILY

16.1. INTRODUCTION

Cocaine use does not only bring both benefit and harm to the user, it also potentially impacts on people around the user. Illicit drug use in general, and cocaine use in particular, takes place in a social context, and those around the user often respond to the use in particular ways. The social contexts of use thus are affected by the use, and in turn influence it. Parents, siblings, partners, fellow workers, and friends are major sources of social responses to illicit drug use, and indeed of efforts to control behavior that is judged as problematic. This chapter explores the patterns of interactions between cocaine users and their family (i.e. parents and/or siblings). The following chapters discuss the interactions between cocaine users and their partners (Chapter 17), their fellow workers (Chapter 18), and their friends (Chapter 19).

In the context of everyday life, the influence of parents and family in the socialization of drug use occupies a special place. To illustrate the family influences on the process of socialization into cocaine use, paragraph 16.2 explores four major family variables that are relevant to the development of controlled drug use, and the effects of the context of the family on the respondents' cocaine use. The effects of our subjects' cocaine use on their family life are described in paragraph 16.3. Illicit drug use is typically taboo within the family, and the respondents' accounts are presented in paragraph 16.4. Some respondents are parents themselves, others may consider having children in a foreseeable future. Paragraph 16.5 describes their views on parenthood and illicit drug use. In paragraph 16.6 we argue that siblings may well be a distinct source of social responses to the respondents' cocaine use.

16.2. EFFECTS OF FAMILY RELATIONS ON COCAINE USE

The interaction of drug use with family life has been much better explored for alcohol than for illicit drugs such as cocaine. Drinking at home under parental supervision often begins during childhood and the early teenage years. During this period, larger and more potent alcoholic drinks generally become available in family-centered activities – a few glasses of wine, a sherry, a couple of glasses of beer – usually on occasions such as birthday celebrations or Christmas. This gradual introduction to, and development of, drinking behavior serves a useful developmental function: *a young person learns to use alcohol in appropriate ways* (Zinberg, 1982: 16-18). During this period the acquisition of fitting drinking behavior is not a problem for the majority of teenagers. A minority report excessive alcohol use and alcohol-related problems. According to Foxcroft and Lowe (1997) four major family variables are relevant to the development of drinking:

- *Modelling/imitation*: In imitating someone else's behavior an individual is simply modelling his/her behavior on that of another, and the salience of the model increases with the significance of the other person, in that individuals are more likely to imitate the behavior of significant others. Within a family, parents and older siblings are typically the most salient significant others on whom individuals model their drinking behavior;
- *Social reinforcement*: Social reinforcement takes place when an individual internalizes definitions and exhibits behaviors and values approved of by significant others. In this context, the attitude of parents' to their offspring's drinking behavior is an important factor. For example, parents may disapprove, approve, or be indifferent toward their offspring's actual or potential drinking behavior.
- *Supportive behaviors* are those aspects of family life which foster in an individual feelings that he or she is basically accepted and approved of as a person by the parents and the family. Supportive families are warm, loving and rewarding. Thus, family support is central to the development of emotional bonds.
- *Controlling behaviors* are those family interactions concerned with rules and rule negotiation, flexibility, power relationships, punishment, authority and permissiveness. Such behaviors generally serve to direct the behavior of the individual in a manner desirable to the parents.

This chapter presents our empirical data on these family variables as a source for 'controlled' or 'moderate' cocaine use. They suggest that modelling and imitation processes regarding illicit drug use are usually non-existent, and that social reinforcement, supportive and controlling behaviors indeed can have an important impact on an individual's cocaine use.

16.2.1. Negative effects

When asked about specific facts in their life that have influenced their pattern of cocaine use, 11 interviewees report that some particular domestic situation may have contributed to an increase in their cocaine use. During the open interviews, another 18 respondents (and some of the former 11) either explicitly or implicitly refer to negative effects of family relationships and domestic situations on their cocaine use.

> *Yes, that my parents kicked me out, that I couldn't use my name anymore, I mean, it really was a disgrace, I was really kicked out. And to work it off, I used more. At first it was nice... but I mean, the first time, it was after a rape by someone I knew, so since then I started to take it out. I couldn't express myself. To work it off, I couldn't be angry with that person, so I worked it off on myself. I had myself tattooed and I started to take a lot of coke.* [H/1/25]

> *Respondent: Actually, it was a really conscious choice to start using. I wanted it deliberately: heroin, cocaine, whatever, speed... I think it had... I had a lot of problems at home, lack of attention, pff... really, it was 'hell'...*
> *Interviewer: Why did you start using consciously?*
> *Respondent: I thought it had something. I wanted to know what it was like to be addicted. I thought it was incredible, when I was 17, so I... and also, even at home I wanted to be a rebel, like: okay, if you're bad, then I'm going to be bad and use a lot of drugs...* [I/1/01]

These stories deal with negative effects of family relations on the respondent's cocaine use. A constant item in all these reports is a *disrupted family life*: the parents are divorced, one or both parents died unexpectedly, alcoholism, sexual abuse and/or physical violence by a parent or a relative, etc. Some of these respondents were separated from their siblings and institutionalized in reform school or a re-educational facility.

My parents were divorced when I was 13. I was only 16 when I realized what was going on, because that divorce had happened, but it was never discussed, and... As the oldest child I somehow got the responsibility over my younger brothers, because my mother started to drink, she has been a very heavy alcoholic. So that's why the education of my brothers was a burden on my shoulders, because my father suggested that I had to take care of my younger brothers. After the divorce he went abroad. He didn't want to have any contact with his children either... But there were very heavy conflicts between him and my mother, big law suits, alimony problems, that stuff... [...] I took advantage of that situation as well because, my mother was drinking, so she was eh... well eh... especially in the weekend, in the week too, but especially in the weekend she was so drunk she didn't have any awareness of time, so she couldn't check at what time we came home. [Q/0/01]

These data are consistent with other studies which have noted significant correlations between variables such as drug and alcohol use by family members, sexual abuse, depressive symptoms, and illicit drug abuse. There are indications that the incidence of childhood sexual abuse and physical violence in populations of drug addicted individuals is high (Benward & Densen-Gerber, 1971; Teets, 1990; Young, 1990). It has been suggested that sexual abuse may be an etiologic factor in women's substance abuse (Davis, 1990).

Furthermore, parental alcohol abuse sets the stage for a form of parenting that is characterized by inattentiveness and lack of parental protection (i.e. a lack of supportive behaviors, see above). This parenting style, which leads to the psychological isolation of the child, can make the child more vulnerable for substance abuse (Miller *et al.*, 1987). Some of the 29 respondents who report on the interrelationship between their cocaine use and family life, say they had lacked a close relationship with their parents or other family members. Some respondents blame their parents for a lax education.[1] They believe their parents did not exert sufficient control over their children, by being too flexible, too permissive and by failing to provide rule setting and rule negotiation (i.e. a lack of controlling behaviors, see above). Others state that family life was characterized by material comfort on the one hand and emotional deficit and communication breakdown on the other. They experienced their families as non-supportive (i.e. cold, not loving, and not rewarding):

My father is managing director of a firm, so he's the rich guy in the story while my mother can just manage. Yes, that is a fact in the whole story: the artificial wealth versus the cozy just-managing. Also towards my friends: my friends know my mother, my father doesn't know my friends. Now it is getting somewhat better, now he has re-married and we decided to leave the past for what it was. Things happened and I still don't know everything about them, but they still work through in today's relationships, but we decided to let it be and to see what we've got left and to go on with that. It was somewhat artificial sometimes, but it's okay. [R/0/07]

For my parents love means giving money. So I didn't really know affection, I think it has to do with that as well, that I am more creative and more socially focused, and they are really productive-minded. They like me and stuff, but a hug? No. [...] I think that's why I went to

these people more and more, and maybe that's why I started to use. It's not like: they do it,
so I have to do that too. [...] What strikes me, is that these are often people who had the sa-
me problem, that they didn't get enough attention at home emotionally. [H/1/18]

For some of these respondents, escapist motives played a role in the start or the continuation of their illicit drug use. Disruptive events in childhood or adolescence, a broken family, or a disturbed relationship with one or both parents may all have negative
effects on cocaine use patterns:

I've always been spoiled, so I have been quite mothered, even when I went to live alone. I
didn't like that, in a way. Not that I didn't love my parents or so, but I wanted to be inde-
pendent, in a way. So then I broke up with my parents, quite suddenly in fact, I broke up with
my background, with my friends, from one day to the next. And then I didn't use for quite a
while, but I think it is also one of the consequences of that breach, like: I can finally do
whatever I want, and fuck the world, they can all get lost, I do whatever I feel like. [...] That
was broken up suddenly, and I think my starting to use was a consequence of that. [H/0/05]

Yes, the emotional pressure, I'm on my own in life, I have very little support from my parents
and stuff, life is hard now. And so there are these moments you say: pff, fuck it! That you just
feel like having a big line and drinking a whisky... [H/1/19]

Between these 29 respondents and the rest of the sample, we do not find any marked
differences for level of use during initial year of use, level of use during period of
heaviest use, life time and last month prevalence of opiate use. But one in three of
these 29 respondents have been in contact with a drug treatment agency (compared to
one in five of the total sample). Furthermore, the proportions of respondents who injected during the first year of use, who injected during their period of heaviest use, and
who combine the use of cocaine and heroin, are larger than in the total sample.

Of the 29 respondents who refer to negative effects of family relationships on their
cocaine use, 13 belong to snowball chain H and 3 to snowball chain F. These snowball
chains also contain larger proportions of respondents who have been convicted for a
felony, who have had contact with drug treatment agencies, who report difficulties
when abstaining or cutting back their cocaine use, who mainly use cocaine intravenously, and who report more criminal activities in order to obtain (money for) cocaine.[2]

16.2.2. Positive effects

The family can also be a source of positive social responses.[3] For example, in Chapter
12 we reported that the source of informal help when trying to quit cocaine most often
mentioned was 'parents'.[4] Five of the 29 respondents who report on the interrelationship between their cocaine use and family life reported seeking help from their parents
when trying to quit. With respect to cocaine the issue of family influence was also
tackled more directly by asking respondents about pressures from family members to
cut down on their cocaine use or to quit. Ten respondents reported having received
comments from their parents that typically referred to the respondent's physical condition, appearance and character changes:

Yes, that I became thin, that I looked bad, they also saw that I didn't eat anymore, my
mother saw it as well, you know, in the end I weighed 53 kilos. [H/0/23]

When I was already using quite some coke, my parents said: this is not right, you have changed. [X/0/01]

About half of these respondents claimed that these comments did not have any effect on their behavior, that they felt indifferent, or reacted by feigning acceptance and compliance, and tended to keep further use hidden:

Unless my mother: 'You don't realize what it does to your health. Go on, go on, I'll have to bury you one day'. [...] It makes me laugh. She's right to talk like that, I can understand that, and often I say I'm not doing it anymore, to please her. Because it hurts her. So I lie. For her it's drugs, and drugs are bad. [C/0/12]

But other respondents report that repeated comments from family members, often combined with efforts at social control by friends, partners and significant others, did have an effect on their cocaine use. In the long run, so these interviewees say, they decided to quit or to cut down on their cocaine use:

Respondent: For a long time I've looked very bad, I lost a lot of weight, I weighed 11 kilos less compared to now, so... I really looked emaciated... Then I started to think about it, when they asked my mother: 'Does she have a kind of incurable disease?' And friends who said to me: 'Look at the state you're in?!', that kind of things, 'It's not possible'.
Interviewer: How did you react the moment you heard those things?
Respondent: I didn't care at that moment. The thinner I became, the more I liked it. I didn't care what they said. And when my parents said: 'You look bad, look at yourself. It went in one ear and out the other. I didn't give a damn.
Interviewer: Did those remarks have any effect?
Respondent: At that moment it doesn't affect you, but when you are alone at home, you think about it, in fact, but you don't want to show anyone else. I must say, when I was alone, I thought about it. [Z/1/04]

Respondent: They told me that I had to go about it in a different way, that I had to drop that guy, and this and that, and that I had to look for other friends, and just, that I had to quit.
Interviewer: How did you respond to it?
Respondent: I was usually angry. I was always like: yes, I want that too, but it isn't that easy, and yes, I was always quite pissed off. But then, once I had quit three, four or five days, I looked at it in a completely different way again. When I had just used, yes, then I went along with them, right? Like: yes, yes, I will quit and this and that, you know. I didn't care much at that moment, right? But later, I did agree with them. [H/1/04]

Much of our knowledge about the impact of the use of cocaine and other illicit (and licit) substances on the family, and about the family's response, has been based on clinical populations, i.e. on families where the drug use of one or more members has been defined as problematic enough to receive clinical attention. However, most respondents quoted in these paragraphs did not have contact with any drug treatment agency. These data give us the opportunity to observe earlier stages in family processes concerning drug use. They bring into focus families where no treatment ever occurs, where problems may have been prevented or controlled or adapted to by the family process itself (and other informal interactions, as discussed in the next chapters). Of course, there is a limit to how far our data can go in understanding the rich diversity of family interaction around illicit drug use, and the sequences of events which result in successful control within the family or which lead to formal treatment. For this, we may need more qualitative studies focusing on particular kinds of family relationships and circumstances.

16.3. EFFECTS OF COCAINE USE ON FAMILY RELATIONS

All respondents were asked if their use of cocaine either improved or worsened their relationship with their family. Table 16.3.a presents our data from the Antwerp sample together with data from the San Francisco sample in 1986-1988 (Waldorf *et al.*, 1991: 166-167).[5] The data from both samples show remarkable similarities. Almost half of all the respondents in both samples state that cocaine had no effect on their relationships with their families. In both samples, more respondents report 'no effect' on family relationships than on other interpersonal relationships (spouse or lover, friends, the people they work with).[6] Thus, cocaine has the least impact on family-of-origin relationships.

The fact that so many respondents in both samples report no effect of cocaine on family relationships is consistent with our findings on control mechanisms and informal rules.[7] It was shown in Chapter 14 that many cocaine users refrain from using cocaine when they are expected to work or to meet family members (parents). Ideally, their cocaine use should not have any effect on their relationship with family members. These data suggest that at least some of our respondents make conscious efforts to ensure that their cocaine use does not interfere with these relationships.

Table 16.3.a   Influence of cocaine on family relations, in two samples

Family relations	Improved	Deteriorated	Both	No effect	N
Antwerp sample (1997)	4.3	43.5	5.4	46.7	92 [*]
San Francisco sample (1986-1988)	3.1	39.5	7.1	50.2	225

[*] N is not 111 due to missing data (19 respondents had 'no opinion' on this issue)

When cocaine does have effects on the relationship with the family, however, these tend to be negative. In both samples, less than 5% of the respondents say cocaine had any positive effects on relationships with family members; less than one in ten report mixed effects on family. Approximately two in five respondents report that cocaine has 'deteriorated' or damaged their family relationships. When asked about their childhood, their upbringing and the relations with their father and mother in particular, eight respondents spontaneously told us about the negative effects of their use of cocaine and other illicit drugs on family relationships. All their accounts contain conflicts and arguments between parents (or one of them) and children over illicit drug use. Typically, the respondent's drug use was not the only subject of discussion, but it was often a factor that intensified existing conflicts and misunderstandings.

In three cases the arguments about drugs caused a (temporary) rupture in the family: one respondent ran away, another was involuntary confined at the request of her parents, and one respondent was barred from her parental home. Respondents say that, as family relations deteriorated because of their cocaine use, they were inclined to use more or with increasing frequency.

Inner void, loneliness... I was really at odds with myself... Especially the period they kicked me out, when I was 17. That period they kicked me out, I used very much. Very much. Lone-

liness. They kicked me out of the house because of those problems with drugs, my parents saw me slipping further and further into it and they were told: 'You'd better kick her out of the house, so she has to decide for herself whether she sinks or swims'. Because I was also destroying the whole family. Sometimes I didn't come home for a week... or I left them worried, right? The stress, and that's how you get arguments... In the end they didn't wash my clothes anymore, I didn't get any food anymore, and at a particular moment, I went out, but I had to be back at one o'clock, but I had just taken a trip. So I came home at five o'clock the next night. And then they said: 'We declare war on you, you're not our daughter anylonger, and we want you to pack your bags and leave.' [H/1/28]

One respondent explains how her relationship with her parents has deteriorated since she decided to tell her mother about her cannabis use. In most cases, however, parents find out about their children's illicit drug use by accident. They either find some cannabis, pills or powder in the house or the respondent gets into some medical or judicial problems.

I haven't been arrested, but I have been grassed on twice, and I had my house searched by the BOB [i.e. special investigation units of the state police, TD], I've been taken in, I sat in jail for one night or one day. But they never found anything. And my dad, who had never cried before, was crying: my son is addicted to a joint. [L/0/02]

At least 4 respondents say that part of the family problems around drugs were caused or intensified by their parents' apparent ignorance about illicit substances. This is consistent with the data presented in Chapter 4, indicating that parents (and non-users and official agencies) are seen as a source of 'false' information about cocaine.[8] Two respondents also believe their parents failed to see the seriousness of their drug problems. Again, we find that some respondents blame their parents for being too permissive and not setting or negotiating rules about illicit drug use.

I will never blame my parents for anything, but when I have kids, I know one thing, you have to keep them, you have to have them under control, and it's true, sometimes it is difficult, but you have to be able to assess things rightly. Because my parents were older, in fact from an older generation than most parents of people of my age, they couldn't assess the situation rightly. My mother comes from a very Catholic family, very religious, educated goody-goody, and then you can't assess the evil in the world, cocaine and drugs... they don't know that, it's taboo. Now they think completely differently, but if they had thought about it then, it would never have happened. But before they realized what was happening and so, that is... Many people close their eyes, right? They don't want to see it, right? It's your own child, you're too emotionally involved, right? You're too close, right? But once they realized it, it was hard for them to accept. [H/1/04]

16.4. THE TABOO OF ILLICIT DRUG USE

During the second interview respondents were asked whether they had ever lied to any one about their cocaine use. Of the 107 respondents, nine respondents (8.4% of the sample) did not answer this question and ninety-eight respondents (91.6%) report ever having lied about it to other people. Seventy-four participants or 69.1% of the sample referred to their relation with their parents or other family members (such as grandparents, aunts and uncles, etc.).[9]

Sixty-one interviewees (57.0% of the total sample) report having lied to their parents about their cocaine use. Most respondents interpret lying about drugs as lying explicitly or denying when parents inquire after their illicit drug use. Some respondents also indicate that they consciously avoid the topic in the company of family members and that they would never bring up the subject themselves.

A white lie. My parents never asked it, they never saw it. So I never had the opportunity to lie about it. [B/0/02]

I never lied, but with some people, it never comes up and I will just do everything to make sure it doesn't come up. Just for security reasons, because I think some people ought not to know. People I work with, people I study with, family. [K/1/03]

Whatever the interpretation given to the term 'lying', all answers indicate that the use of cocaine is strictly taboo in most families. Diaz *et al.* (1992: 301) reached similar conclusions in the Barcelona study. Respondents usually argue that their parents are 'indoctrinated' by the false information from official sources such as the media, the government, school, the police, etc.[10] Furthermore, participants argue that their parents are ignorant about illicit drugs. Often these statements have a reproachful undertone:

No, my parents don't know anything about it. Never. I have come home completely under the influence of coke, of trips, of speed. My parents just don't know that, and they don't see the difference, I guess. [I/1/17]

Yes, to my parents, although I didn't have to lie very much. They preferred that I didn't take it so... they believed whatever they wanted to believe so you don't have to make much effort, right? [H/1/31]

On the other hand, others appear not to blame their parents for being 'indoctrinated' or 'ignorant', but they prefer to hide their illicit drug use because their parents would feel hurt or think they have failed as a parent, because they would panic, or because the respondent would get problems (labeled a problem child, seen as a problematic drug user).

To my parents. Because I preferred that my parents didn't know and because my mother takes it all too seriously, it keeps her awake, and I was like: what you don't know can't hurt you. I'm not open about it because people always make it worse than it actually is. [H/0/16]

To people who shouldn't know anything about it and to people... I know for sure that they will not understand it, or that it will take much trouble to explain it all, and I don't want it. For example, my parents don't know it and I won't try to explain to them, because it will hurt them so much and it will take me so much pain, and in the end they won't understand it anyway. So... I prefer to lie. [L/0/01]

Of those 61 interviewees who report having lied to their parents about cocaine, the majority (56 participants) also report that they also hide or lie about the use of other illicit substances such as cannabis, MDMA ('ecstasy') and amphetamines ('speed'). In most families, the use of all illicit drugs is taboo. This taboo may lead some respondents to conceal their cocaine use from their parents, even if they got into serious trouble with it:

Interviewer: If you had problems with coke, what would you do?
Respondent: Pff, I haven't thought about that yet. First I would try to do something about it
on my own, and if that didn't work, I might go to a treatment agency. And I would make sure
my parents didn't know about it.
Interviewer: Why?
Respondent: Because if my mother knew about it, she would be very disappointed in me. And
I don't want that to happen. [G/0/01]

Five respondents, however, claim that their families ignore the taboo on cannabis use: their parents do not prohibit smoking a joint and it is openly talked about.

For example, my parents smoke a joint every once and a while, so they all know that, and I
think they know me well enough to know that I have it under control. If they saw that I have
no job, that I can't afford to pay my rent, then it would be a problem, but if they ask ques-
tions, and I can explain it properly, I think they wouldn't object. [I/1/09]

Surprisingly, thirteen respondents (12.1% of the total sample) claim their parents know they are regular cocaine users. This does not mean, however, that all these users spontaneously told their parents about their illicit drug use. One respondent was forced to tell his parents about his (excessive) cocaine use because he planned to enter a residential treatment program. Most others told their parents only after some time:

My mother lived through the 'flower power', so she knows how it works. My father would
say: 'Just make sure you don't get addicted to it', because they know themselves, yes, they
lived in that period and tell stories about it, that they tripped once and... there are probably
few parents who dare to say those things, but it's a completely different relationship we
have, right? [I/1/10]

My parents don't approve of it. But I'm telling you: my mother sees it and she knows that
I'm dealing with it in a sensible way at the moment, that I'm not exaggerating with it. Be-
cause the other day, she said: 'I didn't receive any complaints from your boss, so it must be
alright'. But she knows about it, I think she has the right to know what I'm doing. [R/0/08]

Three respondents indicate that they can talk about their cocaine use with one parent but not with the other. Typically, these respondents revealed their cocaine use to the parent who fostered feelings of trust, comfort and belonging:

Let me tell you, my parents knew, I mean, my father didn't, but my mother... I found it nice
to talk about it with my mother, she said: 'Okay, if you just take care', she fully believed in
me, and when someone gives you his trust... yes, well... [I/1/14]

In general, our data indicate that most parents of our respondents are dramatically opposed to illicit drug use and to the possibility of controlled drug use. Ofcourse, a trivial explanation is the fact that most parents get their information about drugs, if any, from the mass media, the government, the police, etc. Most official sources view illicit drug consumption as a plague, a social disease, and it is understandable that parents want to protect their children from such danger. But if parents tell their children not to use drugs because they are harmful (cf. the official discourse), the youngsters disregard that advice because their own experiences have told them otherwise. Their using group and the drug subculture reinforce their own discovery that drug use in and of itself is not bad or evil and that the warnings coming from the adult world are unrealistic. If parents try a different strategy and tell young people that some drugs are all right (alcohol, tobacco, sedatives, hypnotics, marihuana,...) but others have a high risk component and should be avoided (cocaine, heroin, MDMA,...), their position again is vulnerable.

16.5. COCAINE USERS AS PARENTS

In the Antwerp sample twenty-three respondents have one or more children (20.7%). Four of these respondents have children who live elsewhere, and nineteen of them live with (some of) their children at home:[11] During the second open interview six of these cocaine users who have children elaborated on their ideas and experience with their own children. One respondent had given birth to her first baby a few months prior to the interview, another was expecting a second child at the time of interview. Both young mothers indicated they wanted to give their children a supportive family: warm, loving and rewarding. Obviously, they were determined not to let their cocaine use interfere with their duties as a mother. Two other respondents have children of 9 and 10 years old respectively. One of them explains how she informed her daughter about her cocaine use:

Respondent: I don't even lie to the children. I've been very open with the children about smoking joints and stuff, I've never hidden that. I will hide the coke use, because I find it harder to explain it properly to them, they're still quite young... Because I find it another drug than hash... But one moment, my daughter questioned me about it, because she had noticed some things here and there, and then I just told her. Then I don't lie to her.
Interviewer: What did you tell her?
Respondent: The way it was. She had heard someone say: 'Do you have some white?' or something. And she's quite a clever girl, so she asked: 'What is that 'white' you're talking about?' So I just told her: 'That is coke'. Because for them it's... 'Are you addicted then?' and stuff. I said 'no' ... and... that's how I explained her. [H/1/14]

Another two respondents have adolescent children. For them, chances that their children have experimented with illicit substances are quite real. This 32-year-old woman claims to have informed her 14-year-old daughter about her cocaine use, but not her own parents:

Respondent: Well actually it's quite easy now, the other night she [her daughter, TD] went to that 'Thunderdome-party' in the Sports Hall [i.e. a covered stadium, TD] and so I take her there and I pick her up again, and indeed, I tell her 'Don't do this and don't do that'. And then she says 'No, I won't do that, because actually I don't... I've seen it enough with you, I don't like it at all' [she laughs]. In fact I find that a nice concomitant point. And she's really honest in those things, I think.
Interviewer: And what if she told you that she experimented with some drugs?
Respondent: I find that quite difficult, I've already asked myself that question, because I think, I'm very glad with that openness, but I don't know what I would do with that openness when she told me that. On the one hand I wouldn't want to punish her, because she honestly admitted 'I did that', although I have done it myself as well, but I would always tell her: 'Because I know it myself, I know how wrong things can go, and that's why I don't want it for you, maybe I want it myself, but I am bigger and you are smaller, and I don't want it for you, because you're still my child'. I would say that in any case, but I find it a difficult as-

pect. I don't know to what extent you can impose sanctions, or whether you have to control, I find that quite difficult.
Interviewer: Okay. Your parents, do they know you have experimented with some drugs?
Respondent: I know they know that I've experimented with marihuana, but that's all they know, I think. And what they think about it, I don't know exactly. But they are confident about it, I've told them then 'I don't do that because I can't really bear weed because it makes me too tired.' And so they just accepted that.
Interviewer: And what if they would ask you: do you use coke?
Respondent: I think I would say something like: 'I have done it once'. I wouldn't say I do it now, but 'I've done that a few times'. And they would probably fit that into my turbulent past. [K/1/03]

But also respondents who do not have any children talk about their plans for their future children. Most of these interviewees claim they would stop using cocaine or cut down on their use if they had children. As a reaction to their experience with their own parents, they typically want to create a trusting relationship with their children. Instead of avoiding the issue of drugs or panicking when their children ask about illicit drugs, they want to be straightforward with them. These stories show that most respondents have a clear idea of the possible interactions between family relationships and illicit drug use. They are aware of the shortcomings of their own upbringing, and they are determined not to make the same 'mistakes':

When I have kids later, I want to have an honest relationship with my children, I want them to tell me everything, everything. I want them to be able to talk to me about anything, about sex, about drugs, anything... I want them to be honest with me. And when they take drugs: I won't be happy with it of course, not at all, but I will try to give them an education, to tell them in advance what they are starting with and how they are doing. And yes, I just hope they stay off it, but I think a lot depends on the education, and in talking frequently. [...] I think that when they'll ask me about it later, that I will honestly tell them I did it too. So I think it depends on the education how children react to it and which decision they take, right? [Z/1/04]

16.6. THE ROLE OF SIBLINGS

Thirty-two respondents talked about their relationship with their brother(s) and/or sister(s). Of these 32 participants, 24 say at least one of their brothers or sisters knows about his/her cocaine use. Five claim none of their siblings know about it, and four interviewees do not know whether their brother/sister knows about it. Clearly, siblings are usually better informed about the respondent's cocaine use than his/her parents (see also Diaz *et al*, 1992: 302).

Twenty respondents believe that at least one of their siblings has experimented with illicit drugs (in most cases with various types of substances, including cocaine, and in some cases only with cannabis and/or MDMA). Eight participants think none of their brothers or sisters has experimented with illicit drugs and four interviewees do not know. Thus in most cases siblings are familiar with illicit drug use.

Three respondents state that their siblings have never experimented with illicit drugs and do not know anything about their drug use. Typically, these respondents draw a picture of their brother(s) and/or sister(s) as totally different individuals: they perceive them as different in character, part of a different peer group, with other preferences as far as music, leisure time activities, etc. is concerned. There is a big age difference, and they have a different relationship with their parents.

> *A brother and a sister, but they are thirty years older than I am. They are really stupid... they have never used anything, not even alcohol. They are really dry* [patronizing]. *I'm sorry, I'm not a racist* [she laughs], *that's not it, but come on... It is sad, isn't it, people who think the same all their life? It's so narrow-minded, no?* [H/1/24]

> *No, I would never start about that, because my brother drank a lot too, but I don't know anything about him, actually, I didn't know his life. And my sister, she's very conservative, she was like, when I used to go out alone: 'Are you going to a bar alone?!' I said: 'Yes, what am I supposed to do? Do I have to wait until they come and get me?' She was really traditional: she had a boyfriend, and he came to pick her up, and I surely can't tell that to her.* [I/1/02]

Of the 32 respondents who brought up the topic of brothers/sisters, however, 19 claim that their siblings both know that they are regular cocaine users and have experimented with illicit substances themselves. In many cases brothers and sisters have common friends and belong to the same peer group as the respondents. Some respondents had been initiated by an older brother or sister into the use of cocaine or other illicit drugs, or they had introduced (younger) siblings into drug use:

> *The first time I got it from my brother, he was older than me, he had been involved with it for a longer time, and I had already been looking for an occasion to try it, but yes, I didn't dare to ask it, and I didn't know the right people either, especially not then, so until he said: 'Look, you're my brother' and eh, yes, he sees it as psychonautism: the exploration of new worlds, and he wanted to involve me in it, and also from an emotional point of view, and so I started with LSD.* [R/0/01]

> *When my mother died* [a short silence] *I started to go out with my brother. But they had already started going out heavily. And so I started to go along with them. And my first experience was with pills* [i.e. XTC, TD] *and coke. [...] All through my brother. Through my brother and then I came to know his friends and then they immediately became my friends.* [V/1/01]

Most respondents report having used cocaine and/or other illicit substances with their brother(s) and/or sister(s). For some their brother's or sister's heavy use served as a counterexample, but most participants viewed their siblings (who had experience with illicit drug use) as a source of informal help and advice. These brothers or sisters were held to be the only trustworthy members of the family:

> *With my brother I learned to smoke my first joint, you know, in a discotheque. And my brother used to snort coke as well, right? And now he doesn't want to have anything to do with it anymore... But with my eldest brother, I have the best relationship, I always talk with him when I have problems. In that case I call my brother. Never my father or my mother. When I have problems, either with my girlfriend here or with anything else, I always call my brother.* [H/0/23]

> *My brother has always been a good example and... I think if I hadn't had that, it would have been completely different, I would have been deeper down in the dumps,* [she laughs] *I would have gone under even more, I mean, I would have gone the wrong way.* [H/1/32]

Siblings comment a good deal on each others' behavior. These comments may be made with a variety of intentions and effects – they may be instructional, humorous, or devastating- but many of them can be seen as efforts at social control, i.e. efforts to steer future behavior in a particular direction. Comments by siblings about cocaine use or other illicit drug use are often intended to evade problematic behavior.

My sister can understand it, because she also knows that, when I do it now, she knows, okay, he has to work tomorrow, he'll be okay, he'll be able to work too. So I do take it into account a lot. And she understands, and so she lets me do what I want, in a way. Sometimes, when I came from the discotheque, when I had exaggerated with it and so, she told me like: 'Hey, aren't you exaggerating' or so, and sometimes I said: 'Yes, you're right, and it won't happen again', and I was rapped my knuckles then, I like that we get along so well, right? Because sometimes you don't know it yourself, when you're too far. So I listen a lot to people who tell me that I... [X/0/01]

I only talked about it with him, when he knew I used stuff myself. He knew those friends I went out with by face, and when we were all sitting here, he saw what we were doing, he knew well enough what was going on... And then before we talked about it a few times, but especially about friends of his I knew as well and about whom he said: they have had a big problem with it, and so he came to tell me: 'Sister, you've got to be careful with that...' [I/1/12]

During the second interview, we asked our respondents whether they had ever commented on another person's cocaine use. Three respondents had commented to their siblings. One respondent said she had warned her brother that he was too occupied with cocaine. Her brother answered that she might be right about that, but that there was no need to worry. He felt in control of his cocaine use, and he was going to cut down. Another respondent told her sister to be careful because she was using too much. Her sister lived with a dealer who had cocaine available all the time, and she started to freebase. At first this respondent felt her remarks did not have any effect whatsoever, but after a few months her sister had left the dealer and cut down on her cocaine use. And the third respondent tells the following story:

Respondent: To my brother, yes. Well, you try to tackle it subtly, because those people are... it's very... it is very hard to persuade someone who has problems with it. Those people really live in an ivory tower. Little encouraging words and so... and make clear to them that there are alternatives to taking too much coke. And I talked about it with friends of theirs, and then, that we all could exert a kind of social control in the group of friends, that would not come across as paternalizing, because that has a completely contrary effect.
Interviewer: And how did your brother react?
Respondent: Like: 'Yes, yes, I all know that. Absolutely! You're right! I'll cut down.' But yes, usually they don't adhere to it. [R/0/01]

When asked whether anybody else had ever said anything about their own cocaine use, five respondents report having received comments from their brother or sister. Typically, they were urged to quit or cut down.

I sometimes had aggressive excesses. Fighting my sister, or shouting at my mother. My sister took a line of coke every now and then as well, but not that much, and she said: 'Richie, please, calm down, mom and dad might see through it', and stuff. So I said: 'Okay'. When my sister said: 'Calm down, you don't have to beat me', I said: 'Okay, I'll cut down'. [G/1/03]

For example, my sister said: 'Stay off it. You're on coke from the morning until the evening. Tom, slow down, boy. You ought to see yourself'. Well I know, I can't say to her: 'No, it's not true'. I know that cocaine is not the best thing for me, I know milk is healthier. [O/0/01]

16.7. CONCLUSION

The use of cocaine and other (licit and illicit) substances takes place in a social context, and those around the user often respond to the use in a particular way. The social contexts of cocaine use are thus affected by the use, and have an impact on the use. In the social context of everyday life, the influence of parents and family in the socialization of drug use occupies a special place. Unfortunately, the interaction of drug use with family life has been much better explored for alcohol than for illicit drugs such as cocaine. The family plays a formative role in the development of drinking behavior by providing young people with a gradual introduction to, and development of, drinking behavior. their first drinking experiences. Social reinforcement, supportive behaviors, controlling behaviors, and modelling and imitation processes are important factors in the development of appropriate drinking patterns. However, family socialization regarding the use of cocaine (or other illicit drugs) is markedly different from the gradual socialization of drinking behavior.

Parents may smoke tobacco and/or drink alcohol, but parental use of illicit substances is rarely reported by our respondents. Only a few respondents report occasional cannabis use by their parents. Thus, parents may provide their children with their first smoking and drinking experiences, but they do not serve as a role model for cocaine use. Within a family, siblings are the most salient significant others on whom individuals model their illicit drug use. Especially when brothers or sisters are part of the same peer group as the respondent (similar age, same preferences, etc.), they are the trusted family members rather than the parents, and they can play an important part in the onset (or the initiation) of cocaine use, in its continuation and in informal social control over illicit substances.

Gradual socialization of cocaine use by parental monitoring is impossible. First of all, the illegality of the substance has made cocaine use taboo in society in general, and in the family in particular. Most parents have taken over the official discourse from mass media, the police, governmental messages, etc. Most respondents report having lied to their parents about their cocaine use. They deny their illicit drug use, or consciously avoid the topic in the company of family members. Respondents view their parents as ignorant or 'indoctrinated' by official sources such as the media, the government, school, the police, etc.

On the other hand, our data indicate that respondents have internalized the abstinence-oriented definitions and values approved of by their parents to the extent that they prefer to hide their use of illicit drug use in order not to hurt their parents' feelings. Consequently, parents only come to know about their childrens' cocaine use after a considerable period of time, either because the drug use turns problematical (i.e. in need of clinical attention or discovered by the police) or because their children think the time is right for telling them.

Consistent with family systems theory, the sociology of deviance, developmental psychology and community psychology, our data confirm links between family support and control on the one hand and patterns of cocaine use on the other. Several respondents report that a particular domestic situation may have contributed to an increase in their cocaine use. Most stories deal with negative effects of family relations on the respondent's cocaine use. *A disrupted family life* (divorce, unexpected death of a loved one, alcoholism, sexual abuse and/or physical violence, separation, etc.), inattentive parenting, and lack of parental protection and support may have negative effects on cocaine use patterns. For some of these respondents, escapist motives played a role in the start or the continuation of their illicit drug use.

Among the respondents who refer to negative effects of family relationships on their cocaine use, the proportions of those who injected during the first year of use, who injected during their period of heaviest use, and who combine the use of cocaine and heroin, are larger compared to the total sample. More than half of them belong to snowball chain H and F, which also contain larger proportions of respondents who have been convicted for a felony, who have had contact with drug treatment agencies, who report difficulties when abstaining or cutting back their cocaine use, who mainly use cocaine intravenously, and who report a craving for cocaine.

Conversely, illicit drug use can also affect the family relations. When cocaine does have effects on relationships with the family, these tend to be negative. Approximately two in five respondents report that cocaine has 'deteriorated' or damaged their family relationships. These interviewees report about conflicts and arguments between parents (or one of them) and their children over illicit drug use. The respondent's drug use is typically not the only subject of discussion, but often a factor that intensifies existing conflicts and misunderstandings. Again, some respondents say that some of the family problems concerning drugs were caused or intensified by their parents' apparent ignorance about illicit substances.

Some respondents blame their parents for their lack of emotional support and controlling behavior. Furthermore, both respondents with children of their own and childless respondents talk about the future upbringing of their children. Typically, they are determined not to let their cocaine use interfere with their duties as a parent, or to stop using cocaine or cut down when they have children. Their stories show that most respondents have a clear idea of the possible interactions between family relationships and illicit drug use. They are aware of the shortcomings of their own upbringing, and they are determined not to make the same 'mistakes', to be more 'open' and 'honest' with their children.

All this might suggest that the interaction between a respondent's cocaine use and his/her family's efforts at social control is negative by definition. Still, we find that almost half of all the respondents state that cocaine had no effect on their relationships with their families. Compared to cocaine's effect on other interpersonal relationships (spouse or lover, friends, fellow workers), cocaine has the least impact on family-of-origin relations. Indeed, many cocaine users refrain from using, when they are expected to meet family members (parents). Our data suggest that at least some of our respondents make an effort to ensure that their cocaine use does not interfere with relations and other activities that take priority (such as family relations).

Moreover, the family can also be a source of positive social responses. The source of informal help when trying to quit cocaine most often mentioned is 'parents'. Secondly, family members make numerous comments on each other's behavior that serve as efforts at social control. For example, comments on the respondent's physical condition, his/her appearance, and on perceived changes in his/her character, are often intended to steer behavior away from the problematic. Some respondents claim that these comments did not have any effect on their behavior, but others report that repeated comments from family members, often combined with other efforts at social control by friends, partners and significant others, made them quit or cut down on their cocaine use.

Finally, the respondents' relationship with their siblings deserves special attention. Our data suggest that siblings are usually better informed about the respondent's cocaine use than his/her parents. Moreover, in most cases siblings have experimented with illicit substances themselves. In many cases brothers and sisters are part of the respondents' peer group. In these circumstances siblings can play an important role in the initiation into cocaine use, in its continuation, and in the informal social control.

To conclude, these data provide an opportunity to observe families where no drug treatment is involved, where problems may have been prevented or controlled or accommodated by the family process itself. In order to understand the rich diversity of family interaction around illicit drug use, and the sequences of events which result in successful control within the family, we need more qualitative studies focusing on particular kinds of family relationships and circumstances rather than research on clinical populations.

NOTES

1   It must be kept in mind that one drawback of this analysis is the absence of any control or comparison group (e.g. of peers who do not use cocaine). Furthermore, the family relationships are reported by the respondents, who may not be aware of all parenting behaviors or may misrepresent them. Were we to interview our subjects' parents, we might find discrepancies between the parents' and the subjects' accounts.

2   See Chapter 3, p. 86-88; Chapter 6, p. 156; Chapter 12, p. 277; and Chapter 13, p. 300.

3   In Chapter 12, we discussed the reasons for periodic abstinence and quitting. None of the respondents indicated pressure from family members as a reason for quitting. However, some studies have shown that in recalling the reasons for a behavior people tend to attribute them to their own internal decisions rather than to an external cause. Therefore, social reasons such as family influence may be underrepresented. GILPIN, E., PIERCE, J.P., GOODMAN, J., BURNS, D. and SHOPLAND, D. (1992), Reasons smokers give for stopping smoking: do they relate to success in stopping?, 1 *Tobacco Control*, 256-263.

4   See Chapter 12, p. 280-281.

5   No data on this issue were found in other reports on community samples of cocaine users.

6   For data on the effect of cocaine on relationships with fellow workers, see Chapter 18, p. 384-387; for data on the effect of cocaine on partner relationships, see Chapter 17, p. 361-366; for data on the effects of cocaine on relationships with friends, see Chapter 19, p. 396-397.

7   See Chapter 14, p. 306 and 315-316.

8   See Chapter 4, p. 112-114.

9   Many respondents also reported having lied about their cocaine use to friends and/or to a partner. These answers are discussed in Chapter 17, p. 363 and 377-378, and Chapter 19, p. 405-406.

10   See Chapter 4, p. 112-114.

11   See Chapter 3, p. 85.

CHAPTER 17

COCAINE USE, RELATIONSHIPS AND SEXUAL RELATIONS

17.1. INTRODUCTION

First, this chapter addresses the effects of cocaine use on the respondent's relationship with his/her life companion (§17.2). Both quantitative and qualitative data illustrate the positive and negative effects of cocaine on these relationships. A separate paragraph is devoted to the ambivalent reputation of cocaine as an aphrodisiac (the effect of cocaine on the respondent's sexual relations).[1]

Second, the impact of the partner on the respondent's cocaine use pattern is analyzed (§17.3). Obviously, the partner of a drug user responds in some particular way to the use. His/her actions and reactions can stimulate the user to use cocaine (and other illicit drugs), they can curb the drug use, or both. We find a special illustration of these interpersonal processes in the respondents' reactions after a significant relation has broken off.

17.2. EFFECTS OF COCAINE USE ON RELATIONSHIPS AND SEXUAL RELATIONS

17.2.1. Quantitative data

We asked all respondents for whom this was relevant whether the use of cocaine improved or worsened their relationship and their sexual relations. Table 17.3.a presents the findings in both the Amsterdam samples and our data from the Antwerp sample. Respondents in all three samples report both negative and positive effects of cocaine on their relationship, but negative effects are dominant. In all three samples, partner relationships show the largest negative imbalance.[2]

In his 1987 Amsterdam sample, Cohen (1989: 127) found a small positive imbalance for sexual relations. In the 1991 Amsterdam sample, cocaine's negative impact on sexual relations was reported as often as its positive impact (Cohen & Sas, 1995: 99). However, in our sample, we find again an imbalance in the positive direction, and even more marked than in the 1987 Amsterdam I sample. This is consistent with our data in Chapter 11: 20.7% of our respondents mentioned 'better sex' as an advantage of cocaine, versus 8.8% of the Amsterdam I sample and 7.4% of the Amsterdam II sample.[3]

Table 17.3.a   The influence of cocaine on the relationship with a partner and sexual relations, in three samples

Amsterdam I (1987)					
Item	Improved	Deteriorated	Both	Neither	N [*]
Relationship with partner	8.8	33.8	10.1	47.3	148
Sexual relations	15.0	11.1	7.8	66.0	153

[*] N is not always 160 due to missing data or because items were not always applicable
   to respondents' personal situation

Amsterdam II (1991)					
Item	Improved	Deteriorated	Both	Neither	N [*]
Relationship with partner	16	28	4	60	105
Sexual relations	19	19	5	67	106

[*] N is not always 108 due to missing data or because items were not always applicable
   to respondents' personal situation

Antwerp (1997)					
Item	Improved	Deteriorated	Both	Neither	N [*]
Relationship with partner	11.4	41.8	30.4	16.5	79
Sexual relations	40.0	22.7	18.7	18.7	75

[*] N is not always 111 due to missing data (no opinion) or because items were not always
   applicable to respondents' personal situation

As to the relationships with a life companion, we could suspect that partners are supposed to be more tolerant about the respondents' cocaine use. It also goes without saying that cocaine users are less inclined to hide their drug use from their partner (than from parents or fellow workers).

Eventually, if cocaine use really has a negative effect on the relationship with a partner, and efforts to solve this problem fail, the couple can always decide to split up. We also asked whether the use of cocaine had been the cause of divorce (both divorce from marriage and breaking up a relationship). This was the case for 31 respondents of our sample, or 42.5% of those for whom this was relevant. On the other hand, 42 persons did not indicate their cocaine use as a cause of divorce (57.5% of those for whom this was relevant).

17.2.2. Qualitative data

17.2.2.1. Positive effects of cocaine use on the relationship

Our subjects believe there are many ways in which cocaine can improve relationships. In Chapter 11 we showed that cocaine appeals to many respondents because it puts the user in a festive mood, it provides feelings of being high and relaxed, it gives self-confidence, it improves the quality of love making, it gives energy, etc. All these advantages can positively affect social relationships, including those with the spouse, lover or companion. The most important advantage for the Antwerp respondent is that cocaine eases communication and lessens shyness.[4] For many respondents these advantages are positively related to 'sociable' and 'safe' circumstances.[5]

Table 11.3.c (Chapter 11) shows that cocaine effects such as 'talkativeness', 'euphoria' and 'prolonged sex' are regularly experienced by the Antwerp respondents.[6] Again, we assume that these effects also affect relationships in a positive way. Moreover, when asked to describe the most intense experience they ever had with cocaine, many respondents referred to partner relationships. Four respondents referred to a 'good' or 'intimate' conversation with a partner, four respondents described their most positive experience as intense feelings of love and tenderness.

17.2.2.2. Negative effects of cocaine use on the relationship

Cocaine use can have various negative effects on a relationship. Respondents report unpredictable mood changes, lying, irritability, uncommunicativeness, denying drug use, spending long periods in bed, lethargic when not in bed, not keeping arrangements, verbal aggression, neglect of duties, paranoia, nocturnality, moodiness, going missing, reduced sex life, pressure on respondent to take drugs, pressure to be given money, threatening or menacing behavior, physical violence, damage to property, embarassing behavior, etc.

These phenomena can have a variety of negative effects on the partner. He/she may feel lonely, isolated, anxious, depressed, tearful, worried, tense and confused. The relationship (whether only one partner is a drug user or both) can change for the worse, with rows and arguments, deteriorating sexual relations, and a breakdown in trust and communication. Consider this 28-year-old woman's experience:

I really had to leave him, because it was my downfall, I couldn't see it anymore. He also did it behind my back. Yes, in the end, that was the big problem, you start lying and cheating, and I couldn't live with that, right? I went to work from 9 to 6, and he started to fantasize, he really lived in his own world. I came home and he didn't have a job. I asked him: 'Did you apply for a job today?' 'Oh yes, I went there and there' but it was just fantasy, because nothing was true. You find out afterwards, and in the end he believed his own lies. So he had an incredible fantasy world, and then you find out he had just been sitting the whole day in his seat for example, far out from the coke, right? So he indulged in all kinds of fantasies, and afterwards you find out there wasn't a word of truth in what he said. Nothing but lying and cheating, right? And then, he found all kinds of ways to get money, that his car broke down and that he needed to get a spare part, and this and that. Yes, you give him your money, at first you don't realize it, in fact... or you don't want to see he's actually lying for it, but yes, in the end you have to open your eyes and say: 'Hey, actually you are lying and cheating'. And then you confront him with that and he denies, right? Well, you can't live with a person like that. So I left him. In the end he beat me up too, very aggressively, he smashed everything and so. And I always said: when somebody beats me, that's the last thing, and I left. [Z/1/04]

Furthermore, heavy drug use in general can restrict social life, create financial problems, and affect work performance. Under some circumstances, partners of drug users may show a concomitant increase in their own use of drugs, alcohol or some other appetitive behavior such as eating or tobacco use.

When confronted with these negative effects of cocaine use on the relationship, partners may take actions towards eachother. He/she can become angry, or violent, consider leaving or actually leave, reduce the frequency of having sex, or start a new sexual relationship with someone other than the drug-using partner. He/she can try to be firm, by trying to control the drug use, standing up to the user, etc. Any of these methods of coping can in turn influence the drug use and affect the relationship.

Coke has played an important part in my relational problems for a long while: my coke replaced my sex. The kick I got when I came, the kick I had when I had sex was comparable to the kick I had when I freebased. [Q/0/01]

17.2.2.3. Cocaine and sex: an ambiguous relation

Sixteen respondents (14.4% of the total sample) report their most pleasurable experience with cocaine was related to sexual activities. During the second interview, ninety-three interviewees were willing to discuss their personal experiences with cocaine and sex.

Forty-two respondents (45.2% of those who answered the question) had *only positive experiences with cocaine and sex*. They report better sex because the male partner can maintain an erection for a longer time, and both partners can postpone orgasm. Generally, partners feel less inhibited, less shy, and more sensitive, more creative, more relaxed, more open to each other and to sexual experiments. Having sex on cocaine means to have fewer complexes about one's body, having more sexual fantasies and appetite, being more sexually aggressive, and having more intense bodily sensations. Some respondents report better orgasms (including one respondent who had a spontaneous orgasm). Others feel insatiable.

> *It completely disinhibits, it gives a more stimulating feeling, it's much more intense, eh like with most drugs and sex, it is closely related to disinhibition... You have less embarrassment about yourself. You're much more open. More fantasy games. People become what they want to be in bed, I think. [Y/0/01]*

> *You'll be much more creative, and you'll make love more experimentally, and also more at a distance in the sense that you're not only... how can I say... that you are much more concentrated on the inner aspect. [...] You do it in other locations, you do it in more dangerous places, where you can get caught in the act. There is more excitement compared to when you do it without. You come less soon, it takes longer. [H/0/10]*

Thirteen respondents (14.0% of those who answered the question) had *only negative experiences with cocaine and sex*. For them cocaine and sex do not go together because they feel no sexual desire when they are high on cocaine. Cocaine weakens the libido, and its reputation as an aphrodisiac is a myth. These respondents also report that it is difficult to have an erection when they are high on cocaine and that sex is a lot more fun with other substances (such as MDMA, amphetamines, cannabis). The participants either state that cocaine does not affect their sexual experiences at all (i.e. they feel no difference between having sex with cocaine or without cocaine), or that sex and using cocaine are incompatible activities.

> *I'm not myself then and I don't like to make love in that case. I don't like it. There's a bad feeling, for me. When I'm using it, I want to chat and make fun, but not having... [H/1/04]*

> *Sex and coke use, it has happened a few times, but I don't think it's much of a thrill because they are two completely... you can't combine these two, it just didn't work. I want to do both things properly, either I want to do sex very well, or I want to use coke very well. But to do both together very well, it's not possible, I mean, not for me. [Q/0/01]*

Another 25 participants (26.9% of those who answered the question) report *both positive and negative experiences with cocaine and sex*. In general, cocaine improves their sexual relations and the positive experiences they report are similar to those described above. Under specific circumstances, however, respondents have negative experiences such as difficulty in having erection, in reaching an orgasm, or feeling impotent.

Sometimes, sexual encounters take too long. Partners may feel insensitive, 'numbed', and sex is dominated by lust instead of love and tenderness.

> *When it works, it's great* [he laughs], *but usually you can't get a real hard-on anymore, and it's not such a big thing that's hanging there, it takes ages before you come, sometimes it just doesn't work... But when it all works, it's the greatest thing to do.* [C/0/09]

> *It could be so fantastic, making love on coke. But I've had my regrets when I went home with those guys just to get my gram of coke... And, when you use a lot, in the end it's nowhere near it, I think. That penis appeared to shrivel up... so you're doing it for hours, and it's really like: 'Hello there? Are you finished? Just come and go off me, or leave', or... But it can be very nice, I think, yes. You go further, you experiment more, I'm telling you, you feel good, you feel loose, a bit reckless... more experimental.* [H/1/28]

Ambiguous experiences with cocaine and sex were also described by respondents in the Scottish study (Ditton & Hammersley, 1996: 50, 54, and 65-66) and in the Rotterdam study (Bieleman & de Bie, 1992: 40-43). Analysis of users' stories shows that negative experiences of having sex while high on cocaine are affected by a number of drug, set and setting factors. First, some respondents report that sex with cocaine is highly dependent on the quantity used on that particular occasion, on the frequency of use (and therefore on level of use). In their San Francisco report, Waldorf *et al.* (1991: 53) conclude : *'There was great individual variation on this subject, but the majority would probably agree that sex on coke could be enhanced after limited doses, early in their using careers, or when snorted; sex tended not to be enhanced after large doses, late in a heavy use career, or when smoked'.* Second, sex is often 'the final piece' of a night out, and both partners may have consumed alcohol and/or other illicit substances. Third, whether or not the sexual partner has consumed cocaine as well is a decisive factor in the subjective experience of 'having sex on coke'. Fourth, several respondents state that particular routes of ingestion (such as freebasing and injecting) exclude sexual activity because it hampers the complex drug administration rituals associated with these methods. And fifth, whether or not the sexual experience is perceived as positive or negative also depends on the quality of the relationship between both partners.

> *It's only fun when you are with partner who does it too, right, because otherwise it can create problems. Or sometimes it doesn't, it depends.* [H/0/10]

> *You feel much more open and you dare a little more. Especially when you only just know the people, when you haven't been together for a long time yet. But in the end it's almost the same, because you know each other anyway, also when you're sober and so... But when you haven't been so long together with somebody, you dare to do more, and you dare to give it everything you've got actually.* [I/1/16]

Finally, 13 respondents (14.0% of those who answered the question) say they have no experience at all with cocaine and sex. Most of them attributed this to the fact that they did not have a partner at all, that their partner did not use cocaine, or that their partner did not want to experiment with cocaine and sex. Others claim that their cocaine use was limited to parties and going out, and that they never had the occasion to experiment with it. Two respondents indicate that they would never experiment with it:

I also think: making love when you've taken some, I don't know... No, I just don't want to start with it. Sex remains something emotional for me. These things are unrelated. I prefer to make love when I'm sober as well. Sex is something you, I mean, you have to do the 'real' way. [V/1/01]

17.3. THE INFLUENCE OF THE PARTNER ON THE RESPONDENT'S COCAINE USE

Cocaine use brings benefits and harms to the user, but it also impacts on his/her partner. Cocaine use takes place in a social context, and the companion or lover often respond in some way to the use. Not only does the user's cocaine use affect the relationship, but the partner can also influence the user's use. In this paragraph we discuss three major sources of influence of a relationship on our respondents' cocaine use: partner behavior which stimulates the user to use more frequently (§17.3.1), partner behavior which curbs the respondents' cocaine use (§17.3.2), and the effect of breaking off a relationship (§17.3.3).

17.3.1. The partner as a stimulus for cocaine use

The partner can be a stimulus for the respondents' cocaine use in more than one way. Typically, the partner is a regular user of illicit drugs as well. In this paragraph we illustrate some of the mechanisms through which our subjects were encouraged to use cocaine by a partner.

In Chapter 4 we showed that one's first use of cocaine is rarely occasioned by a stranger. Initiation into cocaine typically takes place at parties, in intimate or private settings, and amongst friends. Initiates are usually intimates whom the initiator knows well, trusts and wishes to treat or favor. Therefore, it is likely that some cocaine users have been initiated by their partner. However, when asked during the first interview to state with whom they used their first cocaine, most respondents reported having been with a friend or a group of friends at initiation, and none of them explicitly reported having been with a partner. Nevertheless, we strongly suspect that some of our respondents were actually initiated by a partner, but called their initiator 'a friend'. Indeed, our qualitative data from the second interview illustrate that at least some respondents were initiated by their partner:

> *I started using drugs, because I was with a toxicomane, a junky, who used cocaine and smack* [i.e. heroin, TD]. *I only smoked joints and sometimes took XTC and something like that. I just noticed that there was something, that he was using something, and I asked: 'What do you use?' But cocaine and smack, I didn't know what it was, so I tried, and after two or three weeks, I was completely in it, because I could have it from him.* [H/1/03]

> *For five years I've been with someone who used a lot of coke, and I started to use coke along with him.* [H/1/13]

Also in Chapter 4 we presented data on the circumstances surrounding initiation.[7] When asked whether they had ever seen anybody else use cocaine before they first tried it, four respondents reported having witnessed their partner using cocaine long before they first used it. We also argued that observing more direct modes of ingestion (such as freebasing and injecting) before one's own initiation, typically occurs among intimates (i.e. friends or partners).[8] Furthermore, our qualitative data illustrate that most positive or encouraging information comes from 'friends' or 'intimates' (including partner). All these observations suggest that partners or lovers can and sometimes do play a crucial role as initiators of illicit drug use in general and cocaine use in particular.

> *Of course I preferred –because I had a lot of girls who didn't take anything- but I always found it nicer when it was someone who did it as well, right? I'm telling you, I never pushed it or so. But everyone I met, was already using it... I mean, it's not because of me they started using it... Because in fact, looking at it know, I found it better that they don't use anything, because you cut down then, but yes... it was of course nicer, in the weekend, when I could take a line with my girlfriend.* [C/0/04]

But even a long time after the initial phase of experimentation, the partner can have an important influence on the respondent's cocaine use pattern. To a certain extent, an individual imitates another's behavior or models his/her own behavior on that of others. The salience of the model increases with the significance of the other person, in that individuals are more likely to imitate the behavior of significant others. In other words, the drug use pattern of a partner or lover can have an stimulating effect on an individual, especially in a phase of intense love, attraction and attachment.[9]

> *Meeting particular persons* [she laughs]. *And also, when you have someone who uses a lot, and when you often visit that person, inevitably, you use more, right?* [H/1/24]

> *Before that I had a girlfriend who was very decent, a very decent girl, who drank a glass of wine sometimes, but she lived very consciously. Then yes, I met someone who was ten times as bad than me, yes, she was wild about drugs, so it increased it of course.* [P/0/06]

This modelling and imitation can relate to the quantity used, the frequency of use, or more generally the level of use. It can relate to the company one uses with, the sets or settings surrounding use, the combined use of cocaine with other substances and the preferred route of ingestion.[10]

When asked whether they have ever felt being pushed to use illicit drugs, four respondents refer to former relationships.[11] None of them refer to an ongoing relationship. Three of these interviewees indicate that they felt pushed to use cocaine by the very fact that their partner used it regularly and frequently invited them to join:

> *He used a lot of heroin and cocaine, and it was my boyfriend at the time, and then he really gave me shots, like: 'Yes, common, it's really great together, here, you have to try it.' He kind of pushed me, it was in fact too much injecting. But I did really like it, [...] in fact it was great, but... it was too much in one go. And so it evolved very quickly, in that period.* [I/1/01]

> *With that cocaine, I think my boyfriend liked it when I took it with him because it was more... eh he would get more money from me or I wouldn't tell him off too much...* [I/1/09]

In Chapter 14 we mentioned that the mere fact of talking about cocaine use and cocaine effects can generate an appetite for it.[12] Obviously, when both partners are regular cocaine users, chances are high that the substance is often talked about. These conversations are about previous experiences with the drug, specific effects from cocaine, planning the next occasion of use, advantages and disadvantages of various routes of ingestion, how and where to get acceptable quality cocaine or for a reasonable price, whether there is a budget available for a purchase of cocaine, the frequency of use, other people's cocaine use patterns, advantages or disadvantages of other drugs compared to cocaine, etc. Consider the following stories:

With my friend. We talk about it a lot. When we will do it the next time, and especially, how it makes you feel, and what it does to you, how you felt that night... Sometimes we have deep conversations about it, like: this person react this way, that person reacts that way, and what you've all experienced. I find it very interesting to know what the other person experiences, because it won't be the same things I feel. Oh yes, we talk a lot about it. I find that very pleasant. [R/1/02]

With my friend, that I want to use it infrequently as such. To my liking. So that I don't want to use it anymore before my birthday. And that's only in may. And... I just explained my principles to my friend, like: look, not here anymore, I mean, we will do it again, but not now. [R/1/03]

In some cases, conversations end in conflicts about whether to use or not. Typically the respondent wants to use while his/her partner does not, or vice versa. For example, this woman gave up her attempt to quit using cocaine, after her partner had convinced her to buy again:

There has been a difference of opinion because he really is more hooked to it than me. And then I, let's see, we started again three months ago, something like that, I think, yes, and... Then I said: no X. [her boyfriend, TD]. I said that when you use a lot, that you change: you get depressions, your thoughts change, you see everything too pessimistic. You don't like anything anymore. In the end, you feel inferior, I mean I do, I feel guilty because I could have spent the money to other things. He says: 'Just once'. I say: 'No, I know you, it doesn't not end with once, because when it doesn't work or when you get bad stuff, you'll go out looking for something else. It doesn't end with once, I know that'. And yes, that was the difference of opinion. [H/1/06]

As described above, stimuli for cocaine may be of an erotic nature. Although only few respondents report that sex occurs with cocaine and generates an appetite for it, our qualitative data indicate that the partner's behavior in sexually charged settings and sets can have a marked effect on the respondent's cocaine use.[13]

Finally, the partner can stimulate the level of cocaine use when he/she is a source of supply to the respondent. Several respondents report an escalation of their own cocaine use when they started an affair with another user who was selling cocaine or who had easy access to cocaine. As with cocaine sellers themselves, they had cocaine available to them almost all the time. The (sexual) partner of a dealer usually gets his/her cocaine for free, and most respondents agreed that having constant free supplies on hand carried the risk of consuming too much, too often, and developing cocaine-related problems. A 38-year-old cocaine importer relates how his girl-friend got into trouble with cocaine:

The real reason was that she wasn't familiarized with it, and through her curiosity she ended up with an acquaintance of mine in the Netherlands, while I was away. And the wife of that friend of mine, used it as well and that's how my girlfriend got to know it. Yes, she also used, but mostly XTC and weed and sometimes a sniff. But that friend's wife smoked it as well, she put it in cigarettes and so. My girlfriend experienced it as a nice atmosphere, and eventually she became addicted. One moment, I was involved with drug trafficking, the import. It was not like I bought it here myself. I imported it, and it was 20, 40 and later even 100 kilos, 600 kilos... so it was easy for me. I could just have it, and at a very low price. [...] I was abroad for a couple of months, because I was arranging things, and in the meantime she kept going on. Eventually she ended up with people she didn't know at all, guys who were in business as well. And so she came into contact with their girlfriends, and she conveyed messages like 'This guys wants you' and 'this and that cargo are delivered there and there', and when I came back she had used 3 hectograms [i.e. 3 x 0.1 kilo, TD] in a half a year, she could get it on credit from people I knew, but I had to settle that. That coke was not only for her, she also gave it to friends who came to her, and when I wasn't there. It couldn't go on like that, I said: something is going to burst. Later she ended up in a clinic. When she came out, things went well for a while, but I realize she could get it easily through me as an importer, or through me she could end up with other people so she could relapse. [C/0/03]

But a partner or lover does not have to be an importer or professional dealer to be a source of supply for the user. Some men use cocaine to help them meet or seduce women. In exchange for sexual favors or to bind them to themselves, these individuals pay for their partner's supply. Others become the main source of supply just because they have a lot of money.

I didn't have to do anything to get money. Because first I had a girlfriend who worked, and when she worked for a half a day, she earned 50,000 francs. She was eh... she stole it, I don't know how she did it, she worked in a department store as an employee, and she always paid for us. [J/0/01]

17.3.2. The partner as a curbing factor for cocaine use

A drug user's partner can have a discouraging or a curbing effect on his/her pattern of use in many ways (see also Diaz *et al*, 1992: 302).[14] He/she can make comments on the respondent's use, discuss the pros and cons of illicit drug use, tell the user to cut back or quit using, offer informal help to do so, etc.[15]

As with family members, partners make a lot of comments on each others' behavior. Most of these comments are efforts to influence future behavior in particular directions (i.e. *informal social control*).[16] Respondents were asked whether they had ever received any comments from other people about their cocaine use. Fifteen interviewees (13.5% of the total sample) state their partner or lover had made comments on one or more occasions, such as: 'you become aggressive when you use cocaine', 'you take too much cocaine', 'you look bad', 'you take too large doses', 'you are not a controlled user', 'this is not an occasion for using cocaine', etc.

'The coke or me', my boyfriend said, because I was going too far. I started crying, like: 'Shit, he's right'. You have to watch out with that stuff. He shook me awake, like: 'It's not a toy.' [H/1/18]

That I had to quit, cut down. That I had to refine myself. And yes, that I had to quit with that dirt, right? Or that I had to learn: when it's not there, it's not there. So when you go out, don't start looking for it, like: I want coke, I want coke, that you are calling everyone, that when it's not there, that you can say: okay, it's not there, we just have fun without it. And it worked. [H/1/28]

Almost all of these comments imply implicit or explicit suggestions to cut down on cocaine use, to abstain temporarily or to quit altogether. When asked whether they ever had made any comments about somebody else's cocaine use, nine respondents said they had suggested their partner to cut down or to quit. These comments were all in the same key: 'you are exaggerating', 'you are losing control', 'you are not the same person anymore', 'you need to change your behavior', 'you are taking too much', 'you have to be more careful', 'you spend too much money on cocaine', etc.

Furthermore, several respondents indicate that making remarks about other people's cocaine use only makes sense when they are friends or intimates. Making comments about the drug use pattern of a stranger or a mere acquaintance is useless and can get you into serious trouble.

> *Never with strangers, you only get trouble with it. Even when you say something well intended, you only get trouble. So you better say nothing. People you don't know and who use coke, can get aggressive, or whatever. You can't predict that in advance. [...] But not when I say to a friend: 'Hey, don't you think you should calm down?' When they are friends, they'll accept that. So I don't get involved with strangers. I've done that in an earlier period, I've seen so much, and it was too much. I only do it with people I know. And when I say something to them, they accept it, no aggression or so.* [W/0/01]

These comments are made with a variety of intentions and effects. They may be humorous, instructional, or reproving. And the respondent may react in various ways too. When asked how other people reacted to the comments respondents made about their cocaine use, the reactions most often reported are both positive (compliance, indulgence, agreement) and negative (irritation, anger, indifference, denial). Some respondents feel their remarks produced an effect, in that they succeeded to steer the person's behavior away from the problematic. Other participants state their comments remained ineffective. When asked how they reacted themselves to comments from their partners, respondents report similar reactions. Some respondents countered these comments by saying that they knew what they were doing, and that they did what they wanted to do. Others agreed with the comments and decided to change their cocaine use pattern:

> *Actually, I really felt attacked. Because I knew: okay, I mean, when I think it's too much, I'll see it. I've been doing it for a couple of years, and sometimes I do quit for months, and I know when something goes too far. Okay, maybe not, but I think I still control myself.* [I/1/16]

> *My friend doesn't like it too much, because he would like to do it more often, but... it happened once, that he said: 'Are we going to take another line?' and I said: 'Please, it's not okay. Tomorrow we'll be twisting our lips again, and we won't be able to get up again'. And then, only the next morning you get a thanks for not doing it.* [R/1/03]

Respondents were asked whether they had discussed their cocaine use with other people during the four weeks prior to the interview. Twenty respondents (18.0% of the total sample) reported having discussed their cocaine use recently with their partner or lover. Conversations were about the following topics: the respondent's participation in our study, how to resist feelings of desire for cocaine (craving), negative experiences with cocaine (paranoia, anxiety, etc.), the factors that make an individual lose control over his/her cocaine use, etc. In most cases, these conversations ended in conclusions about possible strategies to control one's drug use. Consider the following stories:

Because my girlfriend works a night shift, and she uses it in a wrong way, to keep awake, because she suffers from her kidney, and then I tried to warn her, and she did admit it, but I can't do more, and I don't want to do more. I mean, it's her decision, I have no authority on that. [I/0/13]

Yes, with reference to this study, I talked about it with my husband and with another friend. We discussed whether my use personally bothers me, and whether you can defend it, and whether you are ashamed of it... that we don't use it often anymore nowadays and so, that it is just because we don't give it a thought anymore. [K/1/02]

Respondent: I regularly talk about it. Just about, about my control. And how you manage to control it, to check that with each other.
Interviewer: What was the conclusion of those conversations?
Respondent: Yes, that you just have to keep a level ahead. [M/1/03]

Despite the fact that partners often comment on each other's cocaine use and thus try to exert informal social control over one another, this is not always effective. We found that partners often lie to each other regarding their drug use, especially when the other is a non-user. We asked respondents whether they had ever lied about their cocaine use to anybody, and 27 of them (24.3% of the total sample) reported having lied to a partner or lover.

Four of these respondents had lied to their partner because they did not want to share their supply of cocaine ('out of greed'). Two interviewees had promised their partner to quit using cocaine, but they had continued anyway. Two participants lied to their partner by not keeping specific promises ('I told her I would not use before she came home, but I did', 'I promised her not to use at that party with those people, but I did'). Most respondents who had a partner or lover *who used cocaine as well*, reported having lied about the quantity used or the frequency of their use. Typically, their partner wanted them to cut down on their use, because they felt the respondent was using too much, too frequently, or because he/she was not in control of cocaine anymore. These respondents say they lied about their cocaine use to avoid lengthy discussions, 'out of laziness', to avoid moral disapproval, because other people would start to interpret the respondent's behavior differently if they knew he/she was high on cocaine, etc. A statement frequently heard was: what the eye doesn't see, the heart doesn't rue.

Nine respondents reported having lied to *a non-using partner*. Most of them had tried to discuss illicit drug use with their partners on previous occasions, but as opinions tended to be incompatible, respondents had decided to avoid discussions and to hide their use. One of these respondents had hidden her cocaine use to her partner because she felt 'guilty' and 'ashamed for doing such unhealthy things'. All other respondents report having lied about their cocaine use because they felt their partner would make problems about something they themselves did not see as problematic. Consider the two following stories:

Respondent: Yes, towards my friend I've toned down the quantity I use, I told him 'I do it every now and then, when I go out, once every two weeks', but in fact I use it almost always when I go out in Antwerp, so I toned it down.
Interviewer: Why?
Respondent: Because he's really frightened about it, yes, that going out in any case, for him that's something, he doesn't do that, and it's difficult for me to explain, so I explain how that feels for me too, I don't feel it as addictive, and for me it could as well be once every two weeks. And it's, yes, because you easily seem like, 'Ho, look, when you use it that often you

must be addicted', and I don't see it that way, because I can also say that 'I have a period that I'm not using it for two weeks, or when I am with you, I don't feel like doing it'. It's hard to explain to someone who has never done it. I understand that because I was afraid myself when I heard other people talking about it, when I was still a non-user, and then you think: 'Oh god, but you take it every time'. That's why... [I/1/09]

To my first girlfriend, I did, because you know that person is very negative about that and okay, it's a white lie, like: you want to avoid the problem because you have decided for yourself: 'Okay, there's no problem, I do it every now and then, but she doesn't have to know about it, because you think differently about it than she does. She looks at it very negatively and you look at it less negatively'. And when you tell her, it will become very difficult, the communication becomes difficult. Just try to convince that person that it is not so bad for you. They won't accept it. They'll immediately see a big problem: 'Come on, why do you use coke? You don't need it?' and that's why you start lying, I think. [P/0/01]

In relationships in which one partner uses illicit drugs and the other does not, communication about drugs can be difficult for both partners. When the deceit about drug use is discovered, conflicts can escalate. Yet, illicit drug use is usually not perceived by our respondents as the cause of a failing relationship with their non-using partner. Relationships typically break off because of differences of opinion about various topics, different life-styles and preferences. In relationships in which both partners are regular users of various types of illicit drugs, the use itself is seldom questioned and carries no taboo. Discussions tend to focus on the quantity of use, the frequency and the circumstances of use. However, most respondents are aware that lying about quantity or frequency can be an indicator of problematic cocaine use. They prefer not to lie:

If I started lying about it, I would, that would be a sign for me: yes, but it's not controlled anymore. Because I know people who do lie about it. They say: 'No, no, I haven't got any' but in fact you can see the stuff sticking in their beard. And I find that so awful that I want to check myself on it. [M/1/03]

One of the clearest indications of a partner's possible discouraging or curbing effect on the respondents' cocaine use, is the fact that so many of them report they have cut back, abstained temporarily or quit using altogether. In Chapter 12 we reported that 'partner raised objections' is mentioned 10 times as a reason for the longest abstinence, and once for abstinences of one month or longer.[17] Furthermore, three respondents stated that the main reason for cutting back on their use was their partner (making problems about it).[18] Finally, five respondents had quit using because their partner raised objections about their cocaine use, because their partner started to use cocaine too, or because he/she started to show characteristics of compulsive drug use.[19]

I quit because I didn't like the life anymore. I had problems, you know, I did a burglary. Doing all kinds of foolish things, I didn't want that anymore. Because the boy I was with then, he didn't want to mend his ways either and it was always the same, and yes, okay, I was four years with him, it wasn't easy, but a relationship between junks doesn't work anyway, and so I bit through it, and I started working, I saved some money and I left the country. [H/1/04]

My wife pointed it out to me as well, she put me in front of a mirror. You can see some people react, they use coke, and suddenly they think they know everything, think everything, and that doesn't fit my pattern, I would like to know it all, but I'm too much of a doubter to be-

lieve that. For me coke is somehow... yes, I started to put things into perspective, I started to... I wasn't so emotionally attached to coke either. [K/0/01]

Similarly, several respondents report they have cut back, abstained temporarily or quit using altogether because of a *pregnancy*.[20] In Chapter 12 we reported that 'pregnancy' is mentioned 6 times as a reason for the longest abstinence, and twice for abstinences of one month or longer.[21] Furthermore, one respondent stated that the main reason for cutting back on his use was that his partner was pregnant.[22] Finally, two respondents had quit using because they were pregnant.[23]

The thirty-two respondents who reported having tried to quit, were asked whether they had ever looked for help while quitting. After family members (50.0%) and friends (46.9%), partners were the source of informal assistance most often mentioned.[24] That fourteen participants (or 43.8% of those who ever tried to quit) had asked for and/or received help from their lover or spouse, indicates again that the partner can (help to) curb the respondent's cocaine use.

17.3.3. After a relationship has broken off

The importance of the partner as a stimulating or curbing factor in the drug taker's pattern of use is also illustrated by the fact that fifteen respondents report a marked increase of their cocaine use after a significant relationship has broken off.[25] When asked for the reasons for the escalation of their cocaine use, respondents tend to report either escapist motives (loneliness, pangs of love, disappointment, etc.) or hedonist motives (regained freedom, more intense participation in the nightlife scene, doing as one pleases, etc.).

I started especially because my relationship had ended, and then I... I mean, before that I didn't take it, he did take it in that relationship, and I didn't, and afterwards, when it was finished, I started using it. And actually, that's how it happened, because I knew it then, and then I thought: 'What the hell, now I'm going to do it too', and that's how it went. [I/1/09]

It increases when a relationship breaks off, not because the relationship broke off, but because you start doing again whatever you want. You can do again whatever you like, without having to take into account anyone else. Now, the last months, August, September, I do whatever I feel like doing. Other than that I haven't been through a lot, no deaths, no heavy stuff, just that. Not the fact that a relationship broke off, but when you have a relationship with someone, I mean, I try to be considerate of it, so my life at night, that it doesn't affect my relationship. And when the relationship is finished, yes, you don't have to bear that in mind anymore, and then it's a party, and you try to keep that party going on as long as possible. [P/0/04]

In some cases the distinction between escapism and hedonism is blurred as respondents report being both brokenhearted and more focused on partying and fun. Furthermore, the respondents who mention escapist motives also tend to report having met heavy or compulsive drug users after their relation broke off and/or having experimented with heroin in that period.

I was just married and my wife already messed around. I had been with her for seven or eight years and I was a good husband, and then I said: 'Now I'm going to start living'. I had friends who used, so it was easy to get it. They gave me some to try. Because I used to say no, I was opposed to drugs, and then I started to snort a line. [C/0/01]

I started in a period that... I got divorced in 1986. So since 1987 I was alone very often, and I went out quite a lot, and then it started. And then in 1990 I went to work in a discotheque in Antwerp, and I think it even increased then. And I decreased when I met my present husband and when I came in a somewhat more stable life. [K/1/03]

17.4. CONCLUSION

Our respondents report both negative and positive effects of cocaine on relationships, but negative effects are dominant. When asked whether the use of cocaine either improved or worsened sexual relations, we find a small imbalance in the positive direction. For 31 respondents of our sample, or 42.5% of persons for whom this was relevant, the use of cocaine had been the cause of divorce (either official divorce or breaking up an affair).

Our subjects report many ways in which cocaine can improve partner relationships. The fact that cocaine eases communication, alleviates relations with others and lessens shyness, can positively affect the relationship with the partner. Other effects such as 'talkativeness', 'euphoria', 'prolonged sex', 'good' or 'intimate' conversations, and intense feelings of love and tenderness can affect relationships in a positive way as well.

Cocaine use can also have various negative effects on the relationship. Mood swings, lying, irritability, lethargy, (verbal) aggression, unreliability, etc. can provoke negative feelings in the partner (loneliness, anxiety, depression, confusion). The relationship between both partners can change for the worse, with rows and arguments, worsening sexual relations, and a breakdown in trust and communication.

Many respondents associate cocaine with better sex. For some respondents their most pleasurable experience with cocaine was related to sexual activities. Almost half of the participants report an exclusively positive impact of cocaine on sex: prolonged sex, sexual stimulation, better orgasms, fewer inhibitions, more creativity, etc.

However, the reputation of cocaine as an aphrodisiac is ambiguous. More than four in ten respondents report a negative impact of cocaine on sex. For some of them cocaine and sex do not go together because cocaine does not affect their sexual experiences at all or because it leads to a lack of sexual interest, temporary impotence, or difficulties in having an orgasm. Users may feel insensitive, 'numbed', and their sex is dominated by lust instead of love and tenderness. Negative experiences of sexual relations while high on cocaine are affected by the quantity used, the frequency of use, the (combined) use of other drugs, the other person, the quality of the relationship, and the route of ingestion.

Cocaine does not only bring benefits and harms to the user, but it also impacts on his/her partner. The spouse, partner or lover respond in some particular way to the use and can either stimulate or curb the use or influence it in some way. First, the partner or lover can be a stimulus for the respondent's cocaine use in more than one way: as an initiator, as a significant other and model, as a pushy user, as someone to talk to, as a sexual partner, as a source of supply, etc.

Second, a drug user's partner can have a discouraging or curbing effect on his/her pattern of use in various other ways: he/she can make comments on the respondent's use (i.e. informal social control), discuss the pros and cons of illicit drug use, suggest to the user to cut back or quit using, offer informal help to do so, etc. These informal control mechanisms, however, are not always effective. About one in four respondents report having lied to a partner regarding their drug use. When the partner is a non-user, most respondents report having lied about their cocaine use because they felt their partner would make problems about something they themselves did not see as problematic. In relationships in which both partners are regular users of various types of illicit drugs, there is no such taboo on drug use. Discussions tend to focus on the quantity, the frequency and the circumstances of use.

Third, the fact that several respondents report a marked increase of their cocaine use after a significant relationship has broken off, illustrates the influence of the partner on the drug taker's pattern of use. The cocaine use of these respondents escalated either for escapist motives or for hedonist reasons.

NOTES

1   In this chapter we use the term 'relationship' to indicate the general bond between life companions, and the term 'sexual relations' to indicate having intercourse, or having sex.

2   Our sample also shows an even stronger negative imbalance for the effect of cocaine on family relationships. See Chapter 16, p. 350.

3   See Chapter 11, p. 246-247.

4   See Chapter 11, p. 246. A total of 63 respondents (56.8% of the total sample) mentioned 'better communication' as an advantage of cocaine. Twenty-one participants ranked it as the most important appealing aspect.

5   See Chapter 11, p. 249-250.

6   See Chapter 11, p. 259.

7   See Chapter 4, p. 107-113.

8   See Chapter 4, p. 109.

9   In Chapter 13 we argued that desire or longing for cocaine is not the result of simple pharmacological effects of the drug. With qualitative data we illustrated that 'craving' is often triggered by set and setting factors, such as the presence of the partner, and specific moods of the user (and his/her partner) as a consequence of the interactions between partners. See Chapter 13, p. 295-297.

10   See Chapter 6, on the choice of route of ingestion, p. 166-169.

11   During the semi-structured interview respondents were asked whether any particular events had had a crucial influence on their cocaine use pattern. Five respondents reported that a relationship with a cocaine using partner had had a stimulating effect on their own use pattern.

12   See Chapter 14, p. 314. See also Chapter 13, p. 296.

13   See Chapter 14, p. 311 and 313.

14   When asked whether any particular events had a crucial influence on their cocaine use pattern, five respondents stated that the start of a relationship had decreased their cocaine use.

15   In Chapter 15 we reported that several respondents state to have an ex-partner as counterexample (i.e. a person they would never want to use cocaine like). See Chapter 15, p. 334.

16   The effect of a partner on the respondents' cocaine use was also illustrated in Chapter 14. Some of the set and setting factors that can interfere with or support informal rules of use indicate the

important role of the partner. For example, some respondents reported that it is more difficult to respect their own principles 'when my partner is not around', 'after an argument or fight', 'when I am emotionally unstable', etc. Others report that it is easier to respect their own rules of use 'when I have a steady partner', when I feel emotionally stable', 'when I am at home', 'when my partner is with me', 'when I see my partner has taken too much cocaine', etc. See chapter 14, p. 317-321.

[17] This reason was not the *main* reason for abstinence. See Chapter 12, p. 268.

[18] See Chapter 12, p. 274.

[19] See Chapter 12, p. 278-279.

[20] When asked about particular events that had had a crucial effect on their cocaine use pattern, three female respondents reported that their pregnancy had had a curbing effect on their cocaine use.

[21] This reason was not the *main* reason for abstinence. See Chapter 12, p. 268.

[22] See Chapter 12, p. 274.

[23] See Chapter 12, p. 278-279.

[24] See Chapter 12, p. 271, 274, 279.

[25] During the semi-structured interview, respondents were asked whether any particular events had had a crucial influence on their cocaine use pattern. Eight respondents reported that a divorce or separation had caused an increase in their cocaine use.

CHAPTER 18

COCAINE USE AND WORK

18.1. INTRODUCTION

Despite cocaine's reputation as a 'party drug' and sex enhancer, some users also find it useful for work purposes. Paragraph 18.2 presents elementary data on (frequencies of) working under the influence of cocaine and other substances in the Antwerp sample. The use (and function) of cocaine in three occupational sectors (the hotel and catering industry, the arts-related professions, and the sex industry) is illustrated with qualitative data. Paragraph 18.3 presents both quantitative and qualitative data on the effects of cocaine on three work-related issues: quality of work, quantity of work, and working relations with co-workers and employers. The negative effects of cocaine use in the workplace are illustrated by the respondents' accounts. Finally, qualitative data on how social modeling and structural factors of the workplace can encourage or discourage illicit drug use are presented in §18.4. If these factors act as a barrier against cocaine use in the workplace, they can be seen as mechanisms of informal social control.

18.2. DRUG USE IN THE WORKPLACE

18.2.1. Quantitative data

We asked respondents if they had been under the influence of alcohol, cannabis, or cocaine during working hours in the last three months. Eighty-four respondents of our sample were employed during the last three months. In our questionnaire the answer categories were 'never', 'once, sometimes', 'often' and (almost) always. In Amsterdam different answer categories were used: 'never', 'rarely', '3-10 times' and '>10 times'. Nevertheless we can compare the categories 'never' and 'ever' in both samples (see table 18.2.a).

In all three samples about 55% had never been under the influence of alcohol, and approx. 45% had been under the influence of *alcohol* during working hours. Almost half of our respondents had been under the influence of *cannabis* during working hours, versus about one third in both Dutch samples (Cohen, 1989: 125-127; Cohen & Sas, 1995: 98-99). This is consistent with the higher lifetime prevalence and last two weeks prevalence of cannabis use in our sample.[1] As for *cocaine*, we find that in all three samples about 30%, or one in three interviewees (who were working at the time of the interview), had been under the influence of cocaine during working hours.

Table 18.2.a   Working under the influence of alcohol, cannabis, and/or cocaine by respondents in employment during the last three months, in three samples, in round percentages

	Amsterdam I 1987 (N=107)			Amsterdam II 1991 (N=86)			Antwerp 1997 (N=84)		
	Alcoh	Cann.	Coke	Alcoh	Cann.	Coke	Alcoh.	Cann.	Coke
Never	52	65	65	55	71	69	57	52	72
Ever	48	34	34	45	29	31	43	47	28
No answer	-	*1*	*1*	-	-	-	-	*1*	-
Total	**100**	**100**	**100**	**100**	**100**	**100**	**100**	**100**	**100**

Table 18.2.b shows frequencies of working under the influence of drugs by the Antwerp respondents (in employment during the last three months). Only a few respondents report having 'often' or '(almost) always' been under the influence of alcohol and cocaine during working hours. The proportion of respondents reporting having often or (almost) always been under the influence of cannabis is much higher (25.0%). The majority of these respondents reporting having been often or always under the influence of one of these drugs are in the artistic or hotel/bar professions (as was the case in the Amsterdam sample).

Table 18.2.b.   Frequency of working under the influence of drugs by respondents in employment in the last three months (N=84) in the 1997 Antwerp sample, in %

	Antwerp					
	Alcohol		Cannabis		Cocaine	
Frequency	**N**	**%**	**N**	**%**	**N**	**%**
Never	48	57.1	44	52.3	61	72.6
Once	14	16.7	11	13.0	13	15.5
Sometimes	15	17.9	7	8.3	5	6.0
Often	4	4.8	10	11.9	4	4.8
(Almost) always	3	3.5	11	13.1	1	1.2
No answer	*0*	*0.0*	*1*	*1.1*	*0*	*0.0*
Total	**84**	**100.0**	**84**	**99.7**	**84**	**100.0**

To find out if the persons who are under the influence of one of the drugs mentioned during working hours are the same, we looked at those who reported having been under the influence *sometimes, often or always* during the last 3 months. We find that 14 respondents have sometimes or more often been under the influence of one drug (16.7% of the total sample of working respondents), 15 respondents (17.8% of the working respondents) under the influence of 2 different drugs (not necessarily at the same time) and 1 respondent under the influence of three different drugs (1.2%).[2]

Looking at the professions of those who have been under the influence of *more than one* drug during working hours, we find 6 bar/hotel employees, 5 artistic professionals, 2 students, 1 social worker, 1 self-employed and 1 unemployed respondent. Again, the high prevalence of the artistic and hotel/bar professions is very similar to Cohen's figures (1989: 126-127).

Nevertheless, these data require caution, as we only checked systematically for the use of alcohol, cannabis and cocaine during working hours. From chapter 8 we know that our respondents were quite experienced with all kinds of drugs.[3] We also asked those respondents who were employed during the three months prior to the interview, whether they had ever been under the influence of other drugs. We found that 13 had been under the influence of amphetamines during working hours (these respondents had all different professions); 7 people under the influence of MDMA (XTC) and 7 respondents under the influence of LSD (each time only two hotel/bar employees and 1 artistic professional), and 5 people under the influence of opiates. Almost of these people reported having been under the influence of these drugs only once.

For being under the influence of cocaine or cannabis or alcohol often or (almost) always during working hours in the three months prior to the interview *per professional category,* we can use different classifications. In Chapter 3 we identified three similar groups of professions (students, arts-related professions and hotel/bar/restaurant employees) like Cohen (1989: 32 and 126) did in the first Amsterdam survey.[4] But we also used a different classification system.[5] In the 1987 Amsterdam I sample the respondents working in the hotel/bar and the artistic professions showed the highest prevalence of being under the influence of some drug during working hours on three or more occasions during the three months prior to the interview (Cohen, 1989: 126-127). Following Cohen's classification, table 18.2.c shows the Antwerp data on these three particular professional groups (artistic professions, hotel/bar employees and students).

Table 18.2.c   Under the influence of a drug sometimes or more often during working hours in a period of three months prior to interview of respondents in employment, in %, in the 1997 Antwerp sample (Cohen's classification of professions)

	Antwerp (1997)			
Under the influence of sometimes or more	**Cocaine %**	**Cannabis %**	**Alcohol %**	**N**
Artistic	5.0%	45.0%	25.0%	20
Students	18.2%	27.3%	9.1%	11
Hotel/bar	27.8%	33.3%	50.0%	18

The hotel/bar employees show the highest prevalence of being under the influence of alcohol and cocaine (sometimes, often or almost always). Arts-related professionals show the highest prevalence of having been under the influence of cannabis (sometimes or more often) during working hours. Within the categories of artists and students, the prevalence of having been under the influence of cannabis is the highest; whereas within the category of hotel/bar employees the prevalence of having been under the influence of alcohol is the highest. [6]

18.2.2. Qualitative data

Drug use at the workplace was not a specific topic during the second interview, but 44 respondents spontaneously told us about drug experiences on the job. The respondents who mentioned cocaine use at or for work during at least part of their cocaine careers, included: 3 waiters, 2 bartenders, a disc jockey, a cook, a model (cover-girl), 2 musicians, a truck driver, 2 actors, 2 photographers, a shop assistant, a market vendor, a travel agent, a trader, a roof constructor, 2 clerks, a hair dresser, a social worker, a tutor, 2 students, a computer expert, an electro-technician, 2 unemployed, a dancer, a fashion designer, a sculptor, a graphic designer, two salesmen, a factory worker, an industrial engineer, an account manager, etc.

Clearly, cocaine use is no longer confined to relatively small circles of illicit drug users, bohemians, and members of a few highly paid, high-pressure professions. Similar to the findings of Waldorf *et al.* (1991: 59) in their San Francisco sample, our data suggest that cocaine users became much more heterogeneous as cocaine use spread through the population. It now occurs across the occupational spectrum and in all sorts of workplaces. Our qualitative data suggest that – contrary to what the official discourse wants us to believe - most of our respondents make efforts to ensure that their cocaine use does not interfere with job performance and working relations. Most resist the temptation of cocaine when their conventional daily life and identity are at risk (compare with Waldorf *et al.*'s (1991: 61-73) case study of cocaine use at "The Company"). Our qualitative data have yielded complete and reliable information about cocaine use in three particular professional sectors: the hotel and catering industry (hotels, bars, restaurants and discotheques), the arts-related professions (actors, photographers, musicians, fashion designers, models, etc.), and the sex industry (prostitutes, escort ladies and their customers). The following paragraphs present the most important findings on cocaine use in these three sectors.

18.2.2.1. Cocaine in the hotel and catering industry

Despite cocaine's reputation as a 'party drug', many of our respondents who are employed in the hotel and catering industry (including discotheques) find it useful for work purposes. As a stimulant, cocaine often makes arduous tasks, late shifts, or long work hours more bearable, indeed pleasurable.[7] For most of these respondents, cocaine use reduces the fatigue that comes with long hours on their feet, boosts their productivity, and improves their mood:

> *So at a certain moment we started working in a discotheque. We worked there almost day and night. They also gave student parties during the day. It was often from ten o'clock in the morning until six o'clock the next morning. Then we could sleep a few hours, but we already had a child, you know. [...] I didn't take it because I liked it, actually, it didn't do much for me, coke and speed. But it was something that when you were working, it kept you going.* [K/0/01]

Waldorf *et al.* (1991: 60) make identical observations with restaurant workers in their San Francisco sample. Typically, respondents working in the hotel and catering industry (such as restaurant workers, bartenders, cooks, discotheque personnel, etc.) find cocaine useful in their jobs. Hard work, constant activity, and long, late hours are instrumental in their using cocaine (for similar observations in Turin, Barcelona and Rotterdam, see Bieleman *et al.*, 1993: 108). During the second interview, three respondents working in the hotel and catering industry indicate that they were initiated by fellow workers and during working hours.[8] This graphic designer used to work in a discotheque as a bartender:

> *I knew coke was being used there, I didn't know... I knew what it was, but I never experienced it... I knew that it was snorted, I had seen it once, that someone was doing it, but other than that I didn't know anything about it. I didn't know how it was manufactured, where it came from... At a certain moment one of those waiters who used it asked me: 'Do you want a line?' And I finished doing the bar, I was just playing some records, and I said: 'Oh yes.' Very spontaneously. I wasn't nervous for it or anything, I took a line then, and I didn't feel much of it. So that was my first time.* [M/0/02]

Furthermore, other respondents who claim *not* to use cocaine on the job in this sector, indicate that even if the actual initiation into cocaine did not take place at the workplace or in the presence of fellow workers, they were at least *mentally* prepared for their first cocaine high by working in a bar or a discotheque:

> *I never used while I was working, you know, never while I was working. [...] But I did get to know it there. [...] I saw people there taking it, I saw people's reaction to it and stuff, I also saw what the reaction was of people on coke, on XTC, on trip, I was able to see it all, I've experienced it, so for me, I mean, if I was to do anything, I preferred to take coke, because people remain themselves when they are doing it.* [C/0/06]

Clearly, in hotels, restaurants, and bars and especially in discotheques and dance clubs cocaine use is facilitated by its *general availability* (as was the case in "The Company", described by Waldorf *et al.,* 1991: 70). Respondents working in these places obtain their cocaine in several ways: some bring their own from outside, others buy it from dealers frequenting the fashionable nightlife centers. Some pool their money with colleagues to buy larger amounts or to get their cocaine at a lower price. For some respondents, the increased availability of cocaine in the catering industry (especially the night jobs) may lead to increased use:

> *In fact, when I was working fulltime in discotheques during the weekends and.. then it is really easy to get it. Then it was drinking and snorting almost every weekend, being completely out.* [M/0/02]

Obviously, the general availability of cocaine in bars, cafés and discotheques is also linked with its reputation as a party drug. Indeed, some interviewees experience cocaine as functional as well as fun. Bieleman *et al.* (1993: 108) also observe that in these settings (the night world), cocaine is easy to obtain and therefore likely to be used. Apart from its fatigue-reducing quality, respondents report other reasons:

> *Yes, it was like standing in the bar like a stranger, it was... completely different compared to when you were serving customers completely sober. Everything was much more smooth, more smooth in contacts, in talking and stuff, you could stand more.* [X/0/01]

A persistent story among many respondents frequenting the Antwerp nightlife scene is that the staff of some bars and discotheques are actively involved in selling drugs (including cocaine). Obviously, personnel in these places are often confronted with clients looking for cocaine and with dealers looking for clients. This is a typical story about discotheque staff protecting dealers:

> *But I think that in large discotheques, those mega discotheques, they should start tackling the staff, and the dealers, and the bouncers and so. Because there are a lot of cops and state police officers who themselves sell in those discotheques. Or that the bouncers and the owner give the state police or the cops an amount of money to turn a blind eye, so that they only, let's say... just to say something, so that they arrest little dealers, but leave the big ones. They earn money on it themselves, you know.* [H/1/28]

Yet, does this mean that drug dealing is tolerated in every discotheque or bar or that every person working in the hotel and catering industry eventually drifts into selling cocaine during the working hours? Only two of our respondents, a waiter and a bouncer, worked in a discotheque and sold cocaine. The waiter told us the following:

That's when I got into contact with XTC and cocaine. There are customers who ask you: 'Where can I get it?' And there are guys who say: 'When you know someone who wants some, just send him to me'. So I got the habit of earning a lot of money by selling cocaine. [H/0/21]

Finally, we do not want to draw strict conclusions from the variety of individual experiences in a complex sector such as the hotel and catering industry. On the one hand, policies to prevent or fight (recreational) use of illicit drugs in the nightlife have been focused to a large extent on trendy discotheques and techno-clubs. On the other hand, policies to prevent or treat drug problems among the hotel and catering industry staff are focused to a large extent on the individual. Restating some observations by Waldorf *et al.* (1991: 69 and 73), we wish to conclude that understanding why some discotheques, bars or restaurants are associated with illicit drug use, 'requires attention to the myriad ways that the characteristics and the culture of employees interact with the structure and the organization of the workplace'. Furthermore, 'certain features of the Zeitgeist or characteristics of organizational culture at some of these workplaces may implicitly or explicitly encourage or discourage drug use'.

Understanding why some respondents use (or abuse) cocaine in the workplace and others do not, requires attention to both the individual and the organizational cultural factors at work. A study of heavy drinking patterns in the restaurant business shows that social modeling and structural factors of the workplace are associated with alcohol consumption (Kjaerheim *et al.*, 1995). Structural factors such as work schedule, type of workplace and company alcohol policy are important prerequisites for the work-related drinking habits in general. Conversely, the modeling factors (such as co-workers taking an end-of-work drink, co-workers going out after work, perceived pressure to drink and modeling by patrons) are predictors for individual heavy drinking.

Similarly, participant observation in the Antwerp nightlife scene supports the hypothesis that structural and modeling factors, which increase co-worker leisure interaction and support positive evaluation of illicit drugs (including cocaine), increase the probability of cocaine use.[9] Structural factors such as co-worker accessibility, teamwork, the company policy on illicit drugs and on-the-job cocaine availability enhance work-related cocaine consumption. Odd working hours or shifts are factors which pull in the same direction. Furthermore, co-workers' drug using levels may be positively related to an individual's cocaine consumption. Some stories of our respondents also suggest that modeling by co-workers and modeling by patrons has influenced their own cocaine consumption, at least to some extent.

18.2.2.2. Cocaine in the arts-related professions

As stated above, cocaine use was at first concentrated among relatively small circles of illicit drug users and members of a few affluent professions. Cocaine first made headlines because of its association with Hollywood celebrities and rock stars. Some of the Antwerp respondents report about cocaine use in the arts-related professions, such as music, the theatre, fashion design, (fashion) photography and modelling, advertising and publicity agencies, etc.:

Yes, in the world of advertising. Yes, it's eh... I won't say it goes without saying there, but it's... it still gives a special cachet to somebody on the job... a coke user... quite a lot of drugs are being used there and coke is one of the main drugs. [...] And then you have the people I came to know in the advertising world, just snobs, who were using coke to... yes, to be 'trendy', or to feel more self-confident, who were using coke as a kind of luxury product. [...] I think that in every job that brings in a lot of cash and that produces people who are creative and who know a lot of people, that coke is a regular thing there... And it's still the same, it's still more interesting than speed or whatever, as they see it. [M/0/02]

I got to know it in Antwerp, yes, by coincidence, I had a few collection pieces that had to be photographed and, it happened at my house at that time, it was kind of a studio, and eh, those models were sitting there, they always went to the back, to cut their stuff, and I got to know them better and that's how it went. [M/0/01]

Most of these stories suggest that in these circles cocaine is typically used for fun, as a party drug, at parties with several fellow workers. Our data do not support the idea of a particular type of user for whom cocaine is more instrumental in intellectual or artistic activities.[10] There are a number of published accounts of individuals who use cocaine in their working lives, and who believed initially that it was a great assistance, particularly in creative activity, before they realized that the assistance rapidly becomes an illusion if not an oppression. This may also explain why cocaine is sometimes reported to have both negative and positive effects on work.

18.2.2.3. Cocaine in the sex industry

Four respondents report having been involved in the sex industry during at least a part of their cocaine career: one woman who has been a striptease artist, one man who has been an escort for female tourists in Mexico, one man who has been involved in the production of porno as a photographer, and one man who was a pimp and body guard for full-time prostitutes. Two other respondents had their girl friend working as a prostitute:

My girlfriend works for erotic fairs, she has been an escort girl, she has gone very far as well, and so, eventually, I think you go very far on coke. There is also a lot of coke use in that scene. It is sometimes asked by the customers. [...] ... in that scene, it is very 'classy', in fact, coke has always had the reputation of being a very 'classy' drug, a very expensive drug, only for people who can afford it, for people who lead a flamboyant life... [U/0/01]

At first the girls entertained them at home. They rented an apartment and then put an advertisement in the regional paper. That's how it works, you know. And so, since then there was of course a lot of money, you know, because there is plenty of money in those circles and there was a lot of cocaine too. That's really typical of prostitution: prostitution and cocaine go along very well. Cocaine and champagne, you often see that. It's a matter of who has a lot of money, is a big spender, and then coke is a very prestigious drug, still because it has little disadvantages as well, a businessman can easily binge a whole weekend long and be on time on Monday, I mean, it fits the picture... [H/0/10]

According to most of these stories, cocaine is used on the initiative of the prostitute's client. Although we did not interview these clients, we suspect that cocaine is typically used to enhance or prolong sexual activity. First, cocaine's reputation as an aphrodisiac suggests it makes sex more intense and more gratifying. Second, users often report that cocaine makes sex less inhibited, more varied and unconventional. Furthermore, most respondents from the Antwerp sample who were involved in the sex industry associated cocaine with exclusivity, top-class, high society, wealth and luxury.

18.3. EFFECTS OF COCAINE USE ON WORK PERFORMANCE

18.3.1. Quantitative data

We asked all respondents for whom this was relevant if the use of cocaine improved or worsened the quality of work done, the quantity of work done, and the relations with colleagues and employers. In table 18.3.a, we present the findings in both the Amsterdam studies and our own data.

Table 18.3.a   Influence of cocaine on work performance, in three samples, in %

Amsterdam I (1987)					
Item	**Improved**	**Deteriorated**	**Both**	**Neither**	**N [*]**
Quality of work	13.3	25.2	18.9	42.7	143
Working relations	5.2	13.3	6.7	74.8	135
Quantity of work done	17.1	16.4	21.2	45.2	146

[*] N is not always 160 due to missing data or because items were not always applicable
   to respondents' personal situation

Amsterdam II (1991)					
Item	**Improved**	**Deteriorated**	**Both**	**Neither**	**N [*]**
Quality of work	20	38	12	54	102
Working relations	10	15	4	78	99
Quantity of work done	24	39	11	48	102

[*] N is not always 108 due to missing data or because items were not always applicable
   to respondents' personal situation

Antwerp (1997)					
Item	**Improved**	**Deteriorated**	**Both**	**Neither**	**N [*]**
Quality of work	22.6	25.0	23.8	28.6	84
Working relations	21.9	32.9	6.8	38.4	73
Quantity of work done	22.6	26.2	25.0	26.2	84

[*] N is not always 111 due to missing data (no opinion) or because items were not always
   applicable to respondents' personal situation

Respondents in all three samples, report both negative and positive effects of cocaine on the quality and quantity of work done, and on working relations. In each sample, however, negative effects are dominant (with the exception of the oddly positive effect of cocaine on the quantity of work done in the 1987 Amsterdam I sample). Overall, the proportion of respondents reporting negative effects is larger than the proportion of respondents indicating positive effects.

The percentages of 'both improved and deteriorated' and 'neither improved nor deteriorated' in all three samples, show similarly marked differences. For each item, the percentage of the 'neither' category is considerably higher than the percentage of 'both'. Although we have to be cautious with interpretations of these strange imbalances, our qualitative data suggest that at least some of our respondents make efforts to ensure that their cocaine use does not interfere with activities that take priority, such as job performance and relations with colleagues. Indeed, the participants reporting neither positive nor negative effects of cocaine on the items above mentioned often add that work and recreational use are two strictly separated spheres of activity (see also Waldorf *et al.*, 1991: 60). We found other indications for this in chapter 14, when we analyzed control mechanisms and informal rules.[11] In other words, cocaine users refrain from the use of cocaine when they are expected to work. Ideally, their cocaine use should not have any effect on their relations with fellow workers. This might explain the imbalances between the categories of 'neither' and 'nor' for these items.

As for *quality of work* done, the number of respondents in both Amsterdam samples who report negative effects is markedly higher than the number of those who report positive effects. In the Antwerp sample we find the same tendency, although much less delineated: 46.4% say cocaine improved the quality of their work, while 48.8% say cocaine deteriorated the quality of their work.[12] In the Antwerp sample 22.6% of the respondents say cocaine has improved the quality of their work at one time or another, which is slightly more than in either Amsterdam sample.[13] Compared to the Dutch samples, more respondents report both positive and negative effects of cocaine on the quality of work done (about one in three in the Antwerp sample) and fewer respondents report 'neither positive nor negative' effects.

As for *quantity of work* done, the number of respondents reporting negative effects is higher than the number of those reporting positive effects in the 1991 Amsterdam II sample and the 1997 Antwerp sample. Again, more respondents report both positive and negative effects (one in four in the Antwerp sample) and fewer respondents report 'neither positive nor negative' effects (about one in five in the Antwerp sample) of cocaine on the quantity of work done, compared to the Dutch samples.

As for *relations with colleagues and/or employer(s)*, table 18.3.a shows that a large majority of the Dutch samples report 'neither positive nor negative effects' of cocaine on their working relations (74.8% in the Amsterdam I sample and 78% in the Amsterdam II sample). In the Antwerp sample this proportion is about half as small (38.4%). Clearly, the Antwerp respondents perceive more positive (28.7% when adding up the 'improved' and 'both'categories) and more negative effects (39.7% when adding up the 'deteriorated' and 'both' categories) of cocaine on their working relations.

These data must probably be interpreted as indications that many respondents experience negative effects of cocaine use the day after at work. When one has been partying all weekend, it can be hard to get up on Monday morning and to go to work. Indeed, even respondents who report never having used any cocaine during working hours (see table 18.2.a) do report negative effects of cocaine use on the quantity of the work done and on relationships with colleagues (e.g. because they are tired and irritable). Thus, like an alcohol hangover, the uncomfortable feelings after 'coming down' from cocaine may have negative effects on the job performance (see also Waldorf *et al.*, 1991: 72).

18.3.2. Qualitative data

As stated above, drug use at work was not a specific topic during the second interview, but some respondents spontaneously told us about their experiences with drugs on the job. Six respondents report extensively on the effects of cocaine on their job performance and working relations. These interviewees distinguish themselves from most other respondents in the Antwerp sample in that they have been using cocaine often or (almost) always at work, and in that they have experienced negative rather than positive effects of their cocaine use on the quality or quantity of the work done, or on the relations with co-workers or superiors. To illustrate the negative effects of cocaine use on work, some stories from each of the three professional sectors described above are presented here. Consider these stories of a bartender and of a bouncer:

It became a very very successful bar, but we mismanaged it completely. Definitely because of coke. [...] It started getting unenjoyable the more we went into the coke. Then I started to have worries, financially, we should have put money away, and we did not, we were just spending, we were spending more than we were getting, and we were getting quite a lot of money, I reckon. So eventually it came to a stage where the two of us were arguing a lot with each other, [...] he was blaming me, and I was blaming him: 'You have to stop with the coke', and I said: 'You have to stop as well'. So, it was kind of like that, we did to a degree, but our business was already very much damaged at that stage, because it could be seen, and it was known. Like lots of people came into the bar and said: 'Hey, where can we get some coke around here?' [...] We never sold coke, never, but I knew dealers who were in there, dealing. [S/0/01]

I couldn't articulate well anymore, and socially you didn't want any contacts anymore, because you were afraid they would notice by your face that you were using. So what do you do then? You turn away your head, you don't speak to anybody. And that's how you get... how other people in any case got the impression I was a very cool guy, to whom you shouldn't say too much. [...] I wasn't sure of myself anymore, when something had to be done I wasn't sure I could take it for a 100%. I became insecure, in the end, and as you are stiff with coke, your muscles become contorted too, and you start shaking on your legs – not because you're afraid- but because of emotions and feelings you can't express because you're blocking, so that nobody would see that you have been using. [Q/0/01]

Of the 17 respondents working in the hotel and catering industry, 7 say cocaine increased the quantity of the work done, versus 4 who say cocaine decreased the quantity of their work. Equal proportions report that cocaine improved and deteriorated the quality of their work (N=8) and their relationships with colleagues (N=6).

As to the arts-related professions, most stories suggest that cocaine is rarely used during artistic performances (by actors, musicians or dancers). These artists may have tried cocaine during working hours (or performances) at a few occasions, but there is a general consensus that it is not done. A jazz musician reports that he quickly felt that cocaine hampered his creativity and virtuosity while playing his instrument. Two actors experimented with cocaine during rehearsals, but quit using during working hours because it hindered their empathy with the characters they were supposed to play and their relations with the other actors. And finally, consider this story of a ballet dancer:

I don't use when I'm dancing. [...] that's what I live for, for me, it's something that makes me very happy: the scene, the rehearsals, the dancers around me, they are people who give a lot of affection, it's a very sensitive environment, very touching, very affective, and also very open sometimes. [...] It's a matter of discipline. I mean: your body, when you use things, you are less able to control your body. When you dance, you have to control your whole body, you have to dominate your whole body, you have to know... what is not good for your body. There are people who take drugs when they dance, but me, I don't think it's right. [...] My choreographer knows very well that I never take drugs during a show. Never! [...] It happened once, during a rehearsal, it's a long time ago, at the cabaret, and I regretted it. I still regret it. I was really ashamed. I couldn't rehearse, I went to sleep, I was afraid. Never again! [H/1/20]

In other arts-related professions cocaine use during the working hours is more acceptable. A photographic model reports that many young, inexperienced girls entering the profession fall prey to heavy cocaine use, through the modeling behavior by more experienced models, photographers and other professionals from the world of fashion. Many models initiate or continue using cocaine (and other substances that suppress appetite) to control or reduce their weight.[14] The next story comes from an adjacent professional sector, fashion design. It illustrates both the attractive (or positive) and unattractive (or negative) sides of cocaine use at work:

> *I worked for X. [i.e. a fashion company annex shop]. It's a fake company to the core. It was an attitude like 'look, we're one big happy, young, hip family' while in fact it was... using, using, using out-and-out. [...] At first it was the first job I really felt comfortable with: I was the kind of guy who did overtime and stuff, who was working incredibly hard... I felt comfortable to a certain extent in that hip thing in that company. But eh... it's all fake. Of course, you only notice that afterwards. In the end, really decadent things happened there, drugs, sex, everything. It was very decadent. There were company parties every now and then, outside the job, and yes... apparently, it didn't have to do anything with the job, but in fact, it was a continuation of the job: all the same 'in-crowd', just everybody from the milieu, who knew each other, who were working for X. as well, and that kind of stuff. [...] But I really was disillusioned. [...] Most people found it fantastic, and they were blinded by it, like: 'Hey, you can address the boss by his first name here, you can speak out here, you can laugh here, and music, and you can live your life the way you want here...' Yes, after a while it had become normal that I was registered as present for a half a day, while they sent me with money from the cashbox to someone to get coke, that was my working day, it just happened after a while. Now I know I never could have stayed there, it was just impossible, but it just happened there. And there was a kind of acknowledgement, like: 'Hey, that's our boss, that's our boss and he uses it too! That's incredible!' Yes, at that moment it really had something. [H/0/30]*

Six of the 20 respondents working in arts-related professions say cocaine has improved the quality of their work. Four of them say cocaine deteriorated the quality of their work, and 3 state it both improved and deteriorated the quality of their work. Half of them report that cocaine deteriorated the quantity of their work, versus 3 respondents who say they produced more work because of cocaine. Seven respondents in the arts-related professions say cocaine had a negative influence on their relations with colleagues, and 5 report cocaine improved these relationships.

As to the sex industry, we have only one account of the effect of cocaine on the perception of the respondent while doing her job. This woman describes how cocaine helped her to be less inhibited while having 'unusual' (i.e. sadomasochist) sex with a client, although only to a certain extent:

> *It's something I would never do if I was clean, because it's something that really doesn't interest me. I'm not at all a sadistic person, but okay, as I was on coke, as I was completely high, and as he wanted to do that, I said: 'Okay, let's try, I'll see how far I can go along'. But I left when he said: 'Piss on me'. That's when, I said, even when I am high as a donkey, I left, because I said: 'No, I can't do that'. [...] These are very rich people. When normal people, who take some coke, okay, when they make love, even on coke, it's true that they will be a little more wild and stuff, but the people who have money, that kind of people, they are businessmen, and they, they are really crazy, you know, they really are not normal, you know, they are wicked, they are really dirty. [H/1/20]*

Most other accounts by people who have been working in the sex industry refer to the effect of cocaine on the behavior of the client. Again, these stories suggest that cocaine is often used on the initiative of the client, in order to make sex with the prostitute more intense, more gratifying, and less inhibited. Furthermore, the general opinion about cocaine use by clients of sex workers is that it brings out people's true nature.

18.4. INFORMAL CONTROL IN THE WORKPLACE

We have shown that understanding cocaine use at work requires attention to the myriad ways in which the characteristics and culture of workers interact with the structure and organization of work. Social modeling and structural factors of the workplace which increase co-worker leisure interaction and support positive evaluation of illicit drugs (including cocaine) *increase* the probability of cocaine use. Conversely, certain characteristics of organizational culture at some of these workplaces may implicitly or explicitly *discourage* drug use. The same processes of social modeling by co-workers and employers that may support illicit drug use, may also act as a barrier against heavy, or any, cocaine use at work. As such, these factors can be seen as mechanisms of informal social control.

First, most of our respondents generally did not use cocaine at or for work. It was shown above that 72% of the Antwerp sample never used cocaine at work. Illicit drug use is taboo in most workplaces (see also Diaz *et al.*, 1992: 303). Most respondents hide their cocaine use for colleagues or lie about it:

> *I lied because of social opportunism. Especially when I know it can have consequences, that I can lose my job... as long as they are satisfied with my work, it would be stupid if they fired me because of their delusions, while they are satisfied with my work.* [E/0/01]

Furthermore, all spoke of their work as vitally important and of careers they aimed to advance. Most people in the sample who worked regularly did not allow their cocaine to interfere with their job performance at all. Most resist the allure of cocaine when their daily life and identity are at risk. Waldorf *et al.* (1991: 73) reached very similar conclusions in their San Francisco study.

Twenty-three respondents (28% of the Antwerp sample) have used cocaine at work. More than half of them (13 interviewees) only did this *once*, usually as an experiment ('to see what it does'), and had never done it again. Only five respondents report using cocaine *often or (almost) always* at work. Five report using cocaine *sometimes* during working hours. Three of them add that this happens occasionally when they go out until the small hours and when they have to go to work the next morning. Another person sometimes uses cocaine to make the repetitive and boring tasks at work more bearable. And finally, one respondent took cocaine for one year because he felt the company demanded more productivity:

> *In the old days, when I went directly from the discotheques to my job, I did. It happened that I couldn't work very well, that I fell asleep, and that I couldn't support too much. Then I dared to take a line of coke to go working. When I was working in Knokke* [i.e. a worldly seaside resort at the Belgian coast, TD], *they knew it on the job. Everybody who worked there, except for the cook and the boss, was taking drugs so...* [G/0/01]

> *I've done that for 1 year, because we were expected to do more for the business and to efface ourselves to obtain better sales figures, whatever, I knew speed, I used it quite a lot, and then I thought, also to stay awake at night of course, until 4 o'clock in the morning, or to work 48 hours on end.* [I/0/13]

Second, cocaine use - and illicit drug use in general – are taboo among the colleagues of most Antwerp respondents. Respondents are afraid that a co-worker blows the whistle on them or that they will be labeled as a drug user. In order to avoid social stigma and/or judicial problems, most cocaine users prefer to keep their use hidden from their colleagues and/or employer:

> *For example, I would never admit it at my job, because first of all, it's none of their business, and they would regard me as an addict, and it would damage my career, and I don't want that.* [P/0/03]

Third, some respondents report they engaged in conversations with co-workers about their drug use. This is particularly the case when most of the employees are a fairly young, liberal and heterogeneous lot. In these stories, the co-workers who are trusted enough to talk to about this sensitive topic are almost exclusively people who are more or less the same age as the respondent and/or who have been or still are using cocaine or other illicit drugs. Waldorf *et al.* (1991: 70) also observed that when other employees have liberal views about most drug use and when these co-workers have at least experimented with illicit drugs in the past or still use marihuana on occasion, chances of discussing cocaine use and its consequences among colleagues are clearly higher. Often respondents also socialize with these co-workers outside the workplace after hours, e.g. in the nightlife scene.

> *In the marketplace yes... there are colleagues market vendors who use as well. You meet them in the nightlife and they say: 'Hey, you take drugs as well? I didn't know that.'* [C/0/11]

> *During my first year at that firm I got a colleague next to me. I was 22-23 years old then, and it was a young guy of about 19-20 years old. It was a very energetic guy, and I had never actually heard about XTC or coke, I had heard about it, but it was the 'none-of-my-business-show', and he talked about it for a very long time, and then I said at a certain moment: 'I want to try that too'.* [P/0/04]

Fourth, respondents of some professional sectors express a laissez-faire attitude about drug use. Similar to our findings, Waldorf *et al.* (1991: 69) observe in their San Francisco sample that some colleagues are inclined to overlook drug use among those with whom they socialize outside work. Especially in the hotel and catering industry, colleagues have an unwritten understanding about tolerance, which means, among other things, that what people do in their own time is their own business. Some decide not to confront anybody else about drugs because they never want to be confronted about their own problems. For others this mutual tolerance serves the business well (flexible work schedules, democratic supervision, etc.). Only when an individual overindulges in alcohol, cocaine or another substance, affecting his/her performance, is there reason to approach that person about the effect his/her drug use is having on his/her productivity:

> *My relationship with my fellow workers is very good, I know a lot of them who use it too. There is a lot being said about it. [...] Not in a negative sense, they just laugh and criticize, like: 'What's up? Did you go out too late again?', or so, 'Yes, you look kinda pale', because we know that in the hotel and catering industry, not only about drugs, but also alcohol, you know. 'Ha, you drank too much yesterday, didn't you?' Like that. But they don't argue about it, because everybody knows: 'You do your thing, and I do mine, when you have a problem with it, yes, watch out, because I may not be the boss, but when the problem be-*

389

comes a problem on the job, I don't agree either that I have to stand in for you five days in a row, just because you have been snorting too much...' I don't like it either when a customer comes up to me and says: 'Hey, that other waiter smells like alcohol, how is it possible?' I don't think that's okay either, you know, but other than that. You're mature enough to find out what is good and what is bad, right? [C/0/06]

To conclude, we have illustrated how some characteristics of organizational culture in some workplaces may implicitly or explicitly discourage drug use. First, it must be kept in mind that most of our respondents did not use cocaine at or for work. Of those who did, most did not allow their cocaine to interfere with their job performance. Unfortunately, illicit drug use is taboo among most of the Antwerp respondents' colleagues. In order to avoid social stigma and/or judicial problems, most cocaine users prefer to keep their use hidden for their colleagues and/or employer. Typically, fellow workers are only trusted if they hold liberal attitudes about most drug use, if they are of the same age as the respondent and if they have at least experimented with illicit drugs in the past. Finally, in some professional sectors respondents express a laissez-faire attitude about their co-workers' drug use. Especially in the hotel and catering industry, colleagues have an unwritten understanding about tolerance, which means, among other things, that what people do in their own time is their own business.

18.5. CONCLUSION

Most of our respondents generally did not use cocaine at or for work: 72% of the Antwerp sample never used cocaine at work. All spoke of their work as vitally important and of careers they aimed to advance. Our qualitative data suggest that most of our respondents make efforts to ensure that their cocaine use does not interfere with activities that take priority, such as job performance and working relations. Contrary to what the official discourse makes us believe, most resist the temptation of cocaine when their conventional daily life and identity are at risk. Indeed, work and recreational drug use are two strictly separated spheres of activity.

Some of the Antwerp respondents find cocaine useful for work purposes. In the Antwerp sample about one in three interviewees (who were working at the time of the interview) had been under the influence of cocaine during working hours. More than half of them (13 interviewees) only did this once, usually as an experiment ('to see what it does'), and never did it again. Only five respondents report extensively on the negative effects of cocaine on their job performance and working relations. These interviewees distinguish themselves from most other respondents in the Antwerp sample in that they often or (almost) always used cocaine at work.

When asked if the use of cocaine either improved or worsened the quality of work done, the quantity of work done, and the relations with colleagues and employer(s), respondents report both negative and positive effects, although negative effects are dominant. Compared to the Dutch samples, more respondents report both positive and negative effects of cocaine on the quality and the quantity of work, and on their working relations, and fewer respondents report 'neither positive nor negative' effects. We believe these data reflect the negative effects some respondents experience on Mondays, when coming down from heavy cocaine use during the weekend. This kind of hangover results in fatigue and irritability, which in turn may lead to negative conse-quences in the workplace.

Concurrent with the data from Amsterdam, we find a high prevalence of artistic and hotel/bar professions among those respondents reporting to have been often or always under the influence of one of these drugs, and among those who have been under the influence of *more than one* drug during working hours. The hotel/bar professionals show the highest prevalence of being under the influence of alcohol and cocaine (sometimes, often or almost always). Arts-related professionals show the highest prevalence of having been under the influence of cannabis (sometimes or more often) during working hours. Within the categories of artists and students, the prevalence of having been under the influence of cannabis is highest; whereas within the category of hotel/bar employees the prevalence of having been under the influence of alcohol is highest.

Qualitative data show that cocaine use is no longer concentrated among relatively small circles of illicit drug users, bohemians, and members of some affluent, high-pay, high-pressure professions. Our data suggest that it is now occurring across the occupa-tional spectrum and in all sorts of workplaces.

For example, many of our respondents in the hotel and catering industry (including discotheques) find cocaine functional in their jobs. As a stimulant, cocaine reduces the chronic fatigue that comes with long hours on their feet, aids their productivity and improves their mood. Clearly, an important factor that facilitates initiation into and continuation of cocaine use in the sector of hotels, restaurants, bars and especially in discotheques and dance clubs is *its general availability*, linked with its reputation as a party drug. Furthermore, staff in discotheques are often confronted with clients looking for cocaine on the one hand and dealers looking for clients on the other. Certain fea-tures of the Zeitgeist or characteristics of organizational culture in some of these work-places may implicitly or explicitly encourage or discourage drug use, and some indi-viduals working in the hotel and catering industry may eventually drift into selling co-caine during working hours.

Structural factors such as co-worker accessibility, teamwork, company policy on illicit drugs and on-the-job cocaine availability, enhance work-related cocaine con-sumption. Odd working hours or shifts are factors which pull in the same direction. Furthermore, co-workers' drug using levels may be positively related to an individual's cocaine consumption. Some respondents also suggest that modeling by co-workers and by employers has influenced their own cocaine consumption, at least to some extent. Conversely, certain characteristics of organizational culture in some of these work-places may implicitly or explicitly discourage drug use. The same processes of social modeling by co-workers and employers that may support illicit drug use, may also act as a barrier against heavy, if any, cocaine use at work. These can be seen as mecha-nisms of informal social control.

Most stories about cocaine use in arts-related professions suggest that cocaine is typically used in these circles for fun, as a party drug, during parties with colleagues. Our data do not support the idea of a particular type of user for whom cocaine is more instrumental in intellectual or artistic activities. Some respondents may have been us-ing cocaine in their working lives, believing it initially to be of assistance (particularly in creative activity) before realizing that the assistance rapidly becomes an illusion, if not an oppression. Cocaine is rarely used during artistic performances (by actors, musicians or dancers). In other arts-related professions (models, photographers and fashion designers) cocaine use during working hours is more acceptable.

Four respondents report having been involved in the sex industry during at least a part of their cocaine career. Two other respondents have witnessed some aspects of the sex industry because their girl friends worked as prostitutes. Most accounts by people who work in the sex industry refer to the effect of cocaine on the client's behavior. Again, these stories suggest that cocaine is often used on the initiative of the client, in order to make sex with the prostitute more intense, more gratifying, and less inhibited. Furthermore, respondents from the Antwerp sample who were involved in the sex industry usually associate cocaine with exclusivity, top-class, high society, wealth and luxury. Their general opinion about cocaine use by clients of sex workers is that it brings out people's true nature (decadence).

To conclude, we have illustrated how some characteristics of organizational culture in some workplaces may implicitly or explicitly discourage drug use. First, it must be kept in mind that most of our respondents generally did not use cocaine at or for work (contrary to what the official discourse tends to make us believe). Of those who did, most did not allow their cocaine to interfere with their job performance. Unfortunately, illicit drug use is taboo among the colleagues of most of the Antwerp respondents. In order to avoid social stigma and/or judicial problems, most cocaine users prefer to keep their use hidden from their colleagues and/or employer. Typically, fellow workers are only trusted if they hold libertarian attitudes about most drug use, if they are of the same age as the respondent, and if they have at least experimented with illicit drugs in the past. Finally, in some professional sectors respondents express a laissez-faire attitude about drug use. Especially in the hotel and catering industry, colleagues have an unwritten understanding about tolerance, which means, among other things, that what people do in their own time is strictly their own business.

NOTES

1 See Chapter 8, p. 197-198.

2 Although not perfectly comparable, Cohen (1989: 125) looked especially at those who reported having been under the influence *more than 3 times* during the last three months. He found that 22 respondents had been under the influence of one drug more often than 3 times (20.6% of the total number of respondents who had employment), 7 respondents under the influence of 2 different drugs (6.5% of the working respondents) and 4 under the influence of three different drugs (3.7%).

3 See Chapter 8, p. 199.

4 See Chapter 3, p. 82.

5 Following our own classification of professions in Chapter 3, we find similar tendencies. The highest prevalence of having been under the influence of cocaine or alcohol is found for the category of skilled workers with a lower secondary school certificate (the category which includes most of the hotel/bar employees). The highest prevalence of having been under the influence of cannabis is found in the arts-related professions. Furthermore we see that among employees with higher education certificate, the prevalence of having been under the influence of any drug is very small or zero. See Chapter 3, p. 81-82.

6 See Chapter 3, p. 81.

7 These respondents often report the use of other stimulant drugs, such as amphetamines ('speed') and Captagon®, on the job to enhance mood or productivity for work.

8   See also the data on the location of initiation and the initiation company, Chapter 4, p. 102-104. For example, 4 of the 10 respondents who reported having been initiated in a bar or café, worked in the hotel and catering industry at the time of interview. Conversely, 6 of the 18 respondents who worked in the hotel and catering industry at the time of the interview, reported having been initiated in a bar or a discotheque. One of the two respondents who reported having been initiated by a fellow worker worked in the hotel and catering industry.

9   However, cocaine use might influence the choice of workplace and work schedule and the perception of the co-worker modeling. This means that selective forces cannot be ruled out as an explanation of the phenomenon. It is likely that the dynamic is dual; structural and modeling factors the influence consumption, which in turn may the influence these factors.

10   In Chapter 11 we did not find a clear relation between the arts-related professions and the frequency of reporting 'more creative' as an advantage of cocaine. Only 5 of the 20 respondents with an arts-related profession reported 'creative' as an advantage of cocaine. Of the 22 respondents who report 'more creative' as an advantage of cocaine only 5 worked in an arts-related profession at the time of the interview (see Chapter 11, p. 247). Of those who did report 'creative', 6 worked in the hotel and catering industry, 3 were unemployed, and 2 worked in the social sector, etc.

11   See Chapter 14, p. 307 and 312-315.

12   These percentages are calculated by adding the percentages of 'both improving and deteriorating' to the percentages of 'improved' and 'deteriorated'.

13   Compare this with the Scotland sample (Ditton & Hammersley, 1996: 55), of whom 33% claimed that cocaine had improved the quality of their work, and a further 24% claimed it had harmed the quality of their work (this included 9 users who had previously indicated that cocaine had also improved the quality of their work).

14   Some authors have suggested that almost half of the women using cocaine did so as a weight control measure. See: COCHRANE, C., MALCOLM, R. and BREWERTON, T. (1998), The role of weight control as a motivation for cocaine abuse, 23 *Addictive Behaviors* 2, 201-207.

CHAPTER 19

INFORMAL CONTROL AND INFORMAL HELP AMONG FRIENDS

19.1. INTRODUCTION

In the previous chapters we discussed the reciprocal effects of cocaine on family, professional, and partner relationships. In this chapter we analyse some effects of cocaine use on friendships, and the influence friends have on the respondents' cocaine use.

Throughout the previous chapters it became clear that friends play an important role in the initiation and the development of cocaine use patterns of our subjects. In paragraph 19.2 the most salient findings regarding the role of friends from other chapters are assembled. Like in the other chapters, we analyze comments from respondents to other cocaine users and remarks from other users to the respondents, to illustrate informal social control among friends (§19.3). Finally, the respondents' accounts about informal help among cocaine-using friends and emergency situations/overdoses are discussed in paragraph 19.4.

19.2. COCAINE USE AMONG FRIENDS

19.2.1. Findings from previous chapters

Friends have a major impact on an individual's drug use. Above we have shown the social character of illicit drug use in general, and the impact of friends on respondents' cocaine use in particular.

In Chapter 4 we showed among others that early experimentation with cocaine generally occurs in the company of a friend or group of friends and that neophyte users receive guidance from friends in the process of 'becoming a cocaine user'.[1] Yet, almost all respondents report that trying out cocaine was their own choice, although they acknowledge that friends or 'peers' play an important role in the onset and continuation of cocaine use.

In Chapter 6 we showed that the respondents' choice of route of ingestion is often influenced by others.[2] The proper technique of preparing freebase cocaine and of smoking it is often learned through observation and imitation of 'experienced' users, usually friends (Chapter 7).[3] Furthermore, friends can also be an important source of supply for the user (Chapter 9).[4]

In Chapter 12 we found that non-using friends can be an important reason for periodic abstinence or cutting back on cocaine use.[5] Furthermore, emotional support from peers can help users to cope with difficulties in cutting back or quitting. Many respondents report avoiding cocaine using friends and seeking help from other friends, in order to quit from cocaine.

In Chapter 13 we presented qualitative data that show that craving (or desire) is often triggered by specific set and setting factors, such as the presence of certain friends, or a specific mood of the user and his/her company.[6] Going out, parties and meeting friends are the three situations in which cocaine use occurs most often (Chapter 14). Clearly, the most suitable situations for cocaine use are those in which people enjoy each other's company.[7] Furthermore, negative and/or positive feelings are often triggered by friends' words, behavior and moods, and can thus indirectly influence the user's cocaine experience. Many set and setting factors that support or interfere with informal control mechanisms relate to the influence of friends (Chapter 14). Respondents report troubles with respect for their principles of use when intimate friends are involved, when they are in an extremely pleasant environment (with friends), when cocaine is offered by friends, when friends talk about it... On the other hand, respect for the user's own rules of behavior can be suppported when he/she is among acquaintances.

In Chapter 15 we stated that forty-seven respondents (43.9% of the total sample) reported having a friend or acquaintance that served as a counter-example, i.e. as a person whose cocaine use they would never imitate.[8] In chapters 16, 17 and 18 we analysed the possible influence of the partner, the colleagues and the siblings on the respondents' cocaine use. Our qualitative data indicate that in some cases respondents classified these persons as 'friends'. Thus, many of the conclusions on informal social control processes may apply to 'friends' as well.

19.2.2. Effects of cocaine use on friendships

We asked all respondents whether the use of cocaine either improved or worsened relationships with friends. Of those respondents who replied to this question, 22.7% report that cocaine improved their relations with friends, 26.7% say cocaine deteriorated them, 29.3% state cocaine had both positive and negative effects on their friendships, and 21.3% report that cocaine neither improved nor deteriorated their relationships with friends.

When asked about crucial events that had an important influence on their cocaine use pattern, 18 respondents (16.2% of the total sample) indicate that their use increased as they made new cocaine-using friends.[9] Conversely, 5 respondents (4.5% of the total sample) report that their cocaine use decreased because their friends cut down or quit using cocaine.

> *Always people I came to know or whom I knew, who had an influence on it, but other than that no. Because of some people I started to use more, and because of other people I started to use less.* [G/1/02]

> *I had some friends who changed completely and stuff. Who didn't dare to step outside anymore. It's kinda scary, really. I didn't come around to those friends anymore, because it wasn't fun anymore, you know. I mean, yes, I used less as well, right?* [H/0/12]

The fact that I had to stop with it has to do with the fact that our friends ditched us. And that really motivated me, because we had very good friends, but in the end they said: 'We're not coming to see you anymore'. Because we slept until 6 o'clock in the evening, and we started to base right away. And that damaged a lot. I think, if those friends hadn't been there, I would still be... [H/1/17]

19.3. INFORMAL SOCIAL CONTROL AMONG FRIENDS

19.3.1. Respondents' remarks to friends

Our respondents were asked to state whether they ever made any remarks about the cocaine use of others. Ninety-two respondents (82.9% of the total sample) report having made remarks to friends about their cocaine use. Table 19.3.a shows the major categories of the respondents' replies.

Table 19.3.a   Types of respondents' remarks to friends, in the 1997 Antwerp sample [*]

Antwerp (1997) N=111		
Remarks	**N**	**%**
On dose and/or frequency of use	63	56.8
On behavioral changes	24	21.6
On route of ingestion	13	11.7
On negative consequences of cocaine use on job, family life, health, etc.	9	8.1
On amount of money spent on cocaine	5	4.5
On technique of using	5	4.5
On price/quality of cocaine	3	2.7
On the person's conspicuous behavior	2	1.8
Other	*3*	*2.7*

[*] More than one answer was possible

Most remarks related to the dose or the frequency of cocaine use. More than half of the Antwerp interviewees (56.8%) report having pointed out to other users that they were 'exaggerating', i.e. using too much cocaine, or too frequently. Typically, respondents had advised their friend(s) to cut down on their use, to abstain temporarily or to quit using cocaine altogether (see also Diaz *et al.*, 1992: 303-304).

Yes, when a friend of mine uses too much, I will tell her. Then I won't say: 'X., stop it.' But I will discuss it. 'You are acting a bit stupid, or you're going too far, are you aware of what you're doing?' [G/1/02]

And with that particular person it was just... not the way he did it, but just the frequency, the quantity... I told him he was overdoing it. We really made it clear to him with a couple of people that it could not go on like that any longer. [R/0/08]

Yea, I've often talked about it. Maybe among friends, for instance, I've seen someone take a line that length [makes a lengthy gesture] . I remember making a remark to someone: 'Just go easy on it, take it fucking easy, or you'll be fucking on it again. You don't need that now. You just had a line'. [S/0/01]

Twenty-four participants (21.6% of the total sample) remarked to a friend that his/her cocaine use had led to negative changes in their behavior: they had become aggressive, ego-centered, introverted, irritable, depressed, insensitive, superficial, paranoid, etc. and consequently they had become unpleasant company for the respondent. Some respondents state that they overtly disapproved of their friends' behavior as these people started to engage in illegal activities to obtain money for cocaine or started selling illicit drugs. Friends who started to lie or cheat provoked comments such as these:

> *Someone I thought was using too much. That it changed his behavior and that it wasn't okay. That his friends didn't like it because he became aggressive.* [C/0/02]

> *I told them they became crazy! That they were paranoid, that they locked themselves in their house, that they didn't open the door anymore, that they were on coke all the time. That they didn't make love anymore.* [H/1/20]

> *Yes, I did, when they can't cope with it, when they become aggressive. Then I tell them they'd better not do it, I mean, when I'm around. When they are planning to do it, I say: 'Yes, but no coke, because I know you're on coke. I prefer you to take XTC'.* [I/1/14]

Thirteen respondents (11.7%) report having made remarks about route of ingestion. Most of them had tried to dissuade friends from freebasing or injecting cocaine, because they felt these routes of ingestion could easily lead to addictive or compulsive drug taking. Two respondents, however, had pointed out to others that freebasing is better than snorting cocaine because it yields more direct and more pleasurable effects.

> *There was someone who just did it in a cigarette, and smoked it. I said: 'Jeezes, if that's gonna give it to you, you may as well throw it in the trashcan! When you do it, you ought to do it right'. I said: 'Have you ever tried it another way? You can also base it, if you're doing it anyway, you'll have more of it'. I'll never encourage anyone to shoot it, I'll never do that...* [H/0/29]

> *To a friend who has injected a few times. I said: 'Come on, are you kidding me?' At first it didn't occur to her, then I told some other friends I always go out with, and then she became aware that she had to be careful with it, that it's dangerous. So first I talked with the girl herself, and then with those other friends as well. And they were also taken alack, and they said too: 'You have to take it easy, it's not good, you never know whether something goes wrong. What would you do then?''* [Z/0/01]

Nine respondents (8.1% of the sample) made remarks about the negative consequences of cocaine use on job performance, on relationships with family members, fellow workers, partner and friends, and on physical health (looks). Five respondents (4.5% of the sample) had pointed out to friends that they were spending too much money on cocaine. Another five respondents had commented on the technique of using: how to prepare freebase cocaine, how to prepare a shot of cocaine, etc. Three respondents made a remark about the low quality of cocaine their friend was using (and where to buy better cocaine), and two respondents had tried to correct other users because their conspicuous behavior might draw police attention.

> *Yes, especially with that friend, I had lengthy conversations about how and why, and the risk of losing all social contacts and especially losing your job.* [Y/0/01]

> *Yes, like the guy who smoked coke and stuff, he never washed his coke with water, so it's still full of ammonia, and his aluminum foil is poisonous too. So I try to make it clear to him, because the guys looks like a wreck.* [H/0/08]

The showing off with 'Look, I'm using', with little boxes, and 'This is my special gear' and so... I mean, the conspicuous use, I make remarks about that. Sure. I don't say it right away, you know, I won't start bullshitting about their showing off when there are other people around, I'll just do it discretely, when we are alone. [...] I think it's stupid to take out something with people you don't know, and to offer them some, to let other people take advantage to take a line, even strangers. Like: 'Yes, but I know that guy'. Yes, it doesn't matter. I find that dangerous. Before you know you're in deep shit. [H/0/30]

19.3.2. Friends' remarks to respondents

Our respondents were also asked whether they had ever received comments on their own cocaine use. Seventy-two participants (64.9% of the total sample) report having had remarks from one or more friends. The kind of remarks made to respondents were very similar to those made by the respondents. Most remarks related to the dose or the frequency of cocaine use. Respondents were told they were 'exaggerating', and advised to cut down on their use, to abstain temporarily or to quit using cocaine altogether. Other remarks related to negative changes in the respondent's behavior and to his/her route of ingestion. Consider the following examples:

- *'It's time you quit, okay, you're playing the fool again, you can't keep yourself under control anymore'.* [B/0/02];
- *'You're doing weird things, you're looking through the window continuously. Come on, there's nobody, just sit down'.* [F/0/03];
- *'You have to quit, you're neglecting everybody from my circle of friends'.* [H/0/11]
- *Yes, that I became thin, that I looked bad, yes, the people also saw I didn't eat anymore. That I was wasting my life.* [H/0/23]
- *About that freebasing I had a remark once. That you're hooked to it right away. That basing was one of the heaviest things, that it is the most addictive...* [H/1/07]
- *That I had to learn: when it's not there, it's not there. So when you go out, don't start looking for it, like: 'I want coke, I want coke!', that you are calling everyone, that when it's not there, that you can say: 'Okay, it's not there, we just have fun without it'.* [H/1/28]
- *That I was using too much. Like: 'What are you doing?' And at the same time, like: 'Maybe you ought to realize that you have to cut back. Don't let it be the center of your life.'* [I/1/04]
- *Yes, that I wasn't the one I used to be, that I had changed in a negative sense. 'Don't let yourself go like that, you used to be a nice guy, and now you're like this.'* [I/1/17]

Although most comments from other users were typically negative, three respondents also claim to have had positive remarks. One respondent reports other users expressed their admiration for her ability to consume small doses on any occasion. Another respondent states that her friends have congratulated her on several occasions because she was able to refuse cocaine when it was offered for free. At the same time, these accounts illustrate subjective indicators of controlled and uncontrolled use.[10] Consider the two following stories:

They sometimes find it weird that I refuse it. When they offer it to me and I say no. They think it's bizarre. You can see it from their reaction, it's not always said in so many words, but you notice it. [H/1/14]

From people who were using a lot, I always got remarks like... encouraging remarks, that my use has always been stable. People who were using more than I was or who were using very frequently, they were jealous about it to some extent, I think. So in that sense it was sometimes said: how strong my character was regarding coke. [Y/0/01]

19.3.3. Talking about cocaine

We asked respondents whether they had discussed their cocaine use with other people during the four weeks prior to the interview, and if so, about what aspects of their cocaine use. Seventy-six respondents answered affirmatively (68.5% of the total sample). Four respondents stated having talked about their cocaine use with non-users:

> *About the use and about coke itself, in the sense that... with a friend of mine who is totally ignorant of the phenomenon of drug use, except the use of cannabis, but other than that she knows little about it. And I had noticed that she had quite a few myths in her head, and I just tried to debunk them, and I told her a bit about my use.* [H/0/27]

> *I've just discussed it with a colleague at work, yesterday. He told me he had never used it, and I gave some explanation about what it feels like, and the price, and that it is very expensive and stuff.* [H/0/29]

The other seventy-two respondents had discussed the following topics with other users during the last four weeks: pleasant and unpleasant experiences with cocaine (good and bad memories), the adverse effects of cocaine, the advantages and disadvantages of cocaine compared to other substances, temporary abstinence from and quitting cocaine, emotional states during cocaine use, the financial consequences of cocaine use, dosage and frequency of use, the quality and prices of cocaine, the sources of cocaine supply, the presence or absence of craving, plans for future use, appropriate and inappropriate reasons for using cocaine, the pattern of use of others, the illegal status of cocaine and its consequences for the user, participation in the present study and its effects on the respondent, etc.[11] These conversations also seem to buttress sanctions and rituals (see also Zinberg, 1984: 104 and 128).

Most of the conversations our respondents report deal with positive and negative experiences with cocaine, and with various methods of controlling the substance. There is a pervasive general concern about whether or not one is 'addicted' or 'in control'.

> *Yes, I think it's a sharing of experiences and also somewhat looking for confirmation. Maybe from that kind of insecurity like: 'It is something that is forbidden, in fact I am doing something illegal every time, and what does someone else think about it?'* [K/1/03]

> *Yes, with reference to the fact that X. [i.e. a key-informant, TD] called about this study, I talked about it with my husband and with another friend. We discussed whether my use personally bothers me, and whether you can defend it, and whether you are ashamed of it...* [K/1/02]

> *Yes, that too, we talk a lot about it, less about the effects, but more about the frequency. In fact, we have built a kind of control towards each other, I mean, built in, it's not like: 'We'll start controlling each other', but it does happen somehow. For example, when I would use coke for two or three days in a row, they would tell me. It can be said laughing, you know, but meanwhile they did tell me, and I know it too. And I find it good that it's done that way...* [R/0/08]

19.3.4. Effectiveness of informal social control

The crucial question here is whether these remarks have a observable effect on the pattern of cocaine use. Whether an individual perceives a remark or comment as well-founded, apt or negligible, depends on many factors: the source or the maker of the remark, its form and content, the situation in which the comment is made and the emotional state of the receiver, etc.

Comments from non-users are often rejected with the argument that they are 'ignorant' of the positive sides and the essence of the drug, and 'hypocritical', because they disapprove of illicit drug use while they themselves use licit drugs such as alcohol, tobacco, sleeping pills etc. Typically, respondents state that they reply to remarks from non-users with a shrug of indifference, with verbal aggression, etc. In some cases they make an effort to explain their investment in cocaine.

> *I always tried to put forward my arguments, and when I thought they would eventually violate my privacy too much, so to speak, I did screen myself off. Then I said: 'Sorry, but I can still decide myself what I do with my body'. In the long run you say that, because you say: 'Guys, I told you my arguments, what more do you want?' There are people who don't want to listen to these arguments, who have a particular idea...* [H/0/27]

> *Even recently I found, for the umpteenth time, that I must not think naïvely that those people can be convinced. I shouldn't try to give an explanation, because the idea is so established in our society, that you can't change it anyway. The only thing that is possible is a lengthy process of talking and talking.* [H/0/30]

> *I try to understand it, in the sense that, because these are remarks that stem from ignorance, and that's why it has little use to argue about it. I do try to explain how the matter stands, without trying to extol coke and coke use, because I don't want to incite anyone to do it. But I do want to inform when I'm asked to. Because I don't want to be seen as a junky, when I'm just using coke every now and then.* [I/0/03]

The respondents' reaction to comments on their cocaine use usually depends on the (perceived) pattern of cocaine use of the commentator. When the latter uses cocaine in higher doses or more frequently than the respondent, the remarks are perceived as inappropriate.

> *When they stay off the coke, it's okay for me, but when they are taking it themselves, the pot is calling the kettle black! That's how it usually is, right?* [H/1/19]

> *It was a really good friend of mine, and we were using at that time the same, we used every day, en sometimes I said to him: 'Oh man, you do too much', and the next day he said the same to me.* [I/0/06]

Furthermore, the effect of the remarks may depend on the form they take. Informal social control can take many forms. Some commentators pick out a discrete and pleasant situation to approach the subject, others just blurt out anything at any moment. Some individuals try to communicate their message in a quiet chat, whereas others become angry, pedantic or paternalistic. Appreciation of another person's behavior can be expressed verbally, or shown with facial expressions. Sometimes, one ignores or avoids a person to make clear one does not agree with his/her behavior. Finally, mutual comments can take the form of a joking discourse.

> *But there are also many people who just don't say it, you know. You can see them thinking like: 'Oh my god.' But they remain silent. And that's often what affects you most. You can defend yourself against somebody who says something about it, and then you deny it and ig-*

nore it and you say: 'Yes, but it's not true, and I'm not using a lot.' But when you see some-one thinking: 'Look at him. He's doing it again...' then you'll say afterwards: 'God damned, I find it quite humiliating, you know.' It's true. [H/0/05]

Sometimes we joke about it, but sometimes it's the best thing to do, just have a laugh with it. You don't blame him, you talk with him, but sometimes you say: 'You with your skinny drumsticks' or so. Just to make them realize, right, that they don't look good, that they don't have that craziness over them, that they know they have to calm down. You can't force those people to stop, you know, I mean, they have to do it themselves. But you have to tell them, and you shouldn't ditch them. I mean, we don't ditch them, but we do joke about it, we make some jokes about it, and usually they'll feel bad about it, and they'll cut back a little. [I/0/11]

Respondent: Not sincerely. I mean, it is like, because the last two or three months I have been using it almost weekly on Friday night, they have said, jokingly: 'Oh boy, you are exaggerating, aren't you?'... You do think about that, you know, and you give it a moment's thought, you try to decide for yourself whether... I mean, I feel comfortable with it, at this moment it isn't problematic yet, but I like it that they keep an eye on it. I keep an eye on them as well.
Interviewer: And how did you react?
Respondent: At that moment I laugh it off, you know. They laugh as well. At that moment it is usually said as a joke, because they actually have about the same frequency like me, so... but in se I find it good that there is this kind of internal control towards each other, that you keep an eye on each other... [R/0/08]

Informal comments can provoke a wide range of reactions, from aggression and indifference, to feigned consent and simulated remorse, to indulgence and behavioral change. Individuals may react differently to similar comments, and even the same individual may react in various ways, depending on his/her mood and on the (perceived) attitude of the commentator:

The one time I was really touched inside, I started to cry, I admitted I was getting addicted, I knew I had to do something about it... those people were shocked of course. And the other time you become angry, right? Because you don't want to face the facts, you just don't want to realize it. [H/1/17]

Some users do not want to listen to these remarks because they feel their cocaine use is nobody's business but theirs, and because they feel in control of the drug. Others pretend to agree with the commentator, but do not change their behavior.

Actually, I really felt attacked. Because I knew: 'Okay, I mean, when I think it's too much, I'll see it'. I've been doing it for a few years, and sometimes I do quit for months, and I know when something goes too far. Okay, maybe not, but I think I still control myself. [I/1/16]

Yes, you keep saying yes, but you don't do it. When you are in a depressive mood, you say yes, but one or two weeks later you've already forgotten it. And you go get some again. At moments that I thought it was too much myself, yes, I agreed with them. But afterwards I trivialized it somehow. [C/0/01]

Still others report that these comments did not affect them initially, because they did not care, but in the long run they came to recognize their friends were right.

> *Respondent: I didn't care at that moment. The thinner I became, the more I liked it. I didn't care what they said. And when my parents said: 'You look bad, look at yourself.' It went in one ear and out the other. I didn't give a damn.*
> *Interviewer: Did those remarks have any effect?*
> *Respondent: At that moment it doesn't affect you, but when you are alone at home, you think about it, in fact, but you don't want to show to anyone else. I must say, when I was alone, I thought about it. [Z/1/04]*

Several participants indicate they readily accept remarks from friends because it stimulates their reflection about their own use and because it keeps them alert to the pitfalls of the drug:

> *Usually I am touched, because when someone says something like that, it is a kind of concern, and so I find it, whatever the reason for it may be, it does confront me at that moment, so that's why I think at that particular moment: 'Actually, it's true'. But the point is you do realize it perfectly yourself, but it is just nice to hear it from someone else as well. Sometimes you just want to hear from another person, while you are aware of it, like: 'hey, you're using too much now, just try to cut back.' [H/0/30]*

When asked whether their comments had any effect on the other person, thirteen participants (14.1% of the respondents who report having made remarks to friends) reply they do not know. Thirty respondents (32.6% of the respondents who report having made remarks to friends) claim the other users reacted *negatively*: careless ('I do not give a damn'), aggressively ('None of your business'), irritably, shocked, with denial, repulsively, denigratorily, etc.

Another thirty respondents (32.6% of the respondents who report having made remarks to friends) state their remarks did have a *positive* outcome. The other users took the comments into account, or they appeared to think about them. They understood the message. They agreed with the maker of the comments and often made efforts to change their cocaine use.

> *In that period, I usually said: 'I'm just going out a bit.' 'Sure', they said, 'but you are going out six days in a row.' At first I said: 'What's wrong with that?'. I didn't care about it. But it became more and more, and talking can do a great deal, I think. So it became more sporadic again. They made me face the facts, like: 'Hup, you're doing it again'. And that's how I came to recognize it... They are right in a way. [Z/0/01]*

Most of the respondents who state their comments had a positive effect add that the other user(s) already 'knew' that he/she was using too much, or too frequently. Most of the respondents' accounts show that a prerequisite for effective informal social control is a strong or intimate bond between the commentator and the object of the comments. Our participants stress the fact that only the remarks of close friends can adjust their cocaine use. Comments by acquaintances, strangers, and non-users in general, go in one ear and out the other:

> *Those people agreed with me, they realized it themselves, they were aware of it themselves. It's also, when I say that to people, I suppose that you can just say the things you think to each other, not only with respect to drugs. I do not condemn those people either, or else it doesn't make sense to me to call these people my friends. When I can't call these people friends, then it's none of my business. Usually, the couple of people I can say that to and who in turn can say that to me, they surely take into account those remarks. [H/0/30]*

But usually they react to it quite well. But it's also because you have known each other for a long time, for years, and now we are all in that users' environment, and then you can put up with quite a lot from each other. We know each other very well, and so it's all possible. [V/1/01]

Fifteen respondents (16.3% of the respondents who report having made remarks to friends) indicate that their remarks were appreciated by some users, but rejected by others. Some of these participants report that comments directed at the same person could have a positive effect on some occasions, and a negative effect on other occasions. When users are under the influence of cocaine they especially are susceptible to comments from others. And finally, four respondents (4.3% of the respondents who report having made remarks to friends) state that, at first, their comments did not seem to have any effect on the other users, but in the long run these remarks resulted in behavioral changes.

At the moment itself when they have been using, when it is in their body, they say: 'Yes, pff, I'll quit some day.' And when they haven't used, you can talk to them better, but yes, they will start thinking and thinking and thinking, and yes... I don't know what it is. It does have an influence when they haven't been using, then it does something, because you talk with them, they have feelings then, they cry... but when they have been using, they don't have any feelings anymore, right? It's like you hit a black wall then. [H/1/17]

I mean, the first reaction was like: 'Come on, I don't have any problem.', but then, by talking more about it, he realized as well that we found him too important the way he was, and that we didn't want to see him pine away. And now, it has been one and a half or two years, he still quotes that, quite often, and he always says: 'Do you remember the time you helped me out of it?' I mean, he says it jokingly, but in fact, it was like that. But his first reaction was like: 'I don't have a problem, what are you talking about?' [R/0/08]

When you hear it from different people, it does help somehow, yes. But from one person... Because to me as well... a person said: 'You've changed.' I said: 'You're kidding me, aren't you?' But then I got that remark from different people, from real friends, because only intimate friends will tell you, and then you start thinking: 'Is there really something wrong?' I'm telling you: you need friends, real friends. Not just anybody from the discotheque, that doesn't help you at all. [Z/0/03]

Finally, the following account by a 30-year-old barkeeper illustrates how informal comments or remarks from others can affect the user, until he/she reaches a stage where he/she is no longer able to conform with others' expectations and starts to lie about his/her cocaine use:

But then, at certain stages, when they say: 'Listen, you've had a lot, you're fucking going down', it affected me. I felt very very very bad, especially when it came from people who were using lower than me. 'Listen, you're fucking going down real quickly, and you wanna cup onto yourself.' It affected me to the extent where I was very depressed. It would be depressing for I don't know how long, and it would constantly be in my head, and it would come to a point: 'Yea, well, I'm gonna finish up'. They would say: 'Ah, do it, you haven't got the bollocks, what the fuck are you talking about, just do it', blablabla. And it came to a fact where I said: 'No, no', when they asked me: 'Well, are you still doing it?' while I had been. They probably knew I was lying on them, because I was afraid, I didn't want to lose their appreciation, which was already gone of course. [S/0/01]

19.3.5. Lying about cocaine

Our respondents were asked whether they had ever lied about their cocaine use. Forty-four interviewees (39.6% of the total sample) report having lied to one or more friends about their cocaine use. Table 19.3.b shows the major aspects of our respondents' lies.

Table 19.3.b   Aspects of cocaine lied about, in the 1997 Antwerp sample [*]

Antwerp (1997)			
Lied about	N	% of total sample (N=111)	% of subsample who lied (N=44)
Cocaine use in general (to non-users)	21	18.9	47.7
Quantity of cocaine available (to users)	14	12.6	31.8
Frequency of use (to users)	10	9.0	22.7
Other	*3*	*2.7*	*6.8*

[*] More than one answer was possible

Almost half of the respondents who report having lied state they had concealed their cocaine use in general from other people. Typically, these interviewees report holding back their illicit drug use from non-using friends to minimize the risk of police attention (i.e. as a means of self-protection), to avoid being labeled a 'drug user' or an 'addict (i.e. being stigmatized and consequently losing friends), or to avoid feelings of concern, anxiety, disappointment, shock, etc. in significant others.

To friends who I don't want to know it, I would lie. Friends who don't ask me any questions, I won't tell either. [...] Because why would you tell it, for a start, you know it's illegal, and secondly, when everybody knows it about you, you can have a lot of trouble. There are people who start looking at you completely differenly because of it, who will condemn you for it, and when they don't know it, or don't see it, they will not condemn you. Usually, the people who don't know it, they will react to it quite weirdly, so from your experience you know: look, you shouldn't tell everyone about it. But the people I know won't tell everyone about it, who know it... I won't hide it for them... [C/0/06]

Yes, to good friends who don't use it themselves, when they asked me: 'Do you use?', I denied it, I said it wasn't true. Because I was afraid that I would lose them if they knew about it. [H/0/16]

Almost one in three of the respondents who report having lied, state they lied about the quantity of cocaine they had with them. Typically, these lies are meant to avoid sharing the drug with others, because it is hard to obtain or expensive, or because they simply want all the cocaine for themselves (cocaine, a greedy drug). Sometimes, these lies are motivated by the wish to respect one's own informal rules: 'If I share this gram of cocaine with others, I cannot control how much I have been using, and I might have to buy an extra gram.' Others denied having cocaine available because they did not want to share with a particular person.

Usually it's always the same people who nag about it, of course, and in the end you say: 'Yes, sorry, I haven't got anything anymore', and also because I want to impose to myself, when I buy something I impose to myself that I have to make do a number of days with it. I always try to stick to my principles and often when those guys come to me, I'm telling you, they are always the same profiteers, so I say: 'Sorry, I haven't got anything'. [C/0/04]

Yes, for example when someone I can't stand – we have a friend like that, he's really disgusting when he uses coke, he becomes very greedy. It's annoying. And when I have some coke, and he asks: 'Do you have any?', then I say no. [K/1/02]

One in five of the respondents who lied (and one in ten of the total sample) acknowledge lying about the frequency of use to friends. These ten respondents indicate that they claimed to have used less cocaine than they had actually used, because they wanted to avoid informal social control from others (social disapproval), or because they wanted to mask their own inability to control the substance. Some respondents say that in fact, they were lying to themselves as much as to others.

Yes, my former friends, you know, I could see that some of them were already quite far with it and... You don't want to admit to yourself, either to those people or to yourself, that you're quite far as well, you know. In a way it is because you want to fool yourself into believing it is not true, right? It is because you lie to yourself and to other people. [H/1/25]

We used to go out and leave at about 12 o'clock, 1 o'clock, and we used to meet at about 10 o'clock, and we always used to make a line or two lines before we left, when we met at the other people's house. But sometimes I had already taken two lines before I arrived there, which they didn't know. Yes, I think everybody has experienced that, that you say: 'No, I haven't taken anything yet', knowing well they can see it but you won't admit. [Z/0/01]

The residual category of 'other' contains three replies: one respondent had lied about his opiate use to his cocaine-using friends because he knew they were anti-heroin; another respondent had lied about prices and quantities to clients when he was selling cocaine; and a third respondent had extolled the positive aspects of cocaine (and denied the negative effects) to another user to obtain cocaine from her. Finally, our data also suggest that lying about one's cocaine use to close friends is often seen as an indicator of uncontrolled use:[12]

But it happened that I entered somewhere, that I saw a friend of mine, and that I said: 'You're snorting, I can see it', and he said: 'No'. 'Why do you lie to me about that, I can't understand that.'. 'But I'm not taking anything.' I said: 'Oh boy, now you're fooling yourself', but he kept lying, [...] I find that really awful. He was bluntly lying to me, and then I say: 'Jeezes, friendship? A good friend of mine is lying about that.' I don't think it's worth it, you know. [C/0/06]

I never hid it. I will never do it secretly because when I do that, yes, you're gone, right? So... [I/1/10]

19.4. INFORMAL HELP AMONG FRIENDS

19.4.1. Helping each other

During the first interview we asked our respondents what advice they would now give to *novice* users (see Chapter 14). During the second interview we asked our respondents whether they had given any advice to other *experienced* users, or whether *experienced* users had given them any advice. The replies to this second question confirm the data from the first interview: respondents report having given advice to other users about mode of ingestion, dose, circumstances suitable to cocaine use, combination of cocaine with other drugs, buying cocaine, disadvantages of cocaine and methods of countering these.

Furthermore, these replies also contain additional examples of informal remarks and comments among cocaine using friends: on the dose and frequency of use, on the amount of money spent, on the negative consequences of cocaine use on other life spheres, on route of ingestion, on techniques of using, on changes in another person's behavior, on the price and quality of cocaine, etc.

Generally, the social factor, i.e. reassurance from close associates, helps the user to overcome his or her apprehension for the effects and the possible consequences of the drug. The desire for social support and interaction predominates with almost every user:

> *With a good friend you feel comfortable, and then the... often a... a lot of, how can I say, stress from the police, but also stress from the illegality, from the general idea that drugs are bad, easily disappears with a friend, when you are doing it with a friend. It's the same as if you are, for example, let's say, suppose you can do that with your father, then you say like: 'Now I am safe, you know, with my dad... what could happen to me now?', you say: 'When he's doing it, there can't be a problem', and so you're very relaxed...* [C/0/06]

The respondents' replies also yield other examples of informal help. We have summarized the data on informal help into eleven categories. The types of informal help most mentioned by our respondents are illustrated in the respondents' stories:

(1)   to warn somebody for the consequences of his/her use;

> *The people I go out with during the weekends all are five or six years older than me, they are people who are 38 years old, so these people know what they are doing, they have been using it for twenty years as well, so they say: 'Listen X., you should do it like that and like that', then they say: 'Ow boy, that's enough, think about what you're doing', and I find that, yes, in my circle of friends it's really like, yes, you'd go through fire and water for someone, I always want to help you. We are with about ten people and we have a kind of control over each other, that we say: 'Hey, that's enough for today, right? Have a beer or... but don't take any more coke because you'll have to go to work next', or so, for example.* [Z/0/01]

(2)   to guide somebody when he/she is coming down from cocaine (including providing tranquillizers or other drugs);

> *When somebody is coming down real bad... I go up to him and I say: 'Hey, come on eh... do this, or try that eh... try to calm down, try to sit down and relax, breathe quietly, nothing's happening... don't be afraid...' that kind of stuff. Just talk about things and don't leave the guy alone with his anxious thoughts... that's sufficient as help...* [W/0/01]

(3)   to cut somebody's supply of cocaine to help him/her cut down or abstain;

> *The others who used it as well, they helped me to keep me off it. They didn't give me anything anymore. Eh, we didn't go out anymore, we didn't go to a discotheque anymore, but just to a bar or so. They threatened other people so they couldn't give me anything anymore.* [C/0/01]

> *That's why those people I buy from, they say at a particular moment, and I've never been angry for that or so, that they say: 'No sorry, you won't get any anymore!' And then I don't*

go looking for other people, although I know people I could get it from. I just let it be. When they say: 'No, just wait for two weeks or so, and then we'll see', that's okay for me. Or: 'You don't get a gram, you can only have a half a gram', that's okay, I accept it. [H/0/30]

(4)   to listen to somebody's problems and worries (to act as a sounding board);

At the moment I do have a friend who is going way too far: but it is mainly because she is totally mentally confused: she has a difficult relationship of two years behind her. And actually, she started to use because she couldn't cope with that. [...] I won't say: 'You can't use anymore, and you have to quit, and stay here, and you don't use anything anymore.' Because I can't. The moment she's out, she'll use anyway. I can be there for her, I can cheer her up, I can listen to her and stuff. [I/1/16]

(5)   to encourage somebody who is trying to quit or cut down (by expressing one's admiration);

(6)   to lend money;
(7)   to stop offering cocaine, or avoid using cocaine in the company of a particular person;

Respondent: In the coke scene it is really like that. People there will easily say... the people who know each other somehow: 'Aren't you going too far and is it still okay?' And so... The coke scene really is a clique and they know about each other that they're using it and they are friends apart from that, in fact.
Interviewer: And how do they do that: to keep an eye on each other?
Respondent: Yes, when that person is really depressed or so, they go up to him and... then you see those people a lot. Or: when they stop by, you talk with them or so. Or when someone says: 'I want to quit for a while', or when a person indicates that, they say: 'Don't use in front of them', or so. Or 'Don't offer it', or, I mean... Like: 'When you want a line, you'll have to ask it yourself...' That makes the threshold higher, they take it into account. When you know someone wants to quit for a while, it doesn't happen in front of him anymore and you won't offer it to him anymore... I mean... Or when someone does ask for a line, like: 'Do you really want that? Because you wanted to quit for a while.' Then they can still make a choice and say: 'Do I really want it or not?'. [I/1/16]

There's also someone who deals a little and she only gives a half a gram or so to a person who is already further gone with it, and she really tells us: 'Don't tell him I have more with me.' Because she doesn't want to have an uneasy conscience because he's using too much. Although she makes a living with it, but... I mean, she does keep an eye on it, she won't give him five grams. So that's what I like about it. And for example sometimes they go to here every now and then and say: 'Stop giving him something because...' [...] I do appreciate it that some people say: 'Hey, did you keep an eye on him this time, because now we have to take care of him, or we have to stay with him...' [M/1/03]

(8)   to refer somebody to a doctor or specialized treatment center;

(9)   to shelter or accommodate somebody temporarily (e.g. to assist in an avoidance strategy);

For example, yes... a friend of mine was at my door and I let him in for a couple of days, like: 'Just come here, leave everything behind, don't go anywhere'. And another friend of mine as well who... sometimes takes care of someone, like: 'Just come and live here for a while, and leave everything behind, so that they can't call you'. Because it's just: when you are at home, next to the telephone, they all call you and you have contact, right? So you need to isolate yourself. So, that's a good example, like: 'Come and live a week with me or so, so that you're gone for a while, so they can't reach you anymore and then...' [H/1/32]

(10) to quit together with somebody to support him/her;

(11) to keep an eye on someone while going out.

I mean, I do have the impression that when someone exaggerates, that there is... I mean, yes, that people are concerned about it. And that people inquire about it, like: 'Are you okay?' I remember for example, I mean, that always stuck in my mind, you know, it was at the Ghent Festival [i.e. one week of parties and cultural activities in the city of Ghent, in July], *at a certain moment it all was too much for me. And I went to sit in a corner at the back, I had to sit down for a while. [...] and I remember that I looked up at that moment and I saw those friends coming up to me, very concerned, like: 'Hey, everything okay? Everything okay?' And at that moment it really touched me, you know, to realize, you know, there still are people who keep an eye on you, on each other.* [R/0/08]

19.4.2. Emergencies and overdoses

The most serious medical complications from cocaine are rapid and/or irregular heartbeat (tachycardia, arrhythmia), cardiac arrest (heart attack, ventricular fibrillation), cerebral hemorrhage (stroke), brain seizure (convulsion with loss of consciousness), respiratory failure (suffocation), and hyperthermia (heat stroke due to elevated body temperature) (Washton, 1989: 29-30). The number of deaths attributed to cocaine use remains relatively small, given the total number of people who use the drug. Even considering the possibility of underreporting, the number of people who actually die from cocaine use remains small (Washton, 1989: 29).

However, there is no reliable 'safe dose' for any single user. Overdoses (and death) have occurred in low-dose users as well as high-dose users, in snorters and freebase smokers as well as intravenous users. The term 'overdose', in fact, is misleading because it implies that below some prespecified dose, toxic or 'overdose' reactions can be avoided. Whenever someone has a serious toxic reaction to a drug, it is, by definition, an 'overdose', even if the dosage taken is considered by accepted standards to have been fairly small. The same person may react differently to the same dose of cocaine taken on different occasions.[13]

Table 19.4.a Overdoses of different substances, suffered and witnessed by Antwerp respondents (1997), in % of total number of reported overdoses

| O.D. from | Antwerp (1997) | | | | | |
| | Suffered | | Witnessed | | Total | |
	N	%	N	%	N	%
Cocaine	7	38.9	15	38.5	22	38.6
Opiates	3	16.6	8	20.5	11	19.3
MDMA	1	5.6	5	12.8	6	10.5
LSD	1	5.6	2	5.1	3	5.3
Amphetamines	2	11.1	-	-	2	3.5
Other [*]	3	16.6	1	2.6	4	7.0
Combinations	1	5.6	8	20.5	9	15.8
Total	*18*	*100.0*	*39*	*100.0*	*57*	*100.0*

[*] The 'other' category contains the following: alcohol (2), cannabis (1) and 'doornappel' (1).

We asked our respondents if they had ever suffered from an overdose of a drug, or had witnessed another person suffer from an overdose. Eighteen respondents (16.2% of the total sample) report having suffered from an overdose (or at least an negative experience after having used too much of one or more illicit drugs). Thirty-nine respondents (35.1% of the total sample) report having witnessed another person having an overdose (or having a negative experience after using too much).

Obviously, as the focus of our interviews was cocaine use, most 'overdoses' reported by our respondents were related to the use of cocaine: 7 respondents had had an overdose of cocaine (and 1 of a combination of cocaine with other substances), and 15 respondents had witnessed other users overdose of cocaine (and 4 of a combination of cocaine with other substances). See table 19.4.a.

It is striking that more than half of the 'overdoses' involved other substances, such as opiates (heroin), MDMA ('ecstasy'), LSD ('trips'), amphetamines ('speed'), or combinations of substances (5 combinations included MDMA, 4 alcohol, 3 amphetamines). Our data are consistent with other literature (e.g. Risser & Schneider, 1994; Wolf *et al.*, 1994: 15). Indeed, certain drug combinations –such as 'snowballs' [= cocaine + heroin], [cocaine + alcohol] or [cocaine and benzodiazepines] tend to increase the chance of causing respiratory or cardiac failures. That is exactly why many respondents report informal rules on the combination of cocaine with other substances (see Chapter 8).[14]

The question is what respondents mean by the term 'overdose'. As to heroin, most accounts of overdoses witnessed by respondents related to serious incidents (mostly fatal), although it must be noted that these stories are often hear-say. The respondents' stories about overdoses involving cocaine show that various adverse effects of cocaine use are interpreted by users as an 'overdose': unconsciousness (5), extreme paranoia (4), palpitations (3), talking gibberish (3), depression (2), epilepsy (2), hyperventilation (2), nausea (1), itching (1), aggression (1), agitation (1), etc.

I really thought I was going to have a heart attack because at first my left arm really hurt and then it was paralyzed, and my heart as well: it was pumping really hard, I had much difficulty with breathing, really out, I was really far out. [H/1/28]

Yes, once we did, when we were going out, and we didn't want to go home yet, and with about ten people we went to somebody's house, and we partied along and [...] at that moment, someone yelled: 'Sarah is in the bath tub! She doesn't talk anymore, she doesn't come to anymore!' We all went to have a look at her, she was foaming at the mouth, she really acted very weird. I mean, we were all very frightened. Because at those moments you can just become sober from seeing someone like that, you know. [Z/1/04]

Most respondents indicate that having an overdose or witnessing another person having an overdose is a shocking experience that can make a deep impression. Some users panic, others try to escape, and still others stay calm and try to find a solution for the 'emergency'. Typically, most of those present are under the influence of cocaine and/or other substances, which intensifies the experience, and may cause the user to misjudge the situation completely. After such a radical experience, some respondents report changes in their own cocaine use pattern:

I think there would be more of a panic. Also because of what I just said: because the coke affects your mind and you easily... But yes, it depends... it depends on the kind of relation between the users present. [H/0/26]

Something did happen that made me cut back as far as my drugs use is concerned [...], it was one night, when a friend of mine fainted. And that was a very... awkward event, because we were under the influence ourselves, and then an event like that is hard to place in the right context, when you are under the influence. And then I looked at myself for a moment and I said: 'You have to be careful now! And: it should not become a habit!' [R/0/07]

What do users do when they witness another user having an overdose? Obviously, the reaction depends on the relationship between the persons present. When a stranger in a discotheque shows signs of overdosing, accidental bystanders might walk away or react indifferently (just like a drunk customer can be ignored by the other café-goers). But when intimate friends get together and use cocaine (and/or other drugs), one should expect solidarity and concern in the case of an emergency. One respondent reports that his friends just waited and did nothing when he had a cocaine overdose:

From the one moment to the next I fell into a coma. I was lying in the seat, and the dog was jumping on me, but I didn't come to. Those friends thought: 'Yes, that's it.'. They said: 'We'll wait another couple of hours and if we can't wake him up then, we'll call the state police.' [C/0/01]

Most respondents, however, report that other users try to reassure the one who suffers an overdose. They try to 'talk him down', give him/her something to drink (a glass of water) or to eat, take him/her for a walk, bring him/her home, put him/her to bed, keep him/her company, etc.

I did react very calmly then, because I had taken some too, but you do take that responsibility, when you have to, you will take it. Something happens to her... And then, at once, you are, you know, sober or whatever, and I put her at ease and I said: 'It's not bad, common, let's have a walk, and lets' talk a little, or just tell me what you feel and it will go away.' And it did go away. [R/1/05]

In my experience the only thing that can help then is to keep on talking to those people, and just in a familiar environment and among friends... absolutely no uniforms or so, or white jackets... As far as I know that has a contrary effect only. [I/0/07]

Three respondents report particular tricks to put someone back on his feet after an overdose of cocaine: to give him/her a glass of milk, an orange or a lemon, or a glass of salted water.

We just, no, we tried, first there was a discussion whether we should give salt or sugar, and milk, because milk is not always the right thing, because you can choke in it. Once drunk a liter of milk myself because I kinda felt that things would go wrong and then I experienced myself that I almost choked in it [she laughs], *in my own puke.* [H/1/28]

These 'detoxification techniques' are probably part of user lore about adverse effects and how to 'treat' them, but they are relatively ineffective. Milk is known to have a slightly tranquillizing effect on very young children, but its effect on adults is negligible. Likewise, drinking a glass of orange or lemon juice is not an efficient treatment for an overdose of any drug. And finally, salt water may cause the person to throw up. As such, it may help if the toxic substance is in the stomach of the user (e.g. after eating a little ball of cocaine or amphetamine). In other circumstances, this folklore solution is ineffective, and may be counterproductive, as the vomit may obstruct the airways.[15] It is striking that most respondents indicate they prefer to look for solutions themselves, rather than appeal to a general practitioner or a first-aid-team, or call for an ambulance.

> *When you are all... a lot of people and they are very much under the influence of coke...*
> *those reflexes are different as well, you know, but there is a reaction of course, it's not like:*
> *we're not interested, there is a reaction to it. But you won't... first you try to solve it your-*
> *self, of course, before looking for help from outside, but when it is necessary, it is done. But*
> *you want to postpone that as long as possible. You try to solve it yourself. [...] You're stuck*
> *with that fear, you know. I mean, pff... because coke has that reputation of... Try to explain*
> *that to other people, right?* [I/1/04]

However, unconsciousness or coma by overdose must always be considered as a medical emergency. Most overdose reactions, such as elevated blood pressure, tachycardia, convulsions, etc. require emrgency medical intervention and sometimes life support maneuvers. According to treatment specialists, witnesses of drug overdoses should call for an ambulance, and report that a respirator is needed. If the users is still more or less conscious, it is advized to keep the person awake with physical movements (Wolf *et al.*, 1994: 15).

Some respondents indicate they would call for a doctor or an ambulance in case of an emergency, irrespective of the possible legal consequences. For them, the physical and psychological well-being of the person having an overdose comes first, and abandoning a friend to his/her own fate is out of the question.

> *If there ever were such a situation, I wouldn't run from it, I would make sure that everything*
> *turns out all right, I would think about the fact that I might get into trouble with it myself.*
> *No, the most important thing is that everything turns out all right for that particular person,*
> *and whatever gets at it, as to police, well that's just bad luck, but it is... of minor importance*
> *at that moment, I mean physical health ranks number one, you have to make sure nothing*
> *goes wrong either physically or mentally, that's' the most important thing, because when*
> *you leave someone to his own devices, that's much worse.* [R/0/07]

However, most accounts illustrate the fear of legal problems in case of an emergency. Some respondents state that they would call for an ambulance when a friend shows symptoms of extreme overdosing, and run off before the emergency service arrives.

> *I would call the emergency services and scarper, I would do that too, I would leave some-*
> *thing or a note to tell what has happened, but I wouldn't stay there, under the influence, and*
> *wait for the emergency services to arrive.* [M/0/01]

Most respondents indicate that they would not call a doctor or an ambulance. In case of an emergency, they panic and do not want to be involved in the aftermath of such an event.

> *Yes, I had such a case last Friday, there was a boy here who got an epileptic attack, and*
> *suddenly I see that coke, here, well I can't call the BOB* [i.e. Special Investigation Unit of
> the state police, TD], *can I? Suppose I call an ambulance for that boy and they see that coke*

here, then I'm in trouble, [...] when they find that in his blood, and he comes from my house, you know, I'm in trouble, right? [H/1/19]

I can imagine that when somebody gets a crisis that you, yes as you say, with the police involved and stuff, so when it happens at your house then you are the one who's responsible, so they will come to your house, and they'll presuppose you gave it to him, and so you have in fact committed an offence because you gave the opportunity to use or something. [I/0/05]

The illegal status of substances such as cocaine and heroin thus causes anxiety in many users when they are confronted with extreme overdosing and emergencies. In these instances, illicit drug users feel the anxiety engendered by society's association of drug use with degradation and criminality. In other words, prohibitionary laws may break up the social bonds between users. In the case of overdosing, users prefer to look for personal solutions rather than to call for external help. Our respondents also indicate this not only applies to other users in distress, but to themselves as well.

That first time I took a pill I had five or six blackouts. My boyfriend wanted to call an ambulance, but I said: 'Ho, jeezes, no!'. I said: 'No, no', I just went crazy, you know, when he said: 'I'm going to call an ambulance' because eh... that would only make it worse. [H/1/17]

One respondent witnessed a friend of his have an overdose of cocaine (and heroin). Another friend present panicked and decided to run off. Our respondent called the ambulance and was convicted later for not rendering assistance to a person in distress. His reaction now:

When I look at it now, what happened to me, I was very stupid to call an ambulance. If I hadn't done that, it would never have been revealed who was involved. I could have gone to the Netherlands, they wouldn't have been able to prove anything. I mean yes, nothing would have happened. And that is exactly why unfortunately a lot of people don't call an ambulance, because they want to get rid of it. The system is not good, that's what it's all about. [H/0/29]

It follows that many users do not call for an ambulance or a doctor in case of an emergency and this may have disastrous consequences.

I had a friend who had an OD, and those guys had, they had tried everything but it didn't work, but they didn't dare to call an ambulance. They waited too long, and now, the guy is 85% handicapped. [H/1/24]

19.5. CONCLUSION

Throughout the previous chapters, it became clear that friends play an important role in the initiation and the development of cocaine use patterns of our subjects. Early experimentation with cocaine generally occurs in the company of a friend or group of friends. Neophyte users receive guidance from friends in the process of 'learning the proper technique of using' and 'becoming a cocaine user'. Cocaine-using friends are likely to be the most important source of information for respondents. Friends can also be an important source of supply.

Going out, parties and meeting friends are the three situations in which cocaine use occurs most often. Clearly, the most suitable situations for cocaine use are those in which people enjoy each other's company. Many set and setting factors that support or interfere with informal control mechanisms relate to the influence of friends. Furthermore, craving (or desire) is often triggered by specific set and setting factors, such as the presence of certain friends, or specific moods of the user and his/her company.

However, the non-use of friends can be an important reason for periodic abstinence or cutting back. Furthermore, emotional support from peers can help to cope with difficulties in cutting back or quitting. For many respondents a particular friend served as a counter-example, i.e. as a user whose cocaine behavior they did not wish to imitate.

Almost one in four respondents report that cocaine improved, and one in four say cocaine deteriorated their relationships with friends. Almost one in three state cocaine had both positive and negative effects on their friendships. When asked about crucial events that had an important influence on their cocaine use pattern, 18 respondents indicate that their use increased as they came to know new cocaine-using friends, and 5 respondents report that their cocaine use decreased because their friends had cut down or quit using cocaine.

Most respondents report having made remarks to friends about their cocaine use. Most of these remarks related to the dose or the frequency of cocaine use, to negative changes in their behavior, to their route of ingestion, and to negative consequences on their job, family life, health etc. Typically, respondents had advised their friend(s) to cut down on their use, to abstain temporarily or to quit using cocaine altogether. More than three in five respondents also report having had similar remarks on their own cocaine use from one or more friends. Although most comments are negative and aimed at correcting another person's behavior, some respondents also claim to have had positive remarks about their ability to control their cocaine intake.

Cocaine use is a regular topic of conversation among respondents and their cocaine-using friends. Conversations typically focus on positive and negative experiences with cocaine, and on various methods of controlling the substance. Discussions are often pervaded with a general concern about being 'addicted' or 'in control'.

The crucial question is whether remarks and conversations are effective. Comments from non-users are often rejected with the argument that they are 'ignorant', and 'hypocritical'. Remarks from non-users are often met with a shrug of indifference, verbal aggression, etc. Sometimes, however, users take great pains to explain their investment in cocaine.

Whether or not a remark or comment from another cocaine user is perceived as well-founded, depends on many factors: the source or the maker of the remark, the (perceived) pattern of his/her cocaine use, the form and content of the remark (serene versus paternalistic, joking versus angry, verbal versus non-verbal), the situation in which the comment is made and the emotional state of the receiver, etc. Informal comments can provoke various reactions, from aggression and indifference, to feigned consent and simulated remorse, to indulgence and behavioral change. Several participants indicate they readily accept remarks from friends because they stimulate their reflection about their own use and because it keeps them alert for the pitfalls of the drug. Furthermore, when users are under the influence of cocaine they are less susceptible to comments from others than when they are sober.

Most of the respondents' accounts show that a prerequisite for effective informal social control is a strong or intimate bond between the commentator and the subject of the comments. Our participants stress the fact that only the remarks by close friends have an impact on their cocaine use. Comments by acquaintances, strangers, and non-users in general, go in one ear and out the other.

However, the user may reach a stage where he/she is no longer able to conform to the others' expectations and starts to lie about his/her cocaine use. Almost half of the respondents who report having lied state they had concealed their cocaine use in general from other people, usually non-users. Typically, these interviewees report holding back their illicit drug use from non-using friends to minimize the risk of police attention, to avoid being labeled a 'drug users' or an 'addict, or to avoid concern, anxiety, disappointment, shock, etc. in significant others.

Almost one in three of the respondents who report having lied state they lied to other users about the quantity of cocaine they had with them. Typically, these lies are meant to avoid sharing the drug, because it is hard to obtain, or expensive, or because these respondents simply want all the cocaine for them. One in five of the respondents who lied acknowledge having lied to friends about the frequency of use, because they wanted to avoid informal social control from others (social disapproval), or because they wanted to mask their own inability to control the substance.

Giving each other advice about mode of ingestion, dose, circumstances suitable to use cocaine, combination of cocaine with other drugs, buying cocaine, disadvantages of cocaine, and methods of countering these, is not uncommon, even among *experienced* users. Generally, the social factor, i.e. reassurance from close associates, helps the user to overcome his or her anxiety for the drug, its effects and possible consequences. However, the respondents' replies also yield other examples of informal help: warning for the consequences of his/her use; guidance when he/she is coming down from cocaine (including providing tranquillizers or other drugs); cutting the supply of cocaine to help him/her cut down or abstain; listening to problems and worries (sounding board); encouraging somebody who is trying to quit or cut down (by expressing one's admiration); loaning money; stopping offering cocaine, or avoiding using cocaine within sight of a particular person; referring to a doctor or specialized treatment center; sheltering or accommodating somebody temporarily (e.g. assisting in an avoidance strategy); quitting together with somebody to support him/her; keeping an eye on someone while going out.

Eighteen respondents report having had an overdose (or at least an negative experience after having used too much of one or more illicit drugs), and one in three respondents report having witnessed another person suffering an overdose (or having a negative experience after using too much). More than half of the 'overdoses' were related to other substances, such as opiates, MDMA, LSD, amphetamines, or to combinations of various substances. The respondents' stories about overdoses involving cocaine show that various adverse effects of cocaine use are interpreted as an 'overdose': loss of consciousness, extreme paranoia, palpitations, talking gibberish, depression, epileptic attacks, hyperventilation, etc. Most respondents indicate that having an overdose or witnessing another person having an overdose is a shocking experience that can make a deep impression and change their own cocaine use pattern.

But the victims of an overdose or an emergency are not left to fend for themselves by their intimate friends. Most respondents report that other users try to reassure the person who suffers an overdose. They try to 'talk him down', give him/her something to drink (a glass of water) or to eat, take him/her for a walk, bring him/her home, put him/her to bed, keep him/her company, etc. Some respondents even report particular 'detoxification techniques' such as a glass of milk, an orange or a lemon, a glass of salted water, although these folklore solutions are usually ineffective or counterproductive. The striking thing is that most respondents indicate they prefer looking for solutions themselves, rather than appealing to a general practitioner or a first-aid-team, or calling for an ambulance.

The illegal status of substances such as cocaine and heroin creates fear in many users when they are confronted with extreme overdosing and emergencies. Some users may call for an ambulance, but run off before the emergency service arrives. Others may not call a doctor or an ambulance, because they panic and do not want to be involved in the aftermath of their action. In these instances, illicit drug users feel the anxiety engendered by society's association of drug use with degradation and criminality. In other words, prohibitory laws may break up the social bonds between users. The conclusion is that many users do not call for an ambulance or a doctor in case of an emergency and this can have disastrous consequences, as user lore on emergencies and overdoses seems relatively incomplete and ineffective.

NOTES

1   See Chapter 4, p. 102-105 and 109-117.
2   See Chapter 6, p. 166-168.
3   See Chapter 7, p. 178-179.
4   See Chapter 9, p. 218-219.
5   See Chapter 12, p. 267 and 274.
6   See Chapter 13, p. 296.
7   See Chapter 14, p. 314.
8   See Chapter 15, p. 333-336.
9   For a discussion of other crucial events reported by the respondents, see Chapter 17, p. 375 (notes 11, 14, 20 and 25).
10   See Chapter 15, p. 328-333.
11   Note that most of these topics were discussed extensively in previous chapters.
12   See Chapter 15, p. 332-233.
13   A very small number of people are unable to tolerate any dose of cocaine, owing to a congenital deficiency of the enzyme, pseudocholinesterase, which metabolizes or inactivates cocaine in the blood. GOSSOP, M. (1987), *Living with drugs*, 165. Aldershot: Wildwood House. WASHTON, A.M. (1989), *op. cit.*, 30.
14   See Chapter 8, p. 208-212.
15   Personal communication from Dr. Sven Todts.

CHAPTER 20

CONCLUSIONS

20.1. INTRODUCTION

Part of the initial impetus for the present study was the observation that drug epidemiology in Belgium is scarcely out of its infancy. Official statistics, population surveys, and utilization studies, are useful indicators of drug use, but they are often biased, partial, and focused on the best known, most visible, accessible, and perhaps most marginalized subgroups of drug users. Moreover, observing or interviewing respondents with the intent of helping, controlling or treating them probably biases the research findings as well. The present study wanted to make an original contribution to the field of drug epidemiology by describing a sample of cocaine users from within their culture rather than from outside, and to present their world as they see it (*the insider's view*).

From the very start the present study assumed a critical attitude towards pharmacocentrism, which is often the subtly implicit paradigm of drug research. *Addiction does not reside in drugs; it resides in human experience.* Overemphasizing the pharmacological effects of any drug may lead to underestimating the importance of set and setting factors. Whether the balance between use and abuse tips to either side, depends not only on the pharmacological properties of a drug, but even more strongly on personality characteristics and socio-cultural factors. Therefore, the *general focus* of this research was on informal control mechanisms or self-regulation by illicit drug users. In order to understand how and why certain users have lost control over the drug or drugs they are using, we tackled the all-important question of how and why many others manage to achieve control and maintain it. Based on the literature survey on informal control mechanisms by illegal drug users (*Chapter 1*), we formulated three specific research goals:

- To locate a minimum of 100 experienced cocaine users, preferably from non-institutionalized, non-captive or hidden populations, and from the metropolitan area of Antwerp;
- To provide a 'thick' description of social rituals and rules (the informal controls) and the processes through which these are transferred;
- To initiate the identification of those factors related to current formal drug policy that might (de)stabilize self-regulation and controlled use.

In this chapter we summarize the main empirical results of our study following these three specific research goals. Paragraph 20.2 describes our sample of 111 experienced cocaine users in general terms. Paragraph 20.3 presents our empirical results regarding informal control mechanisms (rituals and rules) and their socialization. The possible interactions between formal control (the current drug policy) and informal control (self-regulation) are discussed in paragraph 20.4. Finally, some reflections are made in paragraph 20.5, together with some recommendations for policy, for education and treatment, and for future research.

20.2. A COMMUNITY SAMPLE OF 111 COCAINE USERS IN ANTWERP

Given the societal view on cocaine use as deviant behavior and hence the legal and social sanctions, it has proved extremely difficult to identify and specify the correct universe for our study. Based on the essentially social nature of drug use (i.e. the presence of social ties between the drug user and his/her partner, friends, acquaintances, fellow workers, etc.), the present study used chain referral sampling or snowball sampling (*Chapter 2*). Theoretically, random sampling designs are preferable to non-random designs. But because of difficulties in finding and contacting respondents, we decided to omit the randomization in the selection of nominees, and to interview each individual who had been contacted by the respondent and who was willing to cooperate.

To make our sample comparable to the 1987 Amsterdam community sample of cocaine users studied by Dr. Peter Cohen (Centre for Drug Research, University of Amsterdam), we defined identical sample acceptability criteria: (1) cocaine as a main drug; (2) a minimum lifetime experience of 25 instances of cocaine use; (3) a minimum age of 18 years; (4) not having been found guilty of a felony; (5) not having participated in any drug treatment program. Furthermore, some social groups, such as street junkies, prostitutes, professional criminals, secondary school pupils and youth club members were explicitly eliminated as target populations, because we wanted to obtain information about 'hidden' and 'non-captive' subpopulations of cocaine users. Natural congregation areas such as well-known drug copping zones and areas of prostitution were excluded as strategic research sites for the same reason.

Plunging into the Antwerp nightlife started the survey. Mainly through the establishment of approving relationships with high-status indigenous individuals in the nightlife scene, we finally obtained 25 'zero stage' entrances (each one generating a snowball chain). After establishing preliminary contacts with potential respondents during field observations, they were asked to participate in a double interview: a semi-structured questionnaire and an open biographical interview. Eventually, we obtained a total sample of 111 experienced cocaine users from the metropolitan area of Antwerp. This met our first specific research goal.

But did all our respondents come from non-institutionalized, non-captive or hidden subpopulations? Obviously, our non-randomized sampling design had important drawbacks. Comparison of the respondents from different snowball chains showed that the naming of people who share a certain characteristic (cocaine use) is not a random process. Our snowball sampling procedure had the inherent risk of recruiting respondents who are –in unknown, but systematic, ways- similar to the person who nominated them.

Indeed, there are several indications that our choice for a snowball sampling procedure with non-randomized sequences has resulted in a biased sample. Throughout our study, we showed repeatedly that the respondents belonging to snowball chain F and H differed markedly from respondents from other chains. Compared to the rest of the Antwerp sample, both snowball chains contain more 'treated', 'convicted' and 'registered' respondents, more respondents who report difficulties with temporary abstinence or cutting down, more intravenous users, more respondents who report craving, more respondents who report negative effects of their cocaine use on their family relationships, more respondents who report engagement in illegal activities, more respondents who consider themselves 'uncontrolled users', more respondents who report the combined use of cocaine and heroin, etc.

We can identify two sources of bias. First, the particular composition of the zero stage sample has most probably produced respondents within a few networks some individuals of which share certain characteristics. We made use of our personal contacts with the staff of two low threshold treatment institutions in Antwerp to make contacts with drug users who were willing to take us to some bars, or to potential respondents. These contacts led to snowball chains D, F, H and N. Although initially none of these individuals seemed to know each other, it was subsequently found that most of the respondents from these chains frequented the same scene (of rather 'marginal', 'visible' drug users).

Secondly, two of the sample acceptability criteria were that respondents should not have been found guilty of a felony, and that they should not have been in any drug treatment program. These inclusion criteria were not easy to verify before the interview took place. Obviously, asking people in a crowded bar or a noisy discotheque about their police record or treatment experiences is out of the question. Thus, after completing our interviews we found out that some of our respondents had been convicted for a felony and/or had participated in a drug treatment program. Most of them belonged to snowball chains F and H.

But even if more stringent criteria had been applied in the snowball sampling procedure, one can never be sure whether a random sample is truly representative of the population it is drawn from or whether the selection of zero stage respondents reflects the factual population, which is unknown. Furthermore, in our view, it was more important for our sample to show great diversity, since the focus of our research was primarily on the description of new or unknown phenomena.

The sample of 111 experienced cocaine users recruited from the metropolitan area of Antwerp was broadly comparable to samples from other major community studies, in terms of some general social and economic variables such as age, sex, level of education, professional status, and home environment (*Chapter 3*). A large majority of our respondents (80%) had not had any contact with drug treatment agencies or with medical doctors for a drug problem. In general, the interviewees in the Antwerp study were broadly similar in their patterns and experience of cocaine use, as well as in their demographic profile, with those in community studies of cocaine users in Miami, Toronto, Sydney, Canberra, Melbourne, San Francisco, Amsterdam, Scotland, Turin, Barcelona and Rotterdam.

On the other hand, the cocaine users found in Antwerp differed markedly from drug users as they are depicted by the non-using public, health care professionals, law enforcement officials, other research projects (especially in utilization studies), and the media. Drug users who do not conform to the stereotype of 'worst-case scenarios' are less likely to come to the attention of health practitioners or the police, and ordinary citizens rarely identify them as drug users. Our study demonstrates that it is possible to recruit a group of 'invisible' cocaine users who do not fit the stereotype of drug use as heavily associated with deprivation, ill health and crime. Indeed, in other research projects the main barrier to finding such 'hidden populations' may consist in failing to seek them.

Although they are committed to cocaine, the Antwerp cocaine users acknowledge many risks and pitfalls in its use. At the very least, we can say that substantial and sustained cocaine use entails clear risks of problems in many spheres: escalating use, due to a slow increase in tolerance, and the seductive and insidious nature of cocaine (*Chapter 5*), binge use (*Chapter 5*), negative physical and psychological effects (*Chapter 11*), difficulties with cutting back or periodical abstinence (*Chapter 12*), feelings of craving for, and even obsession with cocaine (*Chapter 13*), conflicts and arguments with parents (*Chapter 16*), negative effects on the partner relationship (*Chapter 17*), deterioration of the quality and/or quantity of work done, and of the relationships with fellow workers (*Chapter 18*), negative effects on friendships (*Chapter 19*), overdoses (*Chapter 19*) and other medical complications (*Annex I*), etc.

Most of these risks (binge use, feelings of craving, obsession, unpleasant mental and physical effects, difficulties with periodical abstinence or cutting back,...) are related to *more direct routes of ingestion* such as freebasing or injecting. Furthermore, it was shown that the number of negative *effects increases with level of use* (*Chapter 11*). A level of use higher than 2.5 grams a week definitively alters the balance between positive and negative effects. For high-level users the balance becomes rather negative.

Most Antwerp respondents report knowing such 'risky' or problematic users (*Chapter 3*). They identify overt signs of uncontrolled use as: being unable to stop using (the binge pattern), too large doses and overt signs of 'over'-dosing, financial problems, lying about one's cocaine use, a high frequency of use, active efforts to obtain cocaine, and talking about cocaine incessantly (*Chapter 15*). Indeed, many respondents indicate knowing friends, acquaintances, partners, relatives, and others that serve as examples of how not to use cocaine, for various reasons: because these people use too much, too frequently, and consequently experience negative physical effects; because they engage in illegal activities or behavior looked down upon; because of negative mental effects; because they use cocaine intravenously or possess other 'junky'-like characteristics; etc.

Although a (small) subgroup of our respondents (mainly from snowball chain F and H) displays characteristics which do resemble those found in utilizations studies and the like, the data presented in this study also confirm the findings of other studies on cocaine use outside treatment, that the experiences of cocaine users with problems are highly exceptional rather than typical. Most cocaine users do not develop problems (other than breaking the law) and those whose use has been problematic for a time often moderate their behavior by their own efforts. The Antwerp sample contains many users who depart from the worst-case scenarios known to treatment specialists and law enforcement officials and who do not fit in the simplistic, homogenous image of drug users presented by politicians and in the media:

A large majority of our respondents (80%) did not have any contact with drug treatment agencies or with medical doctors for a drug problem (*Chapter 3*). Only two respondents of the Antwerp sample had sought help for cocaine-related problems.

Fewer than 5% of the total sample report feelings of being 'pushed' and almost all respondents report that trying out cocaine was their own (often conscious) choice (*Chapter 4*). The stereotype of the drug dealer or drug pusher actively recruiting new cocaine users to expand his market did not feature in our sample. Curiosity about cocaine and association with significant others who use it, bring the unititiated in a situation where cocaine is being used.

Cocaine use may escalate, but it does not do so endlessly (*Chapter 5*). About half of all users reach a high use level in their period of heaviest cocaine use, but only 5% had stayed at that level in the three months prior to interview. Almost 1 in 5 Antwerp respondents had not used at all during the last three months. A proportion of cocaine users (18% in the Antwerp sample) is able to maintain a low level of use throughout their whole use career. Furthermore, high-level use of cocaine during certain (top) periods of use does not exclude later abstinence or decreased frequency of use at all.

Respondents experience their cocaine use career as a dynamic, often irregular, pattern, subject to many changes. In all community samples, the proportion of respondents reporting a discontinuous or irregular pattern of use (in the Antwerp sample almost 90%) is larger than the proportion of those reporting a continuous one (*Chapter 5*). Moreover, most respondents report a preference for weekends, and more than 70% report a low rate of use at a typical occasion (non-bingers).

A very large proportion of the Antwerp respondents report having stopped for more than one month (86.5%). Nearly 60% of the total sample report more than 5 abstinence periods of one month or longer (*Chapter 12*). The average duration of the longest period of abstinence was 15 months. Seventy-one respondents (64%) report having cut back on their cocaine use. About half of the respondents who had temporarily abstained or cut back on their cocaine use, did not experience any problems with it. Most others qualify these 'problems' as minor discomforts that manifest themselves initially and fade away after a few days or weeks. Thirty-two respondents (29.7% of the total sample) report having quit cocaine, 6 of whom did so without consciously reflecting on it.

Three in four respondents were 'snorters' at the time of the interview (*Chapter 6*). In all three periods (initial period, period of heaviest use, and most recent period) snorting was practised by an overwhelming majority of the respondents. The proportion of injecting respondents was relatively small. Seventy-three respondents (65.8% of the Antwerp sample) kept a stable route of ingestion (mostly snorting). Thus, the initial snorter (or chaser) is not merely a cocaine user who has not yet injected but will inevitably do so. And the cocaine injector is not bound to continue as an injector for the entire duration of his/her cocaine career.

Our data show that cocaine produces a wide range of positive effects on those who use it in moderation: more energy, a certain intellectual focus, enhanced sensations, and increased sociability and social intimacy (*Chapter 11*). Social, sexual, or recreational activities and work can be enlivened, and many respondents use the drug not only in pleasurable but also in productive ways (*Chapter 16, 17, 18 and 19*). Typically,

421

interviewees perceive the financial consequence of their cocaine use as a more important disadvantage than whatever physical or psychological adverse effect they report. Most participants were prepared to live with the unappealing aspects of cocaine, which were outweighed by its appealing factors.

More than three in four respondents (77.6%) perceive themselves as 'controlled' users (*Chapter 15*). The most important indicators of 'controlled' use according to the Antwerp respondents were: periodical abstinence, refusing cocaine when it is offered (in other words: resisting craving), small doses and/or low frequency of use (and consequently, low level of use), fewer active efforts to obtain cocaine, other activities taking priority over cocaine use, positive reasons for using cocaine. Most respondents report a sense of increased mastery and control over the product. Many users have to go through a period of loss of control over the substance, or to learn about the negative and dangerous aspects, but in the end they are able to use the substance more consciously and to prevent cocaine from interfering with relationships and activities that take priority (such as a job, family life, etc.) (*Chapter 16*).

It has been suggested that the desire for a drug may be so strong that many, if not most, people are unable to resist, even if they have to engage in criminal activities to buy or use it. Yet, three in four respondents had never engaged in any criminal activity to obtain (money for) cocaine (*Chapter 13*). The activities most frequently mentioned by the Antwerp respondents were: tolerating the presence of unpleasant persons to obtain cocaine and selling cocaine (usually to friends). One third of all crimes reported had been committed only 'once', indicating opportunistic and accidental criminal behavior. Most of these crimes had been committed by a small group of 12 respondents, who were mainly recruited from snowball chains with higher proportions of registered respondents, regular injectors, and respondents reporting difficulties with abstaining or cutting back.

20.3. INFORMAL CONTROL MECHANISMS

20.3.1. Drug, set and setting

The research data summarized above document a wide range of possible consequences of cocaine (and crack) use. Clearly, drug use does not always lead down the road to ruin. Our respondents' stories do not imply that negative effects are inevitable repercussions of cocaine use. Whether any given user will experience any one or more of the negative consequences described above, depends upon his/her personality, the length and pattern of use, the characteristics of the setting in which it is used, etc. For example, many of the problems experienced by respondents were related to the illegal status of cocaine, rather than with the pharmacological properties of the substance itself: 46 respondents (41.4% of the Antwerp sample) reported ever having been convicted for a felony, more than half of whom for drug possession only (*Chapter 3*). The quality of cocaine is unstable and difficult to control (*Chapter 10*), and the contacts between buyer and seller always carry the risk of aggression and abuse (*Chapter 9*).

Contrary to the popular fallacy that each drug has the same effect on every user, many important distinctions must be considered when describing the consequences of drug use. Norman Zinberg (1984) has organized the multideterminants of drug effects into three interactive categories: drug, set and setting. The present study contains numerous examples of set and setting factors that interact in producing a response to drug taking.

The typical setting for first use of cocaine tends to be unplanned, and occurs practically always in the company of close friends and/or partner, during parties, or in special conditions of privacy, calm and congeniality in one's own circle of friends (*Chapter 4*). In general it is the initiate him/herself who is the active player in the initiation event. Initiates often have a prejudiced image and expectations of the drug.

Users are able to abstain periodically from cocaine use or cut back on their use, for a variety of set- and/or setting-related reasons (*Chapter 12*): cocaine's high financial cost, no desire for cocaine, negative physical or mental effects, work/study, no cocaine available, pregnancy, no environment for cocaine use, friends do not use cocaine, partner raises objections, traveling, prison/treatment. Furthermore, the difficulties respondents may encounter in abstaining temporarily or cutting back are not insurmountable, especially with informal support from friends or a partner. On the other hand, cutting back or even temporarily abstaining can be hampered if friends or significant others continue to use (at the same level).

Respondents who report having used various routes of ingesting cocaine, indicate some of the determinant set and setting factors in their choice of route of ingestion: the activities engaged in while using cocaine; the other users and/or the company they are in; the quantity of cocaine available; personal preference for a specific route; adverse effects associated with a method; the quality of cocaine available; set-factors (or the emotional state one is in); and who possesses the cocaine... (*Chapter 6*)

What a user feels is to a large extent the result of his or her psychological make-up and expectations (set) and the situational and cultural context (setting) in which the drug is used (*Chapter 7*). Part of that cultural context are the 'stories' about the diabolical drug named 'crack'. However, several studies suggest that crack may not be as overwhelmingly reinforcing as one might guess from examining the minority of users whose problems land them in jail or treatment. Yet, through the mass media these images of cocaine have been diffused into public awareness, and we can expect both the public in general and the cocaine users in particular to be influenced by them. Not only will attitudes and beliefs unfavorable to its use be strengthened in the general public, the exaggerated horrors of crack cocaine may have deterred the Antwerp cocaine users themselves.

Advantages and disadvantages of cocaine are both perceived as related to dose and to circumstances (*Chapter 11*). 87.4% of the Antwerp respondents stated that circumstances influence the perceived advantages of cocaine. The most frequent explanations for the influence of circumstances were in terms of social relations within a group ('pleasant' + 'safe' + 'not alone'). Other important circumstances were: 'relaxed', 'better at home', 'right mood', and 'good music'. 57.7% of the respondents confirmed a relation between circumstances and unappealing aspects of cocaine. Circumstances such as the presence of friends (or non-users or irritating people), the atmosphere (whether there are quarrels or discussions, or not), the (joyful or depressive) mood of the other users, the place (at home or not), etc. play a quite important role as well.

Craving –always 'real' and often quite intense – does not inevitably lead to use of cocaine (*Chapter 13*). This desire or longing is simply not the result of pharmacological effects of an illicit drug. It is often triggered by specific set and setting factors, such as the presence of certain friends, specific mood of the user (and his/her company), conversations about cocaine, etc.

Illicit drug use takes place in a social context, and those around the user often respond to the use in particular ways. The social contexts of use (settings) are thus affected by the use, and in turn influence it. For example, several respondents report that some particular domestic situation may have contributed to an increase in their cocaine use (*Chapter 16*). A disrupted family life (divorce, unexpected death of a loved one, alcoholism, sexual abuse and/or physical violence, separation, etc.), inattentive parenting and lack of parental protection and support may have negative effects on cocaine use patterns. For some of these respondents, escapist motives play a certain role in the start or continuation of their illicit drug use.

The spouse or partner respond in some way to the use and can stimulate or curb the user's use or influence it in some other way (*Chapter 17*). First, the partner can be an incentive for the respondents' cocaine use in more than one way: as an initiator, as a significant other and model, as a pushy user, as a daily conversation partner, as a sexual partner, as a source of supply, etc. Second, the partner of a drug user can have a discouraging or curbing effect in many ways: he/she can make comments about the respondent's use (i.e. informal social control), discuss the pros and cons of illicit drug use, suggest to the user to cut back or quit using, offer informal help to do so, etc.

Structural factors such as fellow worker accessibility, teamwork, the company policy on illicit drugs, and on-the-job cocaine availability enhance work-related cocaine consumption. Odd working hours or shifts are factors which pull in the same direction. Furthermore, fellow workers' drug using levels may be positively related to an individual's cocaine consumption. For example, an important factor that facilitates initiation into and continuation of cocaine use in the sector of hotels, restaurants, bars and especially in discotheques and clubs, is its general availability linked with its reputation as a party drug (*Chapter 18*). Furthermore, staff in discotheques are often confronted with clients looking for cocaine on the one hand and dealers looking for clients on the other. Certain features of the zeitgeist or characteristics of organizational culture at some of these workplaces may implicitly or explicitly encourage or discourage drug use and some individuals working in the hotel and catering industry may eventually drift into selling cocaine during working hours. Conversely, certain characteristics of organizational culture at some of these workplaces may implicitly or explicitly discourage drug use.

Thus, pharmacology is not destiny. Clinical studies on highly selected samples of 'problematical' users are too often used to generate prevalence rates for drug-related problems among the general population of drug users. Our data suggest a critical attitude towards the 'mechanistic' perspectives derived from media images and police claims that focus on the pharmacological properties of a drug only and assume that users are vulnerable biological organisms who can only passively and mechanically obey what the drug dictates. Such views are supported by cases of addicts who have become victims of compulsive use. Some users do become compulsive users. Many more users, however, do not!

20.3.2. *Informal control mechanisms*

The main finding of the present study concerns controlled cocaine users, i.e. users who do not ingest more than they want to and whose pattern of use does not result in any dysfunction in the roles and responsibilities of daily life. Many of the Antwerp respondents were able to maintain long-term control while others reverted from very high levels to controlled use. Our assumption is that it is the social setting, through the development of sanctions and rituals (i.e. informal control mechanisms), that brings the use of illicit drugs under control. Our data show that the use of cocaine (and probably of any drug) involves both values and rules of conduct that define whether and how the drug should be used (social sanctions), and stylized, prescribed behavior patterns surrounding its use (social rituals). The Antwerp sample offered various examples of these informal social control mechanisms:

We found that the number of people reporting advantages and disadvantages of injecting and freebasing is larger than the number of people who have actually tried these methods of ingestion (*Chapter 6*). Apparently, the predominance of disadvantages over advantages for those routes of ingestion is not based on the respondents' own experience, but on negative connotations that intravenous or freebasing user groups have. Users who have never injected associate this route of ingestion with 'junky' type characteristics (such as 'addictive' and 'scary'). These ideas reflect and buttress the informal maxim shared by many of our respondents: 'Stick to snorting as a route of ingestion; never start injecting it'.

In Antwerp freebase cocaine is almost exclusively prepared by the users themselves, and not bought ready-made from dealers (*Chapter 7*). The techniques of making base coke (the Ammonia Method and the Baking Soda Method) require relatively great precision, and must be learnt through direct observation and imitation from peer users. The two main methods of using freebase cocaine are: inhalation of cocaine fumes from an aluminum foil ('chasing the dragon') and smoking freebase cocaine on a glass ('basing'). Especially the latter method often appeared to be a highly ritualized and elaborate technique, although many respondents lack rational knowledge about the functionality and significance of these devices.

The Antwerp sample have a lot of experience with all kinds of drugs (*Chapter 8*). Only a minority use cocaine by itself, whereas most combine the use of cocaine with the use of other drugs. Yet, it would be wrong to conclude that our respondents are permanently taking 'drug cocktails' (i.e. combining several types of drugs at the same occasion of use). They have clear ideas (and informal rules) about which drugs can be combined, and which substances should not be combined! Roughly, we identified nine categories of rules: (1) Rules that aim at continuation; (2) Rules for 'coming down'; (3) Rules to maximize positive effects; (4) Rules for management of finances; (5) Rules to minimize adverse effects while using; (6) Specific taboos; (7) Generalized taboos; (8) Rules to minimize the risk of an overdose; and (9) Rules reflecting a learning process.

Based on the binary oppositions or dual concepts found in the respondents' stories we have tried to reconstruct user lore on 'good' and 'bad' quality of cocaine (*Chapter 9*). This helps the user to decide whether or not he/she will buy 'cocaine' from a particular dealer. As such, user lore on (types of) cocaine and its quality can be perceived as an informal control mechanism. Similarly, we have reconstructed user lore on 'reliable' and 'unreliable' dealers. Most users distinguish between 'honest' and 'rip-off' dealers. Again, this user lore reflects social sanctions concerning the methods of procuring cocaine. Negative experiences, such as being ripped off by a dealer or aggression, lead to some informal rules regarding the purchase of cocaine such as: 'never buy from a stranger', 'never buy from a street dealer', 'never buy from junkies', 'try to find a regular dealer', etc.

More than two in five respondents test their cocaine before they buy it (*Chapter 10*). The testing method most mentioned by the Antwerp sample was 'making a solution' (including the technique of 'cleaning with ammonia'. Other frequently reported methods were 'waiting for freeze', 'boiling in water', 'examining the outlook', 'rubbing between fingers', and 'burning'. Whether these testing methods are as reliable (and healthy) as some users believe, remains questionable. However, they help the user to decide whether or not he/she buys 'cocaine' from some dealer and, as such, can be perceived as an informal control mechanism.

When discussing the advantages and disadvantages of cocaine (*Chapter 11*) two in three respondents claim that disadvantages gradually increase with the *dose* ('not when moderate', 'less when moderate' and 'stronger'). The general rule of use that can be deduced from these findings is that when used moderately, the advantages of cocaine will remain more important than disadvantages. If you do not use moderately, the balance will tip to the side of disadvantages. Both advantages and disadvantages are also perceived as related to *circumstances*. The data show that experienced users have clear ideas about when and where cocaine should be used, and how much of the drug they ought to administer.

The Antwerp respondents describe various strategies and actions for quitting, abstaining temporarily or cutting back on their cocaine use. These behavior patterns can be seen as social rituals concerning the prevention of untoward effects, and we categorized them into avoidance strategies, development of new lifestyle patterns and self-development, or into geographic moves to avoid cocaine, social actions, and health efforts (*Chapter 12*).

Most people see the desire for a drug (in the scientific literature labeled as 'craving') as an inevitable physical or pharmacological effect of the drug (*Chapter 13*). Our findings, however, show that a (strong) desire clearly does not prevent users from regulating their cocaine consumption. In spite of the subjective desire for cocaine, people are able to resist, and to exert power over the drug. Two explanatory factors for this apparent contradiction were discussed: (1) a high level of use (e.g. 2.5 g/week) definitely alters the balance between positive and negative effects. Adverse effects occur more frequently as level of use increases and so compel most users either to abstain or to return to a more pleasurable level of use. Most users manage to do so; and (2) most users apply informal control mechanisms about (un)suitable situations and circumstances for cocaine use, about emotional states that maximize positive effects of cocaine, suitable emotions before use, appropriate dose, etc.

In general, many respondents recognize rules relating to the setting and situations of use, the activities that should take priority, the persons (not) to use with, the maximum number of times one should use cocaine in a given time period, relationships with non-users, frequency of use, appropriate feelings when using, suitable and unsuitable combinations of cocaine with other drugs, route of ingestion, appropriate dose, how to avoid police attention, where and how to buy cocaine, how to manage financial consequences of cocaine use, how to test the quality of cocaine, etc (*Chapter 14, §14.2*). Similarly, responses to questions about advice to novice users may provide indirect access to these regulatory rules (*Chapter 14, §14.3*). These rules can be considered part of the control system that is active when people consume drugs.

Many experienced cocaine users have an implicit theory about how to use cocaine (and/or other drugs) without falling into the trap of abuse: 'never when you feel bad, only when you feel good' (*Chapter 14, §14.4*). Our data indicate that illicit substances are not solely taken for escapist motives (to avoid negative feelings), as is generally believed. Many respondents prefer not to take cocaine when feeling bad. As a set factor, depression may generate an appetite for cocaine, but at the same time, it is regarded as incompatible with cocaine use by a majority of our respondents.

The most suitable situations for cocaine use are those in which people enjoy each other's company: going out, partying and meeting friends (*Chapter 14, §14.5*). Cocaine use is negatively associated with work or study, achievement and the presence of non-users, especially parents and children. Respondents are not prone to using cocaine with just anyone (*Chapter 14, §14.6*). The most frequent categories of persons respondents would definitely not use cocaine with were: family members, non-users, users they don't trust/like, heavy users, etc. Clearly, these respondents have informal rules about the company of use that can serve different goals: (1) to conceal drug use from non-users (because these could be angry, or disappointed, or inform the police or the employer, or because they need to be protected ; (2) To maximize positive effects of cocaine use; (3) To minimize the risk of adverse effects, of becoming dependent on cocaine, of using too much.

More than three in five Antwerp respondents (more than in either Amsterdam sample) stated they put limits to the amount of cocaine they bought per month (*Chapter 14, §14.7*). High-level users (during top period of use) report financial limits significantly less often than medium or low-level users. The average limit on cocaine purchase per month is 4,775.5 BEF, i.e. approximately 2 grams per month. Within the group of Antwerp respondents who report a financial limit on cocaine purchase per month, this limit correlates significantly with level of use during the three months prior to the interview, but not with level of use during top period of use.

Most of the informal rules listed above serve as *boundary protection mechanisms*. They help to prevent disruption of everyday life in which users have invested (jobs, homes, families, communities and identities) and help to maintain or restore the user's balance. As long as everyday life remains a distinct and a paramount reality at the fringes of which drug use takes place, the user maintains control over his/her cocaine use. The fact that many respondents report feelings of shame and regret after having violated their own informal rules or principles of use, illustrates the strength of social rituals and sanctions and their role in the self-regulation of illicit drug use (*Chapter 14, §14.8*). Feelings of remorse may indicate the internalization of rules, norms or values about cocaine use, reinforce the existing informal rules of use, and support rule-awareness and rule-abidance.

More than three in four respondents (77.6%) see themselves as 'controlled' users (*Chapter 15, §15.2*). The indicators of 'controlled' use most frequently reported were: periodical abstinence, refusing cocaine when it is offered (in other words, resisting craving), small doses and/or low frequency of use (and consequently, low level of use), fewer active efforts to obtain cocaine, other activities taking priority over cocaine use, positive reasons for using cocaine. The most important indicators of 'uncontrolled' use were: being unable to stop using (the binge pattern), too large doses and overt signs of 'over'-dosing, financial problems, lying about one's cocaine use, a high frequency of use, active efforts to obtain cocaine, and talking about cocaine incessantly. These indicators of controlled and uncontrolled use serve as boundary protection mechanisms: they keep users from going over the edge with cocaine, or allow them to climb back. These mechanisms help to prevent disruption of the life users have invested in.

Furthermore, counterexamples help the user to draw the line between use and abuse, to set boundaries of appropriate cocaine use, and to develop informal rules to prevent crossing these limits (*Chapter 15, §15.3*). Indeed, friends, acquaintances, partners, relatives, and others can serve as examples of how not to use cocaine, for various reasons: because these people use too much, too frequently, and consequently experience negative physical effects; because they engage in illegal activities or behavior looked down upon; because of negative mental effects; because they use cocaine intravenously or possess other 'junky'-like characteristics; etc.

Most respondents report a sense of increased mastery and control over the product (*Chapter 15, §15.4*). Obviously, the initial hunger (curiosity) for new drug experiences has disappeared and several respondents report the emergence of a (physical or psychological) tolerance for the drug, a steady increase of the dose taken, a greater dependency on the drug, and a transition from snorting to a more direct route of ingestion (freebasing or injecting). However, over the years most respondents have gained better knowledge about the product, its (adverse) effects, the influence of set and setting factors, potential sources of supply, good and bad quality cocaine, other cocaine users, other types of drugs, etc. Many users have to go through a period of loss of control over the substance, or to learn about the negative and dangerous aspects, but in the end they manage to use the substance more consciously and prevent cocaine from taking priority over other activities (such as a job, family life, etc.).

Although a majority of our respondents prefer a cocaine policy that is more tolerant and liberal than the one we have now, many respondents think that while they themselves are able to control their use of these drugs, they are not confident that other people would be so successful in this regard (*Chapter 15, §15.5*). This tendency to be 'tougher' for others can be explained by the fact that they have learned to cope with the dangers of cocaine and with the discomforts caused by the official policy, but at the same time attribute a smaller capacity for controlling cocaine use to others.

The family can be a source of positive social responses (*Chapter 16*). First, the source of informal help when trying to quit cocaine most often mentioned is 'parents'. Second, family members make many comments on each other's behavior, which can be seen as efforts at social control. Some respondents claim these comments did not have any effect on their behavior, but other respondents report that repeated comments from other family members, often combined with other efforts at social control by friends, partners and other significant others, made them quit or cut down on their cocaine use.

The spouse or partner respond in some way to the use and can curb the use or influence it in another way (*Chapter 17*). The partner of a drug user can have a discouraging or curbing effect on his/her pattern of use in many ways: he/she can make comments about the respondent's use (i.e. informal social control), discuss the pros and cons of illicit drug use, suggest the user to cut back or quit using, offer informal help to do so, etc. Furthermore, the fact that several respondents report a marked increase of their cocaine use after a significant relationship was broken off, illustrates the influence of the partner on the drug taker's pattern of use.

Most of our respondents (72%) generally do not use cocaine at work (*Chapter 18*). All speak of their work as vitally important and of careers they aim to advance. Most people in the sample who work regularly do not allow their cocaine to interfere with their job performance at all. Most resist the allure of cocaine when their conventional daily life and identities are at risk. More than half of those who have been under the influence of cocaine during working hours did this only once, usually as an experiment ('to see what it does'). We argued above that structural factors such as co-worker accessibility, teamwork, the company policy on illicit drugs and on-the-job cocaine availability can enhance or discourage work-related cocaine consumption. The same processes of social modeling by co-workers and employers that may support illicit drug use may also act as a barrier against heavy, if any, cocaine use at work. These can be seen as mechanisms of informal social control.

Most respondents report having made remarks to friends about their cocaine use (*Chapter 19, §19.3*). Most remarks to the respondents' friends related to the dose or the frequency of cocaine use, to negative changes in their behavior, to their route of ingestion, and to negative consequences of their cocaine use on their job, their family life, their health etc. Typically, respondents had advised their friend(s) to cut down on their use, to abstain temporarily or to quit using cocaine altogether. More than three in five respondents also report having had similar remarks on their own cocaine use from one or more friends. Several participants indicate they readily accept remarks from friends because they stimulate their reflection about their own use and because it keeps them alert to the pitfalls of the drug. Cocaine use is a regular topic of conversation among respondents and their cocaine-using friends. Conversations typically focus on positive and negative experiences with cocaine, and about various methods of controlling the substance. Discussions are often pervaded with a general concern about whether or not one is 'addicted' or 'in control'.

Giving each other advice about mode of ingestion, dose, circumstances suitable to use cocaine, combination of cocaine with other drugs, buying cocaine, disadvantages of cocaine, and methods of countering these, is not uncommon, even among experienced users (*Chapter 19, §19.4*). Generally, the social factor, i.e. reassurance from close associates, helps the user to overcome his or her anxiety for the drug, its effects and possible consequences. We found illustrations of several types of informal help. Even in the case of an overdose or emergency, people are not left to fend for themselves by their intimate friends. Most respondents report that other users try to reassure the person who suffers an overdose. Some respondents even report particular 'detoxification techniques' to put someone back on his feet after an overdose of cocaine (a glass of milk, an orange or a lemon, a glass of salted water).

20.3.3. Socialization of informal control mechanisms

The processes through which these social sanctions and controls are transferred, vary with the legal status of the substances involved. Unlike the situation with licit drugs, the opportunities for learning how to control illicit drug consumption remain extremely limited. Our study yielded the following observations concerning the socialization of informal control mechanisms:

In the social context of everyday life, the influence of parents and family in the socialization of drug use holds a special place. The process of gradual introduction to drinking behavior by the parents serves a useful developmental function: a young person learns to use alcohol in appropriate ways. However, family socialization regarding the use of cocaine (or other illicit drugs) is markedly different from that of drinking behavior through modeling and imitation processes, social reinforcement, supportive behavior and controling behavior. Parents may provide their children with their first smoking and drinking experiences, but they do not serve as a model for cocaine use. Gradual socialization of cocaine use by parental monitoring is all but impossible (*Chapter 16*). The illegality of the substance has made cocaine use a taboo in society in general, and in the family in particular. Most respondents lie to their parents about their cocaine use. They view their parents as ignorant or 'indoctrinated' by official sources such as the media, the government, school, the police, etc. Within an individual's family, only siblings are the most salient significant others on whom individuals model their illicit drug use, especially when brothers or sisters are part of the respondent's 'peer group'.

Similarly, illicit drug use is a taboo among working colleagues for most of the Antwerp respondents (*Chapter 18*). In order to avoid social stigmata and/or judicial problems, most cocaine users prefer to keep their use hidden from their colleagues and/or employer. Typically, other employees are only trusted when they hold libertarian attitudes about most drug use, when they are of the same age as the respondent and when they have at least experimented with illicit drugs in the past.

Typically, parents and official sources of information (the media, the authorities, the police, medical professionals and the school) have warned our respondents about the negative aspects. These official warnings are mostly perceived as exaggerated, one-sided and faulty, which leads many to throw out the proverbial baby with the bathwater. For example, four in five Antwerp respondents had received false information about cocaine (*Chapter 4*). Most refer to general statements about the addictive characteristics of cocaine, to all kinds of incomplete or biased ideas, the oversimplification underlying the idea that all drugs and any type of drug use must be placed under the common denominator 'bad', or the typical junkie stories about injecting, withdrawal symptoms, criminal users and zombie-like users. Most of this false information is blamed on the newsmedia, official agencies (such as the government, the school, the police, the prevention agents and the medical world), or non-users in general.

Thus, neither the family, nor the school, nor the culture in general provides models for controlled use. As a consequence, the most important, but often inadequate, source is peer using groups. Many of our respondents had a fixed image and expectations of the drug before they first used it (*Chapter 4*). Curiosity about cocaine and association with people who use it lead to the uninitiated being present when cocaine is being used. The stories about pleasurable experiences from cocaine using intimates or friends, and the observations of other users had made our respondents eager to 'know what it is all about'.

Following Becker (1973) we described the social learning process of the use of cocaine in three stages: (1) learning the proper technique (snorting, freebasing, injecting, etc.) by direct instruction or indirectly by observation and imitation; (2) discerning the subtle effects of cocaine; (3) learning to enjoy the effects. Through this learning process, rules or sanctions on the adequate dosage, the preferable route of ingestion, where to obtain good quality cocaine, which safe places to use, good times to use, 'good' people to use with, how to avoid trouble, etc. are passed on from the experienced user to the neophyte. In *Chapter 7* we illustrated this process with the preparation of free-base cocaine, a technique that requires relatively great precision, and must be learnt through direct observation and imitation from peer users. Without doubt, the most important source of precepts and practices for control during initiation is the peer using group. Virtually all our respondents had been assisted by other experienced users in constructing appropriate rituals and sanctions out of the folklore and practices circulating in their drug-using subculture.

Our data indicate that the process of 'becoming a cocaine user' does not end when the user has learned to master the proper technique and to enjoy the effects caused by the drug. Our analysis of subjective indicators of 'controlled' and 'uncontrolled' use, of counterexamples, of perceived changed in cocaine use patterns, and the informal rules developed through the years, shows that the drug user continuously learns from his/her own experience and that of others and the process of 'becoming a controlled cocaine user' approaches completion as knowledge about the product extends (*Chapter 15*). Over the years most respondents have gained better knowledge about the product, its (adverse) effects, the influence of set and setting factors, potential sources of supply, good and bad quality cocaine, other cocaine users, other types of drugs, etc. That is why most respondents report a sense of increased mastery and control over the product.

From their own negative experiences and from other users' stories (the user lore), our respondents learnt to control their cocaine consumption. For example, informal rules about which drugs can be combined, reflect a learning from bad experiences (*Chapter 8*). Similarly, user lore on (types of) cocaine (and its quality), and (types of) dealers, can be perceived as informal control mechanisms (*Chapter 9*). This knowledge helps the user to decide whether or not he/she will buy 'cocaine' from a particular dealer. Furthermore, negative experiences with buying cocaine, such as rip-offs or aggression, lead to informal rules regarding the purchase of cocaine such as: 'never buy from a stranger', 'never buy from a street dealer', 'never buy from junkies', 'try to find a fixed dealer', etc.

Informal rules serve as boundary protection mechanisms. They help to prevent disruption of the everyday life users have invested in (jobs, homes, families, communities and identities) and help to maintain or restore the user's balance. Some respondents refer to a learning process regarding informal rules of use (*Chapter 15, §15.4*): negative experiences after violating their own principles may help them to respect these informal rules on next occasions of use. Many users have to go through a period of loss of control over the substance, or to learn about the negative and dangerous aspects, but in the end they are able to use the substance more consciously and to prevent cocaine from taking priority over other activities (such as a job, family life, etc.). Users see the informal control mechanisms as a part of their personality, and not as learned social sanctions and rituals (*Chapter 15, §15.5*). Many respondents believe that they themselves are able to control their use of these drugs, but they are not confident that other people would be so successful in this regard. This tendency to be 'tougher' for others can be explained by the fact that they have learned to cope with the dangers of cocaine and with the discomforts caused by the official policy, while they attribute a weaker capacity for controlling cocaine use to others.

20.3.4. The effectiveness of informal control mechanisms

The existence of informal control mechanisms does not, however, necessarily imply that they are effective, nor that all sanctions and rituals were devised to aid control. Some social sanctions and rituals may once have served as control mechanisms that gradually became perverted or debased. Others may have originated in erroneous beliefs and ideas. *In many cases, the respondents' knowledge about the product is incomplete or false.* These are the most salient findings in the present study:

Virtually all our respondents had been assisted by other experienced users in constructing appropriate rituals and sanctions out of the folklore and practices circulating in their drug-using subculture. However, this process of knowledge transfer is not always flawless (*Chapter 4*). Users adapt informal control mechanisms to their own personal preferences and demands, or the knowledge being transferred is incomplete. For example, four in five Antwerp respondents have received false information about cocaine. Most of them refer to general statements about the addictive characteristics of cocaine, to all kinds of incomplete or biased ideas, the oversimplification underlying the idea that all drugs and any type of drug use must be commonly labelled as 'bad', or the typical junkie stories about injecting, withdrawal symptoms, criminal and zombie-like users. Most of this false information is ascribed to the newsmedia, official agencies (such as the government, the school, the police, the prevention agents and the medical world), or non-users in general. Distortions about the quality of cocaine are very likely to originate with dealers, while false information about specific effects or the non-addictiveness of cocaine usually comes from other cocaine using friends.

Respondents were asked to list advantages and disadvantages of the three best known routes of ingestion (snorting, injecting and freebasing) (*Chapter 6*). We found that at least some cocaine users, despite their 'experience' with the drug, were badly informed about the possible (adverse) effects and the actual pharmacological action of cocaine on the body.

The terminology of freebase cocaine and the technique of using it, is confusing (*Chapter 7*). There is great controversy among users about whether there is a difference between 'freebase' and 'crack'. Some users believe there is no difference. In any case, it is clear that the users' knowledge about 'crack' is often based on hearsay and (horror) stories, and thus partial, biased and possibly incorrect. While many Antwerp respondents believe it is possible to be a controlled freebaser, that freebasing is not necessarily addicting, they also believe that 'crack' is a distinct product. However, our data suggest that most users have remained unaware of the similarities between 'crack' and 'freebase', or of the fact that 'crack' and 'freebase' refer to similar products. As stated above, much of what a user feels is the result of the situational and cultural context (setting) in which the drug is used. Part of that cultural context are the 'stories' about the diabolical drug named 'crack'. Yet, these images of cocaine are diffused into the public awareness through the mass media, and we can expect both the public in general and drug users in particular to be influenced by them. Not only will attitudes and beliefs unfavorable to its use be strengthened in the general public, the exaggerated horrors of crack cocaine may have deterred the Antwerp cocaine users themselves. But what would happen if we told them that 'freebasing' could be as risky as smoking 'crack', and that in fact, there are few differences between the two?

Some users have acquired their own experimental tools and techniques for 'cleaning cocaine', but the effectivity of those techniques remains questionable (*Chapter 7*). More importantly, two thirds of the respondents reported to omit the phase of rinsing the rock of freebase cocaine with water to remove the ammonia. Yet, ammonia fumes can cause permanent damage to the user's health. Second, although the method of smoking freebase cocaine with a glass ('basing') is a highly ritualized and elaborate technique, we found that many respondents lack rational knowledge about the functionality and significance of these devices.

User lore on 'good' and 'bad' quality of cocaine can help the user to decide whether or not he/she will buy 'cocaine' from a particular dealer, but it is unequally spread among users and it may be incomplete and/or false. The most striking example is the fact that while most experienced cocaine users think that their cocaine is 'always' or 'regularly' adulterated with 'speed' (and even that they are able to feel the presence of amphetamines in cocaine), all prove to be wrong (*Chapter 10*). None of the Antwerp cocaine samples we had analyzed contained amphetamine, contrary to what many users believe. Thus, respondent judgement on purity of cocaine is poor, and most of the reported negative effects of 'speed' in cocaine were cocaine effects, or effects of cocaine in combination with another drug.

Whether the testing methods our respondents report are as reliable (and healthy) as some users believe, remains questionable (*Chapter 10, §10.5*). Reliable testing of the quality is technically difficult and time consuming, and as cocaine is expensive and sometimes scarce, users are not always prepared to sacrifice a part of the precious powder to test it for quality. The contradictory stories on the appearance of cocaine (how good quality should look like) illustrate that the effectiveness of this informal control may be hampered by the fact that it is unequally spread among users and it may be incomplete (and in some individual cases false).

Most participants state that while they are sometimes able to resist temptation and respect their own principles of use, they occasionally violate these rules and 'let themselves go' (*Chapter 14, §14.8*). Respondents often calculate the pros and cons of a given situation and when they 'decide' to betray their own principles it is often because of a combination of interfering set and setting factors. The following set and setting factors that interfere with informal rules of use are most mentioned: increased availability, the inner life of the user, the social character of the occasions of use, the pharmacological actions of cocaine itself or of other drugs.

The spouse or partner can act as a stimulus for the respondents' cocaine use in more than one way: as an initiator, as a significant other and model, as a pushy user, as a daily conversation partner, as a sexual partner, as a source of supply, etc. (*Chapter 16*). Furthermore, the fact that one in four respondents report having lied to a partner regarding their drug use illustrates that informal social control is not always effective. When the partner is a non-user, most respondents report having lied about their cocaine use because they felt their partner would make problems about something they themselves did not see as problematic. When both partners in a relationship are regular users of various types of illicit drugs, discussions tend to focus on the quantity of use, the frequency of use and the circumstances of use.

Informal comments can provoke a wide range of reactions, from aggression and indifference, to feigned consent and simulated remorse, to indulgence and behavioral change (*Chapter 19*). Whether or not a remark or comment from another person is perceived as well-founded, depends on many factors: the source or maker of the remark (non-user or user), the (perceived) pattern of his/her cocaine use, the form and content of the remark (serene versus paternalistic, joking versus angry, verbal versus non-verbal), the situation in which the comment is made, the emotional state of the receiver, whether the receiver is under the influence of cocaine, etc. Most of the respondents' accounts show that a prerequisite for effective informal social control is a strong or intimate bond between the maker of the comments and the receiver. Our participants emphasize that only the remarks of close friends can help to adjust their cocaine use. Comments by acquaintances, strangers, and non-users in general go in one ear and out the other..

However, the user may reach a stage where he/she is no longer able to conform to the others' expectations and starts to lie about his/her cocaine use. Almost half of the respondents who report having lied state they concealed their illicit drug use from non-using friends to minimize the risk of police attention, to avoid being labeled a 'drug user' or 'addict', or to avoid concern, anxiety, disappointment, shock, etc. in significant others. Almost one in three of the respondents who report having lied state they lied about the quantity of cocaine they had with them to other users. These lies are typically meant to avoid sharing the drug with others, because it is hard to obtain, or expensive, or because these respondents simply want all the cocaine for them. One in five of the respondents who had lied acknowledge having done so about the frequency of use to friends, because they wanted to avoid informal social control by others (social disapproval), or because they wanted to mask their own inability to control the substance.

It is striking that in the case of an overdose or emergency, most respondents indicate they prefer to look for solutions themselves, rather than appeal to a general practitioner or a first-aid-team, or call for an ambulance (*Chapter 19, §19.4*). Most bystanders try to reassure the one who has an overdose: they try to 'talk him/her down', give him/her something to drink, keep him/her company, etc. Some respondents, however, report particular ploys to put someone back on his/her feet after an overdose (a glass of milk, a glass of orange or lemon juice, a glass of salty water). These 'detoxification techniques' are probably part of user lore about adverse effects and how to 'treat' them, but they are relatively ineffective and sometimes even counterproductive.

20.4. INTERACTION BETWEEN FORMAL AND INFORMAL CONTROL

An important question is the way in which the user handles conflicts between sanctions. With illicit drugs the most obvious conflict is between formal and informal social controls – i.e. between the legal prohibition and the social group's approval of use.

The positive effects or the appealing aspects of cocaine are usually minimized whereas descriptions of the negative effects or the unappealing aspects of cocaine are classical (*Chapter 11*). All this suggests that the use of illicit drugs only yields positive experiences or advantages in the beginning of a user's career and that –in the end- the balance always tips to the side of the negative effects or disadvantages. We stated above that the official warnings (from the media, the authorities, the police, medical practitioners and the school) are mostly perceived by the respondents as exaggerated, one-sided and faulty, which leads many to throw out the proverbial baby with the bathwater (*Chapter 4*). The worst-case scenario of cocaine that these official sources depict as typical is not likely to match the experience of most current users. For potential users, the credibility of prevention information is drastically eroded once they learn from experienced users that the worst-case scenario is an exception rather than a rule.

When parents, schools, and the media are all incapable of informing neophytes about the controlled use of illicit drugs, that task falls squarely on the new users' peer group – an inadequate substitute for cross-generation, long-term socialization (*Chapter 4*). Since illicit drug use is a covert activity, newcomers are not presented with an array of using groups from which to choose, and association with controlled users is largely a matter of chance. If some individuals, early in their using careers, become involved either with groups whose members are not well versed in controlled use or with groups in which compulsive use and risk-taking are the rules, they might evolve to uncontrolled use.

The official policy complicates the development of controlled use in still another way: by inadvertently creating a black market with drugs of uncertain quality. Wide variations in strength and purity make the task of controlling dosage and effect more difficult (*Chapter 10*). Some users pay more than they should for a poor product. The potency of a buy is unknown, and the risk of an overdose thus increases (*Chapter 19*). If adulterants are present, the risk of infection is heightened when the drug is injected. Reliable testing for quality is technically difficult and time consuming, and as cocaine is expensive and sometimes scarce, users are not always prepared to sacrifice a part of the precious powder to test its quality (*Chapter 7 and 10*). User lore may help the user to decide whether or not to buy 'cocaine' from a particular dealer, but it is unequally spread among users and it may be incomplete (and in some individual cases false) (*Chapter 9*).

The present official prohibition of drug use by legal means would be justifiable if it persuaded some people never to use drugs and led others to abandon them. But, consistent with other studies, the effects of fear of legal consequences on our respondents' cocaine use are either negligible or much less important than extralegal factors (*Chapter 11*). Furthermore, our data on cocaine sellers also suggest that, despite the occupational risks, the law does not have a great deterrent effect and many cocaine sellers manage to keep a step ahead of the police.

In this kind of repressive climate any opinion about illicit drug use tends to be quickly classified as either 'for' or 'against' use, and halfway positions are not acknowledged. Diehard users will dispute any evidence that drug use can be disruptive. Conversely, non-users are eager to show that no one can get away with saying something positive about cocaine or other illicit drugs. A result of the interaction between formal and informal controls is that the gap between users and non-users is getting larger ('us' versus 'them'). Both parties do not communicate, and among illicit drug users there is a code of silence. We showed above that many respondents have informal rules about the company of use that serve to conceal drug use from non-users (because these persons could be angry, or disappointed, or inform the police or the employer (*Chapter 14*).

We showed extensively that cocaine use is a taboo in many circles, and that our respondents took great pains in hiding their use from the people around them. Respondents lie to their parents about their cocaine use because they view them as ignorant or 'indoctrinated' by official sources such as the media, the government, school, the police, etc. (*Chapter 16*). About one in four respondents report having lied to a partner regarding their drug use. When the partner is a non-user, most respondents report having lied about their cocaine use because they felt their partner would make problems about something they did not see as problematic (*Chapter 17*). In order to avoid social stigmata and/or judicial problems, most cocaine users prefer to keep their use hidden from their colleagues and/or employer (*Chapter 18*). Interviewees report holding back their illicit drug use from non-using friends to minimize the risk of police attention, to avoid being labeled 'drug user' or 'addict', or to avoid feelings of concern, anxiety, disappointment, shock, etc. in significant others (*Chapter 19*). In short, the repressive society has minimized the normative influences of family, friends and moderate users. Under such conditions, users can only slowly pass along knowledge of the drug's dangers and the ways to avoid or minimize them. What one generation of drug users learns is difficult to transmit to the next. When social learning is impeded, the tragedies are bound to repeat themselves.

As such, illicit drug use is thus driven into closed and hidden (sub)cultures, where the possibilities for informal social control are limited. The more a deviant group is set apart and put under pressure, the more it will profile itself as a deviant group. Stereotypical deviant behavior, norms and values then become emphasized and reinforced, resulting in a highly separated, intradependent, monofocussed subculture, whose members are very distrustful of the mainstream culture. This phenomenon hinders an open discussion between users and non-users, thus impeding the dissemination of controlling rituals and social sanctions. For example, our data showed that a prerequisite for effective informal social control is a strong or intimate bond between the maker of the comments and the receiver (*Chapter 19*). Our participants stress the fact that only the remarks of close friends are likely to adjust their cocaine use. Comments by acquaintances, strangers, and non-users in general go in one ear and out the other.

When a drug is criminalized, its use tends to be marginalized or pushed out of conventional society into 'deviant' subcultures. In such circles, some users may look for ways to get more 'bang for their buck'. Indeed, the most striking difference of our data with other major community studies lies in the prevalence of freebasing (*Chapter 7*). Many of our subjects believe 'cleaning cocaine with ammonia' and freebasing it is a safe way of consuming a less adulterated form of cocaine. However, communication about the side-effects and other risks tends to remain subterranean and incomplete and therefore ineffective. Most Antwerp respondents believed freebase cocaine and crack to be completely different things. The perceived net merit of freebasing is not as negative as with injecting or smoking 'crack'. However, 'crack' and 'freebase' refer to similar products, but most users remain unaware of the similarities between 'crack' and 'freebase'.

Fearing society's disapproval, as well as its legal sanction, new drug users typically experience high levels of anxiety. Such anxiety interferes with control. In order to deal with this conflict the user may display more antisocial behavior than would have been the case if he/she used licit drugs. The illegal status of substances such as cocaine and heroin causes feelings of anxiety in many users when they are confronted with extreme overdosing and emergencies. In these instances, illicit drug users feel the anxiety engendered by society's association of drug use with degradation and criminality. Consequently, many users do not call for an ambulance or a doctor in case of an emergency, and that can have disastrous consequences (*Chapter 19*).

User lore on 'good' and 'bad' quality of cocaine is unequally spread among users and is often incomplete and/or false (*Chapter 9*). Respondent judgement on purity of cocaine is poor: almost all respondents proved to be wrong about the supposed adulterants in their cocaine (*Chapter 10*). The notion that illicit street drugs are routinely adulterated or diluted with dangerous substances, is an assumption that attains the status of 'fact', because both the drug user and drug commentators of varying persuasions 'invest' in the idea of dangerous adulteration. We have argued that the idea of dangerous adulteration/dilution is a myth that is essentially reliant upon a number of other drug myths for its origin and perpetuation. Without the myth of the evil drug dealer, which itself partially relies upon the image of the depraved drug fiend, which in turn partially relies on the unreasonable exaggeration of the degenerative powers of drugs, the rationale for its existence is difficult to maintain.

20.5. SOME FINAL REFLECTIONS

20.5.1. Getting rid of the ambiguity

All drugs can and sometimes do cause harm. But so do the licit drugs that are freely available for non-medical use. Yet, the overemphasis on the extraordinary pharmacological powers of certain substances has led most health practitioners, prevention workers and policymakers to distinguish between 'soft drugs' and 'hard drugs'. The pharmacocentric perspective predicts a strong, positive association between the 'addictiveness' of a particular drug and the level of destructive use in society. Depictions of particular substances as catastrophic (cocaine and crack) inflate the estimate of their users requiring treatment and related services. Conversely, a 'soft drug' such as cannabis is frequently depicted as a completely harmless substance.

It is truly ironic that our society sets up a firm double standard of behavior in which the use of alcohol and tobacco as pleasure-producing psychotropic drugs is accepted, while the use of any other intoxicant for that purpose is regarded as abusive. The fact that alcohol is psychotropic is easy to dismiss because millions of social drinkers know from experience that an alcohol 'high' can be controlled; abusive use, or alcoholism, is viewed as a disease that is caught by a susceptible minority. This illogical attitude implies that a single use of cocaine or crack is far more likely to be construed as drug abuse than is the heavy ingestion of alcohol. However, our empirical data suggest that even a 'hard' drug such as cocaine can be used in a controlled way...

Nevertheless, the term 'drug abuse' continues to be applied to all styles of illicit drug use, and little or no effort has been made to distinguish abuse from use. There are several reasons for this (for a thorough discussion about the concepts of 'addiction' and other associated terms, see e.g. Gusfield, 1963; Schneider, 1978; Levine, 1984; Peele, 1985; Weil, 1986; Peele, 1989; Kaminski, 1990; Neuhaus, 1991;Peele *et al.*, 1991; Shaffer & Robbins, 1991; Husak, 1992: 127-129; Moore, 1992; Szasz, 1992; Acker, 1993; Neuhaus, 1993; Kaminski, 1997). Given the vagaries of the concepts of 'drug abuse' and 'addiction' in the literature, we have difficulty measuring addiction and categorizing individuals. Moreover, people do not easily fit into neat categories, and their use pattern changes continuously and does not always include the same sets of problems. Trying to fit all drug users into one explanatory system is worse than ineffective. More important than quarrelling over the answers, we would do well to reassess our questions. In this regard, we can ask ourselves when and how it is useful to speak of 'addiction' and 'drug abuse'. What is revealed by speaking of 'addiction' and 'abuse' as a disease, and what is hidden? Would some drug users find new actions possible in a different language set? Does speaking about 'addiction' and 'abuse' promote specific goals and concerns (of the health care system and the regulatory authorities), while inhibiting those of others (drug users)?

It is clear that the greatest problem in studying users of illicit drugs, is that of differentiating between drug use and drug abuse. This difference is fairly evident at the extremes of behavior, but it is by no means that obvious in the gray area where the majority of users find themselves. Anyone can see the difference between those who use no drugs except marihuana, only once a week, and those who inject heroin and cocaine at least two or three times a day. But most drug users fall in between those extremes. The life histories of most of our respondents illustrate this. In our view, most of our subjects fall into the gray area of more or less controlled use. Their stories illustrate the value of approaching the use-abuse problem longitudinally (over time) rather than only cross-sectionally (at a particular point in time). The following observations can be made:

- Although our respondents have used various licit and illicit drugs for longer periods and experienced some adverse effects, only a few of them have felt the need to look for professional help. Even after lengthy cocaine careers, many were able to quit using cocaine without even applying special avoidance strategies.

- Most of these respondents are not known to the police as cocaine users. Although many of them admit having frequented persons or places they did not really like, only because they knew there was cocaine, the majority have never committed any offenses to obtain their cocaine.

- Most respondents do not spend huge sums of money on their drug use: some never bought cocaine themselves, and others only buy every three months.

- Our subjects have a multiplicity of meaningful roles which gave them a positive identity and a stake in conventional daily life (e.g. secure employment, homes, and families). Both of these factors anchor them against drifting toward a drug-centered life.

- All of them acknowledge having regularly experienced adverse effects and indicate some disadvantages of the use of cocaine. Yet, they also report clear advantages.

- When explicitly asked for personal rules of use, some interviewees cannot identify any of such rules of behavior. Nevertheless most seem to be able to restrict their cocaine use to certain settings, and only with certain people.

- Many Antwerp respondents have been able to cut back on their cocaine use or quit temporarily on several occasions.

The Antwerp respondents' drug histories show a complex interrelationship between personality factors and social factors as determinants of the extent and quality of drug use. They illustrate how hard it is to decide when an individual's drug use has crossed the line between use and abuse, and whether the change in either direction is going to be permanent. At some points in time, our subjects' drug use would not be considered a problem if it were not for the current drug policy. At some points in time, their drug use seemed to be controlled; at others, it seemed as if they temporarily lost control.

Almost none of these respondents correspond to the stereotypical drug user. They use several illicit drugs, but they do not use heroin, they do not inject. They are not dressed in filthy clothes, they have normal standards of hygiene and they live in comfortable houses. As we were interviewing them, they did not seem to have distorted images of reality or ways of reasoning. Moreover, none of them commit any socially disgraceful activities in order to acquire money for their cocaine. These respondents do not seem in an 'abnormal' state, nor do they seem to have lost their capacity for voluntary behavior.

On the other hand, these stories illustrate that cocaine use, apart from subjective advantages, may also lead to subjective disadvantages and adverse effects. Patterns of cocaine use vary over time, and the user may at one time quit or cut back on his/her use, and at another time increase the use to a (more) harmful level. It seems to us as if (both licit and illicit) drug users continuously drift on a continuum, while their degree of control over cocaine fluctuates.

In our opinion, drug abuse cannot be defined in the abstract. It must be determined on a case-by-case and moment-to-moment basis. Only after examining each case and reporting in detail on a variety of factors relating to it can the investigator judge whether abuse has occurred and if so, in which particular period. Dropping the term 'drug abuse' is a necessary preliminary to understanding why and when people use drugs, how they use them, and above all, whether they can use them successfully, i.e. in a controlled way. The descriptions of some users clearly shows their use to be excessive, but the histories of other users reveals a complex interrelationship between personal and social determinants of the extent and quality of drug use. Getting rid of the ambiguity of one of the code words intended to indicate what society thinks is wrong with drug use, gives us an opportunity to find and employ clear, precise and realistic terms.

20.5.2. Some recommendations

1. The data of the present study suggest that the view that pharmacology is somehow an instantly addicting destiny is an oversimplification, given the many complex patterns of use and outcomes. *We therefore propose to abandon the classical distinction between 'soft drugs' and 'hard drugs', and to introduce a new distinction between 'soft use' and 'hard use' of any drug.* This approach allows us to assess the overall impact of any substance, without overreacting to the dangers it poses. It does not downplay the pharmacological power of drugs, but it does not consider them the only important factor either. It accepts that drug use does not occur in a social vacuum, and that psychological, social, economic, and cultural factors all play important roles in shaping a person's drug use behavior. Every possible effort should be made –legally, medically, and socially- to distinguish between the two basic types of drug use: the experimental, recreational, and circumstantial, with minimal social costs; and the dysfunctional, intensified, and compulsive, with high social costs. I have labeled these types 'soft use' of cocaine and 'hard use' respectively.

In order to distinguish 'soft use' from 'hard use', greater attention will have to be paid to *how* drugs are used. We should study both the conditions under which dysfunctional or 'hard' use occurs and how these can be modified, and the conditions that maintain control for the 'soft users' and how these can be promulgated. To study the conditions of use for each drug will require consideration of the following topics: dosage, method of administration, pattern of use (including frequency), and social setting, as well as the pharmacology of the drug itself.

Drug policy should encourage the development and dissemination of informal control mechanisms among those who are already using drugs. Any abrupt shift in the present policy would probably be inappropriate. Informal social controls cannot be provided to users ready-made, nor can formal policy create them. The sudden legalization of cocaine, for instance, would leave in limbo those who have not yet had the time to internalize informal social controls. There are, however, several steps that can be taken to demystify drug use and thus to encourage the development of informal control mechanisms. These steps include disseminating realistic information (education), less police activity towards users, decriminalizing all use of any drug, correcting negative attitudes toward drug users, and undertaking legal reform. In the long run a more liberal and tolerant drug policy should remove drugs from their criminal context and make users themselves responsible for their drug use, rather than the State. However, such a tolerant policy must include state-controlled availability and purity of drugs, while at the same time it must discourage the use of drugs in general.

2. The fact that most experienced cocaine users reported receiving mainly false, or at least incomplete, biased, partial or over-simplified, information from the media and the official agencies, leads to questions about the validity of official preventive and repressive efforts. Official sources (including parents) will be dismissed as valid and authoritative sources, as long as preventive efforts ignore the pleasurable effects and advantages of illicit drugs to the user and overexpose the adverse effects and disadvantages. Humans have ingested drugs for purposes of consciousness alteration throughout history. Drugs have many different uses, and for whatever reason they are used, they are experienced as functional as well as pleasurable. The problem is that these benefits (pleasure, insight, comfort, relief, social ease, etc.) some individuals get from some psychoactive drugs are not recognized explicitly. Most people learn to use cocaine from friends who already use it, and these sources remain the only trusted ones. A realistic depiction of cocaine has to be the basis of any professional prevention work.

3. Many, perhaps even most, cocaine users appear able to manage their cocaine use unaided, even if use becomes heavy for a while. This does not mean that the minority who seek treatment should be capable of managing their cocaine use unaided. In a sense, the average drug clinic attender is a victim of his or her failure to make, identify or obey adequate personal rules that govern problematic drug-related behavior. Most people seeking cocaine treatment have tried and failed to manage cocaine use unassisted. These people need help. On the other hand, the misapprehension that illicit drugs are outstandingly addictive, contains a risk that treatment (and judicial) agencies may encourage drug users to attend treatment unnecessarily. Unless drug users know that most of them can stop using drugs unaided, treatment resources will be devoted to treating people who require no treatment.

Our data suggest that drug users have many different reasons for using cocaine and other illicit substances. Particular set and setting factors may be a reason for using cocaine for some subjects, while they are a reason for not using cocaine for others. For whatever reason drugs are used, they are experienced as functional as well as fun. This diversity is also reflected in the idiosyncratic features of informal control mechanisms (Zinberg, 1984: 80). Treatment agencies could develop models of informal control mechanisms, and 'types' of drug users based on the social rituals and sanctions they have adopted. A better understanding of the genesis and transfer of informal control mechanisms among drug users, may help the treatment specialists to draw lessons from those who are able to control their cocaine use ('soft users') for the benefit of those who seem unable to manage their use ('hard users').

4. Devising an appropriate societal response to hard and soft use of substances requires a sound, up-to-date knowledge base. Moreover, the heterogeneity of career patterns found in the present study of experienced cocaine users suggests possibilities for control that are too rarely acknowledged or studied. It is our hope that this research will stimulate other investigators to undertake long-term, longitudinal studies of drug-using behavior as a socially evolving process. Since such studies will require careful selection and special training of researchers, modest budget increases for research may be required. But the focus of the research rather than the budget should be the primary concern.

Finally, we definitely need: (1) more *epidemiological research* into the nature and the extent of drug use in Belgium (not even a general population survey has ever been done). Studies should comprise sufficiently large samples, and focus on different types of substances; (2) There is an urgent need for *qualitative research* that tries to understand drug users' behavior from the 'native point of view'; (3) Future research should also focus on how licit and illicit drugs influence individual health. A topic that deserves special attention is 'drug-related deaths', 'drug-related accidents', and *'overdoses'*; (4) Future studies of *ethnic minorities* may yield interesting data about variations in development and integration of informal control mechanisms. Moreover, the variations in rituals and rules that result from different cultural backgrounds and group affinities may be useful in designing treatment and prevention strategies for these ethnic groups; (5) One of the most striking outcomes of our study is the *high prevalence of freebasing*. Whether freebasing should be considered a significant problem and whether the Belgian setting differs from other European countries should be further investigated; (6) Future research should investigate the possibility for formal education to codify control mechanisms in a reasonable way for those who have been bypassed by the informal process. Does *user lore* contain false and incomplete ideas, and, if so, how can we direct or correct it to avoid problematical drug use? How can we stimulate the development of *informal control mechanisms* and promote their transfer from one user to another, from one generation to the next? (7) To *evaluate the present drug policy,* future studies should investigate the attitudes of both users and non-users toward drug policies, the impact of the media and other official sources on public opinion. Furthermore, we need to know what use is being made of drug research and how its findings influence public policy decisions. There is no need for 'governmental sociology' or scientists who fawn on policy-makers to safeguard research budgets.

REFERENCES

ACKER, C.J. (1993), Stigma or legitimation? A historical examination of the social potentials of addiction disease models, 25 *Journal of Psychoactive Drugs* 3, 193-205.

ADAIR, E.B., CRADDOCK, S.G., MILLER, H.G. and TURNER, C.F. (1995), Assessing consistency of responses to questions on cocaine use, 90 *Addiction* 11, 1497-1502.

AIGNER, T.G. and BALSTER, R.L. (1978), Choice behavior in rhesus monkeys: cocaine versus food, 201 *Science* 4355, 534-535.

ALEXANDER, B.K., COAMBS, R.B. and HADAWAY, P.F. (1978), The effect of housing and gender on morphine self-administration in rats, 58 *Psychopharmacology*, 175-179.

AMBRE, J.J., BELKNAP, S.M., NELSON, J., RUO, T.I., SHIN, S.G. and ATKINSON, A.J. (1988), Acute tolerance to cocaine in humans, 44 *Clinical Pharmacology and Therapeutics* 1, 1-8.

AMERICAN PSYCHIATRIC ASSOCIATION (1994), *Diagnostic and statistical manual of mental disorders. Fourth edition (DSM-IV)*. Washington: American Psychiatric Association.

AMSEL, Z. *et al.* (1976), Reliability and validity of self-reported illegal activities and drug use collected from narcotic addicts, 11 *International Journal of the Addictions*, 325-336.

ANGLIN, D.M. and MCGLOTHLIN, W.H. (1984), Outcome of narcotics addict treatment in California. In: TIMS, F. and RUCHMAN, N. (eds.), *Drug abuse treatment evaluation: strategies, progress and prospects*. NIDA Research Monograph Series. Washington: U.S. Government Printing Office.

ANGLIN, D.M., BONETT, D.G., BRECHT, M.L. and WOODWARD, J.A. (1986), An empirical study of maturing out: conditional factors, 21 *International Journal of the Addictions*, 233-246.

ANTA, G.B., ORTA, J.V., PORTELA, M.J.B. and DE LA FUENTE DE HOZ, L. (1993), The epidemiology of cocaine use in Spain, 34 *Drug and Alcohol Dependence* 1, 45-57.

APSLER, R. (1982), Measuring how people control the amounts of substances they use, 37-51. In: ZINBERG, N.E. and HARDING, W.M., *Control over intoxicant use. Pharmacological, psychological and social considerations*. New York: Human Sciences Press.

ARBER, S. (1993), Designing samples, 68-92. In: GILBERT, N., *Researching social life*. London: Sage Publications.

ARIF, A. (1987) (ed.), *Adverse health consequences of cocaine abuse*. Geneva: World Health Organization.

ASELTINE, R.H. (1995), A reconsideration of parental and peer influences on adolescent deviance, 36 *Journal of Health and Social Behavior* 2, 103-121.

ASHLEY, R. (1975), *Cocaine: its history, uses and effects*. New York: St. Martin's Press.

ATKYNS, R.L. and HANNEMAN, G.J. (1974), Illicit drug distribution and dealer communication behavior, 15 *Journal of Health and Social Behavior* 1, 36-45.

BAILEY, S.L., FLEWELLING, R.L. and RACHAL, J.V. (1992), The characterization of inconsistencies in self-reports of alcohol and marijuana use in a longitudinal study of adolescents, 53 *Journal of Studies on Alcohol* 6, 636-647.

BALE, R.N. (1979), The validity and reliability of self-reported data from heroin addicts: mailed questionnaires compared with face-to-face interviews, 14 *International Journal of the Addictions*, 993-1000.

BALL, J.C. and SNARR, R.W. (1969), A test of the maturation hypothesis with respect to opiate addiction, 21 *Bull. Narcotics*, 9-13.

BALTHAU, M. (1996a), *(Mega)dancings*. Brussels: Gendarmerie (internal police report).

References

BALTHAU, M. (1996b), *Horecadan*. Brussels: Gendarmerie (internal police report).

BARENDREGT, C. and TRAUTMANN, F. (1996), *With a little help from my friends. A survey on nonintentional peer-influences among drug users*. Utrecht: NIAD.

BARNETT, M.L. (1955), Alcoholism in the Cantonese of New York City: an anthropological study. In: DIETHELM, O. (ed.), *Etiology of chronic alcoholism*. Springfield: Charles C. Thomas.

BARRIO, G., DE LA FUENTE, L., ROYUELA, L., DIAZ, A. and RODRIGUEZ-ARTELEJO, F. and THE SPANISH GROUP FOR THE STUDY ON THE ROUTE OF ADMINISTRATION OF DRUGS (1998), Cocaine use among heroin users in Spain: the diffusion of crack and cocaine smoking, 52 *Journal of Epidemiology and Community Health* 3, 172-180.

BAUMAN, K.E. and ENNETT, S.T. (1996), On the importance of peer influence for adolescent drug use: commonly neglected considerations, 91 *Addiction* 2, 185-198.

BEAN, P. (1993), *Cocaine and crack. Supply and use*. New York: St. Martin's Press.

BECK, K.H. and TREIMAN, K.A. (1996), The relationship of social context of drinking, perceived social norms, and parental influence to various drinking patterns of adolescents, 21 *Addictive Behaviors* 5, 633-644.

BECKER, H.S. (1966), *Outsiders: studies in the sociology of deviance*. New York: MacMillan.

BECKER, H.S. (1970), Practitioners of vice and crime, 30-49. In: HABENSTEIN, R.W. (ed.), *Pathways to data*. Aldine.

BELENKO, S.R. (1993), *Crack and the evolution of anti-drug policy*. Westport: Greenwood Press.

BELGISCHE KAMER VAN VOLKSVERTEGENWOORDIGERS (1997), *Verslag namens de werkgroep belast met het bestuderen van de drugproblematiek*, uitgebracht door de heren Maurice MINNE en Jo VANDEURZEN, 1062/1-96/97.

BELGISCHE SENAAT (1998), *Parlementaire commissie van onderzoek naar de georganiseerde criminaliteit in België*. Eindverslag uitgebracht door de heren COVELIERS *en* DESMEDT. Zitting 1998-1999, 1-326/9. 8 december 1998.

BENWARD, J. and DENSEN-GERBER, J. (1971), Incest as a causal factor in anti-social behavior: an exploratory study, *Contemporary Drug Problems* 1, 323-340.

BIELEMAN, B. and DE BIE, E. (1992), *In grote lijnen. Een onderzoek naar aard en omvang van cocaïnegebruik in Rotterdam*. Groningen: Intraval.

BIELEMAN, B. and DE BIE, E. (1994), *Wit, witter, witst. Een onderzoek naar de kwaliteit van cocaïne in Rotterdam*. Groningen-Rotterdam: Intraval.

BIELEMAN, B., DIAZ, A., MERLO, G. and KAPLAN, C.D. (ed.) (1993), *Lines across Europe. Nature and extent of cocaine use in Barcelona, Rotterdam and Turin*. Amsterdam: Swets & Zeitlinger.

BIERNACKI, P. (1986), *Pathways from heroin addiction: recovery without treatment*. Philadelphia: Temple University Press.

BIERNACKI, P. and WALDORF, D. (1981), Snowball sampling problems and techniques of chain referral sampling, 10 *Sociological Methods and Research* 2, 141-163.

BILLIET, J.B. (1990), *Methoden van sociaal wetenschappelijk onderzoek: ontwerp en dataverzameling*. Leuven/Amersfoort: Acco.

BILLMAN, G.E. (1995), Cocaine: a review of its toxic actions on cardiac function, 25 *Critical Reviews in Toxicology*, 113-132.

BLACK, J.A. and CHAMPION, D.J. (1976), *Methods and issues in social research*. New York: John Wiley & Sons.

BLACK, P.W. (1984), The anthropology of tobacco use: Tobian data and theoretical issues, 40 *Journal of Anthropological Research* 4, 475-503.

BLACKWELL, J.S. (1983), Drifting, controlling and overcoming: opiate users who avoid becoming chronically dependent, 13 *Journal of Drug Issues* 2, 219-235.

References

BLANQUART, J. (1996), *De drugproblematiek in Vlaanderen: een kwalitatief onderzoek vanuit agogisch sociaal-humanistisch perspectief.* Doctoral thesis. Dept. of Educational Science. Brussels. Unpublished.

BLALOCK, H.M. (1979), *Social statistics. Revised Second Edition.* New York: McGraw-Hill Book Company.

BLUM, R.H. and BLUM, E.M. (1969), A cultural case study. In: BLUM, R.H. *et al.* (eds.), *Drugs I: drugs and society.* San Francisco: Jossey-Bass.

BOCK, G.R. and WHELAN, J. (1992), *Cocaine: scientific and social dimensions.* Chichester: Ciba Foundation, John Wiley & Sons.

BOEKHOUT VAN SOLINGE, T. (1996), *Heroïne, cocaïne en crack in Frankrijk. Handel, gebruik en beleid.* Amsterdam: Centrum voor Drugsonderzoek.

BONITO, A.N., NURCO, D.N. and SHAFFER, J.W. (1976), The veridicality of addicts' self-reports in social research, 11 *International Journal of the Addictions,* 719-724.

BOURDIEU, P. (ed.), BOLTANSKI, L. and CASTEL, R. (1965), *Un art moyen.* Paris: Minuit.

BOURDIEU, P. (1970), *La réproduction.* Paris: Minuit.

BOURDIEU, P. (1980), *Le sens pratique.* Paris: Minuit.

BOURGEOIS, Ph. (1995), *In search of respect. Selling crack in El Barrio.* New York: Cambridge University Press.

BRADY, M. (1993), Giving away the grog: an ethnography of Aboriginal drinkers who quit without help, 12 *Drug and Alcohol Review* 4, 403-404.

BRAIN, P.F. and COWARD, G.A. (1989), A review of the history, actions, and legitimate uses of cocaine, 1 *Journal of Substance Abuse* 4, 431-451.

BRAUNSTEIN, M.S. (1993), Sampling a hidden population: non-institutionalized drug users, 5 *Aids Education and Prevention* 2, 131-140.

BRECHT, M.L., ANGLIN, M.D., WOODWARD, J.A. and BONETT, D.G. (1987), Conditional factors of maturing out: personal resources and preaddiction sociopathy, 22 *International Journal of the Addictions* 1, 55-69.

BRECHT, M.L. and ANGLIN, M.D. (1990), Conditional factors of maturing out: legal supervision and treatment, 25 *International Journal of the Addictions,* 393-407.

BRODY, S.L., SLOVIS, C.M. and WRENN, K.D. (1990), Cocaine-related medical problems: consecutive series of 233 patients, 88 *American Journal of Medicine* 4, 325-331.

BROWN, E., PRAGER, J., LEE, H.Y. *et al.* (1992), CNS complications of cocaine abuse: prevalence, pathophysiology, and neuroradiology, 159 *American Journal of Roentgenology,* 137-147.

BROWN, J.W., GLASER, D., WARD, E. and GEIS, G. (1974), Turning off: cessation of marijuana use after college, 21 *Social Problems* 4, 526-538.

BSCHOR, F., SCHOMMER, H.G. and WESSEL, J. (1984), Risiken und Perspektiven der Drogenabhängigkeit: Katamnese-Ergebnisse bei 100 Opiatabhängigen der Zugangsjahre 1969-1974, 109 *Dtsch. Med. Wochensehr,* 1101-1105.

BUNTINX, F. *et al.* (1992), Waarom stopt iemand ambulant met heroïnegebruik?, 18 *Tijdschrift voor Alcohol, Drugs en andere Psychotrope Stoffen* 4, 190-196.

BURGESS, R.W. (ed.) (1995), *Computing and qualitative analysis.* London: JAI Press.

CAMERON, D.C. (1971), Abuse of alcohol and drugs: concepts and planning, *World Health Organization Chronicle* 25, 8-16.

CASSELMAN, J. (1996), *Met vallen en opstaan. Motivatiebevordering en terugvalpreventie bij alcohol- en andere drugproblemen.* Leuven: Garant.

CAULKINS, J.P. (1994a), *Developing price series for cocaine.* Santa Monica: Rand Publications (Drug Policy Research Center).

CAULKINS, J.P. (1994b), What is the average price of an illicit drug?, 89 *Addiction* 7, 815-819.

References

CAULKINS, J.P. (1997), Is crack cheaper than (powder) cocaine?, 92 *Addiction* 11, 1437-1443.

CHAISSON, R.E., BACCHETTI, P. OSMOND, D., BRODIE, B., SANDE, M.A. and MOSS, A.R. (1989), Cocaine use and HIV infection in intravenous drug users in San Francisco, 261 *Journal of the American Medical Association* 4, 561-565.

CHAPPLE, P.A.L., SOMEKH, D.E. and TAYLOR, M.E. (1972), A five year follow-up of 108 cases of opiate addiction, 67 *British Journal of Addiction*, 33-38.

CHASNOFF, I.J. (1991), Cocaine and pregnancy: clinical and methodologic issues, 18 *Clinics in Perinatology*, 113-123.

CHITWOOD, D. (1985), Patterns and consequences of cocaine use, 111-129. In: KOZEL, N. and ADAMS, E. (eds.), *Cocaine use in America: epidemiologic and clinical perspectives*. Rockville: NIDA.

CHITWOOD, D. and MORNINGSTAR, P. (1985), Factors which differentiate cocaine users in treatment from non-treatment users, 20 *International Journal of the Addictions* 3, 449-459.

CHRISTIAENSEN, S. and GOETHALS, J. (eds.) (1994), *De illegale drugsgebruiker tussen strafrechtspleging en hulpverlening. Van praktijk naar beleid*. Leuven: Acco.

CHRISTO, G. (1998), A review of reasons for using or not using drugs: commonalities between sociologiacl and clinical perspectives, 5 *Drugs: education, prevention and policy* 1, 59-72.

COCHRANE, C., MALCOLM, R. and BREWERTON, T. (1998), The role of weight control as a motivation for cocaine abuse, 23 *Addictive Behaviors* 2, 201-207.

COGGANS, N. and MCKELLAR, S. (1994), Drug use amongst peers: peer pressure or peer preference?, 1 *Drugs: education, prevention and policy* 1, 15-26.

COHEN, P. (1984), Is heroïneverslaving een vorm van pathologie?, 39 *Maandblad Geestelijke Volksgezondheid* 2, 115-126.

COHEN, P. (1989), *Cocaine use in Amsterdam in non deviant subcultures*. Amsterdam: Instituut voor Sociale Geografie.

COHEN, P. (1991), Junky elend. Some ways of explaining it and dealing with it, 14 *Wiener Zeitschrift für Suchtforschung*, 59-64.

COHEN, P. (1992), Desires for cocaine, 212-222. In: WARBURTON, D.M. (ed.), *Addiction controversies*. Chur: Harwood Academic Publishers.

COHEN, P. and SAS, A. (1993), *Ten years of cocaine. A follow-up study of 64 cocaine users in Amsterdam*. Amsterdam: Instituut voor Sociale Geografie.

COHEN, P. and SAS, A. (1995), *Cocaine use in Amsterdam II. Initiation and patterns of use after 1986*. Amsterdam: Instituut voor Sociale Geografie, Universiteit van Amsterdam.

COOMBER, R. (1997a), Vim in the veins – fantasy or fact: the adulteration of illicit drugs, 5 *Addiction Research* 3, 195-212.

COOMBER, R. (1997b), Dangerous Drug Adulteration – an international survey of drug dealers using the Internet and the World Wide Web (WWW), 8 *The International Journal of Drug Policy* 2, 71-81.

COOMBER, R. (1997c), The adulteration of drugs – what dealers do, what dealers think, 5 *Addiction Research* 4, 297-306.

COOMBER, R. (1997d), The adulteration of illicit drugs with dangerous substances – the discovery of a 'myth', 24 *Contemporary Drug Problems* 2, 239-271.

COTTLER, L.B., SHILLINGTON, A.M., COMPTON III, W.M., MAGER, D. and SPITZNAGEL, E.L. (1993), Subjective reports of withdrawal among cocaine users: recommendations for DSM-IV, 33 *Drug and Alcohol Dependence* 2, 97-104.

COURTWRIGHT, D.T. (1982), *Dark paradise; opiate addiction in America before 1940*. Cambridge: Harvard University Press.

References

CRAMER, E. and SCHIPPERS, G. (1994), *Zelfcontrole en ontwenning van harddrugs*. Nijmegen: University of Nijmegen Research Group on Addictive Behaviors.

CREGLER, L.L. and MARK, H. (1986), Special report: medical complications of cocaine abuse, 315 *New England Journal of Medicine* 23, 1495-1500.

CRISP, B.R., BARBER, J.G. and GILBERTSON, R. (1997), The etiquette of needlesharing, 24 *Contemporary Drug Problems*, 273-291.

CROFTS, N., LOUIE, R., ROSENTHAL, D. and JOLLEY, D. (1996), The first hit: circumstances surrounding initiation into injecting, 91 *Addiction* 8, 1187-1196.

DANCE, P. (1991), Befriending friends. Methodological and ethnographic aspects of a study of a Canberra group of illicit drug users, 2 *The International Journal on Drug Policy* 1, 34.

DAS, G. (1994), Cocaine abuse and reproduction, 32 *International Journal of Clinical Pharmacology and Therapeutics* 1, 7-11.

DAVIES, J.B. (1992), *The myth of addiction*. Reading: Harwood Academic Publishers.

DAVIES, J.B. (1997), *Drugspeak. The analysis of drug discourse*. Amsterdam: Harwood Academic Publishers.

DAVIS, S. (1990), Chemical dependency in women: a description of its effects and outcome on adequate parenting, 7 *Journal of Substance Abuse Treatment* 4, 225-232.

DE BIE, E. and BIELEMAN, B. (1995), Lekker, ingrijpend, teringzooi, 3 *Addictum* 3, 8-9.

DECORTE, T. (1996a), Informele regulering door druggebruikers, 38-45. In: *Peer support en peer education: een methodiek voor AIDS-preventie naar injecterende druggebruikers*. Verslagboek studiedagen VAD-Free CLinic-NIAD.

DECORTE, T. (1996b), Belgische visies op het Nederlandse drugbeleid, *V.A.D.-Berichten* 1, 5-8.

DECORTE, T. (1996c), Informele zelfregulering van illegaal druggebruik, 63 *Streven* 10, 886-899.

DECORTE, T. (1997), Regulering van roesmiddelen, 64 *Streven* 1, 56-60.

DECORTE, T. (1999), Ethnographic notes: informal rules about the combination of cocaine with other drugs, 25-46. In: ENGEMANN, S. and SCHNEIDER, W. (eds.), *The times they are a-changin'*. Internationaler Kongreß über neue und aktuelle Ansätze akzeptierender Drogenarbeit und Drogenpolitik. Studien zur qualitativen Drogenforschung und akzeptierenden Drogenarbeit, Band 22. Berlin: Verlag für Wissenschaft und Bildung.

DECORTE, T. (2000), A qualitative study of cocaine and crack in Antwerp (Belgium): some ethical issues. In: E.M.C.D.D.A. (ed.), *Understanding and responding to drug use: the role of qualitative research* (forthcoming). Lissabon: E.M.C.D.D.A.

DENEAU, G. *et al.* (1969), Self-administration of psycho-active substances by the monkey, 16 *Psychopharmacologia*, 30-48.

DE RUYVER, B., VERMEULEN, G., FRANCK, P. and VAN DAELE, L. (1992), *Kansarmoede, druggebruik en criminaliteit*. Gent : Universiteit Gent.

DE RUYVER, B., VAN DAELE, L. and COOLSAET, M. (1991), *Onderzoek naar alcohol, medicatie, illegale drugs en tabak bij adolescenten tussen 14 en 18-19 jaar in de provincie West-Vlaanderen*. Gent: Academie Press.

DE RUYVER, B. and DE LEENHEER, A. (1994), *Drugbeleid 2000. Gestion des drogues en 2000*. Antwerpen/Brussel: Maklu/Bruylant.

DE RUYVER, B., VERMEULEN, G., DE LEENHEER, A. and VAN DER STRATEN WAILLET, G. (1995) (eds.), *Op weg naar een geïntegreerd drugbeleid in België? Drugbeleid 2000*. Antwerp/Brussels : Maklu Uitgevers/Bruylant.

DE RUYVER, B., VERMEULEN, G., DE LEENHEER, A. and MARCHANDISE, T. (1996) (eds.), *Veiligheids- en medisch-sociale benadering : complementair of tegengesteld. Drugbeleid 2000*. Antwerp/Brussels : Maklu Uitgevers/Bruylant.

References

DE RUYVER, B., DE SOMERE, P., VERMEULEN, G., NOIRFALISE, A. and FIGIEL, C. (1998) (eds), *Het drugbeleid in België : actuele ontwikkelingen. Drugbeleid 2000.* Antwerp/Brussels : Maklu Uitgevers/Bruylant.

DEVRESSE, M.S. (1998), *L'impact des nouvelles orientations 'socio-penales' des politiques publiques sur la trajectoire des usagers de drogues a l'entrée du système pénal.* Intermediairy internal report. Services Fédéraux des affaires Techniques, Scientifiques et Culturelle. January 1998. Unpublished.

DEVRESSE, M.S. (1999), La rencontre entre la police communale belge et les usagers de drogue: en toute discrétion, 23 *Déviance et Société* 1, 59-73.

DIAZ, A., BARRUTI, M. and DONCEL, C. (1992), *The lines of success? A study on the nature and extent of cocaine use in Barcelona.* Barcelona: Ajuntament de Barcelona.

DITTON, J. *et al.* (1991), Scottish cocaine users: wealthy snorters or delinquent smokers, 28 *Drug and Alcohol Dependence* 3, 265-276.

DITTON, J. and HAMMERSLEY, R. (1994), The typical cocaine user, 9 *Druglink*, November-December, 11-14.

DITTON, J. and HAMMERSLEY, R. (1996), *A very greedy drug. Cocaine in context.* Amsterdam: Harwood Academic Publishers.

DOMIC, Z. (1996), Les métamorphoses de coca, 2 *Psychotropes* 3, 57-69.

DUDISH-POULSEN, S.A. and HATSUKAMI, D.K. (1997), Dissociation between subjective and behavioral responses after cocaine stimuli presentations, 47 *Drug and Alcohol Dependence* 1, 1-9.

DUNLAP, E., JOHNSON, B. *et al.* (1990), Studying crack users and their criminal careers. the scientific and artistic aspects of locating hard-to-reach subjects and interviewing them about sensitive topics, 17 *Contemporary Drug Problems* 1, 121-145.

DUVALL, H.J., LOCK, B.Z. and BRILL, L. (1963), Follow-up study of narcotic drug addicts after five years of hospitalization, 78 *Public Health Rep.*, 185-193.

EDDY, N.B., *et al.* (1965), Drug dependence: its significance and characteristics, *Bulletin of the World Health Organization* 32, 721-733.

ELIAS, N. (1990), *Het civilisatieproces. Sociogenetische en psychogenetische onderzoekingen.* Aula Paperback, Het Spectrum.

ELLINWOOD, E.H. and KILBEY, N. (1977) (ed.), *Advances in behavioral biology: cocaine and other stimulants.* New York: Plenum Press.

E.M.C.D.D.A. (1997), *Annual report on the state of the drugs problem in the European Union.* Lisboa: EMCDDA.

ENNETT, S.T. and BAUMAN, K.E. (1993), Peer group structure and adolescent cigarette smoking: a social network analysis, 34 *Journal of Health and Social Behavior* 3, 226-236.

ERICKSON, B.H. (1979), Some problems of inference from chain data, 10 *Social Methodology*, 276-302.

ERICKSON, P.G. (1989), Living with prohibition: regular cannabis users, legal sanctions, and informal controls, 24 *International Journal of the Addictions* 3, 175-188.

ERICKSON, P.G. and MURRAY, G.F. (1989), The undeterred cocaine user: intention to quit and its relationship to perceived legal and health threats, 16 *Contemporary Drug Problems* 2, 141-156.

ERICKSON, P.G. and ALEXANDER, B.K. (1989), Cocaine and addictive liability, *Social Pharmacology* 3, 249-270.

ERICKSON, P.G., WATSON, V. and WEBER, T. (1992), Cocaine users' perception of their health status and the risks of drug use, 82-89. In: O'HARE, P.A., NEWCOMBE, R., MATTHEWS, A., BUNING, E.C. and DRUCKER, E. (eds.), *The reduction of drug related harm.* London: Routledge.

ERICKSON, P.G., ADLAF, E.M., SMART, R.G. and MURRAY, G.F. (1994), *The Steel Drug. Cocaine and crack in perspective.* New York: Lexington Books.

References

ESBENSEN, F.A. and ELLIOTT, D.S. (1994), Continuity and discontinuity in illicit drug use: patterns and antecedents, 24 *Journal of Drug Issues* 1, 75-97.

EVENEPOEL, T. (1996), 2C-B duikt op in Vlaanderen, *Nieuwsbrief Verslaving*, nr. 96/6, 7-8.

FARELL, G., MANSUR, K. and TULLIS, M. (1996), Cocaine and heroin in Europe 1983-1993. A cross-national comparison of trafficking and prices, 36 *British Journal of Criminology* 2, 255-281.

FAUPEL, C.E. (1987), Drug availability, life structure and situational ethics of heroin addicts. 15 *Urban Life*, 395-419.

FELDMAN, H.W. (1977), A neighborhood history of drug switching, 249-278. In: WEPPNER, R.S. (ed.), *Street ethnography: selected studies of crime and drug use in natural settings*. Beverly Hills, CA: Sage.

FINNIGAN, F. (1996), How non-heroin users perceive heroin users and how heroin users perceive themselves, 4 *Addiction Research* 1, 25-32.

FOLTIN, R.W., FISCHMAN, M.W., CORNELL, E.L. and BUTLER, L. (1996), Characteristics of a non-treatment sample of heavy cocaine users volunteering for studies involving cocaine administration in Baltimore (USA), 4 *Addiction Research* 2, 139-149.

FORRESTER, J.M., STEELE, A.W., WALDRON, J.A. *et al.* (1990), Crack lung: an acute pulmonary syndrome with a spectrum of clinical and histopathologic findings, 142 *American Review of Respiratory Diseases* 2, 462-467.

FOSTER, P. (1996), Observational research, 57-93. In: SAPSFORD, R. and JUPP, V. (eds.), *Data collection and analysis*. London: Sage.

FOUNTAIN, J. (1993), Dealing with data, 145-173. In: HOBBS, D. and MAY, T. (eds.), *Interpreting the field. Accounts of ethnography*. Oxford: Oxford University Press.

FOXCROFT, D. and LOWE, G. (1997), Adolescents' alcohol use and misuse: the socializing influence of perceived family life, 4 *Drugs: education, prevention and policy* 3, 215-229.

FREE CLINIC and MODUS VIVENDI (1997), *Hepatitis C. Congresboek*. Antwerpen: Free Clinic.

FREUD, S. (1885), Uber coca, *Zentralbl. Ges. Ther.*, 289-314.

FURNHAM, A. and THOMSON, L. (1996), Lay theories of heroin addiction, 43 *Social Science Medicine* 1, 29-40.

GAWIN, F.H. (1991), Cocaine addiction: psychology and neurophysiology, 251 *Science* 5001, 1580-1586.

GEERTZ, C. (1973), *The interpretation of cultures*. New York: Basic Books.

GEERTZ, C. (1983), *Local knowledge: further essays in interpretive anthropology*. New York: Basic Books.

GEKELER, G. (1983), Ich hab's allein geschafft! Heroinabhängige heilen sich selbst, 10 *Psychol. Heute*, 28-33.

GEORGE, M. (1993), The role of personal rules and accepted beliefs in the self-regulation of drug-taking, 4 *The International Journal of Drug Policy* 1, 32-35.

GERRITSEN, J.W. (1994), *De politieke economie van de roes*. Amsterdam: Amsterdam University Press.

GHYSBRECHT, P., DE RUYVER, B., BRACKE, P., COOLSAET, M. and RÖPCKE, N. (1989), *Onderzoek naar drug-, alcohol- en tabaksgebruik bij adolescenten tussen 14 en 18-19 jaar in de provincie Oost-Vlaanderen*.

GILPIN, E., PIERCE, J.P., GOODMAN, J., BURNS, D. and SHOPLAND, D. (1992), Reasons smokers give for stopping smoking: do they relate to success in stopping?, 1 *Tobacco Control*, 256-263.

GLASSNER, B. and BERG, B. (1980), How Jews avoid alcohol problems, 45 *American Sociological Review* 4, 647-664.

GOLD, M.S. (1993), *Cocaine*. New York: Plenum Publishing Corporation.

GOLDFRANK, L.R. and HOFFMAN, R.S. (1991), The cardiovascular effects of cocaine, 20 *Annals of Emergency Medicine* 2, 165-173.

GOODMAN, L.A. (1961), Snowball sampling, 32 *Annals of Mathematical Statistics*, 148-170.

GORDON, A.M. (1978), Drugs and delinquency: a four year follow-up of drug clinic patients, 132 *British Journal of Psychiatry* 1, 21-26.

GOSSOP, M. (1987), *Living with drugs*, (2nd Ed.). Aldershot: Wildwood House.

GOSSOP, M., GRIFFITHS, P. and STRANG, J. (1988), Chasing the dragon: characteristics of heroin chasers, 83 *British Journal of Addiction* 10, 1159-1162.

GOSSOP, M., GRIFFITHS, P., POWIS, B. and STRANG, J. (1994), Cocaine: patterns of use, route of administration, and severity of dependence, 164 *British Journal of Psychiatry*, 660-664.

GOTTLIEB, A. (1975), *The Cocaine Tester's Handbook*. Manhattan Beach: Kistone Press.

GOYVAERTS, G., VAN HAL, G. and TEUGELS, P. (1991), *Onderzoek naar alcohol, tabak, geneesmiddelen en illegaal druggebruik bij jongeren van het secundair onderwijs in Groot Antwerpen*. Antwerpen: Soda.

GRIFFITHS, P, GOSSOP, M., POWIS, B. and STRANG, J. (1993), Reaching hidden populations of drug users by priviliged access interviewers: methodological and practical issues, 88 *Addiction* 12, 1617-1626.

GRINSPOON, J. and BAKALAR, J.B. (1976), *Cocaine. A drug and its social evolution*. New York: Basic Books.

GRINSPOON, L. and BAKALAR, J.B. (1980), Drug dependence: non-narcotic agents, 1621-1622. In: KAPLAN, H.I., FREEDMAN, A.M. and SADOCK, B.J. (eds.), *Comprehensive textbook of psychiatry*. Baltimore: Williams & Wilkins.

GROOTE, K., VAN HAL, G., VAN DAMME, P. and VAN CAUWENBERGHE, K. (1996), *Registratie en retrospectief onderzoek van druggebruikers in 12 parketten in Vlaanderen en Brussel: 1995*. Antwerpen: Universitaire Instelling Antwerpen/Rechtbank van Eerste Aanleg Antwerpen.

GRUND, J.P., ADRIAANS, N. and KAPLAN, C. (1991), Changing cocaine smoking rituals in the Dutch heroin addict population, 86 *British Journal of Addiction* 4, 439-448.

GRUND, J.P. (1993), *Drug use as a social ritual. Functionality, symbolism and determinants of self-regulation*. Rotterdam: Instituut voor Verslavingsonderzoek.

GRUND, J.P. and BLANKEN, P. (1993), *From chasing the dragon to chinezen. The diffusion of heroin smoking in the Netherlands*. Rotterdam: Instituut voor Verslavingsonderzoek.

GUSFIELD, J. (1963), *Symbolic crusade: status politics and the American Temperance Movement*. Urbana: University of Illinois Press.

HAMMER, R.P. (1995), *The neurobiology of cocaine. Cellular and molecular mechanisms*. Boca Raton: CRC Press.

HAMMERSLEY, R. and DITTON, J. (1994), Cocaine careers in a sample of Scottish users, 2 *Addiction Research* 1, 51-69.

HANSON, B., BESCHNER, G., WALTERS, J. and BOVELLE, E. (eds.)(1985), *Life with heroin: voices from the inner City*. Lexington, Massachussetts: D.C. Heath.

HARDING, W.M. and ZINBERG, N.E. (1977), The effectiveness of the subculture in developing rituals and social sanctions for controlled use, 111-133. In: DU TOIT, B.M., *Drugs, rituals and altered states of consciousness*. Rotterdam: Balkema.

HARDING, W.M., ZINBERG, N., STEMACK, S. and BARRY, M. (1979), Formerly addicted-now-controlled opiate users, *International Journal of the Addictions*, 14.

HARDING, W.M. (1980), Formerly addicted, now controlled opiate users, 15 *International Journal of the Addictions*, 47-60.

HARRINGTON, P. and COX, T.J. (1979), A twenty-year follow-up of narcotic addicts in Tucson, Airzona, 6 *American Journal of Drug and Alcohol Abuse* 1, 25-37.

References

HAYNES, P. and AYLIFFE, G. (1991), Locus of control of behaviour: is high externality associated with substance misuse, 86 *British Journal of Addiction* 9, 1111-1117.

HAYS, R.D. and ELLICKSON, P.L. (1996), What is adolescent alcohol misuse in the United States according to the experts?, 31 *Alcohol and Alcoholism* 3, 297-303.

HEATHER, N. and ROBERTSON, I. (1981), *Controlled drinking*. London: Methuen.

HEATHER, N., MILLER, W.R. and GREELEY, J. (1991) (eds.), *Self-control and addictive behaviours*. New York: Pergamon.

HECKATHORN, D.D. (1997), Respondent-driven sampling: a new approach to the study of hidden populations, 44 *Social problems* 2, 174-199.

HELFAND, W.H. (1988), Mariani et le vin de coca, 4 *Psychotropes* 3, 13-18.

HELLINGA, G. and PLOMP, H. (1996), *Uit je bol. Over XTC, paddestoelen, wiet en andere middelen*. Amsterdam: Ooievaar.

HELMER, J. and VIETORISZ, T. (1974), *Drug use, the labor market and class conflict*. Washington: The Drug Abuse Council Inc.

HENDRICKS, K. (1992), *The party's over: diary of a recovering cocaine addict*. Washington: American University Press.

HENDRIKS, V.M., BLANKEN, P., and ADRIAANS, N.F.P. (1992), *Snowball sampling: a pilot study on cocaine use*. Rotterdam: Instituut voor Verslavingsonderzoek.

HENLEY, J.R. and ADAMS, L.D. (1973), Marijuana use in post-college cohorts: correlates of use, prevalence patterns and factors associated with cessation, 20 *Social Problems* 4, 514-520.

HENRY, B., MOFFITT, T.E., CASPI, A., LANGLEY, J. and SILVA, P.A. (1994), On the "remembrance of things past": a longitudinal evaluation of the retrospective method, 6 *Psychological Assessment* 2, 92-101.

HERMANN, K. and RIECK, H. (1980), *Christiane F. Verslag van een junkie*. Dutch edition. Amsterdam: H.J.W. Becht.

HOCTIN BOES, B. and VISSERS, H. (1993), *Drugs: alcohol, illegale drugs en medicatie: algemene informatie, onderzoek, preventie*. Mechelen: Stad Mechelen.

HOLLAND, R.W., MARX, J.A., EARNEST, M.P. and RANNIGER, S. (1992), Grand mal seizures temporally related to cocaine use: clinical and diagnostical features, 21 *Annals of Emergency Medicine* 7, 772-776.

HOLMAN, B. (1994), Biological effects of central nervous system stimulants, 89 *Addiction* 11, 1435-1441.

HOLSTEIN, J.A. and GUBRIUM, J.F. (1995), *The active interview*. Qualitative research Methods series No. 37. London: Sage.

HONER, W.G., GEWIRTZ, G. and TUREY, M. (1987), Psychosis and violence in cocaine smokers, 2 *Lancet* 8556, 451.

HSER, Y. (1993), Data sources: problems and issues, 23 *Journal of Drug Issues* 2, 217-228.

HUMPHREYS, K., MOOS, R.H. and FINNEY, J.W. (1995), Two pathways out of drinking problems without professional treatment, 20 *Addictive Behaviors* 4, 427-441.

HUNT, D. (1987), *Crack*. New York: Narcotic and Drug Research, Inc.

HUNT, G.H. and ODOROFF, M.E. (1962), Follow-up study of narcotic drug addicts after hospitalization, 77 *Public Health Rep.* 1, 41-54.

HUNTER, G.M., DONOGHOE, M.C., and STIMSON, G.V. (1995), Crack use and injection on the increase among injecting drug users in London, 90 *Addiction* 10, 1397-1400.

HUTCHINGS, D.E. (1993), The puzzle of cocaine's effects following maternal use during pregnancy: are there reconcilable differences?, 15 *Neurotoxicology and Teratology*, 281-286.

HUSAK, D.N. (1992), *Drugs and rights*. New York: Cambridge University Press.

References

IANNOTTI, R.J., BUSH, P.J., and WEINFURT, K.P. (1996), Perception of friends' use of alcohol, cigarettes and marijuana among urban schoolchildren: a longitudinal analysis, 21 *Addictive Behaviors* 5, 615-632.

IMPERATO, P.J. (1992), Syphilis, AIDS and crack cocaine, 17 *Journal of Community Health* 2, 69-71.

INCIARDI, J.A. (1987), Beyond cocaine: basuco, crack, and other coca products, 14 *Contemporary Drug Problems* 3, 461-492.

INCIARDI, J.A. (1988), *Crack cocaine in Miami*. NIDA Technical Review Meeting on the Epidemiology of Cocaine Use and Abuse, May 3-4. Rockville: National Institute on Drug Abuse.

INCIARDI, J.A., POTTIEGER, A.E., FORNEY, M.A., CHITWOOD, D.D. and MCBRIDE, D.C. (1991), Prostitution, IV drug use and sex-for-crack exchanges among serious delinquents: risks for HIV infection, 29 *Criminology* 2, 221-235.

INCIARDI, J.A., LOCKWOOD, D. and POTTIEGER, A.E. (1993), *Women and crack-cocaine*. New York: MacMillan Publishing Company.

INSTITUT DE RECHERCHE ET EPIDEMIOLOGIE DE LA PHARMACODEPENDANCE (IREP) (1992), *Approche ethnographique de la consommation de cocaine à Paris*. Paris: IREP.

INSTITUTE FOR THE STUDY OF DRUG DEPENDENCE (1993), *Drug notes: cocaine & crack*. London: ISDD.

ISNER, J.M., ESTES, M, THOMPSON, P.D., COSTANZO-NORDIN, M.R., SUBRAMANIAN, R., MILLER, G., KATSAS, G., SWEENEY, K. and STURNER, W.Q. (1986), Acute cardiac events temporarily related to cocaine abuse, 315 *New England Journal of Medicine* 23, 1438-1443.

JAFFE, J.H. (1980), Drug addiction and drug abuse. In: GILMAN, A.G., GOODMAN, L.S. and GILMAN, B.A. (eds), *The pharmacological basis of therapeutics*. New York: MacMillan.

JANSEN, P. (1992), *Gereguleerd gebruik van heroïne*. Amsterdam: Instituut voor Sociale Geneeskunde.

JANSSENS, J., MELIS, V., NOOTENS, G., OOMEN, J., RIJNHOUT, L., RIOS, T. and DE VRIES, T. (1993), *De wereld van de kook. Over coca en een 500 jaar oud (mis)verstand*. Amsterdam/Antwerpen: Werkgroep Bolivia (Nederland) / Boliviacentrum (Antwerpen) / Impress (Denemarken).

JELLINEK, E.M. (1952), Phases of alcohol addiction, 13 *Quarterly Journal of Studies on Alcohol* 7, 673-684.

JELLINEK, E.M. (1960), *The disease concept of alcoholism*. New Haven: Hillhouse Press.

JERI, F.R. (1984), Coca paste smoking in some Latin American countries: a severe and unabated form of addiction, 34 *U.S. Bulletin on Narcotics*, 15-31.

KAHN, E.J. (1960), *The big drink: the story of Coca-Cola*. New York: Random House.

KAMINSKI, D. (1990), Toxicomanie: le mot qui rend malade, 14 *Déviance et Société* 2, 179-196.

KAMINSKI, D. (1996), La toxicomanie comme menace pour L'Europe, 287-309. In: TULCKENS, F. and BOSLY, H., *La justice pénale en l'Europe*, Actes des XVèmes journées juridiques Jean Dabin. Bruxelles: Bruylant.

KAMINSKI, D. (1997), The transformation of social control in Europe: the case of drug addiction and its socio-penal management, 5 *European Journal of Crime, Criminal Law and Criminal Justice* 2, 123-133.

KANDEL, D. *et al.* (1985), Cocaine use in young adulthood: patterns of use and psychological correlates, 77. In: KOZEL, N. and ADAMS, E. (eds.), *Cocaine use in America: epidemiologic and clinical perspectives*. Rockville: NIDA.

KAPLAN, C.D., BIELEMAN, B. and TENHOUTEN, W.D. (1992), Are there casual users of cocaine?, 57-80. In: *Cocaine: scientific and social dimensions*, Ciba Foundation Symposium. Chichester: Wiley.

KAROLY, P. (1993), Mechanisms of self-regulation: a systems view, 44 *Annual Review of Psychology* 1, 23-52.

452

References

KEENE, J. and RAYNOR, P. (1993), Addiction as a 'soul sickness': the influence of client and therapist beliefs, 1 *Addiction Research* 1, 77-87.

KEMMESIES, U.E. (1995), *Szenebefragung Frankfurt, Main 1995. Die 'offene' Drogenszene' und das Gesundheitsraumangebot in Ffm – ein erster Erfahrungsbericht.* Munster: INDRO e.V.

KEMMESIES, U.E. (1996), Offene Drogenszene und Druckraum – ein empirischer Beitrag, *Wiener Zeitschrift für Suchtforschung* 3-4, 17-31.

KEMMESIES, U.E. (1997), Compulsive users in the Netherlands and Germany: the open drug scenes in Amsterdam and Frankfurt am Main, 8 *The International Journal of Drug Policy* 4, 187-200.

KERREMANS, S. (1995), *Vlaams Informatiesysteem Drugvrije Centra: statistische gegevens 1988-1994. Verslag van 7 jaar werking.* Antwerpen: ADIC.

KINABLE, H., CASSELMAN, J., TODTS, S. and VAN DEUN, P. (1994), *Aids-risico-gedrag bij injecterende druggebruikers en evaluatie van een preventief project.* Brussel/Leuven/Antwerpen: V.A.D./K.U.L./ Free Clinic.

KIRBY, K.C., LAMB, R.J., IGUCHI, M.Y., HUSBAND, S.D. and PLATT, J.J. (1995), Situations occasioning cocaine use and cocaine abstinence strategies, 90 *Addiction* 9, 1241-1252.

KJAERHEIM, K., MYKLETUN, R., AASLAND, O., HALDORSEN, T. and ANDERSEN, A. (1995), Heavy drinking in the restaurant business: the role of social modeling and structural factors of the workplace, 90 *Addiction* 11, 1487-1495.

KLINGEMANN, H.K.-H. (1991). The motivation for change from problem alcohol and heroin use, 86 *British Journal of Addiction* 6, 727-744.

KOOLS, J.P. and VAN DEN BOOMEN, T. (1997), Bungee jumping on base, *Mainline*, special edition, 12-13. Amsterdam.

KOZEL, N.J. and ADAMS, E.H. (1985) *Cocaine use in America: epidemiological and clinical perspectives.* Research Monograph no. 61. Rockville: National Institute on Drug Abuse.

KRUYER, F. (1997), Crack is een hot item geworden, 1 *Algemeen Politieblad*, 4-9.

LABOUVIE, E., BATES, M. and PANDINA, R. (1997), Age of first use: its reliability and predictive utility, 58 *Journal of Studies on Alcohol* 6, 638-643.

LADEWIG, D. (1987), Katamnesen bei Opiatabhängigkeit, 55-69. In: KLEINER, D., *Langzeitverläufe bei Suchtkrankheiten.* Berlijn/Heidelberg: Springer-Verlag.

LAERMANS, R. (1984), Bourdieu voor beginners, 18 *Heibel* 3, 21-48.

LAMBRECHT, P., ANDRIES, C., DE BOCK, M. and WYDOODT, J.P. (1996), *Middelengebruik in de hoofdstad. De hoofdstad van middelengebruik?* Onderzoek naar het gebruik van de genotmiddelen alcohol, medicatie en illegale drugs in relatie tot de vrijetijdsbesteding van jongeren van 12 tot 22 jaar in het Nederlandstalig onderwijs te Brussel. Brussel: V.U.B.

LANGENAUER, B.J. and BOWDEN, C.L. (1971), A follow-up study of narcotic addicts in the NARA program, 128 *American Journal of Psychiatry* 1, 41-46.

LANZA, G. (1995), 'Coca en cocaine in de Andes', 3 *Noord-Zuid-Cahier. Driemaandelijks tijdschrift voor Ontwikkelingssamenwerking*, 43-55.

LENSON, D. (1995), *On drugs.* Minneapolis/London: University of Minnesota Press.

LEITNER, M., SHAPLAND, J. and WILES, P. (1993), *Drug usage and drugs prevention. The views and habits of the general public.* London: HMSO.

LEVINE, H.G. (1984), The alcohol problem in America: from temperance to alcoholism, 79 *British Journal of Addiction*, 109-119.

LEVY, J.A., GALLMEIER, C.P. and WIEBEL, W. (1995), The Outreach assisted peer-support model for controlling drug dependency, 25 *Journal of Drug Issues* 3, 507-529.

LEVY, P.S. and LEMESHOV, S. (1991), *Sampling of populations: methods and applications.* New York: Wiley.

LINDESMITH, A.R. (1968), *Addiction and opiates.* Chicago: Aldine.

References

LOLLI, G., SERIANNI, E., GOLDER, G.M. and LUZZATTO-FEGIZ, P. (1958), *Alcohol in Italian culture.* Glencoe: Free Press.

MADDUX, J.F. and DESMOND, D.P. (1980), New light on the maturing out hypothesis in opioid dependence, 32 *U.S. Bulletin on Narcotics*, 15-25.

MAES, E. (1995), Effectiviteit van een 'alternatieve' bejegening van heroïneverslaafden binnen de strafrechtsbedeling, 16 *Panopticon* 5, 501-529.

MAGUIRE, K. and FLANAGAN, T.J. (1992) (eds.), *Sourcebook of Criminal justices Statistics: 1991.* Washington, DC: US Department of Justice.

MAHAN, S. (1996), *Crack cocaine, crime and women. Legal, social and treatment issues.* Drugs, Health and Social Policy Series. Thousand Oaks: Sage Publications.

MARLATT, G.A. and GORDON, J.R. (1980), Determinates of relapse: implications for the maintenance of behavioral change. In: DAVIDSON, P.O. and DAVIDSON, A.M. (eds.), *Behavioral medicine: changing health lifestyle.* New York: Brunner/Mazel.

MARLATT, G.A. and GORDON, J.R. (eds.) (1985), *Relapse prevention: maintenance strategies in the treatment of addictive behaviors.* New York: Guilford Press.

MARLATT, G.A., BAER, J.S., DONOVAN, D.M. and KIVLAHAN, D.R. (1988), Addictive behaviors: etiology and treatment, 39 *Annual Review of Psychology* 8, 223-252.

MARZUK, P.M., TARDIFF, K., LEON, A.C., STAJIC, M., MORGAN, E.B. and MANN, J.J. (1990), Prevalence of recent cocaine use among motor vehicle fatalities in New York City, 263 *Journal of the American Medical Association* 2, 250-256.

MARZUK, P.M., TARDIFF, K., LEON, A.C., STAJIC, M., MORGAN, E.B. and MANN, J.J. (1992), Prevalence of cocaine use among residents of New York who committed suicide during a one-year period, 149 *American Journal of Psychiatry* 3, 371-375.

MATZA, D. (1964), *Delinquency and drift.* New York: John Wiley and Sons.

MDHG (1987), *Op eigen houtje afkicken* (Research report). Amsterdam: own publication.

MELIS, B. and WALGRAVE, L. (1993), *Jeugd in de stad: tussentijds verslag van een eerste verkennend onderzoek in de stad Antwerpen.* Leuven: Onderzoeksgroep Jeugdcriminologie (O.G.J.C.).

MERLO, G., BORAZZO, F., MOREGGIA, U. and TERZI, M.G. (1992), *Network of powder. Research report on the cocaine use in Turin.* Ufficio Coordinamento degli interventi per le Tossicodipendenze.

MICHELL, L. and WEST, P. (1996), Peer pressure to smoke: the meaning depends on the method, 11 *Health Education Research* 1, 39-49.

MILES, M.B. and HUBERMAN, A.M. (1994), *Qualitative data analysis.* London: Sage.

MILLER, B., DOWNS, W., GONDOLI, D. and KEIL, A. (1987), The role of childhood sexual abuse in the development of alcoholism in women, 2 *Violence and Victims* 3, 157-172.

MILLER, J. and KORAL, R. (1995), *White rabbit. A psychedelic reader.* San Francisco: Chronicle Books.

MILLER, W.R. and BROWN, J. (1991), Self-regulation as a conceptual basis for the prevention and treatment of addictive behaviors. In: HEATHER, N., MILLER, W.R. and GREELEY, J., *Self-control and the addictive behaviors.* Australia: Maxwell MacMillan.

MILLER, W.R. and ROLLNICK, S. (1991), *Motivational interviewing.* New York, London: Guilford Press.

MOORE, D. (1992), Deconstructing 'dependence': an ethnographic critique of an influential concept, 19 *Contemporary Drug Problems* 3, 459-490.

MOORE, D. (1993a), Beyond Zinberg's "social setting": a processural view of illicit drug use, 12 *Drug and Alcohol Review* 4, 413-421.

MOORE, D. (1993b), Ethnography and illicit drug use: dispatches from an anthropologist in the field, 1 *Addiction Research* 1, 11-25.

454

References

MUGFORD, S.K. and COHEN, P. (1989), *Drug use, social relations and commodity consumption: a study of recreational cocaine users in Sydney, Canberra and Melbourne*. Report to Research into Drug Abuse Advisory Committee, National campaign against drug abuse.

MUGFORD, S.K. (1994), Recreational cocaine use in three Australian cities, 2 *Addiction Research* 1, 95-108.

MURPHY, S., REINARMAN, C. and WALDORF, D. (1989), An 11-year follow-up of a network of cocaine users, 84 *British Journal of Addiction* 4, 425-436.

MUSTO, D.F. (1987), *The American disease. Origins of narcotic control* (expanded edition). New York: Oxford University Press. First published in 1973 by Yale University Press.

MUSTO, D.F. (1992), Cocaine's history, especially the American experience, 14-32 in BOCK, G.R. and WHELAN, J., *Cocaine: scientific and social dimensions*. Chichester: Ciba Foundation, John Wiley & Sons.

NATHAN, P.E. and O'BRIEN, J.S. (1971), An experimental analysis of the behavior of alcoholics and nonalcoholics during prolonged experimental drinking: a necessary precursor of behavior therapy?, 2 *Behavior Therapy* 4, 455-476.

NEUHAUS, C. (1991), Review of 'Diseasing of America: addiction treatment out of control', by Stanton Peele, 23 *Journal of Psychoactive Drugs* 1, 87-88.

NEUHAUS, C. (1993), The disease controversy revisited: an ontologic perspective, 23 *Journal of Drug Issues* 3, 463-478.

NURCO, D.N., BONITO, A.J. *et al.* (1975), Studying addicts over time: methodology and preliminary findings, 2 *American Journal of Drug and Alcohol Abuse*, 183-196.

OBSERVATOIRE GEOPOLITIQUE DES DROGUES (1996), *Atlas mondial des drogues*. Paris: Presses Universitaires de France.

O'DONNELL, J.A. (1964), A follow-up of narcotic addicts, 34 *American Journal of Orthopsychiatry*, 948-954.

O'HARE, P.A., NEWCOMBE, R., MATTHEWS, A., BUNING, E.C. and DRUCKER, E. (1992) (eds.), *The reduction of drug related harm*. London: Routledge.

OM, A., WARNER, M., SABRI, N., CECICH, L. and VETROVEC, G. (1992), Frequency of coronary artery disease and left ventricle dysfunction in cocaine users, 69 *American Journal of Cardiology* 19, 1549-1552.

ONSTEIN, E.J. (1987), Heroïneverslavings-carrières, Hoe is het beloop in de tijd? Heeft therapie effect? Zijn er prognostisch gunstige factoren?, 29 *Tijdschrift voor Psychiatrie* 8, 516-525.

OOSTVEEN, T., KNIBBE, R. and DE VRIES, H. (1996), Social influences on young adults' alcohol consumption: norms, modeling, pressure, socializing and conformity, 21 *Addictive Behaviors* 2, 187-197.

ORFORD, J., MORISON, V. and SOMERS, M. (1996), Drinking and gambling: a comparison with implications for theories of addiction, 15 *Drug and Alcohol Review* 1, 47-56.

OUELLET, L.J., CAGLE, H.H. and FISHER, D.G. (1997) , "Crack" versus "rock" cocaine: the importance of local nomenclature in drug research and education, 24 *Contemporary Drug Problems*, 219-238.

PEELE, S. (1985), *The meaning of addiction. Compulsive experience and its interpretation*. Massachussetts: D.C. Heath and Company.

PEELE, S., (1995), *The diseasing of America* (paperback edition). New York: Lexington Books.

PEELE, S., BRODSKY, A. and ARNOLD, M. (1991), *The truth about addiction and recovery*. New York: Simon & Schuster.

PEETERS, R., MAES, L. and VAN DE MIEROOP, E. (1994), *Jongeren en gezondheid in Vlaanderen*. Antwerpen/Gent: Dienst Epidemiologie en Sociale Geneeskunde (Universiteit Antwerpen)/ Dienst Hygiëne en Sociale Geneeskunde (Universiteit Gent).

455

References

PEREZ-REYES, M., DIGUISEPPI, S., ONDRUSEK, G., JEFFCOAT, P. and COOK, C. (1982), Freebase cocaine smoking, 32 *Clinical Pharmacology and Therapeutics* 4, 459-465.

PERKONIGG, A., LIEB, R. and WITTCHEN, H.U. (1998), Substance use, abuse and dependence in Germany, 4 *European Addiction Research* 1-2, 8-17.

PICKERING, H., DONOGHOE, M.C., GREEN, A. and FOSTER, R. (1993), Crack-cocaine injection, *Druglink*, 12.

PICKLES, A. and RUTTER, M. (1991), Statistical and conceptual models of 'turning points' in developmental processes, 133-165. In: MAGNUSSON, D. *et al.* (ed.), *Problems and methods of longitudinal research: stability and change*. New York: Cambridge University Press.

POLICH, J.M., ARMOR, D.J., and BRAIKER, H.B. (1981), *The course of alcoholism: four years after treatment.* New York: Wiley.

POST, R.M. (1975), Cocaine psychoses: a continuum model, 132 *American Journal of Psychiatry* 3, 225-231.

POWELL, D.H. (1973), A pilot study of occasional heroin users, 28 *Archives of General Psychiatry* 5, 586-594.

POWER, R. (1989), Participant observation and its place in the study of illicit drug abuse, 84 *British Journal of Addiction* 1, 43-52.

POWER, R., GREEN, A., FOSTER, R. and STIMSON, G. (1995), A qualitative study of the purchasing and distribution patterns of cocaine and crack users in England and Wales, 2 *Addiction Research* 4, 363-379.

PREVENTIEDIENST STAD BRUGGE and RAES, V. (1995), *Het alcohol- en druggebruik bij schoolgaande jongeren in Brugge.*

PRINS, E.H. (1995), *Maturing out. An empirical study of personal histories and processes in harddrug addiction.* Assen: Van Gorcum.

PROCHASKA, J.O. and DICLEMENTE, C.C. (1986), Toward a comprehensive model of change, 3-27. In: MILLER, W.R. and HEATHER, N. (eds.), *Treating addictive behaviors: processes of change.* New York: Plenum Press.

PROVINCIE LIMBURG, LIMBURGS INSTITUUT VOOR SAMENLEVINGSOPBOUW (LISO) and CENTRUM VOOR ALCOHOL- EN ANDERE DRUGSPROBLEMEN (CAD) (1995), *Gebruik van tabak, alcohol, drugs, medicatie en gokgedrag bij jongeren, onderzoek naar het middelengebruik in samenhang met ander jongerengedrag, uitgevoerd bij leerlingen uit de tweede en derde graad van het secundair onderwijs in de provincie Limburg.* Hasselt: Marc Martens.

QUINTERO, G. and NICHTER, M. (1996), The semantics of addiction: moving beyond expert models to lay understandings, 28 *Journal of Psychoactive Drugs* 3, 219-228.

RAPOPORT, A. (1957), Contribution to the theory of random and biased nets. 19 *Bulletin of Mathematical Biophysics*, 257-277.

RAPOPORT, A. (1979), Some problems relating to randomly constructed biased networks. In: HOLLAND, P.W. and LEINHARDT, S. (eds.). *Perspectives on social network research.* New York: Academic Press.

RATNER, M.S. (1993), *Crack pipe as pimp: an ethnographic investigation of sex-for-crack exchanges.* Lexington: Lexington Books.

RENSSELAER, W.L. (1990), *The white labyrinth. Cocaine and political power.* New Brunswick: Transaction Publishers.

REUTER, P. (1988), Quantity illusion and paradoxes of drug interdiction: federal intervention into vice policy, 51 *Law and Contemporary Problems*, 233-252.

RHODES, W., HYATT, R. and SCHEIMAN, P. (1994), The price of cocaine, heroin and marihuana, 1981-1993, 24 *Journal of Drug Issues* 3, 383-402.

RICHARD, D. (1994), *La coca et la cocaïne.* Paris: Presses Universitaires de France.

References

RICHARDS, T.J. and RICHARDS, L. (1998), Using computers in qualitative research, 211-245. In: DENZIN, N.K. and LINCOLN, Y.S., *Collecting and interpreting qualitative materials*. London: Sage Publications.

RILEY, K.J. (1996), *Snow job? The war against international cocaine trafficking*. New Brunswick: Transaction Publishers.

RISSER, D. and SCHNEIDER, B. (1994), Drug-related deaths between 1985 and 1992 examined at the Institute for Forensic Medicine in Vienna, Austria, 89 *Addiction* 7, 851-857.

ROBINS, L.N., HELZER, J.E., HESSELBROCK, M. *et al.* (1977), *Vietnam veterans three years after Vietnam: how our study changed our view of heroin*, Problems of Drug Dependence, Proceedings of the 39th Annual scientific Meeting, Committee on Problems of Drug Dependence. Boston.

ROBINS, L.N., HELZER, J.E., HESSELBROCK, M., WISH, E. (1979), Vietnam veterans three years after Vietnam. In: BRILL, L. and WINICK, C., *Yearbook of Substance abuse*. New York: Human Sciences Press.

ROBSON, P. and BRUCE, M. (1997), A comparison of 'visible' and 'invisible' users of amphetamine, cocaine and heroin: two distinct populations?, 92 *Addiction* 12, 1729-1736.

RONALD, P. and ROBERTSON, J. (1993), Initial and current drug use: how are they related?, 88 *Addiction* 9, 1225-1231.

ROOM, R. (1983), Sociological aspects of the disease concept of alcoholism. In: SMART, R.G., GLASER, F.B. *et al.* (ed.), *Research advances in alcohol and drug problems*. New York: Plenum Press.

ROUSE, B.A., KOZEL, N.J. and RICHARDS, L.G. (eds.) (1985), *Self-report methods of estimating drug use: meeting current challenges to validity*. Washington: NIDA Research Monograph.

RUTTER, M. (1989), Pathways from childhood to adult life, 30 *Journal of Child Psychology and Psychiatry* 1, 23-51.

RUTTER, M. (1996), Developmental psychopathology as an organizing research construct, 394-413. In: MAGNUSSON, D. (ed.), *The lifespan development of individuals: behavioral, neurobiological and psychosocial perspectives*. New York: Cambridge University Press.

SABBAG, R. (1976), *Snowblind. A brief career in the cocaine trade*. New York: Avon Books.

SAHIHI, A. (1989), *Synthetische drugs*. S.l.: Uitgeverij Elmar.

SASSE, A., VAN RENTERGHEM, H. and VAN DER HEYDEN, D. (1996), *De epidemiologie van AIDS en HIV-infectie in België. Toestand op 31 december 1995*. Brussel: Instituut voor Hygiëne en Epidemiologie.

SATEL, S.L. and EDELL, W.S. (1991), Cocaine-induced paranoia and psychosis proneness, 148 *American Journal of Psychiatry* 12, 1708-1711.

SATEL, S.L., SOUTHWICK, S.M. and GAWIN, F.H. (1991), Clinical features of cocaine-induced paranoia, 148 *American Journal of Psychiatry* 4, 495-498.

SAUNDERS, B. and ALSOP, S. (1992), Incentives and restraints: clinical research into problem drug use and self-control. In: HEATHER, N., MILLER, W.R. and GREELEY, J. (eds.), *Self-control and the addictive behaviours*. Australia: Maxwell MacMillan.

SCHALER, J.A. (2000), *Addiction is a choice*. Chicago: Open Court.

SCHMIDBAUER, W. and VOM SCHEIDT, J. (1989), *Handbuch der Rauschdrogen*. Frankfurt am Main.

SCHNEIDER, J. (1978), Deviant drinking as disease: alcoholism as a social accomplishment, 25 *Social Problems* 4, 361-372.

SCHNEIDER, W. (1988), Zur Frage von Ausstiegschancen und Entwicklungsmöglichkeiten bei Opiatabhängigkeit, 34 *Suchtgefahren* 6, 472-490.

SCHOFIELD, J.W. (1993), Increasing the generalizability of qualitative research, 200-225. In: HAMMERSLEY, M. (ed.), *Social research: philosophy, politics and practice*. London: Sage Publications.

References

SCOTT, P.D. and MARSHALL, J. (1991), *Cocaine politics. Drugs, armies and the CIA in Central America*. Berkeley: University of California Press.

SCOTTISH COCAINE RESEARCH GROUP (1993), 'A very greedy sort of drug': portraits of Scottish cocaine users, 76-98. In: BEAN, Ph. (ed.), *Cocaine and crack. Supply and use*. New York: St. Martin's Press.

SEGAL, B. (1988), *Drugs and behavior, cause, effects and treatment*. New York/London.

SHAFFER, H.J. and JONES, S.B. (1989), *Quitting cocaine. The struggle against impulse*. Lexington/Massachusetts: Lexington Books/D.C. Heath and Company.

SHAFFER H.J. and ROBBINS, M. (1991), Manufacturing multiple meanings of addiction: time-limited realities, 13 *Contemporary Family Therapy*, 387-404.

SHANNON, M. (1988), Clinical toxicity of cocaine adulterants, 17 *Annals of Emergency Medicine* 11, 1243-1247.

SHAPIRO, H. (1994), The crack report, *Druglink*, 13-15.

SIEGEL, R.K. (1982), Cocaine smoking, 14 *Journal of Psychoactive Drugs* 4, excerpted in SIEGEL, R.K. (1992), Cocaine smoking, 24 *Journal of Psychoactive Drugs* 2, 183-212.

SIEGEL, R.K. (1983), Cocaine: new issues for defense and prosecution, 1 *Drug Law Report* 5, 49-60 cited in COHEN, P. (1989), *Cocaine use in Amsterdam in non-deviant subcultures*. Amsterdam: Instituut voor Sociale Geografie.

SIEGEL, R.K. (1985a), New patterns of cocaine use: changing doses and routes, 204-220. In: KOZEL, N.J. and ADAMS, E.H. (eds.), *Cocaine use in America: epidemiologic and clinical perspectives*. Rockville: NIDA.

SIEGEL, R.K. (1985b), Changing patterns of cocaine use. In: GRABOWSKI, J., *Cocaine: pharmacology, effects and treatment*. Rockville: NIDA.

SIJMONS, R. (1997), 'De politieapotheker', *Vrij Nederland*, June, 14th 1997, 44.

SILVERMAN, D. (1993), *Interpreting qualitative data. Methods for analysing talk, text and interaction*. London: Sage.

SIRKIN, R.M. (1995), *Statistics for the social sciences*. Thousand Oaks: Sage Publications.

SLUTSKER, L. (1992), Risks associated with cocaine use during pregnancy, 79 *Obstetrics and Gynecology* 5, 778-779.

SNOW, M. (1973), Maturing out of narcotic addiction in New York City, 8 *International Journal of the Addictions*, 921-938.

SOBELL, L.C., SOBELL, M.B. and TONEATTO, T. (1991), Recovery from alcohol problems without treatment, 198. In: HEATHER, N. MILLER, W.R. and GREELEY, J. (eds.), *Self-Control and addictive behaviours*. New York: Pergamon.

SPOTTS, J.V. and SHONTZ, F.C. (1980), *Cocaine users: a representative case approach*. New York: Free Press.

SPREEN, M., Rare populations, hidden populations, and link-tracing designs: what and why?, 6 *Bulletin de Méthodologie Sociologique*, 34-58.

SPRINGER, A. (1989), *Kokain, Mythos und Realität. Eine kritische dokumentierte Anthologie*. München.

STEDELIJK OVERLEG PREVENTIE VERSLAVING (1994), *Vrijetijdsbesteding en het gebruik van genotsmiddelen bij de Lommelse jeugd*.

STEPHENS, R. (1972), The truthfulness of addict respondents in research projects, 7 *International Journal of the Addictions*, 549-558.

STEPHENS, R. and COTTRELL, E. (1972), A follow-up study of 200 narcotic addicts committed for treatment under the Narcotic Addict Rehabilitation Act (NARA), 67 *British Journal of Addiction* 1, 45-53.

References

STERK-ELIFSON, C. and ELIFSON, K.W. (1993), The social organization of crack cocaine use: the cycle in one type of base house, 23 *Journal of Drug Issues* 3, 429-441.

STIMSON, G.V., OPPENHEIMER, E. and THORLEY, A. (1978), Seven year follow-up of heroin addicts: drug use and outcome, 1 *British Medical Journal* 6121, 1190-1192.

STRANG, J., GRIFFITHS, P., POWIS, B., ABBEY, J. and GOSSOP, M. (1997), How constant is an individual's route of heroin administration? Data from treatment and non-treatment samples, 46 *Drug and Alcohol Dependence* 1-2, 115-118.

STRANG, J., BEARN, J., FARRELL, M., FINCH, E., GOSSOP, M., GRIFFITHS, P., MARSDEN, J. and WOLFF, K. (1998), Route of drug use and its implications for drug effect, risk of dependence and health consequences, 17 *Drug and Alcohol Review*, 197-211.

SWIERSTRA, K. (1987), Heroïneverslaving: levenslang of gaat het vanzelf over?, 13 *Tijdschrift voor Alcohol, Drugs en andere Psychotrope Stoffen* 3, 78-92.

SWIERSTRA, K. (1990), *Drugscarrières: van crimineel tot conventioneel.* Academisch Proefschrift Rijksuniversiteit Groningen. Groningen: Onderzoekscentrum voor Criminologie en Jeugdcriminologie.

SYKES, G.M. and MATZA, D. (1957), Techniques of neutralization: a theory of delinquency, 22 *American Sociological Review* 6, 664-670.

SZASZ, T. (1992), *Our right to drugs. the case for a free market.* Westport: Praeger.

TEETS, J. (1990), What women talk about: sexuality issues among chemically dependent women, 28 *Journal of Psychosocial Nursing* 12, 4-7.

THOMPSON, T. and PICKENS, R. (1970), Stimulant self-administration by animals: some comparisons with opiate self-administration, *Federation proceedings*, 6-12.

TIMS, F. and RUCHMAN, N. (1984) (eds.), *Drug abuse treatment evaluation: strategies, progress and prospects.* NIDA Research Monograph Series. Washington: U.S. Government Printing Office.

TIMS, F.M., FLETCHER, B.W. and HUBBARD, R.L. (1991), Treatment outcomes for drug abuse clients, 93-113. In: PICKENS, R.W., LEUKEFELD, C.G. and SCHUSTER, C.R. (eds.), *Improving drug abuse treatment.* Washington: NIDA Research Monograph 106.

TIMS, F.M. (1993). *Drug abuse treatment outcomes: two decades of research.* Lecture October Meeting Gelders Centrum voor Verslavingszorg. Arnhem.

TRAUTMANN, F. and BARENDREGT, C. (1994), *European Peer Support Handbook. Peer support as a method for AIDS prevention among IDU's.* Utrecht: NIAD.

TURNER, C.F., LESSLER, J.T. and GFROERER, J.C. (1992), *Survey measurement of drug use: methodological studies.* Washington: Department of Health and Human Services.

VAILLANT, G.E. (1966), A twelve-year follow-up of New York narcotic addicts: IV. Some characteristics and determinants of abstinence, 123 *American Journal of Psychiatry* 4, 573-585.

VAILLANT, G.E. (1973), A 20-year follow-up of New York narcotic addicts, 29 *Archives of General Psychiatry,* 237-241.

VAN BILSEN, H. and VAN EMST, A.J. (1989), Motivating heroin users for change. In: BENNETT, M.G. (ed.), *Treating Drug Abusers.* Tavistock: Routledge.

VAN CAUWENBERGHE, K., VAN DAMME, P. and VAN HAL, G. (1991), Registratie-onderzoek van druggebruikers door het Parket Antwerpen, 12 *Panopticon* 6, 615-618.

VAN CAUWENBERGHE, K., VAN DAMME, P. and VAN HAL, G. (1993), Registratie-onderzoek van druggebruikers door het Parket Antwerpen 1991, 14 *Panopticon* 6, 526-535.

VAN DAELE, L., CASSELMAN, J., DEBBAUT, D., DE RUYVER, B., ETIENNE, M., GILLET, I., NOIRFALISE, A. and PASSCHYN, L. (1996), *Gathering and availability of drug related epidemiological data in Belgium and in some neighbouring countries. A preliminary study.* Brussels : Federale Diensten voor Wetenschappelijke, Technische en Culturele Aangelegenheden.

VAN DAELE, L. and CASSELMAN, J. (1997), Epidemiologie van drugsgebruik in België, A 5600-3 to A 5600-19. In: *Handboek Verslaving.* Houtem/Diegem: Bohn Stafleu Van Loghum.

References

VAN DE GOOR, L.A.M., GARRETSEN, H.F.L., KAPLAN, Ch., KORF, D., SPRUIT, I.P. and DE ZWART, W.M. (1994), Research methods for illegal drug use in hidden populations: summary report of a European Invited Expert Meeting, 26 *Journal of Psychoactive Drugs* 1, 33-34.

VAN DER STEL, J.C. (1995), *Drinken, drank en dronkenschap. Vijf eeuwen drankbestrijding en alcoholhulpverlening in Nederland*. Hilversum: Uitgeverij Verloren.

VANDERWAEREN, L. (1992), Overheidsinformatie over criminaliteit, criminaliteitsbeheersing en de bredere veiligheidsproblematiek IV, 13 *Panopticon* 3, 264-279.

VANDERWAEREN, L. and VAN KERCKVOORDE, J. (1993), Overheidsinformatie over criminaliteit, criminaliteitsbeheersing en de bredere veiligheidsproblematiek V, 14 *Panopticon* 3, 248-259.

VAN EPEN, J.H. (1988), *De drugs van de wereld, de wereld van de drugs*. Alphen aan den Rijn/Brussel.

VAN HAL, G., VAN DAMME, P., VAN CAUWENBERGHE, K. and HEREMANS, T. (1995), *Vijfde drugsregistratie via de parketten van Vlaanderen en Brussel*. Antwerpen: Universitaire Instelling Antwerpen.

VAN LAETHEM, W., DECORTE, T. and BAS, R. (1995), *Private politiezorg en grondrechten*. Leuven: Universitaire Pers.

VAN REE, J.M. (1986), Farmacologische werking van cocaine. In: VAN LIMBEEK, J. (ed.), *Cocaine*. Bilthoven.

VAN SCHAREN, H. (1997), *De cannabisconnectie*. Antwerpen: Hadewijch.

VEREBEY, K. and GOLD, M. (1988), From coca leaves to crack: the effects of dose and routes of administration in abuse liability, 18 *Psychiatr. Annals*, 513-520

WAEGE, H., BRACKE, M. and DEGROOTE, A. (1993), *Genees- en genotsmiddelen bij de Leuvense studenten in 1993*. Leuven: Studentenvoorzieningen KULeuven.

WALDORF, D. (1977), *Doing coke: an ethnography of cocaine users and sellers*. Washington: Drug Abuse Council.

WALDORF, D. and BIERNACKI, P. (1981), Natural recovery from opiate addiction: some preliminary findings, 11 *Journal of Drug Issues* 1, 61-74.

WALDORF, D. and BIERNACKI, P. (1982), Natural recovery from heroin addiction: a review of the incidence literature, 173-182. In: ZINBERG, N.E. and HARDING, W.M., *Control over intoxicant use. Pharmacological, psychological and social considerations*. New York: Human Sciences Press.

WALDORF, D. (1983), Natural recovery from opiate addiction. Some social-psychological processes of untreated recovery, 13 *Journal of Drug Issues* 2, 237-280.

WALDORF, D., REINARMAN, C. and MURPHY, S. (1991), *Cocaine changes. The experience of using and quitting*. Philadelphia: Temple University Press.

WARBURTON, D.M. (1992) (ed.), *Addiction controversies*. Chur: Harwood Academic Publishers.

WASHTON, A.M. (1987), Outpatient treatment of cocaine abuse, 106-117. In: WASHTON, A.M. and GOLD, M.S., *Cocaine: a clinician's handbook*. New York: Guilford Press.

WASHTON, A.M. (1989), *Cocaine addiction. Treatment, recovery and relapse prevention*. New York: W.W. Norton.

WATTERS, J.K. and BIERNACKI, P. (1989), Targeted sampling: options for the study of hidden populations, 36 *Social Problems* 4, 416-430.

WEBER, G. and SCHNEIDER, W. (1990), Herauswachsen aus der Sucht: Kontrollierter gebrauch illegaler Drogen und Selbstheilung, 22 *Kriminologisches Journal* 1, 50-55.

WEBSTER, R.A., HUNTER, M. and KEATS, J.A. (1994), Peer and parental influences on adolescents' substance use: a path analysis, 29 *International Journal of the Addictions* 5, 647-657.

WEIL, A. (1979), *The green and the white. The coca leaf and the cocaine papers*. New York.

WEIL, A. (1986), *The natural mind* (revised edition). Boston: Houghton Mifflin Company. First published in 1972.

References

WEITZMAN, E.A. and MILES, M.B. (1995), *Computer programs for qualitative data analysis: a software sourcebook.* Thousand Oaks, CA: Sage.

WEST, R.W. and KRANZLER, H.R. (1990), Craving for cigarettes and psychoactive drugs. In: WARBURTON, D.M., *Addiction controversies.* London: Harwood.

WEST, R. and GOSSOP, M. (1994), Overview: a comparison of withdrawal symptoms from different drug classes, 89 *Addiction* 11, 1483-1489.

WHITE, H.R. and BATES, M.E. (1995), Cessation from cocaine use, 90 *Addiction*, 947-957.

WIEBEL, W.W., (1990), Identifying and gaining access to hidden populations. In LAMBERT, E.Y. (ed.), *The collection and interpretation of data from hidden populations.* Rockville MD: National Institute for Drug Abuse.

WIEPERT, G.D., BEWLEY, T.H. and D'ORBAN, P.T. (1978), Outcomes for 575 British opiate addicts entering treatment between 1968 and 1975, 30 *U.S. Bulletin on Narcotics* 1, 21-32.

WILLIAMS, T. (1990), *Cocaine kids. Un ethnologue chez des dealers adolescents.* Paris: Editions Gallimard.

WILLIAMS, T. (1992), *Crackhouse: notes from the end of the line.* Reading: Addison-Wesley Publishing Company.

WILLMS, D.G. (1991), A new stage, a new life: individual success in quitting smoking, 33 *Soc. Sci. Med.* 12, 1365-1371.

WILSON, M. (1996), Asking questions, 94-120. In: SAPSFORD, R. and JUPP, V. (eds.), *Data collection and analysis.* London: Sage.

WINICK, C. (1962), Maturing out of narcotic addiction, 14 *U.S. Bulletin on Narcotics*, 1-17.

WINICK, C. (1964), The life cycle of the narcotic addict and of addiction, 16 *U.S. Bulletin on Narcotics.*

WOLF, H., TODTS, S., VAN DER KREEFT, P. and VAN CAUWENBERGHE, K. (1994), *Drugs en gebruik. Duidelijke antwoorden op uw vragen.* Antwerpen: Icarus.

WOLFE, H., VRANIZAN, K., GORTER, R.G., KEFFELEW, A.S. and MOSS, A.R. (1992), Crack use and human immunodeficiency virus infection among San Francisco IV drug users, 2 *Sexually Transmitted Diseases*, 111-114.

WYDOODT, J.P. (1994), Legale en illegale drugs: een overzicht, 7-32. In: GOETHALS, J. and CHRISTIAENSEN, S., *De illegale drugsgebruiker tussen strafrechtspleging en hulpverlening.* Leuven: Acco.

WYDOODT, J.P. and LENDERS, F. (1995), *Alcohol, illegale drugs en medicatie. Recente ontwikkelingen in Vlaanderen.* Brussel: V.A.D.

WYDOODT, J.P. and NOELS, B. (1996), *Alcohol, illegale drugs en medicatie. Recente ontwikkelingen in Vlaanderen.* Brussel: V.A.D.

WYDOODT, J.P. and BOOMS, B. (1997), *Alcohol, illegale drugs en medicatie. Recente ontwikkelingen in Vlaanderen.* Brussel: V.A.D.

YOUNG, E. (1990), The role of incest issues in relapse, 22 *Journal of Psychoactive Drugs* 2, 249-258.

ZINBERG, N.E. and DELONG, J.V. (1974), Research and the drug issue, 3 *Contemporary Drug Problems*, 71-100.

ZINBERG, N. and JACOBSON, R.C. (1976), The natural history of "chipping", 133 *American Journal of Psychiatry* 1, 37-40.

ZINBERG, N.E., HARDING, W.M. and WINKELLER, M. (1981), A study of social regulatory mechanisms in controlled illicit drug users, 277-300. In: SHAFFER, H. and BURGLASS, M.E. (eds.), *Classic contributions to the addictions.* New York: Brunner/Mazel.

ZINBERG, N.E. and HARDING, W.M. (eds.) (1982), *Control over intoxicant use. Pharmacological, psychological and social considerations.* New York: Human Sciences Press.

461

References

ZINBERG, N.E. (1984), *Drug, set and setting: the basis for controlled intoxicant use*. New Haven/London: Yale University Press.

SUBJECT INDEX

AUTHOR INDEX

ANNEX : QUESTIONNAIRE

SECTIONS

Introduction

Have you used cocaine more than 25 times so far?
1   Yes
2   No

I. INITIATION TO USE

1   How old were you when you first used cocaine? (number of years and, if possible, months) Or do you still remember the year (month and year)?

    a. age first used ... years ... months   *or*   b. month .... of the year 19....

2   Who were you with when you first used cocaine?

    1   alone
    2   with a friend
    3   with a group of friends
    4   with one or more colleagues
    5   with others. Specify:.........

3   Where did you first use cocaine?

    1   bar/café
    2   disco
    3   night club
    4   coffeeshop
    5   in a friend's house
    6   in my own house
    7   at work
    8   at a party
    9   at school
    10   elsewhere. Specify:..........

4   How did you first use cocaine?

    1   snorting
    2   injecting
    3   eating
    4   rubbing on genitals
    5   freebasing
    6   smoking
    7   other. Specify ....

5   When you first used cocaine, was it offered to you for free, did you ask for it, or did you buy it?

    1   offered (unasked, for free)
    2   asked for it (got it free)
    3   bought it myself

6a   How many lines do you normally extract from 1 gram of cocaine?

6b   For this research we have defined an average standard line of coke as ca 25 mg. This means that there are about 40 lines in one gram of cocaine. Based on this assumption, can you remember how much cocaine you used that first time (in lines, packets, small balls, grams or milligrams)?

II. LEVEL OF USE

These questions are about your level of cocaine use, divided into three periods:

       a   level during your first year of use
       b   level during your heaviest period of use (the length of this period doesn't matter)
       c   level in the last three months

7   This card shows some frequencies of use. Which frequency for cocaine was the most appropriate to you? *(Card 1: Frequency)*
a During my first year of use
     1   daily
     2   not daily, but more than once a week
     3   once a week
     4   less than once a week, but at least once a month
     5   less than once a month
b During my heaviest period of use
     1   daily
     2   not daily, but more than once a week
     3   once a week
     4   less than once a week, but at least once a month
     5   less than once a month
c During the last three months
     1   daily
     2   not daily, but more than once a week
     3   once a week
     4   less than once a week, but at least once a month
     5   less than once a month
     6   none

8   This card shows various methods of use. Which method is most appropriate to you? *(Card 2: Methods)*
a During my first year of use
     1   snorting
     2   injecting
     3   eating
     4   rubbing on genitals
     5   freebasing
     6   other. Specify:..........
b During my heaviest period of use
     1   snorting
     2   injecting
     3   eating
     4   rubbing on genitals
     5   freebasing
     6   other. Specify:..........
c During the last three months
     1   snorting
     2   injecting
     3   eating
     4   rubbing on genitals
     5   freebasing
     6   other. Specify:..........

9.   For this research we have defined a standard cocaine line as 25 mg. This means there are 40 of these standard measures in 1 gram of cocaine. How many of such lines of cocaine did you use in a normal day when you were using cocaine?

       a   During my first year of use: .... lines
       b   During my heaviest period of use: .... lines
       c   During the last three months: .... lines

10   What was your maximum dosage of cocaine per day during the last 4 weeks?
     .... lines

11   How often did you use this maximum daily amount during the last 4 weeks?
     .... times

12   What was your minimum dosage of cocaine per day during the last 4 weeks?
     .... lines

III. PATTERNS OF USE OVER TIME

13   How much time was there between your first and your second use of cocaine?
     ..... years/months/weeks/days

14   How old were you when you started to use cocaine regularly? (We define regularly as:
     with relatively short intervals, e.g. mostly every weekend or every week)
     .... years old

15a How old were you when you used most heavily (years and, if possible, months)? Or do
     you remember the year?

     .... years, and .... months old   *or*   in .... month of 19....

15b How long did this period last?   ... years/months/weeks/days

16   To get some idea about your use of cocaine over the full period in which you have used,
     I have a card here with some statements and graphs on them. Could you tell me which
     one comes closest to your use pattern in terms of regularity and frequency? *(Card 3:
     Patterns of use over time)*

     Pattern 1: I immediately started using large amounts after I first tried cocaine, but have gradu-
                 ally decreased since then.
     Pattern 2: My cocaine use has gradually increased over the years.
     Pattern 3: I started using cocaine at the same level that I still use, and the amount and fre-
                 quency haven't changed.
     Pattern 4: My use increased gradually until it reached a peak, then it decreased.
     Pattern 5: I have started and stopped using cocaine many times.
     Pattern 6: My use pattern has been very varied over the years.

17   Have a look at this card. Which sentence best describes your experience over the last 4
     weeks? *(Card 4)*
             1   I use cocaine only at weekends
             2   I use cocaine more at the weekends than during the week
             3   On weekdays I use as much cocaine as on weekend days
             4   On weekdays I use more cocaine than at the weekend
             5   I use cocaine only during the week
             6   Never

18   Now have a look at this card. Which sentence best describes your use? *(Card 5)*
             1   I use a little, wait, then use some more
             2   I use some cocaine, then stop
             3   I use cocaine without stopping until there is no more left

IV. TEMPORARY ABSTINENCE AND DECREASED USE

19a   Have you ever decreased your cocaine use (without being totally abstinent)? *(stress difference with question 22a)*
   1   Yes
   2   No *(if no, go on to Q22a)*

19b   If yes, how often has that happened?
   1   once
   2   twice
   3   three times
   4   four times
   5   five times
   6   more than five times
   7   don't know

20   Can you name some of the most important reasons why you decreased your cocaine use?

21a   Did this abstinence period create any problems for you?
   1   Yes
   2   No *(if no, go to Q22a)*

21b   Could you expand on that?

22a   Have you ever been abstinent from cocaine for longer than a month since your first period of more or less regular use (temporary abstinence)?
   1   Yes
   2   No *(if no, go on to Q26)*

22b   If yes, how often did that happen?
   1   once
   2   twice
   3   three times
   4   four times
   5   five times
   6   more than five times
   7   don't know

23   Can you name some of the most important reasons why you were abstinent from cocaine for a month or longer?

24a   Did this abstinence period create any problems for you?
   1   Yes
   2   No *(if no, go to Q25a)*

24b   Could you expand on that?

25a   How long was the longest period that you used no cocaine?   .... months/years

25b   When was that?

25c   What were your reasons for ending for this period?

26   Are there specific life events that have influenced your pattern of cocaine use (start, decrease, temporary abstinence, quitting)?

27   Have you ever tried to quit cocaine definitely?
   1   Yes
   2   No *(if no, got to Q38)*

28   What were the main reasons for your decision to quit?

29   Was it on a particular day that you decided to quit?
    1   Yes
    2   No

30   Was it a conscious (well-considered) decision to quit?
    1   Yes
    2   No

The next questions are about techniques for quitting cocaine use. You can answer each of them by 'yes' or 'no'.

31a These techniques relate to moving away from the city:

    1. Did you move to another city or country?   Yes/No
    2. Did you move to another neighborhood?   Yes/No
    3. Did you take a long vacation?   Yes/No
    4. Did you get out of town to avoid using?   Yes/No

31b Some people have other techniques to quit:

    1. Did you make conscious efforts to avoid cocaine-using friends?   Yes/No
    2. Did you stop going to specific places where coke was used?   Yes/No
    3. Did you seek new, non-drug-using friends?   Yes/No
    4. Did you look for new interests?   Yes/No
    5. Did you get involved in sports?   Yes/No

32   Can you remember if you used one of these techniques?

    1. Did you get more concerned with your physical health?   Yes/No
    2. Did you change your eating habits?   Yes/No
    3. Did you start a program of physical conditioning?   Yes/No
    4. Did you start taking vitamins?   Yes/No

33   When you wanted to quit cocaine, did you get any help from these agencies?

    1. Financial help, welfare ('O.C.M.W.')   Yes/No
    2. Help for physical health   Yes/No
    3. Help for mental health   Yes/No
    4. Legal help   Yes/No
    5. Family or child care   Yes/No
    6. Telephone help line   Yes/No
    7. Other. Specify:....   Yes/No

34   Did you ever seek or get any help from

    1. Your family   Yes/No
    2. Your spouse or lover   Yes/No
    3. Your friends   Yes/No
    4. Your employer   Yes/No
    5. Others. Specify:....   Yes/No

35   Since you quit cocaine, have you used any cocaine?

    1 No, not once
    2 1 to 5 days
    3 more than 5 days
    4 don't know

36   How many grams did you use on that occasion?

    1 None
    2 Less than 1 gram
    3 1-2 grams
    4 more than 2 grams
    5 don't know

37   When you were quitting cocaine,

    1 Did you smoke more cigarettes?   Yes/No
    2 Did you drink more alcohol?   Yes/No
    3 Did you start using drugs you had not used before?   Yes/No

V. Methods of use (routes of ingestion)

38   This card shows some ways in which cocaine can be used. Can you indicate which sentence best describes how you mostly use cocaine? Do so both for your total period of cocaine use and for the last 4 weeks. *(Card 6)*

A snorting	total period	last four weeks
1 always 2 mostly (75% yes/25% no) 3 sometimes (50% yes/50% no) 4 mostly not (25% yes/75% no) 5 rarely 6 never		

b injecting	total period	last four weeks
1 always 2 mostly (75% yes/25% no) 3 sometimes (50% yes/50% no) 4 mostly not (25% yes/75% no) 5 rarely 6 never		

c eating	total period	Last four weeks
1 always 2 mostly (75% yes/25% no) 3 sometimes (50% yes/50% no) 4 mostly not (25% yes/75% no) 5 rarely 6 never		

d rubbing on genitals	total period	Last four weeks
1 always 2 mostly (75% yes/25% no) 3 sometimes (50% yes/50% no) 4 mostly not (25% yes/75% no) 5 rarely 6 never		

e free basing	total period	last four weeks
1 always 2 mostly (75% yes/25% no) 3 sometimes (50% yes/50% no) 4 mostly not (25% yes/75% no) 5 rarely 6 never		

f smoking	total period	last four weeks
1 always 2 mostly (75% yes/25% no) 3 sometimes (50% yes/50% no) 4 mostly not (25% yes/75% no) 5 rarely 6 never		

39 If you have ever smoked or freebased cocaine, can you explain

    39a   What you call this product?
    39b   Was it already prepared by the dealer?
    39c   If not, who prepared it and how?
    39d   How you use this product?

39d What do you think is the difference between 'crack', 'cooked cocaine' and 'freebase'? Keep in mind that we do not evaluate your answer to be right or wrong; we only want to know your opinion.

39e Do you have any other remarks about this specific technique of cocaine use?

40 If you have different methods of cocaine use, what does your choice depend on?

41 Can you suggest the advantages and disadvantages of the following three methods of use (you needn't have tried them)
    a. snorting   advantages   disadvantages
    b. injecting   advantages   disadvantages
    c. freebasing   advantages   disadvantages

VI. USE WITH OTHER DRUGS

42 Have you ever used any of the following substances?

    a. alcohol   b. cigarettes
        1   yes   1   yes
        2   no   2   no
    Also during the last two weeks?   Also during the last two weeks?
        1   yes   1   yes
        2   no   2   no
    c. tranquilizers   d. sleeping pills
        1   yes   1   yes
        2   no   2   no
    Also during the last two weeks?   Also during the last two weeks?
        1   yes   1   yes
        2   no   2   no

e. hash or marihuana
    1   yes
    2   no
Also during the last two weeks?
    1   yes
    2   no

g. solvents (ether, glue, thinner)
    1   yes
    2   no
Also during the last two weeks?
    1   yes
    2   no

i. amphetamines ('speed')
    1   yes
    2   no
Also during the last two weeks?
    1   yes
    2   no

f. LSD
    1   yes
    2   no
Also during the last two weeks?
    1   yes
    2   no

h. opiates (opium, methadone, heroin…)
    1   yes
    2   no
Also during the last two weeks?
    1   yes
    2   no

j. MDMA ('ecstasy')
    1   yes
    2   no
Also during the last two weeks?
    1   yes
    2   no

43   Do you use cocaine with other substances? If so, how often have you done so in the last three months? *(ask first for combination with other substance, then for frequency)*

a. with alcohol
    1   yes, often
    2   yes, sometimes
    3   yes, but seldom
    4   no, never

c. with tranquilizers
    1   yes, often
    2   yes, sometimes
    3   yes, but seldom
    4   no, never

e. with hash or marihuana
    1   yes, often
    2   yes, sometimes
    3   yes, but seldom
    4   no, never

g. with solvents
    1   yes, often
    2   yes, sometimes
    3   yes, but seldom
    4   no, never

i. with amphetamines ('speed')
    1   yes, often
    2   yes, sometimes
    3   yes, but seldom
    4   no, never

b. with cigarettes
    1   yes, often
    2   yes, sometimes
    3   yes, but seldom
    4   no, never

d. with sleeping pills
    1   yes, often
    2   yes, sometimes
    3   yes, but seldom
    4   no, never

f. with LSD
    1   yes, often
    2   yes, sometimes
    3   yes, but seldom
    4   no, never

h. with opiates
    1   yes, often
    2   yes, sometimes
    3   yes, but seldom
    4   no, never

j. with MDMA ('ecstasy')
    1   yes, often
    2   yes, sometimes
    3   yes, but seldom
    4   no, never

VII. PURCHASE OF COCAINE

44a   Can you tell me as accurately as possible the value of the cocaine you have used in the last 4 weeks?
    .... Belgian francs

44b How much of this has been self-financed?
.... Belgian francs

45 What is the price per gram that you have paid in the last 4 weeks? (or would have had to pay)
.... Belgian francs per gram

46 Who do you mostly buy your cocaine from?
1 The same one dealer
2 A number of dealers
3 Friend(s)/acquaintance(s)
4 Other. Specify:....................

47 Where do you mostly buy cocaine?
1 Bar/café
2 Disco
3 Coffeeshop (in the Netherlands)
4 Dealer's house
5 Other. Specify:..................

48 If you ever get cocaine for free, who do you get it from?
1 The same one dealer
2 A number of dealers
3 Friend(s)/acquaintance(s)
4 Other. Specify:...........................

VIII. CIRCUMSTANCES OF USE

49 Now I would like to ask a few questions about the circumstances, places or events where you have used cocaine over the last 3 months.

49a Can you think of any situations in which you have used cocaine? For example, 'when I go to a football match', or 'when I do some work in the garden', etc.
49b How often do these cocaine using situations occur?
49c Can you tell each of the circumstances you mentioned gives you a desire to use cocaine?

a	Situations	b Regularity	c Arouses desire
1	situation 1:.....................	1 often 2 sometimes 3 seldom	1 yes 2 no
2	situation 2:.....................	1 often 2 sometimes 3 seldom	1 yes 2 no
3	situation 3:.....................	1 often 2 sometimes 3 seldom	1 yes 2 no
4	situation 4:.....................	1 often 2 sometimes 3 seldom	1 yes 2 no
5	situation 5:.....................	1 often 2 sometimes 3 seldom	1 yes 2 no

50a Are there particular emotions which arouse the desire to use cocaine? (For example, 'when I feel creative')
1   yes
2   no *(if no, go to Q51)*
50b Can you list these emotions?
50c Also mentioning how often you feel them?

a	emotion	b	regularity
1	emotion 1:....................	1	often
		2	sometimes
		3	seldom
2	emotion 2:....................	1	often
		2	sometimes
		3	seldom
3	emotion 3:....................	1	often
		2	sometimes
		3	seldom
4	emotion 4:....................	1	often
		2	sometimes
		3	seldom
5	emotion 5:....................	1	often
		2	sometimes
		3	seldom

51 Are there any distinct situations in which you simply wouldn't want to use cocaine? Specify:...............

52 Are there any emotions that definitely do not combine with the use of cocaine? Specify: ....

53 Do you ever use cocaine when you are alone?
1   yes
2   no

54a Are there people with whom you definitely wouldn't use cocaine?
1   yes
2   no *(if no, go to Q55)*

54b If so, who are they?

The next questions are about possible personal rules that you apply when using cocaine. For example, some people have rules for drinking alcohol such as 'no alcohol at lunchtime', 'not if you have to get up early in the morning', 'wine during dinner only', etc....

55a Do you apply any similar rules with cocaine use? Could you tell me something about such rules?

55b Are there any specific situations in which it is more difficult for you to respect these rules?

55c Do you respect these rules in those situations?

55d Are there any specific situations in which it is easier for you to respect your rules?

IX. ADVANTAGES OF USE

56   Now I want to find out if cocaine has any definite advantages for you. Could you:
     a   list any distinct advantages, and
     b   then rank them in order of importance to you

     a   advantages   b rank order
           advantage 1:.................   ......
           advantage 2:.................   ......
           advantage 3:.................   ......
           advantage 4:.................   ......
           advantage 5:.................   ......

57a Does the actual amount of cocaine that you use on an occasion affect any of these advantages?
     1   yes
     2   no *(if no, go to Q58)*

57b Can you say something more about this, and give one or more examples?

58a Do the circumstances in which cocaine is used have any effect on these advantages?
     1   yes
     2   no *(if no, go to Q58c)*

58b Can you give further details?

58c Are there any combinations of cocaine with other substances that you find advantageous (suitable combinations)?

X. DISADVANTAGES OF USE

59a Now I want to find out if coke has any definite disadvantages for you.
     Could you: a   list any distinct disadvantages, and
                       b   then rank them in order of importance to you

     a   disadvantages   b rank order
           disadvantage 1:.................   ......
           disadvantage 2:.................   ......
           disadvantage 3:.................   ......
           disadvantage 4:.................   ......
           disadvantage 5:.................   ......

60a Does the actual amount of cocaine that you use on an occasion affect any of these disadvantages?
     1   yes
     2   no *(if no, go to Q61b)*

60b Can you say something more about this, and give one or more examples?

61a Do the circumstances in which cocaine is used have any effect on these disadvantages?
     1   yes
     2   no *(if no, go to Q61c)*

61b   Can you give further details?

61c   Are there any combinations of cocaine with other substances that you find disadvantageous (unsuitable combinations)?

62   I am now going to read out a long list of physical symptoms. For each one please answer
      a   whether you have experienced it
      b   if so, whether you experienced it the last year
      c   if that was connected with cocaine use

symptom	experienced ever yes/no	last year experienced yes/no	as a result of coke use yes/no/don't know
High blood pressure			
Jaundice			
Pneumonia			
Respiratory problems			
Stomach ulcer			
Infections			
Diabetes			
Lack of sexual interest			
Lack of appetite			
Sleeplessness			
Impotence			
Inability to reach orgasm			
Gynecological problem			
Runny nose			
Nasal infections			
Depressive (> 1 month)			
Restlessness			
Anxiety			
Delirium tremens			
Heart diseases			
Venereal diseases			
Kidney diseases			
Bad physical condition (> 1 month)			
Skin infections			
Fight wounds			
Accidents or serious injuries			
Nose/septum problems			
Hemorrhages			
Minor operation (e.g. tonsils)			
Drug overdose			

63   I now want to ask you about the direct effects of using cocaine. I am going to read out a list of possible side-effects (after-effects), and if you have ever experienced any of them after using cocaine, please tell me how frequently.

Symptom	never	seldom	regularly	often	always
Dry mouth					
Faster/irregular heartbeat					

Feeling energetic					
Feeling self-confident					
Thinking faster					
Sweating					
Visual distortion					
Headache					
Hand tremors					
Dizziness					
Lack of concentration					
Overly suspicious					
Nausea					
Teeth grinding					
Meaningless actions					
Skin bugs					
Cold/impersonal to other people					
Feeling of power					
Mystical experience					
Forgetting worries					
Breathing difficulties					
Hallucinations					
Depression					
Insomnia					
Changes in menstrual cycle					
Nasal irritation / bleeding nose					
Difficulty in achieving orgasm					
Convulsions					
Losing consciousness					
Restlessness / nervousness					
Unexplained fear					
Loss of appetite					
Clearer thought					
Feeling separated from body / environment					

64   I have got some more possible side-effects (after-effects) here. If you have ever experienced any of these after using cocaine, please tell me how frequently.

Symptom	never	seldom	regularly	often	always
Dilatation of pupils, sensitivity to light					
Tightness or pain in the chest					
Local stupefaction					
Yawning					
Weight loss					
Sensitivity through allergies					
Diarrhea / greater intestinal activity					
Reverberating sounds in the ear					
Epileptic attack					
Flashing lights during cocaine use					
Feelings of wellbeing, euphoria					
Feeling that everything is perfect					
'don't care' attitude					
Spontaneous orgasm after using					
Greater talkativeness					
Painlessness					
Less interest in work / lack of ambition					
Longer sexual intercourse					

Heightened sexual response
Better orgasm during cocaine use
Fear, panic
Motivation to carry weapons
Desire to escape imaginary enemies
Tendency to become physically violent
Urinate more often

65a Are there any other consequences of cocaine use which haven't been mentioned yet, but which you think are important? *(interviewer: note verbatim)*

65b If so, how frequently have you experienced these effects?

66 What is the strongest effect that you have ever had of using cocaine? *(interviewer: note verbatim)*

XI. PRESENCE OF ADULTERANTS

67a Do you know whether the cocaine that you use contains adulterants?
    1   yes
    2   no *(if no, go to Q69a)*

67b How often do you estimate adulterants are present in the cocaine you use?
    1   always
    2   often
    3   regularly
    4   hardly ever
    5   never

68 Which adulterants can be found in the cocaine you use?
    1   ....
    2   ....
    3   ....
    4   ....

69a Can you notice if there is any speed (amphetamines) in the cocaine you use?
    1   yes
    2   no *(if no, go to Q70a)*

69b How do you know?

70a Do you check the purity of the cocaine that you buy?
    1   yes
    2   no *(if no, go to Q71a)*

70b How do you do that?

71a Compared to six months ago, do you think that the quality of the cocaine you use
    1   has improved
    2   has deteriorated
    3   has remained unchanged, stable
    4   has been better at one time, and has been worse at another.
    5   I don't know

71b Could you estimate the quality of the cocaine you have used on the last occasion?
1   ….. %
2   I don't know *(if no, go to Q72a)*

XII. OPINION FORMATION OF COCAINE

72a Can you remember your opinion about cocaine and its users before you started using it yourself?
1   yes
2   no *(if no, go to Q73a)*

72b Tell me about the opinions you had at that time.

72c Do you remember how you got this information?

72d Did your opinions change after you started using cocaine?
1   yes
2   no *(if no, go to Q73a)*

72e What has been the most significant change in your opinion about cocaine?

73a Which of these sources had an influence on forming your opinion about cocaine?
1   news   yes/no
2   books   yes/no
3   non cocaine using friends   yes/no
4   cocaine using friends   yes/no
5   doctors   yes/no
6   addiction treatment agencies   yes/no
7   parents   yes/no
8   teachers   yes/no

73b Did you ever get false information about cocaine?

73c Where did this information come from?

74   What advice would you give to someone who is starting to use cocaine?

75a To how many people have you ever offered cocaine (users and non-users)?

75b Who were they?

76a Did you discuss certain aspects of your cocaine use with other people lately?
1   yes, during the last week
2   yes, during the last month
3   no *(if no, go to Q77)*

76b Which aspects of your cocaine use did you discuss on that occasion?

76c Who did you discuss these aspects with?
77   Who did you see using cocaine, before the onset of your own use?

78a Did you ever get discouraging or negative information about the use of cocaine, before the onset of your own use? If so, which information?

78b Who from?

78c Did you ever get encouraging or positive information about the use of cocaine, before the onset of your own use?

78d Who from?

79a Have you ever made any remarks about other people's use? If so, which remarks?

79b Who to?

79c How did these people react to your remarks?

80a Have other people ever made remarks about your cocaine use to you?

80b Who?

80c How did you react to these remarks?

81a I want to ask you about this country's cocaine policy. Do you think that cocaine use should be treated in the same way as hash and marihuana in the Netherlands, or more like heroin, or just like alcohol?
1   like cannabis (in the Netherlands)
2   like heroin (in Belgium)
3   like alcohol (in Belgium)

81b Please explain your view.

XIII. DEPENDENCY

82 Do you smoke?
1   yes
2   no *(if no, go to Q83a)*

82a Have you ever tried to stop smoking?
1   yes
2   no *(if no, go to Q82c)*

82b If so, did you succeed?
1   yes
2   no

82c Have you ever tried to reduce your smoking?
1   yes
2   no *(if no, go to Q83a)*

82d If so, did you succeed?
1   yes
2   no

83a Have you ever found yourself longing for cocaine?
    1   yes
    2   no *(if no, go to Q84a)*

83b In what year did that first happen? Or, how old were you?

    Year: 19......   *or*   your age then: ..... years ..... months

83c How often now do you feel this longing for cocaine?
    1   never
    2   seldom
    3   every now and then
    4   often
    5   (almost) always
83d Do you feel a longing for cocaine also when it is not available?
    1   yes
    2   no

84a Has cocaine ever been an obsession for you?
    1   yes
    2   no *(if no, go to Q85a)*

84b When was that?

85a Do you have a limit to the amount of money that you are prepared to spend on cocaine per month?
    1   yes
    2   no *(if no, go to Q86)*

85b What is that limit?
    .... Belgian francs per month

86 I now want to read out a list of different ways people have used to get cocaine. All these ways were actually reported by respondents studied by researchers in America. For each one, I would like you to tell me if it
    1   never occurred to you
    2   occurred to you once
    3   occurred to you sometimes
    4   occurred to you often
    5   occurred to you (almost) always

	never	once	some-times	often	(almost) always
1 getting a second job					
2 getting a loan					
3 selling personal possessions					
4 taking things or money from family, friends to sell					
5 shoplifting					
6 selling cocaine					
7 breaking in (burglary)					
8 stealing money from a person					
9 forging checks					
10 stealing cocaine					
11 involved in prostitution					
12 running con games					

13 stealing a car
14 stealing from a car
15 trading sexual favors
16 hanging around with people/ being in a situation you didn't like in order to get cocaine
17 other. Specify:....

XIV. COCAINE USE AT THE WORKPLACE

Now I'd like to ask you some questions about work.

87a Are you employed at the moment?
    1   yes, full-time
    2   yes, part-time
    3   yes, moonlighting
    4   no, unemployed
    5   other. Specify:......................

87b How many hours do you usually work per week?   .... hours

87c How many months have you been unemployed in the last two years? .... months

88   How many different jobs have you had in the last two years?   .... jobs

89   *(if respondent has been employed in the last three months)*
Have you ever been under the influence of any of these substances when at work: *(Card 7)*

	never	once	sometimes	often	(almost) always
a alcohol					
b cocaine					
c cannabis					
d other drug. Specify:......					

90   Some people say that the use of cocaine affects the way one performs in work or other areas, like relationships with family, friends, partner, etc. I have some statements of possible influences here. Please indicate for each of these statements whether:
    1   you fully disagree,
    2   you disagree to some extent,
    3   you neither agree nor disagree,
    4   you agree to some extent,
    5   you fully agree,
    6   you have no opinion,
    7   this statement does not apply to your personal situation.

a   Cocaine has improved the quality of my work.

fully dis-agree	Disagree to some extent	Neither agree nor disagree	Agree to some extent	Fully agree	No opinion	Not applicable

b   Cocaine has deteriorated the quality of my work.

Fully dis-agree	Disagree to some extent	Neither agree nor disagree	Agree to some extent	Fully agree	No opinion	Not applicable

c   Cocaine has harmed my relationship with my supervisor or my colleagues.

| Fully dis-agree | Disagree to some extent | Neither agree nor disagree | Agree to some extent | Fully agree | No opinion | Not applicable |

d   Cocaine has improved my relationship with my supervisor or my colleagues.

| Fully dis-agree | Disagree to some extent | Neither agree nor disagree | Agree to some extent | Fully agree | No opinion | Not applicable |

e   Cocaine has helped me do more work.

| Fully dis-agree | Disagree to some extent | Neither agree nor disagree | Agree to some extent | Fully agree | No opinion | Not applicable |

f   Cocaine has made me work less.

| Fully dis-agree | Disagree to some extent | Neither agree nor disagree | Agree to some extent | Fully agree | No opinion | Not applicable |

g   Cocaine has improved my relationship with my partner.

| Fully dis-agree | Disagree to some extent | Neither agree nor disagree | Agree to some extent | Fully agree | No opinion | Not applicable |

h   Cocaine has deteriorated my relationship with my partner.

| Fully dis-agree | Disagree to some extent | Neither agree nor disagree | Agree to some extent | Fully agree | No opinion | Not applicable |

i   Cocaine has been the cause of a separation, divorce (or splitting up).

| Fully dis-agree | Disagree to some extent | Neither agree nor disagree | Agree to some extent | Fully agree | No opinion | Not applicable |

j   Cocaine has improved my sexual relationships.

| Fully dis-agree | Disagree to some extent | Neither agree nor disagree | Agree to some extent | Fully agree | No opinion | Not applicable |

k   Cocaine has deteriorated my sexual relationships.

| Fully dis-agree | Disagree to some extent | Neither agree nor disagree | Agree to some extent | Fully agree | No opinion | Not applicable |

l   Cocaine has deteriorated my (family) budget.

| Fully dis-agree | Disagree to some extent | Neither agree nor disagree | Agree to some extent | Fully agree | No opinion | Not applicable |

m   Cocaine has improved my family relationships.

| Fully dis-agree | Disagree to some extent | Neither agree nor disagree | Agree to some extent | Fully agree | No opinion | Not applicable |

n   Cocaine has deteriorated my family relationships.

| Fully dis-agree | Disagree to some extent | Neither agree nor disagree | Agree to some extent | Fully agree | No opinion | Not applicable |

o   Cocaine has improved the relationship with my friends.

| Fully dis-agree | Disagree to some extent | Neither agree nor disagree | Agree to some extent | Fully agree | No opinion | Not applicable |

p   Cocaine has deteriorated the relationship with my friends.

| Fully dis-agree | Disagree to some extent | Neither agree nor disagree | Agree to some extent | Fully agree | No opinion | Not applicable |

91   Did you ever miss one or more days of work after the use of cocaine?

XV. GENERAL INFORMATION

92a   What is your age?   .... years

92b   Sex?   1. male   *or*   2. female

93a   Your marital status?
  1   married
  2   divorced
  3   unmarried
  4   widow/widower

93b   Do you have a steady partner at the moment?
  1   no
  2   yes, less than a year
  3   yes, more than a year

94   What is your living situation at home? *(try to record as accurate as possible: living alone, with a partner, with or without children, with other people, with parents, etc...)*

95   Do you have any children? If so, where do they live?
  1   no children
  2   children living with you
  3   children living elsewhere
  4   some children living with you, some elsewhere

96a   Which country were you born in?
96b   And your father?
96c   And your mother?

97a   *(if employed)* What is your main job?
97b   *(if unemployed)* What welfare benefits do you get?

98a   What is your educational level?
  1   none
  2   elementary education
  3   lower vocational education
  4   lower technical education (A3-level)
  5   lower level high school
  6   higher vocational education
  7   higher technical education (A2-level)
  8   higher level high school
  9   non-university college (A1-level)
  10   university
  11   Other. Specify:........

98b   Did you finish these studies, did you quit before taking a degree, or are you still studying?
  1   finished
  2   quit
  3   still studying

99   What was your average monthly net income last year (Belgian francs)?
  1   <20,000 Belgian francs
  2   20,000-30,000 Belgian francs
  3   30,000-40,000 Belgian francs
  4   40,000-50,000 Belgian francs
  5   50,000-60,000 Belgian francs
  6   60,000-70,000 Belgian francs
  7   70,000-80,000 Belgian francs
  8   80,000-90,000 Belgian francs
  9   >90,000 Belgian francs

100a Have you ever had any contact with an alcohol or drug treatment facility?
   1   yes
   2   no *(if no, go to Q101)*

100b Have you had any contact during the last two years with an alcohol or drug treatment facility?
   1   yes
   2   no

100c For what kind of drug problems did you seek help, and how did you experience those contacts?

101a Have you ever been convicted for any criminal offence?
   1   yes
   2   no *(if no, go to Q102)*

101b Have you been convicted for any criminal offence in the last 2 years?
   1   yes
   2   no

101c What kind of criminal offence(s)?

XVI. KNOWLEDGE OF COCAINE USE

102 Could you tell me how many people you know who use cocaine (including casual users).
   .... persons

103 Of those people, what proportion are male, and what proportion female?
   ..... % male and ..... % female

104a I would like to know if anybody among the cocaine users you know uses cocaine in a way you would consider 'risky'?
   1   yes
   2   no *(if no, go to Q105)*

104b How many?   .... persons

105 Do you want to mention anything about the use of cocaine not covered by this interview?

XVII. CARDS

Card 1 *(Question 7)*   1   daily
                                  2   not daily, but more than once a week
                                  3   once a week
                                  4   less than once a week, but at least once a month
                                  5   less than once a month
                                  6   none

Card 2 *(Question 8)*   1   snorting
                           2   injecting
                           3   eating
                           4   rubbing on genitals
                           5   freebasing
                           6   other. Specify:..........

Card 3 *(Question 16)*

    Pattern 1   I immediately started using large amounts after I first tried cocaine, but gradually decreased since then.
    Pattern 2   My cocaine use has gradually increased over the years.
    Pattern 3   I started using cocaine at the same level that I still use, and the amount and frequency haven't changed
    Pattern 4   My use increased gradually until it reached a peak, then it decreased
    Pattern 5   I have started and stopped using cocaine many times
    Pattern 6   My use pattern has been very varied over the years

Card 4 *(Question 17)*   1   I use cocaine only at weekends
                           2   I use cocaine more at the weekends than during the week
                           3   On weekdays I use as much cocaine than on weekend days
                           4   On weekdays I use more cocaine than in the weekend
                           5   I use cocaine only during the week
                           6   never

Card 5 *(Question 18)*   1   I use a little, wait, then use some more
                           2   I use some cocaine, then stop
                           3   I use cocaine without stopping until there is none left

Card 6 *(Question 38)*   1   always
                           2   mostly (75% yes / 25% no)
                           3   sometimes (50% yes / 50% no)
                           4   mostly not (25% yes / 75% no)
                           5   rarely
                           6   never

Card 7 *(Question 89)*   1   never
                           2   once
                           3   sometimes
                           4   often
                           5   (almost) always

499